Amy Beach

Passionate Victorian

Amy Beach

Passionate Victorian

THE

LIFE AND WORK

OF AN

AMERICAN COMPOSER

1867–1944

Adrienne Fried Block

New York   Oxford   •   Oxford University Press   1998

Oxford University Press

Oxford   New York

Athens   Aukland   Bangkok   Bogotá   Buenos Aires   Calcutta
Cape Town   Chennai   Dar es Salaam   Delhi   Florence   Hong Kong   Istanbul
Karachi   Kuala Lumpur   Madrid   Melbourne   Mexico City   Mumbai
Nairobi   Paris   São Paulo   Singapore   Taipei   Tokyo   Toronto   Warsaw

and associated companies in
Berlin   Ibadan

Published by Oxford University Press, Inc.
198 Madison Avenue, New York, New York 10016

Oxford is a registered trademark of Oxford University Press

Library of Congress Cataloging-in-Publication Data
Block, Adrienne Fried.
Amy Beach, passionate Victorian : the life and work of an
American composer, 1867–1944 / Adrienne Fried Block.
p.   cm.
Includes bibliographical references and index.
ISBN 0-19-507408-4
1. Beach, H. H. A., Mrs., 1867–1944   2. Composers—United States—
Biography.   3. Women composers—United States—Biography.
I. Title.
ML410.B36B56   1998
780'.92—dc21   97-2710
[B]

The MacDowell Colony, Inc., heir to the unpublished materials of the Estate of Amy
Beach, has generously given permission to reproduce photographs, manuscripts,
and memorabilia from library collections.

The following publishers have given permission to use quotations from copyrighted
works. "Night Song at Amalfi," in the Collected Poems of Sara Teasdale, copyright 1937 by
Macmillan Publishing Company; copyright renewed 1965 by Morgan Guarantee
Trust Company of New York, reprinted by permission of Simon and Schuster.
"Rendez-vous," by Leonore Speyer, in A Canopic Jar, copyright 1921 by E. P. Dutton &
Co., reprinted by permission of A. A. Knopf and Bankers Trust Company, New York.
"Hillcrest," in The Collected Poems of Edwin Arlington Robinson, copyright 1916 by Macmillan
Publishing Company, renewed 1944 by Ruth Nivision, reprinted by permission of
Simon and Schuster. The Poems of William Ernest Henley, copyright 1898 by Charles Scrib-
ner's Sons, renewed 1926, reprinted by permission of Scribner, a division of Simon
and Schuster.

Publication of this book was supported in part by a grant from the H. Earle Johnson
fund of the Sonneck Society for American Music.

1 3 5 7 9 8 6 4 2

Printed in the United States of America
on acid-free paper

To

my

daughters

PREFACE

[H]ow inevitable it was that music should be
my life's work. Both in composition and piano
playing, there seemed to be such a strong attraction . . . that no other life than that of a musician could ever have been possible for me.
(Amy Beach to Mrs. Edward F. Wiggers, 24 August 1935).

IN 1917 AMY BEACH TURNED FIFTY. If in that year someone had proposed a full-
scale biography, people would have found it a perfectly reasonable thing to
do. The only objection might have been that it was too soon to be definitive,
that her life's course was only partially run. Over the preceding thirty years,
feature articles and interviews giving biographical information appeared in
newspapers and music journals with considerable frequency, whetting the
public's appetite for more. To women she was a heroine, not as glamorous as
a diva perhaps, but all the more remarkable for having ventured into a field of
composition thought to be the exclusive preserve of men—and having succeeded. To some, Amy Marcy Cheney Beach was thoroughly admirable; to
others, one who overstepped her boundary; but to both groups, an object of
interest if not curiosity.

The earliest evidence of public interest in Amy Marcy Cheney was an article
written when she was seven, reporting a private recital that included two unnamed works, one by Chopin and one by her. It marked her for the public as
a child prodigy. There is a mythic aura about a child who instinctively knows
how to play the piano and compose.

Amy Cheney was fortunate in that her family had moved from Henniker,
the small New Hampshire town where she was born, to Boston, an ideal place
for a gifted child to grow up. As she said, Boston was a "very musical" city; it
also took pride in and supported its own performers and composers. Together
with professional musicians, members of Boston's social and cultural elite
heard her play in drawing rooms and salons and adopted her years before her
debut. They found the girl irresistible and the teenager gifted and charming
and with enormous potential. Part of her attraction was that she was one of
their own, a Yankee like them, and a girl with extraordinary promise.

Her musical gifts undergirded her ambition, which was strong enough to
launch a performing career despite parental opposition. She became the first
American concert pianist to succeed with local training. Thus she helped de-
molish notions that only those trained in a German conservatory could make

a go of it. Her debut at sixteen, which took place in Boston's main concert hall, had outstanding reviews; thereafter, she had a devoted concert audience of Bostonians.

Her early success took place against a background of contention over women's roles as musicians. Despite this, Beach's life in music was defined by two quests: a global audience for herself as performer and composer and for solutions to compositional problems. Those dual quests meant living a public life and a life devoted to work. As Carolyn Heilbrun notes, it was a narrative women were rarely empowered to pursue and even more rarely lived. Beach eventually lived this narrative but only after surmounting some sizeable obstacles.

Her parents' opposition to a concert career was the first. They allowed her a debut but not the necessary next steps for building an international career. The second was marriage, which put an end to her career as a local recitalist, but had the effect of focusing her energies on composition. Now instead of Amy Marcy Cheney, her professional name for most of the rest of her life was Mrs. H. H. A. Beach, thus masking her former identity in the distinguished name of her new husband, Henry Harris Aubrey Beach, M. D.

Both parents and husband opposed her studying composition with a teacher, to her great disappointment. She turned that defeat into a triumph by teaching herself whatever she needed to know about composition and orchestration. Wisely, she also continued to practice piano, giving one or two public performances a year, occasionally playing a concerto with orchestra. She soon added her own piano solos and chamber works to her concert repertory. Critics reviewed her programs as much for her new works as for her playing. Thus, in a limited way, she circumvented the agreement with her husband to abandon her concert career after marriage.

Her first recognition as a composer came when at age twenty-one, she played Beethoven's third piano concerto with the Boston Symphony Orchestra. For the occasion she had written her own cadenza, a lengthy essay on Beethoven's themes. Critics hailed it as substantial evidence of her promise as a composer. When her Mass, op. 5, was played, critics and public could finally take her measure as a composer. The work, which takes over an hour, was given by 349 members of the leading American chorus, the Boston Handel and Haydn Society, and accompanied by members of the Boston Symphony Orchestra. It was so successful that her name became known well beyond Boston and immediately generated two commissions. The first was for a concert aria given its premiere by the New York Symphony, conducted by Walter Damrosch; the other was for chorus and orchestra and conducted by Theodore Thomas at the World's Columbian Exposition in Chicago in 1893.

Her second even bigger success, the "Gaelic" Symphony, op. 32, premiered by the Boston Symphony Orchestra in 1896, moved an audience to intense displays of approval and the critics to much praise—not unmixed with caveats. A letter to Beach after the premiere from Boston composer George Whitefield Chadwick made her acceptance official in the so-called Second New England School of Composers. The symphony produced amazement in late nineteenth-century minds because a woman had written for orchestra, taming the unwieldy medium with mastery. All but one of the major American orchestras performed it during the next two decades. Her fame was then truly national.

Its spread was helped substantially by the timely publication of everything she wrote between 1885 and 1914 by the firm of Arthur P. Schmidt, as part of his commitment to support Boston's composers. This in turn encouraged many more performances. Boston's musical establishment and Amy Beach herself were responsible for the majority of performances of her works during her Boston years. As a composer, she needed such exposure to further the development of her craft as well as to build the fine reputation she earned even before turning thirty.

Press criticism helped as well in establishing her as a composer. Even their occasional attacks on aspects of her compositions served to show how seriously they took her music. However, Beach learned early to let the audience be her guide, valuing its response to her music more than that of any professional reviewer. And respond people did—to her emotional depths, her lyricism and, if sophisticated listeners, to her solid compositional designs. Performers loved her work as well. Her reputation rippled out from Boston as the divas of opera's Golden Age adopted her songs. Her chamber music found illustrious players and enthusiastic audiences not only in the United States but also in Europe, as later her orchestral pieces would.

Amy Beach was truly an American pioneer as a composer and the first successful woman in the field. Being the token woman in the composition of high art music had its advantages and disadvantages. On the one hand, it helped spread her fame; on the other, it suggested that as a woman composer she was an aberration. Nevertheless, weighed in the balance against doubters and detractors were her great gifts, her concentration on work, her location in Boston, and her timing: she was able to ride the crest of the first feminist movement. The next generation of women composers found courage in Beach's record as a pathfinder and model, formalizing her role with the honorific title of dean of American women composers.

Personal tragedy struck in 1910 with the accidental death of her husband, effectively ending her life in Boston. Grieving and alone but also newly in charge of her life, Beach decided to return to her career as a performer while promoting her own works on the concert stage. She was free to go to Europe, where she stayed for three years and found enthusiastic reception for her major chamber and orchestral works and for her playing. She placed her career on the line in Germany and won, despite the traditional hostility of local critics toward Americans and women. A manager made sure that her European successes were regularly reported in the American press. Returning reluctantly to the United States at the outset of World War I, she had a heroine's welcome in Boston. Outstandingly successful years followed during which she crisscrossed the country giving recitals. Beach told the press that she enjoyed nothing more than traveling to a new place and conquering a new audience.

All that touring left little time for creative work. To compose she needed a place out of the city and surrounded by nature. Beach tried out one locale after another, and in 1921 she found the ideal solution: her favorite place, where she composed almost everything from that time on, was the MacDowell Colony in Peterborough, New Hampshire. Although she spent only one or two months there each year, she composed quickly once she sat down with pencil and manuscript paper and greatly increased her productivity over that of the previous decade. For her winter residence she eventually settled in New York, where she found a pied-à-terre in 1930, taking full advantage of the city's rich musical life as participant and auditor.

During the second half of her life, her style became more adventurous in response to the revolutionary changes in twentieth-century music. Yet Beach rejected the ultra-modern and searched successfully for a middle way, out of a belief that music must be the product of both intellect and emotion. That ideology grew naturally out of her own persona, a combination of strong feelings and Bostonian propriety. Indeed, except for music, her attitudes were class-bound and conservative. Yet she was a warm, giving person, much concerned about others, and particularly involved in helping younger women musicians through their organizations and directly as a loving friend.

Amy Beach believed that music must be shared and lived her life by that principle. In writing her life, I have tried to place it in context, to show what it meant to straddle two centuries from her birth during the expansive Victorian era through two world wars and a depression. In sharing her life, I hope most of all to help others share in her music.

A NUMBER OF PEOPLE HAVE raised objections to the name "Amy Beach" on the grounds that she was known after her marriage as Mrs. H. H. A. Beach. That is the truth, but not the whole truth. There was a handicap to that name which she herself recognized: in later life it marked her as a Victorian holdover at a time when she wished to be viewed as a contemporary composer.

In Europe after her husband died, Beach changed her name to Amy Beach. She also published an autobiographical article under that name in an American magazine, thus taking the first step toward renaming herself back home. When someone asked her if she were the daughter of Mrs. H. H. A. Beach, however, she suddenly realized how indelibly her identity back home was tied to the latter name. On her return to the United States at the beginning of World War I, she again called herself Mrs. H. H. A. Beach.

Small indications of her continuing desire to change the name surfaced: the name on her bookplate (Amy M. Beach) and on stationery she used late in life (Amy Beach). But evidence that she wished to be remembered as Amy Beach is in her last will and testament. In it she set up a fund for the MacDowell Colony to receive royalties and performance fees earned by her music—they were and are now substantial—called the Amy Beach Fund. Those who honor her memory do so by respecting her final wish.

New York City   A. F. B.
1997

ACKNOWLEDGMENTS

WORK ON THIS BOOK OFFICIALLY began in 1986 with a fellowship from the National Endowment for the Humanities that supported a year's research at major Beach repositories as well as many smaller collections and at the places where Beach lived and worked. The Sonneck Society for American Music also supported this book with a generous publication subvention. A grant from the Sinfonia Foundation supported computerization of the data with the expert assistance of Andrea Goodzeit. A brief residency at the Newberry Library in Chicago permitted the exploration of documents relating to the World's Columbian Exposition of 1893. I express my thanks and gratitude to all four institutions.

Unofficially, however, this book owes its beginning to work done ten years earlier on *Women in American Music: A Bibliography of Music and Literature* (1979) compiled and edited by Carol Neuls-Bates and myself. During the book's preparation, Amy Beach's commanding position as America's first successful woman composer of art music became apparent; examination of her music made clear that she was a major American composer.

After I did some preliminary research and publishing an article on Beach and her music, three colleagues—Nancy B. Reich, Judith Tick, and Elizabeth Wood, all of whom were writing biographies of women in music—convinced me that a full-scale biography of Beach should be my next project. I am especially grateful for their ongoing encouragement and expert advice.

I wish to acknowledge the education in the craft of biography that I have gained from members and presenters of the Biography Seminar at New York University and from Women Writing Women's Lives, a seminar held at the Graduate Center of the City University of New York. Archival research was facilitated greatly by the able genealogist Melinde Lutz Sanborn.

To the many librarians and curators whose invaluable assistance often extended beyond the call of duty, I offer my sincere appreciation. Special thanks go to Wayne Shirley and Gillian Anderson of the Music Division of the Library of Congress; Barbara White, Elizabeth Witham, Tim Dodge, and most recently William E. Ross and his staff at the Dimond Library of the University of New Hampshire; Peter Munstedt, formerly at the Library of the University of Missouri in Kansas City; and Jeanne Morrow, head of the Library of the New England

Conservatory of Music in Boston. The staff of the MacDowell Colony in Peterborough, New Hampshire, has been generous, accommodating, and endlessly helpful.

In addition, I am grateful to the staffs of the Music Research Division and the Main Reading Room of the New York Public Library, Astor, Lenox and Tilden Foundations; the music libraries at Brooklyn College, Hunter College, City College, and the Graduate School and University Center of the City University of New York; and the Pierpont Morgan Library, the New-York Historical Society, the Metropolitan Opera Archives, the Juilliard School of Music, the New York Academy of Medicine, the Franklin D. Roosevelt Presidential Library, the Chautauqua Institution, and the Sibley Library of the Eastman School of Music.

I have been much assisted by librarians at the California Genealogical Society; the California Historical Society; the Sacramento State Library; the Art and Music Department of the San Francisco Public Library; the Music, Bancroft, and General Libraries of the University of California, Berkeley; the Ira F. Brilliant Center for Beethoven Studies of the San Jose State University; the Tomás Rivera Library of the University of California, Riverside; the Riverside Municipal Museum; and the San Diego Historical Society.

Major assistance came from numerous research organizations and libraries in New Hampshire: the New Hampshire Historical Society, the New Hampshire State Library, the Fuller Public Library of Hillsborough, the Tucker Free Library of Henniker, and the Peterborough Historical Society. I also extend my thanks to the Bagaduce Music Lending Library and Kneisel Hall in Blue Hill, Maine, and to the George and Helen Ladd Library of Bates College.

I am grateful for the help of staff members of the Andover-Harvard Theological Library, the Countway Medical Library, the Eda Kuhn Loeb Music Library, the Gray Herbarium, the Houghton Library, and the Widener Library, all of Harvard University, as well as the Arthur and Elizabeth Schlesinger Library at Radcliffe College. I also thank the librarians and archivists at Boston University Library, at the Library of the New England Conservatory of Music, the Boston Symphony Orchestra, the Church of the Advent, the Massachusetts General Hospital, the Harvard Musical Association, the Boston Athenaeum, New Bedford Free Public Library, the Worcester Historical Museum, the Werner Josten Library at Smith College, and the Centerville Historical Society.

I gratefully acknowledge the assistance of the libraries of the National League of American Pen Women and the Daughters of the American Revolution in Washington, D.C.; the public libraries of Atlanta, Chicago, Cleveland, Huntington (California), New Orleans, Pittsburgh, and San Francisco; the Fleisher Collection of the Free Library of Philadelphia; the libraries of the University of Virginia, the University of Washington, the Atlanta Historical Society, and the Georgia Department of Archives and History. Special thanks also are owed to the Marcella Sembrich Memorial Association, Inc.

I also express my gratitude to librarians at the Bibliothek der Bayerischen Staatsoper and the Bayerische Staatsbibliothek, Munich; the Musikverlag of B. Schotts Söhne, Mainz; the Staats- und Universitätsbibliothek, Hamburg; and the Rigsarkivet, Copenhagen.

Special thanks go to those who granted me interviews: first and most important, the late David Buxbaum and his sister, the late Lillian Buxbaum Meredith; also Robert Baker, the late Jeanne Behrend, Shirley A. Bentley, Willa Brigham, Radie Britain, Pearl Morton Bates Brodrick, Jane F. Broughton, Elna Chase, Wallace Dailey, Eugenie Limberg Dengel, Vernon de Tar, Ann P. Duggan, Frances Brockman Farrier, Sally Gallagher, the late Anna Hamlin, Charles N. Henderson, Andreas Holm, Harry Johnson, Dorothy L. Kelley, Geoffrey Levey, Sr., the late Margaret W. McCarthy, Marella MacDill, Norma Mellen, Virginia Duffey Pleasants, Paul Scruton, Carl E. Schroeder, Helen K. Smith, the late Julia Smith, and the late William Strickland. Correspondents who answered my author's query in the *New York Times* include Vincent de Sola, Sally J. Faria, Marie Thérèse Fleming, Ann Mathews Holand, Ruth Jeffrey, and Claire M. Warner.

My thanks as well to John Baron, Burton Benedict, Cyrilla Barr, Elizabeth Block, Ira F. Brilliant, Betty Buchanan, Wilma Reid Cipolla, Susan C. Cook, Blanche Weisen Cooke, Martha Cox, Richard Crawford, Liane Curtis, Mary Wallace Davidson, Rodney Dennis, J. Michelle Edwards, Wayne Eley, John A. Emerson, Dena Epstein, Virginia Eskin, Brice Farwell, Aloys Fleischmann, Sylvia Glickman, Andrea Goodman, Eric Gordon, Jane Gottlieb, Michael Griffel, Marion Groce, Terry Guptill, Lydia Hailparn, Franz Hajek, Marnie Hall, David Hildebrand, Helga Heim, H. Wiley Hitchcock, Monika Holl, Elizabeth Hostetter, Dorothy Indenbaum, Alfreda Irwin, Carol Jacobson, Walter S. Jenkins, Joy Kestnbaum, Elise K. Kirk, John Koegel, Orly Krasner, Clare Le Corbeiller, Steven Ledbetter, Margery Morgan Lowens, Roberta Lukes, Geoffrey and Mary McGillen, David Margolick, Honor Moore, H. Vincent Moses, Michael Ochs, Carol J. Oja, Natalie Palme, Frank Pendle, Marian Peterson, Leslie Petteys, Joan T. Phipps, Samuel Pogue, Joanne Polk, Percy Preston, Carolyn Rabson, Mary Riley, Angela Robinson, Deane L. Root, Judith Rosen, Wayne Schneider, Mary Scanlan, Doris Schrekengaust, Arnold T. Schwab, Elizabeth Ann Sears, Kay Kaufman Shelemay, Catherine P. Smith, Margaret Steger, William K. Tinkham, William Trafka, Judy Tsou, Judith Vander, Channan Willner, and Victor Fell Yellin.

I particularly want to express my gratitude to those who have read the completed manuscript, Dena Epstein, Stuart Feder, Nancy B. Reich, Wayne Shirley, Ruth Solie, Joseph N. Straus, and Judith Tick. Others who have given wise counsel include Joseph Bankman, Barbara H. Fried, Linda P. Fried, and Joseph Margolick. To Arthur L. Block, especially, I am grateful for the innumerable ways he has aided this work, including his editorial help and his generous and loving encouragement.

Special thanks go to my editors at Oxford University Press, Sheldon Meyer, MaryBeth Branigan, and Maribeth Anderson Payne. Barbara B. Heyman's fine copy-editing has made this a better book.

My apologies and grateful thanks go to any who have generously assisted me, but whose names are inadvertently omitted here.

CONTENTS

Photos follow p. 122

Amy Beach

Passionate Victorian

A PRODIGY'S

NEW ENGLAND

UPBRINGING

PRODIGIES ARE AT ONCE A JOY and a trial to parents. Watching them leap over barriers, telescope the learning process, and work with the intense concentration that is the mark of the gifted makes parents both proud and grateful for their children's gifts. However, these very gifts may make parents feel diminished in size, in authority, in competence. Even if gifted children do nothing but follow their bent and never challenge their parents' authority, their amazing displays of genius give them authority and power. If parents treat them as if they were normal, never admitting to anyone that their children are special, the children know better. If the child's musical perceptions are of great depth and intensity, prompting urgent and imperious demands for satisfaction, then the parents worry that the child may be abnormal, untamable, even monstrous. If the parents' religious beliefs place the children's salvation ahead of earthly gratifications, the problems intensify. If, in addition, the child is a female and born into a tradition that denies women freedom to develop their talents to the full, then the problems multiply—for both parent and child. Clara Imogene Cheney may have had all these thoughts and feelings when she realized that her child was a musical prodigy. The realization came early.

Amy Marcy Cheney was born between noon and 1 P.M. on 5 September 1867 in West Henniker, New Hampshire, just nine months after her parents were married.[1] At that time the family included Amy; her father, Charles Abbott Cheney, age twenty-three; her mother, Clara Imogene (Marcy) Cheney, twenty-one; her widowed maternal grandmother, Amy Eliza Marcy, age forty-seven; and her paternal grandfather, Moses Cheney, forty-five.[2] Amy's maternal aunt, Emma Francis (Marcy) Clement, age twenty-five, who married six months before Amy was born, was a frequent visitor with her husband, Lyman Hinkley Clement, age twenty-seven, probably remaining for an extended period.[3]

The land on which their house at 102 Western Avenue still stands now lies fallow; however, in the late nineteenth century it was a working farm.[4] The farm did not, however, provide the family's main support. Across from their home runs the Contoocook River, and if you follow the river two miles to the west, you come to the former site of Moses and Charles Cheney's paper mill. Father and son were the third and fourth generations of Cheneys who milled paper.[5]

The two-story white clapboard house where the Cheney family lived may have lacked the second story at the time Amy was born. Even with the later addition of an entire floor this is a modest farm-house. There is no front porch. Rather, two or three steps lead from the outside directly into the front room, one of several small rooms and a kitchen. Upstairs are three or four small bedrooms. Behind and connected to the house are a workshop and barns.

The house, despite its modesty, contained a piano, a weighty emblem of middle-class status. But in the Cheney household it was more than a symbol. Amy's mother was a talented pianist and singer, and her grandmother Marcy was a high soprano who sang in the church choir as well as at home.[6] Thanks to these women, and to visits by Amy's Aunt Franc, there was constant music making at home.

Amy, a fair-haired child with large blue-violet eyes, was small for her age. She became a participant in music making even before she could speak: by the time she was one year old, she hummed forty tunes accurately and always in the key that she first heard them.[7] Her mother, aware of the remarkable talent this evinced, made a list of the tunes, which has not survived,[8] although three are named in Cheney's biography of her daughter: "Old Dog Tray," "Sweet Face in the Window," and Amy's favorite hymn, "The moon shines full at His command / And all the stars obey."[9]

Amy soon proved strong-willed and demanding, especially of music. The toddler insisted on a constant diet of songs, which at times had to be supplied in relays: as her mother's voice tired, her grandmother would take over, or there would be tears.[10] Any change from Amy's first hearing of the song would upset her; after she learned to speak, she would order them to " 'sing it clean.' "[11]

Not only did the one-year-old child control how music was sung but she also determined what was sung. When Amy's mother or maternal grandmother rocked her to sleep, "if we sang a song that she didn't want to hear," Mrs. Cheney wrote, "she would show such anger that we would gladly make a change."[12] Such willfulness poses a serious threat to parental authority.

The child's sensitivity was not only musical but global. From infancy, sounds that suggested a lack of control—loud laughter, for example—moved her to tears, even painful sobs. Indeed, when company came, "her lip would quiver at the first signs of mirth," and she had to be carried out of the room. Rain hitting the windows also moved her to tears, as if the sight of nature "crying" was threatening; she demanded that her mother wipe away nature's tears as she did her own.[13] Thunder was especially disturbing to Amy, a reaction that persisted throughout her life.

Her remarkable memory and accurate singing startled friends and neighbors as well as her family. In 1869, thousands of choristers in New England were practicing to take part in Patrick Gilmore's "Grandest Musical Demonstration that the world has ever witnessed," a giant National Peace Jubilee held in Boston to celebrate the end of the Civil War. The high point would be the triumphant entrance of President Grant to the singing of "See, the Conquering Hero Comes" by a chorus of ten thousand, accompanied by bands and orchestras and introduced by an artillery salute. The conductor was Boston's Carl Zerrahn, who would be an important person in Amy's early musical career.[14]

Among those practicing for the performance was the local photographer W. G. C. Kimball of Concord. As he prepared to take the two-year-old's picture, she suddenly burst out at the top of her voice with "See, the Conquering Hero Comes." Kimball, who was amazed at the clarity and accuracy of her rendition, said, "That is more wonderful than anything we shall see at the Jubilee."[15] The photo suggests that he caught her in the act of singing, for her mouth is open and her expression is one of fierce intensity. The pose would have required remarkable control on her part, since subjects at that time had to remain still for an entire minute.

Her concentration on music was extraordinary for so young a child: Clara Cheney's piano playing was the joy of Amy's life, and when her mother accompanied a local violinist, Amy would listen for hours without moving.[16] All these signs of a musical gift gave both equal portions of pleasure and concern, the latter prompting a strong reaction: from the moment Amy reached up to try to touch the piano keys, her mother made it clear that the piano was out of bounds for the toddler.

The child, who wanted nothing as much as she wanted to play the piano, did not accept the restriction placidly. Rather she begged, coaxed, and tried to climb on the piano stool or on her mother's lap at the piano. But nothing moved her mother to change. Amy could hear music, and nothing and no one could stop her from thinking music. She could order others to sing, sing herself to sleep, and find the apt song for any event, including the stray cat scratching at the window or the moon shining through it. But she could not touch the piano keys. Resourceful and determined yet accepting, the child found another outlet for her musicality: she sang original melodies to Mother Goose rhymes while playing an imaginary keyboard.

On occasion, even Clara Cheney was startled. Before Amy was two, when her mother rocked her to sleep, she exhibited a new skill, that of improvising "a perfectly correct alto to any soprano" that her mother might sing.[17] There is something threatening, even uncanny about the little child cradled in her arms taking charge of music making in this way. Clara Cheney, who identified this feat as a display of compositional ability, responded to it not by relenting the ban on piano playing but rather by reinforcing it, explaining that she was afraid that too early access would cause the child to tire of music. She followed what the popular essayist Gerald Stanley Lee called the "top bureau-drawer principle," of placing the desired object just out of reach. Children must learn discipline early, and the best way to teach it is to withhold whatever the child wants most.[18] Besides, Cheney did not want Amy to become a prodigy, with all that that implied, and was not about to allow behavior that would induce others to treat her daughter as one.[19]

Her decision seems both harsh and inflexible by present-day standards. Why, for example, did not her curiosity lead her to allow the child to experiment at the instrument, merely to find out what she could do? But no, Clara

Cheney held firm, animated perhaps by more profound motives than the ones she expressed.

Charles and Clara Cheney were determined that their daughter grow up as much as possible as a normal child.[20] Part of the standard education of middle-class girls was to teach them to be modest, not to take undue pride in their accomplishments, and certainly not to be boastful or arrogant. Amy soon learned that her prodigious talent was a gift of God, an idea that preserved her modesty while suggesting the magnitude of the gift.

Her parent's decision undoubtedly had deeper roots than even the issue of proper female modesty. If Clara Cheney needed other reasons for keeping her child from the piano, her religion may have provided them. Amy's parents both came from colonial stock. Charles Abbott Cheney (1844–1895) was the son of Freewill Baptists, a liberal sect that, unlike other Baptists, did not believe that infants were born depraved.[21] A genial and easygoing man, he seems to have had less direct influence on his daughter than his wife, especially during the many years when he traveled as a salesman of imported paper stock, beginning in 1870.

Clara Imogene Marcy (1845–1911) was a Congregationalist, that is, a Calvinist, although probably a moderate one.[22] Calvinists believed that children were born depraved, that to save their souls they must be taught piety early, and that earthly life was but a preparation for heaven. Horace Bushnell's influential book, *Christian Nurture*, appeared between 1847 and 1863, the years when Clara Cheney was growing up.[23] He was important as a reformer, rejecting the harsher aspects of Calvinist training, particularly that of breaking a child's will. Instead, he.recommended genial warmth and love, "a good life, the repose of faith, the confidence of righteous expectation [of salvation, and] the sacred and cheerful liberty of the spirit."[24] It is likely that Clara Cheney followed Bushnell's teachings.

But he also believed in discipline. Infants, Bushnell asserted, have "blind will," perhaps their strongest characteristic, and one that must be curbed. "Is this infant child to fill the universe with his complete and total self-assertion, owning no superior, or is he to learn the self-submission of allegiance, obedience, duty to God?"[25] It is easy to see how the mother of such a demanding child might worry that Amy would turn into a monster of self-assertion. How comforting then to know that someone of the Reverend Bushnell's authority had a cure for such willfulness: between the ages of ten months and three years, gently, lovingly train the child to submit to the parent's will,[26] advice Clara Cheney apparently followed. The recommended means was the consistent control of what the child wanted most—food, for example—or in Amy's case, the piano.

Indulgence of any kind corrupts, according to Bushnell. "A child can be pampered in feeding, so as to become, in a sense, all body; so that, when he comes into choice and responsible action, he is already a confirmed sensualist."[27] Similarly, with the powerful and sensual medium of music, the child must first learn to do without; later, limited experiences could be safely offered because the child has learned that even such a privilege may be taken away for cause. For the first four years of Amy's life, Clara Cheney taught her daughter submission by withholding the piano, and later by controlled relaxation of the ban: "I was to be as carefully kept from music as later I would be helped to it."[28]

Clara Cheney's second response to these feats was a long-term decision that Amy "was to be a musician, not a prodigy."[29] Since the child already was a prodigy, it could only mean that she would not be allowed to act nor, indeed, to live like one. Gender considerations also entered in. Because she was female, she must learn early that her adult life would be centered on home, husband, and children, not music. Careers for women outside the home were hardly the accepted practice in the years immediately following the Civil War. With few exceptions, a professional artist-musician class, in which the performing traditions were handed down from parent to child, did not yet exist in the United States.[30] Middle- and upper-class women gifted in music were turned from any thought of such a life plan because of the stigma attached to those who appeared as performers on the public stage. The attendant social degradation was not something that a middle-class family like the Cheneys desired for a daughter. A musical girl could perform as a private person; but child prodigies were often the victims of exploitation and notoriety. For the next sixteen years, this decision of Clara's (and probably Charles's as well) circumscribed Amy's musical life.

In 1869, the year that Amy turned two, the paper mill burned down. Thereafter, her grandfather devoted himself to farming; the following year, her father found a position with a Boston firm as a paper stock salesman.[31] His wife and child soon followed him, moving in 1871 to Chelsea, a suburb of Boston. Thereafter, they may have moved with some frequency, but their earliest known address was 36 Marlborough Street, probably rented quarters.[32]

At age four, Amy finally got to the keyboard. This happened despite her mother and through the intervention of Aunt Franc, who was visiting from her new home in San Francisco. Beach described the signal event, her first vivid memory of her beloved aunt:

> At last, I was allowed to touch the piano. My mother was still opposed, but I can remember my aunt coming to the house, and putting me at the piano. I played at once the melodies I had been collecting, playing in my head, adding full harmonies to the simple, treble melodies. Then my aunt played a new air for me, and I reached up and picked out a harmonized bass accompaniment, as I had heard my mother do.[33]

The very first piece she played on that occasion was a Strauss waltz that she had learned by hearing her mother play it. "The difficulty for me was the tiny size of my hands which made it necessary to omit octaves and big chords, but I seemed to have an uncanny sense of knowing just which notes to leave out, so that the result sounded well."[34] But there were times when the frustration of not being able to recreate the sounds she heard in her head made her fly into a rage. Her mother described her reactions: "Tears of grief and anger, screams of mingled sorrow and wrath would issue from the child's throat . . . but this would soon pass away as she yielded to the soothing influence of the music."

Otherwise, from that day on she played whatever she heard from others or whatever music she imagined in her head.[35]

In all but very large houses, the person at the piano keyboard controls the aural space. There is no escaping the sound. Suddenly, the piano belonged to Amy as much as to her mother. Clara Cheney responded to this stunning demonstration by limiting the time her daughter could spend at the piano, thus still maintaining control over music in her home. Moreover, Clara Cheney withheld music as punishment, the way other parents might withhold food or treats. If Amy Cheney misbehaved, her mother refused her access to the instrument.[36] Or, since "music in the minor keys made her sad and disconsolate," Clara Cheney would play something in the minor mode as punishment.[37] "When the little fingers were getting into mischief, this always had the desired effect. No other punishment was needed than the playing of Gottschalk's *Last Hope* [*méditation religieuse*]," op. 16 (ex. 1.1). Indeed, Clara Cheney had only to play what she termed the "theme" of *Last Hope* — probably the highly chromatic and dissonant passage in the introduction — and "the little hands would drop whatever had been grasped and tears would immediately flow."[38] Here was a child of great aural sensitivity, whose very gift was turned into her greatest vulnerability.

Amy's intellectual development kept pace with her musical growth, for at three she taught herself to read. Her first and favorite book, *A Child's Dream of a Star*, by Charles Dickens, was undoubtedly read many times.[39] The book deals with death and the child's journey along the shining path to a star, that is, to heaven. The first to die in a family of four was the youngest, a little girl. Morbid, yes, but not when considered from the point of view of mid-nineteenth-century Protestant belief. A mother's duty was to teach her young children not only that God "look[s] upon sin . . . with abhorrence," but also promises salvation to the righteous. Mothers were told to "excite the gratitude of the child by speaking of the joys of heaven . . . There is enough in the promised joys of heaven to rouse a child's most animated feelings."[40] This was the message the Dickens tale delivered with clarity. There is no way of knowing whether Amy identified with the little girl who died or whether her joy in the hope of heaven outweighed any terror at the threat of damnation. Both parts of the lesson had to be learned, and their imagery would reverberate throughout Beach's life and music.

She attended Sunday School at the Central Congregationalist Church in Chelsea and fell in love with her teacher — the only teacher other than her mother that she would have during the next few years.[41] At age five she took to reading the Scriptures aloud, which she did with the clarity and emphasis of an adult. Her remarkable memory was not only for music, for she was able to recite extended and difficult poems in Sunday School or at church meetings.[42]

Amy was still four when she composed her first piano pieces while spending the summer with her grandfather in West Henniker.[43] "[W]hen I reached home I told my mother that I had 'made' three waltzes. She did not believe it at first, as there was no piano within miles of the farm. I explained that I had written them in my head, and proved it by playing them on her piano."[44] Clara

EXAMPLE 1.1 Louis Moreau Gottschalk, *The Last Hope, méditation religieuse,* op. 16 (1854).

Cheney's reaction to this new achievement was to restrain displays of her own enthusiasm as well as that of others. As friends and relatives soon learned about Amy's precocious abilities at the piano and in composition, her mother went to great lengths to keep Amy's accomplishments from turning her daughter's head. She made no fuss over these waltzes, nor would she allow others to do so in the child's presence.[45]

Amy named one piece "Snowflake Waltz," because she made it up during the hot days of summer; "Marlboro Waltz" was named after the street in Chelsea where she lived; there were eventually two more, "Golden Robin Waltz" and "Mamma's Waltz." This last survives in a copy probably written out by her mother; it is a lengthy piece that shows a remarkable sense of form and key structure, and includes some sophisticated harmonies (see chapter 4). All four pieces were composed in her head and away from the piano, a practice she continued throughout her life.[46]

Evidence that the child had perfect pitch surfaced early, although her parents did not recognize it until later. She would ask for music by its color: "Play the pink or blue music," she would demand. Her mother erroneously thought the child was referring to the colors on the cover page, but eventually she discovered that Amy was referring to the key of each piece. Her color associations for the major modes were C, white; E, yellow; G, red; A, green; A♭, blue; D♭, violet; E♭, pink. She named only two minor keys, F♯ and G♯, both black.[47] While the list is incomplete—she identified only nine correspondences out of a possible twenty-four—the colors strongly suggest mood and will later help to explain some of Amy Beach's compositional practices.

By age five, Amy had an "allotted time each day for practice," limited by her mother.[48] She taught herself to play various pieces by ear, including chorales from Mendelssohn's oratorio St. Paul.[49] She also insisted on knowing what musical notation meant, and her mother told her only enough so that she soon figured out the entire system and could sight-read. One of the pieces she learned was the "Spirit Waltz" (wrongly attributed to Beethoven), which she played during a visit with the children of friends.[50] On her return, she told her mother that she was distressed to discover that the piano was a half tone lower than her mother's. In compensation, Amy had transposed the piece. "It sounded all wrong," she said, "I had to change it to a half tone higher to bring it right."[51] Her memory of a musical work was so indelibly wedded to its key that it was only acceptable when heard in the original key.

Later that year, parents and child found themselves once more at crosspurposes. Her father mentioned to her mother that the famous soprano and opera impresario Clara Louise Kellogg could identify any pitch she heard. When Amy piped up, "'Oh that's nothing. Anybody can do that. I can do that,'" her father reprimanded her for being "'pert,'" aiming to teach her both manners and humility. As the conversation continued and Amy was again scolded for interrupting, her mother recalled the incident with the "Spirit Waltz." At that point they decided to take the child seriously, tested her, and learned that she, too, had absolute pitch.[52]

Of her parents' discovery, Amy Beach wrote that "It helped [my mother] to patience later, when her child appeared only pert."[53] *Patience?* One needs patience to educate a slow child. But here was a child who soaked up everything around her, whose musical feats, on top of intellectual gifts, kept family and friends amazed. But patience and consistency are needed also to train a child to accept the values parents espouse and the limits they impose. For her part, Amy soon learned to cloak her self-assurance and pride in her achievements in a modest mien.

Such modesty was particularly important for a girl to learn. According to nineteenth-century practice, during a child's first few years, issues of gender socialization were not a concern because all children were treated like girls. Both sexes wore long dresses that limited gross motor movement and were taught to be pliant and submissive. By the age of five or six, however, differential treatment of boys and girls began when, during a ceremonial rite of passage, boys were "breeched," or put into trousers.[54] For boys, the freedom and autonomy that were withheld since birth—like access to the piano—were now offered in a limited and controlled manner along with their first masculine clothing. For girls, however, there was no ceremonial equivalent of breeching. Even limited freedom was withheld: their clothing continued to restrict their movements, they remained confined at home, were often given less food than their brothers in order to remain "slender and delicate," were expected to avoid vigorous physical activity advocated for boys, and were educated in domestic skills whether or not they also studied academic subjects.[55] Most important, they were expected to remain pious, self-abnegating, humble, and modest.

Up to the age of five or six, girls and boys also were expected to have no wills of their own. Thereafter, although boys were still under parental discipline, in practice they had greater latitude. Boys were not taught the same kind of submissiveness as girls; the "stronger wills of male children would in the end make them more manly men . . . [with] a taste for ruling which is the germ of their future character."[56] Amy Cheney, a passionate and strong-willed child, demanded the more flexible treatment granted to boys. However, her very striving against limits may well have driven Clara Cheney to greater efforts to conform the child to standards for girls.

Yet Clara Cheney was far from being entirely repressive. As we have seen, during the earliest years she was often solicitous of her daughter's feelings and intense reactions, trying to shield her from emotional trauma. She also did not wish to overburden the child with information and instruction before she believed Amy was ready to receive it. Although she tried to keep Amy's talents more or less hidden, privately—in a biographical sketch of her daughter—she revealed immense pride in her daughter's achievements while omitting any mention of their battles of wills.[57]

When Amy was six, Clara Cheney finally agreed to teach her piano. She had three lessons a week and could only practice during the time her mother allotted to her. Beach later commented that "the piano was still, theoretically, in the top bureau drawer."[58] At the same time, her mother began her daughter's general education, tutoring her at home rather than sending her to a school. Perhaps this was an economy measure or sprang from a prevalent nineteenth-century belief that organized school activities were too regimented for "delicate and sensitive" girls,[59] which frequently led mothers to tutor their daughters at home. An additional benefit of home tutoring was that the mother continued to have total control of her child's experience, including that of shielding her from people who might make a fuss over her talents. From the child's point of view, however, this was a claustrophobic way of living that deprived her of companions of her own age. Later, Beach displayed a marked talent for friendship and pleasure in social contact, as if to make up for this unfulfilled early need.

Her progress in music was swift. Within a year after beginning lessons, she had mastered the Boston Conservatory Method, which, although advertised "for beginners," required—especially in its closing pages—considerable technical facility and grasp of theory and harmony.[60] Her mother proudly listed other pieces Amy was playing then, including works by Handel, Mozart, Mendelssohn, Chopin, and Beethoven.

When she was seven, Amy played her first pieces by Bach; she especially liked the fugues. Beethoven, however, was her favorite, and she only interrupted the playing of his works when she was forced to leave the piano. Her hand size was still a problem, and occasionally—to her extreme and loudly voiced distress—she had to omit the lowest notes. With that exception, everything was played accurately and with feeling.

By now, Amy Cheney was ready and eager "to give serious recital programs."[61] When the opportunity arose, it was her mother who bent once again, although Beach thought "the consent was unwilling."[62] As with Amy's first session at the piano, outside intervention plus the child's intense campaign to perform may have caused Clara's change of heart. Nevertheless, Clara Cheney simply stated that she gave her permission.

At one recital, a benefit for the Unitarian Church, the performers waited their turn in the library, where Amy, who was to play a Chopin waltz and one of her own waltzes as encore, immediately became engrossed in a book. Her mother reported:

> When her number on the programme came and I went to take her to the conductor of the concert, she spoke very impatiently[:] "Wait, please[,] until I have finished my chapter." She put the book down very reluctantly with the command that "no one should lose her place." She didn't approve of the encore as it kept her from the book.[63]

Yet it was Amy who had insisted on performing. Headstrong, impetuous, imperious—those characteristics in the child arouse the reader's sympathy for Clara Cheney.

At a musicale in a private home in Boston, Amy repeated the Chopin waltz and also played Beethoven's easy sonata, op. 49, no. 1, and one of her own waltzes.[64] That event resulted in what was probably her first review: *The Folio,* a journal of the arts, reported that she "played with an accuracy and style which surprised every listener. . .the young pianist is exciting much surprise by the precocity of her musical talent."[65]

As a consequence of this recital, two or more concert managers, attracted by the combination of precocious talent and extreme youth, offered contracts. Indeed, Beach noted that she looked even younger than her seven years because she was "small for her age, fair, and slight." She wrote, "it would have been merely play to enter upon the career of a travelling pianist, but my father and mother both agreed it would have been the worst possible thing for me mentally and physically."[66]

Clara Cheney then announced that there were to be no more recitals—even at private or Sunday school events—and that in raising Amy, "due regard must be paid to a judicious expenditure of health and energy."[67] Unquestionably, a recital tour would be a strain on a young child; indeed, it often is on adults. The outcome of that little recital, a press notice and offers from concert managers, was what Clara Cheney had hoped to avoid, along with the "corrupting" power of such a heady experience, one that would lead the child to dream of a concert career. Nevertheless, years later Beach agreed with her parents' decision: "I shall always have the deepest gratitude for my inexperienced young parents that they did not allow me to be exploited by managers."[68]

In early fall of 1875, they moved even closer to the hub when they settled in Roxbury at 63 Clifford Street.[69] Now they were a short trolley ride from Beacon Hill, the center of upper-class Boston, where Unitarians and Transcendentalists rejected harsh Calvinist practices and where women's public activism as abolitionists and feminists suggested new ways of raising children, especially girls.[70] Even though public performance would remain just out of reach, Amy Cheney's world would expand in new and exciting ways.

$$2$$

THE CHENEYS

AND

THE MARCYS

THE APPEARANCE OF A PRODIGY may send the family on a search for its roots, for the source of their child's gift. Perhaps the search is done to show that this special talent did not spring from ordinary clay, thus reducing the asymmetry between subject and parents; or it may lend verisimilitude to what essentially is a latter-day reconstruction, a family romance.

Something of both impulses may have been at work in Clara Cheney's genealogical investigations reported in a letter to a cousin and summed up as follows: "So many people have asked me if Amy is not of foreign parentage [because of her musical gifts], I reply if being one of the tenth generation of the Dearborns, the eighth generation of the Marcys and no-end-of generations of Cheneys in New England doesn't make her an American, I do not know what will."[1] The statement reflects the dominance of European music and performers in America's art music and Americans' cultural insecurity vis-à-vis Europeans. But even more, there was the widespread notion that real musicians came from Europe and that real Americans, that is, those with Anglo-Saxon ancestors who settled here in colonial times, could not be real musicians. But Amy Beach defied the stereotype: she was both a fine musician and, by her mother's definition, one hundred percent American.

Biographies of Amy Beach cite three early eminences in her extended family. The first is on the Cheney side: General Henry Dearborn (1751–1829), related through Beach's paternal grandmother, Rebecca Dearborn (Rundlett) Cheney. A hero of the Revolutionary War who was at the Battle of Bunker Hill and Valley Forge under Washington, Dearborn also served as a representative in Congress and Thomas Jefferson's secretary of war.

The other two luminaries were on the Marcy side. William Larned Marcy (1786–1857) was a United States senator who resigned from the Senate on his election to the governorship of New York, in which office he served for three successive terms. Later he was secretary of war under President Polk and secretary of state under President Pierce. The second notable Marcy was Charlotte Cushman (1816–1876), of Boston, an actress who made her debut in New Orleans in 1836 as Lady Macbeth. She became one of the great tragediennes and a favorite on the English stage, performing for Queen Victoria in

1848. She retired from the stage in 1852 and finally returned to Boston in 1870, where she became a member of Annie Adams Fields's literary salon.[2]

But the direct line of Cheneys and Marcys that ended with Amy consisted of hardworking New Englanders of more modest callings. The first Cheney in the colonies was John, a Puritan who came from England in 1635 and settled in Newbury, Massachusetts.[3] He and his wife were progenitors of a line of farmers and grist, corn, and paper millers that reached to Amy Marcy Cheney's father Charles.

Amy's great-grandfather Moses Cheney began as an apprentice in the family paper mill, progressed to journeyman after marrying in 1816, and took over the mill in 1822. An original member and deacon of the Freewill Baptists,[4] the liberal wing of a sect that abhorred slavery, he made his home a station on the underground railroad, sheltering Frederic Douglass, among other escaped slaves. He acted on principle and despite the stiff fine of $1,000 that the federal government imposed for such activities.[5]

He and Abigail Morrison Cheney had three sons, two of whom were illustrious. Oren Burbank Cheney (1816–1903) became a Freewill Baptist minister and was the founding president of the Maine State Seminary in Lewiston, Maine, where Charles Cheney was a student. The Reverend Cheney remained president after it was renamed Bates College, "the first . . . in New England to give equal advantages to men and women."[6] The second son, Person Colby Cheney (1828–1901), first joined his father at the paper mill but then went into his own paper business, fought in the Civil War, and was elected governor of New Hampshire in 1875; in 1892 he served in the administration of President Benjamin Harrison.[7]

The third son was Amy's grandfather, Moses Cheney, Jr. (1822–1889). He remained a farmer and paper manufacturer, beginning in Ashland in his father's mill. In 1843, he married Rebecca Rundlett of Stratham, New Hampshire.[8] Moses purchased water rights and property on the Contoocook River in Henniker in 1863, built a paper mill, and moved there the following year.[9] In 1869, there was a startling development for that era that partially explains Charles and Clara Cheney's subsequent move to Chelsea. On 1 June, Moses sued Rebecca for and was granted a divorce on the grounds of abandonment.[10] Two years later, on 26 October 1871, he married Martha Smith, a native of Henniker, probably about the time when Amy and her parents relocated.[11]

The assertions about Charles Abbott Cheney (1844–1895), Moses and Rebecca Rundlett Cheney's only surviving child, made in family genealogies and published biographies of his daughter are somewhat overblown.[12] The *Cheney Genealogy* states that Charles Cheney "was educated at Phillips Exeter Academy and Bates College."[13] Charles's school records suggest that this was part truth, part exaggeration, and part suppression of the facts.

Charles did attend Phillips Exeter for three semesters, walking eight miles a day back and forth to school. However, he did not take a full course. Rather he studied only Latin, which he passed the first two semesters but failed the third.[14] That might explain why "his fondest recollections of the Academy were the great pleasure of playing baseball at the noon hour."[15] From there he entered not Bates College but its predecessor, the Maine State Seminary.[16] He was fourteen, not sixteen as claimed, when he enrolled in 1858, perhaps in the Preparatory Department, which was "open to students of any age or rank of scholarship," rather than in the Seminary proper. In order to qualify for admission to the seminary, students had to be "well versed in Geography, Arithmetic, English Grammar, History of the United States, and Latin Grammar." Although Charles Cheney is listed among the seminary students,[17] his weak academic record suggests that special treatment was accorded to the nephew of the president of the seminary.[18] Charles attended the seminary for two years, not the four required for a degree. He then joined his father at the paper mill and probably helped run the farm in West Henniker as well. However, according to his daughter, he was gifted in mathematics and in languages—although obviously not in Latin—and retained his scholarly interests in later years.[19]

After the mill burned down on 8 February 1869,[20] Charles Cheney found employment as a traveling salesman of paper stock with successive Boston firms; he eventually went into business for himself in 1887, selling imported paper stock on the road.[21] He undoubtedly was a man of some charm and warmth. The word used to describe him is "genial," and he had many friends among his business colleagues. As a salesman, however, Charles was modestly successful, as he acquired over his career only a small amount of money and never owned property.

There is little that can be gleaned regarding his relationship to his daughter. The incident that established Amy as having perfect pitch suggests that Charles and Clara Cheney agreed on the matter of discipline. Yet he may have appeared less strict to his daughter, merely because most of the training devolved on his wife. There may have been a special bond between father and daughter: they certainly looked alike—the same wide face, large eyes, ample mouth, and broad nose.

The Marcys had deep colonial roots, although not quite so deep as the Cheneys: John Marcy emigrated to the colonies some time before 1685. Son of the high sheriff of Limerick, Ireland, and thus probably Anglo-Irish, he married Sarah Hadlock of Roxbury, where he settled.[22] Amy's direct ancestors on the Marcy side, like those on the Cheney side, were hardworking people—farmers, lumber dealers, and homemakers. Later, in Hillsborough, New Hampshire, the family prospered as millers of cotton products and wood, and manufacturers of bricks. Amy's grandfather, Chester Marcy (1818–1849), worked in the family's cotton mill, and married Amy (Ann?) Eliza Waterman (1820–1895) in 1842.[23] Seven years later gold fever lured him to California, but he never had a chance to pan gold. Heading west on the Overland Trail, he stopped at Missouri's Fort Independence, where an epidemic of cholera had broken out. He stayed to nurse the ill and died there of cholera on 9 May 1849.[24] At the time of his death, he left a wife and two daughters, Emma, age seven, and Clara, age three. Beach inherited his clarinet; she reported that he "was a good performer and a great admirer of the instrument."[25]

As Hillsborough and Henniker are neighboring villages, it is not surprising that Charles Cheney and Clara Marcy knew one another, although there is no information about their courtship. The two were married at the Congregational church in Hillsborough on 2 January 1867 and afterward lived with Charles's father in the farmhouse on Western Avenue in West Henniker.[26]

Colonel Leander Cogswell, who had served in the Union army, gave Henniker's Independence Day address in 1876. He reported on how the town, with a population of about 1200, had changed in the years since its establishment in 1768, especially emphasizing the growth of manufacturing. Its products—shoes, boxes, woodenware, and lumber—went by rail to Concord and south through Manchester to Boston. The Cheneys' mill, Cogswell bragged, turned out "some of the very best paper . . . in all New England."[27]

Cogswell rhapsodically recounted the progress of the entire nation three years after the end of the Civil War, a nation where among many other triumphs "the arts and the sciences [have been] carried to a state of perfection."[28] In Henniker, there was a musical life both outside and within the home. Early in the century, singing schools, in which instrumental as well as vocal music was taught, were common. Choirs flourished, singing at public celebrations as well as in church. But "the violin, the bass-viol, the trombone, the clarinet and the flute" that enhanced church services in the 1820s were by the 1860s replaced by the organ to the regret of some:

> But songs and songsters now are dead;
> Those Sabbath days have long since fled.
> The strings are broken, mute the tongue,
> That then God's praises sweetly sung.[29]

Instrumental music was heard elsewhere, however. Henniker's brass band became famous, if only locally. One organized in 1857 was in demand not only in Henniker but in neighboring towns as well, playing "at promenade concerts, celebrations, funerals" and accompanying sleighing parties.[30] Eventually, the band had few rivals in the state, said Cogswell, who spoke in the same vein about Henniker's smaller string band.[31]

Nearby Concord offered more music, including the Lyceum concerts, at which local and visiting talent combined to produce programs of piano and vocal solos and duets.[32] One of the best known Concord musicians was Clara Marcy's teacher, John Holmes Morey (1834–1895), pianist, organist, bachelor, bon vivant, and factotum of music, who came to dominate musical life in Concord. In 1864, together with two other men, he inaugurated the first of twenty-two annual Concord State festivals.[33] A reporter congratulated Morey for the festival's eminent success, a result of two years of "self-sacrificing efforts to assemble the musical talent of New Hampshire in a convention which should do honor to the state."[34] Clara Marcy and her sister probably took part as choristers.

A trip to Manchester by rail or buggy offered even more variety. Musical events in 1865 included concerts by the Peak Family Swiss Bell Ringers, Cotton and Murphy's California Minstrels Brass Band and Burlesque Opera Troupe, "The Original and Only Raymor's Christy Minstrels and Brass Band composed of 20 first class artistes," and the Manchester Cornet Band. In addition, there was a rehearsal of the Beethoven Musical Association and a notice that I. F. Whitney would conduct a singing school in Manchester using *The Harp of Judah* as text, for a fee of $1.25 for twenty lessons.[35]

In 1866, L. S. Whitney, "a public school music teacher of Manchester, initiated the first music festival in the city," for which he secured the services of several Boston musicians including Carl Zerrahn, eminent conductor of the Boston Handel and Haydn Society.[36] The May Festival held that year in Manchester attracted choruses from all over the state as well as the usual celebrities from Boston. The *Daily Union* noted that the program for the evening of 3 May offered the "Overture" to Boieldieu's opera *The Caliph of Bagdad*, vocal solos by Boston and local singers, a set of variations on a Swiss Air for clarinet and orchestra, and two choral excerpts—"Achieved is the Glorious Work," from Haydn's *Creation*, and the "Hallelujah" chorus, from Handel's *Messiah*. A reporter lamented that while the women choristers managed to make the trip to Manchester—Clara and Franc Marcy may have been among them—few men attended, which "rather detracts from the grandeur" of the effect.[37] Undoubtedly, spring planting had taken its toll on the event.

Music in the home flourished as well. Back in Henniker, Cogswell boasted of the instruments found in well-appointed homes in that town, probably grander than the Cheneys':

> The dwellings . . . are, most of them, large and spacious, painted, and with blinds, surrounded by capacious barns and out-houses, the whole circled with neat and tasty fences. Inside of your dwellings you have carpets upon your floors, pictures upon your walls, sofas and lounges in your parlors and your sitting-rooms, and instead of the music of "the loom, the wheel [and] the distaff" you have that of the sewing machine, the piano, and the organ.[38]

The *Concord Monitor* of 25 November 1865, in a column on the "Influence of Pleasures in the Home," stated that a farmer might make

> a good investment in a piano, a melodeon, or some other instrument, to accompany the voice of his wife and children, provided always that practice on these instruments be not allowed to interfere with the practice at the kneading trough, the wash-board, or any other duty that a true woman, be she daughter, sister, wife, or mother, ought to understand.

As in thousands of other homes in the United States, in the parlors of Henniker the piano was the center of amateur music making, and girls and young women learned to play that instrument so that they might enhance their status on the marriage market. Some, of course, were genuinely talented, and by the testimony of her daughter, Clara was among that group.

Music was important to the Marcy family.[39] "Franc" Marcy, Clara's older sister, a contralto, sang at the local Universalist church and also taught voice, piano, and painting in water colors—all favored accomplishments for young and unmarried women.[40] Clara Marcy began teaching music before her marriage and continued for a year or so thereafter.

Although the suggestion in Beach biographies that Clara Cheney had a career as a performer of some local fame remains undocumented, she was an active amateur pianist.[41] She wrote, "When I was playing over new music I have known [Amy] to drop her play outdoors and run into the room where I was at the piano and ask, 'What new piece is that, you are playing in such a key?' naming the key correctly." On occasion she brought her daughter with her when she played chamber music: "One evening at the house of a friend where there was to be instrumental music, the 1st violinist and the others tuned their instruments by her singing to them the tuning pitch A. As he said, *she* would give them the *correct pitch*."[42] Other than that, very little is known of Clara Cheney's life outside of her relationship to her daughter.

Music helped forge a powerful bond between them. After Amy began playing the piano, however, the relationship of mother and daughter may have taken on competitive aspects, as each claimed time when she would be in charge of the aural space. When Amy was six and her mother assumed responsiblity for her daughter's musical and general education, Clara Cheney would have had less and less time for her own music making. It is not known whether the pleasure in watching her child's rapid development was sufficiently gratifying to the teacher to make up for her own loss.[43]

Photographs of Clara Marcy taken in Concord, New Hampshire, before her marriage show an unsmiling and stern woman of some intensity, with chiseled features and a rather narrow face. Her dress appears plain, with a simple stand-up collar.[44] The look accords with her severity, strength of character, and consistent discipline of her daughter.[45] Of the Marcy sisters, Clara was the stay-at-home; and after her marriage, she took her mother into her home, thus incorporating into the household an earlier and possibly even stricter approach to child rearing.

Clara's older sister, Emma Frances ("Franc") left home before marriage to live in Boston, where she taught music.[46] While there, she met Lyman Hinckley Clement (1840–1922), the son of a minister and sometime lumber dealer and conductor on the Massachusetts railroad.[47] Within two years after they had married in 1867, the couple put a continent between themselves and Henniker, settling for a half century in San Francisco. After they were established in San Francisco, Lyman became increasingly successful. He first had the lowly job of a drayman, a driver of a horse and wagon. Soon, however, he was teaching bookkeeping and mathematics in a business school; he became a bookkeeper himself, then a bank teller, and, at the height of his career, the chief clerk of the United States Mint.[48] An indication that the couple had a more luxurious lifestyle than the Cheneys was their ownership of a sailboat, called—out of affection for Franc's sister—"The Clara." The family was probably more than comfortable, indulging in occasional luxuries in addition to the boat.

Franc Clement was a young woman with strikingly large dark eyes, exuding a warmth that must have made her an especially attractive vocalist. Of the two sisters, it was Franc, not Clara, who gained a reputation as a singer. Franc was selected by San Franciscans to represent them at Boston's Peace Jubilee of 1872, at which she sang in the so-called Bouquet of Artists, a *chor favori*. Such a role did not confer solo status on Franc but nevertheless was a distinction setting her apart from those in the massed choirs of some twenty thousand voices, an honor not accorded her sister.[49] Franc continued to teach music and give recitals, despite having a child.

Indeed, becoming a mother did not clip Franc's wings. Her only child, Ethel, who was born in 1874, displayed a talent for art; and in the 1890s, Franc— leaving her husband at home—took her to study in New York, Boston, and twice to Paris. Thus Aunt Franc's masculine sounding nickname matched a considerably more adventurous and independent, perhaps even rebellious, life. Such distribution of the roles between sisters may have been usual, as noted by Marianne Hirsch: "One sister leads the more conventional life so that the other may be free to break away from it."[50]

Despite their differences and the distance between the two families, there obviously was affection between them. Travel between coasts was made easier by the direct rail link from Boston to San Francisco established in 1869 by the Central and Union Pacific Railroads.[51] It was during one of Franc's visits to the Cheneys that she placed Amy for the first time at the piano, with results already noted.

In 1875, the Cheney family moved to Boston, where Amy's musical world opened up in ways that neither Henniker nor Chelsea could ever offer. Boston, considered by its civic leaders the Athens of America, boasted a rich cultural life and one of the finest musical communities in the country. Indeed, with the move from Chelsea to Roxbury, a musical feast was in store for Amy Cheney.

3

A PRODIGY

DESPITE

HER MOTHER

IT WAS EXCITING TO BE IN BOSTON, a city whose leaders were devoted to the arts and to the city itself as a work of art. Boston used the years following the Great Fire of 1872 not merely to rebuild but to improve, to enhance, to make crooked streets straight, plan for broad avenues and parks, and to decorate with fanciful terra-cotta carvings, ornamental ironwork, and Victorian elaborations in wood. The enormous work of transforming the mud flats of Back Bay into elegant streets of town houses was on its way. The hub, the "modern Athens," grew more handsome than ever, dominated by a State House with a dome now covered in gold leaf. Of course, no further away than the far side of Beacon Hill was an Irish slum, from whence came many of the day laborers who carried out the plans to beautify the city and the domestics who toiled in Beacon Hill and Back Bay mansions.

The year 1875 was important for Boston's musical community. John Knowles Paine (1839–1906) was appointed Harvard's first professor of music; Arthur Foote (1853–1937) earned a master's degree in music at Harvard, one of the earliest awarded by an American university; and George Whitefield Chadwick (1854–1931) defied his father by giving up his job in the insurance business to go into music, accepting a position to teach music at Olivet College in Michigan.[1] The year brought important developments for Amy Cheney as well.

The new Cheney home at 63 Clifford Street in middle-class Roxbury was close to the flourishing centers of musical life in Boston and Cambridge. The previous year, Clara Cheney had joined the soprano section of the Handel and Haydn Society Chorus, which practiced in the Lowell Institute on Boylston Street, now only a brief trolley ride from home.[2]

As helpful as the move was to Clara Cheney, it was even more so for her daughter. Soon Amy would be embraced by Boston but in ways that her mother could not have predicted. The first step toward recognition of the child's musical endowments grew out of a search for a new piano teacher. Clara Cheney had decided that her daughter, who had just turned eight, had outgrown her tutelage on the piano. In the course of their search for a new teacher, the child played for some of Boston's leading German-trained musicians. They were so impressed that they recommended study in Europe for Amy, confident that despite her extreme youth, any first-rate German conservatory would accept her on the spot.[3] Their appraisal was both a recognition of the child's outstanding talent and a compliment to her mother's training. The auditions also had an important if unintended side effect: they created a circle of Bostonians who were excited by Amy's promise and would monitor her progress for the next eight years until her debut.

Despite "the devoted sympathy" Amy attributed to her parents, they did not support her ambitions for a career—and certainly not European study, a crucial pathway to such a career.[4] Being in the company of musical peers who planned to be professionals was the very experience a gifted girl needed in order to imagine a public life for herself.[5] But a young child usually was taken to Europe by her mother, thus separating husband and wife, often for years at a time. Maud Powell, born the same year as Amy Cheney, later became America's first native-born concert violinist. Her mother chaperoned her from the time she entered Leipzig Conservatory at age fourteen through her debut and then on international tours until she was over thirty. Powell's illustrious career was won at the cost of a major disruption of family life, all but destroying her parent's marriage.[6]

At the time of Amy's audition, had she gone to study abroad, she would have been six years younger than Maud Powell was when she left for Europe. Predictably, Amy's parents "wisely decided to keep her at home for her general education, with such musical instruction as could be combined with it."[7] While there was some mention of study in Europe, the Cheney's decision to postpone that plan to the distant future may have been made with consideration of the probable strain on family life and the family's limited financial means. Yet even when Amy Cheney entered her teens, her parents still opposed European study for their daughter.

Their attitude regarding her need for a general education is a linguistic sleight-of-hand, since her education to that time had consisted of her mother's tutelage, something Clara Cheney could have continued in Europe. On the other hand, Amy would soon have but two years of formal schooling, hardly enough to satisfy their expressed concern. This was despite the educational opportunities Boston offered girls.[8]

These decisions may also have been a means of keeping the lid on their daughter's musical ambitions out of concern for her health, at the very least. Looking forward to her 'teens, they determined to pay "due regard . . . to a judicious expenditure of health and energy." This statement resonates with late-nineteenth century concern about the health of girls. Physicians warned that females were delicate and prone to disease, especially beginning at puberty.[9] To nineteenth-century eyes, talent and intellectual interests in a girl were cause for alarm; no exertions should be allowed to divert essential energy from a female's most important physical function—one that could easily destabilize her entire life—that of sexual maturation.[10] If that were true for normal girls, what then were the risks for a gifted child who, moreover, was intensely emotional?

Thus for the foreseeable future, Amy Cheney was to remain at home in Boston and study with local piano teachers. This accords with accepted practices for a middle-class girl, whereby limited musical training might enhance her chances for an advantageous marriage and afterward for "expanding in her offspring that love for the divine art which is more or less inherent in every human being."[11] Viewed from this perspective, the child's drive toward a professional life may have been read by her mother as a rejection, a "repudiation of the domestic role [the mother] . . . had so faithfully followed."[12]

The choice of German-trained Ernst Perabo, one of Boston's finest pianists and teachers, was far from a compromise solution, however, for he furthered Amy's growth as a pianist and artist.[13] Her work with her new teacher began in 1876 and continued until 1882. Perabo, who taught both privately and at the New England Conservatory, was highly regarded; over the years he had a thousand students. He believed that "the development of the mind requires slow growth, assisted by the warm sun of affection, and guided by conservative teachers with honest and ideal conceptions who understand how to so load its precious cargo, that it may not shift during life's tempestuous vicissitudes."[14] If he radiated that "warm sun of affection" while imposing high standards of work, he must have been a fine teacher for Amy Cheney and she, in turn, a source of enormous satisfaction for him.

Perabo paid several of his pupils the compliment of dedicating piano pieces to them. On 24 November 1882, he played a program in Chickering's Rooms in Boston that included a short piece he wrote "for a talented little girl." Recalling Beethoven's *Für Elise*, he gave it the title, "For Amy: A Musical Sketch."[15] Boston's cultural elite—especially Perabo's patrons and friends John Sullivan Dwight and Henry Wadsworth Longfellow—did not need to be told who "Amy" was.

Despite the excitement and stimulus of a new teacher, Amy Cheney still spent most of her time at home with her mother.[16] Clara continued to teach her general subjects and probably supervised her four hours of piano practice. Amy studied with Perabo privately and thus missed the social and musical companionship of other students. This was a lonely life for a girl of eight, relieved only by her mother's decision in 1875 to allow her to attend concerts at night.

During Amy's first year of concert going, Boston offered her a musical feast. On Christmas Eve of 1875, at the Music Hall, Clara Cheney sang with the chorus of the Handel and Haydn Society in their sixty-fifth performance of *Messiah*. The soprano soloist was the great prima donna Teresa Tietjens. That season they also gave the performances of Handel's *Joshua*—its premiere in the United States—Mendelssohn's *Elijah* and *Hymn of Praise*, Haydn's *Creation*, Rossini's *Stabat Mater*, and, on Palm Sunday, 9 April 1876, a three-hour version of Bach's *Passion According to St. Matthew*. After hearing her mother practicing her parts at home, Amy probably attended all the performances as well as some of the rehearsals.[17]

Other choral organizations were also active that season; the Cecilia Society, conducted by Benjamin Johnson Lang—who also was the organist for the

Handel and Haydn Society—gave a Bach cantata, and Theodore Thomas led his touring orchestra in a performance of Bach's *Magnificat*. Six years before the establishment of the Boston Symphony Orchestra, Boston did not lack for orchestral music. Theodore Thomas's orchestra and the orchestra of the Harvard Musical Association, led by Carl Zerrahn, both offered symphony series.

This was also the year for pianists. On 18 October 1875, the famous German pianist Hans von Bülow opened his American concert tour in Boston, playing a group of solos as well as the Beethoven "Emperor" Concerto with orchestra. By the end of the month, von Bülow had played six different programs in seven concerts, all from memory—something not usually done at the time —and had given the American premiere of Tchaikowsky's First Piano Concerto, which was dedicated to the pianist. Boston audiences were demonstrative in their appreciation, so much so that at one point von Bülow addressed them, "Ladies and Gentlemen, this is the Athens of America. You are Athenians. I am proud of your good opinion."[18]

Amy Cheney, who attended von Bülow's Boston concerts, wrote perceptively:

> There was one afternoon that I recall especially when he transposed several of his numbers with such a roguish air. The Chopin "Tarantelle" in A-flat he played in B major, and it was infinitely more brilliant; the "Impromptu" in G he played in G-flat, and it was more poetic. I do not believe that he did this on the spur of the moment, but to secure his effects, trusting to the chance that it would not be noticed. . . . [T]he critics, apparently, had no inkling of it, for the fact was not alluded to by one of them at the time. But what a comical air Von Bülow assumed when he was busy with it.[19]

Amy Beach, who had the same facility, was known to transpose songs on the spot in concert, but there is no record of her transposing piano works during a recital.

A number of female musicians found a warm welcome in Boston. The American-born Julie Rivé (later Rivé-King), who was on her first tour of Boston, gave a solo recital on 29 October 1876, followed by three concerts with orchestras in the month of December. Another American pianist Amy Cheney may have heard that year was Amy Fay (1844–1928), fresh from six years in Germany and one of the earliest of the native-born women to study abroad. Her vivid epistolary account of her life as a music student in Germany, published in 1880, inspired hundreds of American girls and women to do likewise.[20] If Amy Cheney had read Fay's very popular book, her sense of deprivation would have been acute. Fay describes not only lessons with musical luminaries, including Liszt, but also concert life in Berlin, Leipzig, and Weimar, where she heard and met Clara Schumann and von Bülow, among many others. Amy Cheney had to wait half a lifetime before she could partake of that rich cultural atmosphere. Meanwhile, she made the most of being in Boston.

At that time, American-born concert artists like Fay and Rivé were few indeed; rather the field was dominated by visitors and immigrants. The most important of these was the Venezuelan pianist Teresa Carreño (1853–1917), to whom Beach later dedicated her piano concerto, op. 45. Carreño had blossomed after her New York debut as a child prodigy in 1862 and became a favorite in Boston and soon an international star. Her career was typical of virtuosi in that she also composed, mainly the expected display pieces for the piano, although later in life she wrote as well for string quartet and orchestra. Had she been free to do so, Amy Cheney probably would have chosen such a life for herself.

But if Carreño was a positive model for Amy Cheney, she was a negative model for those who, like Clara Cheney, objected to exploitation of prodigies—Carreño made her debut in New York at age nine and for some years was the support of her family—and for those who felt that the stage was no place for a lady. By the time Carreño was twenty-three, she was divorced and remarried; in the end, she married four times—not the kind of life that middle-class Americans like the Cheneys found acceptable.[21]

On 6 March 1877, Amy collected the autograph of the Russian pianist Annette Essipoff, thus beginning an album that includes signatures of some of the great writers, actors, and musicians of the time.[22] Essipoff gave a recital that evening, one in a remarkably successful series begun by the pianist a year earlier. Pupil and, for a time, wife of the famous teacher Theodor Leschetizky, Essipoff came from St. Petersburg, where her beauty and talent made her a favorite of the Russian nobility. Along with Carreño and Clara Schumann, she was considered by one critic to be among the leading female concert artists of the world.

On 12 May of that year Essipoff gave an American program, offering works by Arthur Foote, William H. Sherwood, John K. Paine, William Mason, Richard Hoffmann, Louis Moreau Gottschalk, and Amy Cheney's teacher Ernst Perabo. It may have been that very evening that Essipoff listened to Amy Cheney play and responded with enthusiastic praise for the eleven-year-old's private performance.[23] The following year Amy played for Rafael Joseffy, a leading European pianist who had recently settled in this country.[24]

For the Cheneys, family ties were sometimes stronger than the attraction of musical life in Boston. Thus, on 12 May 1878 Clara and Amy Cheney traveled to San Francisco to spend what Amy later called a "blissful year" with Aunt Franc, Uncle Lyman, and cousin Ethel, then four years old.[25] Just before they left Boston, Clara Cheney had sung in the final concert of the Handel and Haydn Society's season. This was the important and eagerly awaited American premiere of Verdi's "Manzoni" Requiem. As usual, Carl Zerrahn conducted the chorus and orchestra, the four soloists—Eugenie Pappenheim, Adelaide Phillips, Charles R. Adams, and Alwin Blum—and the organist, B. J. Lang.

Zerrahn was an important figure not only in Boston's musical life; he was frequently called out of Boston to conduct mammoth music festivals, so much favored at the time, in Manchester, Salem, and Worcester and, in late May 1878, in San Francisco.[26] That is how it happened that, on his way to San Francisco for its "Grand Musical Festival," he was on the same train as the Cheneys.[27] The child made a profound impression on Zerrahn, as he recalled thirteen years later when their professional lives crossed.[28]

San Francisco's May Festival took place in the Mechanics' Pavilion, a barn of a place with poor acoustics. But two thousand choristers and the accompanying band labored valiantly to compensate, and the climactic performance of the Anvil chorus—with local blacksmiths playing the anvils—may have overridden the acoustical deficiencies of the hall.[29] Another event of the festival presented "100 young ladies on 40 pianos"—the numbers may have been a bit of puffery—playing Liszt's *Rákóczy March* under the direction of Hugo Mansfeldt, a former pupil of the composer.[30] The *Daily Alta California* proclaimed this "one of the most magnificent successes ever had on this Coast."[31] Such an event could hardly have been passed up by Amy and Clara Cheney or the Clements. It is not clear whether Clara Cheney remained there for the year or returned home to Boston soon after arriving.[32]

That year the Clements lived at 405 O'Farrell Street, a few blocks from Market Street and from the center of town where the Mechanics' Pavilion stood. Uncle Lyman was the receiving teller of the First National Gold Bank and Trust Company, and Aunt Franc was teaching voice and piano. Music making with her aunt and time spent with her four-year-old cousin Ethel were part of Amy's wonderful year. Both cousins were without siblings, and it was the closest Amy came to having a sister. Her five-stanza poem, "Lullaby to My Baby," written while she was in San Francisco, suggests that she enjoyed taking care of Ethel. The last stanza of her ditty shows that her poetic models were sentimental Victorian hymns:

When as through life you go wisely
And other babes you see
Remember it was Mother
Who always prayed for thee.[33]

Perhaps that "blissful year" in San Francisco gave her a taste of a freer and more relaxed—even indulgent—way of living than she had at home. A photo taken in San Francisco shows Amy Cheney in an elaborate and fashionable dress of velvet, with lace collar and cuffs and a bustle, the like of which is not seen in photos taken back East.[34]

While she was in San Francisco, her quick ear and tonal memory served the cause of ornithology. She met the poet Edward Rowland Sill, professor of English literature at the University of California in Berkeley, who was collecting bird songs for a colleague's book.[35] When he learned that Amy had absolute pitch, Sill asked her to help him "steal from the birds!" As she describes the spring morning,

[T]he poet and I sat down behind a stone wall. It is a sweet memory of the kindly poet, of California, of the spring flowers, of the unconscious birds. With pencil and paper, we took their melodies. We got twenty of their airs that morning.[36]

Thus begun, Amy Cheney continued collecting bird songs for many years, using them later in several compositions.[37]

After her return from San Francisco, the Cheneys rented quarters at 1 Hancock Street and the following year at 21 Pemberton Square, both in Boston. In those days the square was an island of repose edged by town houses.[38] Nearby, at 16 Pemberton, was the Harvard Musical Association, headed by John Sullivan Dwight, for years the leading music critic and journalist in the United States.

This may have been the time when Amy Cheney played for Dwight and his friend Otto Dresel, a German immigrant musician. Both men had a strong antipathy to the music of Brahms. Without announcing the composer's name, Amy played a capriccio of Brahms that was new to these shores. "The Boston musicians were enchanted and eager to learn who had written the piece. When she announced that it was by Brahms, there were coughs and mutterings that it was the best piece yet to come from his pen."[39] Amy Cheney's independence of spirit and courage to make her own judgments about music shine through this encounter.

Up the hill from Pemberton Square was the state house that crowns Beacon Hill. The Cheneys' centripetal progress had brought them ever closer to the center of Boston's cultural life. This progress was further abetted by the family decision to send Amy to Professor William L. Whittemore's preparatory school —thought by some to be Boston's most successful school—which was located a few blocks down the other side of Beacon Hill at 52 Chestnut Street.[40] Amy Cheney probably began school in 1879, attending full time for two years.[41] This was the most momentous change in her education since beginning to study with Perabo. The school's organized curriculum challenged and stimulated her. Fascinated as much by the natural sciences as by the study of foreign languages and mathematics, she excelled in all. And she finally was in a child-centered world where she had daily contact with others her own age.

She also joined a girls' literary club, the Attic Club, which flourished from 1879 to 1953—seventy-five years. Two girls of about twelve had begun the club "for fun and to write stories," in imitation of their mothers' literary clubs. They met regularly on Saturday mornings, during which members came in with stories and poems, all of them later carefully copied by the club secretary into the book of minutes.[42] Many years after she joined, Amy Beach wrote to Edith B. Brown, one of the founders, to say that she hoped to be able to attend the sixtieth anniversary of the Attic Club. She added, "I recall so vividly our meetings in those early days, for they meant so much enjoyment to me in the life I had to lead, with little companionship of friends near my own age."[43]

The club historian wrote of Amy Cheney, "One of our happiest memories is of the music which filled our rooms when we could persuade her to play for us at the close of the meeting. She was studying hard . . . at the time and our club was one of her few relaxations. She wrote interesting stories too."[44] If "exceptional girls [like Amy Cheney] need exceptional companions,"[45] then this was the closest she came to such associations. Nevertheless, while there was much that Amy could share with her sisters of the Attic Club, she may have been unique among them in wanting a professional career.

Her autograph album offered a way to move close to figures in public life. One of the most influential of those figures was Henry Wadsworth Longfellow. During the Attic Club's early years, "Longfellow was living in his Cambridge home, whither certain [Attic Club] girls, unbeknownst to their parents, went to call upon him and obtain his flowing autograph."[46] Amy and her piano teacher also visited Longfellow in his home, Craigie House, where she played for him. His generous praise of her playing was followed by a letter with his autograph. In it he wrote, "[I take] this opportunity to thank you again for your beautiful music on Saturday."[47] Amy Cheney soon set to work putting Longfellow's poem, "The Rainy Day" to music:

> Christmas time was near and I, of course, was very short of pocket money. I said to my mother, "What shall I give Aunt Franc for Christmas?" Mother suggested I write her a song. My aunt was a singer, so I wrote the little setting, copied it and sent her the manuscript for a Christmas gift. She sang it on many of her concert programs.[48]

Three years later, in 1883, Amy Cheney's first published composition appeared under the imprint of the distinguished old Boston firm of Oliver Ditson.[49] She was then sixteen. The work is rich in associations—with her Aunt Franc, with the poet, and with teardrops, rain, and the minor mode.

In another outcome of that visit to Longfellow, the poet wrote to thank Perabo for "the great pleasure" in hearing "Miss Cheney" play. Longfellow predicted a bright future for her and hoped that Perabo would succeed in his plan to send her to Europe to study, to which end "all musical people should come to your aid."[50] Perabo may have planned to raise a fund to send Amy to Europe like one that had been raised for his own support earlier. It is not surprising that this idea was abandoned, for of course the Cheneys would have turned it down had support been offered. It may also explain why, not too long after, Amy had another piano teacher. However, all was not lost, because Longfellow, as a result of that visit, became an enthusiastic supporter of the young pianist and Amy was another step closer to the upper-class world he inhabited.

The violinist Teresa Liebe also signed Amy Cheney's autograph album, on 3 October 1881.[51] This may have been the time when Liebe tested Amy's abilities as a musician. At the violinist's request and in the presence of writer and music critic Louis Elson, Amy not only played fugues from Bach's *Well-tempered Clavier* from memory, but "transposed them into any required key." Indeed, her ability and natural gifts plus the musicality of her playing and her enthusiasm led her teachers to conclude that she was "the greatest musical prodigy of America."[52]

In 1882, fifteen-year-old Amy Cheney changed piano teachers, leaving Perabo for Carl Baermann. At first a pupil then a close friend of Franz Liszt, Baermann became Royal Professor of Music at the Munich Conservatory, where he and von Bülow taught the most advanced piano students. He had recently taken musical Boston by storm, playing the Beethoven G-major concerto with the Philharmonic Society. "[T]he critics lavished enthusiasm unbounded upon him; the public could talk of no one else." Given such a marvelous reception and with some urging by Boston musicians, Baermann decided to make Boston his home; he went on to become "Boston's most eminent pianist and teacher."[53] The lineage from Liszt to Baermann to Cheney conferred on her an inheritance from Europe's most brilliant pianist.

About the time Amy began studying with Baermann, her mother came to a most momentous decision, to allow Amy to make her debut as a pianist. Beach earlier used the word *allow* in reference to her mother's grudging consent for her to play a few recitals when she was seven; now she used it again regarding the debut.[54] There is no indication of how her mother made this important about-face. Any parent who has ever pitted herself against a determined and perservering child, however, can picture the campaign waged by the child: pleas, demands, tears, arguments, combativeness—the child uses them all. But now Amy was not alone. She had a powerful ally in her teacher, and in Bostonians who believed she would become a fine musician, provided that she study in Europe.[55] On the other hand, she had an adversary who—in this regard at least—had long ago determined the course of Amy's life, and nothing —not even a debut—deflected Clara Cheney from her plan. Clara Cheney may have rationalized giving permission for a debut on other grounds. A debut would lay the groundwork for a career as a piano teacher, should Amy not marry, or limited public exposure might attract a suitor. If the latter, she was prophetic.

With her debut in mind, Amy spent her third and last year at Whittemore's School studying only French and German, a change that suggested hope for future study in Europe. Even so, managing time for study and four hours of piano practice challenged her ingenuity. She therefore made a practice of propping her German or French textbooks up on the piano desk and studying them while doing technical exercises at the piano.[56] Otherwise all her energies went into music and the preparation for her debut.

When the debut took place on 24 October 1883, it was the high point of an eventful year in which her first composition was published. At her debut she was a month past her sixteenth birthday. Among the audience in Boston's main hall, the Music Hall, Attic Club members "sat in an enchanted row as she, with two heavy plaits of hair hanging down her back, sat at the great piano, dealing with it already with a master's hand."[57] It was a very rainy Wednesday night; nevertheless the hall was well filled. Boston had come to hear a homegrown prodigy play two major works, Moscheles's Concerto No. 2 in G minor and Chopin's *Rondo* in E♭, op. 16, works that would allow the critics to take her measure as a pianist and an artist.

This was not the sort of solo debut recital that became the rule in the twentieth century. Rather it was a variety program typical of the time and a much kinder way to introduce a debutante. The concert was organized by Alfred P. Peck in celebration of his twentieth year as manager of the Music Hall. The conductor of the orchestra, Adolph Neuendorff, came to this country from Germany at the age of eleven. A child prodigy in violin and piano, he later became a conductor, composer, and theater manager in New York. In 1871 he had conducted the first American performance of Wagner's *Lohengrin*.[58] Now he was about to begin a stint in Boston as conductor of the Promenade Concerts at the Music Hall.[59]

Top billing—quite rightfully—went to Clara Louise Kellogg (1842–1916), the woman with absolute pitch to whom Charles Cheney had referred years earlier.[60] Other performers included Clarence Hay, the bass, an occasional singer for the Handel and Haydn Society; the contralto Hope Glenn, who would make her debut two months later as soloist with the society in the Christmas performance of *Messiah*; and Timothée Adamowski, a Polish-born violinist (1858–1943) at the beginning of his career in Boston.[61] Altogether they were good—and in case of Kellogg, illustrious—company for a debut.

All the principal performers except Adamowski and Amy Cheney volunteered their services. Just why they did so is not stated, but one possible explanation might be their desire to bolster an orchestra threatened by the Boston Symphony Orchestra, now two years old.

The reviews do not mention that Cheney played from memory, but since this was her practice for her entire life, she may well have done so at her debut.[62] Although there are sections in the Moscheles concerto that recall Mozart, there also are brilliant and extended octave runs, figurations in thirds and sixths—a good bit of flashing passage work, well calculated to demonstrate her technical skills. The Chopin rondo is a musically demanding as well as highly technical piece with more brilliant passage work calling for velocity and the ability to stretch a tenth (an octave plus two). Amy had then and continued to have small hands in keeping with her small stature, but she also said that her hands were quite flexible, as they must have been to stretch so wide an interval.

Her own pleasure in the event was intense:

> The presence of that throng of people was an inspiration. And as for the orchestra . . .(it was my first experience with one), no words can tell the pleasure I felt performing with a band of instrumentalists, each member of it himself such a musician as to sense my wishes more quickly and surely than the greatest conductor could convey them. I can only compare my sensations with those of a driver, who holds in his hands the reins that perfectly control a glorious, spirited pair of horses. One must live through such an experience to properly appreciate it.[63]

This inexperienced child, totally devoid of stage fright and playing with orchestra for the first time, had vied with the conductor for control and won.

At least nine Boston papers as well as a monthly and the *New York Tribune*, which sent its Boston correspondent, covered the concert. All agreed that the chief event of the evening was Amy Cheney's debut. The critic for the *Gazette* summed it all up:

> Her natural gifts and her innate artistic intelligence were made apparent in the very first phrases she played. Her manner is winningly modest, though it lacked nothing in easy self-possession. She has a brilliant and remarkably fluent technique, of which the grace and refinement are delightfully conspicuous. Her playing is wholly without affectation, and is surprising in the maturity of taste, the delicacy, warmth and propriety of expression, the largeness and beauty of phrasing, the thorough musicianly understanding, and the exquisite purity of style that characterize it throughout. A special charm was added to her performances by the freshness, the artless simplicity, and the thorough grasp of the composer's meaning that signalized them.[64]

It is hard to imagine a more positive critical reaction to a debut. The audience too was "enthusiastic in the extreme, and flowers were heaped upon her in lavish profusion."[65] This was a coming-out party *par excellence*.

Because of the close association of musicians and writers in Boston at that time, it is likely that the critics, along with others in musical circles, had been aware for years of Amy Cheney's reputation as a *Wunderkind* and of her mother's opposition to her career as a pianist; and they may even have had heard her play at private gatherings. Unfortunately, there are few records of such informal events.

Another striking aspect of the reviews is the total absence of any reference to her gender as a limitation. Her youth and Boston's traditional respect for women artists precluded such comments, although only for a few years. Nor did the critics subject her to the subordination by gender, by which each woman is compared only to other women. For Amy Cheney, this was a total triumph.

The issue of future promise as well as present success loomed large in the review of one influential critic, who recommended only an occasional performance, backed by slow, patient study and growth "for a good while yet; and then the ultimate successes will be greater and more true than any applause won by performance."[66] His advice, however, was not taken and she began preparing for her next appearance almost immediately.

With her debut her life changed, as it would have had she been a social debutante. Although her mother continued to chaperone her, at least now she was out in the world. Amy had become a public figure who was known to her audiences; she had made a strong impression as a performer and was part of the musical circle of Boston. This was a sudden release from the isolation of the studio and the relative anonymity of the student. Indeed, as she reported later, "Life was beginning!"[67]

Amy Beach's first public recital was on Wednesday afternoon, 9 January 1884, in Chickering Hall, Boston.[68] The hall was full, and according to one critic, there was "a fine audience, representing . . . the best musical and critical talent in Boston." The reviewers agreed that the recital "justified fully all the expectations" aroused by her debut.[69] One noted, however, that she was not the most powerful of players, another that her naïveté, her innocence displayed in interpretations of the Chopin Nocturne, and the "somewhat too honeyed sentiment" of the Henselt were utterly charming and the essence of "sweet sixteen."[70] All else was high praise and further predictions of a great future. One critic gave a finely detailed description of her playing:

> The almost imperceptible poising over a note, and the almost imperceptible pausing upon it; the caressing touch in a melodious phrase, or the airy turn of an ornament; the sharpness or the softness of a trill; the justness of taste which keeps feeling from crossing the narrow line into exaggeration or bathos—these are the characteristics which . . . we recognize in Miss Cheney, and which qualify her, not as a precocious child, but as a young player of artistic nature, large early acquirement and rarest promise.[71]

She then took the program on the road with Loeffler the assisting artist. They gave two afternoon recitals: in Andover on 19 February and in Bradford, New Hampshire, the following day. The earlier recital may have been the time described by Clara Cheney when mother and daughter went to Abbot Academy where Amy Cheney gave a solo recital. "The grounds of this seminary are beautiful and, arriving there, she tossed her hat in the air and ran down the tree bordered path, laughing with all the glee of a happy child, bent on play." Minutes later, smiling but dignified, she gave a recital.[72]

Not a month after, she appeared again in Chickering Hall, presenting an entirely new program. Although there were critical disagreements on details, all praised the high quality of her performance. The *Boston Globe*, however, expressed concern, stating "[t]hat Miss Amy Marcy Cheney may not be spoiled by her surprising success as a pianist is the earnest wish of all the musical people in Boston." His and other critics' comments also indicated how proprietary were the feelings for her in her adoptive city.[73]

Amy Cheney's second appearance in one of Peck's Annual Concerts at the Music Hall was on 23 April 1884. In this program of light classics, Cheney played the *Polacca brillante* of Carl Maria von Weber and two works of Anton Rubinstein. Again she shared the program with distinguished colleagues, among them three stars of opera: the tenor Charles Adams and the sopranos Sofia Scalchi and Marcella Sembrich (the latter had recently made her debut with the Metropolitan Opera). Over two decades later, Amy Beach, in a letter to Sembrich, recalled the precious memory she had of sharing a concert with the great artist: "In your generous life you must have forgotten the great kindness which you then showed to a sixteen-year old just beginning her public work, but you may be sure that I shall never forget it while life lasts."[74] Three recitals in nearby towns completed Amy Cheney's second season of performing.

The pianist found support among a number of women artists and writers on whom she had made a strong impression. Celia Thaxter, Elizabeth Porter Gould, and Nora Perry wrote poems celebrating her achievements. In this quatrain inscribed in Amy Cheney's autograph album, Perry captured the passion of the seventeen-year-old pianist:

Wild waltzes with a dying fall
In every note, a plaintive call
Of passionate entreating pain
Inwoven with each mirthful strain.

Perry, in her admiration, noted that this "child prodigy . . . in her short dress, with her long braided hair . . . [was] a girl such as one might meet any day on the Common going to school." When she played, however, she was still a child, but one comparable to Liszt and Mendelssohn.[75]

Two orchestral engagements capped the climax of two successful years of performing following her debut: Cheney's first appearances with the two leading American orchestras. The last concert of the Boston Symphony's 1884–85 season took place at the Music Hall on 28 March, with Amy Cheney playing Chopin's Concerto in F Minor, op. 21. The *Traveller's* critic noted that "being chosen to play at the last concert of the season" was compliment indeed and one she fully deserved.[76] An immense audience attended, in part because of public approval for the orchestra's conductor, Wilhelm Gericke, then completing his first season. The audience recalled her to the stage twice, filling her arms with flowers each time, and Cheney responded with "several encores."

Praise for her playing was remarkable in its virtual unanimity. One critic would have liked a little more power, but that was the only reservation in otherwise superb reviews.[77] On the other hand, the Transcript's reviewer used praise of Cheney's playing to put down other women, saying that she displayed a "totality of conception that one seldom finds in players of her sex."[78] A few days later, a reviewer wrote that her "really wonderful performance of the Chopin F-minor concerto . . . has been the talk of the musical part of the town almost ever since."[79]

Another major concert engagement brought the young prodigy into collaboration with America's most important conductor, Theodore Thomas (1835–1905), with whom she played the Mendelssohn Concerto No. 2, in D minor, op. 40. Thomas had made as his aim the elevation of musical taste in the United States, and with his own traveling orchestra, he had gone a long way to achieving it. Among his many concerts in Boston was a matinee—"A Young People's Popular"—on 29 April 1885. Critics commented that, as a children's program, it was rather heavy going for it included Beethoven's Symphony No. 1 in addition to the Mendelssohn. The conductor's choice of Amy Cheney as soloist provoked the comment that it was "an authoritative indorsement of Miss Cheney's abilities and attractions."[80]

At the rehearsal, Thomas decided that, in consideration of her youth, he would take the brilliant last movement of the concerto at a slower tempo than usual, and he began the orchestral introduction accordingly. When the time came for the piano to enter, however, Cheney was not content simply to follow: "I did not know that he was sparing me, but I did know that the tempo dragged, and I swung the orchestra into time." The astonished conductor had no choice but to take her tempo for the rest of the movement. Later he found the incident amusing.[81]

The critic for the Advertiser noted her continued growth as an artist. A review in the Beacon mentioned that the Mendelssohn was "played to perfection." The only negative note was again from the Transcript. Its critic suggested that females striving for strength of tone overstep the limits of their abilities in the pressure to prove their power as players, as Cheney did in the second theme of the last movement. Yet despite this "slight blemish," her playing was "worthy the highest praise."[82]

As extraordinary as this year had been so far, by the time it ended it would usher in important, even profound changes in her life. But for the present, the progress Amy Cheney achieved "in her art . . . upheld the prophecies made in private and in public by the young musician's friends."[83] If her importance was still very much a local one, she now had a secure place in Boston's musical life.

THE MAKING

OF A

COMPOSER:

I

AT SEVENTEEN, AMY CHENEY HAD achieved her first aim. She was established as a pianist in Boston with nothing but the highest public expectations for her continued artistic growth. Now she wished to have a composition teacher who would build on the work she had begun as a small child. Composition was as natural to her as playing the piano. She saw no reason why she could not pursue both.

In 1884 her compositions—the juvenilia that survive—consisted of a number of piano pieces and vocal and choral works. One song, "A Rainy Day," had been published, and another, "With Violets," would come out the following year. Short as they are, these early pieces demonstrate her ability to process and synthesize everything she heard into works of her own. Part of that ability related to her prodigious musical memory. Several years after she composed "Mamma's Waltz" and "Snowflake Waltz" in her head, Amy Cheney wrote them out from memory.[1] Two years later, after hearing another Perabo pupil play a Beethoven sonata, she played it herself without having seen the music.[2] Her extraordinary memory explains why she regularly composed away from the piano, even without pencil and paper; when she did write out her compositions, they usually had already been composed, and she merely took dictation from her inner hearing of the recalled work.

"Mamma's Waltz" is the earliest surviving work composed before her fifth birthday. It is remarkable in several ways. First, its length is 180 measures. Second, its formal organization comprises an opening section, which is repeated twice in the course of the piece, and two contrasting sections, one of which is in a near-related key. Third, her use of harmony—untaught and undoubtedly intuitive—is correct, sure, and occasionally even sophisticated; see, for example, mm. 27–29, in which she modulates to F major and then returns to C major through a diminished seventh chord (ex. 4.1). Finally, the piece, written in her head, "works" as a piano solo; even when she first touched the piano, she instinctively knew how to make the instrument "sound."

From 1877, there survive holographs—an "Air and Variation," a "Minuetto" that she later used as the theme of her "Minuet italien," op. 28, no. 1, and a "Romanza"—all for piano.[3] The "Romanza"—with its juxtaposition of

EXAMPLE 4.1 "*Mamma's Waltz*," [1872], copyist's manuscript, mm. 1–35. (Used with permission of University of Missouri-Kansas City Libraries, Special Collections, and the MacDowell Colony.)

D major with F♯ minor and major—is a harbinger of musical practices to come. She already had a sure sense of how to move from key to key, including distantly related ones. Another adumbration of a feature that would characterize her later practice is its chromaticism. Also among these manuscripts are a very pretty "Petite Waltz" of 1878 and an exercise in which Amy added a vocal line to Chopin's *Trois nouvelles études*, no. 3, in A♭, with a text used by Schubert, "Whither" ("Wohin").[4]

Her first published work, "The Rainy Day," a setting of the famous poem by Longfellow that she wrote after her visit to the poet in 1880, is in F minor. Her choice of key recalls her earlier tendency to cry when she heard pieces in the minor mode and her childish association of raindrops with tears. The song pays homage to Beethoven, for she borrows both melody and accompaniment from the opening of the last movement of Beethoven's Sonata *Pathétique*, op. 13, for her opening phrase. She adapts it for the first line, "The day is cold and dark and dreary." But the continuation is original and shows not only her lyric gift but also a fine feeling for how to prolong a line as well as how to use harmony to build tension (ex. 4.2).

While many of these compositional devices are in the music she studied or heard at home and in concert, or perhaps found explained in the *Boston Conservatory Method*, her ability to use them properly in her own works at such an early age reveals a significant creative gift. This gift was undoubtedly assisted by her musical memory, which, combined with her perfect pitch, meant that she had as a compositional resource much of the music she had heard.

Amy Cheney's course in harmony with Junius Welch Hill lasted for a year (1881–82) while she was a pupil at Whittemore's school and studying piano with Perabo.[5] At that time, Hill was a church organist and teacher of piano, voice, and organ, both privately and at the Boston Conservatory of Music. Fortunately for Amy Cheney, he believed in giving women a first-class musical education.[6]

During her year of study with Hill, she wrote four chorales for four voices, an excellent way to learn four-part harmony. The settings are more than merely correct, for their musical qualities recommend them for use today; they are polished and show careful study of Bachian models. Her mother may have helped make the fair copies of the chorales; the music is in Cheney's immature hand, the title and hymn texts in her mother's. These are the only examples that remain from that course.

The following year, she wrote a song that, when it was published in 1885, became her opus 1, number one, "With Violets." Her model here may have been Robert Schumann's opening phrase of "Aus meinen Thränen spriessen" from his song cycle, *Dicterliebe*, op. 47, which is echoed in the opening vocal line and piano accompaniment. For a text she chose a sentimental poem by Kate Vannah, typical of the parlor song of the time:

> The violets I send to you
> Will close their blue eyes on your breast;
> I shall not be there, sweet, to see,
> Yet do I know my flowers will rest
> Within that chaste white nest . . . .
>
> If you could speak! Yet she will know
> What made your faces wet, although
> I fain would follow you and tell.
> There, go and die, yet never know
> To what a heav'n you go.[7]

EXAMPLE 4.2 Amy Marcy Cheney, "The Rainy Day," mm. 1–14 (Oliver Ditson, 1883).

Cheney turned it into an art song, using the asymmetrical structure of the stanzas to create long and flowing—and highly vocal—lines. Her feeling for prosody, the fit of word and music, is clearly apparent. Theorist and teacher Percy Goetschius found the song so remarkable for a fifteen-year-old "that many a full-fledged composer might envy her much that it contains; particularly the exquisite and strikingly original modulation with which this Op. 1, No. 1, terminates."[8] Although the opening clearly established G major as the tonality, Cheney soon flirts with the relative minor, E. The final verse begins in E minor, moves through F major to Db, and then, with remarkable ease, climbs back to G major, a sudden emergence from the dark to the bright realm of heaven (ex. 4.3).

Her request for permission to dedicate the song to Adelina Patti was as daring as the harmonies at the end of the song. The dedication may have grown out of Amy Cheney's two encounters with Patti. The composer touchingly recalls a trip to New York in June 1885 to attend her first opera performance, starring Adelina Patti: "I have never forgotten hearing her in Traviata when I was a young girl. I can hear some of her delicious low tones now, near the end, when she was so pathetic! How I cried!"[9] At some time, perhaps during her trip to New York, Amy played Chopin and Liszt for Patti, who was quite impressed and later accepted the dedication with pleasure.[10] Patti's name at the top of the title page of a song was a validation of Cheney as a composer.

While early pieces give evidence of unusual gifts, there is nothing of major proportions to prove that her abilities in composition matched those in piano. The time had come for serious study of composition. All but one of the other composers of the Boston School had formal lessons in composition, most of them completing their studies in Germany. That one was Clara Kathleen Rogers, who had studied at the Leipzig Conservatory in the 1860s. Even though she had composed a string quartet as a teenager, she, like other women, was barred from the conservatory's composition class. After an opera career under the name of Clara Doria, she returned to composition but lamented her inadequate training, especially when tackling works of large dimensions.[11] Helen Hopekirk, a graduate of the Leipzig Conservatory who had a successful career as a concert pianist, turned to composition as an adult, studying privately.[12] Margaret Ruthven Lang, born the same year as Amy Cheney, was the daughter of a professional musician who taught her theory and harmony and later sent her to Munich to study violin as well as counterpoint and fugue. On her return, she studied orchestration with Chadwick and later with John Knowles Paine and the composer and organist James Cutler Dunn Parker.[13] If the Cheneys had been professional musicians, they probably would have managed Amy's musical training differently and perhaps followed a plan similar to the Langs'.

Since her only training in theory had been the year with Junius Hill, the Cheney family sought advice about a composition teacher from Wilhelm Gericke (1845–1925), who had recently arrived from Vienna to become the conductor of the Boston Symphony. Gericke was a conscientious musician who demanded high levels of performance from the orchestra and very soon was able to shape it to his requirements.[14] He included on his programs the stan-

EXAMPLE 4.3 "With Violets," op. 1, no. 1, mm. 29–39 (Arthur P. Schmidt, 1885).

dard works by European masters and occasionally offered works by Boston composers, among them Paine, Chadwick, Foote, and MacDowell.[15]

Sources do not shed light on the details of this consultation other than its outcome. Gericke's attitude toward women composers is not known; as a European, he may well have been less supportive than some Americans. He knew about study in Europe but little if anything about American conservatories and teachers of composition. The Cheneys might also have asked the advice of Paine at Harvard or Chadwick at the New England Conservatory,[16] both of whom had studied composition in Europe and taught it in Boston. But apparently Gericke's advice was authority enough; as conductor of the symphony and a distinguished European musician, he was the ranking professional in Boston.

His recommendation—which they accepted—was that Amy Cheney teach herself composition by studying the great masters. Would he have given the same answer if she had been young, gifted, and male? Was Gericke less impressed with her promise as a composer than with her achievements as a pianist? Did he wonder if there would ever be a great woman composer and assume the negative?

Considering that Amy Cheney had been compared with Mozart,[17] Gericke's recommendation seems especially ill-advised. Chadwick believed her to be the most gifted of the Boston composers and that Gericke was wrong.[18] His advice must be seen in the context of prevailing opinions about women, however— not only in Europe but in this country as well—that intellectually they were less highly evolved than men and, as a result, less able to respond to training.[19] This may explain Gericke's advice.

But music, the language of the emotions, seems on the surface more "feminine" than "masculine." How then do we explain women's perceived failure to achieve as serious composers? Although Gericke probably did not know about this, a debate about whether women could create art works of value had begun in 1880 with the publication of George Upton's book, *Woman in Music*.[20] An influential critic for the *Chicago Tribune* who identified women's primary role as muse to male creative artists, Upton set the boundaries of the controversy for decades. While music was a language of feelings, he proposed, it could only be transmuted into great art by intellect and the ability to think in abstract terms, the latter supposedly found wanting in women.[21]

In the 1890s, women did develop counter-arguments, pointing out, on the one hand, the social and professional limitations on women and on the other, the achievements of European women composers of the past and present. In other words, feminists attributed women's lesser achievements not to nature but to nurture. Alice Stone Blackwell commented in the *Woman's Journal* on the superficial nature of girls' training in music and the low expectations of the results of that training. But, she wrote, when the climate of opinion, the support, and the training were the same for women as men, and when those equal conditions endured for decades if not centuries, then such comparisons would be apt if women did not rise to men's levels as composers.[22]

By the mid-nineties, it would be Amy Beach whom defenders of women cited as proof that an American woman could compose—successfully—large-scale art music. But this was 1884, and she knew of no American pioneer to serve as model. Undaunted by negative ideology, Amy Cheney followed Gericke's advice and started on a multi-year process of self-education. Her studies at Whittemore's school having ended by 1883 and her debut behind her, she began by studying counterpoint and fugue, working with enormous concentration and purposefulness. The regime she set for herself demanded determination, resourcefulness, and the ability to carry on without the regular criticism and validation that a teacher might offer. In addition, she had a busy performing schedule. Later she wrote, looking back on the long process she had begun in 1884, that composition self-taught was not something she would recommend to others; it was simply too difficult.[23]

In 1885, the publication of "With Violets," soon to be followed by a second song, marked the beginning of a thirty-year-long exclusive relationship with the publisher Arthur P. Schmidt. Born in Altona, Germany, Schmidt (1846–1921) emigrated to Boston when he was twenty. Ten years later he went into business as a music importer, soon adding publications of his own, and in 1880 he issued his first works by American composers. Grateful for the opportunities he found in this country, Schmidt was determined to show his gratitude by supporting native composers, especially by publishing their large as well as their smaller compositions. Beginning with John Knowles Paine's "Spring" Symphony, op. 34 (1880), he published dozens of works for orchestra by Bostonians Chadwick, Parker, Foote, Beach, MacDowell, and Henry Hadley as well as Paine.[24] For Schmidt that meant taking sizeable financial risks that usually were paid for by profits from the composer's smaller works. Singlehandedly—other publishers took many years to follow suit—Schmidt gave crucial support to two generations of American composers, thereby nurturing an American school of art music where none had previously existed.[25]

Schmidt apparently made no distinction between women and men but rather gave to all the identical royalties of ten percent of the retail price. He published songs by Clara Kathleen Rogers beginning in 1883, by Amy Cheney in 1885, by Helen Hopekirk in 1886 (the previous year G. Schirmer had published one of her piano works), and by Margaret Lang in 1889. For the next twenty-five years he published every composition that Amy wrote within a short time of its completion. Such a service was crucial for a composer. Coming events would only strengthen her relationship with her publisher.

5

TWO WAYS OF

LOOKING AT

A MARRIAGE

AMY MARCY CHENEY'S MARRIAGE TO Henry Harris Aubrey Beach was, like other human events, a mixed blessing. A May-to-September marriage, not uncommon in the late nineteenth century, the bride was just past eighteen, the groom a widower just short of forty-three, a little older than her father. An eminently successful man, Henry Beach (1843–1910) was a surgeon at Massachusetts General Hospital who taught surgery at Harvard Medical School and had a large general practice among Boston's social and cultural elite.[1]

Although the date of the engagement is not certain, the wedding took place on 2 December 1885.[2] The minister, the Reverend Phillips Brooks, rector of Boston's Trinity Church and favorite preacher of Boston's Brahmins, was Henry Beach's friend and patient.[3] The ceremony, which took place at five in the afternoon, was a quiet one. "The bride, who wore a white satin costume, with tulle veil fastened by sprigs of orange flowers, entered the church with her father, Charles A. Cheney, and was received at the altar by the bridegroom, according to the English custom." George Whitefield Chadwick and Arthur Whiting, among Boston's leading young composers, were the organists, and two physicians, former students of Henry's and now colleagues, were the ushers.[4]

The contrast between bride and groom as they stood before Phillips Brooks must have been striking. Only five feet tall, she had a rosy complexion and fair hair that she had wound into a large coil on top of her head for the first time. She was not beautiful, but her warmth and vitality charmed many, as did her "quick and infectious smile." Dominating her face were her eyes: large, bright, and an intense blue-violet.[5] Henry by contrast was five-feet-nine-inches tall, with grey expressive eyes and dark brown hair, a high forehead, and drooping moustache.[6] Some might have considered him handsome.

After their honeymoon in New York, the couple lived in Henry Beach's home at 28 Commonwealth Avenue, next door to the Saltonstalls and half a block from the Public Garden. Their home, which still stands, was one of a row of elegant attached town houses on Back Bay's most fashionable street; of red brick with cream-colored stone framing the doors, windows, and front stoop, it had a bay window on the second floor. His medical offices filled the ground floor.[7] The spacious second floor consisted of a combined drawing and music room that looked down on the street and a dining room that faced the service road at the rear. Above were two floors of bedrooms. Kitchen and pantries were in the basement, and quarters for their three servants were on the mansard-roofed top floor. The interior was elegantly finished, with fruitwood panelling, handsome fireplaces, and wrought-iron banisters on the stairways.

The music room, according to a visitor who came a dozen years later, was decorated in yellow and white, with a marble mantle, and Turkish rugs scattered over a floor of inlaid oak. Among the decorations were a bronze death mask of Beethoven by St. Gaudens, which was a gift of Phillips Brooks, and water colors by Henry Beach himself. There also was "an engraving of Brahms, autographed, sent from Ischel [sic], the famous German watering place where the great composer spent much time; Rosenthal's gift of a small lamp for sealing wax, once used by Mozart, are there together with original manuscripts given by well-known composers from every part of the world."[8] Another visitor wrote that the room had "an old-time elegance" rather than "that unpleasant newness about everything which boldly announces the absence of family relics."[9] In fact, all the so-called old-time elegance was newly acquired; for Henry's parents, like Amy's, lived modestly and had little to spare.

His grandfather, Amasa Beach of Hebron, Connecticut, had fought in the War of 1812.[10] On 29 May 1842, Amasa's son Elijah married Lucy Smith Riley of Middletown, Connecticut,[11] where they settled and Elijah had his tailor's shop. Their first son, Henry Harriss [sic] Beach (Aubrey was not on the birth certificate) was born 18 December 1843;[12] his brother William Niles Beach was born five years later.

Sometime before 1854, the Beach family moved to Cambridge, Massachusetts, where Elijah had a tailoring shop, in which he sold as well as repaired men's clothing.[13] Henry revered his father, describing him as "a man of unusual amiability and dignity of deportment."[14] Modest as the family's station was, there were distant relatives on the Beach side who were connected by marriage to the Roosevelt family, a relationship Amy Beach claimed later in her life.[15]

While still a boy, Henry exhibited the dual interests in medicine and music that he carried through life.[16] Musically talented, he made the crucial choice of his early life when he became a boy chorister at the Church of the Advent, the first Anglo-Catholic Church in the United States. Within a few years of its establishment in 1844, the church introduced "the beautiful English Cathedral service in all its musical glory," sung by a choir of men and boys. The first church in Boston to have such a choir, Advent soon had a reputation for having the best liturgical music in the city.[17] Henry Beach probably traveled to the church from Cambridge "in a jangling horse-car," earning a stipend for his services as a choirboy.[18] In addition to singing in the choir—he eventually became a baritone—Henry Beach studied organ and piano at the church.

Because his family could not afford to pay for his education beyond high school, he went to work, probably with his father, and saved money for tuition. He nevertheless found time to sing in the chorus of the Handel and Haydn Society, joining on 18 February 1863.[19] On the following 29 November 1863, he was baptised at the Church of the Advent, adding the name of

Aubrey, after one of his sponsors at the baptism, the organist Edmund Aubrey Matson.[20] Henry Harris Aubrey Beach was a name to conjure with, the Aubrey adding a touch of English elegance. Renaming himself, it would seem, was part of his progress toward becoming a self-made man. Furthering his religious commitment, the following year he was also confirmed at Advent.[21]

Henry would soon have to choose between medicine and music for his life's work, and his membership at Advent may have helped him decide. Three physicians, adherents of the Oxford Movement in England, had established the church in 1844.[22] One of them, who was also the church's initial financial supporter, was George C. Shattuck, Jr. (1813–1893), descendant of a long line of physicians in his aristocratic Boston family. A member of the faculty of medicine at Harvard, Shattuck would become its dean from 1864 to 1869, including the very years when Henry Beach would be a student.[23] Being a fellow parishioner with Shattuck could only help Henry Beach along in his career and may have influenced his choice.

An opportunity soon arose that would make the pathway to his career easier. On 23 July 1864, he enlisted in the Union army as a clerk and was immediately assigned to Readville Hospital, located at the southern edge of Boston. Given the rank of sergeant of ordinance, he had the job of hospital steward, probably at the recommendation of the physicians at Advent.[24] For a twenty-year-old, this was a position of responsibility in that he supervised the medical, surgical, and apothecary departments. There he served his apprenticeship before entering medical school.

He soon took part in a historic event. In late 1865, under the supervision of Dr. Henry J. Bigelow, of Harvard and Massachusetts General Hospital, Henry Beach made the first application in America of antiseptic to a surgical incision, a procedure inaugurated in Edinborough by Lister.[25] Bigelow, a preeminent surgeon who in 1846 had helped arrange for the first use of ether at Massachusetts General Hospital, served on the faculty of Harvard Medical School from 1849 to 1882. Like Shattuck, he came from a socially prominent medical family in Boston.[26] Beach and Bigelow also developed a warm friendship.

At the time of Henry's honorable discharge from the army on 15 September 1866,[27] his performance at Readville Hospital under the stress of caring for wartime casualties led to an offer of an appointment as surgical officer at Massachusetts General Hospital. He was the unanimous choice for the position and was thus able to pay for his medical course at Harvard.

For the three years following his graduation in 1868, Dr. Beach had his office at home on Dwight Street in Cambridge.[28] He very soon acquired a reputation as a gifted surgeon and was appointed assistant demonstrator and eventually demonstrator for the famous anatomy lectures of Oliver Wendell Holmes at Harvard Medical School.[29] During the fifteen years Beach served in that capacity, he and Holmes became close friends as well as colleagues.

Oliver Wendell Holmes (1809–1894) is remembered today as the poet and author of *The Autocrat of the Breakfast Table*. However, he was an extraordinarily influential physician whose discoveries—especially that child-bed fever was a contagious disease—changed the practice of medicine in this country.[30] A witty and brilliant conversationalist, he dominated a circle that included Emerson, Longfellow, and James Russell Lowell.[31] It was Holmes who invented and applied the term Brahmin to Boston's upper class.[32]

For Henry Beach, the medical profession offered the best opportunity for economic and social advancement, even acceptance into high society: "patients of fashionable doctors have always been available to open the right doors" for them.[33] Among his patients was Holmes himself, who thought "very highly of him [Dr. Beach] as a careful and able practitioner of most agreeable manners and one whose presence inspires confidence and hope." Indeed, Dr. Holmes also entrusted Henry Beach with the medical care of his family.[34] Nothing could have established Dr. Beach's medical credentials more convincingly than Holmes's recommendations—and his social credentials than his friendship with Holmes. Dr. Beach's articles in medical journals soon earned him a reputation as one of the world's leading surgeons.[35]

If professional success came fairly quickly to Henry Beach, affluence eluded him. There is a longstanding tradition that a doctor of modest circumstances[36] needs a wealthy wife whose family can furnish an office and people it with wealthy patients. While the doctor "marries up," his wife has the distinction of marrying a physician, who in Victorian times carried even more social weight than today. Henry Beach followed this pattern.

On 7 June 1871, the New Bedford Evening Standard reported on a "Fashionable Wedding" in the Unitarian Church; Henry Beach married Alice C. Mandell at a ceremony "on a scale of magnificence befitting the wealth of the bride's family," and a display of gifts that were equally lavish.[37]

Following Henry and Alice's marriage, which was childless, Henry's career quickly blossomed, with articles in journals, appointments to Massachusetts General Hospital, election to the presidency of the medical society of Harvard, appointment to the editorial board of the Boston Medical and Surgical Journal, and—topping it off—to the Harvard Medical School faculty.

A joiner, Beach belonged to a number of other medical societies as well as to the American Association for the Advancement of Science and the Biological Society of Washington, D. C. In retrospect, it is easy to see that Henry Beach, a man of personal charm and magnetism, had many talents, not least that of being in the right place at crucial moments of his life.

On the first of March 1879, Henry Beach purchased the handsome town house at 28 Commonwealth Avenue, where he lived to the end of his life.[38] A considerable part of the purchase price for the house came from a substantial mortgage held by Massachusetts General Hospital.[39]

Commonwealth Avenue, Boston's Park Avenue, is a broad expanse with islands of greenery running down its center, punctuated by an occasional piece of monumental sculpture. Paved walks on the islands are lined with benches. Samuel Eliot Morison, naval historian, wrote that purchasing a house on Commonwealth Avenue "where the swells lived" was a way to win a place in Boston society, provided that one entertained often enough.[40]

Henry and Alice Beach lived together in their new house only a year. On 30 July 1880, Alice Beach died of a stroke at the early age of thirty-three.[41] When

Henry married again five years later, he must have felt secure enough in his professional work, if not financially, to choose a wife without regard to money.

There are conflicting stories about how Henry and Amy met. One relates that Clara Cheney took Amy, aged ten, to see Dr. Beach about an injured finger.[42] The second repeats the same story but gives the consultation the unlikely date of the summer of 1885, the time when they probably announced their engagement and just a few months before they were married.[43] It is possible that Henry heard Amy play at her debut, or perhaps earlier in someone's salon, and was so taken with her gifts that he thereafter followed her career. Indeed, a newpaper account reported, well after the fact, that "among the many admirers of Miss Cheney's playing, it was soon whispered there was none more enthusiastic than the prominent surgeon."[44]

Such interest grew naturally out of his musical training and participation and his many associations with musicians as both physician and friend. In addition to singing in the Handel and Haydn Society,[45] Henry Beach was a member of the Harvard Musical Association, which presented chamber and orchestral programs,[46] and the Euterpe Club, which sponsored string quartet concerts,[47] and he was a founding member of the St. Botolph Club, a men's club devoted to literature and the arts.[48]

A letter to Henry Beach dated 3 October 1884 from William Mason, one of this country's leading pianists and teachers of piano, gives an idea of just how interested Henry was in Amy. Mason began by thanking Henry for his letter and the piece of music enclosed. He described to Dr. Beach, his physician, an attack of gout he suffered during the summer. Next, he described meeting Amy's piano teacher, Carl Baermann, and finally Amy herself at the Baermann's house in Cambridge, where he heard her play. His verdict: she was "a young lady of remarkable talent and attainments."[49] It is not difficult to imagine from this letter, which Amy Cheney saved in her autograph album, what the contents of Dr. Beach's letter to Mason had been: he must have written to ask Mason's opinion of Amy Cheney's talents as a pianist and a composer and at the same time enclosed a newspaper clipping with a review of one of her performances. He may even have enclosed a copy of her first published song, The Rainy Day, or of a manuscript song entitled "Jeune fille et jeune fleur," which Henry sang at a recital of voice students the following January.[50] Because the latter song was still in manuscript at the time, it is reasonable to conclude that he had received the copy directly from the composer.

Confirming Henry's initial interest in Amy as a musician, a columnist describes their courtship in a passage rich in Victorian hyperbole:

> As Dr. Beach says, in speaking of his gifted wife, he blesses his deep love for and knowledge of the divine art of music which led him to take an interest in the early musical development of the little maid whose friendship finally ripened into the affection that made them one in the highest sense of that misused word.[51]

THE MARRIAGE HAD IMPORTANT advantages for Henry, not least the cachet of having a resident professional musician in his elegant home at a time when the choice was between live music and none at all. Perhaps even more enticing was the prospect of playing Pygmalion to her Galatea, by supporting and directing her development as a fledgling composer, functioning as critic and enabler, and masterminding her career.

Obviously the marriage had important advantages for the bride. Henry now planned to further enhance the stature Amy had gained on her own, helping her along the path he had followed to professional eminence and social acceptance, the two intimately connected in the Boston of Back Bay and Beacon Hill. Many of Boston's patrons of the arts were his patients as well as his friends, a fact that would be of assistance in her musical career. In a symbolic act that recognized the importance of his position, Amy Marcy Cheney now became Mrs. H. H. A. Beach, both socially and professionally. It was a name she was pleased to bear.

Their home provided an elegant backdrop for social and musical events. Amy must have been dazzled and overwhelmed at becoming mistress of so grand a home. It is not surprising that she made an occasional faux pas. Soon after their marriage, in an attempt at domesticity, Amy had the servants set the table with ornamental plates, pierced and decorated with gold leaf, perhaps wedding gifts to Henry and Alice Beach. Henry had to explain to her that these were museum pieces, for display, not for use.[52] That might explain why, in the beginning, Henry continued to manage the household. But Amy was a quick study in all things, and gradually she took over its management. Even so, with two chambermaids and a cook, she was able to continue to fully concentrate on her music. Probably this arrangement was what Clara Cheney had hoped for, as she had not trained her daughter in household arts. And so the Beaches were soon entertaining "handsomely" and mingling with society "as much as their busy lives" allowed.[53]

Along with her marriage vows, Amy Beach had made a number of agreements with her husband to live according to his status, that is, function as a society matron and patron of the arts. She agreed never to teach piano, an activity widely associated with women and which usually provided "pin money." Because he was old-fashioned and believed that a husband should support his wife, he also requested that any fees she earned as a performer be donated to charity.[54] As a result, her subsequent annual recitals were prominently identified as benefits, each for a specific charity.

Regarding the curtailment of Amy Beach's public performances, we can only guess at the nature of their agreement by its results. Following their marriage, Amy gave one solo recital a year, a far cry from her busy recital schedule of the past two years. She was not limited to one public performance a year, however, for when invitations came to play a concerto with the Boston Symphony or to appear with a string quartet, she accepted. As her catalogue of compositions grew, she was able to introduce some of her own works on these programs.

The change in her life that was most important and with far-reaching consequences was that from giving recitals to composing. Henry wanted her to devote her time to composition, for which he believed she had an important gift. Indeed, he was in awe of her talent and was in a position to support its re-alization wholeheartedly. That support was not merely financial but personal as well. As an added inducement, he agreed to allow her to collect royalties on her music; apparently such commerce was not incompatible with being a society matron, because the work was done in private, not on a public stage. This contrasts with earlier social strictures placed on women who wished to publish their works: having one's name in print previously invited notoriety and was considered unwomanly. However, by 1880, Ednah Dow Cheney could proudly report that "in literature, the progress of women has been so rapid that now a woman's name on the title page of a book hurts neither its accep-tance with the publisher nor its sale to the public." She also noted that "young aspirants in art, however wealthy, seek to sell their pictures, that they may be classed as artists, not as amateurs."[55] The name that appeared on the published music was not "Amy M. Beach," of course, but "Mrs. H. H. A. Beach," itself a shield of propriety and a public affirmation of her husband's role in her cre-ative life.

At the end of each day of hard labor—he in surgery, teaching, and seeing patients in his office; she in the music room, studying, composing, and prac-ticing—Henry Beach would greet his wife with the question, "What did you compose today, dear?"[56] If it was a song, there would be a further collabora-tion in the offing: after singing the song to his wife's accompaniment, he would give her his opinion about it.[57] Instead of a teacher, Amy now had two critics. She wrote:

> Very often he and I would discuss works as I was preparing them. He might differ as to certain expressions and so would my mother, with the result that I had two critics before facing a professional critic. And Dr. Beach could be very impartial and hard-boiled.[58]

It was Henry Beach who urged her to create the big works that would es-tablish her as a professional composer. Three months after their marriage, and at her husband's "incitement,"[59] Amy began work on her first large-scale com-position, a mass for solo voices, chorus, organ, and orchestra—an audacious undertaking for a fledgling composer. Beach recalled later:

> It was he more than any one else who encouraged my interest upon the field of musical composition in the larger forms. It was pioneer work, at least for this coun-try, for a woman to do, and I was fearful that I had not the skill to carry it on, but his constant assurance that I could do the work, and keen criticism whenever it seemed to be weak in spots, gave me the courage to go on.[60]

If she missed the heady life of a concert artist after their marriage, she did not say. Of her change from piano to composition, she later wrote, "Though I had not deliberately chosen, the work had chosen me. I continued to play at concerts, but my home life kept me in the neighborhood of Boston. My com-positions gave me a larger field. From Boston, I could reach out to the world."[61] The statement reveals how ambitious she was for an international reputation as a composer, even as she was denied one as a pianist.

Henry may have had something to do with the publication of her op. 1, no. 1, "With Violets," which Arthur P. Schmidt issued before they married. Being Schmidt's friend, as well as his physician, Henry may have brought the song to the publisher's attention, thus leading to Amy's contractual agreement.[62] It is likely that Schmidt would have published Amy's music even without his close friendship with Henry, but the friendship between the two men smoothed the way.

At the same time and despite that friendship, Henry drew on his own experience as editor of a medical journal to teach his wife how to keep a publisher toeing the line, a lesson she learned well indeed. Schmidt regularly sent two or three sets of proofs for her corrections, for which she had a sharp eye. He also consulted her about cover designs; and, as their voluminous correspondence shows, she soon learned to keep a tight control over publication. Beach boasted that among the "countless blessings he conferred" on her, Henry trained her carefully in business matters.[63]

Year after year, on his birthday, Amy presented Henry with a new song in manuscript with the dedication "To H." Occasionally her birthday presents to him were settings of his own poems, a double compliment. To these private dedications must be added the dozen songs published with dedications to him. On their second anniversary, Amy presented him with her arrangement for four hands of the Largo from Beethoven's Piano Concerto no. 1. At the top of the page was her habitual dedication.[64] In making the arrangement, she carefully reserved all the more technical passages for the *primo*, leaving the *secondo* easy enough for a nonpracticing amateur, such as Henry Beach, to play.

He in his turn gave her jewelry, creating a collection that eventually grew to considerable size. Among the pieces were three of Henry's own design that Beach described in her will as, "my large cross of miscellaneous jewels; also my large brooch of deep red jacinths and diamonds with a large aquamarine in the center; and my ring with large green diamond and two small diamonds."[65] Although she may have had reservations about wearing the flamboyant cross, the other jewels she wore with pleasure, sometimes several at a time.[66]

Amy gained from the marriage not only love and security but assistance in career building from a master of the art. The years of their marriage were for Amy Beach years of rapid growth and substantial achievement. For his part, Henry gained not only her devotion but the pleasures of a Pygmalion who created a composer—out of most promising stuff, to be sure—along with satisfaction and pride in her achievements. But nothing can compare to the tremendous gift of time and support in becoming a composer. For Amy, Henry was husband, patron, sponsor, musical mentor, and—with her mother—critic.

At the time of their marriage, Henry was at the height of his career, Amy at the beginning of hers. While her youthful success and enormous talent as a pianist had already captured the public imagination, afterwards his achievements added luster to hers and his position in society advanced her career as a composer. All in all, there can be but one view of the marriage: it was an ideal partnership.

OR CAN THERE BE A SECOND VIEW? One can only wonder how Amy Cheney felt about marrying a man slightly older than her father. Still in her teens and without ever having left her mother's careful oversight, she went typically from her parents' control to that of her husband. It is clear that she never had autonomy, nor did she make a habit of challenging authority; what is not clear is whether she wanted to do so. The religious training that she had from her mother, which stressed humility, docility, and submission to the will of parents and God, tended to discourage rebellious behavior.

As a male in a patriarchal society and a physician who typically exercised enormous control over his female patients, as a man who had built a lustrous career out of his own talent and ambition, and as one who arrogated to himself the role of artistic adviser and critic, Henry Beach had considerable authority over his wife. It was exercised in a number of ways, some of them relating to only small matters, yet telling in the way they defined Amy's relationship to Henry as a dependent one.

Soon after their marriage, she told him she would like to have a dog. Fulfilling her request while also denying it, he presented Amy with a large and rather ugly statue of a Boston bulldog.[67] Eventually they compromised on a cat, Tiger, a long-haired Persian that kept her company in the music room while she worked.

Other decisions were of more consequence to her life and work. Amy Beach mentioned in an interview that she regretted not having a child. There is no way of knowing whose decision this was, or whether there was even a choice, since both of Henry's marriages were childless. His age and medical authority suggest that if a decision were to have been made, it would have been more his than hers. He also was protective of her physical well-being, something that childbirth could and often did threaten. Finally, for Henry, Amy was both child and wife, and thus he may have felt less need for a family than she. While such a decision was far from unusual at a time when over half the married women who were professionals did not have children, remaining childless might well have been a part of Henry's strategy to keep her concentrated on her work.[68]

As a man of her parents' generation, he brought to their marriage attitudes and standards similar to those of her parents. Had she married a man of her own generation, the new couple, reinforcing each other's desire for separation from parental ways, would have, perhaps haltingly, found a modus vivendi appropriate to their own generation. With a middle-aged husband and without regular contact with contemporaries, any tendency toward rebellion against parental values was the more easily stifled.

But nothing made as much difference to Amy Beach as did the decision to give up her professional career as a pianist and concentrate on composition. Concerning this decision, she wrote that although Henry believed that her true career was in composition, "I didn't believe him, for I thought I was a pianist first and foremost."[69] The change was wrenching for one who had said that life began at her debut. She exulted in performing, finding it an intense and unalloyed pleasure, a heady challenge. She also loved her audiences and received a full measure of love in return. Henry simply continued her mother's decision against a full-scale concert career.

Both her withdrawal from frequent performance and refusal of fees when she did so deprived her of her former status as a professional pianist. Furthermore, by taking Henry's name and being known only as Mrs. H. H. A. Beach, she completely obliterated her own, which had gathered considerable luster in two years, and cloaked her identity in her husband's, thus erasing the reputation she had built as Amy Marcy Cheney. Her new name also suggests the amateur status that in fact she now had as a pianist. Compared to the life of a traveling performer, that of composing at home was more ladylike — even though the role of serious composer was considered a masculine one.

Her prolonged absences from the concert stage, however, may have taken a toll on her playing, as one critic suggested:

> It may be doubted whether any executive talent . . . can reach its largest development without the stimulating and enhancing influence which springs from the magnetic contact with the public . . . [A concert artist] must work by insufficient light and with insufficient enthusiasm if he tries to perfect himself in his closet or in the circle of his own friends.[70]

Here, the critic no doubt refers to Beach's private performances at home and in the homes of friends. Since the Beaches' social circle included musicians and patrons of music as well as critics, Beach was able in part to compensate for her all-but-retirement from performing. The reviewer ended by wishing that the conditions of Beach's life allowed for more frequent public appearances so that her expressive abilities might be able to grow toward the freer and the grander.

Her agreement with Henry never to teach music meant that she surrendered another possibility for professional status and for collegial associations with peers, something denied her because she never studied at a conservatory. Her professional contacts with other musicians, especially those of her own age who were at the start of careers, were limited to collaborations on her infrequent recitals or to those under the controlled situations of salons.

During their first year of marriage, Amy discontinued her lessons with Carl Baermann, the man who had prepared her for her debut. She reported that from that time on, her only teacher was the public. But the result was the cessation of regular contact with the one professional musician in a position to give her objective criticism of her playing. Most important, Henry did not approve of a composition teacher for her, preferring that she teach herself so as to keep her style unchanged: women were assumed to be more impressionable and less able to survive such training and remain in control of their own creativity.[71] In addition, out of an acute awareness of their age differences, he may have feared that a male composition teacher might form a strong, perhaps even threatening, bond with his young and passionate wife. Clearly, he wanted to remain in control of this musical treasure. But it is important to remember that because Henry's musical tastes were formed a generation earlier than Beach's during the height of the Romantic era, he may have pulled her back from experimenting in new forms and styles, something she might have pursued had she been in contact with other young composers.

This lack of outside contact was especially important because—perhaps unknown to Amy—Henry may have believed in protecting her from the critics during the years when she was teaching herself composition. This, too, would have been a mixed blessing. Although critics were inclined to favor her because she was one of Boston's most eminent daughters, a local girl who made good with local training, Henry was reported to have censored the reviews, showing her only favorable notices while quietly setting the others aside.[72] If that were true, it meant that while she was protected from destructive criticism at a formative time in her life as a composer, she was also cut off from the constructive kind as well.

There is no reason to assume that, had she remained unmarried, Amy Cheney would have concertized but not composed. As she pointed out, she moved with ease from her desk to the piano and, since she both composed and learned works quickly, might well have combined the two careers, working out the balance between the demands of composition and concertizing, something others have done. Amy Beach's comments about this decision are suggestive of a certain amount of resistance on her part, as well as pressure by Henry and her mother to convince her to give up her professional career as a pianist. She probably was referring to the time between her debut and marriage when she wrote:

> I gave recitals and played a good deal of chamber music, in concerts, and in the intervals worked at my compositions. I had not then divided my enthusiasms; the work was complementary. It had not come to me that there was a choice to be made; that where many many people play music, few write music; that creation is higher than interpretation.[73]

Perhaps without outside assistance, such an idea would never have come to her. Indeed, later in life after she resumed performing, she wrote that she profited from the alternation of roles:

> I have literally lived the life of two people, one a pianist, the other a writer. Anything more unlike the state of mind demanded by these two professions I could not imagine. When I do one kind of work I shut the other up in a closed room and lock the door, unless I happen to be composing for the piano, in which case there is a connecting link. One great advantage, however, in this kind of life is, that one never grows stale, but there is always a continual interest and freshness from the change back and forth.[74]

Whatever their devotion to her, it seems regrettable that Henry Beach and Clara Cheney, rather than a professional composer, were the closest she came to having a composition teacher. There is evidence in her music of unsolved compositional problems: occasionally a work displays a certain lack of discipline, a tendency to go on too long and to introduce unnecessary complications, practices that a vigilant composition teacher might have helped her overcome. That she succeeded otherwise without one was remarkable. Even so, her success came at a high price through hard and lonely work, work that might have gone faster and easier with professional help. Amy Beach wrote that the outcome of their agreements was that "I was happy and he was content."[75]

But as we have seen, there are occasional clues, subtle suggestions that she had thoughts that ran counter to her husband's and even longed for an autonomy she never had. Henry's requirements dovetailed so well with Clara's that one wonders whether the two of them, with the agreement of Charles as well, worked out the marriage arrangement together or simply were of one mind about Amy's future. The effect, in either case, would have been no different. She continued to live the protected life that she had before marriage. Except for those few occasions when there were out-of-town performances of her works, Henry carried on Clara's policy of excluding concert tours and limiting engagements to the Boston area, and he took that policy to its inevitable conclusion: she was to be a composer, not a pianist, "a musician, not a prodigy."[76]

There is no reason to blame husband or parents for their actions. All three were products of their time and training, acting in ways that they believed were for Amy's own good. Nor can Amy Beach be blamed for the path she took in response to their pressures. If, for her, the marriage was bought at the cost of a professional performing career, it may also have been a mixed blessing; for those who enjoy and value her music now are indebted not only to her but also to Henry Beach for his support and encouragement of her work as a composer, which then took a stellar path.

THE MAKING

OF A

COMPOSER:

II

NOW THAT THE MARRIAGE CHANGED the focus of her musical life from performance to composition, Amy Beach had the enviable good fortune to be able to compose without concern for money and with only the infrequent pleasure and distraction of a concert date. Alone in the music room, she left her desk to practice the piano when she felt "written out" and needed a break from composing. If the daytime hours spent working alone recalled the isolation of her life before her debut, she could look forward to the evenings' social diversions during which she might even play for assembled guests.

The physical surroundings and her agreement to focus on composition provided an atmosphere conducive to work. Yet much of that discipline was self-imposed: Amy Beach said that "very few people would be willing to work so hard. It may be that it kept for me my individuality—at any rate, I enjoyed it immensely."[1] To support the work, she collected every book she could locate on theory, composition, and orchestration. Eventually, she claimed to have a collection that was unexcelled in America. Hidden from view by antique, gold silk curtains, the books were on low shelves along the east and west walls of the music room. The shelves also housed her music, including orchestral scores that she had collected from Europe and the United States, sometimes from the composers themselves. She was reported to be especially pleased to have the scores of Wagner's operas and a prized French edition of [Gluck's?] *Alcestis*.[2]

She taught herself, successively, theory, harmony, counterpoint, fugue, and orchestration.[3] Considerable insight into her working habits may be gained from study of the manuscript workbook that she kept from 1887 to 1894.[4] In it she entered musical terms and technical details about rhythmic and pitch notation and copied important quotations from her various texts, arranging the entries alphabetically. In addition, for each step of the way, Beach used musical works as authoritative tutors: "I memorized [Bach] fugues and similar works, until I could write them down from memory, writing each 'voice,' or part, on its own separate staff," she said.[5] That way she laid bare their contrapuntal structure.

The largest part of the workbook is devoted to copies of passages—often extensive — on how to write for orchestral instruments. Here is a description of effective writing for the harp:

> Liszt (Faust [Symphony]) has used this exquisitely near the close of the "Gretchen" [movement], just picking out the tonic chord slowly, one note at a time, in the *medium* [register]. The notes here given in this way are full and sweet in tone. . . . Beautifully used as a solo inst[rument] at the beginning of Goldmark's "Sappho" overture. Full, rich chords in the medium and low register, slow enough to be well and strongly played. Key, G flat. An exquisite acc[ompaniment] to oboe, flute, & solo viola in turn.[6]

She copied into the workbook not only descriptions of the sound capabilities of individual instruments but also ways of combining two or more orchestral instruments. Under letter B in the workbook are entries entitled "Brass Instruments," "Beginning on fractional beats," and a description of the effect of the bassoon when combined with strings:

> The bassoons are the habitual companions of the celli. They do not sensibly increase the strength of the celli when the latter are united to the [contrabass]; in a rapid figure without melodic significance the addition is superfluous if not reprehensible. A sympathy none the less close unites the bassoons to the altos [violas]. Celli, altos and bassoons form together a male voice, full & of the most beautiful character.[7]

Gevaert's and Berlioz's treatises on orchestration, which feature excerpts from orchestral scores, with explanatory texts that discuss the effects of various instruments, were most composers' bibles. Because there were no English translations of the two books at the time, Beach wrote that she translated them from the French; in the workbook, she entered — with some crossings out and corrections — translations of occasional passages from these texts, and then memorized entire chapters.

Beach knew that the study of orchestration depended on knowing the distinctive sound of each instrument. Although the best way of learning orchestration might be to play every orchestral instrument — as did Paul Hindemith — Beach relied on her very acute ear, her textbooks, and the orchestra itself as tutors.[8]

Her next step was to look at complete orchestrations: "I copied and memorized whole scores of symphonies," she said, "until I absolutely knew just how they were made. It was like a medical student's dissection. I began to know instrumentation *on paper*."[9] Finally, after she could look at a score and hear in her head the sounds of the instruments singly and in combination, she took her studies to the concert hall. She brought orchestral scores to each performance of the Boston Symphony; that way, she said, "I learned to know each voice as intimately as I know the voices of my own family." Later, having learned a score, she would write it out from memory and then bring her work to the concert in order to "compare it with the playing of the orchestra. In this way," she said, "I learned whole movements from symphonies by heart. Thus I feel that the knowledge I have acquired has been by my own effort; and what I compose is a part of myself."[10]

Another of her methods of study involved writing reviews of orchestral and chamber compositions following performances that she had attended. Beach entered her reviews in a small notebook, carefully numbering pages and providing a table of contents. Although volume 1 is lost, volume 2, begun October 1894, provides substantial insight into her perceptive hearing, analytical abilities, and musical memory.[11] She describes symphonic and chamber works by contemporary composers—only Smetana was no longer alive—recalling keys and tempo, themes, details of instrumentation, and manner of development and assessing the overall quality and effect of each work. With endearing candor, she notes that some themes or other aspects of a movement are beyond her recall. But what she remembers is nonetheless impressive.

Her description of the first movement of Dvorak's Cello Concerto in B Minor, including the themes,[12] offers a typical example of her postperformance analyses:

> The first movement opens with a rather long "tutti" in which the orchestra set forth the main themes of the movement in the old-fashioned way. The 'cello enters ditto, but instead of playing straight through, it varies and diversifies the themes with many free passages, some of considerable interest. Here is the first theme, which is treated with *great* variety:

> It is effective at the beginning of the movement when given out by the low clarinet notes with a pizzicato accompaniment then with bassoons added to the clarinet. It is good, too, for the cello when its turn comes. The second theme occurs in D major, both when first given by the tutti and when followed by the solo instrument. It begins:

> It is sweet, suave and borders on the commonplace, yet it suits the cello cantabile well. Of course, it does not bear working as does the first theme, nor does Dvorak attempt it. There is considerable "squealy" passage work before the working-out is reached, of the usual unsatisfactory and all but impossible kind, excepting that here the arpeggios etc. mean more musically than in other concertos and seem to blend with the orchestral harmony. In the working out [development] a beautiful effect is produced by the first theme taken very slowly in A-flat minor and developed by the cello and orchestra in the most pathetic manner.[13]

Her astute critical faculties are apparent, as is, also, a hint of the arrogance and inexperience of youth.

Beach's ten commandments for young composers, written two decades later, cast further light on her autodidactic method (see appendix 2). She emphasized the student's need to become technically proficient in the craft of composition and recommended that he or she work diligently on small compositions until they are perfect, analyze string quartets, choral music, and symphonies by master composers, and hear these works in concert. Several of her "commandments" are especially relevant to her own practice: polish small forms before tackling the larger ones, choose a model for each genre from among the master works, and seek perfection in technique in order to better convey meaning, especially intense emotion.[14] But Beach was careful to qualify these suggestions, stating that:

> I do not recommend my system of study to the average student. It requires determination and intensive concentration to work alone, and those who are not equipped for it will go seriously afield. I have the greatest respect for formal educational guidance in music, though I have been able to assert myself without it. The average student needs guidance.[15]

Proud of her ability to work alone, this was how she carried out Gericke's prescription for self-education in composition.

Beach did not put off composing until her studies were behind her; however, she began turning out small works with some regularity, which Schmidt in turn issued soon after their completion. Of her very first published set of songs (1885–87), "With Violets," as discussed earlier, was notable for the expressive use of tonality in its remarkable close (see chapter 4). Opus 1, no. 2, "Die vier Brüder" (The Four Brothers), to a text by Schiller, is about the four seasons—the passage of time may have been important to Beach, especially since her husband was a full "season" older than she. Musically, it is an exploration of tonality. Each season is assigned a different key: lighthearted spring is in D; summer is harmonically richer and in Beach's pink key, E♭ major; autumn continues the same feeling but is, appropriately, in Beach's yellow key, E major; the last season opens with the barest unisons of voice and piano, moves through a dark chromatic descent, and finally returns to D major and its springlike opening. These modulations do not fulfill the traditional role of exploring near-related tonal areas; indeed, moving from D to E♭ to E denies rather than supports the tonic, and anticipates Beach's later tonal practice.

In the third song, "Jeune fille et jeune fleur," Beach gives each verse a contrasting setting, but sets the closing line of each as a refrain, thus providing a unifying element (see chapter 12). In contrast, the last song of the set shows Beach unifying all the verses of a song. "Ariette," op. 1, no. 4, displays her growing skill in prosody. A setting of Shelley's "To Jane," this asymmetrical, evocative poem describes "a lady singing to her accompaniment on the guitar."[16] As in "With Violets," so in this song, too, the persona of the one who sings is male. It is significant that in "Ariette" the composer's role as the singer of the song is not a direct one: Shelley's voice in the poem is that of the presumably male poet describing the woman who sings, not of the singer of the serenade herself. Was Beach more comfortable setting the words of a male rather than a female poet; did she need the cover of a male voice to sing her own song? Was this because, for her, empowerment as a composer derived from another male voice, Henry's, and not her own?[17]

Young as she was, Beach demonstrates in "Ariette" that she already knew how to spin out a long line, how to write a melody that singers would love to sing. An example of tone painting is displayed in an affecting dip into the minor for the phrase "O'er the faint cold starlight of heaven." She also demonstrates in this lovely song her understanding of the role of the piano accompaniment: to set the mood, support the voice, and provide a unifying element while illustrating a salient aspect of the text — the strumming of a guitar.

As if in confirmation of her dependence on a male voice, her next songs, opus 2 (1887–1891), are set to poems by her husband. Henry, who had a modest talent for poetry, had collected a set of ten lyrics, publishing them in a pamphlet under the title *Sketches*, with the attribution "H. H. A. B."[18]

For her opus 2, the composer chose from the booklet three poems about night.[19] The second, "When Far from Her," opens with a long descent beginning in the piano's treble register and ending on a low G, as if to illustrate the idea of the speaker's distance from the beloved. The rhythmically distinctive motive introduced by the piano in the opening measures permeates the song and is picked up by the voice at the high point of each of the two verses and later is heard more and more persistently in the accompaniment, building tension to the final cadence. As might be expected, given the poetic source of this highly integrated song, the narrative voice is male.

Although most of Beach's songs were fully composed before she wrote them down, for some she might write several versions and then choose among them. Occasionally a song required considerable reworking where the verses were "cranky," she said, that is, they contained "faulty meters" and were "badly constructed." Nevertheless, they were so pleasing to her that she decided to set the poem anyway, despite all the work needed.[20] Beach also described the mental work that goes on before a note is written: "The key is the first thing to suggest itself to me, and after that it comes, phrase by phrase, until the whole has taken shape."[21]

But Beach stated that song writing was recreation for her, a respite from other, more demanding work. "Then I just drop the larger work for the day and write a song. It freshens me up; I really consider that I have given myself a special treat when I have written a song," she said.[22] Perhaps she intended these remarks to distance herself from the genre — as a way of separating herself from women who compose only songs — and underscore the importance of her larger instrumental works. In this way, during the first three years following her marriage, Beach wrote over a dozen songs, many of them little gems. These in turn became a storehouse of musical ideas for use as themes in larger instrumental works.

The compositional procedure differed when writing for instruments without voice. Then her ideas for formal structure and for themes and their development were generative. She suggested the extent of the mental processes behind some instrumental compositions: "All original art workers must have various plots and schemes docketed away in the 'pigeon holes' of their brains, undergoing a kind of mental digestion, an unconscious growth, until the day that they shall be called for. I have many such plans waiting for me to develop them."[23]

Several of Beach's early works were written to fill practical needs: music for the church—including an anthem for the ordination of the Reverend Phillips Brooks as Bishop of Massachusetts—and piano works as well as songs that could be presented at recitals or during musicales at home. A special possibility arose when Beach was asked to play Beethoven's Third Piano Concerto with the Boston Symphony on 21 April 1888. She decided to write her own cadenza to the first movement.[24] A brilliant essay in virtuoso writing, the cadenza's length is an eyebrow-raiser—longer than one third of the movement. While it might have used some judicious cutting, one critic stated that "the unusual length of this cadenza may be easily pardoned in view of its great musical beauties."[25] Because Beach based it entirely—and correctly—on themes from that movement, the cadenza connects seamlessly with the body of the movement, deemphasizing its length. The voice is that of Beethoven, with a bit of extra chromaticism the only hint of Beach's late Romantic style.

The review in the *Beacon* reported that Beach "illuminated" the concerto "not only with her sustained and yet splendid style of playing, but also by a bold, large and shining cadenza of her own composition."[26] The *Home Journal* indicated the interest of the musical community in this first evidence of her ability to deal in large-scale abstract forms, calling the cadenza "a masterpiece that is entitled to rank with some of the most important productions of its class."[27] In addition to unanimous acclaim for the cadenza, every critic praised her performance of the concerto, which was received by the audience with "wonderfully unbroken silence."[28]

As her catalogue of works grew, Beach included her own piano works, songs, and chamber music on her annual recitals. In 1889 she presented not one but two completely new programs, the first on 24 January and the second on 21 March; both were benefits for the Marine Biological Laboratory, a favorite Boston charity. On the second program, Beach gave the premiere of her *Valse-Caprice*, op. 4. The piece, while light and fanciful, makes great technical demands on the player. The music critic for the *Beacon* called it "elegant in its shaping and . . . delivery"[29] and another, "a charming and dainty bit of writing, especially noteworthy for the fine effect of climax with which it is rounded off."[30] It became a favorite encore piece for the eminent pianist Josef Hofmann (ex. 6.1).

Beach's next composition for piano, *Ballad*, op. 6 (1894), has a most explicit narrative. It is a reworking of her art song "O my luve is like a red, red rose," op. 12, no. 3 (1889). Whereas the opus number suggests the primacy of the piano piece, copyright dates make clear that the song was published five years earlier than the piano work. The song's text is by Robert Burns, and the voice is that of a man who declares to his beloved that he will remain true "though he go ten thousand mile." The melody, however, is unrelated to the Burns song and original with Beach.

Placing Beach's art song and piano solo side by side illuminates her compositional procedures and gives clues as to the dramatic line of the *Ballad*. The

EXAMPLE 6.1 *Valse-Caprice*, op. 4, mm. 1–20 (Arthur P. Schmidt, 1889).

EXAMPLE 6.2 (a) "My Luve Is Like a Red, Red Rose," op. 12, no. 1, mm. 43–48 (Arthur P. Schmidt, 1889). (b) *Ballad*, op. 6, mm. 91–96 (Arthur P. Schmidt, 1894).

melody of the song is threaded through the piano work, and the accompaniment is expanded but still recognizably based on that of the song. The key of both the song and the piano work is Db major, but in the *Ballad* Beach repeats the entire first section in the darkest possible key of Db minor. This then leads to the section of the *Ballad* that greatly expands on the song's B section and intensifies exponentially as she explores musically the idea of the destruction of the world suggested by "Till a' the seas gang dry, my dear, and the rocks melt with the sun" (ex. 6.2a). The section begins with the broadly declamatory Allegro con vigore that soon turns threatening, even cataclysmic (ex. 6.2b). That leads to a powerful reassertion of the original melody in the original key, a passionate and even broader climactic statement of the theme. The result is that the *Ballad* is the song writ large, in the style of Lisztian transcriptions.

But neither the composition of songs, piano music, and occasional short choral works nor the preparations for an isolated performance were Beach's main interest. Only a few months after the marriage and her commitment to composition, while still a fledgling composer, she was "incited" by Henry to work on an audacious project, a mass for solo quartet, chorus, organ, and orchestra, which would be her opus 5. In it she would test all her newly acquired skills, putting some to use even as she was learning them.

BECOMING

MISTRESS OF

HER CRAFT

THERE IS A TRADITION OF COMPOSING for the Mass that goes back to the Renaissance, during which composers used the work to demonstrate their skills, to create the "master piece" that placed them in the company of master composers. That tradition continued after the Reformation for both Catholic and Protestant composers, as epitomized by the great B-Minor Mass by Bach, a Lutheran. But Beach did not have to go outside of Boston to find a precedent: John Knowles Paine, also a Protestant, wrote a mass in 1865. His first large-scale work, it was composed while he was a student in Germany and almost as young as Beach was when she began hers.[1] Paine's Mass—like Beach's—has impressed its hearers by its beauty, craftsmanship, and fine use of the orchestra.

Amy Beach had a different and more difficult set of challenges than did Paine. Although she had the support and "incitement" of her husband to tackle a mass, it is also clear that she knew of no other woman who had written one.[2] That so few are known to date is hardly a surprise considering the church's historical limitations on women's activities in liturgical music.[3] Thus Beach believed herself to be a pioneer in the genre.

Perhaps the most significant difference between the two composers lay in their training. Paine had fine composition teachers in the United States and Europe; Beach was an autodidact. As a result, she needed courage and support, as well as a belief in her own capabilities, in tackling her first large-scale work and her first composition for orchestra. When she questioned the enormity of the task, Henry Beach buoyed up her spirits, assuring her that she was ready for such a challenge.[4]

She was resourceful and used whatever support she could find. For the new challenges she may have followed the rules she herself later laid down in her "Ten Commandments," especially with regard to the use of models when writing in a new genre.[5] It is likely, therefore, that as Beach planned her first major work, she looked for at least one model, perhaps beginning with choral works in her own extensive score collection. The collection, unfortunately, is dispersed, most of it lost.[6] There remains, however, a detailed record of performances by the Handel and Haydn Society, at whose concerts she was a regular attendee.

Between the time of its establishment in 1815 and the late 1870s, the soci-

EXAMPLE 7.1 (a) Luigi Cherubini, *Messe solemnelle* in D major, Kyrie, mm. 21–25 (©1985 Henry Litolffs Verlag. Reprinted by permission of C. F. Peters Corporation, New York). (b) Beach, Mass in E♭, op. 5, Quoniam tu solus, mm. 9–16 (Arthur P. Schmidt, 1890).

ety had never presented a Latin mass.[7] The first solemn mass that the Handel and Haydn Society gave was Luigi Cherubini's *Deuxième messe solemnelle*, in D minor, on 2 May 1883. A second work may also have been an important influence on Beach. In the fall of 1886, about the time she began work on her mass, the Handel and Haydn Society began rehearsals for its first performance of Bach's B-Minor Mass, from which they offered selections on 27 February 1887.[8] Amy Beach probably heard both these works with score in hand, studying them in advance.

EXAMPLE 7.1 (continued)

Although the very length of a mass is daunting, its clearly defined text sections offer structures that composers can use to build individual movements. The composer must first decide on the divisions of the text, especially for the Gloria and the Credo; as they are long, they are usually divided into several movements. In Bach's B-Minor Mass the Gloria and the Credo are each divided into eight movements. In Beach's Mass in E♭, the Gloria is in four parts, the Credo in one, with four clearly segmented subdivisions. Thus, Bach's B-Minor Mass could not be her model in this regard; but Cherubini's could, for it has precisely the same text divisions with but one minor change.[9]

Thematic similarities tend to confirm Cherubini's mass as a model. The opening Kyrie has characteristic double-dotted rhythms that were similarly used by Beach in her "Quoniam," of which the rhythmic figure recurs throughout in both the orchestra and the chorus (ex. 7.1). There is an even closer resemblance: in Cherubini's Credo, there is a striking dactyllic rhythm for the opening acclamation that Beach probably borrowed for the choral opening of her Credo (ex. 7.2). There are no such thematic similarities to the Bach's B-Minor Mass, with the possible exception of the "Dona nobis pacem" (ex. 7.3).

But the differences are in the end more important than the resemblances. Beach wrote her Mass in E♭ in late Romantic style, lush in harmony and wide-ranging in tonality. Her expressive use of tonality, with individual movements in third-related keys as well as in the dominant, B♭, is far removed from either

EXAMPLE 7.2 (a) Cherubini, *Messe solemnelle*, Credo, mm. 6–8. (b) Beach, Mass in E♭, Credo, mm. 1–4.

(a)

Do - na no - bis pa - cem, pa - cem

(b)

Ky - ri - e e - lei - son, Ky - ri - e

(c)

Ky - ri - e e - lei - son

(d)

Do - na no - bis pa - cem

EXAMPLE 7.3 (a) J. S. Bach, Mass in B Minor, "Dona nobis pacem," mm. 1–4. Beach, Mass in Eb, Kyrie: (b) mm. 3–6, (c) mm. 19–22; (d) Agnus Dei, mm. 171–74.

Bach's late-Baroque or Cherubini's classical practice.[10] Within movements as well, there are frequent modulations to third-related keys. For example, the "Laudamus te" opens in Eb major and changes key signature to Gb major for the "Gratias agimus tibi." The latter is a key Beach frequently uses for music of intense affect, in this case for thanking God for His great glory. On "Gloriam tuam," Beach modulates to the relative minor, Eb, while the section beginning "Domine Deus, rex coelestis" is a further third lower, in the key of C. In Beach's tonal lexicon, a modulation to C major often indicates heaven or light or, as in this instance, divinity (ex. 7.4). The tonality returns to Eb minor on "omnipotens," before the movement ends in its second key, Gb major.

Her well-honed skills in setting the texts of songs were applied directly to the vocal lines of the Mass in Eb, which carry her usual intensity and lyric beauty. There is evidence of unfamiliarity with Latin accentuation: a number of words, such as *peccata, patris, altissimus, adoratur,* and *nostram,* are incorrectly accented. In addition, one might question the many repetitions of such unimportant words as *quoniam* (since).

Beach builds her climaxes with dramatic effectiveness, giving singers the melodic lines that allow them to open up vocally. She also demonstrates her ability to build a large scale dramatic structure in her Mass. The chorus and soloists in the Kyrie, which is lightly accompanied by organ plus woodwinds and

EXAMPLE 7.4 Mass in E♭, "Laudaumus te," mm. 66–76.

strings, are quietly luminous. In the second movement, following the opening tenor solo of the "Gloria in excelsis Deo," the chorus enters accompanied by brass in a burst of vivid and brilliant writing that appropriately builds on the word *excelsis*. After a quieter middle section, Beach returns to the opening text and music for a climactic finish to the movement. After the more lyrical "Laudamus te" and "Qui tollis" movements, Beach completes the first half with the marchlike "Quoniam tu solus Dominus," with dotted rhythms, trumpets, and drums that evoke "the church militant." Beach sought out and found the dramatic values in the text and, with her usual intensity, underscored these values.

The orchestra consists of pairs of woodwinds, four horns, three trumpets, three trombones, timpani, harp, strings, and organ. One of the reviewers made note of the contrast that Beach achieved in instrumentation and was especially admiring of the solos for oboe, English horn, cello, and harp.[11] The Mass also demonstrates her resourceful use of solo voices and chorus and rich harmonic palette.

According to Clara Cheney, who may have monitored this creative project as closely as did Henry Beach, Amy Beach wrote the vocal and choral parts in 1886 and 1887 and completed the orchestral score in 1889.[12] Arthur P. Schmidt published the vocal score with piano accompaniment in 1890. Its issuance two years before the work's premiere created a stir. A work of this magnitude allowed critics to affirm that this was a significant creative talent. The *Boston Beacon* printed a lengthy review of the piano-vocal score on 27 June 1891, an indication of the interest—indeed the investment—the Boston musical community had in Beach. The writer described the work in detail from the Kyrie to "Dona nobis pacem," praising "the beautiful human spirit, the true ecclesiastical feeling, and the sincere sympathy" that he found in the work. Word also came back from Germany that Wilhelm Gericke, who had recommended that she teach herself composition, had "warm praise" for Beach's mass.[13] Most gratifying to Beach were the words of Carl Zerrahn, conductor of the Handel and Haydn Society, who wrote to her publisher that he remembered Beach well from the cross-country train trip they had shared when she was ten and was delighted to see this evidence of her gifts; he stated that he would give the premiere of the mass in the winter of 1892.[14]

Zerrahn's decision was made even before he saw the full score. Beach is reported to have said that she made "slight revisions" to the full score during the time between the publication of the vocal score and the premiere in 1892.[15] A comparison of the two scores shows no changes in the number of measures, in the harmonies, or in the choral parts. She did, however, make some minor adjustments in the orchestration, through octave transpositions of the solo cello part in the "Laudamus te" at "Gloriam tuam" and the rescoring of the "Crucifixus" with the addition of muted strings to the organ accompaniment of the soprano solo.[16]

The *Boston Commonwealth* was among several papers that heralded the coming production as "one of the chief musical events of the season," not only for Boston but for other music centers as well, and a celebration of a woman's important achievement in music.[17] The Handel and Haydn Society began rehearsals for the Beach Mass in the autumn of 1891. The musical preparation of the chorus was most thorough. Zerrahn scheduled more rehearsals than usual, drilling the large chorus with care. The choristers not only worked hard but were invested in and charmed by the work. The result was that the chorus "never sang better."[18] Zerrahn hired four first-class soloists: Jennie Patrick Walker, soprano; Mrs. Carl Alves, alto; Italo Campanini, tenor; and Emil Fischer, bass.[19] The orchestra consisted of players from the Boston Symphony with Franz Kneisel in his usual role as concertmaster and B. J. Lang as organ-ist.[20] In addition, Zerrahn offered Beach an opportunity to perform, engaging her as piano soloist in Beethoven's Choral Fantasia to "crown the eventful evening."[21] The Beethoven work, which has an extended solo for piano, is about eighteen minutes in duration, while Beach's Mass takes almost an hour and a half. Together they made a full program. Despite her dual involvement, Beach received no fee.[22]

An unusual feature of Beach's mass is her inclusion of a "Graduale," a tenor aria with a text that is a proper for the Feast of the Immaculate Conception on 8 December.[23] This is a movement found in neither the Cherubini nor the Bach masses. It was written in response to a request from the society that the com-poser add an extra solo for the tenor and star performer, Italo Campanini.[24]

The "Graduale" is in two sections. Unlike the "Laudamus te" described above, its tonality is relatively stable. The first part opens in G minor with an introduction for solo oboe and bassoon accompanied by strings that is at once reminiscent of the opening of the Mozart *Requiem* and, in Beach's employment of instruments in the introduction, of Bach arias. The solo voice enters in praise of the Virgin Mary, *Benedicta es tu*, with occasional interjections by the solo instruments. The second part of the "Graduale," *Tu gloria Jerusalem*, in G major, is accompanied by the entire orchestra. It is operatic in its triplet-driven progress to a climax before the final, quietly sung Alleluias. Admirably suited to Campanini's voice, temperament, and operatic style, it was the hit of the evening. In the performance, the "Graduale" began the second half after inter-mission, preceding the Credo. It was published separately in 1892, two years after the piano-vocal score of the mass appeared, and had several performances after the premiere.[25]

The program booklet for the concert has a front cover with medallions on its ornate border, each bearing the name of a composer: Handel, Bach, Haydn, Beethoven, and Beach, a fine compliment for the young composer and indica-tive of the support given to her by the Handel and Haydn Society. The public was intrigued by the novelty of a large work by a woman, especially one as young as Beach who was also Boston's own. Despite bad weather, the perfor-mance on Sunday evening, 7 February 1892, in the Music Hall, drew an "im-mense audience." Their response to the mass was intense: following the per-formance, Beach's entrance to play the Beethoven was "the signal for a royal ovation, the chorus rising at her [appearance] 'en masse,' with waving of hand-kerchiefs and clapping of hands," even stamping of feet. She was overwhelmed with flowers as well. It is no wonder that she seemed a bit nervous in the opening passages of the Beethoven.[26] But the nervousness passed and her play-ing was, according to the critics, exemplary—a triumphant event and, best of all, a validation of Beach as a composer and particularly of her writing for large forces in an extended work.

The press was there in force;[27] there were reviews in at least eighteen Boston papers and nine out-of-town papers and journals. They noted that the soloists were of high caliber and sang beautifully except for a single flaw: the solo trio that opens the "Laudamus te" had pitch and ensemble problems. One critic explained that this was the result of insufficient instrumental support for a difficult passage—not, as he might have said, because this was a first performance.[28] Otherwise, there was praise for her vocal and choral writing.

Her mastery of orchestration and of the "deeper resources of the science of music," that is, the intellectual aspects of composition such as counterpoint and fugue, were for some "difficult to associate with a woman's hand."[29] One declared that she "has shown considerable ability in her orchestration and her generally judicious use of the instruments and the resultant effect was somewhat of a surprise to the majority of the audience."[30] Such words as *virility, mastery* and *scholarly*, and phrases as *command of the modern orchestra* suggest the extent to which critics considered writing for orchestra a masculine affair.[31] Nevertheless, some critics evaluated the work as the product of a woman.[32]

Philip Hale, however, was of two minds. He wrote in the *Journal* that the Mass "is a work of long breath. It shows knowledge, skill and, above all, application, patience and industry." He found Beach's orchestration uneven but attributed that to inexperience, writing that while "the composer [has] not yet learned . . . that orchestral effects are gained by economy rather than by extravagance," the work deserved the exuberant demonstrations of approval given by the audience. In general, critics agreed that Beach's Mass was a noble work that placed her—as one said—"among the foremost rank of American composers."[33] But another, after praising the work, could not explain how Beach was able to rise so far above her limitations as a woman.[34]

Those working for women's suffrage and advancement generalized from Beach's Mass to all women. Julia Ward Howe (1819–1910) wrote in *The Woman's Journal* that the Mass in E♭ "made evident the capacity of a woman's brain to plan and execute a work combining great seriousness with unquestionable beauty." She finished her review by stating that "'the eternal womanly,' cited by Goethe, received a new and happy illustration."[35]

Howe also wrote to Henry Beach, her physician and friend, asking that he convey her thanks to Amy for sending her the tickets and stating, "I was astonished to find a work of genius, conceived and executed with real mastery. . . . How well she deserved her 'royal ovation'! and, how awfully proud you must be of her."[36] How striking that the letter is addressed not to the composer herself, but to Henry, as if he were the guardian of a minor.

That same year, heavy artillery against women was moved into the battle in the comments of the great pianist Anton Rubinstein: "The growing increase of women . . . in music . . . I consider . . . as one of the signs of the downfall of our art." Women lack "subjectivity and initiative." They imitate rather than create, lack "courage and conviction . . . depth, concentration, the power of thought, breadth of feeling, freedom of stroke." Having denied women any of the attributes usually considered masculine, Rubinstein then denied them feminine ones as well, claiming that no woman had ever written a love duet or a lullaby of "sufficient artistic value to be stamped as type."[37]

After the production of the Mass in E♭, Beach became a salient part of the argument in defense of women as composers. At times she herself went to some lengths to defend women. In December 1892, less than a year after the premiere of the Mass, Antonín Dvořák—three months after he arrived in this country to assume the position of director of the National Conservatory of Music in New York—stated in an interview that, although in the United States there was ample talent that might be trained to become professional composers, that talent was male, not female. The reason, he made amply clear, lay in women's intellectual inferiority. As a result, women had nothing to contribute to the development of American music.[38]

A few days later, a Boston newspaper printed rebuttals by musicians and feminists in the hub, among them Chadwick, who as both composer and teacher of composition rushed to women's defense:

> Mr. Dvořák doesn't know. When he has been here a year he will change his mind about women, and when he has been to Chicago and seen the things they are doing there he will talk differently. There is no doubt about the ability . . . of women. There is plenty of precedent for women composers. . . . There is the case of Mendelssohn's sister, who wrote as good a trio as Mendelssohn ever composed.[39]

The Chicago Fair was at that time five months in the future, but Chadwick may well have seen two of the works by Boston's women that would be heard at the fair, Beach's *Festival jubilate*, which was published in the fall of 1892, and Margaret Lang's *Overture Witichis*.

In preparing her response to Dvořák, Beach did her homework. Her first source probably was Upton's *Woman in Music*, in which the author argues that a woman's main function in the arts is as muse to men. In an appendix, however, Upton lists European women active as composers of stage works from the seventeenth to the second half of the nineteenth century.[40] With the names of women as a starting point, Beach could then look them up in the first edition of Grove's *Dictionary of Music*.[41]

Her rebuttal to Dvořák began with some conciliatory words, noting that he was very much engaged in his work at the National Conservatory of Music and too new to this country to know about the work of women. "Otherwise it would have occurred to him that from the year 1675 to the year 1885 women have composed 153 works, including 55 serious operas, 6 cantatas, 53 comic operas, 17 operettas, 6 sing-spiele, 4 ballets, 4 vaudevilles, 2 oratorias [sic], one each of farces, pastorales, masques, ballads and buffas."[42] She then went on to name dozens of female European composers.

Concerning the future, she noted that works by Cécile Chaminade, Augusta Holmès, and herself would be heard on programs given during the coming World's Columbian Exposition in Chicago and that "[m]ore women are interested in the serious study of the science of music as well as the art than formerly." The key word is *science*, a reference to the use of learned techniques of thorough-bass and counterpoint. Thus, she rebuts claims that women were incapable of mastering the intellectual aspects of composition. About her own work she wrote modestly, "Coming down to the present it would be unbecoming in me to allude to my own work, and I should, therefore, prefer to leave the record I have made in the hands of musical historians and critics."[43]

To her newly won status as America's leading woman composer, she now added the role of advocate and spokesperson for women, roles she would continue to fill for many years.

In a published interview, however, Beach demonstrates her sense of being a token, of being unlike other women:

> I frankly confess that I have never been able to determine the reason [why women have not created great music]. I have often thought of the strangeness of such a fact, but can find no thorough explanation of it. It is certain that in the high flights of musical creation women do not begin to compare with men.[44]

Beach then points out the limitations women live with by virtue of their gender: "[M]usic is the superlative expression of life experience, and woman by the very nature of her position is denied many of the experiences that color the life of man." She also believed that women were inferior to men in physical endurance, an idea that stems from the theory of Social Darwinism that had wide currency in the late nineteenth and early twentieth centuries. According to Beach, woman does not have "the necessary strength to sustain the tremendous pressure involved in carrying through the problems involved in composition—mental labor exhausting enough to react with far-reaching physical effect."[45] Thus Beach suggested that not only were women relatively weak but also that their life experiences left them emotionally immature. She concurred with the prevailing belief that women were physically more vulnerable than men, a belief that statistics on life expectancy for the late nineteenth century did not bear out. Yet she herself apparently suffered no adverse physical effects from her concentration on composition. Did she consider herself unique, different in that regard from other women because of her enormous gifts and therefore not to be measured by the same standards?

Meantime, evidence of a larger reach came a week after the performance of the Mass—her first commission. C. Katie Alves, the contralto soloist for the Handel and Haydn Society performance, requested a dramatic solo with orchestra to sing with the Symphony Society of New York, conducted by Walter Damrosch.[46] *Eilende Wolken, Segler die Lüfte* ("Wandering Clouds, Sail through the Air"),[47] op. 18, dedicated to Alves, would be the first work by a woman given by that orchestra.

The choice of a text was crucial. Beach chose an excerpt from Schiller's play *Marie Stuart*, a fictionalized rendering of the last days of Mary Queen of Scots.[48] The subject was a tragically heroic woman to whom the composer could relate. In the opening of the third act, the Scottish queen imprisoned for treason by Queen Elizabeth I is briefly allowed out of the dungeon of Fotheringay Castle to roam its grounds with apparent freedom—freedom so close she could see it, hear it—even as she was still imprisoned. The English translation begins:

> O thanks to these trees so green and friendly,
> that from my eyes the prison walls conceal!
> I now may dream, once more in happiness and peace.

Ah why awaken me from my fading sweet illusion?
Surrounds me not the azure vault of Heaven?
Unfettered, and free, my wandering eyes may range
O'er endless space, in everboundless freedom.[49]

The queen, in her boundless ambition and desperation, has reached out from her prison to her countrymen, her French allies, and her co-conspirators who planned to overthrow Elizabeth I and place Mary on the throne of England. Mary's story has a certain resonance with Beach's—her need to "reach out to the world" with her music. With the success of her Mass in E♭, Beach could now envision a life as a composer, imagine new countries and new audiences to conquer, although as a performer she was still confined to Boston.[50]

Beach may have had Damrosch's devotion to Wagner's operas in mind when she chose Schiller's play as the source for her setting. Her harmonic vocabulary and her assignment of thematic material to the orchestra while the voice declaims above it are Wagnerian. The darkness of a contralto's voice suited the tragic heroine's role. Wagner, however, was not the only influence. The dramatic *scena ed aria* consists of an introduction for orchestra laced with Verdian pathetic accents and an accompanied recitative and aria in which Mary laments her imprisonment, the opening of which gives the work its title. This is followed by a climactic cabaletta that is accompanied by the sounds of galloping hooves and hunting horns depicting the excitement of the chase, a memory that recalls Mary Stuart's lost freedom. A coda returns briefly to the earlier aria, restoring the desolation of the beginning as Mary again faces the reality of her imprisonment and the threat of execution.

While Damrosch's devotion to German opera was well known, it is less likely that Beach knew that Damrosch's principal backer, Andrew Carnegie, loved Scottish folk songs; her quotation of Robert Burns's "Auld Rob Morris" probably was a happy coincidence (ex. 7.5a).[51] The Burns song functions as a *leitmotif*: it is played first by the oboe, then joined by all the woodwinds (ex. 7.5b) just before Mary sings "There, where yon misty mountains rise in grandeur, / I can my empire's border see."[52] The musical reference to Scotland is emblematic, much as Puccini's quotation of the "Star Spangled Banner" in *Madama Butterfly* would later be, although without the irony. Beach thereafter weaves the song into the score; it is heard twice more, in an oboe solo during the hunting scene (mm. 233–40) and by strings in the coda (mm. 296–301), following Mary's farewell to Scotland, the land of her youth. The first of many works in which she quoted folk music, *EilendeWolken* is thus a landmark in Beach's oeuvre.[53]

By the end of April 1892, Beach was well on her way to finishing *Eilende Wolken*. At that time her second commission intervened, but by mid-July the concert aria was completed and her publisher soon issued a vocal score.[54] C. Katie Alves sang it with the Symphony Society, Walter Damrosch conducting, on the second and third of December 1892 in the new and handsome Music Hall, soon renamed Carnegie Hall after its donor.

Critical reception was mixed: The *New-Yorker Staats-Zeitung*'s review correctly praised the work as a perfect embodiment of the moving scene, and the *American Art Journal*'s critic described it as "a powerfully written work of decided dra-

EXAMPLE 7.5 (a) Robert Burns, "Auld Rob Morris" (*Songs of Robert Burns*, London, 191?), mm. 52–53. (b) Beach, *Eilende Wolken, Segler die Lüfte*, op. 18, mm. 79–95 (Arthur P. Schmidt, 1892).

matic feeling and expression and one that would do credit to any composer."[55] Other reviews were less positive, as, for example, one from *Harper's Weekly*:

> Judging from this composition, which, on the whole, proved decidedly disappointing, Mrs. Beach has talent, considerable technical aptitude, refined taste, and a nice feeling for contrast and dramatic effect. This work . . . gives evidence of more future promise than present fulfillment."[56]

Soon after the premiere, Beach programmed the work twice, accompanying the vocal soloists on the piano, and within several years following, she gave at least three additional performances with piano as well.[57] In Baltimore in 1901 there was a second performance with orchestra at a festival of women's music.[58] The work's undeserved neglect subsequently may be ascribed to the following: the undervaluation of works by the New England composers and American composers in general, Beach's gender, and the dismissal of late Romantic works as bearers of emotional excess.

Nevertheless, Beach's first commissioned work had the advantage of a performance by a major orchestra in America's leading musical city. Her second commissioned work would be heard by an international audience, command international attention, and have a sturdier performance record.

8

REACHING

OUT TO

THE WORLD

AMY BEACH'S SECOND COMMISSIONED WORK was heard by an international audience at an event that climaxed the end of the century. The World's Columbian Exposition, held in Chicago in 1893, celebrated the four hundredth anniversary of Columbus's landfall in the New World and ushered in the American century. The commission to compose a festive piece for the dedication of the Woman's Building at the fair was an honor that demonstrated how widespread was the reputation Beach had gained from the Mass.

Landmark events in a nation's history, world's fairs encapsulate past and present and offer visions of a nation's future. To some visitors, the fair was an event that "evinced cooperation instead of competition, idealism instead of materialism, beauty instead of ugliness, social responsibility instead of individual avariciousness, and art instead of business";[1] to others, the fair's leading message was the celebration of America's coming of age as a world power and, concomitantly, its claims of the cultural and intellectual superiority of white Americans, discussed below.

The fair was a watershed event for women as well, a landmark in their struggle to participate in the public life of their country as well as a powerful impetus for future advancement. The Woman's Building, a symbol of women's newfound status, was the creation of the Board of Lady Managers of the fair, headed by the reigning queen of Chicago society, Bertha Honoré Palmer. Granted a toehold at the fair by an act of Congress, the board, under Palmer's leadership, succeeded in expanding the original mandate and won an imposing physical presence at the Exposition. The Board of Lady Managers raised money and hired a woman to design the structure, a first for world's fairs.[2] Overlooking a lagoon, the handsome building in Renaissance style was among the most popular at the fair.[3] Nevertheless, its location at the edge of the White City, the official section of the fair, symbolized women's marginal position there. To sharpen the point, directly behind it was the entrance to the "dark city" of the fair, the Midway Plaisance—one half an anthropological display of so-called primitive peoples, the other a carnival and side show.[4]

For those in the arts, and for music in particular, the fair was a signal event. One of its aims was to convince the nation that "life consists of more than wealth and material gain," and to demonstrate that Americans no longer had to look to Europe for artistic direction.[5] By including the universe of music in its broadest terms, Theodore Thomas, head of the fair's Bureau of Music, hoped to prove to millions of people that art music was at the pinnacle of the Darwinian evolutionary ladder.[6] To that end, he scheduled symphonic, chamber, and choral and folk music concerts in two specially constructed buildings, the Music Hall and the Festival Hall.

For women in music the fair was an especially significant event, bringing together for the first time composers, performers, teachers, and representatives of the burgeoning music club movement. The programs given at the Women's Musical Congress, the Woman's Building, and several of Theodore Thomas's concerts became a showcase for women as performers and composers. As a result of the performance of her works at the fair, Amy Beach's musical career gained momentum, thus helping to realize her aim to "reach out to the world" with her compositions.[7]

On 19 March 1892, more than a year before the fair opened, Palmer wrote to "Mrs. H. H. W. Beech" [sic] asking for a specially composed celebratory ode that would be sung at the dedication of the Woman's Building in October 1892; she offered to have a poem written for Beach.[8] She explained, however, that because of limited funds, no fee could be offered: she understood that Beach was "not dependent upon [her] talents for a livelihood." Despite her belief in fair pay for women, when faced with a limited budget Palmer trimmed wherever possible, even at women's expense.[9] Beach for her part was delighted to accept an honor—with or without fee—that would further her reputation as the leading women composer of the United States.[10]

Palmer was an extraordinary woman who combined great beauty and charm with drive and business acumen.[11] Bolstered by her husband, Potter Palmer, the wealthy Chicago real estate magnate and vice-president of the directory of the fair, she above all others made it possible to realize the very ambitious plans for a women's building and programs and displays to be held there. But it was far from easy, for she and her board ran into considerable conflict with the governing directory, despite her husband's position on it. This was especially true concerning the commission to Beach.

Palmer must have consulted both with Theodore Thomas and his assistant, the choral conductor William L. Tomlins, about the commission.[12] Thomas knew Beach as a performer and undoubtedly had heard of the success of the Mass; he now knew her work as a composer, for she had recently sent him three works with orchestra—the Mass, *The Minstrel and the King*, op. 16, and the Mary Stuart aria—with the hope that he would present them at the fair.[13] Although he featured several compositions by women on his orchestral programs, Thomas's forced resignation in mid-August precluded the presentation of these works by Beach.[14]

Once in receipt of Bertha Palmer's letter, Beach set to work immediately, postponing the completion of the Mary Stuart aria. Rather than waiting for an ode, Beach chose the celebratory Psalm 100, "Oh, be joyful in the Lord, all ye lands."[15] As she noted, its text weaves together past and present, Catholic and

EXAMPLE 8.1 Chant, first tone, termination on A (Desclée, 1947). (b) Beach, *Festival jubilate*, op. 17, mm. 3–7 (Arthur P. Schmidt, 1892).

Protestant, thus combining the dominant religious traditions of fifteenth-century Spain and nineteenth-century America.[16] To close the work, Beach added the traditional "Gloria patri."

Her opening theme, which was drawn from both Catholic and Protestant sources,[17] is a cadential formula, or ending of a psalm melody (ex. 8.1a). The first phrase of the fugal subject, "O be joyful in the Lord," (ex. 8.1b) uses the same theme which appears again in the "Gloria patri." A phrase from a Protestant canticle for Easter Day, *Christ Our Passover*, may have been Beach's source for the lyrical fugue subject, "O go your way into His gates with thanksgiving" (ex. 8.2a, b).[18]

Beach wrote much of the piece in broad strokes. The outer celebratory sections are in D major, a key associated with festive trumpets and drums. Each succeeding section is introduced by a choral declamation, or by passages in a slow harmonic rhythm. There are two short fugues for chorus, however, that require the clarity of a concert hall, features that Beach's work shares with George Chadwick's *Ode*, written on commission for the dedication ceremonies for the fair as a whole. Beach, keeping her part of the bargain, finished in only

(a)

(b)

EXAMPLE 8.2 (a) "Christ Our Passover," canticle for Easter Day, no. 682 (*Hymnal of the Protestant Episcopal Church in the United States*, 1940). (b) Beach, *Festival jubilate*, mm. 268–72.

six weeks.[19] At the end of May she informed Theodore Thomas that her *Festival jubilate*, op. 17, for chorus and orchestra, was in the hands of the publisher.[20]

Unfortunately, the politics surrounding the work soon began to unfold. The Board of Lady Managers planned a dedication ceremony for their own building, which would be held on 13 October 1892 and feature Beach's *Festival jubilate*.[21] But members of the directory rejected the plan, saying that the building could not accommodate enough people and the budget would not allow them to hire an orchestra for this event alone.[22] The women then proposed that Beach's work and "The Battle Hymn of the Republic," set to the words of Julia Ward Howe, be presented on 21 October 1892 during the main dedication ceremonies for the fair.[23] The performance would take place in the Manufactures and Liberal Arts Building—perhaps the largest building in the world—with an elaborate program of speeches and presentations and specially commissioned works by Beach's Boston colleagues, Paine and Chadwick.[24]

Tomlins, who had approved of the *Festival jubilate*, changed his mind, saying that "as a woman [composer Beach was] very good, [but] . . . of ordinary merit as compared to men," that the work lacked "majesty and breadth," and was too elaborate to be heard in that huge space.[25] No one explained how, if Beach's work for a chorus of over 5,000 would be a "mere chirp" in that vast hall, works by Paine and Chadwick could be better heard. Besides, the eight-minute slot that the Council of Administration offered the women was less than half the time needed for Beach's work alone.[26]

The directors then suggested that Palmer use the time for an address. Angry at the rebuffs, Palmer was doubly reluctant to speak because she also knew that her voice would not carry. But given the historic importance of the occasion, she finally agreed. In her address, printed in full in the daily press and entitled "Works of the Lady Managers," Palmer congratulated the United States Congress for the unprecedented step of creating the Board of Lady Managers, which she said represented interests of women from all over the world. Congress, she rejoiced with not so subtle irony, had "discovered" women.[27] For Palmer and the Board of Lady Managers, the controversy over Beach's music brought home the fact that their position vis-à-vis the men of the directory— despite Potter Palmer's membership in that group—was as marginal as the position of the Woman's Building at the edge of the White City and that the men "intended to snub them at every opportunity."[28]

After the work's rejection for the dedication ceremonies, the Board of Lady Managers decided to have festivities in the Woman's Building on opening day, 1 May 1893, since "Mrs. Beach might feel that she was not fairly treated if her cantata was not played at a time when it would be well advertised and made very prominent."[29] The board of directors agreed, for the performing forces would then be on payroll.

Amy Beach probably remained quite innocent of the controversy over her music. The Beaches arrived at the fair to confront nothing but pleasures, especially at the amazing vistas and dazzling white structures. Indeed, the fair was a watershed in urban design.[30] Known as the White City, its gleaming buildings, illuminated at night by electricity—a startling novelty to many—and bordering on canals in which gondolas glided, soon set the style for the design of official Washington. It also gave Americans a vision of "the city beautiful," rather than the ugliness, haphazard planning, and hodge-podge architecture of many urban areas. Its dazzlement moved Hamlin Garland to instruct his mother to "sell the cookstove if necessary and come. You must see this fair."[31] There were over twenty-seven million admissions to the fair at a time when the population of the United States was sixty-three million. Clearly, a large number of Americans followed Garland's advice.

Opening ceremonies for the fair as a whole, on 1 May, featured an address by President Grover Cleveland. Festivities in the rotunda of the Woman's Building followed at three o'clock that afternoon. Conditions were far from ideal. The air in the building, which like all others at the fair was unheated, was cold enough to set teeth chattering. At the last minute, a platform was erected for speakers and honored guests, but not for the musicians; the placement of chorus and orchestra at floor level in the north side of the building made the music difficult to hear.[32] Nevertheless, the event was a thrilling one for the two thousand people who crowded into the rotunda.

The program opened with the *Grand March* of Ingeborg Bronsart (von Schellendorf), followed by Frances Ellicott's *Dramatic Overture*.[33]

Palmer, in her address, made a powerful statement about the inequities faced by women in the name of keeping them on their pedestals. The majority, she asserted, had no pedestals; rather they needed to work for their own and their families' survival, while being penalized by limited opportunities and low pay. Therefore, she advanced a program for "the thorough education and training of woman to fit her to meet whatever fate life may bring." In order to demonstrate women's competence, Palmer declared that the board has brought together "evidences of her skill in various industries, arts, and professions as may convince the world that ability is not a matter of sex."[34]

Soon thereafter, the three hundred singers of Tomlins's mixed-voice Chicago Apollo Musical Club joined the orchestra to give Beach's *Festival jubilate* under the baton of Theodore Thomas. In a review of Beach's piece, a critic for the *Chicago Tribune* wrote that, acoustics aside, the work was "dignified and elevated in style, cleverly conceived, and skillfully constructed."[35] The Chicago *Inter-Ocean* found the work "a fitting climax to [Palmer's] address which was in itself a jubilate over the emancipation of women."[36] Another writer called it "a clarion of triumph—the cry of a Balboa discovering a new sea of opportunity and emotion."[37]

Beach's *Jubilate* was "the success of the afternoon," declared Lauder, the reporter for the *Musical Courier*. But he could not refrain from taking back some of the praise by suggesting that Beach used as a model Chadwick's *Columbian Ode* given at the dedicatory ceremonies.[38] In fact, Beach completed her work two months earlier than "George W." and thus could not have modeled her work on his.[39]

For Beach the affair was a triumph. A Chicago writer, reviewing Beach's role at the fair, noted that in the past "some fugitives from Mrs. Beach's pen have floated westward, but little was known of this composer in Chicago" until the performance of the *Festival jubilate*.[40] Interest in Beach was especially high, prompting the first of many feature articles about her.[41]

Amy and Henry Beach not only attended on opening day, but they made a second trip to Chicago when she participated in the Woman's Musical Congress held from 5 to 7 July.[42] The sessions took place in the newly built Memorial Art Palace, soon renamed the Art Institute of Chicago. So many women responded to the call that the sessions were moved to the largest hall in the Art Palace.[43] Singers were represented by Luisa Cappiani, Octavia Hensel, and the celebrated Lillian Nordica. Highly successful opera singers like Nordica were the culture heroines of the day. Not only were they paid the highest fees of any concert artists, but the press regularly reported on their personal lives as well as their professional activities. Leading members of America's first generation of female professional instrumentalists also had a prominent place in the proceedings both as speakers and performers, including the concert violinists Camilla Urso and Maud Powell.

In addition, the Woman's Musical Congress presented songs and piano and chamber works by fifteen women.[44] Beach played on each of the three days, offering on the first day two compositions from her recently published set of four piano *Sketches*, op. 15 —"Autumn Leaves" and the brilliant "Fireflies." On the second day, Maud Powell, with Beach at the piano, gave the first performance of Beach's *Romance*, op. 23, for violin and piano, which is dedicated to the violinist. The *Chicago Times* reported that "the audience cheered [*Romance*] to the echo"; the *Record* noted that "the selection was listened to in sympathetic silence . . . at the close tears glistened in many eyes," and it had to be given an encore.[45] On the final day Beach and the singer Jeannette Dutton presented "Sweetheart, Sigh No More," the song on which her *Romance* is based.[46] In offering these two compositions, Beach demonstrated to her colleagues how she developed and expanded a musical idea. The relationship between the two works, however, was nowhere recognized.

Boston papers celebrated the important role that their own composers played at the Woman's Musical Congress, among them Clara Kathleen Rogers, Margaret Ruthven Lang, Helen Hood, Adele Lewing, and Mary Knight Wood in addition to Beach. A reviewer in *Harper's Weekly* singled out Beach, calling her "the shining light among American women composers."[47] She was the only composer whose works were heard at all three sessions. Another reviewer commented on the discrepancy between Beach's appearance and her musical achievements: "The composer . . . instead of being imposing and antique, was just a fresh-faced, pretty young woman, in a stylish gown, who didn't look a bit like the regulation genius!"[48]

The women's meetings were among several musical congresses that took place that week. Sessions on musical education, music journalism, folk music, sacred music, and music in higher education, which were given at meetings of the American College of Musicians, the Music Teachers National Association, and the Illinois Music Teacher's Association, helped to fulfill the fair's aim to present an ingathering of knowledge about music.

At the orchestral concerts conducted by Theodore Thomas, Maud Powell played the Bruch and Mendelssohn concertos with the Exposition Orchestra; both were enthusiastically received.[49] Pianist Fannie Bloomfield Zeisler (1863–1927), then an international star on the concert circuit, played twice with the Exposition Orchestra under Thomas—in Beethoven's Triple Concerto on 12 May and the Schumann Piano Concerto on 9 June.[50] A critic reported that she played the latter "very beautifully" but without the power shown by Paderewski.[51] It was to Zeisler that Beach had dedicated her *Ballad*, op. 6. Urso, Powell, and Zeisler were important models inspiring the next generation of American women to pursue professional performing careers.

Thomas also scheduled several works by women for the orchestral concerts: Helen Hood's "Summer Song," on an all-American program given for the Music Teachers' National Association on 7 July; Margaret Ruthven Lang's *Overture: Witichis*, op. 10, for orchestra on 29 July and twice thereafter; Bronsart's *Grand March* on 8 August; and Augusta Holmès's symphonic poem *Irlande* the following day.

Had Theodore Thomas been able to complete the season, he would have offered more American music. Unfortunately, the orchestral music component foundered in August and died the following month, a victim of ongoing controversies between Thomas and the directors and of the financial panic that summer that led the directors to cut off the large payments to the musicians in the Exposition Orchestra.[52] Thomas resigned on 10 August and the symphony orchestra was disbanded in early September, weeks before the fair closed.[53]

Bands, however, continued to play, offering a mixture of art and popular music in as many as ten concerts a day in the several bandstands erected in the White City. These were free and drew large crowds.[54] Offerings of folk music added greatly to the varieties of music at the fair and were of particular interest to Beach. In the White City, traditional music was presented at concerts and in encampments of Native Americans and sung and discussed at meetings of the World's Folklore Congress held from 10 to 16 July.[55]

Even greater varieties of traditional music entertained visitors daily on the Midway Plaisance. Dominating the Midway was the Ferris wheel. From its top the tourist could see the mile-long fair street connecting Jackson and Washington parks. On either side, specially constructed environments imitating ethnic neighborhoods were peopled by natives of countries from Ireland to Dahomey who brought their crafts, food, theater, dance, and music. As a result, the World's Columbian Exposition was an unequaled resource for studying world music, and none could have been more aware of this than the American composers who came to the fair to perform or hear their music or simply to visit. They included, in addition to Amy Beach, Margaret Ruthven Lang, Arthur Foote, and Edward MacDowell, as well as Charles Ives and John Alden Carpenter,[56] still in their teens.

The visitor who strolled the length of the midway must have felt like a world traveler, but with the world viewed from the wrong end of a telescope. The effect was overwhelming to many. Yet there was a negative side to these displays, one that distanced the viewer from the performer, making the latter an object rather than a fellow human being. Indeed, anthropologists who designed the fair expected white American visitors to measure themselves against the peoples of color and conclude that they were at the pinnacle of civilization, while those they watched perform were well below them.

Without a record of Henry and Amy Beach's stay at the Exposition, we cannot know whether they too strolled the length of the midway, stopping to hear the music offered on either side. Perhaps they attended one of the sensational and deliberately violent performances by the Dahomeyans. Purportedly imports from Central Africa, the Dahomeyans had become by default the ethnological stand-ins for black Americans, who were rejected as participants in the fair's exhibits.[57] If the Beaches saw their performance, they may have come away with mixed reactions to both the music and the musicians.

Interest in the fair's offerings of folk music could only have escalated as a result of the controversy over nationalism in music that was initiated in the New York press on 21 May 1893 by Antonín Dvořák; the controversy touched on the troubling ethnic problems confronting America's increasingly diverse population. This was especially so because Dvořák recommended that composers draw on the music of African Americans to create a truly American art music. Given the powerful lessons in racism—pervasive in society at large and reflected by the fair—questions might have arisen in Beach's mind about Dvořák's recommendations to borrow from a people placed by contemporary anthropologists at the low end of the evolutionary ladder. When Beach, along with other composers, returned from the fair's opening events that May to read about Dvořák's proposal, they might have wondered how his recommendation could lead to musical progress.

For those who, like Beach, agreed with Dvořák in principle if not in detail, however, the fair offered a unique opportunity for a universal musical feast and one of which Antonín Dvořák himself partook not once but three times during that summer.[58] For them, the Bohemian composer's words—and very soon his music, too—would validate the use of folk idioms in art music, whether or not they followed his specific recommendations. Responding to Dvořák, and nourished musically by the research of proto-ethnomusicologists, over the next fifty years a number of American composers, among them Amy Beach, would create a distinctive body of music using ethnic sources.

9

"ONE OF

THE

BOYS"

SYMPHONIES, LIKE HEROIC FEATS, are enacted in public. Composing a symphony means challenging the heights of art and taking a monumental risk. Beach had already taken one in the Mass in E♭ and won. But with the Mass, she could take her cues from the text itself and from the accretion over the ages of musical treatments of that text, its divisions, its piety, pathos, and tragedy. She also drew on her skills in text setting that had been learned from her songs. A symphony, however, grows not out of words but out of musical ideas.

She began her symphony sometime in January 1894. By this time Beach was steeped in the symphonic tradition, having studied and reconstructed from memory many of the symphonic works performed by the Boston Symphony, for example. But she, like many nineteenth-century composers, had to confront the looming shadows of Beethoven's symphonies. If Brahms had delayed until he was over forty, what should a twenty-seven-year-old woman do?

Whereas a mass had been the traditional proving ground in earlier times, the symphony was the contemporary test for composers. Whether Beach felt the urgent need for such a test or was challenged by her husband, she had to face the prevailing assumption that women were not equipped to deal with "the theoretical intricacies, the logical sequences, and the mathematical problems which are the foundation principles of music" deemed necessary for the creation of high art.[1]

Beach may have been countering that assumption when she told the press that she inherited her musical gifts from her mother, "while her strong taste for the scholastic and mathematical side of her art seems like a reflex of her father's mental qualities."[2] As the possessor of an androgynous combination of intellectual and emotional qualities, she transcended "feminine" limitations and was fully equipped for the task. Nevertheless, her socialization as a girl and woman hardly prepared her for such work. A symphony, considered the ultimate in "man-tone" music, required that a conductor and a large body of musicians—then, usually all male—take directions from the composer, in this case a female.[3] Beach needed courage and Henry's strong support to take this step. But under a modest exterior were two powerful streams: the first, her talent and musical imagination and the second, her determination to master compositional problems—including orchestration—unaided. Her success at this task was a matter of great pride.[4]

Beach, in her search for role models, had found no symphonists. Ironically, the information she had sought while she worked on the "Gaelic" became public as a result of its premiere. Critic Philip Hale began his review of the symphony with a discussion of women who composed symphonies, naming among others Louise Farrenc (1804–1875) of France, Alice May Meadows White (1839–1884) of England, and two Germans, Emilie Mayer (1821–1883) and Aline Hundt (1848–1873).[5] Without knowledge of these women as she worked on her symphony, Beach believed that she was once again navigating in uncharted waters.

Two events involving Antonín Dvořák influenced the way Beach composed the symphony. The first was his recommendation for the creation of an American national music, issued in May 1893 when he was putting the finishing touches on his Symphony in E Minor, "From the New World."[6] The Czech composer generalized from his own experience in writing that symphony when he told the press, "I am now satisfied . . . that the future music of this country must be founded upon what are called negro melodies. . . . There is nothing in the whole range of composition that cannot be supplied with themes from this source."[7] Dvořák named plantation melodies and minstrel show music as sources for the American art music of the future. Critics were quick to point out that much minstrel show music was written by whites.

On 28 May 1893, the *Boston Herald* published responses by leading Boston musicians. That they published the comments of Beach, the youngest respondent to Dvořák's proposal and the only woman, suggests her growing importance as a composer and her emerging role as the token woman in music. Replying at some length to Dvořák's statements, Beach began by noting that the plantation songs he recommended were "deeply rooted in the heartbreaking griefs" suffered by African Americans. Nevertheless, she objected to Dvořák's ideas, believing that blacks were no more "native American" than "Italians, Swedes or Russians." It is significant that Beach omitted Americans of Anglo-Saxon origin from this list. The sense that the New England composers should be the ones to define an American style is implicit in Beach's and others' responses.[8] Rather she believed that composers should look to their own heritage, that "[w]e of the North should be far more likely to be influenced by the old English, Scotch, or Irish songs, inherited with our literature from our ancestors." Songs from Scotland and especially Ireland had been part of the American musical mainstream for a century.[9]

Dvořák's challenge may well have been the impetus that spurred Boston composers Chadwick, Foote, Margaret Lang, and Beach to draw more heavily on Scottish and Irish traditional songs. The related question of national identity, an issue that arose in the late nineteenth century because of the perceived threat to Anglo-Saxon hegemony from the Northeast's large immigrant population, may also have figured in their choice of vernacular music from the British Isles.[10]

The second influence on Beach and her symphony was Dvořák's "New

World" symphony, premiered in New York on 16 December 1893 and in Boston on the 29th and 30th of that month by the Boston Symphony under Emil Paur's direction. Themes for the outer movements, either in the idiom of or fragmentary quotes from African-American spirituals and work songs, feature the gapped scales and syncopations associated with black music. By the time of the premiere of the "New World," Dvořák cited the influence of Native American music on the middle movements of the symphony. He then recommended the music of Native Americans, as well as that of blacks, as sources for American composers.[11]

Beach recorded her reactions to the "New World" in her manuscript book of music reviews, vol. 2. Here is her conclusion:

> The symphony as a whole made a far better impression on me than at its first performance last year. It is interesting throughout, the machinery of it admirably managed, the orchestral and harmonic coloring done by a master. It seems to me light in calibre, however, and to represent only the peaceful, sunny side of the negro character and life. Not for a moment does it suggest their suffering, heartbreaks, slavery.[12]

Beach determined not to repeat in her symphony what she considered this failing of Dvořák's.

Before a month had elapsed following the Dvořák premiere, Amy Beach had begun a symphony that was both inimitably her own and at the same time influenced by the "New World" Symphony's use of folk idioms and perhaps her recent exposure to folk and traditional music at the Chicago Fair. She began work on the symphony by reading Irish history, exploring articles on Gaelic life and art in *The Citizen*, a nationalist magazine published in Dublin in 1841. Included in each issue of the short-lived publication were several Irish folk songs and instrumental music. Not only did Beach study and absorb the characteristic melodic gestures of the idiom, she investigated the compositional potential of specific songs, orchestrating one or more of them. Years later she wrote that the songs "sprang from the common joys, sorrows, adventures and struggles of a primitive people. Their simple, rugged and unpretentious beauty led me to 'take my pen in hand' and try to develop their ideas in symphonic form."[13]

In calling the folk tunes "old," Beach was at least partially accurate: one is attributed to the blind bard Carolan (1670–1738). Their age undoubtedly attracted her, for at the time it was widely believed that the more ancient a folk tune, the more "authentic" it was, thus ignoring all the permutations—early and late—brought about by oral transmission. Beach neither named the borrowed tunes nor identified her source. However, the four melodies in the "Gaelic" Symphony as well as five melodies she later used in her *Suite for Two Pianos Founded upon Old Irish Themes*, op. 104, are among the folk tunes published in *The Citizen*.[14]

Beach's aim was to live up to her title and create a Gaelic symphony. She explained that the last theme of the first movement, the only theme of the second, and the two themes of the third were based on Gaelic melodies. Unlike

Dvořák, Beach used three of the four tunes in their entirety, probably to guarantee that the sound would be authentically Gaelic. There were models for this as well, including Tchaikovsky's use of the Russian folk song "The Birch Tree" in his Fourth Symphony (1877) and Vincent D'Indy's *Symphony on a French Mountain Air* (1886). Her original themes, she said, were written in the Gaelic style.

There are other similarities between the "New World" and the "Gaelic": both were written according to their composer's own recommendations for creating an American national style; and they are both in the same key, use pentatonic themes, feature oboe and English horn solos in the slow movements, and combine folk idioms with late-Romantic, that is, German, harmonies. Although this last characteristic may seem contradictory, in fact most so-called national music at the time—whether by Dvořák, Grieg, D'Indy, or Beach—consisted of an infusion of selected folk elements into the German Romantic idiom, then the dominant language of Western art music.[15]

Beach began by composing the second movement, to our confusion entitled "Alla Siciliana" because of its $\frac{12}{8}$ meter. A slow movement is compositionally less demanding than a first movement in sonata-allegro form with its requisite development section. She orchestrated as her theme the entire Gaelic folk song, "Goirtin Ornadh" (The Little Field of Barley), assigning the melody to the woodwinds, which imitate a bagpipe. The folk tune occupies the entire first section of this tripartite movement (ex. 9.1a,b). In the central section, marked *Allegro vivace*, the folk melody is transformed into a scherzo, thus setting the form on its head (ex. 9.1c). In a further modification, this section is in duple rather than the convential triple meter. Both aspects, however, have a number of precedents,[16] the most likely model being the scherzo of Brahms's Second Symphony, op. 73, which not only reverses the usual order of scherzo and trio, but also, like Beach's has a central *Presto ma non assai* in duple meter that is a variation of the opening *Allegro grazioso*.

Beach completed the second movement on 22 March 1894, just two months after she began. Later, probably after she had completed the third and first movements, she added a brief introduction to the second movement using fragments of the main theme.[17] This is the shortest movement of the symphony and one that many critics found the most appealing, undoubtedly for its vivacity, clarity of form, and tuneful theme.

The slow third movement took longer to compose and is unusual in that it is the longest movement of the four. It is also unusual in its double construction: the first folk theme is stated, developed and recalled, and then Beach goes through the same process with the second folk theme. There is a link between the two sections, for a fragment of the second theme appears early in the first part. The orchestration of both attractive themes is beautifully managed, with solos for cello, violin, oboe, and clarinet and careful husbanding of orchestral resources.

The first section is based on a lullaby dated c. 1800, "Paisdin Fuinne" (The Lively Child) or "Cushlamachree" (ex. 9.2a).[18] Beach quotes it in its entirety, first with solo cello and then with woodwinds and strings (ex. 9.2b). The second tune is "Cia an Bealach a Deachaidh Si" (Which way did she go?),[19] which

EXAMPLE 9.1 (a) "Goirtin Ornadh," mm. 1–8. Beach, Symphony in E Minor ("Gaelic"), op. 32, holograph, II. (b) mm. 5–12; (c) mm. 35–39. (University of New Hampshire, Durham).

(c)

EXAMPLE 9.1 (*continued*)

was sung by a woman from Kerry "as she wandered in her grief and melancholy . . . . [The song became] the solace of every peasant [who] felt the sorrows of this distracted country" (ex. 9.3a).[20] Its fullest statement is given in example 9.3. The tunes are at times somberly lyrical, at others heroic—expressing, in the composer's words, "the laments of a primitive people, their romance and their dreams."[21] She completed this affecting movement on 11 November 1894, seven months after she began it.

Beach found time for a number of other activities during the two years she worked on the symphony. She wrote nine songs, three sets of piano pieces, and two sacred and two secular choral works, seeing them through publication as well.[22] She also remained active as a performer. On 22 January 1894, she was the featured soloist with the Kneisel Quartet playing Schumann's Piano Quintet and her *Romance* with Franz Kneisel. She introduced her three songs from op. 21 at a benefit concert three days later, accompanied a violinist in her *Romance* at a concert of the Cecilia Society, gave five recitals with assisting soloists—four of them devoted to her own works exclusively—and played the technically dazzling and fiercely difficult Saint-Saens Second Piano Concerto with the Boston Symphony on 16 February 1895. In the fall of 1894 she was unanimously elected as Boston's honorary corresponding secretary for the New York branch of the Manuscript Society.[23] This was an unusually busy time for a retired performer.

On 21 November 1894, Beach began work on the first movement of the symphony. For her first and second themes, she turned to her own "Dark Is the Night!," a song with an atmospheric text by the British poet William Ernest Henley (1849–1903).[24] Of the several sea songs that Beach set, none is more tempestuous, "recalling Schubert's 'Erl-king' . . . but highly original and tremendously fierce and eerie."[25] Indeed, the song, marked *Allegro con fuoco*, has a melodic line at once heroic and ominous; its accompaniment, which Beach describes as a "murmuring chromatic figure" drives the song with accumulating intensity (ex. 9.4a).[26] Too turbulent for its brief sixty-six measures, the song demands the recomposition and development that Beach gave it in the symphony.

But Beach did not use the song as a unified theme as she had the folk melodies in the second and third movement. The piano accompaniment that

EXAMPLE 9.2 (a) "Paisdin Fuinne." (b) Beach, Symphony in E Minor ("Gaelic"), holograph, III, first theme, mm. 20–39.

(a) (continued)

(b)

EXAMPLE 9.2 (continued)

EXAMPLE 9.3 (a) "Cia an Bealach a Deachaide Si." (b) Beach, "Gaelic" Symphony, holograph, III, second theme, mm. 95–98.

EXAMPLE 9.4 (a) "Dark Is the Night!" op. 11, no. 1, mm. 1–6 (Arthur P. Schmidt, 1890).
(b) "Gaelic" Symphony, holograph, I, mm. 1–5.

(a)

(b)

EXAMPLE 9.5 "Dark Is the Night!" mm. 43–45. (b) "Gaelic" Symphony, holograph, I, first theme, mm. 17–21.

opens the song was recast for the opening measures of the symphony, in which its chromatic whizzing evokes the turbulent sea surrounding the Emerald Isle (ex. 9.4b). She uses it throughout the movement as an accompaniment to the first theme and an introduction to subsequent sections. It is both a driving and a unifying element. For her first theme, which is stated by trumpets and then French horns, Beach chose a phrase of the song with the text "A wild wind shakes the wilder sea" (ex. 9.5a). The result is a marchlike heroic theme that sets the tone for the Allegro movement (ex. 9.5b). Her second, lyrical theme is based on the melody from the middle section of "Dark Is the Night!" to the words "Where are the hours that came to me, so beautiful, so bright" (ex. 9.6a, b).

For the closing theme of the exposition, Beach quotes a sprightly dance tune, "Conchobhar ua Raghallaigh Cluann" (Connor O'Reilly of Clounish), that offers relief from the turbulent music that precedes it and recalls the bucolic sounds of the bagpipe's chanter and drone (ex. 9.7a). Its first appearance presents a short version of the melody; in the recapitulation the melody appears complete[27] (ex. 9.7b). As material for the extended development section, however, Beach uses only the first two themes, not the dance tune. A recitative on the clarinet, an instrument that Beach favored, introduces the recapitulation. The movement is long but absorbing because of its many contrasting moods of drama and lyricism. She finished the movement in seven months, on 9 June 1895, and with hardly a break she began work on the last movement,

(a)

(b)

EXAMPLE 9.6 (a) "Dark Is the Night!" mm. 28–33. (b) "Gaelic" Symphony, holograph, I, second theme, mm. 114–18.

EXAMPLE 9.7 (a) "Conchobhar ua Raghallaigh Cluann" (b) Beach, "Gaelic" Symphony, holograph, I, closing theme of recapitulation, mm. 443–60.

probably after the Beaches had left for their new summer home in Centerville on Cape Cod.

After summers spent in New Hampshire, the Beaches had settled in Centerville. With royalties from the sale of her most successful song to date, "Ecstasy," op. 19, no. 2 (1892), Amy herself purchased five acres of property (later increased to eleven) in a wooded area bordering on Long Pond. Henry provided the funds for a modest house that lacked running water and other amenities.[28] "We wanted to live in a tent . . . and we could have stood it well enough but the piano couldn't, so we built a cottage around the piano."[29]

(a)

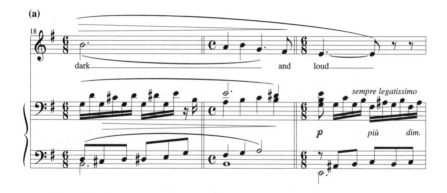

(b)

EXAMPLE 9.8 (a) "Dark Is the Night!" mm. 18–20. (b) "Gaelic" Symphony, holograph, IV, first theme, mm. 19–27.

There, surrounded by woods and close to the ocean, they both relaxed and worked, as Beach reported: "I spend much of my time digging in the dirt and cultivating flowers. At home I make composing my work, down there I do it at will. The doctor studies, and we are uninterrupted in our little home on the outskirts of the village."[30] They named their summer home "The Pines."[31]

Beach completed the symphony in early March 1896. Of the Finale, she wrote that it "tries to express the rough, primitive character of the Celtic people, their sturdy daily life, their passions and battles, and the elemental nature of the processes of thought and its resulting action."[32] Clearly she was thinking of the Ireland of the peasant class, from whom the most authentic folk music was assumed to stem.[33]

Like the first and third movements, the last is in sonata form. However, the themes are Beach's own. She derived its first theme from a fragment in the first movement—which in turn came from "Dark Is the Night!" (ex. 9.8a, b). Other themes were developed out of the first, as Beach stated: "There is no subsidiary theme or phrase that is not the direct outcome of the principal subject in some of its modified forms."[34] The second theme, given by the violas, is Romantic in its soaring length, its wide range, its prominent falling and rising sixths, and its rhythmic suspensions. Beach wrote that the end of the fourth

movement, in E major, has "fanfares of trumpets, horns and trombones surrounded by rapid fortissimo figures in the strings and full chords in the wind
instruments," bringing the symphony "to an energetic close."[35] She finished
the movement on 16 February 1896 but probably added some final touches
thereafter, for she told the press two weeks later, "only today I wrote the last
notes of my new symphony."[36] The symphony is a full-blown late Romantic
work strongly influenced by Brahms, who died a year after Beach finished her
symphony. Highly effective, like all her early major works, it carries the passionate intensity we have come to expect from her music.

Eight months later, the work was presented to Boston audiences. The open
rehearsal was given on the afternoon of Friday, 30 October, and the official
premiere was given the next evening by the Boston Symphony conducted by
Emil Paur, to whom it was dedicated. Interest was high indeed. William
Apthorp in his dual role of program annotator for the symphony and music
critic for the *Transcript*, stated that he had attended all the rehearsals, as well as
the two performances of the work, before writing his review.[37] At the final
open rehearsal, the "usually undemonstrative rehearsal audience broke away
from tradition and applauded with uncontrolled enthusiasm."[38] "Modest and
pretty," Beach took a bow, wearing "a dark costume, with black coat and a
closely fitting toque with rosettes of dark red."[39] The audience at the premiere
was similarly demonstrative.

Critical response reflected both the complexity of the score and the work's
unusual length of forty-plus minutes. While there was the expected disagree-
ment among experts on detail, there was unanimity on the general effect and
musical value of the symphony. Benjamin Edward Woolf, the critic for the
Herald, wrote that the work "never falls into triviality, but is steadily high-
reaching, dignified and virile, and of an able musicianship that is beyond all
question."[40] Philip Hale wrote that Beach "is a musician of genuine talent who
by the imagination, technical skill, and sense of orchestration displayed in this
symphony has brought honor to herself and the city which is her dwelling
place."[41] The most elaborate praise came from C. L. Capen, who rhapsodized
that the "Gaelic" was "a genuine symphony—a real, soulful masterpiece" elegantly formed "into a structure no less full of intellect than of vocative power."
He likened its virtues to the "physical and corporeal beauty" of Correggio, the
"spiritual beauty" of Angelico, and the sincerity and truthfulness of Rubens.[42]
The first movement was viewed by two critics as occasionally noisy and over-
elaborated, problems that Beach might correct in a revision. Although she may
have done some minor rescoring, no draft score survives to confirm this. Two
other reviews remarked on the unifying and fascinating effects of the "chromatic whizzing" heard first in the introduction.[43]

While every critic admired the second movement—one called it "a masterpiece"—the third movement had mixed reviews, on the one hand attacked for
its length and supposed weakness, on the other praised for its "deeply emotional" qualities and "moments of positive exaltation" as well as for its "strikingly original and effective combinations of instruments."[44] Regarding the Finale, Hale praised its vigor of conception in a "grand design," its "mastery of

climax," and "heroic spirit." Some thought it the best movement of the four, but the *Brooklyn Eagle*'s critic wrote, after a performance there by the Boston Symphony, that Beach was all written out by the time she reached the Finale.[45]

Critics also differed about how effectively Beach conveyed its Gaelic spirit. Krehbiel, who knew a great deal about folk music and was a strong supporter of Dvořák's proposal for a national style of American music based on ethnic tunes, failed to recognize that Beach quoted actual tunes. He, like others, wrote that the themes were not as interesting as her treatment of them (but that could be said of many Classical and Romantic works). He went on: "She has called it 'Gaelic' and justified the epithet by the use of some melodies with Irish rhythms and turns, but the task of stamping the whole work with a [Gaelic] spirit . . . seems to have been beyond her powers."[46] Some Boston critics changed their minds after Paur conducted the work again on 11 February 1898.[47] The *Boston Herald*'s critic noted that the work "improves mightily upon better acquaintance," and with one exception he "could find none of the weak points that struck us at the first hearings." The work, he concluded, "has earned a place in the repertory."[48]

Not one of them, however, included a discussion of the "Gaelic" as an example of musical nationalism, even though as time went on there was a wider recognition that Beach quoted actual folk tunes. Following the Boston Symphony's fourth performance of the work in 1898, the critic of the *Boston Courier* (probably Louis Elson) came close, recognizing that Beach quoted Gaelic tunes in the two middle movements but stating that "it was not intended to imply that the composer had attempted to represent either the spirit of the ancient Gael or his possible notions of musical expression."[49] As we have seen from Beach's own comments, however, that was precisely what she intended.

It took twenty years for a critic to recognize the nationalist implications of the work, but his was a lonely voice. On 5 April 1916 a Kansas City reviewer wrote, following a performance by the Kansas City Symphony conducted by Carl Busch, that the work was "fundamentally Gaelic, full of Celtic fire." Yet its Gaelic quality did not preclude its being an American work: "It is a grievous mistake to assume that American writers must confine themselves to 'high-brow coon songs' or American Indian melodies in order to preserve their nationalism."[50] In other words, one could write "American" music by drawing on the musical traditions of any ethnic group among this country's population. Dvořák's symphony was greeted as an exemplar of American musical nationalism; Beach's "Gaelic" deserved to be as well.

Perhaps the critics might have considered this as a nationalist work if they had not been distracted by their search for masculine or feminine qualities—or both—in Beach's work. Philip Hale praised her skill in orchestration, then continued, "[O]ccasionally she is boisterous, but the boisterousness is healthy, not merely vulgar. The only trace of woman I can find in this symphony is this same boisterousness."[51] Another agreed with Hale that the work "has not the slightest trace of effeminacy, but is distinctly and thoroughly masculine in effect," yet found its "noisy orchestration" characteristic of "the scoring of most women composers."[52] How many symphonic works by women composers could these critics have known?

Following the Boston Symphony's first performance of the symphony in Brooklyn on 27 March 1897, the reviewer for the Brooklyn Eagle praised its "strong writing" as "manful." But a year later, after Emil Paur conducted the symphony in New York on 17 February 1898, there was an intemperate review in a German-language paper in New York that was infected with the politics of the Spanish-American War as well as by anti-Boston feeling. The passage was translated from the German by Beach herself: "The last movement begins so full of strength, as if the world, or at least Cuba, were to be conquered, and the orchestration is as thick as if it were pasted on with Boston pork and beans. Musically this movement is the weakest."[53] Another type of negative review appeared in the New York Sun, which viewed the work as "four movements of graceful writing, music that flowed along spontaneously, whose chief characteristics were two—serenity and feminine persuasiveness."[54] To characterize the symphony as *graceful* and *spontaneous* is to use code words that are usually applied to women's smaller works, in particular parlor songs and piano pieces, marking them as expressions of the "eternal feminine." *Spontaneous* is especially belittling, for it suggests that such a composition by a women is an instinctive product, the writing of which has no intellectual component.[55] It is remarkable that these last reviews were the only ones that did not take the work seriously. On balance and after only a single hearing, most critics treated "the Gaelic" well.

While it was not usual for critics to denigrate all other male composers in comparison with one they considered gifted, this practice was applied to women in some criticisms of Beach's symphony. Considering that little was known of symphonic works by women, the logical approach would have been to place the work in the context of what male composers were writing at the time. But only a few did so by comparing her symphony to those of Raff and Saint-Saëns or to Charles Villiers Stanford's Irish Symphony. Sometimes this response was wedded to pride that a woman could create such a work: "Right here in this city of Boston there lives another Clara Schumann, a lady with striking originality in composition, rare skill in orchestration, and a finished artist in pianoforte playing."[56]

Women recorded Beach's triumph with pride. A review in the suffragists' Woman's Journal stressed the intellectual and "scientific" aspects of the work as it had with the Mass, referring to its more lyrical side only at the end: "We recognize with profound respect and admiration the intellectual power in conception, the technical skill in orchestration, and that rare inner sense of tone-color and picturesqueness belonging only to the sensitive musician, which united have produced a composition dignified and in many aspects touchingly beautiful and inspirational."[57] The poet Elizabeth Porter Gould published a poem entitled "Mrs. H. H. A. Beach," in which she compares Beach's music to "the heavenly harmonies of angel-choirs."[58]

Whether reviews were positive or negative, the big news was that a woman had written a symphony and one of this country's leading orchestras had given its premiere. Beach was "an epoch maker who has broken through old bound-aries and presented an enrichment and extension of woman's sphere in art such as has not been surpassed or even equalled by any contemporary of her sex."[59]

When George Whitefield Chadwick wrote to Beach after the premiere, he mixed high praise and gender bias:

> I want you to know how much Mr. Parker and I enjoyed your symphony on Satur-day evening. It is full of fine things, melodically, harmonically, and orchestrally, and mighty well built besides. I always feel a thrill of pride myself whenever I hear a fine work by any one of us, and as such you will have to be counted in, whether you will or not—one of the boys.[60]

Chadwick undoubtedly intended the last statement as a compliment, although it also served to remind Amy Beach of the prevalent belief that composition of high art music was not the business of women. Beach took him at his word, however, treasuring the letter for its unqualified praise of her "Gaelic" Sym-phony and rejoicing in her acceptance as a composer by her Boston colleagues.[61]

AMY BEACH'S

BOSTON

TOWARD THE END OF HER LIFE, Beach looked back gratefully to her early years in Boston, that "happy period" in a city that was "very musical indeed."[1] It is hard to imagine another city—or indeed another time—that would have been as supportive of her as a woman and a musician. The special bonding that took place between patrons and artists, the high value that its Brahmin aristocracy placed on music as an art, and the support its individuals and musical institutions offered to its resident composers and performers resulted in a thriving community of musicians and helped create America's first school of high art music. When George Whitefield Chadwick called Amy Beach "one of the boys," he was welcoming her into that school. When the leading performing organizations in Boston—the Boston Symphony, the Handel and Haydn Society, and the Kneisel Quartet—presented her as a pianist and gave the premieres of her compositions, they were providing a woman a level of support that few, if any, other cities began to match.

The three people who were most supportive of Beach were themselves composers. Pride of place belongs to John Knowles Paine (1839–1906), a highly gifted composer trained in Germany who had "massive attention" paid to his major works by Boston's leading ensembles. As professor of music at Harvard, he taught two generations of composers and critics.[2] George Whitefield Chadwick (1854–1931) was a prolific composer, conductor, and influential teacher. His works reflected his European training but also displayed distinctly American vernacular elements. He taught composition at, and later became director of, the New England Conservatory of Music. Chadwick not only praised but also conducted Beach's music.[3] Arthur Foote (1855–1937), composer, teacher, organist, and pianist was, similar to Beach, a leading composer in Boston whose musical training was wholly American. After receiving a master's degree in music at Harvard, the first that institution awarded, he had an active career as a recitalist and church organist. Brahms was the major influence in his music, which includes instrumental, vocal, and orchestral music, much of the latter given performances by the Boston Symphony.[4] Foote was an ardent admirer of Beach's music and often included her piano works on his recitals.

There were also other musicians who supported Beach as a performer by joining her in her recitals, among them George Henschel, the first conductor of the Boston Symphony; Charles Martin Loeffler, violin soloist and member of the Boston Symphony as well as a leading composer; Franz Kneisel and Wulf Fries, members of the Kneisel Quartet and concertmaster and first cellist of the symphony respectively. Boston churches also presented Beach's music, among them Trinity, Old South, and especially the Emmanuel Church.

Nor was Beach the only woman welcomed into that circle. Also included were Clara Kathleen Rogers (1844–1931), a native of England and a graduate of the Leipzig Conservatory who became an opera and concert singer, performing in Italy and England under the name of Clara Doria. After she came to the United States, she married the Boston lawyer Henry Munroe Rogers, and in 1902 she joined the faculty of the New England Conservatory of Music, where she taught voice. Her music, primarily songs of lyric beauty and drama, were widely sung by recitalists. Margaret Ruthven Lang (1867–1971) had strong connections to Boston's musical community through her father, Benjamin Johnson Lang, a musician at the center of music making in Boston. She had a thorough musical education both in Boston and in Europe and devoted her life to composition, turning out mainly songs and choral works as well as works for orchestra and for solo instruments. In 1893 the Boston Symphony introduced her "Dramatic" Overture, the orchestra's first performance of a work by an American woman; they later played two more of her compositions. Lang stopped composing about 1919, when only half her long life was lived out.[5] Helen Hopekirk (1856–1945), whose career as a concert pianist was primarily based in Europe, was born in Edinburgh, Scotland. She studied at the Leipzig Conservatory and gave her debut performance there in 1878. Tours of Europe followed, and in 1883 she made her Boston debut as soloist with the Boston Symphony. She settled in Boston in 1897 after accepting an offer from Chadwick to teach at the New England Conservatory. Her commitment to composition grew over the years, and her original works reflect her interest in Scottish folksong, which she collected and published in her own arrangements.[6] The Boston Symphony presented music by all these composers with the exception of Rogers, and Arthur P. Schmidt published the music of all six. The inclusion of women in the Boston circle, apparently without reservation, may have resulted from the group's need for a critical mass that would support its position as the leading composers' group in the United States. Its members shared not only an ideology but—even more important—a musical language.

Music had not always been Boston's primary artistic concern. Its first preoccupation was with the word, as taught at Harvard and as preached from Boston pulpits. Boston's great preachers—from Cotton Mather to William Ellery Channing and Theodore Parker—fed a stream that grew into the mid-nineteenth-century American Renaissance in literature. The movement spawned such Transcendentalist lecturers and writers as Emerson, Thoreau, and Fuller, as well as Hawthorne, Longfellow, Harriet Beecher Stowe, Harriet Prescott Spofford, John Greenleaf Whittier, Celia Thaxter, Emily Dickinson, Oliver Wendell Holmes, James Russell Lowell, Henry Adams, and finally Sara Orne Jewett and

Henry James. Long before the end of the century, however, Boston ceded its primacy in letters to New York.

Next after literature came the development of the Boston school of art, which was led by William Morris Hunt, a Harvard graduate who studied in Europe. Leading painter and teacher of art, including an entire class of women, Hunt also influenced Brahmin collectors to buy the works of Millet and other members of the Barbizon School, at midcentury the most progressive school of European art. Supported by Brahmin donations of money and art works, the Museum of Fine Arts was established in 1870, its School of Art seven years later. Its students and faculty soon constituted the leading school of art in this country.

Music was the last to flower in Boston. The most remote from "the word" because it was the most abstract of the arts, its very abstraction allowed critics to call it the divine art. The earliest nineteenth century bearer of music's "divine" message was the Handel and Haydn Society, whose choristers, beginning in 1815, presented "the word" set to music. John Sullivan Dwight (1813–1893), above all, led Bostonians to turn to absolute music, especially that of Beethoven, as the bearer of "things eternal."

In his writings, Dwight set forth "a complete system of Transcendental thought about music."[7] Not only did he believe in human perfectibility, but he wrote that music—especially that of Beethoven—was "one of the great divine agencies by which humanity even now is led toward the fulfillment of its glorious destiny."[8] The gradual ascendency of chamber and orchestral music over choral works, culminating in the establishment of the Boston Symphony Orchestra, reflects in part Dwight's influence on Boston's musical community and on its patrons.

Late in the century there was a gradual ideological shift as members of Boston's cultural elite came to believe that moral education of the public would come about in the concert hall through exposure to the divine art, providing, of course, that the public was protected against the "debilitating effects of bad music."[9] Even Dwight modified his expectations of the efficacy of the best music: listening to it would not lead to perfection, but rather uplift, educate, and refine the souls of the uncultivated among the middle classes, and the philistines among the rich. In other words, the meliorist idea of music's role had replaced that of the Transcendentalists.[10]

It was through music especially that the lower, as well as upper, classes were to be educated in moral and spiritual values. This ideology created among Brahmin patrons a sense of responsibility toward composers and musical organizations to further their work of moral education through music.[11] When Henry Lee Higginson organized the Boston Symphony Orchestra, he specified that the price of tickets be kept "low always, and especially where the lighter concerts are in question, because to them may come the poorer people; 50 cents and 25 cents being the measure of prices" to hear the message of the divine art.[12]

Beach, too, believed in music's redemptive power, a belief she actively promoted over her long lifetime, clinging to this dogma long after others in the arts had repudiated it both in words and creative acts. Her earliest statement, in *The Music Lover's Calendar* of 1905, was called "The Uplift of Music." In it, she quoted Ruskin, saying that "music is the first, the simplest, and the most effective of all instruments of moral instruction." She goes on to warn, however, that "the noblest attributes of so great an educational force may be . . . frittered away by its degradation to the purpose of mere amusement."[13] Thus, she ruled out listening to anything but the best, and carried into her later life the principles espoused by late-nineteenth-century Brahmin society.

Boston was, as Beach noted, much smaller in the 1890s than it would soon become, and its cultural community was a tightly knit mix of artists of all kinds, along with critics, publishers, Harvard faculty, and Brahmin patrons. These were interlocking circles, inbred in the case of the Brahmins—it is said that all of them were related to each other—but also crossbred to other circles.[14]

The mingling of culture and wealth in Brahmin Boston was strongly bonded through marriage. On his return from Europe to Boston, the artist William Morris Hunt married Louisa Perkins, a Brahmin heiress. In 1850, the widowed Harvard naturalist Louis Agassiz married the Boston heiress Elizabeth Cabot Cary, later founder and first president of Radcliffe College. In the next generation, Louis's second daughter from his earlier marriage, Ida Agassiz, married Henry Lee Higginson, financier and sole patron of the Boston Symphony Orchestra from 1881 to 1918.[15] Henry Wadsworth Longfellow, who came from Portland, Maine, married into the Appleton family, whose fortune had been made in the textile mills; and the daughter of Ralph Waldo Emerson married a Forbes, whose wealth came from the China trade.[16]

Still another expression of the Brahmins' social acceptance of artists and intellectuals was the St. Botolph Club, one of several such clubs for men of the social and cultural elite.[17] Established in 1880, the purpose of the founders of the St. Botolph was "the promotion of social intercourse among authors and artists, and other gentlemen connected with or interested in literature and art."[18] The roster of founding members reflects the commitment of Boston's upper class men to the support of the arts. Among them were Brahmins Henry Lee Higginson, Henry Cabot Lodge, the Reverend Phillips Brooks—"the most eloquent and inspiring preacher Boston has ever heard"[19]—and Harvard professor Charles Eliot Norton. There were also America's leading landscape architect, Frederick Law Olmsted; the sculptor Augustus St. Gaudens; and the critic John Sullivan Dwight. Not least among the founding members was the adoptive Brahmin Dr. Henry Harris Aubrey Beach.[20]

The club served as more than a casual meeting place. Artist members Frank Benson, William Paxton, Maurice Prendergast, Childe Hassam, and John Singer Sargent all exhibited there, while several women exhibited as guests, among them Ellen Day Hale, Lillian Westcott Hale, and Lilla Cabot Perry, student and disciple of Monet, who in 1897 gave her first solo exhibition at the club.[21]

Most of Boston's leading male musicians were members. Several of them found a hospitable working space at the club. Arthur Foote fondly recalled sessions he shared with composer colleagues Chadwick, Horatio Parker, and Arthur Whiting at which, he wrote, "We each offered manuscript compositions for criticism, sometimes caustic, always helpful. The talk was honest and frank to a degree, and one was constantly up against the unadorned truth. I learned a lot from it."[22] Women composers might have benefited as well, but this after all was a men's club.[23]

On the other hand, gifted people like Henry Beach and Amy Cheney, who also were of the right ethnicity, found a welcome from Boston Brahmins even though they married each other and not into proper Boston families. This was part of a long tradition among proper Bostonians of welcoming into their society intellectual and artistic creators of culture. Thomas Bailey Aldrich, the author, wrote in 1866, "The humble man of letters has a position here which he doesn't have in New York. To be known as an able writer is to have the choicest society opened to you. . . . In New York—he's a Bohemian! Outside of his personal friends he has no standing."[24]

One of the givens among the Boston elite was their responsibility to pay the cultural bill for the entire city. Along with this support came control over cultural expression, most conspicuously in the infamous Watch and Ward Society, established in 1878 as the New England Society for the Suppression of Vice by the Reverend Phillips Brooks, rector of Trinity Church and later the Episcopal bishop of Massachusetts (1891–93). On the board were the Reverend William Lawrence, Endicott Peabody, and Godfrey Lowell Cabot, self-appointed keepers of the public morals. Their first act was the banning in 1878 of Walt Whitman's *Leaves of Grass*, a fact which may have influenced Beach against setting any of Whitman's poetry.[25] Henry Beach's long association with the Reverend Brooks as friend and physician would have made such a step unthinkable.

In 1897, in another controversial act, the Watch and Ward induced the trustees of the Boston Public Library to remove the sculpture by Frederic MacMonnies, "Bacchante with an Infant Faun," from its courtyard. The censors declared that in depicting a nude female in an attitude of wanton joy—with a bunch of grapes in one hand and a chubby infant in the other—the sculpture glorified "that which is low and sensual and degrading."[26] This was not the vision of the eternal feminine they wished to deliver to the public.

The vision they no doubt approved, and one that had profound implications for Amy Beach, was the dominant image of women in the works of contemporary Boston artists. The idea of Goethe's "eternal feminine"—often given by Boston writers in its original German as *das Ewig weibliche*—was especially realized in art works by members of the Boston School of painting. Such paintings as Paxton's "The New Necklace" or Edmund Charles Tarbell's "Girl Crocheting" or Lillian Westcott Hale's charcoal "The Old Ring Box" depict women as the physical embodiments of the Anglo-Saxon type as well as decorative objects, passive, enclosed, domestic, passionless, and sexually innocent. Such images were soothing to the prospective buyer—usually male—precisely because they suppressed the conflicts between upper-class men and women in fin de siècle Boston.[27] The woman in her traditional role was the object not the subject, "the model not the painter, the character not the author."[28] Rarely is there an indication, in Boston artists' portraits, of female discontent with their enclosed lives or, indeed, of the active public lives of an impressive number of Boston women.

Among them were the very women artists who portrayed their female subjects exactly as did the men. A few, however, such as Marion Boyd Allen in her portrait of the sculptor Anna Hyatt (later Huntington) at work, and Ellen Day Hale and Gertrude Fiske in their self-portraits, defied the stereotype in their portraits of women.[29] Yet all sought a professional role for themselves despite the assumption that such a role was not natural for a "true woman."[30]

The issue of true womanhood affected women in music as we have seen—those who appeared on the public concert stage and those whose names appeared in print on their music, both stances evincing command. For Beach, this first became apparent in several reviews of the "Gaelic" Symphony, which sought to reconcile the conflicting roles of woman and symphonist. Beach herself was of two minds on the issue, accepting the designation of "true woman" as a valid representation of her position vis-à-vis her husband. She may also have welcomed it as a social convenience to mask or at least balance her ambition as a professional composer and her impetuous and passionate nature, a quality in women rarely depicted by Boston artists or indeed accepted as a Victorian norm.

As we have seen, Beach's search for female models of musical creativity yielded only Europeans. Boston, however, offered her many models in fields other than music, perhaps more than any other American city. A distinguished group of Boston women had long histories of social activism, before and during the Civil War as Abolitionists, during the Civil War as organizers of and workers on the Sanitary Commission, and later as suffragists and social reformers as well as professionals in a variety of callings. Their public lives gave the lie to the image of women as isolated, passive, and domestically contained.

Ednah Dow Cheney (1824–1905) describes Brahmin women in her chapter in The Memorial History of Boston (1880) as a mixture of the puritannical and the proactive: "more intellectual than passionate," chaste, highly moral.[31] Even more significant, she celebrates those women who seized the new opportunities for education and training to become professional teachers, lawyers, physicians, theologians, and artists—but not musicians.

Cheney herself was a prime example of Boston's active women. A disciple of the Transcendentalist and early feminist Margaret Fuller, she "sought to bring about an enlargement of the share which women have in the political, social and economic life of the nation."[32] In 1851 Cheney set up a school of design for women, in order to train them to earn their own living. In 1862 she founded and for many years was president of the New England Hospital for Women and Children. An abolitionist, after the Civil War she was active in the New England Freedmen's Aid Society, which sent teachers south to educate the freed slaves. She also contributed money to Tuskegee and Hampton institutes. Back in Boston, she helped to establish the Latin School for Girls and, along with other women, worked for and won the right of women to be elected to the school's board. Together with Julia Ward Howe, she was an active member of the Association for the Advancement of Women, working on women's issues on a national level for twenty-five years from 1874 to 1899.[33]

Women's clubs provided a place in which strong bonding occurred among members, as Cheney noted about her many friends in the New England Women's Club, among them Howe and Lucy Stone. Beach, too, was a member of a club, although one less political and more informal; it had no clubhouse but rather met at various members' homes for lunch on Wednesdays. The mix of professionally active and socially prominent women was similar to that found in the all-male St. Botolph Club. Because of its informal nature, however, there is no extant list of its members. Fortunately, in a letter to Beach, the popular novelist Margaret Deland (1857–1945) provides a few names. Deland recalled the time when

> you and I and Mrs. William James were, because we were "agreeable young women"—invited to become members of a luncheon club of charming ladies. . . . Of our little group, you were the youngest and also the most important because of your professional distinction. Mrs. James was the eldest, and as delightful a conversationalist as her husband. Those were the days of sitting at the feet, so to speak, of Mrs. Henry Higginson—do you remember the smile in her starry eyes? and how gentle dear Miss Georgiana Lowell was, and the brilliancy of Mrs. Bell![34]

Deland was probably referring to Helen Choate Bell, who "reigned supreme over the city's smart set" and was known as the "complete Boston woman."[35]

Distinguished as this group was at the time Beach joined, it became even more so when Annie Adams Fields (1834–1915), Boston's leading salonière, and the novelist Sarah Orne Jewett (1849–1909), best known for The Country of the Pointed Firs (1896), joined the club.[36] But Deland was modest when she stated that Beach was the most distinguished new member of the group. While her major works were still to come, Deland had already had a novel published as well as short stories in the Atlantic Monthly and Harper's Bazaar. From one of Deland's earliest publications, The Old Garden and Other Verses (1886), Beach had chosen three poems that are at once sentimental yet comment wryly on love and betrayal.[37] She set them as part-songs for women's voices, calling them Three Flower Songs, op. 31, the conventional title masking the irony of the texts.[38]

Despite their professionalism and social activism, many women remained ambivalent about women's roles. Hopekirk publicly accused women in general of being ill prepared as teachers of music.[39] Deland, who preached independence and active lives for women, for example, was antisuffrage, something she noted ironically in a letter to Beach in which she nevertheless solicited support for women running for election to the Boston School Board.[40] Others remained completely wedded to traditional roles for women, among them the militant upper-class antisuffragists who organized the Remonstrance Movement out of concern that women's involvement in politics would sully their purity and innocence.[41]

Beach exemplified that ambivalence. At once commanding as a performer and composer, she also accepted—with all its attendant implications—the mantle of true womanhood that was laid on her shoulders by interviewers and columnists. Unlike her colleague Helen Hopekirk, who was a strong supporter of female suffrage, she was never active in political movements of any kind until 1915 when she rode in a suffrage parade in Boston.[42] How much of this stance may have been attributed to Henry Beach's position on these matters— Amy Beach said that he was old-fashioned—is speculative. The headstrong and impetuous girl had turned into a Victorian lady under her mother's and then her husband's influence and tutelage. Yet Beach's music continued to contradict this image.

The glue that created a tightly knit social group uniting Brahmin patron and music lover with the establishments in literature, art, and music carried with it contradictions that mirrored those experienced by Beach herself. The years from 1880 to 1910 that were remembered by Foote, as well as Beach, as golden years of music in Boston, and the years when Beach was part of the musical mainstream in a city that valued music perhaps more than any other art form, also carried the seeds of change. Not only the old life but the old verities would soon be challenged.

THE COMPOSER AT

THE KEYBOARD

Beach Plays Beach

AT FIRST GLANCE, AMY BEACH's performing schedule seems an active one, much more so than the Beaches' marriage agreement—whether explicit or implicit —would have indicated, suggesting that despite all she had a concert career. The appearance, however, is deceptive. During her twenty-five years of marriage, Beach made on average one guest appearance and played one or occasionally two recitals each year. She had no concert manager and made no national or international tours; in fact, she hardly ever left Boston. As she said, her husband wanted her at home.

She managed her yearly recitals herself, hiring the hall and assisting artists. The halls were often small by concert standards. For example, Steinert Hall, the elegant oval-shaped concert hall in the basement of Morris Steinert's piano showrooms, where she played many times, seated about eight hundred people. Typically, she filled the hall, for she had an enthusiastic following.

The balance between composition and performance, however, had shifted 180 degrees. Her national reputation as a composer now far outstripped that as a pianist, which was mainly confined to Boston. The painful truth for Beach was that her natural pianistic flair, her marvelous ability to grasp a piece of music quickly, and her daily three hours of practice were not enough to make a concert pianist. Only frequent performance does that.[1]

Yet Beach could no more give up playing in public than she could breathing. She had three engagements in 1886, probably arranged before her marriage. With the Boston Symphony on 20 February, she played Mozart's Concerto in D Minor, K. 466. Everything about her playing was praised—beauty of tone, sense of structure and form, and tenderness and power.[2] Soon thereafter, a charity event for the benefit of the Perkins Institute for the Blind brought her out of the study once again. At the "Authors' Readings and Musicale" held at the Beacon Hill home of socialite Robert Treat Paine, Amy Beach shared the program with two authentic Brahmin poets, Oliver Wendell Holmes and James Russell Lowell. The authors read a number of their poems and dramatic excerpts, and later two little blind girls demonstrated the newly developed Braille system of reading. Amy Beach's contributions were Prelude and Fugue by Mendelssohn, three pieces by Chopin, and a technically dazzling transcription by Liszt, the "Rigoletto" Fantaisie. The audience of over fifty people included governors and ex-governors, Harvard professors, musicians, critics, and assorted society people, and of course, Henry Beach, all of whom remained for dinner after the program.[3] At this early stage in her career, it was a distinct honor to be included on a program with Boston's leading poets.

On 31 March she played the first of her postnuptial annual recitals, a benefit for the Children's Hospital. Featured on her program was Chopin's brilliant and extended Scherzo no. 4. The review in the Evening Transcript found nothing to criticize in her playing, yet the writer could not resist warning her against "that besetting sin of pianists of her sex — superficiality." That aside, he saw "no reason why she should not rise, step by step, to real greatness."[4]

The following year, her only performance was her annual benefit recital on 9 March, in which she presented a most ambitious program, including sonatas by J.C. Bach, Mozart, Scarlatti, Beethoven—the "Appassionata," op. 57—and Chopin, the B-minor Sonata, op. 58. Evidently there were some acoustical problems in Association Hall, "where the basso continuo of horse cars, and the frequent obbligati in locomotive bells and hand organs furnish additional accompaniments never contemplated by composers." But even the curmudgeon who reviewed for the Transcript found much to praise: "Her exquisite technique seemed more finished than ever, and her fine musical instinct showed itself as convincingly as ever."[5]

Beach's appearances with the Kneisel Quartet provided important opportunities, not only to play the piano but to introduce her own works as well. In the first concert, on 22 January 1894, she was the pianist in Schumann's Quintet, op. 44, and earned superb notices. In addition, with Franz Kneisel, Beach gave the second performance of her Romance, op. 23, for violin and piano (the program incorrectly lists it as a premiere). Its origin in the song "Sweetheart, Sigh no More," op. 14, no. 3, (on a text by Thomas Bailey Aldrich) is made clear by the identity of the opening phrase, which Beach then uses sequentially and developmentally. The appoggiatura-laden violin melody, together with the pulsating accompaniment, conveys the longing appropriate to a piece entitled Romance.

On her next appearance with the Kneisels in Association Hall on 4 January 1897, she presented a new major work of her own, one that was very different from Romance. Interest in the Sonata in A Minor for Piano and Violin, op. 34, was so high that some listeners choose the new Beach over the opening night of a new play starring John Drew, this country's leading actor.[6] Beach had composed the sonata between 11 March and 6 June 1896, immediately following the completion of the symphony.[7] It is a strenuous and impassioned work in four movements. In the opening movement, she developed the first theme extensively, beginning at m. 17 (ex. 11.1). Motives from the theme supply material for the second theme, which Beach initially gives to the violin; when the piano repeats the second theme directly, it is again varied substantially (ex. 11.2). Indeed, Beach's opening theme serves as seed material for themes in three of the sonata's four movements.

EXAMPLE 11.1 Sonata in A Minor for Piano and Violin, op. 34, I, first theme and development, mm. 1–41 (Arthur P. Schmidt, 1899).

EXAMPLE 11.1 (continued)

The second movement is, like the second movement of her symphony, a sparkling scherzo in duple rather than triple meter. In the traditional form, with the trio in the middle, the sonata's scherzo has a persistent motoric rhythm as well as close imitation between piano and violin (ex. 11.3a). Drawing on a fragment of the opening theme of the first movement, the Scherzo theme successively outlines two seventh chords, as does the theme of the Trio. Extended passages of parallel-moving chords in the Trio suggest an acquaintance with contemporary French music. The piano is subtended by the violin's

EXAMPLE 11.2 Sonata for Piano and Violin, I: (a) second theme, mm. 65–72; (b) second theme elaborated, mm. 84–95.

eighteen-measure pedal point on low G, after which the two instruments explore the theme together (ex. 11.3b).

The songlike slow movement, *Largo con dolore*, is at once expressive and dirge-like. The lyrical theme is long-breathed, its sustained tones propelled by persistent dissonance that results in sharp harmonic clashes. A sudden and dramatic shift from E minor to C major at measure 5 provides a moment of simple consonant harmony and a welcome ray of light, recalling her previous use of C major to signify redemption (ex. 11.4). Urgency and romantic longing are written into the ever-present forward movement toward a resolution of dissonance that comes only with the last note.

The introduction to the final movement, which is in sonata form, has an energetic series of upsweeping passages, mainly on the piano, that soon serve as both transitional and climactic material. The first theme is a model of economy, starting with a two-pitch cell and gradually expanding upward: here development takes place within the theme itself (ex. 11.5a), as it also does in the quieter and more lyrical second theme, marked *Più tranquillo* (ex. 11.5b). The development section proper begins with a statement of both themes, followed by a fugue based on theme 1, which is initiated by the piano. The texture and surface rhythm of the fugue recall the light, crisp quality of the Scherzo. The recapitulation seems at first to be a false one, since the first theme returns in D minor, but before the second theme enters the key changes to A major, which is retained to the end. As ever, Beach feels the need to end a piece that begins

(b)

EXAMPLE 11.2 (continued)

in the minor by moving into the tonic major, achieving both resolution and transcendence. Here was a major work, highly effective and moving. Louis Elson had nothing but praise for the first movement's "stern and majestic chief theme and . . . subordinate theme of ineffable beauty." He also praised its "good sonata-allegro form," ignoring the avoidance of the tonic at the recapitulation—a typical late Romantic revision of classical sonata form.[8]

Critics disagreed about the slow movement. One called it "the most musical, the theme suggesting a song without words, a passion of grief and longing

EXAMPLE 11.3 Sonata for Piano and Violin, II: (a) Scherzo, mm. 1–8; (b) Trio, mm. 74–81.

EXAMPLE 11.4 Sonata for Piano and Violin, III, mm. 1–8.

. . . it might well be the setting for the saddest words ever written by a Byron or a Burns."[9] Indeed, the songlike quality of Beach's adagio melodies, usually marked *espressivo*, reveal the lyrical source of much of her musical thought. In contrast, Elson wrote that "the elegaic and passionate Largo had very little to say . . . on first hearing; it seemed made up of modern vagueness and finally of an apotheosis of ecstasy."[10] That, however, was not the audience response: "At the close of the movement came one of those pauses most flattering to an artist, the pause of an audience spellbound and fascinated. Then came the burst of well-deserved applause."[11]

Schmidt's publication of the sonata in 1899 moved Percy Goetschius to note that Beach adopted "the methods of development peculiar to Brahms," something composer Arnold Schoenberg later called "developing variation."[12] That is, Beach took a simple melodic germ, developed and varied it, transforming it into a contrasting theme, and in the end spun an entire movement out of a mere scrap of a melodic idea, something she had done as well in the last movement of the "Gaelic" Symphony.

On 26 March 1899 when Beach and Kneisel gave their fifth performance of the violin sonata and the first in New York, local critics were as usual harder to

EXAMPLE 11.5 Sonata for Piano and Violin, IV: (a) first theme, mm. 13–20; (b) second theme, mm. 47–54.

EXAMPLE 11.5 (continued)

please than Bostonians.[13] Krehbiel wrote that the Sonata "is wofully [sic] immature and one sided," while Henry T. Finck complained that Beach's obvious eagerness to follow the compositional rules for sonatas laid down in German textbooks robbed her work of individuality.[14] However, Beach did not follow all the rules for sonata form in either the first or the last movement. Finck also noted that "[a]ll the material it contains could have been condensed—to great advantage—into one movement lasting ten minutes."[15] Would he have said that of one of Haydn's monothematic movements? But William J. Henderson prefaced his remarks by proclaiming that Beach "has proved that it is possible for a woman to compose music which is worthy of serious attention." He then attacked all other women composers both abroad and at home where "Mrs. Beach stands almost alone."[16] He found the slow movement the most beautiful, the Scherzo the most successful, and the finale the weakest of the four. In the face of negative comments, Percy Goetschius reiterated his support of the work: "One must be blind, indeed, not to discern the noble qualities of your writing, and contemptible not to acknowledge them."[17]

If the Beaches were unhappy over the violin sonata's critical reception in New York, three well-received performances in Europe came as soothing balm. The first was in Berlin by pianist Teresa Carreño and violinist Carl Halir on 28 October 1899. Carreño wrote an admiring letter after their performance:

I assure you that I never had a greater pleasure in my life than the one I had in working out your beautiful sonata and having the good luck to bring it before the German public. . . . [I]t really met with a *decided success* [emphasis Carreño's] and this is said to the credit of the public.[18]

The second European performance was by the famous Belgian violinist Eugène Ysaÿe and the pianist Raoul Pugno on 4 April 1900 in Paris. Ysaÿe and

Pugno "chanced upon the sonata in a bundle of music, scanned it, liked it, and added it to their repertory." They then gave the work "without suspecting that the composer was a woman or knowing that she was an American." Yet the name on the title-page in letters a half-inch high was, of course, Mrs. H. H. A. Beach. It is hard to understand how they missed the Mrs. in her name. The report, however, may have been less than candid: the name of the composer was given on the program as "H. A. Beach."[19]

The third overseas concert was by violinist Sigmund Beel and pianist Henry Bird in St. James's Hall in London on 28 November 1901. The *Times* of London called it "a sonata of remarkable beauty," while the *Graphic* noted that "a good, new sonata for violin and piano is something of a rarity, and Mr. Sigmund Beel is to be congratulated most heartily on having produced one at his concert."[20]

It was after this performance that Henry Beach took action to counteract the impact of Krehbiel and Finck, the leading New York critics, by asking Schmidt to obtain copies of the London reviews. Upon receipt, he wrote to Schmidt that "[i]t is a great satisfaction to have justice on our side once in a while."[21] The London reviews were soon reprinted in Boston and New York papers.[22] Despite conflicting critical opinion, the work had dozens of performances during Beach's lifetime, and many years later was featured on one of the recordings that began the recent Beach renaissance.[23]

After all the success of the violin sonata, the time had come for Beach to produce a new major recital piece. Up to the turn of the century, her catalog of piano works had remained surprisingly small for a pianist, and all the compositions were relatively short.[24] Outstanding, however, are two intensely lyrical pieces with long-breathed melodies, the *Ballad*, op. 6, and "Dreaming," op. 15, no. 3, from her *Four Sketches*.[25] Her first piano solo of the new century was a concert transcription of Richard Strauss's "Ständchen" (Serenade), op. 17, no. 2.[26] The song, which had quickly become a favorite of singers, has an expressive melodic line and an atmospheric piano accompaniment that are close to Beach's own style. While much of Beach's transcription is a straightforward arrangement for piano, the final section extends the work, adding a *fortissimo* climax not found in the original, thus dramatizing the last lines of the poem when the light of dawn illumines the rapture of the lovers. Beach gave several performances of the transcription, her op. 49 [bis], beginning with a recital on 15 March 1902 at the Brooklyn Institute of Arts and Sciences.[27]

Her recital programs, however, demanded longer and more substantial works to set off the shorter ones. In 1904 Beach completed her first large-scale piano composition, *Variations on Balkan Themes*, op. 60, her longest and most important solo work. Its composition grew out of her abiding interest in folk music. Unlike Scottish and Irish melodies, Balkan folk songs were not a part of the American musical mainstream. Nevertheless, the region was much on the minds of the American public at the time; a recent uprising by Macedonian nationalists had provoked cruel and repressive measures by the ruling Turks.

Because of the timeliness of the subject, in the spring of 1904 Beach assembled an audience including Elizabeth Sprague Coolidge to hear the Reverend William Washburn Sleeper, Wellesley professor and Protestant missionary to

Amy Marcy Cheney's birthplace on Western Avenue, West Henniker, New Hampshire, c. 1900. (*Special Collections, University of New Hampshire Library, Durham.*)

Amy Marcy Cheney, two years old, Concord, New Hampshire. (*Special Collections, University of New Hampshire Library, Durham.*)

Clara Imogene Marcy. Concord, New Hampshire. (Special Collections, University of New Hampshire Library, Durham.)

Charles Abbott Cheney. (*Special Collections, University of New Hampshire Library, Durham.*)

Left: Emma Frances "Franc" (Marcy) Clement, San Francisco. (*Special Collections, University of New Hampshire Library, Durham.*)

Right: Clara Imogene Marcy, Concord, New Hampshire. (*Special Collections, University of New Hampshire Library, Durham.*)

Amy Marcy Cheney, about
ten years old, San Francisco.
(*Special Collections, University of New
Hampshire Library, Durham.*)

Amy Marcy Cheney, sixteen years old,
Boston. (*Special Collections, University
of New Hampshire Library, Durham.*)

Program for debut of Amy Marcy Cheney, Boston Music Hall, 24 October 1883. (*Special Collections, University of New Hampshire Library, Durham.*)

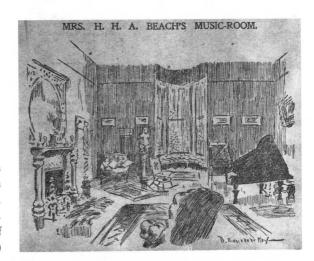

MRS. H. H. A. BEACH'S MUSIC-ROOM.

Sketch by B. Englebert Key, in "America's Chief Woman Composer," *Sunday Times-Herald*, 26 November 1897. *(Special Collections, University of New Hampshire Library, Durham.)*

Henry Harris Aubrey Beach and Amy Marcy (Cheney) Beach. *(Special Collections, University of New Hampshire Library, Durham.)*

House at 28 Commonwealth Avenue. (*Music Division, Library of Congress.*)

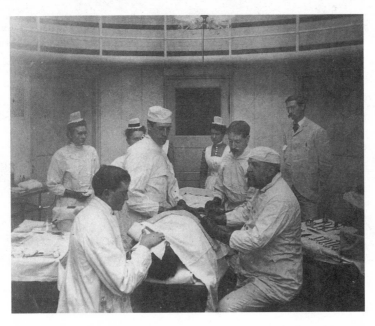

Henry Harris Aubrey Beach, M.D., operating on patient. (*Archives of the Massachusetts General Hospital.*)

Amy Beach. (Elizabeth Porter Gould Photographic Collection, Department of Rare Books and Manuscripts, Boston Public Library, by courtesy of the Trustees of the Boston Public Library.)

Program booklet, Boston Music Hall, 7 February 1892. Premiere of Amy Beach's Mass in E-flat, op. 5, by the Handel and Haydn Society of Boston; Beethoven Choral Fantasia, op. 80; Beach, piano solo, Carl Zerrahn, conductor. (*Special Collections, University of New Hampshire Library, Durham.*)

Amy Beach, cameo portrait, c. 1903. (*Music Research Division, New York Public Library.*)

Beach's bookplate,
in Lawrence Gilman,
Wagner's Operas.
(Fuller Public Library,
Hillsborough,
New Hampshire.)

Henry Harris Aubrey Beach. (*Archives of
the Massachusetts General Hospital.*)

Marcella Craft as Salome. (*Courtesy of Deutsches Theatermuseum, Munich.*)

Amy Beach and Marcella Craft in Munich. (*Craft Collection, Tomás Rivera Library, University of California, Riverside.*)

Theodore Spiering. (*Music Research Division, New York Public Library.*)

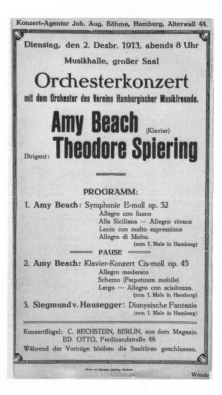

Program, Musikhalle, Hamburg, 2 December 1913. (*Special Collections, University of New Hampshire Library, Durham.*)

Amy Beach. (*Courtesy of the Peterborough Historical Society, Peterborough, New Hampshire.*)

Composers whose works were played at the American Composers' Day Concert, Festival Hall, Panama Pacific International Exposition, 1 August 1915. (*Special Collections, University of New Hampshire Library, Durham.*)

Amy Beach at the Panama-California Exposition, San Diego, Beach Day, 1916. (*Musical Courier*, 25 May 1916.)

Left: Lyman H. Clement, San Francisco. (*Special Collections, University of New Hampshire Library, Durham.*) Right: Arthur Sewell Hyde. (*Courtesy of St. Bartholomew's Episcopal Church, New York.*)

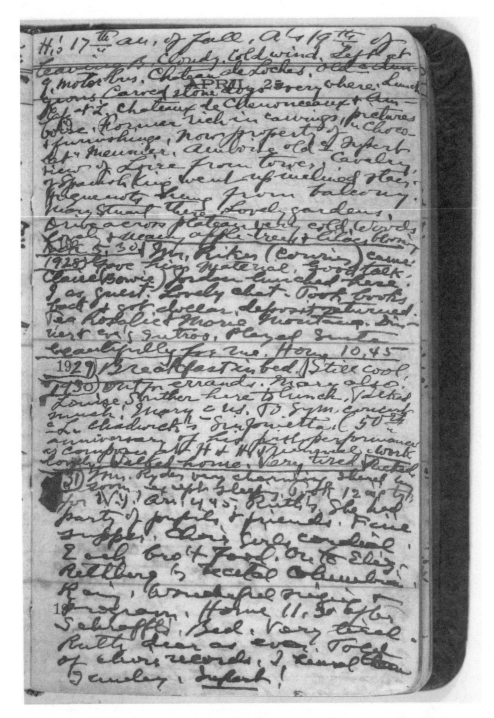

Page from Beach's diary for 25 April 1927 to 1931. (Special Collections, University of New Hampshire Library, Durham.)

Regina Watson Studio, MacDowell Colony, Peterborough, New Hampshire. (Courtesy of the MacDowell Colony.)

Amy Beach with the Junior and Juvenile Beach Clubs, Hillsborough, New Hampshire. (Special Collections, University of New Hampshire Library, Durham.)

The Centerville group: (left to right) Fannie Lord, Eugenie Limberg, unknown, Amy Beach, Mabel Pierce, and Lillian Buxbaum. (*Special Collections, University of New Hampshire Library, Durham.*)

Amy Beach on board ship. (*Courtesy of Virginia Duffey Pleasants.*)

David McKay Williams,
choirmaster and organist,
St. Bartholomew's Episcopal
Church, New York. (*Special Col-
lections, University of New Hampshire
Library, Durham.*)

Ruth Shaffner, Eugenie Limberg, and Virginia Duffey, Caracas, Venezuela, 1938.
(*Courtesy of Virginia Duffey Pleasants.*)

Composer members of the National League of American Pen Women attending its biennial meeting on 22–28 April 1932 in Washington, D.C. Seated left to right, first row: Francesca Vallejo, Mrs. H. H. A. Beach, Mrs. Ernest Thompson Seton, President of the League, Dorothy de Muth Watson, Chair of Music, Mary Carr Moore, Mary Howe, and Dorothy Radde Emery; second row: standing, Reah Jackson Irion, Margaret McClure Stitt, Pearl Adams, Phyllis Fergus (Hoyt), Bonita Crow, Marianne Genet, Annabel Morris Buchanan, Helen Matthews, Josephine Forsyth, Gena Branscombe, and Louise Crawford.

Amy Beach. (Courtesy of
Eugenie Limberg Dengel.)

Bust of Amy Beach by Bashka Paeff,
photo by Peter A. Julley & Son.
(Courtesy of Virginia Eskin.)

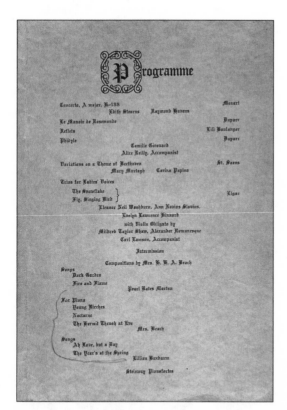

Program in honor of Nadia Boulanger, Hotel Vendôme, Boston, 23 February 1938. (*Special Collections, University of New Hampshire Library, Durham.*)

Amy Beach with members of the Tollefson chamber group, Neighborhood Music School, Brooklyn, New York, 1940. (*Special Collections, University of New Hampshire Library, Durham.*)

75th BIRTHDAY ANNIVERSARY
CELEBRATION

FRIDAY
November 27, 1942, 8.30 p. m.

PROGRAM

SONATA op. 34 for Violin and Piano
Allegro Moderato — Scherzo
Largo con dolore — Allegro con fuoco

SONGS for Baritone
a) Across the World
b) My Star
c) The Wandering Knight

THEME and VARIATIONS for Flute and Strings
Theme—Lento di molto — L'istesso tempo
Allegro giusto — Quasi Valzer lento
Largo di molto — Presto leggiero
Allegro giocoso — Tempo di Tema

First Performance in Washington

VARIATIONS on BALKAN THEMES for Piano
Adagio malincolico — Più mosso — Maestoso
Allegro ma non troppo — Andante alla Barcarole
Largo con espressione — Poco più mosso
Quasi Fantasia — Allegro all'Ongarese
Vivace — Valse lento — Con Vigore
Allegretto — Marcia funerale

First Performance in Washington

SONGS for Soprano and Piano
a) STELLA VIATORIS } (Violin, cello obbligato)
b) MIRAGE
c) RENDEZVOUS (violin obbligato)

ARTISTS:

Mme JULIA ELBOGEN, pianist   ELENA de SAYN, violinist
BERNICE RICKMAN GORDON, soprano WILLIAM LEACH, baritone
KENTON F. TERRY, flutist

SAYN STRING QUARTET

Elena de Sayn } violinists
Myron Kahn
Louise Ehrman, violoncellist
Harold Niessenson, violist

SATURDAY
November 28, 1942, 8.30 p. m.

PROGRAM

TRIO op. 150 for Piano, Violin and Cello
Allegro — Lento espressivo
Presto — Tempo primo — Allegro con trio
First Performance in Washington

ROMANCE op. 23 for Violin and Piano
STRING QUARTET op. 75 in one movement
Grave — Allegro molto
Manuscript First Performance

SONGS for Soprano
a) I Sent My Heart Up to Thee
b) Ecstasy (words by Mrs. H. H. A. Beach)
c) June

QUINTET for Piano and Strings
Adagio — Allegro moderato
Adagio espressivo — Allegro agitato, Presto

ARTISTS:

Mme JULIA ELBOGEN, pianist
ELENA de SAYN, violinist
BERNICE RICKMAN GORDON, soprano
LOUISE EHRMAN, cellist

SAYN STRING QUARTET

Elena de Sayn } violinists
Myron Kahn
Louise Ehrman, violoncellist
Harold Niessenson, violist

Mrs. H. H. A. Beach is a native of New Hampshire. At the age of 4 she displayed a precocious gift for music. Not unlike Mozart, she began to compose at when she made her debut as pianist-prodigal. At 17 she appeared as soloist with the Boston Symphony Orchestra and played extensively thereafter in concerts and with orchestras on both sides of the Atlantic. Her compositions, featured on these programs, received world wide acclaim having been performed by famous European and American artists. She is considered to be the greatest woman composer in the world.

PHILLIPS MEMORIAL GALLERY
1600 Twenty First Street, N. W.
Washington, D. C.

Programs for 75th Birthday Celebration of Amy Beach, 27–28 November 1942, Phillips Memorial Gallery, Washington, D.C. (DeSayn-Eversman Collection, Music Division, Library of Congress)

Bulgaria, and his wife lecture on Balkan life and customs.[28] As part of the presentation, the Reverend Sleeper played for Beach a set of folk tunes he and his wife had collected in various Balkan countries. One struck her as having possibilities for development, and the Sleepers promised to send her a copy. With Beach's total recall, of course, that was hardly necessary; after waiting a few days for the copy, she wrote four of the melodies down from memory, then used them as themes for her variations, which she completed in eight days. "When the copy of the [principal] melody arrived, there was but one note, and that an unimportant one, which needed to be changed."[29]

The use of four themes was unusual for a variation form (ex. 11.6). The Serbian song "O Maiko moyá" is used as the principal theme and appears in each of the eight variations as well as in the cadenza and the coda. Its text, as translated for Beach's edition, reads:

> O my poor country, to thy sons so dear,
> Why art thou weeping, why this sadness drear?
> Alas! thou raven, messenger of woe,
> Over whose fresh grave moanest thou so?[30]

The words refer to the lives taken by the Turkish rulers of Serbia during their five-century domination of what later became part of Yugoslavia.

Beach wrote that she introduced the other melodies for their dramatic effect and to set off the melancholy character of the principal theme.[31] The distinctive elements in these Balkan melodies lend an exotic flavor to almost every variation: the pathos-laden augmented seconds in both "O Maiko moyá" and "Stara planina"; the changes from minor to major in "O Maiko moyá," which ends on the fifth degree of the relative major, and from major to minor in "Nasadil e dado"; the alternation of duple and triple meters in "Stara planina" as well as its ending on a tonic a fourth below the opening; and, finally, the Dorian minor scale of "Macedonian!" with its lowered seventh degree (ex. 11.6a-d). Beach retained many of the folk elements but reinterpreted the modes of "O Maiko moyá" and "Stara planina" to conform to what Western ears would assume are the tonalities (ex. 11.7), much as she had done with the Irish fiddle tune she quoted as the closing theme of the first movement of the "Gaelic" Symphony. As a result, despite the exotic coloration, Beach's lush late-Romantic harmonies locate the piece in Western rather than Eastern Europe. Nevertheless, the work's tragic quality fits the subject.

It is, by turns, a lament, a dramatically gestural polonaise, a scherzo, a barcarole, a spirited *perpetuum mobile all'ongarese*, a slow bittersweet waltz, and a funeral march that rises to a dramatic climax. About twenty-five minutes in duration, its climaxes in a long Lisztian cadenza in which three of the four themes are recapitulated. The work closes with the final statement of the theme. The *Variations on Balkan Themes* is her most effective and affecting solo piano work.

Beach gave the premiere while the variations were still in manuscript, on 8 February 1905 at a recital at Huntington Chambers Hall in Boston, as a benefit for the Faelten Piano School. The music critic for the *Transcript* was most impressed: "These themes from folksongs of that long harassed borderland be-

EXAMPLE 11.6 (a) "O Maiko moyá"; (b) "Stara planina"; (c) "Nasadil e dado"; (d) "Macedonian!" Variants between titles and texts are as in Beach's manuscript collection of Balkan folk songs.

EXAMPLE 11.7 *Variations on Balkan Themes*, op. 60: (a) opening of theme based on "O Maiko moyá"; (b) var. 3, based on "O Maiko moyá"; (c) variation 4, based on "O Maiko moyá"; (d) var. 6, introduction, based on "Stara planina"; (e) var. 6, closing section, based on "Nasadil e Dado"; (f) var. 8, introduction, based on "Macedonian!"

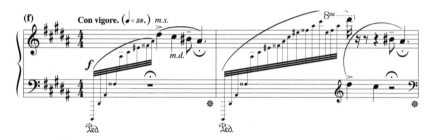

EXAMPLE 11.7 *(continued)*

tween Christian and Moslem Europe are in general of a melancholy character, and from them Mrs. Beach has developed a series of compositions marked by deep feeling, and great variety and richness."[32] The following year, she received an enthusiastic letter from Percy Goetschius after he had studied the published edition:

> At one of our music evenings at home, your "Balkan Variations" were the central topic of display and discussion. I wish you could have been with us to witness the enthusiasm with which the endless beauties of the work were greeted . . . for the half dozen friends who were present were artists whose critical judgment is to be respected. . . . You know very well how I "gloat" over such admirable technical excellencies. It is, naturally, an exposition of the maturing process and ever increasing mastership . . . surely your best effort.[33]

In 1907 Beach performed the variations three times, beginning with her annual recital on 6 February in Steinert Hall. On the 28th of that month she gave the variations a second time on an all-Beach program for the Thursday Morning Musical Club of Boston, the group that, under the direction of Arthur Hyde, had given performances of her *Sea-Fairies* and *Chambered Nautilus*.

On 22 May 1907 she played the Balkan Variations for a third time at the spring meeting of Arthur Farwell's American Music Society at the Hotel Somerset, Boston. Only one work on the program, Stanley R. Avery's "Eskimo Love Song," continues Farwell's earlier preoccupation with music on Native-American themes. May Sleeper-Ruggles, a singer and voice coach as well as the sister of the Reverend Sleeper, ended her solo group with a set of Balkan folk songs, perhaps the very ones Beach used as themes. Beach then followed by playing the variations.[34]

Two other works for piano appeared in 1907. The suite for children, entitled *Eskimos*, op. 64, consists of four short pieces—"Arctic Night," "The Returning Hunters," "Exiles," and "With Dog-teams." In them, she quotes a total of eleven Inuit melodies. This was Beach's first use of Native American themes, possibly inspired by the music of Farwell and other Indianist composers.[35] Their use represented an about-face for Beach. In 1893, when she had replied to Dvořák, she insisted that the music of African Americans was too remote from her experience as a New Englander to be useful as themes for a distinctive American music. Now she found these even more remote tunes a challenge; later she would base one of her finest works on Inuit tunes.

Her source for the songs was an early monograph on the Alaskan Inuit by the anthropologist Franz Boas.[36] In *Eskimos*, Beach gave these stark melodies a harmonic treatment similar to the Balkan tunes; as she said, she "enriched" this music, which the Inuit sang unaccompanied, with late-Romantic harmonies.[37] Although the suite was intended for teaching purposes, Goetschius found it extraordinary and congratulated Beach for a new "individuality" that placed her among the "*real creators.*"[38] His favorable comments may have led her to include the suite on recital programs despite its intended use for teaching.

It is a far cry from the world of the Inuit or the sufferings of Serbs and Macedonians to *Les Rêves de Colombine: Suite française*, op. 65, Beach's next extended work for piano. The five movements are "La Fée de la fontaine," about "a capricious, a fierce and sullen as well as gracious fairy"; "Le Prince gracieux," a gavotte danced by an elaborately dressed gallant; "Valse amoureuse" based on Beach's song, "Le Secret," op. 14, no. 2, in which "Columbine dreams of a sweetheart with whom she is dancing"; "Sous les étoiles," which suggests music for a romantic *pas de deux*; and "Danse d'Arlequin," in which Beach recapitulates earlier movements as well as adding "a new dance-tune."[39] Although Beach did not say, she may have had classical ballet in mind as she composed this work.

She began the composition in the autumn of 1906, completed it the following March, and a month later on 17 April 1907 gave its first performance while the suite was still in manuscript. The occasion was a morning recital of her songs and piano music at the Hotel Tuileries on Commonwealth Avenue.[40] Thereafter, Beach often included the piece on programs for musically less sophisticated audiences.[41] On her all-Beach programs, however, the work served as a foil for the gravity and intensity of the *Variations on Balkan Themes*.

Beach's next major chamber composition after the violin sonata was the Quintet for Piano and Strings, op. 67, which offers perhaps the clearest indication of Brahmsian influence. In 1900 Beach had played the Brahms Piano Quintet, op. 34, with the Kneisels.[42] Five years later, when she wrote her own piano quintet, she adapted the second theme of the last movement of the Brahms quintet, presenting it in successive transformations as themes in all three movements of her own work (ex. 11.8a).

Beach's quintet is in F♯ minor, one of her two "black" keys. The jagged descending theme that she borrowed from Brahms is chromatic and dark in color. In the introduction to the first movement, there is a long-held F♯ in the strings that descends gradually and by chromatic steps to C♯; the motion outlines a Phrygian cadence (F♯-E-D-C♯), which for hundreds of years has been associated with death and grieving. The last two notes, D to C♯, constitute a pathetic accent that appears in various transpositions throughout the movement (ex. 11.8b).

The first theme of the *Allegro moderato* that Beach states initially in the first violin part, has the same chromatically descending line, although it is rhythmicized to give it a distinct profile (ex. 11.8c). The second, brightly lyrical theme is heard first in the alto register of the piano against repeated F♯s that later become the bridge to the development section. For all its chromaticism, its frequent changes of key, and its lush harmonies, the structure is close to the textbook model for a sonata-allegro movement.

EXAMPLE 11.8 (a) Johannes Brahms, Quintet in F Minor, op. 34, IV, second theme, mm. 53–66 (C. F. Peters, 1918). Beach, Quintet in F♯ Minor, op. 67: (b) I, mm. 8–19; (c) I, first theme, mm. 27–31; (d) II, first theme, mm. 1–9; (e) III, allegro agitato, mm. 14–17 (Arthur P. Schmidt, 1909).

The slow second movement is in a three-part form and has a contrasting middle section. The theme, which is in D♭ major, outlines a Phrygian cadence in its descent from the sixth to the third degrees of the major, thus emphasizing the darker minor quality found within the major scale (ex. 11.8d).[43] The third and final movement, which returns to F♯ minor, also repeats the Phrygian cadence in its opening theme, while pathetic accents mark its continuation (ex. 11.8e). Thus, the lament quality permeates the entire work. This characteristic, however, is not the sole distinguishing affect in the quintet; what stands out in all three movements is its intensity.

The premiere of the Beach Quintet for Piano and Strings took place in Boston's Potter Hall on 27 February 1908, with the Hoffmann Quartet and Beach at the piano.[44] The audience was unusually large, drawn by interest in Beach's latest work. Boston critics, in an instance of unanimity, greeted the work as an important contribution to the literature.[45] In the longest and most detailed review, Henry Taylor Parker called the work "truly substantial, free, variously imagined and restlessly expressive music." Writing of her style, he declared it "distinctly, but without obvious and toilsome striving . . . in truly modern and nonacademic vein." His negative comments were few: he believed—perceptively—that she might have found more variety of tone color among the strings. Parker added that while Beach adhered to sonata form, she made it "flexible and responsive to her musical thoughts and imaginative moods." Louis Elson in his review believed that the work, while not quite a match for the piano quintets of Schumann, Franck, or Brahms, was nevertheless a fine one.[46]

One critic complained about a typical late-Romantic feature that presents a challenge to performers, that Beach "courted, perhaps a little too often, the slowly mounting, expanding and finally breaking climax in broad sweep of warm tone."[47] In the second movement, Beach builds two climaxes in which the piano part becomes orchestral with repeated triplet chords in the high treble; in the finale, there are two more such high points. A more modern evaluation, however, gives the work high marks:

> The quintet is very Brahmsian; there is, indeed, scarcely a turn of phrase, a rhythmic figuration, or a harmonic progression throughout its three movements that does not recall something similar in Brahms. Yet the whole thing hangs together— it has integrity and style, and one can listen to it with pleasure for its own values. It is a little smaller in scale and concept than the chamber works of the Master, but it stands up alongside them without apology.[48]

During Beach's lifetime, the work had well over forty performances, in dozens of cities, over the radio, and by many string quartets. A large number of those performances were with the composer at the piano, most notably during a lengthy tour in 1916 and 1917 with the Kneisel Quartet.

Beach, who would turn forty-three on 5 September 1910, could look back over the past twenty-five years with a good deal of satisfaction. She had produced a number of important works: the mass, the symphony, the sonata, the piano concerto, the *Variations on Balkan Themes*, and the piano quintet. The hard work had paid off, for it established her as a creator of high art music, not merely the songs and piano works associated in the public's mind with "woman's work." She had, of course, turned out those smaller works as well— choral, chamber, and piano works and songs that alone would have made her famous.

By playing her compositions, she had simultaneously kept her hand in as a performer. Her prowess at the instrument was demonstrated dramatically when she played the premiere of her Piano Concerto, op. 45, in 1900. A work of large dimensions with powerful autobiographical overtones, it constitutes her most impressive bid for renewed recognition as a concert artist as well as a composer.

"A VERITABLE

AUTOBIOGRAPHY"?

The Piano Concerto

IN THE LAST YEARS OF THE nineteenth century, Amy Beach composed a piano concerto.[1] The genre had changed since it was created by Mozart, evolving into a contentious form in which the soloist usually emerges victorious over the orchestra. Part of that evolution was the work of Liszt, whose persona as the *virtuoso assoluto* became the standard for those aspiring to heroic pianism. The other crucial change was the replacement of the piano's wood frame with a steel one, creating a louder and more brilliant sound. The combination of extraordinary technique and ringing sound allowed the great pianists to dominate the orchestra, despite being one against many.

Beach had experienced that range as a soloist in concertos by Mozart, Beethoven, Mendelssohn, Chopin, Moscheles, Saint-Saëns, and perhaps Schumann.[2] She also was thoroughly aware of the power struggles that may occur among conductor, orchestra, and soloist during a performance. Even as early as her debut, as was noted in chapter 3, she had exulted in taking control as soloist. Later, at a rehearsal of the Mendelssohn D-minor Concerto, conducted by Theodore Thomas, she changed the tempo of the last movement when Thomas's did not suit her. More recently, with the Boston Symphony in February 1895, Beach had played the Saint-Saëns G-minor Concerto, in which the piano dominates so brilliantly throughout that the conductor Emil Paur had no choice but to follow the soloist. Thus, in the late-Romantic concerto the successful soloist exerts power over the orchestra, over the conductor, over the audience—a heady mix to contemplate.

Another superlative example of the concerto as a virtuoso vehicle is Tchaikovsky's first, in B♭, which Beach never played but surely knew—the Boston Symphony had already presented it three times beginning with the premiere in 1885. She may have used it, as well as the Saint-Saëns, as a model for contentiousness.[3] Beach would make the struggle between forces the central issue of her concerto. As soloist *and* composer, the pianist's lead could hardly be challenged.

Having reveled in playing with orchestra, Beach found composing a concerto the most natural thing to do. But because of the special place of the piano in her life, the years of deprivation she had endured as a pianist and now the

EXAMPLE 12.1 (a) "Jeune fille et jeune fleur," op. 1, no. 3, mm. 1–7 (Arthur P. Schmidt, 1887). Concerto for Piano and Orchestra, op. 45: (b) I, mm. 1–5; (c) I, Cadenza for piano solo, mm. 42–53 (Arthur P. Schmidt, 1900).

fact that the time between her concerto engagements had grown increasingly long, she may have felt that her piano career was withering on the vine. Beach may have referred to that feeling when she wrote: "[A] composer might remain apparently unaffected by even the most terrific onslaught upon all that was deepest in his life, and years afterward give expression in music, perhaps unconsciously, to all that the experience had cost him." Thus, she concluded, a musical composition may be "a veritable autobiography."[4] The concerto offered Beach a medium to "give expression in music" to the central conflict with husband and mother over control of her musical life. A full-blown late Romantic work for virtuoso pianist and large orchestra,[5] her Piano Concerto in C♯ Minor was also a bid to return to the concert stage that she so missed. She soon had assurances that she would do so; before the work was completed, Maestro Gericke engaged her to play it with the Boston Symphony.[6]

Specific evidence of a hidden narrative in the concerto is found in Beach's choice of themes. That she quoted three songs from her opp. 1 and 2 is especially significant because, as she said, her songs were highly personal and came from the depths of her being.[7] The three songs used in the Concerto in C♯ Minor were all written shortly before or after her marriage, after which she gave up her career as a pianist.

"Jeune fille et jeune fleur," op. 1, no. 3, quoted in the first movement, is intimately connected with her husband, who had sung it nearly a year before they were married. A setting of a poem by the French Romantic poet Chateaubriand, its opening lines, which describe the descent into the grave of the coffin of a very young woman as her father grieves, could not be more melodramatic. The poem may well have been heavy with symbolism for Beach: her suitor, then husband, a bit older than her father, had "buried" her ambitions as a pianist even as he obliterated her name and replaced it with his.[8] The absence of a grieving mother in the poem may also have been significant in Beach's choice of a text.

In the first movement of the concerto the orchestra opens with the broodingly eloquent and portentous first theme, which closely resembles the music for the introduction to the song (ex. 12.1a, b): both are in C♯ minor, both have the same "serious" affect, and both feature falling modal scales. When the piano enters, it strikes out with its own material in a short but powerful cadenza (ex. 12.1c). With its second phrase, the piano is gradually drawn back

EXAMPLE 12.1 (continued)

EXAMPLE 12.2 Concerto for Piano and Orchestra, I, mm. 69–72.

into the orchestra's orbit as it loudly repeats the first theme—now in F major and harmonically restructured—only returning to the tonic at the end of its solo.

The tonic is briefly reinforced by the ensemble. Thereafter, a contentious relationship between soloist and orchestra is especially apparent. Although the orchestra subsequently develops thematic material, it is overwhelmed by the piano's heroic figurations, which feature horn fifths, first *piano*, later *forte* (ex. 12.2). Faced with such a conflict, the conductor ordinarily brings the theme into the foreground. However, in this passage Beach thwarts convention by requiring the first violins to play it *pianissimo* in their lowest register.

Beach follows tradition when she has the piano take the lead in introducing the second theme, which is based on the third quatrain of the song (ex. 12.3a):

> Tu dors, pauvre Elisa, si legère d'années!
> Tu ne sens plus du jour le poids at la chaleur;
> Vous avez achevé vos fraiches matinées,
> Jeune fille et jeune fleur.

Here the relationship between the song and the concerto movement emerges unmistakably. Although the theme in both song and concerto is in the major mode, its emphasis on modal degrees (the second, third, and sixth notes of the major scale) creates considerable pathos. This is also one of the few passages in the movement where the orchestra is supportive of the piano (ex. 12.3b). For the remainder of the movement the contentious relationship between piano and orchestra predominates. As Beach described that relationship, "The first [movement], 'Allegro', is serious in character, piano and orchestra *vying* with each other in the development of the two principal themes" (emphasis mine).[9]

Although a concerto often moves across the spectrum from collaboration to contest, Beach chose to treat her concerto as a competitive enterprise. The

EXAMPLE 12.3 (a) "Jeune fille et jeune fleur," mm. 39–43. (b) Concerto for Piano and Orchestra, I, second theme, mm. 132–35.

"vying" in the first movement continues throughout the work as a whole, as the piano increasingly dominates the orchestra. In light of the programmatic nature of the thematic material quoted in the first movement, it is possible that Beach treated the piano part as a personifying element as well—to be played by her in a public performance that the premiere of the work afforded, but also to function as an autobiographical symbol.

Who then might the opposing orchestra represent? Certainly not the professional world of music as Beach knew it; for Boston had not only supported her as a composer but proudly claimed her as its own, and local critics, who had earlier predicted a distinguished career for the New England piano prodigy, now lamented her retirement from the concert stage. As for the larger world outside Boston, Beach had experienced little opposition from it since, as a performer, she had hardly been allowed to test its waters. It seems quite plausible that the symbolic presence emerging from the work's treatment of the duality in the genre points to Beach's private life and to the struggles she encountered from opposing forces in her home. Further aspects of the work's design make this supposition a likely one.

The second movement, in A major, behaves much like the first, but with the contest now more weighted in the piano's favor. In addition, thematic material continues to resonate with autobiographical meaning. The second movement is derived from Beach's "Empress of Night," op. 2, no. 3 (1891). Of her more than one hundred published songs, this is the only one that involves the two primary figures in the composer's life—her husband as author of the text, and her mother as the song's dedicatee. In fact, this is the only song Beach ever dedicated to her mother. She may have chosen a limited range and low tessitura with her mother's no longer fresh voice in mind.

Texts of songs were not only very important to Beach but generative. Because this poem is one of Henry Beach's pedestrian efforts, she probably did not choose it for its poetic quality. It begins:

> Out of the darkness, / Radiant with light,
> Shineth her Brightness, / Empress of Night,
> As granules of gold, / From her lofty height,
> Or cataract bold / (Amazing sight!).

The image of the moon, traditionally a female symbol, is highly suggestive. Emphasizing the moon's role, Beach published the song as "Empress of Night" rather than use her husband's bland title, "At Night." A striking feature is the dominating piano accompaniment, which moves constantly in sixteenth-note patterns in the same register as the slower-moving voice. Such practice is unusual for Beach, who, from her very first published songs, knew how to write more conventionally balanced piano accompaniments. Why in this song did Beach write such an intrusive accompaniment? With mother as singer and daughter as composer-accompanist, the personifications are easily found (ex. 12.4a).

When she transformed "Empress of Night" into the concerto's second movement, a scherzo marked *Perpetuum mobile*, the song's piano accompaniment became the soloist's sparkling figurations. The recomposed and developmentally elaborated vocal line of the song is presented at the onset by the orchestra an octave lower than the piano, even more deeply buried in the texture than it was in the song (ex. 12.4b). Thus, in the second movement as in the song, the piano is not merely an obbligato to the orchestra's receding theme but remains the dominant element. Could Amy Beach, who in 1884 heard the great Marcella Sembrich sing the Queen of the Night's aria "Der Hölle Rache" at a variety concert in Boston at which Beach, too, was soloist, have associated the "Empress of Night" with the Queen of the Night's ice-cold rage and, by her settings of both the song and the scherzo movement, overwhelmed that voice?[10] If so, the song's dedication to her mother was hardly a compliment.

Her mother was very much on Amy Beach's mind when she was working on the concerto. Clara Cheney had moved in with the Beaches following the death of her husband in 1895. Tragedy had struck when Charles Cheney suddenly took ill during a business trip. He was diagnosed as having a prostatic abscess for which he was operated a few days later. Septicemia set in, and eight days later he died, on Friday night, 26 July, at the Beaches' home on Commonwealth Avenue.[11] He was just one month short of his fifty-first birthday. Funeral services were held the following Tuesday at the Chapel of the Forest Hills Cemetery in Roxbury, where Henry Beach's parents were buried. He left no property and the modest sum of $3,200 in cash to his widow, who soon gave up her home to move in with her daughter and son-in-law.[12]

The adjustment must have been difficult all around, as much for daughter

EXAMPLE 12.4 (a) "Empress of Night," op. 2, no. 3, mm. 1–5 (Arthur P. Schmidt, 1891). (b) Concerto for Piano and Orchestra, II, mm. 9–19.

as mother. As Clara and Henry were of the same generation, a triadic relationship was set up similar to that of Beach's childhood. While her husband had taken over her mother's former role as arbiter of her career—deciding how Amy made music and lived her life—they both served as her musical mentors and critics. Such a relationship was at once supportive and oppressive.

Furthermore, Clara Cheney liked to sit in the wing chair in the music room while Amy was composing or practicing, so she was physically present at least part of the time when her daughter was at work on the concerto.[13] Beach's comments on the problems facing married women who compose at home may have been inspired by a tension between her mother's needs and her own:

> The constant interruptions that beset one who needs repose and time for reflection in such a career require much patience and considerable diplomacy to prevent their distracting influence from devitalizing and unnecessarily wearying the spirits that are so essential to commanding work. One must learn early in life . . . to concentrate all our powers, so far as is possible, on the serious work in hand. . . .When we have found the courage to do this we are a long way on the road to the accomplishment of our chosen task.[14]

In the second movement of the concerto, Beach may have both recognized and suppressed her mother's voice as she had learned to do while composing.

(b)

EXAMPLE 12.4 (continued)

The third movement is based on Beach's op. 2, no. 1, a setting of her husband's poem, "Twilight." Like the song, the concerto movement, a largo—in Beach's words, "a dark, tragic lament"—is in the key of F♯ minor, a key Beach associated with the color black.[15] The text of the song is somewhat more poetic than is usual for Dr. Beach:

No sun to warm
The darkening cloud of mist,
But everywhere
The steamy earth sends up
 A veil of gray and damp
To kiss the green and tender leaves
And leave its cool imprint
In limpid pearls of dew.

The blackened trunks and boughs
In ghostly silhouette
Mark grimly in the coming eve
The shadows of the past.
All sounds are stilled,
The birds have hushed themselves to rest
And night comes fast, to drop her pall
Till morn brings life to all.

The music's pathos leaves the words far behind (ex. 12.5a). The accompaniment for the lackluster words "But everywhere" becomes the orchestra's darkly portentous opening motto (ex. 12.5b), which is used as a brief refrain throughout the movement. The movement begins as a meditation on the first two lines of the song (see mm. 24–25), eventually incorporating all but the song's last phrase.

Piano and orchestra no longer vie with one another in this slow movement, but rather they alternate the roles of orchestral tutti and solo (or accompanied solo), each participant now clearing aural space for the other. As a result, the melody that in the concerto soars free of the words is revealed in all its tragic intensity, more keenly reflecting the poem's association of nightfall with death.

The music of the last line of the song, "Till morn brings life to all," is the focus of the last movement, "a bright vivacious rondo" in a waltzlike $\frac{6}{8}$ meter, a veritable burst of energy and *joie de vivre*. Now the emphasis is on an exuberant life, on the daily rebirth with the sun, as promised in the last line of the song. For the opening theme, Beach uses the rising third that begins the last line, extends it through figuration and a rising scale into an expansive gesture encompassing three octaves (ex. 12.6).

Unlike the earlier movements, the finale, which opens in C♯ minor, belongs almost exclusively to the soloist. In assigning the first statement of the theme to the piano, Beach again follows tradition.[16] But the soloist also initiates each subsequent theme as well as most changes of key and mood. Furthermore, the two main themes are both virtuosic, so that the piano dominates with thematic material rather than with unrelated gratuitous virtuosic passages as in the first

EXAMPLE 12.5 (a) "Twilight," op. 2, no. 1, mm. 1–9 (Arthur P. Schmidt, 1887). (b) Concerto for Piano and Orchestra, III, first theme, mm. 21–25.

two movements. Finally, except in tutti passages, in which the main themes are repeated, the orchestra's role is that of a discreetly supportive accompanist.

The second theme, introduced by the piano at measure 45, is a free inversion of the first (ex. 12.6). Marked *con grazia*, it is as ebullient as the first theme yet somewhat more relaxed. The two bright themes, in effect, balance the two dark themes of the first movement. In an extended passage, however, the tempo slows to *lento* as the piano recalls the tragic theme of the Largo (ex. 12.7). But the piece ends in D♭ major with brilliant virtuoso flourishes on the piano.

Considering Beach's characterization of the concerto as a struggle between soloist and orchestra, it is possible to trace the evolving role of the piano in the

(b)

EXAMPLE 12.5 (continued)

four movements from unequal to equal contestant and finally to victor. This evolution suggests a plot that encapsulates the most important issue of Beach's life, her struggle for the freedom to play whenever and wherever she chose.

The piece is a tour de force for the soloist, and its difficulties may have discouraged some performers from learning it, since it requires a considerable investment of time by both soloist and orchestra and, like many American works, was rarely given more than once by any single orchestra. As a result, most of the performances of the concerto were by Beach; she succeeded therefore in writing a vehicle for herself.

Her dedication of the concerto to Teresa Carreño was at once a response to Carreño's enthusiasm for the earlier Violin Sonata and a hope that the Venezuelan-born pianist would become a champion of Beach's concerto as she had been for those of Edward MacDowell.

EXAMPLE 12.6 (a) "Twilight," mm. 47–53. Concerto for Piano and Orchestra, IV: (b) mm. 1–4; (c) second theme, mm. 46–49.

EXAMPLE 12.6 *(continued)*

The first performance of the concerto was in the old Music Hall on 7 April 1900, toward the end of the Boston Symphony's last season in that house before moving to its new home, Symphony Hall. Wilhelm Gericke, who had advised Beach to teach herself composition some sixteen years earlier, was the conductor. Critical opinion was more evenly divided than in the past. Beach's stalwart supporter, Howard Malcom Ticknor, wrote of the work that it was representative of the composer's continuing growth: "[E]ach new year sees a fresher, richer and more spontaneous melody, alike in simple salon songs and in works for the chamber or the orchestral musician, while the variety, surety and strength of instrumentation develop logically and agreeably."[17]

Louis C. Elson, usually in Beach's corner, gave a mixed review. Initially, he complained that in the first and second movements the orchestra often overpowered the piano, explaining that "the solo instrument is not employed in sounding forth bold themes. . .but in giving constant fioriture, scales and ornate passages against rather vague themes in the orchestra." The last movement, he believed, was the best and most original of the four.[18]

EXAMPLE 12.7 Concerto for Piano and Orchestra, IV, recall of opening theme of third movement, mm. 125–28.

The most negative review came from Philip Hale, who declared that the work was "a disappointment in nearly every way" and went on to complain that "[i]t is a pity that she has never had a thorough, severe drill in theory and orchestration. Her symphony led one to believe that natural talent, self-study, close observation, might do much without painful labor under a pedagogue, but this piano concerto does not encourage any such belief."[19] Hale's opinion of the concerto was seconded by the reviewer for the *Herald*, who said, "The fault was in the remorseless heaviness of the instrumentation, that no skill or care on the part of conductor and orchestra" would help.[20] Perhaps, the writer suggested, she should have composed a series of shorter works for orchestra in order to gain more skill. For Beach this was quite a blow. It was bad enough to criticize the work in this way, but even worse to cast doubt on her training and skill as a composer. However, this was the first performance, and it is likely that more than one was needed before the texture could be clarified and the correct balance established; perhaps with more hearings, critics could make more carefully considered judgments.

There is evidence that Henry Beach no longer withheld negative reviews from his wife—if he ever did—and that she saw such reviews of the concerto. The following letter from Teresa Carreño, in which she thanks Beach for the concerto and its dedication, suggests that Beach may have complained to her about the critical reception. Carreño wrote:

> [A]ll that you tell me about the first appearance of this "godchild" of mine has greatly interested me, and as to the controversy in the matter of criticism, it is not exceptional for, with every work of importance, criticism finds itself rather uncertain as to what to say. How can it be otherwise? How can anyone, whilst listening to a musical, important, complicated and long work be able to form a final opinion from one hearing? Or even two?. . .From the moment a work is *serious* and based on deeper thoughts and feelings we must *study it* each one for ourselves, and try and grasp it into *our* mind and into *our* soul and then we can do it justice.[21]

Despite Carreño's support in this letter, she never performed the concerto. Although she did plan to give it at a concert with the Berlin Philharmonic in 1901, her manager was opposed, and in the end she played an Anton Rubinstein concerto instead.[22] Later, two other pianists, neither of whom had reputations at all comparable to Carreño's, gave the work with orchestra.[23] On the other hand, thirteen years later the concerto became Beach's own vehicle, for between 1913 and 1917, she performed the concerto nine times, playing with several major orchestras including a second performance with the Boston Symphony.[24]

The last four years of the nineteenth century brought Amy Beach a secure if occasionally uncomfortable niche as the token American woman composer, and an international public for her music. She also had developed a style that had its roots in the works of late nineteenth-century giants, especially Wagner and Brahms, yet was distinctively her own in its lyricism and harmonic daring.

THE

COMPOSER'S

WORKSHOP

FOR MANY YEARS BEACH WAS one of the most successful composers of art songs in the United States.[1] For everyone who knew her instrumental works, there were dozens of singers who—in their search for contemporary vocal repertory—found her songs wonderfully effective and sympathetic to the voice; there were hundreds, perhaps thousands, of listeners who were deeply moved by her songs. By 1910, Beach had composed seventy-three songs in three languages and a broad range of moods. The few songs selected for discussion here are representative of the variety and expressive features of Beach's writings. They show the influence of language—English, French, and German—on her compositional style and, on occasion, suggest autobiographical content as well.

The central mystery of artistic creation will always remain just out of reach no matter how we try to close in on it through carefully assembled evidence. In the end, we must be content with ambiguity. Beach, however, left many clues about the genesis of her creativity, not only in her choice of texts but also in her musical settings. And finally, her own words cast a reflected light on her creative process.

Beach claimed that song writing was recreation for her; when she felt herself going stale while working on a larger piece, she would stop and finish the day's work by writing a song. "It freshens me up," she claimed, "I really consider that I have given myself a special treat when I have written a song."[2] Nevertheless, a song's creation was no casual event; for indeed, the wellsprings of Beach's creativity lay in song. We have seen how folk and art songs—whether her own or others'—were musical sources for otherwise abstract works, among them the symphony, the concerto, and her chamber and piano music. There would be many more such self-borrowings in later years. Her lyrical impulse was unfailing and her feeling for the human voice was acute; for her, the first requirement was "that the song shall be *singable*."[3] Beach also said that her songs came from the depths of feeling, which may explain their emotional immediacy. She may have been describing herself when she wrote about "a sensitive soul with musical depths underlying life itself, though apparently hidden."[4]

Beach cast a broad net for her poems. Among the English poets she chose were Shakespeare, Shelley, Tennyson, and the two Brownings; among the French were Perronet and Chateaubriand; among the Germans, Goethe, Schiller, and Heine. But the largest number of her poets were Americans, many of them Bostonians whom she knew: Thomas Bailey Aldrich, Phillips Brooks, William Ellery Channing, Margaret Deland, Oliver Wendell Holmes, Henry Wadsworth Longfellow, Alice Meynell, Harriet Prescott Spofford, and Sara Teasdale, as well as two poets from California, Edward Rowland Sill and, in later years, Ina Coolbrith. A few of her choices reflect her interest in vernacular idioms, especially those of the Irish poet Thomas Moore and the Scotsmen William Black and Robert Burns. Two of her texts were her own—her very successful "Ecstasy," op. 19, no. 2, and "Within Thy Heart," op. 29, no. 1. Later there would be two more, "When Mama Sings," op. 99, no. 1, and I Sought the Lord, op. 142. However, the largest number of texts from any single author—second only to the eight texts by Robert Burns—were the seven by Henry Beach, beginning with op. 2 and ending with "A Prelude," op. 71, no. 1. This last song is from 1910, the year of his death; thereafter, she set no more of her husband's poems. But their collaboration on songs had lasted twenty-five years, their entire married life.[5]

When Beach chose a poem by her husband, the urge to please him may have been as strong as her affinity for the poem. She selected texts by other poets, however, for the special resonance that they held for her. She would further appropriate the poem by changing or adding a title, omitting a verse, or repeating a word or phrase in order to change the emphasis or equalize musical and poetic time. She then would add melodic, rhythmic, and harmonic accents that bring to the foreground certain images—or suppress others—and compose an accompaniment that added its own meaning, thus changing the meaning of the vocal line. In this way, Beach effected "a transformation of poetic and dramatic content," in the words of Edward Cone, that makes a poem her personal statement.[6]

Beach composed quickly, often completing a song in a few hours. Behind this quick birth, however, there was usually a longer gestation period that began with memorizing the poem, then saying the text over and over to herself until, she said, "the music takes a definite shape in my mind."[7] During this process she was able to underscore and dramatize key words that bore the sense and emotional content of the poem, deciding which words to prolong and which to move through quickly.

Prolongations give expressive life, allowing the singer to invest emotional weight in important ideas. As an example, see the song "The Western Wind," op. 11, no. 2, set to a text by William Ernest Henley, the British poet and critic (1849–1903). The breathless accompaniment figure in the piano's right hand moves toward the downbeat but does not achieve it; stated in the first two measures, it recurs many times. The piano introduction soon arrives on the treble note D, the dominant of the key of G (colored bright red by Beach), where it stays for three measures. That same D is then prolonged by the singer for an additional two measures on the first word of the opening line, "Bring her again, O western wind," thus dramatically embodying the lover's longing and impatience for the return of the beloved (ex. 13.1a).

EXAMPLE 13.1 "The Western Wind," op. 11, no. 2: (a) mm. 10–15. Upper staff shows implied counterpoint in vocal line; (b) mm. 61–69 (Arthur P. Schmidt, 1889).

This phrase also shows Beach's early mastery of the long melodic line. There are large intervals, yet paradoxically, the melody holds together because it implies not one voice but two. By connecting the high points of the line that suggest an upper voice and the low points that suggest a lower, there emerges a perfectly coherent and balanced counterpoint. The large intervals at the beginning of the phrase that do the expressive work of the line are answered by the lyrical scalewise motion that ends it. These vertical and horizontal balances are typical of Beach's melodies and explain in part why they are so pleasing.

Beach's long lines are the product of melodic and harmonic means. In the second part of this example (ex. 13.1b), the voice has a long, decorated descent from high A down to low G in three phrases that nevertheless create one sweep; a typically active harmonic vocabulary colors the line and drives it forward without, in this case, changing key.[8]

Many of the poems she set reflect her love of nature; and their texts connect natural elements—the sea and birds, trees and flowers, the moon and the sun, and the cycles of the day and the year—with earthly and heavenly love and with life and death. Her love of nature led her to keep a sketch book in which she notated bird songs that she had heard.[9] Edward Rowland Sill, the poet who started her on this investigation, is the author of a poem Beach set in 1891 as "The Thrush," op. 14, no. 4. The piano accompaniment recalls the silver fluting of the thrush in its repetitive figuration. She also makes expressive use of register by reserving her lowest and highest notes for the psychological low and high points of the text. These occur in the last strophe, which describes a carefree bird that remembers no sorrow:

He has lost his last year's love, I know,
He, too, but 'tis little he keeps of woe,

EXAMPLE 13.1 (continued)

For a bird forgets in a year, and so,
No wonder the thrush can sing.

Beach began this quatrain with a turn to the dark B♭ minor, then set "He, too" to the song's lowest notes, *pianissimo*. The piano interlude that follows underscores the subject's loss by bringing the bird calls down in a mournful chromatic descent.

Beach's most impassioned songs are triplet-driven and orchestral in sound. *Villanelle: Across the World*, op. 20, marked *Allegro appassionato*, has a powerful text by Edith M. Thomas (1854–1925) from her *A NewYear's Masque and Other Poems* (1885). It begins:

Across the world I speak to thee;
Where'er thou art (I know not where),
Send thou a messenger to me!

The singer, a contralto or baritone, declaims in trumpetlike, dramatic upward leaps of a fourth. The vocal line pits eighth-notes against the piano's triplets to create further tension. At the end, the change from minor to major may be a symbolic representation of the beloved moving from the realm of the living to that of the dead, from mortal to eternal life:

Whether in yonder star thou be,
A spirit loosed in purple air,
Send thou a messenger to me.

Intermingled with the compelling emotion in Beach's music is another strain. Beach refers in her credo, "The Uplift of Music," (published in 1905 in *The Music Lover's Calendar*) to "the moral influence and uplifting power of music" that leads to "all that is good, just and beautiful." But she also approves of music's role as the inspiration for "good manners." She attributes the idea to Luther, but to modern ears it sounds Victorian. Indeed, there is much of the Victorian lady about Beach, "one of the old school" whose "old-fashioned courtesy" and observation of social amenities defined her relationships. "You minded your manners around her, but she imposed this in a nice way."[10] The feeling came first and the Victorian training followed; nevertheless, the lady-like attitudes—far more than a thin overlay or a defensive strategy—remained with her for a lifetime.

A manifestation of Victorian attitudes may be found in Beach's occasional choices of sentimental poems that to modern ears sound romanticized and unrealistic, with musical settings that may seem disproportionately intense. Yet, at the same time that the modern listener thinks "Life is not like that," an unbidden tear comes to the eye. An example, "Chanson d'Amour," op. 21, no. 1, appears with Victor Hugo's text in French and a translation, probably by the composer.[11] Beach creates the propulsive intensity of this song—as she did with "Villanelle"—by the ever present triplets in the accompaniment. The final verse especially recalls the sentimental parlor song tradition:

I adore thee, I love thee truly;
God, who has filled my life with thine,
Created mine eyes for thy beauty,
And for thy soul this love divine.[12]

The climax comes in this final refrain and is prepared by an accelerando and crescendo during which the piano's pulsating triplets are thickened to six, even seven, notes per chord, played *fortissimo*; the sustaining pedal provides full resonance.

Her most famous song, "The Year's at the Spring," uses the same triplet figuration to express youthful ardor and exuberance. Its time signature is $\frac{3}{4}$, but the quarter notes are divided into triplets throughout the accompaniment. The Boston Browning Society commissioned Beach to set this text from Robert Browning's *Pippa Passes* for a celebration of the poet's birthday. While on a train, Beach found herself saying the words over and over until the song sang itself into her consciousness against the persistent rhythm of train wheels. "I listened to the melody—it was the only melody, after that, for that burst of joy and faith. I wrote it down as soon as I got home."[13] The poem reads:

The year's at the spring,
The day's at the morn,
Morning's at seven,
The hillside's dew-pearled;

The lark's on the wing;
The snail's on the thorn;
God's in His heaven;
All's right with the world![14]

The short phrases suggest a breathlessness that matches the spring morning, and the rhyme scheme postpones closure until the end of the last line. Beach sets the short lines as anacruses, each one leading to the downbeat, and each downbeat a scale-degree higher, climbing up five degrees, then dropping back down to climb an entire octave. Crescendo and accelerando increase the triplets' drive from beginning to climactic end. The result is a single emotional sweep that is extraordinarily powerful.

Because of its very directness, the song became the best-seller among American art songs for many years. Such divas as Marcella Sembrich and Emma Eames often sang the song as an encore, with the audience demanding its immediate repeat. Eames wrote to Beach that she had sung the song for two years, and that "it has never failed to carry away [the audience] by storm." So it was when Eames sang the song as an encore at a Metropolitan Opera Sunday Evening Concert (12 February 1905) to Beach's orchestration, written on short notice at the singer's request.[15] Another such accolade was given in Florence, Italy, when Eames sang the song for Browning's son, who, she reported to Beach, "was intensely moved by it and said. . .that one could not imagine anything more perfectly 'married' than his father's words and your music."[16]

In certain other instances, Beach uses reiterated triplet chords to build an orchestral-sounding climax, even when the song—or the instrumental work—does not begin with triplet figurations. Rather the accompaniment breaks out of its frame at the climax, almost as if that climactic passage were imported from another composition.[17]

Two settings of French poetry, "Le Secret," op. 14, no. 1, and "Elle et moi," op. 21, no. 3,[18] create a very different emotional climate from "The Year's at the Spring," a difference that can in part be ascribed to the language itself. "Le Secret," a lilting waltz, suggests by short phrases in the vocal line a flirtatious conversation while dancing. Later, Beach confirmed that impression by reworking the song as the "Valse amoureuse" of *Les Rêves de Colombine*, op. 65.

"Elle et moi" is stylized, decorative, objective. The poem by Félix Bovet characterizes the beloved as the seductive flame and the lover as the butterfly who recklessly singes his wings in that flame. While the speaker is a man, the song is written for a coloratura soprano, suggesting that the singing voice embodies not the man's voice but the movements of the butterfly or the flickering of the flame. The accompaniment, which is to be played *con delicatezza* and nonlegato, invokes both images in a recurring rhythmic pattern and is transferred to coloratura passages for the voice.[19]

Beach also set a number of German texts, beginning with Schiller's "Die vier Brüder," op. 1, no. 2 (discussed in chapter 6). Three of the four songs in her op. 35 are to German poems and demonstrate a strong connection to the *Lied*. The first of the set, "Nachts" (Night), to a text by Christian Friedrich Scherenberg (1798–1881), is an utterly peaceful and lovely song. The text of the second of the set, "Allein," by Heine, was made doubly famous by Schubert's "Ihr Bild," which Beach probably knew.[20] When the tempo marking of a Beach composition includes the word *espressivo*, as many do, one expects a work of considerable intensity. For "Allein," however, Beach used the stronger word *addolorato* (with grief and pain). The poem depicts a lover who weeps as he beholds the portrait of his late beloved. As he gazes, the image comes to life, a smile on her lips and tears in her eyes.

In Beach's setting, the vocal soloist's opening phrase features accented dissonances on downbeats and ends with the oppressive interval of a diminished fourth on the word *Träumen*. The second phrase repeats the same pattern a third higher (ex. 13.2a). In the first ten measures, prominent sigh figures emphasize grief. Throughout, dissonance prevails, further underscoring grief, with few moments of consonant harmony. Yet the tonality is quite stable and rarely in doubt—perhaps a reflection of the stasis the poem projects. The final line, "Und ach! Ich kann es nicht glauben, Dass ich dich verloren hab'" (Alas, I cannot believe that I have lost thee), suggests utter dejection or perhaps even denial in the Schubert setting, but in Beach's song the effect is of intense sadness. The climax is reached on "Alas," the singer's highest note, sustained over a dissonant and volatile augmented-sixth chord in the piano accompaniment (ex. 13.2b). The song ends *pianissimo* as the piano recalls the opening strain. "Allein" appears in an instrumental version as the *Lento espressivo* of the second movement of Beach's Piano Trio, op. 150, composed years later.

Time signatures also have special meanings for Beach. Compound meters like the $\frac{6}{8}$ of "Allein" or the $\frac{12}{8}$ of *Villanelle* are often used for emotionally charged texts. Beach, however, chose duple meters, especially $\frac{2}{4}$, for her scherzo movements, as we have seen, or a scherzolike song, such as "Elle et moi" or "O Mistress Mine," op. 37, no. 1. Written to a lyric of Shakespeare, the latter is a fresh-sounding composition in G major, *Allegretto grazioso*, with coloratura passages similar to those in "Elle et moi." Dissonances are few and the texture is transparent. Momentary shifts in key move to the brighter, dominant, D major, rather than to the darker, third-related key as in "Allein" and other serious songs.

Beach's sense of music as "the divine art" and the immanence of the divine in humans finds expression in the many love songs that invoke God through the joining of mortal souls in spiritual love. It was the common coin of the late nineteenth century to speak of music as the divine art, "the language of natural religion."[21] By the end of the century, the idea of music as natural religion was a bit out of date, but the term *the divine art* remained. The critic Henry Edward Krehbiel, however, redefined the relationship as a new trinity consisting of God, nature, and music.[22]

Amy Beach's bookplate of her later years encapsulates this trinity. It depicts an outdoor scene framed by tall trees, their topmost branches meeting in a Gothic arch. On the grass—front and center—is a woman seated at a grand piano with the lid up. Emanating from the piano are vibrations moving heavenward and led by a dove, the traditional symbol for the Holy Spirit. In Beach's bookplate, the "Spirit" comes from the music and is an offering to God.

EXAMPLE 13.2 "Alone!" op. 35, no. 2: (a) mm. 4–8; (b) mm. 37–42 (Arthur P. Schmidt, 1897).

EXAMPLE 13.3 *When Soul Is Joined to Soul*, op. 62: (a) mm. 1–3; (b) mm. 25–37 (Arthur P. Schmidt, 1905).

Nature played a significant role in her creative life. "I like to sit out of doors, I want to be in the midst of nature when I write," she said. "If it is cold or bad weather when I write, I try to have a room with wide windows or a balcony."[23] She also believed that she received messages from the infinite, given a natural setting and a quiet place to "hear" them.[24]

A number of Beach's songs begin with nature images or human love and end by invoking the divine, exemplifying Krehbiel's trinity. No poem of her choosing comes closer to that Apollonian ideal than *When Soul Is Joined to Soul*, commissioned by Emma Eames. She was so taken with "The Year's at the Spring" that she asked for another Browning song.[25] Beach chose a poem not by Robert but by his wife, Elizabeth Barrett Browning. It begins:

> Oh, wilt thou have my hand,
> Dear, to lie along in thine?
> As a little stone in a running stream,
> It seems to lie and pine.
> Now drop the poor pale hand,
> Dear, unfit to plight with thine.[26]

Beach's setting of the poem, her op. 62, presents musical analogues for its main ideas. The first is that of delayed gratification, achieved by postponing the resolution of the dissonance from the beginning to the very end of the song: the soprano's opening phrase rises from tonic to leading tone, leaving a melodic dissonance of a seventh unresolved to the octave tonic (ex. 13.3a). By a variety of means, Beach denies that resolution again and again, arriving at the high G♭ on the down-beat and supported by tonic harmony only for the singer's very last note.[27]

Another expressive procedure in this song is the use of key changes for lines that demand a distancing of the lovers: "Now drop the poor pale hand" and, in the second verse, "Now leave a little space," where the music moves briefly from G♭ major to the remote D major at mm. 12 and 31, respectively (ex. 13.3b). The final two lines of the third verse, "Nor hands nor cheeks keep separate/When soul is joined to soul," open in G♭, modulate again to D major,

(b)

My cheek is white, my cheek is worn, by— ma-ny a tear— run down. Now leave a lit - tle space, Dear,— lest— it should wet thine own.

EXAMPLE I3.3 (continued)

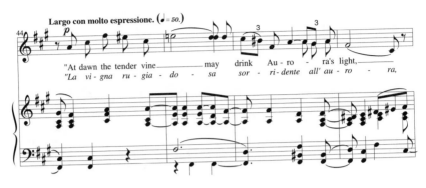

EXAMPLE 13.4 *Jepthah's Daughter*, mm. 44–48 (Arthur P. Schmidt, 1903).

but return to G♭ via D♯ minor, its enharmonic relative minor, thus easing the final return to the tonic for the last line and the tonality-affirming coda. Such tonal shifts suggest that the sensual is sanctioned only with the creation of an idealized love. Nevertheless, emotion deferred is not emotion defeated, as the final ecstatic burst of music suggests. This is one of many examples of Beach's use of modulation not for structural but for expressive purposes.

A few songs written after 1900 suggest a dark underside of an apparently happy and productive life. Her tragic concert recitative and aria for soprano and orchestra, *Jephthah's Daughter*, op. 53 (1903), a biblical paraphrase, recalls the pathos of her earlier "Jeune fille et jeune fleur," in which a father buries his daughter, with a narrative voice that objectifies both the quick and the dead. In this aria, however, the daughter is the singer throughout, expressing her own despair over the imminent sacrifice of her life to save her father's. Nature and time are again invoked in the contrast between her death and the ever-renewing cycle of day and night. The reference to Jephthah's daughter, who would die childless, had resonance for Beach's life: after seventeen years of marriage, there were still no children, nor would there be any, something she may have regretted.[28]

For her setting of *Jephthah's Daughter*, Beach called forth her most tragic musical vocabulary: the key is again F♯ minor; the melodic lines present pathetic accents, dissonant and diminished intervals, and descending chromatic scales as the singer imagines the darkness of death closing in. The aria, a *Largo con molto espressione*, opens with a decorated descending tetrachord, or Phrygian cadence, its twists and turns illustrating the text. This is a musical progression which Beach also used as a defining motif in other works, especially in her Piano Quintet in the same key (ex. 13.4). The phrase ends a dramatic octave and a half lower than its high point of F♯, its downward thrust also contributing to a sense of doom. While the melody of the next phrase rises, its bass line descends chromatically from tonic to dominant, the most pathos-laden version of a Phrygian cadence.

The song "I Know Not How to Find the Spring," op. 56, no. 3 (1904), in its contrast between the eternal renewal of life in spring and human mortality,

EXAMPLE 13.5 "I Know Not How to Find the Spring," op. 56, no. 3, mm. 5–15 (Arthur P. Schmidt, 1904).

may also be related to Henry's turning sixty; for in choosing this poem by Florence Earle Coates, Beach anticipates her long widowhood:

I know not how to find the spring
    Though violets are here,
And in the boughs high over me
    The birds are fluting clear;
The magic and the melody,
    The rapture all are fled
And could they wake, they would but break
    My heart now you are dead.[29]

Beach again uses modulations for expressiveness. The song is in D minor, but at the line "The birds are fluting clear," she moves to F major, then immediately repeats the line in A major, with sixteenth-notes suggesting a snatch of bird song (ex. 13.5). The effect is enchanting. It also makes the return to D minor on the line, "The rapture all are fled," all the more poignant. The climax on "now you are dead" is forceful, if somewhat melodramatic.

Whether spontaneous or the result of careful shaping through several versions, Beach's songs deserve a permanent place in the vocal repertory. Their emotional content, sensitive matching of word and tone, long lines that allow the singer to open up vocally, and accompaniments of great artistry affirm their value as exemplars of the genre. Products of the first creative period of her life, many of the songs reflect her youthful enthusiasm and high spirits and, ultimately, upper-middle-class optimism before World War I. They also express the security of being in the mainstream of music—a security that would soon be challenged.

CHORAL

MUSIC

AN ART SONG IS INTENDED for the privacy of the salon or the intimacy of a lone singer's Lieder recital. Choral compositions, however, have a public function involving a corporate body of singers usually assembled before a large audience for civic or ritual celebrations. We expect much less of the personal in choral music, although Beach managed to put her private stamp on the most ceremonial works.

The most public and ceremonial compositions were for world's fairs. From 1893 to 1940, fairs loomed large as a venue for her choral works, providing her with mass audiences and wide publicity. The success of the *Festival jubilate* at the World's Columbian Exposition prompted a second commission to compose for a world's fair: a choral ode for the opening exercises on 1 June 1898 of the Trans-Mississippi International Exposition in Omaha, Nebraska. The request came at short notice; nevertheless, she agreed to fulfill the commission immediately, producing in one week her *Song of Welcome*, op. 42, for chorus and wind band.[1]

Set to a poem by Henry M. Blossom, Jr., *Song of Welcome* is from a world far from her more intimate music.[2] Entire pages of the chorus remain relentlessly diatonic, the work as a whole all but devoid of chromaticism. A rousing piece, it resembles the "Star-Spangled Banner" but is a lot more comfortable to sing. Indeed, one report suggested that Beach had been instructed to "'make it easy'" and did so. "The average church choir would take it up on Saturday night for the first time and sing it without a mistake Sunday morning."[3] Expansive and four-square, its occasional affecting features—lyrical phrase extensions and expressive changes of key—mark the work with Beach's personal style.

As the *Musical Courier* noted, it was Omaha's ambition to be the center of fine arts and music for the region—so prestigious a center that only those looking for advanced training need go to New York or Europe.[4] The fair bolstered this claim by offering programs by local choral groups and orchestras but at the same time imported the Chicago Symphony and the Apollo Society chorus—both of which had been important at the Chicago Fair—to ensure quality performances. American pride led to renewed claims that we in the United States need no longer be dependent on Europe for music or any of the arts, as one stanza of the *Song of Welcome* assures us:

Here science weaves her wonders for the mind,
Here stands arrayed the golden pride of art,
And commerce hath searched the world to find
The treasures rare of many a far-off mart.
   Welcome, welcome to the people of the world.

The poem also celebrated the winning of the West and America's further growth as a colonial power.

On opening day, Beach's "broad and inspiring" *Song of Welcome*, was sung by a chorus of two hundred to the accompaniment of the Marine Band conducted by Willard Kimball.[5] The *Boston Home Journal* of 7 June 1898 reported with pride that Beach's chorus was "a notable feature of the opening ceremonies," and, while an occasional work, its worth far exceeded the occasion.

In 1901 Schmidt published the piano-vocal score of Beach's *Sylvania: A Wedding Cantata*, op. 46, a full-scale multimovement work for five soloists, double chorus, and orchestra. There is no indication that Beach had a particular wedding ceremony in mind when she wrote it; perhaps the poem itself evoked musical images. The text is freely adapted from the German by Frederick W. Bancroft. It includes solos for a nightingale, a bridesmaid, a sibyl, a watchman, and the "Spirit of the Night." There are choruses for men's, women's, and mixed voices, representing brownies, skylarks, students, bridesmaids, forest trees, and villagers. "Redolent. . .of the whisperings of the forest, the caroling of birds and songs of elves and fairies," both music and text recall Mendelssohn's *A Midsummer Night's Dream*.[6] This is one of Beach's sunniest works, with most of the numbers in the major mode. Those sections that are in minor seem to play at being tragic in order to make the celebratory choruses even brighter. The prevalence of dominant harmony—which Beach usually avoids in favor of modulation by thirds—adds to the bright, festive quality. It is notable that the work begins in G minor but ends in D major, anticipating her later use of progressive tonality (see chapter 22).

Its premiere in Boston by the Amphion Club of Melrose, Massachusetts, on 7 April 1905 took place in Chickering Hall, with Beach at the piano. Also on the program were several of Beach's songs and the *Romance*, op. 23, for violin and piano. Although the event was private, an audience of six to seven hundred had been invited that included Wilhelm Gericke, George Chadwick, and John Knowles Paine among Beach's usual loyal following.[7]

Critical reviews were few because of the private nature of the concert, but Beach heard promptly from Paine and Chadwick. The concert is "a triumph," wrote Paine, and the cantata "one of the finest works you have created."[8] Chadwick prefaced his appreciation with an attack on modern French composers and their "unhealthy new concoctions, painfully grubbed out of the scale of whole tones."[9] For Beach's music, however, he had nothing but praise: "I heard the concert of your compositions with the greatest pleasure and pride. I say pleasure because your music is in every way sympathetic to me, and pride because an American and a woman can produce such strong and beautiful musical ideas and express them with such thorough mastery."[10] Small wonder that Beach saved their letters.

(a)

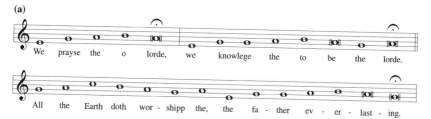

EXAMPLE 14.1 (a) *Te Deum*, Ambrosian chant. (b) Beach, *Service in A*, op. 63, "Te Deum," mm. 1–12 (Arthur P. Schmidt, 1905).

Most of Beach's compositions for mixed choir during this period were sacred. For her, the very process of composing religious music was spiritual: "There can be no greater experience than the act of entering into the great religious texts with the intimacy that we must feel in order to put such words into adequate music." She treasured the time spent in such creative work, even though her "musical efforts must fall so far short of the glorious words."[11] Having grown up hearing and studying choral music, she knew much of the repertory and brought both tradition and turn-of-the-century sensibility to her own choruses.

Her second major choral work from this decade is the *Service in A*, op. 63, consisting of five large-scale compositions for mixed chorus, soloists, and organ.[12] Schmidt issued the "Te Deum" and "Benedictus" in 1905, and the "Jubilate," "Magnificat," and "Nunc Dimittis" the following year. In writing this service, Beach reached back a century to draw on elements of Anglican cathedral music. Because all five movements have the half note rather than the quarter note as the beat, visually the work resembles the music of William Boyce and William Croft.[13] Beach's deliberate archaism is also apparent in the opening movement, in which she quotes the "Te Deum" chant from Marbecke's *Booke of Common Praier noted* (London, 1550), an early Anglican version of the famous Ambrosian melody (ex. 14.1a).[14]

Her note on the first page of the holograph of the "Te Deum" states, "Ambrosian theme has been used as cantus firmus." The theme indeed is prominent; however, it is not used as a cantus firmus in accordance with medieval or Renaissance practice, but rather in contemporary style as an opening theme for further development and recall. The chorus, singing in unison and octaves, intones the opening phrases of the chant, which later recur as themes (ex. 14.1b). There is very little imitative writing. Rather, like Anglican service music, rhythmicized chanting on recitation tones lead to harmonized cadences, chant, or four-part block harmony, all alternating with free solos.

The four movements that follow the "Te Deum" contain occasional reminiscences of the chant but are freer and more contemporary in sound. The five movements—from the joyous phrases of the "Jubilate" to the contemplative "Now let thy servant depart in peace" of the "Nunc dimittis"—are among Beach's best and most dramatically effective choral pieces. Perhaps the most striking passage of all comes in the "Gloria patri" of the final movement, where

EXAMPLE 14.1 (continued)

EXAMPLE 14.2 *Service in A,* "Nunc dimittis," mm. 61–70.

the choir chants on a single pitch while the organ changes harmony, a brilliant illustration of the text "As it was in the beginning, is now, and ever shall be" (ex. 14.2).

Individual choruses from the *Service in A* were heard in many churches over the years. The "Te Deum" and "Benedictus," were given first performances at Emmanuel Church, Boston, on Palm Sunday and Easter of 1906, conducted by Arthur Hyde.[15]

BEACH ALSO WROTE WORKS for all-male and all-female choirs. Her compositions for male chorus are few and include the following: a "Ballade" entitled "The Minstrel and the King," op. 16 (1901), with original German text by Schiller, for soli, male chorus, and orchestra, dedicated to Theodore Thomas;[16] Te Deum, op. 84; and three male choruses to texts by John Masefield, op. 126, nos. 1 and 2, and op. 127.[17]

Beach's works for women's voices were almost as numerous as those for mixed choir. The demand for such music grew exponentially, beginning in the late nineteenth century, as a result of the growth of the women's club movement. This movement has yet to find its place in the history of music in America. A few all-female choirs flourished in the women's academies, but the mainspring of their growth was the women's and music club movement. Following the initial gathering of their representatives at the Chicago Fair in 1893, more and more women joined music clubs, doubling their membership by the time of the establishment of the National Federation of Music Clubs in January 1898.[18] Many of them had choruses.

Before that time, women's choruses were a rarity. Rather they were auxiliaries organized to serve when men's choruses and *Singvereins* required their help in such presentations as *The Creation* or *Messiah* or *Elijah*. Typically women had no say in the running of men's choruses, either in the choice of repertory or in performers or in the disbursement of assets. But with the formation of independent choruses, women took charge of their own musical activities.

Beach credited the clubs with major responsibility for the expansion of musical taste and more frequent performance of music by women. Club members celebrated the work of women—although not exclusively—through study sessions and recitals. Beach, beloved by club members personally and as a composer, was a special heroine to them. Her music was often chosen for National Federation of Music Clubs competitions. A few clubs were moved to rename themselves in her honor: members of the Ladies' Choral Society of East Stroudsberg, Pennsylvania, voted in 1897 to change their name to the Beach Choral Society; a Providence music club changed its name to the Beach Club, as did one in Beach's mother's birthplace, Hillsborough, New Hampshire.[19] Thus, her name was added to the list of composers memorialized by the women's music clubs, a list that began in 1868 with the Rossini Club of Portland, Maine, and included Mendelssohn, Robert Schumann, Bach, and Rubinstein as well as Clara Schumann and Chaminade. Beach's following among women, established first at the Chicago Exposition in 1893, now increased manyfold. Despite criticism from the likes of Henry Krehbiel,[20] the influence of women's clubs was highly constructive, for they were leading factors in the growth of a nationwide audience for art music.[21]

The demand for women's choral music grew during the first decade of the new century.[22] Men as well as women responded to that need, but women seem to have a special affinity for the medium. Beach, Margaret Lang, Gena Branscombe, and Chaminade contributed to the repertory, while publishers, including Schmidt and G. Schirmer, instituted women's choral series to serve the growing nationwide market.

Between 1891 and 1944, the year of her death, Beach wrote nearly thirty compositions for women's voices. Her first was the four-part unaccompanied chorus *The Little Brown Bee*, op. 9, the music of which is far better than Margaret Eytinge's saccharine and anthropomorphic poem. For the text of her next work for women's voices, Beach chose another sentimental poem, "The Rose of Avon-Town," by Caroline Mischka of Buffalo. It is based on a favorite Victorian conceit, the equation of a woman's life cycle with that of a flower.[23] A bride picks a rose to wear at her wedding. Like the rose, the bride begins to fade soon after the ceremony, which is described in the third stanza. In the fourth stanza, grief overtakes her; and in the fifth stanza, she is old and grey, a flowerless stem sustained by memories of love.

Beach took seriously the text of *The Rose of Avon-Town*, her op. 30 (1896), as she did all the words she set.[24] Beginning in a bright and lilting F major with a series of upthrusting phrases, the music becomes more lyrical as it moves into darker key areas. Energy and color diminish as the bride ages, while the survival of love is celebrated through a sedate return to F major. In the end, the music contentedly fades away.

The commission for *The Rose of Avon-Town* came from the Caecilia Ladies' Vocal Society of Brooklyn, about the time Beach was putting finishing touches on the symphony. The cantata, for four-part chorus and soprano soloist, was completed at the end of March 1896, several weeks before its first performance on 22 April at the Lee Avenue Congregational Church in Brooklyn. The singers were obviously quick studies.

A Brooklyn critic considered the work "fine. . .musicianly, and strong," adding that "one never thinks of classing Mrs. Beach among 'women writers,' since her work does not show. . .'feminine characteristics.'"[25] But Philip Hale, reviewing its third performance and the first in Boston, referred to the "inexorable sweetness" of the text: "The emotion is gentle and becomingly womanly, for passion in this sentimental bride who on her wedding day could moralize genteelly over the fate of a rose would be incongruous." He did, however, find words of praise for Beach's skill as a composer and for the women of B. J. Lang's chorus, the Cecilia, who gave the work on 4 February 1897 at the Boston Music Hall.[26] The cantata became increasingly popular among women's choruses from Newark to Los Angeles, from Beloit to Birmingham. When George Chadwick decided to give the cantata at the Worcester Festival on 28 September 1898, Beach orchestrated the piano accompaniment for double woodwind quintet and timpani.

The two other large-scale choral works for women's voices reflect Beach's special fondness for sea imagery: earlier, she had written a set of three vocal duets entitled *Songs of the Sea*, op. 10, followed by her powerful "Dark Is the Night!" op. 11, no. 1, the song she quoted so extensively in her symphony. In 1904, she set another sea poem, Tennyson's "The Sea-Fairies," which became her opus 59, for soprano and contralto solos, four-part women's chorus, and piano accompaniment. The orchestration, which she completed on 5 November 1904, is for two flutes, two clarinets, two French horns, harp, and strings.[27] She dedicated the work to the Thursday Morning Musical Club of Boston, conducted by Arthur Hyde.

The poem tells of the sirens who tempt mariners to their destruction. Beach's setting has harmonic echoes of Debussy: augmented triads and sixth chords, parallel sixth chords and chromatic progressions. Especially effective is the a capella passage beginning at m. 41 ("Whither away, fly no more")—the sirens' voices disembodied, floating (ex. 14.3a). Following is a choral waltz ("Day and night to the billow the fountain calls") which, despite its flowing accompaniment, is sheer Vienna (ex. 14.3b).

Beach's last major secular choral work for women's voices written before 1910, *The Chambered Nautilus*, op. 66, is a setting of the famous poem by Oliver Wendell Holmes (1809–1894), which appeared in his first book of conversations, *The Autocrat of the Breakfast Table* (1858). Holmes claimed that the poem was

EXAMPLE 14.3 *The Sea-Fairies,* op. 59: (a) mm. 45–56; (b) mm. 98–106 (Arthur P. Schmidt, 1904).

"suggested by looking at a section of one of those chambered shells to which is given the name Pearly Nautilus." He wrote, it has "a series of enlarging compartments successively dwelt in by the animal that inhabits the shell, which is built in a widening spiral. Can you find no lesson in this?"[28] Clearly, Holmes did. While the poem—considered by some to be Holmes's poetic masterpiece—recounts the life cycle of the animal that enlarges the shell as it grows, it also suggests the expansiveness of New England life in the mid-nineteenth century. Indeed, it is more in harmony with the Romantic ideas of the Transcendentalists than with those of Holmes the rationalist, the careful scientific observer.[29] Nor was it typical of Holmes in his role as the witty and satiric conversationalist who dominated the talk of the famous Saturday Club, whose members included only men: Louis Agassiz, Phillips Brooks, John Sulli-

EXAMPLE 14.3 (*continued*)

van Dwight, Ralph Waldo Emerson, James T. Fields, William Dean Howells, Henry James Sr., Henry Wadsworth Longfellow, James Russell Lowell, Lawrence Lowell, and John Greenleaf Whittier.[30]

In the winter of 1883, when Amy Cheney was sixteen, with her light brown hair in a thick pigtail down her back and looking like a school girl, she had asked Oliver Wendell Holmes to sign her autograph album. Along with his name, he inscribed the last stanza of "The Chambered Nautilus."

> Build ye more stately mansions, O my soul,
>   As the swift seasons roll!
>   Leave thy low-vaulted past!

Let each new temple, nobler than the last,
Shut thee from heaven with a dome more vast,
   Till thou at length art free,
Leaving thine outgrown shell by life's unresting sea.

Amy Cheney might well have made a setting for Holmes's poem even if their paths never again crossed. But following her marriage to Henry Beach, their paths crossed frequently—for example, at the benefit program at the home of socialite Robert Treat Paine when Holmes read "The Chambered Nautilus." The poem was no doubt registered in Beach's marvelously retentive memory, waiting for the appropriate opportunity to arise for a musical setting.

That opportunity came twenty-one years later when Victor Harris, the conductor of the St. Cecilia Club of New York asked Beach to write a work for his women's chorus. The sea imagery of her recent composition, The Sea-Fairies, surely was on her mind then; the new work would offer the opportunity to further explore and develop those ideas. Moreover, the connection between the French modern musical style and the sea might have been a preoccupation following the Boston Symphony premiere on 1 March 1907 of Debussy's La Mer.

Beach worked on the new commission over the summer of 1907.[31] By 31 October, The Chambered Nautilus, op. 66, was in print, and she again wrote Schmidt, this time to congratulate him for having done such a beautiful printing job in "so marvelously short a time."[32] Less than two weeks later, Beach sent Schmidt a list of people who were to receive professional copies, among them Percy Goetschius.

In his letter to Beach dated 15 December 1907, Goetschius writes, "I have just spent a most delightful hour with your truly exquisite 'Chambered Nautilus' and wish to tell you, warm from my first glowing impression, how keenly I have enjoyed it." He could rejoice in the work especially because, "in this day of the dreadful disease which. . .one might call the Debussy-disease —or Strauss or Max Reger-disease,. . .I am so glad that we have at least one American composer who is not affected by the plague. God bless you!"[33] Beach, who saved the letter, must have appreciated the compliment, although she did certainly did not agree about "the plague." Indeed, the comment makes one wonder how Goetschius the theorist explained those floating first-inversion, augmented, and diminished chords, and the chromaticism, all creating the Debussy-like sound of many passages.

Beach scored The Chambered Nautilus for women's chorus, contralto and soprano soloists, woodwinds, horns, piano, organ, and strings. A work of generous proportions, it takes about twenty minutes to perform. In her setting, the musical divisions follow the structure of the poem, the five verses of which describe the progress of the nautilus through its life cycle. Beach opens with a piano solo of sixteenth-note patterns that suggest both the ever enlarging spiral of the nautilus shell and the glittering sea, first peaceful, then rolling (ex. 14.4a). The chorus enters with the "ship of pearl" theme, which threads its way through the entire work—sometimes simply repeated at the beginnings and endings of verses, as frequently varied and developed; sometimes given by

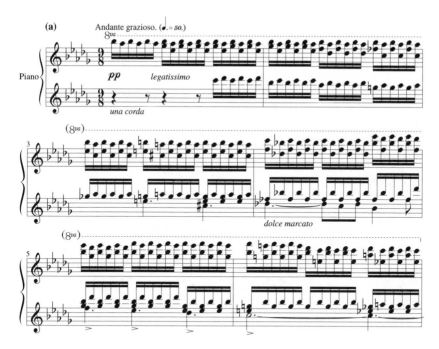

EXAMPLE 14.4 *The Chambered Nautilus*, op. 66: (a) mm. 1–6; (b) mm. 13–16 (Arthur P. Schmidt, 1907).

voices, sometimes embedded in the orchestral texture. The theme also serves as a marker, enclosing stanzas (ex. 14.4b). The first verse describes the nautilus's sea journeys to "gulfs enchanted where the siren sings" and "the cold sea-maids rise to sun their streaming hair," concluding *pianissimo* with the refrain. In the second verse, "Wrecked is the ship of pearl" calls for a quickening of tempo and more dissonance; and the lines "Its iris ceiling rent, its sunless crypt unsealed" are marked by increased chromaticism.

The third verse describes the former life of the nautilus in its spiral shell, each cell of which becomes in turn its new dwelling-place. Beach's setting offers here a contrasting theme for contralto solo—lyrical yet energetic—beginning "Year after year beheld the silent toil" (ex. 14.5). For the fourth stanza, she introduces a rising melody that includes a bright horn call at the words, "From the dead lips a clearer note is born"; it too is a further development of the "ship of pearl" theme (ex. 14.6). The organ is introduced in the hymnic final stanza, "Build thee more stately mansions, O my soul." The transformed theme is sung by the soprano soloist, then echoed by the chorus, bringing the work to a majestic conclusion (ex. 14.7).

The first performance of *The Chambered Nautilus* was in New York on 21 January 1908 by the St. Cecilia Club; thereafter, the work became a staple of their repertory and of many other women's choruses as well. In 1909, a year after the premiere, the St. Cecilia repeated the work with Beach at the piano. Goet-

EXAMPLE 14.4 (continued)

EXAMPLE 14.5 *The Chambered Nautilus*, mm. 129–32.

EXAMPLE 14.6 *The Chambered Nautilus*, mm. 213–18.

EXAMPLE 14.7 *The Chambered Nautilus,* op. 66, mm. 238–41.

schius made sure to attend, and afterward he wrote again, saying how he "reveled in every one of the distinguished beauties of this master work. . .You always were a singularly expert and original harmonist (with absolutely none of the taint of the French school. . .)."[34] About the quality of the work, if not its harmonic vocabulary, many others agreed, for it was among the most popular of Beach's many choral compositions.

THE

CHAMBERED

NAUTILUS

"THE CHAMBERED NAUTILUS" IS AN APT metaphor for Beach's Boston life. Her personal "shell" was the house on Commonwealth Avenue. But she was also comfortably lodged in the bosom of Boston's Brahmin society and was established as a composer in its musical community. Regarding the time in her life that was now coming to an end, Beach would later write, "I belonged to a happy period that may never come again."[1]

Following the turn of the century, Boston found a number of ways to honor her. The Chromatic Club of Boston, founded by Edward MacDowell, with a membership of professional musicians who had been trained in Europe, made Beach an honorary member and on 8 March 1901 presented her in a program of her own compositions including the Mary Stuart recitative and aria, *Eilende Wolken, Segler die Lüfte*.[2] A number of other Boston groups presented all-Beach concerts, among them the College Club, the Amphion Club, and the Thursday Morning Musical Club, which also made Beach an honorary member.[3] The Boston Browning Society made Beach an honorary member in 1903 and elected her to its Hall of Fame in 1915.[4]

With the dedication of the Boston Opera House, Beach's achievements were recognized in still another way. Overcoming its puritan rejection of vain show, Boston finally succumbed; on 30 November 1908, the cornerstone-laying ceremonies for its first opera house brought together celebrities of the music world, patrons, such as Isabelle Stewart Gardner and Eben Jordan, and politicians, led by Governor Curtis Guild. Jordan, head of the department store Jordan Marsh Company was the president of the new Boston Opera Company; Henry Russell, the son of the composer of "Woodman, Spare that Tree," was its impresario.[5] The building, which opened for its first performance on 8 November 1909, was designed to match Symphony Hall both architecturally and acoustically. The result was outstanding on both counts. Its exterior, of "chaste red brick, grey limestone, and white terra cotta," earned it the nickname "the first Unitarian Opera House."[6]

Encased in the cornerstone was a bronze box containing documents from Boston's musical life, concert programs of the Cecilia Society, the Handel and Haydn Society, the Boston Symphony, and the Kneisel Quartet among others;

copies of the leading music periodicals, and newspaper articles about the Opera House. Music was there as well—recordings by singers of opera's Golden Age, and printed scores of vocal and choral works by leading Boston composers Paine, Chadwick, MacDowell, Hadley, Converse, Loeffler, and Beach, who was represented by her Mass, op. 5.[7]

Another important support for Beach's developing career came from Morris Steinert (1831–1912), a piano dealer. He had designed and furnished her with an unusual instrument that she used both at home and in recitals. A well-known collector of ancient instruments, Steinert exhibited them at the Paris Exposition of 1889 and the World's Columbian Exposition in Chicago in 1893.[8] During the 1890s, Steinert invented a piano action called the Steiner-tone that allowed for extremely rapid repeated notes, giving the effect of a vibrato and replicating the special expressive capabilities of the historic clavichord. After Beach's Steinway was fitted out with the action, she became its enthusiastic supporter and promoter. It is not hard to understand why Beach was attracted to such an instrument, for long before she began playing on a Steinertone she produced "fine gradations in shading" and a singing tone that drew from the string "all its tone and none of its jar."[9]

On 14 March 1899, Beach had introduced the instrument to the public at a concert of the Kneisel Quartet at Sanders Theater, Harvard, in which she and Franz Kneisel played her Violin Sonata. At the same time, Beach published an article on the Steinertone, in which she stated that the piano gave the artist better control of the sound and an even tone from top to bottom.[10] The following year, Beach again used the Steinertone for the premiere of her concerto with the Boston Symphony Orchestra. The critic Howard Malcom Ticknor wrote: "The fine Steinertone with Mrs. Beach's exquisite touch upon the keys brought out a wonderful depth of tone, and responded to her call, whether for a dreamy softness, sparkling vivacity, or broad maestoso effects."[11] The action, however, did not hold up under repeated playing; sometime after 1906 Beach gave up its use at concerts, and Steinert stopped producing it.

At Beach's annual recitals in Steinert Hall from 1907 to 1910, she was assisted each time by Carl Faelten, head of the Faelten Piano School. On 6 February 1907 she gave a program featuring her Balkan Variations, op. 60, and closed with the two-piano work, Liszt's *Rhapsodie espagnole*. She also included a group by MacDowell, in a gesture of sympathy for the composer who was terminally ill.[12] On 12 February 1908 she again featured piano works by Mac-Dowell, this time as a memorial, together with her own *Suite Française*, op. 65, and closed the program with the Saint-Saëns *Variations on a Theme by Beethoven*, op. 35, for two pianos.

At her annual recital on 17 February 1909, Beach offered a series of solos including, most notably, Debussy's *Clair de lune* and *Toccata* and Gottschalk's *Berceuse*, op. 47. To close the program, Beach and Faelten joined forces once again, this time to play the two-piano version of Beach's Piano Concerto, a choice that may have been dictated as much by a desire to remind the public of its existence as for reasons of program building. As the critics noted, although the pianists gave an artistically impressive rendering, it could not be entirely satisfactory: "The piano, however skillfully played, cannot be substituted [for the orchestra] without a loss of color, re-enforcement, and contrast. The sympathetic performance, however, went far to display the qualities of Mrs. Beach's music, and to make it the chief feature of the concert."[13]

The following year on 11 February, Beach and Faelten again gave a recital, to a full house. "Interest centered principally in the first performance of her own two-piano suite, 'Iverniana,'" wrote Gertrude F. Cowen. She noted that the suite is based on old Irish themes and commented further on "the unique value of the pure folk theme as a basis for genuine expression in music."[14] That the work was never published and the manuscript is still missing makes Cowen's description of the suite especially valuable. When Beach later issued a two-piano suite in which Irish folk melodies were prominently quoted, it was possible to establish a tentative identity between the two works with the help of Cowen's description. The balance of the program consisted of solo piano works by Bach, Franck, Reger, Gottschalk, Paine, Debussy, Max Fiedler, and Chopin, all of which Beach played with much "spiritual insight" and "served up intact, quietly, with none of the personal element, no thought of anything save the loving service rendered by one composer to another. The audience felt and appreciated this and rewarded the modest artist enthusiastically."[15]

But Beach had long wished for a larger reach for her compositions, in both the United States and Europe. She had already achieved that to a limited degree. On 15 March 1901, the Baltimore Symphony Orchestra, conducted by Ross Jungnickel, presented the "Woman in Music Grand Concert," which was sponsored by the United Women of Maryland. The program included Beach's *Eilende Wolken* (its second performance with orchestra), as well as the "Graduale" for tenor solo from her Mass. Also on the program were Margaret Ruthven Lang's last piece for orchestra, the *Ballade in D Minor*, op. 36, now lost; Chaminade's *Concertstück* for piano and orchestra and *Suite de Ballet*; and the song cycle, *In a Persian Garden*, by the English composer Liza Lehmann (1862–1918), to poems from Omar Khayyam's *Rubaiyat* in Edward Fitzgerald's translation.

A reviewer noted Beach's primacy among women composers in the United States, perhaps in the world as well. He credited Lang with "originality of thought and conception," although he thought her orchestration lacked color; he considered Chaminade's music pleasing and graceful but shallow; and he found Lehmann's songs the best of all. Presented with works by several women, this critic picked only one to praise. This was a species of gender bias Beach had encountered before and would again. It is also significant that the compositions singled out were songs, which the reviewer considered women's best works, perhaps because most suited to women's "limited" abilities.[16] Thus, the critic replaced Beach with Lehmann as the "token" woman, or exception in music.[17]

In 1905 Beach made a considerable stir in Pittsburgh when Emil Paur conducted the Pittsburgh Orchestra in the "Gaelic" Symphony, which he had introduced with the Boston Symphony nine years earlier. Beach played the Saint-Saëns G-minor Piano Concerto. Press coverage was extensive, including advance notices, many reviews of the concert, and several feature articles.[18] Another instance of a continental reach was an all-Beach recital on 1 April 1910 by faculty members of the Whitman Conservatory in Walla Walla, Washington. The performers offered songs, instrumental works, and *The Rose of Avon-Town.*

International recognition was accorded to her as well. Her music was included in an exhibit at the Paris Opera House; and as "a prominent representative of American culture," she was invited to participate on a committee sponsoring a monument to Wagner that would be unveiled in Berlin on 3 January 1903, twenty years after his death.[19]

Interest in Beach and her music stimulated interest in her personal life, a not unusual response to celebrity at home and abroad. In 1910 the *Musical Courier* displayed Beach's picture on the cover; in the same issue is a biographical sketch that includes much of the "official" information, undoubtedly prepared in consultation with Beach. The stress is on her life as a musician and the tone is dignified and professional.

In the same *Musical Courier* article are carefully placed references to Beach as a "true woman" and a brief sketch of Henry Beach's life, even mentioning their courtship. The flowery conclusion of the article assures the reader that, despite all her hard work and productivity, she was no virago. Rather these experiences leave

> her beautiful womanly nature as sweet and as unspoiled as though she had not already completed the wonderful amount of splendid work which one less nobly gifted never could had accomplished in such a short space of life. Today Mrs. Beach stands forth pre-eminently [as] the great composer, and highly gifted pianist, while over and around her hangs the crown of beautiful womanhood, which, like a halo, illuminates all it touches to the highest ethical and artistic responsiveness.[20]

Beach worked hard to keep such interviews focused on her music, but interviewers often had other agendas. One interviewer noted that she was more interested in discussing music than housekeeping, but there was "ample proof" of her concern in the spotlessness of her home.[21] The implication is of course that she only practices and composes *after* she fulfills her role as homemaker in her "stately mansion" on Commonwealth Avenue. Indeed, Beach herself, in an article on music and motherhood, places music second: "All the [musical] training in the world during early life might easily be annulled by the imperfect or bad administration of the home. . .a woman must be a *woman* first, then a *musician.*"[22] But her advice was probably for amateur musicians rather than for professionals like herself.

Beach's right to wear the mantle of "true womanhood" soon was put to the test. While Clara Cheney had been seriously ill for two years, Henry, a year older than Clara, remained well, although his moustache and goatee had turned white and a late portrait of him shows other signs of aging. On or about 25 April 1910, he had a serious fall. According to hearsay evidence, Dr. Beach, who usually carried keys to the homes of his elderly patients, had let himself into one to make a house call, took a wrong turn in the dark, and fell down a flight of stairs.[23] Whatever the cause, he had torn some muscles and was confined to bed.

Soon thereafter in a letter to her publisher, Beach thanked Schmidt for the flowers and get-well message, and reported that Henry was recovering "as well as could be expected after such an accident." The x-ray showed no broken bones, but there were serious injuries to muscles and ligaments. Bandages and splints were applied, and he was kept immovable while tissues healed.[24] Doctors anticipated a quick recovery. The cure, immobilization, however, turned out to be worse than the disease, for on 16 June he developed an abscess and on the 20th septicemia, a fatal illness in the years before antibiotics.[25]

Henry Beach died on 28 June 1910 at the age of sixty-six, his death attended by his wife and mother-in-law.[26] Dr. Elwood Worcester, of Emmanuel Church, presided over the funeral two days later. No doubt at Amy Beach's request, no music was played. Honorary pallbearers included several physicians from Massachusetts General Hospital. Henry Beach was cremated and his ashes buried in the plot he had purchased in Forest Hills Cemetery in Jamaica Plain, Boston, alongside Charles Cheney and his parents, Lucy and Elijah Beach.

The *Boston Medical and Surgical Journal* printed an obituary notice that included, along with a biographical sketch, an evaluation of his importance:

> In the death of Dr. Beach, Boston loses a surgeon long associated with the best traditions. . .For many years he combined hospital work with a very extensive private practice which was both exacting and absorbing. Although his activities had been somewhat modified [he was consulting, rather than attending, surgeon at Massachusetts General Hospital] during the past few years, he was still active preceding his final illness.[27]

An obituary in the *Musical Courier* stated that Dr. Beach "always stood in the vanguard for everything that was humane, progressive, and wide reaching in the theoretical, literary and practical side" of medicine. It mentioned, also, that it was "difficult indeed to find a closer and more ideal companionship than existed between Dr. and Mrs. Beach."[28]

Amy Beach was not even allowed the luxury of an undisturbed mourning period following the funeral. Her mother by then had become very ill. Drastic steps were required, and Beach responded decisively. By fall, she and her mother had moved out of their vertical house and into the Hotel Brunswick. There—unencumbered by the management of servants—she devoted herself to her mother's care, offering every possible comfort "to help her bear her great pain and increasing feebleness."[29]

Beach now had pressing financial concerns. Henry left her about $25,000 mainly in securities plus a house valued at $30,000.[30] There was a mortgage on the house, however, of $25,000.[31] This may have been the first Amy Beach knew of the heavy debt: typically husbands kept their wives ignorant of family finances. The facts suggest that the couple might have been living somewhat above their means. Thus, the received information that Amy Beach was left a rich widow is something of an exaggeration.

Beach complained to Schmidt that finances had become difficult because of heavy expenses, "and no brave husband to work and fight for me," and asked that he put on a campaign to increase the sales of her music. Schmidt, in response, offered instead to give her an advance on her royalties. Beach thanked him but turned down the offer, saying that she was managing at present and would prefer not to accept advance royalties. She added, "My dear husband trained me very carefully in business matters (one of the countless blessings he conferred on me) and I am trying to do and plan everything as he would have wished me to do." She stressed, however, that the income from royalties would be particularly important "until I am strong enough to take up other musical work."[32]

That other musical work would be, at long last, performing. Schmidt soon proposed that she engage a manager to arrange a concert tour during which she would promote her own works, but this she could not do even though the expected result, concert fees and an increase in sales of her music, was "vitally important" to her. Her mother was simply too ill to be left alone, and she indicated that her own health was in jeopardy as well, probably from grief and the stress of her mother's illness.[33]

Meanwhile, Beach made other important changes. One decision had long-range personal, religious, and musical consequences: she joined a church. It was not the Church of the Advent, at which Henry had been a communicant for many years until 1902 or later; the Beaches had attended together, but Amy had never joined. At 11 a.m. on Friday, 4 November 1910, she was baptized at Emmanuel Church, an Episcopal congregation on Newbury Street, where her father's and husband's funeral services had taken place.[34] She probably was influenced in her choice by the quality of the Reverend Worcester's sermons. After the baptism, she attended classes at Emmanuel in preparation for her confirmation, which took place on 2 April 1911. Her decision, made so soon after her husband's death, suggests a need for the consolation offered by religious observance, as well as for a new meaningful relationship, now that she had lost her primary one and knew that her mother's days were numbered.

Beach, looking ahead, made plans to go to Europe even before her mother died and despite her unfounded belief that she was a poor sailor.[35] Her offer to return objets d'art given to her husband by her publisher suggests that she wished to unburden herself of some of her possessions in advance of her trip and even during her mother's waning days. She wrote to Schmidt that "it naturally occurs to me that you might like to have them back again, enriched as they now are by association with the life of your old friend"; for, since she would be "wandering about," she would have to place them in storage.[36] In a later letter to Schmidt, she again reminded him of her offer to return his gifts to her husband unless she heard otherwise. Although his reply is lacking, in fact he must have declined both offers, since Beach's heirs now own the art works from Schmidt. The deterioration of their relationship may have begun at this time, for Schmidt could only have felt that her offer to return the gifts was a rejection of the giver.

Clara Imogene Cheney died at age sixty-four on 18 February 1911 at the Hotel Brunswick. The funeral service was again held at Emmanuel Church, and she was buried, after cremation, at the foot of her husband's grave in the family plot in Forest Hills Cemetery.[37] She left a very modest sum to her daughter and sole heir.[38]

Suddenly, Amy Beach was alone and mistress of her life. Except for a brief interval, Beach never again lived at 28 Commonwealth Avenue. Now her travels began.[39] By March she was in Readville with her childhood friend Amy Brigham;[40] the following month she was at a cousin's home in Washington, D. C., "for a short rest." Meanwhile she "was looking forward with keen anticipation to her contemplated European journey and her hope of resuming her work in Germany and other countries."[41] At this time also Beach laid the groundwork for her future life as a pianist by acquiring a concert manager, Richard Newman of Boston, in expectation of her return to the States a year later.[42]

This is not to suggest that Beach's grief over the loss of her husband and her mother was not profound. She would spend well over a year grieving before she could resume performing, and even then she would find the regime of a traveling pianist too stressful. Nevertheless, she went through with her plans to go to Europe. The freedom to make her own choices must have been a heady new experience that she fully welcomed.

The text of The Chambered Nautilus, the last major choral work she wrote before the close of her Boston life, has a peculiar resonance for Beach. Her personal shell, the house on Commonwealth Avenue, had been her "low-vaulted" chamber for a quarter of a century, and it was a symbol of both the advantages and the limitations of her life. The speed with which she left that home suggests the heavy burden it had become with Henry's death. Like the chambered nautilus of Holmes's poem, she was leaving her "outgrown shell," her last stately mansion on life's unresting shore, but not to die, like the inhabitant of the shell; but to begin a freer yet riskier, less encumbered yet lonelier life.

EUROPE

AND A

NEW LIFE

ON 5 SEPTEMBER 1911, AMY BEACH sailed for Europe, beginning a new life on the very day she turned forty-four. After the early failed promise of study in Europe, after years of watching others leave for European study, after years of waiting for her turn, the trip was finally a reality. But instead of going to Europe as a student, she was going as an established composer with a national reputation—and even something of an international one. Now she must convince European audiences, who were likely to reject Americans and women, to take her work seriously and to give it a fair hearing.

Her second and equally urgent purpose was to reestablish herself as a concert artist. After years of appearing before friendly audiences as an amateur and occasional performer, Beach must convince strange—perhaps hostile—audiences of her authority at the keyboard. She had taken many chances in her life, but this one was the biggest challenge of all.

The very trip was a hurdle in spite of her keen anticipation. In an interview that she gave before leaving, she claimed to be a poor sailor: "I have never quite summoned the requisite courage until this year to attempt a voyage across the ocean. Indeed I had almost concluded that until the journey could be made by some other way—perhaps by a flying machine—I should have to forego the pleasure of travel in Europe."[1] But if she never before had made an ocean voyage, how did she know that she was a bad sailor? Although Beach made several subsequent crossings, there is no further word about the "problem." Perhaps Henry Beach had had other reasons—financial, for instance—for not going to Europe during their twenty-five years of marriage. Once afloat, she quickly discovered that she loved ocean travel.

Beach did not travel alone. Her companion on board and during much of her sojourn in Europe was Marcella Craft (1874?–1959), the American soprano and prima donna of the Munich Royal Opera.[2] In 1896 Craft had come to Boston from Riverside, California, to study with the famous tenor and teacher Charles R. Adams. Beach and Craft met in 1898 when she sang for Beach, who later wrote in her "Musical Visitors" diary that Craft had a "beautiful lyrical style and remarkable dramatic warmth and expressiveness." Her singing of "Chanson d'amour" and the humorous "Wouldn't That Be Queer" was the best Beach "*ever* heard."[3] Craft responded with equal enthusiasm to Beach's warmth and generous appraisal of her voice. "From that moment she was one of my great inspirations. Little I dreamed at the time that the famous Mrs. Beach would one day be among my most intimate friends."[4]

In 1900, following the death of her teacher, Craft continued her studies in Italy—changing her name from Marcia to Marcella—and made her debut with a provincial opera company as Leonora in Il *Trovatore*.[5] In 1904, while Craft was looking for a position with a major opera company in Europe, Henry Beach, in the hope of getting her an audition, wrote a letter to Nahan Franko, concertmaster and the first native-born conductor of the Metropolitan Opera, whose wife he had recently seen as a patient. After inquiring about Mrs. Franko's health, he described Craft's voice, personality, and experience in Italy in the most glowing terms. Unfortunately for Craft, the letter did not win her an audition, although Franko had the authority to arrange one.[6] For an American singer to appear at the Met, she had to have made a mark in Europe first.

Craft soon did just that. The following year she began a decade of starring roles with German opera companies.[7] Her efforts were crowned in 1909 when she signed a five-year contract with the Royal Opera in Munich, one of the great houses of Germany.[8] While there, she sang more than twenty roles, including Mimi to Caruso's Rodolfo in *La Bohème* and the lead in *Salome* under Richard Strauss's direction. In September 1911, when Beach and Craft set sail, the soprano was returning to Munich to begin her third year at the Munich Opera.

It is likely that Craft had something to do with Beach's decision to choose Munich as her base while in Europe. The singer, long a champion of Beach's songs, was in a perfect position to be the instrument of the composer's acceptance into German musical life and thus return the Beaches' earlier favors to her. Indeed, the tables were turned: now Beach was the newcomer and Craft the successful professional performer on European stages. Their friendship was for Beach—as Heilbrun might have characterized it—an "enabling bond that not only supported risk and danger but also comprehended the details of a public life and the complexities of the pain found there."[9] Perhaps most important, the two women not only enjoyed making music together but liked each other's company as well.

After landing, Beach may have spent four days in England. From there, she went to her new studio in the Pension Pfanner at Finkenstrasse 2 in Munich, where Craft had an apartment. Craft regularly had "at homes" at teatime where European and American musicians met, among them the American tenor George Hamlin and the honeymooning Olga Samaroff and Leopold Stokowski, all three of whom presented Beach's music in concert. An American reporter recalled that "[a] pleasant feature of [one] afternoon was the singing by Miss Craft of several songs by Mrs. H. H. A. Beach with the composer accompanying."[10] There probably were many more such occasions.

Once settled in Munich, Beach discovered that music was "universally recognized and respected by all classes and conditions [of Europeans] as the great art that it is." Such "tremendous respect," she wrote, "is almost impossible to convey. . .to persons who have never been outside of America."[11] And music seemed to be ubiquitous. Near her pension in the Old Town of Munich was the *Residenz*, the palace of the Bavarian kings of which the Opera House was a part. Also nearby was the Hofgarten, where a military band played a popular concert twice weekly. "The other day when I was enjoying a cup of coffee under these delightful circumstances, the first numbers on the program of this 'popular' concert were the Overture to Mozart's *Magic Flute* and a long selection from Wagner's *Parsifal*, which lasted certainly twenty minutes."[12] Just past the Hofgarten is the Odeon Platz, where another military band gave concerts every noon, playing "standard musical compositions" to hundreds of people who gathered there daily.

Beach planned to stay in Europe for a year in order to launch her second career as a pianist as well as gather European reviews of her major works. But she did not reckon with her own grief and the toll on her health and stamina that had been taken by the terminal illnesses of her husband and her mother. After she arrived, she found that she was not ready to play in public. "Even in private," she wrote, "to hear the music for which I cared wrung my heart for a while."[13] Clearly she needed more time to grieve.

Soon after her arrival, wanderlust overtook Beach, and she resumed the pattern of frequent travel that she had begun after her mother's death and that would continue until she was seventy. Her first stop was Garmisch-Partenkirchen, in the Bavarian Alps, where she saw friends and went sightseeing. From there she traveled to Berlin for a week, where she visited with her friend Lillie Hegermann-Lindencrone, the amateur singer from Cambridge, Massachusetts, who had recently married the Danish ambassador to the United States. By 1911 he was serving as ambassador to Germany. Lillie Hegermann-Lindencrone had long been an admirer of Beach's music, singing her songs in courtly salons and promoting performances of her vocal and orchestral music. Now she gave a musicale in Beach's honor in her Berlin residence, where a "notable company" heard Beach play her own works.[14]

Beach's networking skills helped her enormously in Europe. While in Berlin, she saw the concert pianist and composer Adele Aus der Ohe, whom she had met in Boston. Aus der Ohe, a champion of women's music, had praised Beach's violin sonata, which had been given at the Deutsche Lyceum Club in 1909, and recently she had invited Beach to submit music to the exhibition of works by women that she was organizing at the club for February and March 1912.[15] Next, Beach went to Meran in the Austrian Alps, where she visited with a Dr. and Mrs. Coit, with whom she planned a song recital for Craft and herself. From there she traveled to Lake Garda and then to Rome to rest, enjoy its "colorful atmosphere," see friends, and meet other musicians.[16] She was especially excited about meeting Giovanni Sgambati, a leader in the revival of instrumental music in Italy:

> I saw a good deal of Sgambati, and had some beautiful times at his house. One
> evening I was playing for him and his wife, and he entreated me to play some of my
> own work. So finally I did, and he said some things charming to hear. "Now," I said,

"I'll play you something I wish I had written"—and I did that wonderful nocturne
of his. . . . He was so pleased and his wife simply came over and kissed me.[17]

Afterward, Sgambati sent Beach a copy of the nocturne with his autograph and
a warm dedication.

Beach also spent a week at the Roman villa of the family of the late novelist
F. Marion Crawford, son of the expatriate sculptor Thomas Crawford and
nephew of Julia Ward Howe, an old friend of the Beaches.[18] She ended her
Italian stay in Venice, to her as to many others the most colorful of Italian
cities. Perhaps it was the atmosphere or simply a matter of time, but during the
two months she spent in Italy she reported that she "was composing nearly the
entire time. . .Even though I was supposed to be resting," she said, "I couldn't
help it; it's in the air somehow. . . . After I got back to Germany I went right on
with it."[19]

In Munich, she also took in musical events with her childhood friend from
the Attic Club days, Amy Johnson Brigham. They attended a production of *Salome* conducted by Strauss with Craft in the leading role.[20] A woman with an
elfin face and slim figure, she also insisted on dancing the role, the first singer
to do so, and became Strauss's favorite for the part.

The morning after the performance Beach, still overwhelmed by Craft's performance and by the evening's music, wrote to the singer:

> The acting throughout was a marvel—the dance a *dream*—and the singing! Oh my
> dear, that delicious voice! . . . The quality of tone was like white velvet and pearls!
> . . . I was amazed at. . .the *beauty* of the music, for which I was not prepared from
> what I had heard of it and from "Electra." Orchestrally it is a glowing mass of beau-
> tiful color, like a rich tapestry or stained glass window. The weaving of the motives,
> with the transcendent beauty of the modulations, was overwhelming.[21]

It is no accident that Beach, herself a master of modulation, should single out
those of Strauss.

By spring 1912, Beach had been in Europe for months without giving a single concert; clearly she needed to stay another year. The *Musical Courier* of 19
June put the best face on the matter: "So great has been the personal and artistic success gained by Mrs. Beach in Europe and so flattering have been the
many offers from different Continental managers, that she has decided to remain abroad next year in order to concertize. . .prior to making a tour of this
country in 1913–14." In the early fall of 1912, she reported to Schmidt that she
had a European concert manager, a Mr. Hensel, and that he had arranged
recitals in Dresden, Leipzig, and Munich for the fall and early winter.[22]

Perhaps it was Hensel who convinced Beach to change her name, not an
easy step for her to take. Having left the small world of Boston where Henry
was famous, she must have known that his initials carried no weight in Germany. While she liked using Henry's name better than her own, she was nevertheless willing to change it if a billing as Amy Beach would help her career.[23]

Her European debut took place on 28 October in Dresden, where she performed her Violin Sonata. On a program, Beach wrote, "Audience large, very

attentive and enthusiastic. Dr. B[ülau] played beautifully."[24] A Dresden review stated that the sonata had "a fine romantic feeling worked out in clear, readily understandable form" and that Beach was "a splendid pianist."[25] That and other similar reviews from Dresden were a fine beginning. At the second recital, in Leipzig on the 30th, she again played only the Violin Sonata.

Back in Munich after the Leipzig concert, Beach wrote to her publisher, asking him to send publicity materials and copies of printed music including the Piano Concerto. She also asked for his advice on concert giving; it was her intention, she wrote, "to make each appearance of benefit to my work in future American tours. . . . Even a limited number of European appearances will help at home." But, she continued, touring was "fatiguing, with the necessary travelling etc., and I am not yet very strong, as the new life is hard and exhausting to me in many ways." She decided, therefore, to give few recitals but do everything to insure each one's success.[26]

At the third concert in Munich, on 17 January, Beach gave a much more ambitious program that included not only the Violin Sonata but also three sets of songs—two by herself, one by Brahms—and piano solos by Bach, Beethoven, and Brahms: a program by the four B's. Assisting artists were the violinist Richard Rettich, former concertmaster of the Kaim orchestra, and the alto Marianne Rheinfeld.

A review of the Munich recital by the *Münchener Zeitung* was reprinted in the *Musical Courier*, which quoted only the favorable words of the German critic. Writing about the first two movements of the sonata, he said, "[It is] an earnest work, worthy of all respect. It shows a thorough musical knowledge and the composer is evidently completely in sympathy with the works of Brahms, without in any way being a copyist."[27] Omitted were the negative comments about other works; indeed, the critic disliked the rest of the program: "It remains a riddle why the composer so completely forgets her lofty goals in her songs and how she could write in the light, sentimental style of the salon music of Hildach and Meyer-Helmund—of which there is only a light but tolerable trace here and there in the Sonata. Only the song 'I dreamt I loved a star' ["My Star," op. 26, no. 1] remains above this level." His review of her piano playing also was mixed: "Her pianistic talents are not as perfected as her musical talents; her technique is not always clear, and the touch lacks sensitivity. But in terms of phrasing and rhythm, she remains the good musician, and for those reasons one listens to her with interest."[28]

Another Munich critic was harsher. He found her technique adequate and her playing sensitive; but her tone was hard and without resonance, her interpretations charmless and without individuality. Her accompaniments to the songs drowned out the singer, he said, because she kept the piano lid up, while her playing of the Brahms "Rhapsodie," op. 119, no. 4, was not exactly clean technically. The critic apparently thought more of her as a composer than a performer, that her works were worthy of respect. Nevertheless he found Beach's eight songs "kitschy," nauseatingly sweet, and monotonous in their sameness. Her violin sonata was another matter, technically praiseworthy but in terms of content, empty of value. The reviewer ended by questioning Beach's judgment in bringing such works to a German audience.[29] Beach, however, was pleased to report:

> The audience was large and very enthusiastic, and there were quite as many Germans as Americans present. I was gratified also at the unexpectedly large sale of tickets, which paid the larger part of my expenses, and these were rather heavy, owing to the high character of my associates. . .[It was] a brilliant success.[30]

She had hoped to give a concert with orchestra during the 1912–1913 concert season but had to put it off until the following fall because she could not obtain the hall and orchestra that she wanted for any good dates that season.[31] As a result, she committed herself to spending a third year in Europe.

Her next appearance, however, may have earned her a fee. On 22 January 1913 Beach appeared at one of a series of concerts given by the Munich Quartet, an ensemble composed of first desk players from the Munich Symphony Orchestra, conducted by Richard Strauss.[32] A music critic found words of praise, if not for her playing, at least for her piano quintet.

> As far as her piano playing is concerned, it is only necessary to repeat what was said on that earlier occasion: it is very skilled and technically brilliant, but the touch is cold and rough. The quintet shows Mrs. Beach at her best as a composer. Just as the violin sonata is. . .musically far superior to the songs, so one may obtain from this quintet—which may be a bit superior to the sonata—an impression of quite respectable ability—and since the composer does not have very high ambitions for her music, and her composition has middling pleasant moments and always remains within the boundaries of immediate pleasantness and easily accessible, she can always be sure of a certain external effect.

Thus, the reviewer seems to have considered this work on the level of entertainment music. He concluded on a nationalistic note:

> But one must ask whether it really was really necessary for the Münchener. . .to accept the work of an American [woman] who is quite good as a composer, as well as a pianist, but is not especially significant in any manner of speaking and, in any case not more significant than dozens of composers to whom we feel closer because they are Germans.[33]

Xenophobia rears its head, with intimation of events to come.

Despite the trashing her songs had from Munich critics, they had made an impact. Requests for copies had multiplied as a result of her recitals, outstripping the inadequate supply sent to Europe by Schmidt. In a letter to her publisher, Beach again asked Schmidt to make sure the songs could be bought in Germany. The question remains why Schmidt was not eager to sell more of her works.[34] For whatever reason, this did not happen. As a result, Beach felt herself poorly served, and the relationship soured on her part.

Schmidt, who would retire three years later, may not have had much energy to pursue foreign sales. Or perhaps the death of Henry Beach, Schmidt's close friend, affected his relationship with Amy Beach. She and Arthur Schmidt might not have gotten along too well if it had not been for the friendship between the two men. Schmidt could be difficult, as Mabel Daniels testified:

> Schmidt has the kindest of hearts but how he loved to bluster. He always began by bewailing the fact that certain of my choral pieces had practically no sale, the difficulties of a publisher making both ends meet, the high price of paper, etc—but as he invariably ended by accepting anything I brought, I listened patiently.[35]

Perhaps Beach, whose sales were substantial, had less tolerance for his bluster. Whatever the reasons for the poor relationship, from 1914 to 1921 the New York firm of G. Schirmer, not Arthur P. Schmidt, was her publisher. That did not mean that her relationship with the Schmidt company was severed; they continued to publish her extensive catalog of music, profit from the sales, and pay her royalties during the period she was under contract with Schirmer.[36]

Probably as a result of the unfavorable reviews in Munich, Beach offered fewer songs in her next recital, which took place in Breslau on 14 February 1913. She repeated three works by Bach, Beethoven, and Brahms; and Elisabet Christian, a well-known mezzo-soprano from Berlin, sang just three of her songs. Instead of the sonata, she gave a set of four short piano pieces: two from her French suite, op. 65; the "Scottish Legend," op. 54, no. 1; and as a finale, the brilliant "Fire-flies," op. 15, no. 4. The critics found her outstanding as solo pianist, accompanist, and composer.[37] The concert season for Beach ended with a joint recital with Craft in Meran, a winter resort in Austria.

In early March, Arthur Abell, the Berlin correspondent for the *Musical Courier,* gave a reception in Beach's honor at which she and Christian repeated works they had given in Breslau. Abell reported that her music was "received with great acclaim by the large number of musical notabilities who were present."[38] This was one of the weekly musicales the Abells gave in their elegantly furnished Berlin home, with the purpose of bringing together leading figures in music. No doubt it was also a way for Abell to gather material for his columns in the *Musical Courier.* Beach made it a practice to attend whenever she was in Berlin. Among the previous guests of honor had been composers Max Bruch, Ferruccio Busoni, Engelbert Humperdinck, and Xavier Scharwenka; violinists Jascha Heifetz and Fritz Kreisler; singers Lillian Nordica and Ernestine Schumann-Heink; pianists Leopold Godowsky and Vladimir de Pachmann; and conductors Frederick Stock and, most important to Beach, Theodore Spiering.

The solution to the problem of presenting her orchestral works to the German public came in the person of Theodore Spiering. Beach and Spiering arranged for three concerts in fall 1913 in which Spiering would conduct the "Gaelic" Symphony and the Piano Concerto with Beach as soloist. An American violinist and conductor who had studied with the great Joseph Joachim, Spiering had an impressive career. Most recently, he had been brought by Mahler from Europe to become concertmaster of the New York Philharmonic; he replaced Mahler as conductor during the composer's final illness. At the time Beach met Spiering, he had been engaged for three concerts with the Berlin Philharmonic for the 1913–14 season. Thus it is likely that Beach was spared the expense of hiring a hall and orchestra, and might even have collected fees.

Beach was very fortunate to find an American conductor who was sympathetic to both American composers and women, and who agreed to champion her works.[39] With these concerts arranged, she was free to travel during the summer of 1913. In late June and early July she made a trip to Scandinavia; she traveled by boat through the Norwegian fjords and on 2 July crossed the Arctic Circle.[40] By mid-July she was back in Munich to "spend the summer quietly, composing and preparing for her next season's concert work."[41] But in the early fall she was on the road again to visit Dresden, Prague, and Vienna, where she heard outstanding performances of *Tannhäuser* and *The Marriage of Figaro*.[42]

Early in November Beach went to Berlin to begin the concert season, using that city as her base for the next two months.[43] Receptions, at which she also performed, were given in her honor at the American Women's Club and at Aus der Ohe's German Lyceum Club.[44] She then left for Leipzig and the first orchestral concert on 22 November 1913 with the Winderstein Orchester. Perhaps the best of the reviews, which were all excellent, was one reported by Eugene R. Simpson to the *Musical Courier*: "[In her symphony] the composer has earned the profound respect of musicians by sketching in long lines, holding her discourse together with a firm hand. . .the instrumentation throughout is singularly characterful and [effective]. . . . Everything sounds and has color in keeping with the general musical content."[45] There were good words about the Piano Concerto, as well, in the *Leipziger Abendzeitung*: "The piano concert [sic] has beautiful material and indicates the sure, steady hand, particularly in the cheerful scherzo and the effectively built climax of the finale."[46]

Ten days later, on 2 December, a similar program was given in Hamburg with the Orchester des Vereins Hamburgischer Musikfreunde. It was here that Beach had her greatest triumph, as she recalled:

> In Germany before the war they were sceptical enough about woman's creative ability. I was summarily warned of the fate that probably awaited me when my "Gaelic" Symphony and my piano concerto were played in Hamburg. The audience would be cold, the critics hostile. . . . The Symphony was splendidly played but had only a courteous reception. . . . Immediately thereafter, I was to play the piano part of my Concerto. But I rejected the invitation to discouragement, "got my mad up," as we put it in New England, and determined to force the audience to like it. My resolve won the victory, and a very considerable one. The critics wrote well, and even the worst bear of all, Dr. Ferdinand Pfohl, was eulogistic.[47]

Pfohl began by dismissing the notion that women cannot compose, calling Beach

> a possessor of musical gifts of the highest kind, a musical nature touched with genius. Strong creative power, glowing fancy, instinct for form and color are united in her work with facile and effortless mastery of the entire technical apparatus. To this is added charm of poetic mood, delicacy and grace of melody, and a gift for rich, soulful harmonization. Her symphony is a work that compels the highest respect, perhaps in the coloring of the end movements somewhat too much weighted down by trumpets and trombones, but free from trivialities, and at times

enthralling the listener by the uncommon intellectual content of its thematic work.[48]

Of the piano concerto, Pfohl wrote that

> the opening allegro [is] a surpassing movement, rich in ideas, in the romantic element, and marked by its refined treatment not only of the solo instrument but of the orchestra. The scherzo also, in form and content a piquant etude with orchestral accompaniment, entertains in no small degree by its tireless movement and vivacity. A Largo of genuine value leads over to the Finale, a movement preeminently suggestive of Chopin, full of playful charm and grace.

He also had strong words of praise for her playing: "an excellent pianist with brilliant technic and contagious rhythm. Amy Beach had the satisfaction of participating as a virtuoso in the big success of her interesting work."[49] Other Hamburg critics wrote enthusiastically, but none topped Pfohl in his positive appraisal of the two works. Beach had his review translated and her manager featured it prominently along with other Hamburg reviews in advertisements in American music journals.

In Berlin she faced her last trial by fire, the third performance of the Concerto for Piano and Orchestra. Before the Berlin concert there were more festivities in her honor, with informal recitals at Arthur Abell's and at Spiering's.[50] The concert on 18 December, with Spiering conducting the Berlin Philharmonic, was attended by "practically every resident musician of importance."[51] The Berlin correspondent for *Musical America* was enthusiastic but with reservations: he found the first movement admirable, the subsequent movements, however, weaker, but thought Beach better as a composer than as a pianist.[52]

But this time the reviewers for Berlin papers were her champions. Beach's performance of the piano concerto, said one critic, was the high point of the program and an "extraordinary success." Reviewers praised the composition, the orchestration, the themes and their working out, and the balance between piano and orchestra. Her playing was described as brilliant, having "great depth of feeling and expression, and with a purling technic," especially in the scherzo. Finally, a review in the *Berliner National-Zeitung* gave one of those double-edged compliments that successful women often receive: "Robert Schumann said very prettily, 'The names of the true woman composers may be written on a rose leaf.' Let us add to these the name of Amy Beach."[53]

This was a far cry from the response of the Munich critics to her recital the previous year. Had her playing improved? Had she finally hit her stride? Or was it the critics who learned to expect music making on a high level and responded accordingly? Whatever the reason, Beach achieved a substantial victory, one that would launch her new career back home as a touring composer-pianist. This was exactly why she had come to Europe. She had hoped to "reach out to the world" with her own compositions, to conquer new audiences.[54] Indeed, she believed that "Nowhere in the world are there more critical audiences—nowhere audiences more generous with their applause when you have won them."[55] In celebration Beach treated herself to a trip to Italy to enjoy its sunshine.[56]

EXAMPLE 16.1 (a) Franz Liszt, *Fantaisie und Fuge über das Thema B-A-C-H* (Budapest: Editio Musica, 1983), mm. 1–3. (b) Beach, *Prelude and Fugue*, op. 81, Prelude, mm. 1–6 (G. Schirmer, New York, 1946).

Marcella Craft gave her final performance of the season on June 26 — it also was her last with the Munich Opera. She left Munich to visit her former dramatic coach in Milan, and from there went to Paris where she planned to spend six weeks studying voice.

Activities for Beach had wound down, but instead of returning home immediately, she moved into Craft's apartment for the summer where she completed work on the compositions she had agreed to write. These included the songs Craft would sing during their planned joint tours in Europe in October and in the United States in November.[57]

Beach's compositional output during her time in Germany comprises eleven songs, "Panama Hymn," commissioned for the Panama Pacific International Exposition to be held in San Francisco in 1915; six sacred choruses; and two large-scale piano solos. All were published by G. Schirmer.[58] Although several works are outstanding, the most important is the *Prelude and Fugue*, op. 81, which she began in Garmisch in 1912, inspired by the majestic mountains she viewed from her hotel room. Both the prelude and the fugue share the same craggy theme, which Beach created from her name: A-B-E-A-C-H (B in German is the note B♭, H the note B♮) — perhaps suggested by Liszt's *Fantaisie und Fuge über das Thema B-A-C-H*. Note that the Beach and Liszt themes have four of the six notes in common (ex. 16.1). This similarity suggests that Beach's work was a double homage — to Liszt and Bach.

The prelude is one of the few compositions that Beach wrote at the piano. Claiming that she wanted to give it the character of an improvisation, she varies the theme freely.[59] At the onset the theme is stated in octaves; each of the following sections has a distinctive texture: chordal, arpeggiated, parallel thirds, octaves, arpeggiated, and finally chordal. The sectionalization by figuration suggests that she may have modeled the works on Liszt's composition.

The influence of Liszt is apparent also in the chromaticism and bravura octave passages in the fugue. In A minor, it has two subjects: the first, the A B E A C H theme, has an extension that becomes the countermelody (ex. 16.2a). The second subject, presented in the lowest register, is rhythmically modified and a tonal inversion of the first (ex. 16.2b). Beach stays close to A minor tonality, moving only to near-related keys and ending with a section in A major. Typically, the fugue builds from beginning to end, thickening in tex-

EXAMPLE 16.1 (continued)

ture, while also speeding up the surface rhythms. Toward the end, the two subjects are presented simultaneously in augmentation against octave passages in a third voice (ex. 16.2c). Both the prelude and the fugue demand a virtuoso technique.

The *Tyrolean Valse-Fantaisie*, op. 116, an extended piano work, was sketched out in Garmisch-Partenkirchen in the Tyrol in 1911 and completed in 1914.[60] The introduction—a free *Lento quasi improvisata*—is followed by a fantasy based on three themes: the first may be original (ex. 16.3a); the second and third themes are based on two folk songs, "Kommt ein Vogel geflogen" and "Rosestock Holderblüh" (exx. 16.3b, and 3c).[61] Set forth separately in the main body of the work, the melodies are infused with chromatically distorted intervals and dissonant harmonies. Beach then combines and recombines the themes in quodlibet fashion, building to a brilliant climax (ex. 16.3d). Only toward the end—and briefly—do the themes appear stripped of distortion,

EXAMPLE 16.2 *Prelude and Fugue*: first subject of fugue, (a) mm. 1–12; (b) second subject, mm. 48–52; (c) mm. 96–99.

(c)

EXAMPLE 16.2 (continued)

fully revealing their folk qualities. If the *Valse-Fantaisie* is reminiscent of Richard Strauss, this is no surprise: As composer and conductor of both the Munich symphony orchestra and the opera, Strauss and his music were very much presences during Beach's stay in Munich.

Two songs written during this period also stand out. "The Lotos Isles," op. 76, no. 2, a setting of the opening eleven lines of Tennyson's "Song of the Lotos Eaters," was Beach's first full-length experiment with the modern French style. The gentle melody with its slow ascents and descents is subtended by an accompaniment with long-sustained harmonies in the bass and an undulating treble section subtly driven by dissonance (ex. 16.4). The song never breaks out of its frame, but becomes in its final lines more and more somnolent, as if the poppy that "hangs in sleep" is a double presence.[62]

For Marcella Craft, Beach wrote "Separation," op. 76, no. 1. The text suggests that Beach chose it in anticipation of their final departure from Munich; the threat of war also reverberates in John L. Stoddard's poem:

Who knows if we shall meet again?
　Behind each parting lurks a fear;
We smile to hide the haunting pain—
　The rising tear.

EXAMPLE 16.3 *Tyrolean Valse-Fantaisie*, op. 116: (a) theme 1, mm. 66–72; (b) theme 2 ("Kommt ein Vogel geflogen"), mm. 98–103; (c) themes 2 and 3 (3 in tenor voice), mm. 116–22; (d) themes 1 and 2 ("Kommt ein Vogel geflogen" and "Rosenstock Holderblüh), mm. 156–63 (Oliver Ditson, 1926; used by permission of Theodore Presser Co.).

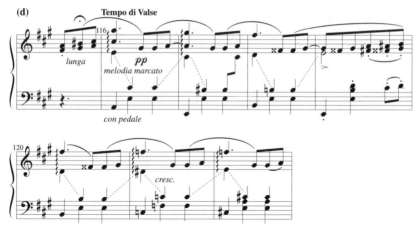

EXAMPLE 16.3 (continued)

The poet's words—*fear, pain*—are heightened through well-placed dissonances. Especially expressive is the third verse with an opening that reads, "You say that we shall meet, but how?" The word *say* is underscored by an unprepared modulation, emphasizing the uncertainty in the question. As the phrase proceeds against a continually dissonant and increasingly agitated accompaniment, the outer lines move further and further apart by chromatic progression—a musical analogue of separation (ex. 16.5).

Beach finished the song shortly before Craft left Munich. The timing, dedication, text, and musical quality of the work all suggest a personal narrative. Even though the two women had planned tours of Europe and the United States, their lives would no longer be centered in one location: their new careers in the United States would require them to go their independent ways. Thus Beach's friendship with Craft could no longer satisfy her need for intimacy.

World events led to the cancellation of their tour of Europe. On 28 June, the Archduke Ferdinand of Austria was assassinated in Sarajevo, and a month later a declaration of war was made by Austria-Hungary on Serbia. Germany followed, declaring war on Russia on 1 August and then on France and Belgium a few days later. During the ominous July days, their American concert manager, M. H. Hanson, advised Beach and Craft, who was in Paris, to leave Europe. Craft took his advice immediately; arriving in New York on the SS *New York* on 10 August, she took an apartment for the winter. Beach, however, refused to leave Munich.[63]

On 10 August, Beach wrote to Mrs. Herman Lewis of the Hanson Concert Management in New York reporting that, despite "tremendous excitement," she was safe and comfortable. She did not know when she would return to the states. Meanwhile she was assisting the Red Cross.[64] *Musical America* reported that musical life was paralyzed by the war. Beach worried about the safety of the young American women who were studying music and for whom she had be-

EXAMPLE 16.4. "The Lotos Isles," op. 76, no. 2, mm. 1–9 (G. Schirmer, 1914).

come a mentor. She also worried about Teresa Carreño, whose whereabouts she did not know, and Fritz Kreisler, who was reportedly "defending bridges" with the German army.

Preparations for war came closer and closer to the Pension Pfanner, where Beach was living. She recalled: "All day and night the tramp, tramp of marching feet could be heard and the sound finally got hold of me so that I don't believe I shall ever be able to forget it."[65] Beach saved a special free issue of the *Frankfurter Zeitung und Handelsblatt* devoted to "Das deutsche Weissbuch über den Krieg." Dated 3 August 1914, it justified Germany's declarations of war. Beach wrote her name and address on the copy, which suggests that she probably gave it to others to read.[66]

EXAMPLE 16.5 "Separation," op. 76, no. 1, mm. 23–26 (G. Schirmer, 1914).

Later, at home, both Beach and Craft made strongly pro-German statements to the American press, although Beach declared that her allegiance was to the musical not the militaristic Germany. Like Craft, she defended the kaiser, stating that neither he nor his army wanted the war and that he had done everything to avert it: "[T]he situation is pathetic for Germany. She is fighting for existence, hemmed in on all sides by enemies. Understand, I am not pro-German, or pro-anything except pro-American. . . .all I ask is that we keep out of it. But I do wish that our German friends could be understood here."[67] In fact, Germany had been building up its armed forces to a point of unprecedented strength.

Concerned for the safety of her unpublished music, Beach decided against trusting it to the mails and instead gave some manuscripts to Craft to take back to the states. She packed other music in a trunk and entrusted it to another friend who left Munich by train:

> Before reaching the Belgian frontier, however, the train on which [the friend] was travelling was stopped, the passengers unceremoniously ordered out by the German soldiers and literally driven across the border, while their luggage was abandoned. The trunk containing Mrs. Beach's manuscripts shared the fate of the other possessions of the hapless voyagers and was not recovered.[68]

With the escalation of World War I, Beach finally faced the inevitable and made plans to leave Europe in September. A potentially dangerous overland journey out of Germany and across the ocean loomed. Beach, however, stayed until the Germans offered Americans the last train out, with all conveniences at government expense. "Advised to go," Beach reluctantly left her German friends and made her way to Liverpool.[69] She sailed on the SS *Cretic*, a steamer of the White Star Line that the frightened and impatient Americans on board called the "Creeping Cretic."[70] Arriving in New York on 18 September 1914, she made her way to Boston and a triumphant reception after three long years of absence.[71]

"LION OF

THE HOUR"

ON 13 JANUARY 1915, A PHOTOGRAPH of a jubilant Amy Beach, head thrown back, face lit by a broad smile, appeared in the *Musical Courier*. Her concert manager had caught her walking in the Boston Common the morning after a recital of her compositions that celebrated her return to Boston.[1] Perhaps she had already read the excellent reviews. Perhaps she had an inkling that the next few years would be the most successful of her entire life. One music magazine, reflecting on plans for performances of her works and her many invitations to play, recognized her as the "lion of the hour."[2]

Fresh from Europe and in her forty-seventh year, Beach was plainly delighted with her German triumphs and her American prospects. She looked forward to a new life in the United States as a traveling composer and pianist. Her manager had already booked her for thirty concerts across the country for the 1914–15 concert season: "I have now enough dates to be quite satisfied, especially as I want some of my time left for composition," she said.[3] But the windfall of invitations to give recitals that came from women's clubs threatened to usurp her time for creative work.

She had allowed herself to be billed as Amy Beach while in Europe; however, after someone in Europe had asked her whether she was the daughter of Mrs. H. H. A. Beach, she decided that rather than build a reputation all over again under the new name, on her return to the United States she would revert to the name that appears on her music. Besides, she told the press, she liked using her husband's name.[4] Whatever the long-term effects of that decision, for the immediate future it appears to have had no negative impact on her career.

Once again, Beach made her permanent headquarters in Boston.[5] After reopening her house at 28 Commonwealth Avenue, she was soon entertaining friends, preparing for upcoming concerts, and attending festivities to celebrate her return. One of the first programs, on 18 November at Copley Hall, was sponsored by the MacDowell Club, an organization of professional musicians. Beach, with the singers May Goodbar and Blanche Hamilton Fox, performed eight songs—five were new—and the *Romance*, op. 23, with violinist Marie Nichols.

Beach described the concert as an emotional scene to Ethel Clement, beginning her postcard, "Shena dearest":

> The MacDowell Club was simply *wonderful*. 700 people & the whole audience *rose* as I stepped on to the stage! Program went beautifully. Lots of flowers and the loveliest tokens and words of welcome from musicians and everyone. I spoke to everyone after the music while *other* people had tea etc.[6]

After shaking hands with everyone, an exhausted Beach asked that her car be sent around to take her home. But instead "she was carried off. . .to the Copley Plaza Hotel" to join seventy women for lunch.[7] That week, despite a heavy cold, she practiced and rehearsed, attended two dinner parties, three receptions in her honor, and played four concerts.

In early December, her touring schedule began with recitals in Pittsburgh and Kansas City, where she shared billing with Marcella Craft. Beach then returned to Boston for a more public welcome at an all-Beach program in Steinert Hall on 16 December; there she was assisted by the singer Karola Frick and the Hoffman Quartet, who, with Beach, had introduced her Piano Quintet in 1908. Boston's leading musicians, among them Chadwick and Foote, and critics Olin Downes, Philip Hale, and H. T. Parker, turned out to hear her play and to listen with interest to her new compositions.

The two new piano works, however, had a less than enthusiastic reception from the critics. Only the reviewer in the *Transcript* had words of praise for the *Prelude and Fugue*, which, he declared, "runs in large, coordinated and contrasted design, in free and clear outline, and in ample sonorities."[8] The *Valse Fantaisie*, as it was named for this program, was less successful, according to the same critic: "The bedecked waltz is more fantastical in ornament and imagery, but less free and firm-handed and interspersed with those filling passages Tchaikovsky aptly called 'head-work.'" The most positive comments were about the now familiar piano quintet. Olin Downes wrote that "the ideas have value and contour, and their development is both musicianly and effective"; the *Transcript* agreed, stating that Beach "shone clearest [in the quintet, where she] has something to say and says it with her own voice."[9] There were generally enthusiastic reviews for her playing, which had "more emotional variety, more authority."[10] Her more frequent performances had paid dividends in polish and command at the keyboard. Perhaps her newfound autonomy also contributed to the change.

In addition, Beach had the compliment of an entire recital of her music by May Goodbar.[11] A former protégée of Beach's, Goodbar had begun singing her songs well before she joined forces with the composer at Beach's annual recital in 1909;[12] now she became Beach's regular soprano soloist for the Boston area, filling in when Craft was otherwise engaged. Thus, Boston welcomed Beach for her performance, her compositions—albeit, with some reservations about the new ones—and her warm and generous self.

Despite the welcome attention, the loneliness of the big, empty house, together with the expense and responsibility of maintaining it, would surely have weighed heavily on Beach each time she returned from a concert tour.[13] Equally important, Boston's first generation of art composers was all but gone by 1915: Paine had died in 1906; Horatio Parker had left for Europe in 1882 and, except for one year, never returned to Boston; MacDowell had left in 1896 and died in 1908; Foote believed that the golden age of music in Boston was over; and that very same year Chadwick wrote his last important work, *Tam O'Shanter*.

Beach, who was totally revitalized by her European experience and ready to begin the second half of her life, undoubtedly found that Boston no longer reflected her energetic mood. These feelings, the experience of living three years in Munich, a leading center of European music, and being a part of an international circle of musicians, may have all contributed to Beach's decision to move to New York in February 1915.

In New York Beach stayed at the Marlton, at 5 West 8th Street, just off Fifth Avenue. She explained the move to the *New York Sun*: "Nowhere else is there a keener appreciation of the highest in music. . . . New York has grown to be such a centre of music that all are bound to come here and give of their best."[14] Among the satisfactions for her were the many performances given of her sacred works at St. Bartholomew's Episcopal Church, whose choir was under the direction of Arthur Hyde.

Hardly was she settled in New York when she was off to Philadelphia to hear the first American performance of the "Gaelic" since 1905. In a pre-concert interview, Beach shared her anticipation of the event, saying, "I'm fond of going places where I am a stranger and having my work appreciated for itself."[15] Seated with Olga Samaroff-Stokowski in a box at the Academy of Music, Beach was delighted with the performance and its reception. Stokowski wrote to Beach soon after, expressing his great pleasure in the symphony, a pleasure shared by orchestra members and audience. The work is "so full of real music," he said, "without any pretense or effects that are plastered on from the outside, but just real, sincere, simple and deep music; and one can only say that of about one percent. of contemporary music."[16] Other conductors agreed with him. When Stokowski repeated the symphony in 1918, it would be the fifth performance of the work in four years.[17]

Reviews of the Philadelphia premiere were mixed. One reviewer declared Beach a genius. Two others labeled the "Gaelic" a "woman's symphony," one that "glows and scintillates. . .is graceful and charming"[18]—this, despite its contrasting drama and lyricism. Yet another critic found "difficulty in picturing this bright-faced, energetic, enthusiastic little woman as a composer and a pianist who in three years playing in German cities never once received a derogatory comment" [!]. This last would have been the opinion of anyone reading the extensive—and selective—quotations from her German reviews that were published as advertisements in American music journals. The *Musical Leader* reported that Stokowski's reading was a "tremendous success" and that the symphony was greeted by the audience with intense enthusiasm.[19]

New York was still to be conquered. Surely the local critics could not be less inclined in her favor before hearing her works than the German critics had been and whom nevertheless she had won over. But not so; New York's critics turned out to be harder to please than any had been in Philadelphia or, indeed, in Leipzig, Hamburg, or Berlin. Although this was an all-Beach program, there was considerable variety among the works given at Aeolian Hall on 16 March 1915; included were songs, piano solos, the violin sonata, and the piano quintet. Assisting artists comprised the Olive Mead Quartet, Theodore Spiering, and a young tenor, George Sheffield.

The quintet and the sonata, which, like her symphony and concerto, had had excellent reviews in Germany and in Boston, had mixed reviews in New York. That of the *New York Times* was in large measure positive; but the critic found her style derivative.[20] Sigmund Spaeth, who wrote for the *Evening Mail*— he was later dubbed the "Tune Detective"—found echoes of César Franck in the Violin Sonata, of Rachmaninoff in the prelude and Bach in the fugue of op. 81, of Grieg in one of the encores, and of Strauss's "Zueignung" in the affecting song "Separation." That aside, he viewed Beach's music as "generally melodious. . . .with evidence of good honest workmanship" even though occasionally dull; and he noted that she was a pianist "of more than the usual composer's ability." Finally, he could not resist alluding to Beach's gender: "One feels instinctively that her mince pies are quite as good as her minor chords."[21] He had no way of knowing that Beach never cooked a meal in her entire life![22] After such disappointing reviews, it may be no accident that while she played many times in New York thereafter, she never again played there at a public concert. That, however, is an unfortunate reaction on her part: many performers have built followings without wholehearted critical approval.

These reviews may have reflected a recent heated controversy about "woman as composer" that had been set off, according to the critic Emilie Frances Bauer, by Beach's return to the United States.[23] The argument turned into a firestorm when Walter Damrosch, conductor of the New York Symphony Orchestra, wrote that it was not in women's nature to write great music.

> [I]t seems impossible for woman to create a beauty that must come from the soul and encompass a comprehension of the supernatural beauty that is given to us through the master artist. True, America has Mrs. Beach and France Cécile Chaminade. . . . But we have not opera, concerto, symphony, oratorio, or string quartet from womankind. Their work is light and frothy; it lacks weight and profundity, sentiment and philosophy in comparison with men's masterpieces. . .they have not produced any thing that could even be called near great.[24]

Bauer answered by citing German reviews of Beach's symphony and concerto, implying that, if Damrosch was looking for great—or even a near-great— works, indeed Beach had produced two.

Damrosch's article also provoked responses from several others, including Beach herself. She disagreed with Damrosch's contention that musical training and opportunity were lavished on girls and women rather than boys and men, noting that "woman has indeed been handicapped and always will be at an enforced disadvantage" by not having access to the orchestra.[25] But the plain fact is that, faced with fine works by women, Damrosch and others dismissed them out of hand as trivial.

Yet even Beach herself could not give a wholehearted defense of women as composers. She later responded to the question of why a woman composer "never scales the heights attained by men" by asserting that women's experiences in both private and public life do not have the emotional impact of men's public endeavors; her statement reflected the small value society placed on women's activities.[26] Perhaps she felt that she herself was not a part of the controversy because of her gifts and achievements and because she had not lived the conventional life of a woman.

Shortly after the Aeolian Hall recital, Beach left New York for California. Her departure was not a result of a sudden change of plans, however; she had engagements to fill on the West Coast. Her first stop was the Mission Inn in Riverside—Marcella Craft's hometown—at which she stayed for the month of April. While at the Inn, Beach composed the song "Wind o' the Westland," op. 77, no. 1. She unintentionally incorporated into the accompaniment the cooing of doves that awakened her every morning, stating that "the words of [Dana] Burnett's poem seemed to fit against this background of sound."[27] The tenor George Hamlin, who commissioned the song, premiered it at a New York recital on 28 November 1916.

Beach and Craft shared a number of events honoring one or both women. One such event was especially memorable: on 3 April, Easter morning, Beach and Craft, along with some fifteen thousand persons on foot and in motor cars, ascended nearby Mt. Rubidoux where they took part in an Easter morning service, "undoubtedly the most remarkable outdoor religious service in America."[28] Just after trumpets announced the first light of dawn, Marcella Craft and the chorus of the Methodist Church sang Carrie Jacobs-Bond's *Anthem to the Easter Dawn*. Then, to the surprise and delight of the worshippers, Beach accompanied Craft in "The Year's at the Spring."[29]

Her month of comparative rest in Riverside over, in early May Beach left for San Francisco for a long awaited reunion with the Clement family, now her closest living relatives. She stayed with them at their home at 1088 Fulton Street, opposite Alamo Park. Her aunt and cousin joined in the many events celebrating her arrival in town. At this time, she was also able to visit the Panama-Pacific International Exposition in San Francisco, where at last she heard her *Panama Hymn*, op. 74, in its intended setting.[30]

Then in its fourth month, the fair, occupying 635 acres on the bay, marked San Francisco's phoenixlike emergence from the earthquake and fire of 1906. A poster that announced the exposition suggests that the Panama Canal had been built by nothing less than brute force, an idea mirrored, too, in the text of Beach's hymn. Wendell Phillips Stafford's words begin, "We join today the East and West," and continue:

> Thou didst give our land the might
> To hew the hemisphere in twain,
> And level for these waters bright
> The mountain and the main.

Beach's powerful strophic setting—its march rhythm, fanfare opening, strong harmonies, and direct simplicity—illustrate once more her consummate skill in composing a rousing and singable anthem (ex. 17.1). Opening day ceremonies at the fair had begun with the singing of "The Heavens Are Telling" from *The Creation*. Following presentations and addresses by dignitaries, Beach's *Panama Hymn* was sung.[31] To close the event, a connection was made to President Wilson in Washington on the newly installed long-distance telephone lines. From there, he pressed the button that transmitted electrical current to the exposition grounds, and the fair was opened.[32] The *San Francisco Examiner* reported that the *Panama Hymn* "was splendidly fitted to express the universal spirit of jubilation."[33] It was sung often during the ten months duration of the fair and frequently in other venues across the country.

Like the Chicago fair of 1893, the San Francisco fair presented high art music as emblem of the evolutionary advancement of white, Western culture and civilization. In nine and a half months, the music department presented 2,206 concerts and recitals, including eighty performances by the exposition orchestra, and a series by the Boston Symphony conducted by Karl Muck. Unlike the earlier fair, the exposition included little music by Americans. Popular American culture, however, had its place in the band concerts, which were given as many as twelve times a day.

Beach's San Francisco welcome was not confined to the fair, for she was immediately inundated with invitations to private receptions.[34] There were so many fetes given in her honor that Beach's concert manager claimed, "I am doing my best to prevent this hospitable Coast from wrecking the health of one of my stars, Mrs. H. H. A. Beach. I felt that she needed a guardian who could say 'no' to at least 75 percent of the beautiful invitations Mrs. Beach receives."[35] Just in case any of those honoring Beach were not fully aware of the composer's achievements, Alfred Metzger's article in the *Pacific Coast Musical Review* filled in the details: "Mrs. Beach is not only one of the first American musicians, but one of the foremost composers in the entire world of music today." Included in his story was a brief biographical sketch and a detailed discussion of her major compositions.[36]

San Francisco could not hold Beach for long. As she pointed out in an interview, she was "too enthusiastic a traveler to settle down"—anywhere.[37] At the beginning of June she traveled north, pausing briefly to visit Muir Woods, then on to Portland for a recital; and at the end of the month she headed south to Los Angeles for the biennial meeting of the National Federation of Music Clubs (NFMC), which ran from 24 June to 3 July.

That meeting—in contrast to the San Francisco exposition—featured the music of American composers.[38] During the conference, a number of works by Beach were heard: on 26 June at a concert of American orchestral music, Adolf Tandler conducted Beach's piano concerto with the composer at the piano, her fifth performance of the work with orchestra and her second in the United States; singers from three music clubs presented her choral arrangement of "The Year's at the Spring"; the Brahms Quartet of Los Angeles gave her piano quintet; and the Chicago pianist, Walter Fry, played the *Variations on Balkan Themes*.

Beach reported in a postcard to her cousin: "The concerto went grandly Saturday night and I had 4 big recalls & shouts of bravo & waving of hdkfs. Loads

EXAMPLE 17.1 *Panama Hymn*, op. 74, no. 1, mm. 1–8 (G. Schirmer, 1915).

of flowers. Orchestra *stood* as I came in! Good notices!"[39] One reviewer believed that the first movement of the concerto was a trifle long, but as it was "stocked with an abundance of material, there should be no difficulty in cutting it," a suggestion Beach later put into practice.[40] In an overview of orchestral music given during the biennial, Edwin F. Schallert found the music of Chadwick and Carl Busch outstanding but none as fine as Beach's concerto, "one of the most vital and convincing messages of all the festival composers." After heaping praise on the quintet and the Balkan variations, he concluded that "everything that is modern is not progress, and Mrs. Beach in her music more than once shows that she realizes this."[41]

One of the high points of Beach's California stay took place in San Diego: 28 June 1915 was "Mrs. H. H. A. Beach Day" at California's second fair, the Panama-California Exposition in Balboa Park. With San Francisco, this city had taken on new importance after the opening of the Panama Canal. The selection of these port cities for the sites of expositions was symbolic of America's expanding empire, which then extended over the Pacific, embracing Guam and the Philippines.

The recitals and festivities given in Beach's honor on "her day" were elaborate. Her hostess, the contralto Loleta Levette Rowan, sang some of Beach's songs. Beach described the events on a postcard to her cousin Ethel:

> Yesterday "my" day. Began with Coronado Beach drive & more visit to the Exposition, Ethnological & Indian exhibits especially. Big lunch by Ladies of the Board, including the wife of Exposition President. Concerts by Hawaiian & Spanish singers & dancers specially arranged for me. Organ recital at 4. Dr. Stewart played Scot[tish] Legend and Mrs. Rowan sang 2 songs. . . . Reception at Women's Reception Room. More songs & flowers![42]

Music at the San Diego fair was more modest than at the San Francisco fair —offering mostly organ and solo recitals—but there was more music by Americans.

Beach returned to the NFMC meeting in Los Angeles, which closed with three performances of Horatio Parker's new opera, *Fairyland,* under the baton of Alfred Hertz, conductor of the Metropolitan Opera from 1902 to 1915 and currently the music director of the San Francisco Symphony. *Fairyland* had won the NFMC competition and $10,000 prize. Beach was there especially to hear Marcella Craft, who created the role of Rosemund, a novice unhappy in her novitiate who falls in love with a young king, Auburn. There was a great deal of praise for the opera from critics and fellow composers, including a full-length review by Beach, who nevertheless suggested that Craft's role gave her little opportunity for acting; another reviewer, however, found the music outstanding but the libretto weak and unconvincing.[43]

Beach then returned to San Francisco for a quiet summer of composition, interrupted only by another performance of her concerto on 1 August, American Composers' Day at the San Francisco fair. Alfred Metzger, writing for the *Pacific Coast Musical Review,* found Beach's piano concerto "the most delightful musical offering of the program. . .[and] of the utmost musical magnitude."

While he approved of the program because of the quality of the music, he disapproved of segregating works by American composers. Rather, he said, such performances should be everyday occurrences.[44] This, however, was the only program of American works, in spite of the fact that by 1915 there was a significant harvest of music by Americans.

The program included not only Beach's piano concerto but also Mabel Daniels's concert aria, *Desolate City*, conducted by the composer. For the balance of the exposition, however, women's music was all but ignored, even though many more women were writing not only in the United States but also in France and England. According to Beach, women had "advanced in technique, resourcefulness and force, and even the younger composers have successfully achieved some effects which the great masters themselves would never have dared to attempt."[45] For Beach, however, the fair was a personal triumph and one that added to her national reputation. The *Pacific Coast Musical Review* reported that her music was being played all over the United States, demonstrating once again that performances of Beach's works did not depend upon her presence.[46] The *Musical Leader* affirmed that her name was now a national household word.[47]

A high point of her fall schedule was her performance of her piano quintet with members of the San Francisco Quintet Club—soon renamed the Chamber Music Society of San Francisco—on 28 October; she was described as "brilliant" by the reviewer for the *Chronicle*.[48] As a result, flautist Elias Hecht, the leader of the ensemble, gave Beach a commission that she fulfilled the following year with one of her finest works, the *Theme and Variations for Flute and String Quartet*, op. 80.[49]

In December 1915 Beach was back East for a winter tour that took her to Pittsburgh and Sewickley, Pennsylvania, for two recitals with Craft and one in Philadelphia with the singer Cecil Fanning. On 15 January at the Washington Irving High School, New York, there was a program by the St. Cecilia Club, considered by critics to be the nation's most polished chorus of women's voices. The featured work was Beach's *Chambered Nautilus*, by then a staple of their repertory. Just as the chorus was about to start the "Nautilus," a figure emerged from the alto section and seated herself at the piano. Beach, as a surprise to chorus and audience, was there to play the accompaniment for her work. Moved by the "loving care" lavished on her work by conductor and singers, Beach wrote to the group's conductor, Victor Harris, "For absolute beauty of tone and fine qualities of gradation, I cannot imagine the superior of your club, nor should I know where to look for its equal."[50]

The climax of the season, however, was her appearance with the Chicago Symphony under the direction of Frederick Stock on 4 February 1916. Theodore Thomas, who founded the orchestra in 1891, had made it into one of the best orchestras in the country; and Stock, who became music director on Thomas's death in 1905, built on the founder's fine beginning. For Beach, no performance, perhaps not even of the "Gaelic" Symphony, offered her the satisfaction of playing her concerto with a first-rate ensemble like the Chicago Symphony Orchestra.

Reviews were plentiful and full of the usual contradictory evaluations. Felix

Borowski's narrowly focused review began by citing music by women whose works had been previously performed by the Chicago Orchestra: there were only two, Chaminade's *Concertstück* in 1895, and the Comtesse de Grandval's oboe concerto in 1908. Recalling that other women had written now-forgotten concertos—among them Dora Bright, Rosalind Ellicott, Leopoldine Blahetka, Luise Adolpha LeBeau, Marie Jaëll, Alice Mary Smith, and Mary Wurm—he implied that their neglect was deserved, even though there is no indication that he examined their works. On the other hand, Beach, he said, had written a concerto that deserved repetition since it "makes an appeal to connoisseurs who exact much from musicians who handle symphonic material and who are not disposed to look leniently upon a composer merely because she is attired in petticoats." But he found the work uneven, the first movement "broad, dignified, masterly," the second "clever and effective," the third "somewhat lacking in conviction," and the finale "trivial—albeit brilliant." He praised her orchestral writing, however, as demonstrating "admirable understanding of orchestral effect."[51] Karleton Hackett, on the other hand, liked the second movement best; he found the themes strong but thought the orchestration was inadequate.[52] Edward C. Moore approved the balance between the piano and orchestra and viewed the work as structurally strong but thematically weak; her playing he found restrained, clean, but not brilliant.[53] Eric de Lamarter, like other reviewers, wrote that, as a pianist, she was far better than most composers, yet the composition's strength lay in "melodic facility and on its approved effects of the salon composer at work."[54]

Stanley K. Faye's review delighted her. In a letter to the critic, Beach expressed her deep appreciation and asked for twenty-five copies.[55] Could it be that she liked the masculine images he found to describe both the work and her performance? "Her concerto commands admiration equally with respect," he said, "for with its spirited construction, its fearlessness and its triumphant force is combined a richness of material that is unusual." Faye also praised her compositional skill in weaving together a rich tapestry of music. Remarking on her "superb" technique, he stated, "Mrs. Beach will satisfy most people who demand that a woman play the piano like a man. The virile force with which she attains to an enormous tone is remarkable, the more so because she does not merely pound the piano, but seeks for effects with the pedal." Faye compared her to men and found her their equal.[56]

Beach was not able to attend the performance of the "Gaelic" Symphony on 4 April 1916, by the Kansas City Symphony Orchestra, conducted by Carl Busch, but she was pleased to read the excellent reviews. Back in San Francisco that spring, she attended a meeting of the YWCA during which Helen Hoburn Heath sang "The Year's at the Spring" over the telephone to a similar gathering in Newark. This was the first time that music was transmitted by wire across the continent.[57] Caruso is credited with that "first," but in fact he sang over the phone a few weeks later, on 30 April.[58]

On 2 May 1916, Beach was again the honored guest of the San Diego fair for a second "Beach Day," which she called "one of the prettiest events of my musical life."[59] At the California building a crowd, including a number of musicians, waited to greet her and hear a serenade for Beach by the Spanish Singers. Then at the organ pavilion, which had a narrow stage and minimal protection from the elements, Beach sat at the piano, looking like a veritable club woman in her "Queen Mary" hat, while the large audience listened in the rain; the lucky ones had their umbrellas with them. Beach played two solos— her "Scottish Legend" and "Gavotte fantastique," op. 54—and accompanied local soloists in a selection of her songs. Her "day" concluded with a second recital program, also devoted to her works. This time she did not have to write to Ethel, for her cousin was with her.[60]

Sometime during the year, Beach became a San Franciscan. The welcome given her by Californians and the joy she found in being near her family, must have gradually led to her decision to establish a permanent base in San Francisco. She moved into a frame house at 1104 Fulton, opposite Alamo Park and a half block away from the Clements. When registering to vote in the 1916 election, she gave her occupation as composer and her party as Republican.[61] (California had passed a woman's suffrage act in 1911.)

Beach settled into her new home, where she spent the summer composing. California's birds were the inspiration for "Meadowlarks" and "In Blossom Time," op. 78, nos. 1 and 3. The lyrics were by California's poet laureate Ina Coolbrith (1841–1928), who became a special friend of Beach's.[62] About the first song, Beach said, "In the southern part of the state I heard the meadow lark singing and I have not only made use of its florid song, but even in its own tonality. And, if the poets and the birds of California are an inspiration, its Sierras, the music of its woods and the thunder of the surf are not less so."[63] Indeed, for Beach "Meadowlarks" was emblematic of her happiest days in San Francisco.[64]

In July, she completed the *Theme and Variations for Flute and String Quartet* for the San Francisco Chamber Music Society. Beach again returned to her own compositions for thematic material, in this instance choosing as her theme the beautifully lyrical part song for women's voices on an anonymous poem "An Indian Lullaby," op. 57, no. 3:

> Sleep in thy forest bed
> Where silent falls the tread
> On the needles soft and deep
> Of the pine.

The poem is not authentically Native American; even the invocation to "Mother pine" in the last verse is considered by experts to be atypical of Native American usage.[65] Not only that but the music, which is original with Beach, sounds more European than American, even though the flute suggests the frequently used Native American instrument.[66]

For the theme of the quintet, Beach retains the four-voice setting of the part song, assigning it to the string quartet alone. Whereas the melody in the first violin is essentially unchanged, there are some significant changes in the accompanying parts. Beach increases the contrapuntal voice leading in the other three strings, and most importantly, she develops the "sigh" motive or its in-

EXAMPLE 17.2 *Theme and Variations for Flute and String Quartet*, op. 80: (a) theme, mm. 1–8; (b) var. 1, mm. 1–4; (c) var. 1, mm. 19–21; (d) var. 5, mm. 1–9 (G. Schirmer, 1920).

version, which now appears in one or more parts on virtually every beat of the theme. As a result, she greatly intensifies the elegiac quality of the theme (ex. 17.2a).

The flute enters at the beginning of the first variation with an exotic-sounding cadenza, its augmented seconds in sharp contrast with the theme (ex. 17.2b). The strings resume as before, but aspects of Beach's "clever scheme" of musical interchange between the flute and strings slowly emerge.[67] The rhythmic motive ♪♫♫ from the cadenza gradually invades the four string parts (ex. 17.2c), while the flute picks up a phrase from the strings. This exchange increases in the variations that follow, expecially in the elegiac fifth variation (ex. 17.2d).

(b)

VARIATION I
L'istesso tempo (♩. = 48)

Flute

dolce

cresc.

(Flute Solo, strings tacet)

(c)

Fl.

Vl. I

Vl. II

Vla.

Vlc.

sempre marcato

EXAMPLE 17.2 (continued)

210

(d)

EXAMPLE 17.2 (continued)

211

After attending a rehearsal of the work, Beach wrote in admiration to Elias Hecht, stating that their wonderful playing was "deeply" moving and "unforgettable."[68]

The premiere took place on 28 September 1916 in the Palace Hotel in San Francisco—but without Beach.[69] On or about the sixth of August, she suddenly left San Francisco with her cousin Ethel and Aunt Franc; her Uncle Lyman remained behind. Whatever the mysterious, unexplained crisis was in the Clement family, the result was that a family was shattered and a fifty-year-old marriage broken apart. Beach's only surviving comments on this sudden development are in her letters to Ina Coolbrith. On the third of August, she had written of her imminent departure from San Francisco, while recalling the pleasure of their recent visit, which "brightened these last sad days of our life together in our beloved San Francisco." She doubted that she would return, she said, except perhaps on a concert tour. Beach gave Coolbrith her new address as Hillsborough, New Hampshire.[70] This precipitous change on the part of Beach was one more failed attempt to find a milieu that offered her both intimacy and rich musical gratification. Leaving California was a move she would forever recall with sadness.[71]

Was their hasty departure in some way due to Lyman Clement? Was he dishonest in his work, violent toward his wife or daughter, incestuous? adulterous? There are no answers at this time. The following year Clement was settled in the Veterans Home of California in Yountville, outside of San Francisco where he stayed until his death in 1922.[72] Apparently Beach deliberately avoided mentioning the break; one newspaper reported that she left because of professional commitments,[73] which she surely had in abundance.

On their way east, the three women stopped for only a few hours in Seattle. There, before taking a boat to Vancouver, they saw Beach's friend, the poet and journalist Agnes Lockhart Hughes, and her son and Beach's godson, Lockhart Beach Hughes.[74] The journey ended in Hillsborough, the town where Aunt Franc and Beach's mother were born.[75] Beach, her cousin, and her aunt moved into rented quarters in Jesse and Helen Parker's house on Church Street.[76] Thereafter, Hillsborough was Beach's official residence: there she voted in presidential elections and there she lived in between concert commitments. This was a most unhappy ending to her years in San Francisco. But she was together with family and could look forward to the exhilarating and professionally fulfilling years ahead as a composer and pianist.

MY OLD

NEW HAMPSHIRE

HOME

WITH THE MOVE TO HILLSBOROUGH, Amy Beach began a decade of loving service to her cousin and her aunt, now her immediate family. But why leave San Francisco, a cosmopolitan city with an active cultural life? Beach had been welcomed there as she had never been welcomed before, and, ever after, she spoke of her "beloved San Francisco." If the three women decided that they must put many miles between themselves and Lyman Clement, there were other cities to choose from. Why settle in Hillsborough, a town of a mere two thousand souls, a fair distance away from Boston, and far from other principal cultural centers?

Perhaps they sought roots in the town where Clara and Franc Marcy were born and brought up, where Franc had taught school during the Civil War and both sisters had taught music.[1] It was Beach's homecoming as well, for Hillsborough is the very next town to Henniker, her birthplace. Perhaps they needed to connect with the Marcys and Cheneys living in the region. Perhaps the three women wished to escape the complexities and especially the expenses of urban life. Perhaps it was Beach's choice; she needed close contact with nature to compose, something that Hillsborough offered her: "For composition, I need absolute quiet. To work in a large city I find is impossible. I cannot chain myself down to a creative task and really lose myself in the problems connected with it if I am haunted with the desire to hear some concert or opera performance."[2] Hillsborough would not present such enticements.

Soon after their move, Ethel Clement's life seemed promising: she had a position as a drawing teacher in the Hillsborough Public Schools.[3] In contrast to her cousin's life, Ethel's had hardly been a successful one despite her extensive training at the Art Students Leagues in San Francisco and New York, at the Cowles Art School in Boston, at the Julian Academy in Paris, and with Georges Laugée in Picardie. She had won awards at California state fairs, exhibited in Boston, and in 1908 had the honor of having a portrait of her mother hung "on the line" (that is, at eye level) at a Paris salon. There is no way of knowing if she was able to sell her art, and her professional positions were few and far between: she had worked a year as an art teacher at Miss West's School in San Francisco (1906–7), and two years as superintendent of the San Francisco

Reading Room and Library for the Blind (1912–14).[4] It is possible that hers was a modest talent; the contrast between the two cousins may have been painful for all three women. For Ethel Clement, Hillsborough offered a chance to begin a new but quiet life.

Beach must have considered the issue of her own professional isolation, especially after having lived earlier in New York. On the other hand, as a touring musician she could live anywhere. There were other compensations in addition to being close to nature. Beach entered into Hillsborough life as both a neighbor and the town's greatest celebrity. In addition, she developed close relationships with relatives and friends in the area.[5] She was soon touched by the devotion to her displayed by her fellow townspeople, who on occasion invested themselves in the performance of her music. In preparation for an entire program of her works, Beach noted that there were many rehearsals; "for all the dear girls and women taking part are so anxious to do their best," she wrote to Coolbrith, "and I have 'coached' them and shall play all the accompaniments in addition to solos."[6] If she was a bit condescending in her attitude toward the musical life of Henniker, she nevertheless gave generously of her talents on numerous occasions.

Living in Hillsborough with her aunt must have intensified her sense of connection to her mother. Beach reported on an "old-fashioned tea" given by a church benevolent society for which women wore dresses "several generations old." For music, Beach chose two pieces that her mother played when a girl in Hillsborough and followed with two that her mother had taught her when she was six, so small that her mother had to pedal for her. Among the pieces was *The Old Oaken Bucket with Variations*.[7]

Her 1916–17 touring schedule, however, required that she spend many months away from Hillsborough; more than twenty concerts were planned from October to May. On tour with the Kneisel Quartet, then in their thirty-third and final season, she played her piano quintet in Boston, Brooklyn, Chicago, and Philadelphia. Beach also played the quintets with quartets in Baltimore, Evanston, and Toronto.[8]

Performances of the Piano Concerto with the St. Louis Symphony Orchestra, Max Zach conducting, were given on 12 and 13 January at the Odeon Theater. Critical reception of the concerto, heard for the first time in St. Louis, was highly favorable. Richard L. Stokes of the *Post-Dispatch* admired her innovative orchestration, especially the several orchestral solos and the duet for piano and timpani—"perhaps explained by Mrs. Beach's confession that her loftiest ambition as a girl was to be a kettle drummer."[9] He also wrote that Beach was a "composer of brilliant genius, irrespective of sex," and "one of the great virtuoso pianists of the day." Another reviewer faulted her playing—it was "musicianly" but "not consistently" that of a concert artist of the first rank.[10] The audience, however, was entranced, applauding each movement and giving her an extended ovation at the end.[11]

The performance was the prelude to an even more important one, her return engagement to play the concerto with the Boston Symphony on 2 and 3 March.[12] The *Advertiser* announced that "Boston is proud of Mrs. Beach and will show its pride at her home-coming Friday."[13] Her very appearance as she walked on the stage touched off a long ovation; and at the conclusion of her performance the audience again and again recalled "the sumptuous and stately figure in purples."[14]

Many who attended recalled the premiere of Beach's Piano Concerto in 1900. Now, more than a decade and a half later, the critics, hearing the work with fresh ears, found much to praise. Henry Taylor Parker, whose columns signed H. T. P. earned him the sobriquet "Hell-To-Pay," wrote that the concerto had sturdily weathered the intervening years, was eminently worth the re-hearing, and that Beach had never before played with "such ready resource and ample range, felicity of touch, ardor of tone and freedom of rhythm and progression." While he did not think the concerto a masterpiece, he found it "expertly, sensitively and fancifully written. . .at the golden mean that treats a concerto neither as a virtuoso piece for solo instrument with accompanying band or as a symphonic piece that happens to add a piano to the other instru-mental voices."[15] Parker also commented on the fine work of the conductor and the orchestra who, he believed, "enkindled" Beach's performance. Karl Muck had brought the Boston orchestra to a point close to virtuosic perfection, and Beach, ever sensitive to the conductor's and players' responses to her inter-pretations, was doubly inspired.[16]

Muck, a naturalized Swiss of German origin, retained the admiration and confidence of many Bostonians at a time when anti-German feeling was on the rise in the United States following the declaration of war on 6 April 1917.[17] Emotions reached fever pitch the following fall. Both the press and the public in Providence, Rhode Island, accused Muck of pro-German behavior, which eventually led to in his internment as an enemy alien on 25 March 1918.[18] Beach's sympathies, as well as the sympathies of all those who retained a sense of fairness, must have lain with the conductor. Nevertheless, her allegiances had undergone considerable change in the three years since her return from Germany. By the time the United States entered the war, Beach responded with patriotic intensity. She soon decided that her country was ready to challenge even the musical hegemony of Germany:

> For many years the country was in bondage to the idea that music, in order to be good, must come from abroad, especially from Germany. . . . Little by little has come the change and the realization that good things were being produced here in our own land. At last came the climax of separation from Germany. We broke off far more than "diplomatic relations" even with our first blow. We broke a long past of submersion in German ideas, musical and otherwise. . . . In time we shall regain our old love of the classics which belong to the world more than to any one coun-try, but our old slavery to a mistaken theory will be swept away in the "limbo of forgotten things."[19]

Like other recitalists, Beach had a repertory heavy with music by German and Austrian composers. Her favorite opening solo group for the more serious audiences included a Bach prelude and fugue, Beethoven's *Variations*, op. 34, and a Brahms rhapsody. Now however, Beach sought new repertory among the works of Italian, French, English, and Russian composers. She also noted that during the coming season she would be playing "'real American' music—some Zuñi Indian melodies" arranged for piano by Carlos Troyer and Homer Grunn.[20] Although she did not mention it, she also would be playing her own suite on Inuit themes, *Eskimos*, op. 64, at a recital given just a few miles from Hillsborough, in Concord, New Hampshire, on 28 July 1917; she introduced the work with a brief lecture on Eskimo music.[21] Beach also expressed her support for American composers by becoming vice-president of the Society for the Publication of American Music, headed by John Alden Carpenter.[22]

The war swept her patriotic hymn of 1902, *Song of Liberty*, op. 49, back into popularity. After Schmidt republished it, the hymn was sung all over the country during the war.[23] In a wartime review of the hymn, A. Walter Kramer, the composer and critic, wrote, it "expresses America's feeling at this time more potently than any patriotic song that has come to my notice" since the United States entered the war.[23] He viewed the hymn as "a fine healthy piece of diatonic writing, with something of the majesty and dignity we find in the Prelude to the *Meistersinger*." To Kramer, Beach was "one of the best composers this country has ever produced, a woman who understands her craft, knows how to deliver her message, be it in peace or war, with loftiness of purpose and adherence to her high ideals."[24]

Beach spent the summer of 1917 composing and preparing for the next season's recitals. She was now intensely involved in the social life of Hillsborough, as well as of nearby Henniker and Concord, the state capital a few miles away. That and her recital schedule may explain why Beach had no immediate plans for any extended compositions, even during her summer vacation:

> For anything large scale I need a path quite clear of more or less distant concert duties and obligations. After a few more years of travel and recital-giving, I may settle down for a big, sustained effort—an opera, perhaps, if I can obtain a fine libretto. But I am much too enthusiastic a traveler yet to settle down, too fond of my audiences to give them up.[25]

In fact, her recital schedule for the coming season was relatively light.[26] Outstanding was her December engagement with the Minneapolis Orchestra, conducted by Emil Oberhoffer, which gave the symphony and the concerto with Beach as soloist in St. Paul and Minneapolis. Reviews offered good words about both. The symphony was found to be "full of youthful fire and charm," its first and last movements "virile, not feminine."[27] About the concerto, a second critic wrote that "the long first movement is more symphonic than the symphony itself and filled with engaging subjects as engagingly handled," while the second movement is "sheer delight."[28] She could not know at the time that this would be her last performance of the concerto.

In January 1918 there were two concerts, one of which was for the Saint Cecilia Society of Grand Rapids, Michigan, and devoted entirely to Beach's compositions. In Toronto, for a return engagement with the Academy Quartet, she played her *Prelude and Fugue*, two groups of songs, and again her Piano Quintet. There were several receptions for Beach, including a large one in which members of the Musical Club gave *The Sea-Fairies*. Beach had become a great favorite with Torontonians.

Suddenly, upon her return to Hillsborough, she published the following announcement:

> Mrs. H. H. A. Beach. . .has decided to devote her energies exclusively to Red Cross and other war relief work until the end of the war. She is available for concerts for these purposes and will present not only her own music, but programs of the music of Allied countries.[29]

She also announced a drastic curtailment of her own performance schedule and her itinerary, and the dismissal of her concert manager: "Those wishing to present Mrs. Beach in concert or recital for patriotic purposes may make arrangements with her directly at her home, Hillsborough, N. H. For the remainder of this season Mrs. Beach wishes to confine her activities to the New England States."[30]

In addition to the war, there was another compelling reason for the abrupt cancellation of her concert plans—her cousin's health. Ethel Clement had developed a terminal illness; during the next two years she became increasingly ill. Beach's presence at home was required, since her seventy-five-year old aunt could hardly care for Ethel by herself. She now chose the traditional female nurturant role at the expense of her career. With the help of a local resident who relieved her, however, Beach was able to get away to Boston during the spring of 1918, first to play at the Peabody Institute and then to pack up the contents of her house at 28 Commonwealth Avenue in preparation for renting it. By the end of April, Beach returned to her aunt and cousin in Hillsborough.

It is a measure of the stress Beach was under that she did virtually no composing during the time of Ethel's illness. She wrote a violin obligato for a new edition of "The Year's at the Spring" and revised the *Valse-Caprice*, op. 4, for a new edition, which she planned to use extensively in recital.[31] Nevertheless, over the next few years G. Schirmer brought out several of her earlier works: in 1917, the women's chorus, *Dusk in June*, op. 82; in 1918, the brilliant *Prelude and Fugue*, op. 81; and in 1920, *Theme and Variations for Flute and String Quartet*, op. 80, which the Chamber Music Society of San Francisco continued to feature on their programs.

In the autumn of 1918, Beach received a personal invitation from Elizabeth Sprague Coolidge to attend a historic event, the First Berkshire Festival of Chamber Music given 25–27 September 1918 in the Temple on South Mountain in Pittsfield, Massachusetts. Coolidge, a fine amateur solo and ensemble pianist and occasional composer herself, had decided that chamber music would be the focus of her philanthropies. Her sponsorship of festivals and her support of music and musicians through numerous anonymous gifts has been continued through her endowment of the Elizabeth Sprague Coolidge Foundation, which awards commissions to composers. Coolidge's campaign to promote chamber music, however, began with the founding in 1918 of the Berkshire Festival.[32] Beach, alas, was forced to decline.

Beach and Coolidge may have met for the first time in 1893 at the World's

Columbian Exposition in Chicago when Coolidge played the second and third movements of the Schumann Piano Concerto with Theodore Thomas and the Exposition Orchestra.[33] Beginning in 1902, in Boston, she showed her original songs to Beach for her evaluation. Beach was encouraging and found much to praise, yet she clearly believed that Coolidge had a long way to go toward mastery of her art. Eventually, Beach recommended that Coolidge study with Percy Goetschius.[34]

For the 1918–19 season, in accord with her announced plan, Beach curtailed her concerts and only played close to home, postponing all other engagements. She missed two acclaimed performances of her Symphony: on 26 February 1918, a second performance by the Philadelphia Orchestra under Stokowski;[35] and in December, a performance by the Detroit Symphony, conducted by Ossip Gabrilowitsch, who afterwards wrote of its "fine success."[36]

Most of the winter of 1919 she spent in Hillsborough.[37] For the season of 1919–20, Beach canceled nearly all her recitals; she was under tremendous strain because of Ethel's illness.[38] Finally, on 1 April 1920, after a winter of intense suffering, Ethel died. In a letter to the California poet Ina Coolbrith, Beach described her own and her aunt's emotional devastation: "The long winter of agony at last ended, and ever since I have tried to make life at least bearable for my poor stricken aunt. She has been wonderfully brave, but her heart lies buried with the body of her dear one."[39]

A year after Ethel's death, in another letter to the poet, Beach reported that she had returned to composing and was working on a "Te Deum," op. 84, for men's voices "and some new piano pieces," but not songs: "Somehow the *song* has gone out of my life of late!" She wrote, "The past month has taken four of my good friends, and last spring my losses were heavy indeed in addition to my cousin's going."[40]

The second heavy loss of spring 1920 was—and still is—one of Beach's best-kept secrets. Cryptic clues in her diaries, which chronicle the years from 1926 to 1944, consist of repeated remembrances of "A"—of his birthday, his death, his leaving Boston, and other signal events of his life. Finally, in one entry she names him as "Arthur" but still does not provide his last name. There is no question, however, that he was as important to her as Henry Beach had been and as David McKay Williams would later be. It would seem likely that "A" was Arthur Sewell Hyde (1875–1920); his dates match those Beach memorialized in her diaries, and she was well acquainted with him as early as 1906 when he was organist and choirmaster of the Emmanuel Church in Boston and conductor of the Thursday Morning Club chorus. Both ensembles performed Beach's choral music, with her assistance at the piano for the secular works.[41] After Hyde assumed his new post at St. Bartholomew's Episcopal Church in New York in 1908, he gave many more performances of the "Te Deum" and "Benedictus" from Beach's *Service in A*,[42] and on 4 April 1915 he introduced her *Panama Hymn*, op. 74, with its new sacred text and title, "All Hail the Power of Jesus' Name." The fact that the choir sang it months before its publication suggests that Hyde received the music directly from the composer.

Beach's continuing contact with St. Bartholomew's and Hyde is confirmed in her "Night Song at Amalfi," which was composed on or before 1916[43] and dedicated to Grace Kerns, Hyde's soprano soloist at St. Bart's.[44] Its text by Sara Teasdale—perhaps a message to the organist through Kerns—suggests that Beach's feelings for Hyde were not reciprocated. Below are the first and last stanzas:

I asked the heav'n of stars,
What should I give my love?
It answered me with silence,
Silence above....

Oh, I could give him weeping,
Or I could give him song,
But how can I give silence,
My whole life long?[45]

The paucity of evidence of a relationship beyond the references in her diary suggests that Hyde's only interest in Beach lay in the performance of her music.

Born in Bath, Maine, on 21 February 1875, Hyde was a bachelor, eight years younger than Beach and a cousin of Emma Eames, the opera diva. A gifted organist, after graduating from Harvard in 1896 he studied with Charles-Marie Widor in Paris.[46]

His portrait reveals a man with a handsome and sensitive face and soulful dark eyes. He had a beautiful though untrained baritone voice and occasionally gave recitals. On 16 January 1915 at a concert by the Rubinstein Club in New York's Waldorf Astoria Hotel, Hyde sang a group of songs accompanied by David McKay Williams, his eventual successor at St. Bartholomew's. As a surprise, Hyde offered "The Year's at the Spring" "with fire" to Beach's stirring accompaniment.[47]

A description of Hyde as organist and man suggests why he was so appealing to Beach: "In his playing he possessed a warmth, a quality of pure sweetness and beauty, which was always a delight. In his control and training of boys he was a master, but a master greatly loved."[48] His death in 1920 was tragic and untimely. After war was declared, Hyde, single and without dependents, became a captain in the infantry; on 13 January 1918 he left for France, where he was twice gassed with serious damage to his lungs: he would never sing again. He resumed his post at St. Bartholomew's in May of 1919. On 21 February 1920, having succumbed to the influenza epidemic, he died of pneumonia at age forty-five.[49]

Beach consoled herself over her losses, writing, "I realize that I still have much to be thankful for!. . .Yet, when my time comes to go on further, I shall be happy!"[50] Later, Beach wrote in her diary an epigram that suggested how intense was her grief: "Memories make life beautiful, forgetfulness makes it possible."[51]

Aunt Franc was her next worry. She was feeble, quite nervous, suffered from a weak heart and persistent pain and discomfort, and needed constant care. Beach reported, "I have not left her this winter, except for the month of

December up to Christmas, when I was giving concerts in the middle West."[52] Although an old friend gave her the best of care in Beach's absence, it was her niece that Aunt Franc wanted at her side.[53]

Fortunately, a measure of consolation arrived that would make a positive difference in Beach's life as a composer—she was to become a fellow at the MacDowell Colony, a place for which she soon had infinite affection.

AT THE MACDOWELL COLONY

"Solitude in Silence"

He may by contemplation learn
A little more than what he knew,
And even see great oaks return
To acorns out of which they grew.

He may, if he but listen well,
Through twilight and the silence here
Be told what there are none may tell
To vanity's impatient ear . . .

Edwin Arlington Robinson

THE ONLY SOUNDS THAT PENETRATED the silence at the MacDowell Colony were the sounds of nature. One morning soon after Beach's arrival at the colony in Peterborough, New Hampshire, that first summer of 1921, one of nature's sounds was so insistent that she stopped her work to have a conversation—with "a most voluble thrush." A longtime collector of bird songs, she decided to record his "lonely but appealing" music. "I took the songs down at the bird's dictation, and oh, how hard I worked!" she said, "Even the most expert stenographer would have had difficulty keeping up with him! I took them exactly, even as to key (except for a few intervals too small to be transcribed) and rewrote and corrected as he sang them over and over. Then I played them back to him and he would answer."[1] Out of his songs Beach then fashioned "A Hermit Thrush at Eve" and "A Hermit Thrush at Morn," op. 92, among her most original and successful piano pieces. Soon thereafter Beach played the "Hermit Thrush" pieces for fellow colonists, first telling the story of her morning's conversation.[2]

The hermit thrush became Beach's metaphor for the MacDowell Colony, a place where she could hear her own musical thoughts, could "learn a little more than what she knew" to quote the poet, friend, and fellow colonist Edwin Arlington Robinson.[3] It was "through the innermost silence," Beach wrote, that we receive communication "from some source outside ourselves."[4] The colony also offered her a place to heal after the wrenching early deaths of Ethel Clement and Arthur Hyde, to work through her grief in her music, and to find respite from concern over her aunt's deteriorating condition. Composition once more became the focus of her musical life, especially because performance, under the force of home circumstance, had again become a subordinate one.

The MacDowell Colony offered Beach another crucial benefit—daily contact with other workers in the arts. Among the fellows that summer were Bashka Paeff, the sculptor who later did a plaster bust of Beach;[5] Katharine Adams, whose poems, "The Moonpath," and "Christ in the Universe," Beach set;[6] and Padraic Colum, who that summer worked on translations of old Irish songs and provided the melody that Beach arranged for piano as *The Fair Hills of Éiré, O*," op. 91.[7]

Colonists brought more than the stuff of new compositions to her life, however. Beach's gratitude to Marian MacDowell, who, after her husband's death built the artists' retreat with her hard work and determination, was enormous. The two women became close friends over the years when Beach worked at the colony. This was a culmination of a long history, beginning in 1888 with the MacDowells' years in Boston, where they moved in the same musical circles until Edward MacDowell's appointment to Columbia University took them to New York in 1896.

When Edward MacDowell was dying, Beach was extremely supportive, making a special point of including his music on her 1907 and 1908 recital programs.[8] Following a memorial concert for the composer given two months after his death in March 1908 by the Boston Symphony Orchestra, Beach wrote Marian MacDowell, praising the Second Suite for Orchestra, "Indian."[9] She also encouraged Mrs. MacDowell in her initial fund-raising efforts to set up a working retreat for artists. During the years before 1921, Beach found various ways to support the colony, contributing money and manuscripts for fund-raising events and playing at benefit concerts.

Marian MacDowell personally picked the colony fellows. It is no surprise, considering her broad support among women musicians, that so many of the colonists were women. During Beach's first month at the MacDowell Colony there were twenty-three women and twenty-two men. Seven of the eleven composers were women: Emilie Frances Bauer, Marion Bauer, Mabel Daniels, Fannie Charles Dillon, Helen Dyckman, Ethel Glenn Hier, and Beach.[10] All were or became long-time friends of Beach's; a generation or so younger, they called her Aunt Amy at her request.

The MacDowell Colony became her main point of contact with male artists, several of whom she counted as friends. Edwin Arlington Robinson, who that year won a Pulitzer Prize for his *Collected Poems*, was one whom Beach fondly cheered on as she watched him play billiards during evenings at the colony. Later, Beach had a warm relationship with the playwright Thornton Wilder, whose play *Our Town* would memorialize Peterborough, under the pseudonym "Grovers Corners." The young composer Walter S. Jenkins was a Beach admirer who in the late 1930s joined her in recreational activities at the colony. He had sought her out early in the 1930s and owed his residencies at the colony in part to Beach's recommendations.[11] Her friendship with a group of fellow artists—female and male—somewhat compensated Beach for the deprivation of living in a small town away from cultural centers.

Nevertheless, generational and gender divisions were evident. "Reportedly everyone [at the Colony] was fond of her, some a touch patronizingly, because she (or her work or both) [was] no longer fashionable. Mrs. Beach ignored the patronizing of others because of her. . .sense of her own worth."[12] It was at the colony that the name "Mrs. Ha-ha Beach" was coined by some unnamed person; according to artist Prentiss Taylor, colonists used the name "with a range of feeling from affection to denigration." Although he was fond of Beach and appreciative of her remarkable gifts and record of achievements, Taylor did not show her his own works for fear that they were too modern for her taste.[13]

Each day began at breakfast with other fellows at Colony Hall, but thereafter the colonists were completely alone and, by fiat, uninterrupted in their studios—even at midday when basket lunches were silently set at their studio doors. During her first month and in subsequent years, Beach worked in the Regina Watson Studio, a miniature "Greek temple out of Tara," with a colonnaded open porch; its grey and white exterior enclosed a room twenty by thirty feet "done in Impoverished Nobility: gilt chandelier. . .splendid concert grand, immense rococo work table, sofa by the fireplace."[14] Among its mementos are a chest of drawers that Beach donated to the colony and wooden wall plaques that the colonists referred to as "tombstones," into which successive occupants of the various studios carved their names and years of occupancy.[15] Beach, like the other colonists, did not sleep in her studio but rather at the Eaves, the dormitory for women hard by Colony Hall. Her room on the ground floor is now identified by a plaque as the "Mrs. H. H. A. Beach" room.

Dinner was at six o'clock in the dining room at Colony Hall. However, on nights when employees had time off, colonists ate at the Colony's inn, the Nubanusit Tea Barn, and on Sunday evenings at Hillcrest, Marian MacDowell's home. The latter dinners were "simple, early affairs. . .Mrs. MacDowell helping to wait on everyone, and all the guests and Colony members seated. There was a friendly and charming quality to it."[16]

In the evening, after dinner at Colony Hall, colonists shared ping-pong and talk, billiards, and informal presentations of their work in the large hall with its immense fireplace and dark-beamed ceiling. There were also recitals and readings in the Savidge Library nearby, where Beach played on occasion for fellow colonists. One unforgettable evening, she and Albert Spalding played two violin sonatas of Beethoven, the C minor and the F major. The famous violinist apparently neglected to bring the piano score of the Mendelssohn Concerto, but Beach was able to play the accompaniment to the slow movement from memory, having learned it for another violinist.[17]

Departures from the colony were always wrenching because of the bonding that took place among residents during their stay. Although, like Beach, many returned year after year, no group of colonists was ever the same. Thus, when the time came to leave, there was a sense of closure, of finality, and of pending loss.

In 1921, during the month Beach spent at the colony, music poured out of her that had been all but dammed up. In the following five years, nearly fifty works appeared (opp. 83–117), twice as many as in the previous ten years,

EXAMPLE 19.1 "The Hermit Thrush at Morn," op. 92, no. 2: (a) mm. 5–10; (b) mm. 43–46 (Arthur P. Schmidt, 1922). Composer's note at the bottom of the first page of music: "These bird-calls are exact notations of hermit thrush songs, in the original keys but an octave lower, obtained at the MacDowell Colony, Peterborough, N.H."

thanks to the MacDowell Colony. From 1921 on, almost all of her music would be written or at least sketched there. Among the first were "The Hermit Thrush at Eve" and "The Hermit Thrush at Morn," op. 92, nos. 1 and 2. The quotations at the head of each piece evoke Krehbiel's "new trinity" of God, nature, and music: in "Eve" Beach cites John Vance Cheney's "Holy, holy!—in the hush/Hearken to the hermit thrush; All the air/Is in Prayer." In "Morn," she quotes John Clare's "merry thrush" that sings "hymns of joy."

Bird song, like other sounds of nature, helped her to find new musical directions. These two pieces are securely anchored in their keys, "Eve" in a dark Eb minor and the waltz-like "Morn" in a brighter while still somewhat mournful D minor. "Eve," however, is marked by chromaticism, and "Morn" contains patches of tonal ambiguity, momentarily touching on a key, only to abruptly change to another, yet always connected through the logic of voice leading—a typically post-Romantic procedure. In the following example, the song of the thrush temporarily led her into remote tonal bypaths (ex. 19.1a, b).

Change was in the air at the MacDowell Colony, and this may have been the catalyst for Beach's stylistic changes. Most of her fellow colonists were younger, and some of them, like Marion Bauer, were searching for solutions to artistic problems posed by the modernist movement in the arts.[18] Beach, who rejected the more extreme compositional practices of Varèse, Stravinsky, or Schoenberg, was moved—despite her more conservative pronouncements—to experiment with modern idioms. Indeed, she wanted to be thought of as an up-to-date composer and took steps, largely unrecognized, to change with the times.

Although she said the song had gone out of her heart when Ethel died, still she continued to write songs, finding poems with themes that expressed her

(b)

EXAMPLE 19.1 (continued)

grief: death and messages from the dead, lamentation and mourning assuaged only by God, and the making of music as the only answer to emotional isolation. She also sought out poems that suggested a more expressionistic style wherein dissonance and harmonic excursions are used to destabilize tonality, with the home key affirmed only at the final cadence.

One such work is In the Twilight, op. 85, which Beach wrote for Emma Roberts to sing at a music festival in Buffalo in the early fall of 1921. Longfellow's poem describes a fisherman's wife and child who fear for the father's safety on a storm-tossed sea. Marked Allegro tempestoso, the music is dissonant, tonally unstable, and rich in chromaticism (ex. 19.2a)—expressive of the turbulent sea and escalating terror of the mother. Beginning in the tonic key of F# minor, one of Beach's two "black" keys, an enharmonic spelling of the leading tone E# as F♮, in m. 4, initiates a series of fleeting tonal excursions.

The last quatrain is especially dramatic: the piano's abrupt silence leaves the voice naked for the final words, "drives the color from her cheek." A chilling conclusion to the song, it recalls the deathly hush at the end of Schubert's "Erlkönig" where the narrator, unaccompanied, sings "In seinem Armen, das Kind war todt" (In his arms, the child was dead). Unlike the "Erlkönig," however, "In the Twilight" ends not in the tonic but on the leading note, E#—its final melodic dissonance left hanging, like the fate of the fisherman (ex. 19.2b).

Nature is present in the titles of all but two of the eighteen piano works Beach wrote between 1921 and 1925. That first summer at the colony, she also wrote the piano suite From Grandmother's Garden, op. 97. This is another instance of Beach's words contradicting her music: the title of the suite suggests a sentimental look backward, whereas its music is contemporary if not forward-looking. In it, her lyrical voice returns but, despite the Victorian title, only in the context of dissonance and chromaticism. Each piece is named for a flower. The first is "Morning Glories," whose opening to the sun is depicted in an

EXAMPLE 19.2 In the Twilight, op. 85: (a) mm. 1–9, (b) mm. 105–14 (Arthur P. Schmidt, 1922).

etudelike design of rapidly rising arpeggios with dissonant nonchord tones. The piece begins and ends in E minor, but the parallel motion throughout, the passages of non-functional harmony, the persistence of seventh and augmented chords, the unresolved dissonances, and the chromatic progressions, mark it as a modern piece.

"Heartsease" has a cantabile melody set off by chromatically shifting harmonies. "Mignonette," a minuet (the title perhaps a musical pun) with staccato parallel fourths and strange juxtapositions of keys, also plays on the meaning of *mignon* (dainty, pretty, tiny, and graceful). The flowers for which "Rosemary and Rue" is named suggest remembrance and regret while its successive falling chromatic lines and bittersweet overlapping dissonances create tension (ex. 19.3). Finally, "Honeysuckle," is a fast waltz with twisting melodic lines and abrupt modulations.

(b)

EXAMPLE 19.2 (continued)

EXAMPLE 19.3 "Rosemary and Rue," op. 97, no. 4 (from the suite *From Grandmother's Garden*, Arthur P. Schmidt, 1922), mm. 7–16.

Other piano works that refer to nature include "Farewell Summer" and "Dancing Leaves," op. 102; *Old Chapel by Moonlight*, op. 106, "inspired by the painters' studio at the colony (the Alexander studio)";[19] and *By the Still Waters*, op. 114, its title a reference to the Twenty-third Psalm as well as to a mood of calm inspired by "still waters." Thus, explains Beach, while the title is biblical, the piece is secular and a depiction of nature.[20] The new trinity again!

Folk songs also invoke nature, especially when patronizingly considered the creation of a people who live close to the soil, and are thus nature's "children."[21] Beach's description of the Irish people whose songs she quoted in the "Gaelic" Symphony reflected this idea. She produced two works based on Irish folk melodies in the 1920s, indications of her continued fascination with this traditional music. The first, *The Fair Hills of Éiré, O!*, op. 91, is a setting of "Beautiful and Wide Are the Green Fields of Erin," the song given to her by Padraic Colum.[22] Haunted by the folksong, Beach could only get it out of her mind by giving it a setting "that brings out its full pathos," using a harmonization that is expressionist rather than folk-like.[23]

In 1924 Beach published a four-movement work, the *Suite for Two Pianos Founded upon Old Irish Melodies*, op. 104. Although she never stated that her new work was a revised version of "Iverniana," which was withdrawn soon after its premiere on 10 February 1910—there is considerable evidence that it is.[24] Beach may have planned to revise "Iverniana" after its second and final performance on 30 March 1910, but the deaths of the two people closest to her and the demands of her life thereafter intervened. The absence of manuscripts for both *Iverniana* and the suite may be explained by Beach's practice of revision, whereby she entered changes and additions directly into the original manuscript, which she then sent to the publisher.[25]

One of the strongest arguments for connecting these two piano works may be found on a handlist of Beach's works compiled by the composer in 1937.[26] The list begins with the entry, "op. 70, 'Iverniana,' Suite for 2 pianos. MS." The opus number is changed to 104, "Iverniana" and MS are crossed out. Further down the list and in opus number order, the revision is also entered as "Op. 104. Suite for 2 pianos on Irish Melodies," with the publisher's name, "John Church."

Further evidence supporting the relationship between the suite and "Iverniana" is found in the fact that folk themes appearing in the suite match Beach's own description of tunes quoted in "Iverniana": she told an interviewer that the latter "is constructed upon a set of melodies of Ivernia, old Ireland, given to [her] many years ago."[27] The melodies used as themes in the suite, op. 104—like those of the "Gaelic" Symphony—are found in the January to June 1841 issues of *The Citizen* which is most likely the source for the themes of op. 70 as well.[28] See, for example, the second movement of op. 104, "Old-time Peasant Dance," in which she quotes two of the melodies from *The Citizen* precisely (ex. 19.4a, b). A review of the unpublished "Iverniana" viewed the second movement as "a genuine bit of rollicking Irish humor in dance form," which is also an apt description of the second movement of op. 104.[29] The same is true of the other movements of op. 104, which alternate slow and fast tempi, songs and dances. Beach, however, is quoted as saying that she had "the pull of tides and

EXAMPLE 19.4 "Old-time Peasant Dance," second movement of *Suite for Two Pianos Founded upon Old Irish Melodies*, op. 104: (a) theme 1, *secondo*, mm. 17–21; (b) theme 2, *primo*, mm. 83–87 (John Church Co., 1924; used by permission of Theodore Presser Co.).

the rhythms of big bodies of water" constantly in her mind as she worked on the suite, an imagery that suggests a complex narrative.[30]

Beach gave the *Suite for Two Pianos* an opus number that was current in 1923–24; and when she signed the contract for its publication, she clearly wanted it to be considered a new work.[31] This would explain her suppression of information that might suggest that the suite was a revision of an earlier work, even if it were. Without access to the manuscript of "Iverniana," however, there is no way of knowing how close the two works are; yet the evidence suggests that they are nearly identical.

The publication of the suite op. 104, was greeted with enthusiasm by music critics. Sydney Dalton, of *Musical America*, stated that "nothing that Mrs. Beach has done for many a day surpasses in beauty, technical finish and sustained interest this finely conceived work." He noted further that when the two-piano team of Rose and Ottilie Sutro, to whom the work is dedicated, gave the premiere in Paris at the Salle des Agriculteurs on 25 October 1924, the work was "exceedingly well received. . .[and was] an important contribution to the none too plentiful stock of music for two pianos."[32] The Sutros also performed the suite on subsequent American tours.[33] Mary Howe, the Washington pianist and composer, joined Beach in the American premiere of the suite at an all-Beach recital on 7 March 1925 to benefit the MacDowell Colony; they played the work again at a private concert at Chickering Hall, New York, on 9 April 1926. Altogether there were more than a dozen performances during Beach's lifetime, an impressive record for a work with proportions and challenges to match a piano concerto. Indeed, it became in her later years her "concerto without orchestra"—easier to arrange for a performance yet expansive enough to serve as the major component of a program.

Music for worship was, of course, an important aspect of the new trinity, to the extent that the text evoked the natural world as God's creation. During the first five years at the MacDowell Colony, Beach turned out a number of sacred choral works. For the composer, who believed that all "good" music is sacred, the act of composing devotional music had especially deep personal meaning: "Though we fall far behind in the attempt to express what is often far beyond expression, and though our musical efforts must fall so far short of the glorious words, the uplifted hours through which we pass can be compared to no others in our musical life," Beach claimed. She continued, "the greatest function of all creative work is to try to bring even a little of the eternal into the temporal life. . . to uplift" ourselves and others with our music.[34]

It is in Beach's sacred works that some feeling of peace and repose resides. Several—but not all—are in relatively conservative styles, although she characteristically uses tonality for expressive rather than merely for structural purposes. I *Will Lift Up Mine Eyes*, op. 98 (1923), a setting of Psalm 121 for unaccompanied mixed chorus, is striking in its use of modulation. Beach moves to C-major at the apex of four phrases: on the word "heaven" in "who hath made heaven and earth"; twice on the phrase, "the sun shall not burn thee"; and at the end of the eight-measure ascent for the phrase, "from this time forth forevermore," before a quiet final return to E-flat. In so doing Beach joins Haydn and Wagner, who in *The Creation* and *Parsifal* used modulation to C major in their depictions of light.

During her early years at the MacDowell Colony, Beach sketched out three of her finest works, bringing them to completion in the second half of the decade: the obbligato song *Rendez-vous*, op. 120, and the sacred chorus *The Canticle of the Sun*, op. 123, both published in 1928; and her *Quartet for Strings in One Movement*, op. 89.[35]

Leonora Speyer (1872–1956), poet, ex-violinist, friend, and fellow colonist in Peterborough, was the author of the poem and the dedicatee of *Rendez-vous*.[36] One of the imagist poets and a friend of Amy Lowell's, Speyer won a

EXAMPLE 19.5 *Rendez-vous*, op. 120: (a) mm. 6–10; (b) mm. 105–11 (Oliver Ditson, 1928; used by permission of Theodore Presser Co.).

Pulitzer Prize in 1927 for her *Fiddler's Farewell*. Like a number of other poems set by Beach, *Rendez-vous* associates nature—here the month of June as it bursts into blossom—with death. Its refrain, "June, my June," recalled for Beach a time when she lived in the woods, in Peterborough or Centerville, when the joy of her own creative work matched that of nature's (ex. 19.5a). But June was also the month when Henry died, an anniversary she marked throughout her life, as Speyer's poem suggests:

> I bring to you
> Still near to me,
> Still dear to me
> My ancient grief still new (ex. 19.5b).

The refrain, "Wait for me, June," anticipates nature's lushness. But that intense longing is mixed with dread that the speaker might not survive for the

EXAMPLE 19.5 (continued)

EXAMPLE 19.6 (a) Richard Wagner, *Parsifal*, act 1, scene 2, "Procession of the Knights of the Grail." (b) Beach, *The Canticle of the Sun*, op. 123, mm. 3–6 (Arthur P. Schmidt, 1928; used by permission of Warner Publications).

"one more month, so soon." Beach inscribes in the music the sense of impatient, unfulfilled yearning through persistent dissonance, delaying all resolution until the final measure. The vocal line is chromatic yet lyrical. The violin obbligato foreshadows, then echoes, the voice, following a suggestion in the poem, "wrapped in a shadowed harmony." The piano's surging, arpeggiated figuration that opens the song persists throughout, sweeping toward its final climax. Of all the songs she wrote on poems with this theme, this is the most intensely moving and effective. Its first performance was at a program of the Society of American Women Composers, a group Beach founded and headed at the time.[37]

Her second important work from the early 1920s, the *Canticle of the Sun*, op. 123, is a setting of Matthew Arnold's translation of the twelfth-century sequence by St. Francis of Assisi. Dr. Howard Duffield, a friend and pastor of the First Presbyterian Church in New York, gave her the text in 1915, at a time when she was too involved in playing and traveling to work on it. Years later, she found it by accident just after she arrived at the MacDowell Colony. She was "forcibly" struck by it: "I went out at once under a tree, and the text took complete possession of me. As if from dictation, I jotted down the notes of my 'Canticle.' In less than five days, the entire work was done."[38] Beach put the work away to let it "cool" for several years until she received a request from H. Augustine Smith, conductor at Boston University and also of the Chautauqua Choir, for a sacred work with specifications that matched the *Canticle* exactly. Then all she had to do was make a fair copy and orchestrate the *Canticle* before sending it off to the Schmidt company, who agreed to accept it.[39] The work is about twenty-five minutes long and calls for a mixed chorus, solo quartet, and orchestra or piano reduction.

Beach may have had Wagner's *Parsifal* in mind when she wrote *The Canticle of the Sun*, for the prominent four-note ostinato that is heard in the bass throughout the opening section and recalled at the end resembles the orchestral ostinato for the procession of knights and squires in the opera's first act (ex. 19.6a, b).[40] Similarly, the modulation from B♭ minor to C major at the words "our brother, the Sun," mirrors Wagner's modulation to C major, as the light of the Holy Grail is uncovered.

The text invokes the "new trinity" in powerful language, depicting St. Fran-

EXAMPLE 19.6 (*continued*)

cis's veneration of nature and God's creatures. This is reflected in the personifications not only of "our brother, the sun," but also "our sister, the moon," as well as the stars, wind, water, fire, and "our mother, the earth." The elements are described in separate sections, some powerful and dramatic—like those about the sun and fire—some lyrical, referring to the moon and stars. With the lines,

> Praised be the Lord for our Sister,
> the death of the body from whom no man escapeth.
> Woe to him who dieth in mortal sin.

the music turns tragic, pressing downward in chromatic steps (ex. 19.7). Recurring augmented and diminished intervals and seventh chords heighten the affect.

Although Beach dedicated *Canticle* to the Chautauqua Choir, the first performance, on 8 December 1928, was given by the choir of St. Bartholomew's Episcopal Church in New York, conducted by David McKay Williams, who also accompanied the work on the organ. Thereafter, Williams conducted annual performances of the work at the church.

Beach also orchestrated *Canticle* for woodwinds, four horns, two trumpets, timpani, and strings. The first performance of this version took place in Toledo on 12 May 1930. Mary Willing Megley conducted the Toledo Choral Society, the Children's Chorus of Webster Junior High School and the Chicago Symphony.[41] A reviewer wrote that "[t]he serene, unquestioning adoration of the celebrated medieval religious glows in every phrase of the lucid musical setting of his words."[42] Albert Stoessel conducted the work with orchestra at Chautauqua on 14 August 1930[43] and again at the Worcester Festival on 8 October 1931, when Beach was finally able to hear the orchestral version. Another performance with orchestra took place in Chattanooga in 1937.[44] Added to these performances were many others given with organ in New York churches. These, in turn, spurred organists across the country to present this appealing work.[45]

Amy Beach's most innovative work of the early 1920s was the *Quartet for*

EXAMPLE 19.7 *The Canticle of the Sun,* mm. 347–54.

Strings in One Movement, op. 89.[46] She never explained her decision to write a string quartet, a work that, like the flute quintet, had no role for her as a performer. Of course, a composer does not need a reason to write a quartet beyond the wonderful possibilities of the medium. Her attendance at chamber music concerts of the Berkshire Festivals in 1919 and 1920 may have been the inspiration and Elizabeth Sprague Coolidge's chamber music competitions the enticement. Beach may have decided to compete in the string quartet competition announced for 1922. Although there is no direct evidence to support this conjecture, the timing of the work's composition suggests a relationship between it and the Coolidge string quartet competition.

The composer, whom Coolidge regularly invited to the festivals, had attended in 1919, when Coolidge herself broke the judges' tied vote in the competition for a viola work: the winner was Ernest Bloch (1880–1959), the Swiss-born composer; the runner-up, to everyone's amazement, was a woman—Rebecca Clarke (1886–1979), an English composer and professional violist. Both composers had arrived in the United States in 1916.[47] The following year at the festival, Beach heard the prize composition for that year, *Rispetti e Strambotti*, a string quartet by the Italian composer Gian Francesco Malipiero. She wrote an appreciative letter to Coolidge, praising everything about the festival except Malipiero's quartet, merely saying, "I hope to hear the Prize Quartet again and be able to become better acquainted with its Italian atmosphere."[48]

Beach took two actions to win her music a place on the festival programs. Early in 1921 she wrote to Coolidge, announcing the recent publication of her *Theme and Variations for Flute and String Quartet*, op. 80, and asking permission to send her a copy, which permission Coolidge granted.[49] The quintet, alas, was never included on the festival programs, for reasons that can only be guessed. Beach may not have been aware, then, that Coolidge tended to choose avant-garde pieces; the flute variations may have been too conservative to be included in a festival program.

Beach's second move was to compose a string quartet. Like Malipiero's, her string quartet is in one movement and is dissonant in a new and very modern way; she used—with adaptation—some of Malipiero's techniques, despite her implied dislike of his work.[50] Beach's work, however, is very different from *Rispetti e Strambotti*.

First attempts at composing in a new medium often require more work than usual. With the quartet, Beach had to not only master a new medium but also create a new style. She worked hard on the quartet, as the two manuscripts in her hand suggest. The first, a pencil draft, shows her progress during the first summer at the MacDowell Colony. It contains multiple corrections and additions as well as several passages that Beach replaced by sewing new versions over the originals.[51] It bears two dates: the first, probably marking the completion of the first draft, is "July 15th 1921"; the second, marking the completion of one or possibly two revisions, is "Peterboro Aug. 9/21."[52] Such extensive reworking of a composition was unusual for her. By the end of her stay at the colony, Beach apparently had not revised the quartet to her total satisfaction. Conditions at home in Hillsborough did not allow the concentration needed to complete it. Perhaps, having missed the deadline for submission to the 1922 Berkshire competition, Beach felt less urgency about finishing the quartet. In any case she set the work aside. It may be significant that Beach never attended another Berkshire Festival. Giving as reasons her aunt's illness and her own work, Beach turned down all Coolidge's subsequent invitations.[53]

Eight years later, in Rome for the winter of 1929, Beach returned to the string quartet and completed it; she made final revisions and prepared a fair copy between 16 and 22 January.[54] She was able to work quickly because the changes between the 1921 and the 1929 versions were minor. Nevertheless, the revisions that she made in Rome are significant, involving several additions and deletions, altered key signatures, and the transposition of long passages. Two days after completing a fair copy, Beach gave the quartet to a copyist who had a "fine Italian hand" and worked quickly to produce the third manuscript.

EXAMPLE 19.8 *Quartet for Strings in One Movement*, op. 89, mm. 1–14 (*Music of the United States of America*, vol. 3, ed. Adrienne Fried Block; A-R Editions, 1994; used by permission of the American Musicological Society).

Beach, who proofed the copyist's score and parts, was very pleased with their accuracy and appearance.[55]

Although the quartet is in one movement, it has three divisions: Grave-Più animato, Allegro molto (the main body of the quartet), and a reprise of the Grave. It is in the symmetrical form of an arch (ABCB¹A¹)—unusual for Beach—and has a duration of about fifteen minutes. The introduction, which is freely composed and dissonant, has a strong suggestion of grief, and immediately establishes that this work is in a new style. It is not merely that it is dissonant; Beach has normalized dissonance by eliminating the tonal imperative of consonant resolutions for the dissonant harmonies (ex. 19.8).

The central portion of the quartet has themes based on three Inuit melodies (ex. 19.9). Beach found the tunes in the same monograph on the Alaskan Inuit by Franz Boas from which she had years earlier borrowed eleven tunes for her piano suite *Eskimos*, op. 64. Following the opening Grave of the quartet there is a recitativelike statement of the first Inuit tune, "Summer Song," followed by a long passage based on the lyrical first strain of "Playing at Ball," with an ostinato accompaniment on the violoncello (ex. 19.10a). This section is recalled at the end of the work. In the B section, following an introductory passage based on "Ititaujang's Song," a fragment of that song is combined with the second strain of "Playing at Ball," with considerable development of both. Section C, the climax of the work, is a fugue based on rhythmically transformed melodic fragments from "Ititaujang's Song" (ex. 19.10b).

These "meager" melodies seem more stark in the quartet than in *Eskimos*—even bleak. In the later work, Beach found a compositional idiom that grew out of the themes themselves: all four string parts have musical lines derived entirely from motives found in three Inuit tunes. Indeed, the Inuit melodies that are the basis for the contrapuntal lines saturate the texture. In addition, through the use of unresolved dissonances and lean textures, Beach's music suggests the frozen north of the Inuit. Throughout she creates a distinctly more modern sound than in any previous work of hers. Beach also alternates nontonal and tonal sections, the latter usually a free floating, constantly mutating structure.

On 11 April 1929 at the American Academy, Beach heard her quartet performed by "very good players" and reported only that it "sounded well."[56] In the 1930s, Beach's quartet had a series of private performances, beginning with one by the LaSalle Quartet, an "eager" young New York group who played it at the studio of composer Ethel Glenn Hier during an informal program for the Society of American Women Composers on 24 January 1931.[57] The string quartet was played in 1932 in Cincinnati on an all-Beach program for a club of professional musicians; the event was arranged by Emma C. Roedter, a local leader of music and, according to Beach, a "strong friend" with whom she had been "closely associated."[58] Beach missed that recital but attended one that she wished she *had* missed, by the Lewis Reed Quartet of Dorchester, Massachusetts, in June of 1933.[59] In 1937, Roy Harris, then concert director for the National Association of American Composers and Conductors of which Beach was a member, arranged for a performance of the quartet in March. After attending a rehearsal supervised by Harris and his wife Johana, Beach reported that the musicians sight-read the quartet and played badly. She decided to skip the concert but may have regretted it, for friends who attended reported that the performance was well received.[60] Yet Beach stated that no performance did the work justice, another unfortunate reason why the quartet did not make the mark she hoped it would and never became part of the repertory of any leading ensemble. The best performance during the composer's lifetime no doubt was given in Washington, D.C., in 1942, when Beach was too ill to attend.

In 1940 Burnet C. Tuthill, author of a major article on Beach and her music, singled out the quartet for praise:

EXAMPLE 19.9 Three Inuit melodies: (a) "Summer Song" (b) "Playing at Ball," mm. 1–9; (c) "Ititaujang's Song."

EXAMPLE 19.10 Quartet, op. 89: (a) mm. 15–27, (b) mm. 273–82.

EXAMPLE 19.10 (continued)

> The String Quartet. . .is unlike anything else of Mrs. Beach's in its basic feeling, although all her usual technical skill is in evidence. There is a little resemblance to her customary harmonic writing in the slow introduction and its repetition at the close. . . . Throughout, the writing for strings is handled with technical mastery and fine effect. The work deserves publication and frequent performance.[61]

Tuthill further noted the quartet's unusual thematic material: "The main theme is quite Amerind in feeling if not in derivation and it is treated with a harmonic bareness that is suitable and gives the resulting sound a feeling of the open spaces of the great West."[62] Indeed, Beach's choice of Inuit tunes for the string quartet's thematic material was central to her creation of a new style. It was by her engagement with them in 1921 and 1929 that she found her answer to the dilemma regarding modern music. Despite Tuthill's recommendation, the work was neither published nor given frequent performances. Completed on the eve of the stock market crash of 1929 and the onset of the Great Depression, Beach's string quartet remained in manuscript until 1994, fifty years after the composer's death.

Being at the MacDowell Colony was important for Beach, possibly crucial to her creation of the quartet and other music as well. Marian MacDowell, by her invitation to Beach to become a fellow at the colony, had rescued the composer at a time when her creative efforts were languishing, and the renewal of her fellowship each year after 1921 undoubtedly revitalized Beach's work. Exulting in her first "wonderful month of work" at the colony, she declared that she loved the place "beyond words." There she had found the ideal place for one who wished to "hear a little more than what she knew."

CARING

"QUITE MADE OVER BY THE JOY OF returning to [creative] work after a long absence," Beach went back to Hillsborough after her first month at the MacDowell Colony to confront once again the sad reality of Aunt Franc's physical decline.[1] Her aunt had urged her to fulfill her concert commitments; Beach, however, was reluctant to leave her.[2] As a result, she remained in Hillsborough during the next four years, leaving only for a few short concert tours to the Midwest. For Beach, that constituted a sea-change in her performing career.

Significantly, because of illness, she cancelled the one engagement that might have given her some exposure, to play her concerto in Cincinnati. But even more important, while requests for recitals from women's and music clubs, and women's academies and colleges kept coming in, sustaining her during this decade, mainstream support disappeared. The contrast to the heady excitement of her years from 1912 to 1918 was considerable and only partially accounted for by her lengthy retreat to New Hampshire.

Widespread shifts in music were taking place during the 1920s. Those like Beach, who believed that music's role was to provide moral and spiritual uplift, had to navigate between the Scylla of the Jazz Age and the Charybdis of the avant-garde. Beach considered this a choice between the visceral and the dryly intellectual, and she rejected both. In addition, with the advent of the "new music," many women felt marginalized, crowded out by European men such as Varèse and Milhaud and by American men who rejected works that conveyed even a hint of late Romanticism.

Beach did what she could to counter this new climate. Asked for her opinion of jazz following the first performance of Gershwin's *Rhapsody in Blue* in New York in 1924, Beach said, "I should hardly class it among . . . influences for good." She stated that "it would be difficult to find a combination more vulgar and debasing" than the combination of the music, the lyrics, and the dances. At the same time she made a plea for music "that will inspire and strengthen," reiterating her advocacy of music as spiritual uplift.[3]

She, of course, believed that her own music constituted the strongest argument for her values and wanted her latest works made available to the public. Her contract with G. Schirmer had run out after they published the *Theme and*

Variations for Flute and String Quartet, op. 80 (1920). The death of Arthur P. Schmidt in May 1921, however, made a return to that firm a possibility. Beach had written a condolence letter to his former firm: "In the cultivation and diffusion— the creation, indeed— of American music, he has been a great force, by his interest and encouragement as well as by his good judgment and keen criticism. He will be missed in many ways, but he will be long remembered for the fine work he has done."[4] This was an appropriate appreciation for Schmidt's important role in American music but also remarkable for its impersonal tone and for what Beach did not say about her long association with Schmidt or his role in promoting her music.

Following her first productive stay at the MacDowell Colony, Beach wrote to Harry Austin, head of the firm since 1916, asking if he would be interested in seeing her new music. This resulted in a contract and the immediate acceptance of four piano works. The two "Hermit Thrush" pieces had big sales.[5] Although never again was Schmidt her exclusive publisher, the firm now became her principal one.[6]

She was invited to play and discuss her teaching pieces before the Piano Teachers Society of Boston. Earlier, her composition of teaching pieces may have been obligatory, to provide Schmidt with music that would yield a profit. Now, however, Beach was also impelled by her own agenda, that of offering children attractive artistic alternatives to jazz and other popular music.[7] Her concern is reflected as well in the several articles published in *Etude* in which, drawing on her own experience, she gives advice to serious young students of piano and composition, that the best music is a "source for spiritual growth."[8]

She had another way of expressing her concern for the musical education of children. Sometime in 1922 Beach, together with two local music teachers, established a Beach Club for children in Hillsborough.[9] The club, which met on the second floor of the Fuller Public Library, was organized under the guardianship of the women of the Hillsborough Music Club. The following year the children's club was subdivided by age into the Junior and the Juvenile Beach Clubs.

The children regularly played for one another, and when Beach came to the meetings she listened to them play and gathered them around the piano as she played for them. She shared her personal experiences with them as well— telling about her career and her wonderful husband and reporting on her tours in the United States and her trips to Europe. The children responded to her kindness and warmth and bragged about her importance as a composer. One of them wrote a letter to *Etude* that described the club and suggested that all children should "have a Beach Club, and of course they can, but there is only one Mrs. Beach and she belongs to us."[10] Sixty years later, surviving club members remembered with pleasure their trip with Beach to the MacDowell Colony, where they visited Edward MacDowell's grave and met his widow.

Beach also dedicated a suite of teaching pieces, *From Six to Twelve*, op. 119 (1927), "[t]o the Junior and Juvenile Beach Clubs of Hillsborough, N. H."[11] The pieces seem childlike in their phrasing but are complicated by chromaticism and changes of texture and register, which suggest that at least some of the young pianists in the Beach clubs had reached a level of moderate technical proficiency. The composer remained involved until the clubs disbanded in 1934.

Ever the networker, Beach welcomed opportunities to reach out to others. In recognition of her past support of the MacDowell Colony, as well as her new status as a fellow, she was elected to membership in the Allied Members of the MacDowell Colony, a group sponsored by the board that included colonists and others interested in raising money and supporting its functions. Even while Beach was most worried about her aunt, she was ready to solicit funds and new members. On 6 February 1925 Beach played music composed at the colony in a benefit recital in Boston arranged by her protégée Margaret Starr McLain.[12]

The following month, on 7 March, a second benefit took place in Washington, D. C.; an all-Beach recital, sponsored by the Washington Alumni Club of the music sorority, Mu Phi Epsilon, was given in the grand ballroom at Rauscher's restaurant.[13] The First Lady, Grace Coolidge, with whom Beach had had tea at the White House, headed the list of patrons, which also included members of the new administration and the diplomatic corps. Beach played through the entire program of her works, which comprised songs and a solo piano group that included her newly composed By the Still Waters, op. 114. The climax of the evening was the Washington premiere of the Suite for Two Pianos Founded upon Old Irish Melodies, with Mary Howe at the second piano.[14] The audience and critical reception were enthusiastic, especially for their performance of the technically dazzling suite, and the benefit to the MacDowell Colony was substantial.[15]

Beach took a number of steps to support women, both singly and in groups. Soon after signing a contract with Schmidt, she presented to the company an ultimately unavailing request that they consider publishing the music of Ethel Glenn Hier, a fellow colonist whom Beach praised as very talented, noting that she recently heard her "Prelude" for piano and found it "original" and "full of charm."[16] Among the most modern composers of the MacDowell Colony group and a former student of Alban Berg and Malipiero, Hier wrote in a style that might well have been too modern for the Schmidt company, which had recently terminated a contract with Marion Bauer for that reason.[17]

Beach found organizational means of support for her own music at the same time that she supported other women, as for example, when she joined the National League of American Pen Women, probably in 1922.[18] At the next biennial meeting of the league held in Washington, D. C., on 23–26 April 1924 at the Shoreham Hotel, Beach played her own works all through the convention; she also spoke at the authors' breakfast at which she, the popular writers Fannie Hurst and Gertrude Atherton, and the poet Edwin Markham were honored.[19]

At that meeting, a group of members formed the Composers' Unit, the first such organization of women in the United States. Its very formation was a testimony to the marginalized position of women composers and their resolve to do something about it. Beach, long acknowledged as the Dean of American

Women Composers, was unanimously elected chair. The criterion for membership in the group was modest indeed, and certainly not one that guaranteed the professionalism of its members, as these words from *Musical America*, 19 May 1924 suggest: "Anyone wishing to join . . . must be able to write her own manuscript." Nevertheless, to mark the inauguration of the Composers' Unit, two "brilliant" concerts were scheduled as part of the Pen Women's meeting on 23 and 25 April 1924.

The Pen Women also gave a concert of music by the American composers Gena Branscombe, Pearl Curran, Mary Turner Salter, Lily Strickland, Harriet Ware, and Mana Zucca, as well as Beach; performers included singers from the Monday Morning Music Club and, last, the Rubinstein Club, a choral society of Washington, gave a program on 10 March that included solo songs arranged by Beach for women's voices.

On 28 April the Composers' Unit presented the American Women Composers First Festival of Music at the Women's City Club in Washington. The program included violin and piano sonatas by Mary Howe and Gena Branscombe, works for two pianos by Ulric Cole,[20] songs by Mary Turner Salter, a piano trio by Elizabeth Merz Butterfield, and two songs with violin, cello, and piano, op. 100, by Beach. The program's emphasis on chamber music suggests that the group decided to establish themselves as composers of high art music.

Dissatisfied with the nonprofessional requirements of the Composers' Unit, several women made plans to set up a women composers' group independent of the Pen Women, to be called the Society of American Women Composers.[21] In a letter calling prospective members to an organizational meeting, Beach wrote, "this Society may come to mean much in the future of American music, if we go about the work in the right way."[22] At the meeting on 11 October 1925 at the Beethoven Association in New York, Beach was elected president, Gena Branscombe, first vice-president, and Helen Sears, second vice-president. The by-laws that the attendees drew up specify that to gain membership in the society, a composer must be proposed by a member who submits the candidate's personal and professional qualifications; then, subject to approval by a majority, the candidate is admitted by invitation of the executive board. The by-laws further provide for stringent control of activities under the new group's aegis. Together with the by-laws is a list of twenty founding members,[23] among them Marion Bauer, who may have been in France at the time to study composition.[24] She would soon be considered the most distinguished member after Beach.

During the following six years, the group gave a series of recitals in New York and Washington, many reviewed in newspapers and journals.[25] In 1928 Beach, replaced as president by Gena Branscombe, became honorary president; Mary Howe was elected first vice-president and F. Marion Ralston, second vice-president. Although the Great Depression forced the society to dissolve in 1932,[26] the group had undoubtedly, during its few years of existence, kept the music of its members in the public ear and, via reviews, the public eye.

On 23 September 1924 Beach was elected to the American Society of Composers, Authors, and Publishers, which provided quarterly payments of fees for radio and public concert performances of her music. These fees grew larger with the passage of time, eventually amounting to a substantial income and offering evidence that Beach's music had an extensive audience during her later years.[27] Also momentous was the sale of her house on Commonwealth Avenue on 27 December 1924; finally, her connection to this emblem of her former life was severed. She realized a large sum for the house as she had paid off most of the mortgage since Henry's death and was more secure financially than ever before.[28]

In 1924 Aunt Franc's increasing senility required a full-time companion, thus allowing Beach more freedom. By April 1924 she was able to fulfill postponed engagements in the Midwest, and that summer she returned to her Centerville house—probably the first time since 1911—which "did wonders" for her.[29] On 12 November 1925, Emma Frances Clement died in their home in Hillsborough, a month short of her eighty-third birthday. Thus ended Beach's seven years of attendance on two terminally ill, close relatives. Now, her second family gone, she was again alone.

Beach must have stayed in Hillsborough for the probate, which took place a week later. Aunt Franc left her niece an inheritance of $25,000.[30] Beach was now financially secure if also grief-stricken and exhausted and in need of a long rest. Even so, a mere week after Aunt Franc's death she left Hillsborough for Marion, Indiana, to fulfill concert commitments made a year earlier.[31] Following that brief tour, she remained in Hillsborough for most of the winter and spring of 1926, during which she was diligently fussed over and cared for by many townspeople.

Beach kept for herself two rooms at the Parkers' house, for which she paid a modest monthly rental year round.[32] The Parkers provided her with meals, transportation, and undoubtedly other services as well, since they were friendly and generous neighbors.[33] She continued to be active in the music and women's clubs and the Beach clubs for children, even when performances by her neighbors and their children tested her tolerance: "My smile will get a bit tired, but it will stay on, as the people and children *are* so dear. Their *intentions* are *wonderful!*"[34] She attended church services and meetings at the Benevolent Society, the local chapter of the National Federation of Music Clubs, and the state chapter of the National League of American Pen Women.

A new colleague and friend appeared in Beach's life, the mezzo-soprano Lillian Buxbaum, whose voice Beach admired and whom Beach chose to be her assisting artist in local recitals after May Goodbar moved to California in late 1923.[35] Beach was supportive of Buxbaum's career; she wrote recommendations for her, advised her on professional matters, coached her in the songs that they performed together, and dedicated a song to her, "Spirit of Mercy," op. 125, no. 1.[36] They gave their first recital together on 1 January 1924, an all-American program for the Women's City Club of Haverhill, Massachusetts. The two soon became close friends as well, visiting each other's summer homes—Beach reopened her house in Centerville the following summer—where they soon spent extended time together.[37] Later, Lillian Buxbaum's family would become Beach's adoptive family and, eventually, heir to a substantial portion of her estate.[38] The caring was reciprocal.

While Beach and Lillian Buxbaum were on a first-name basis, with Isidore Buxbaum, Beach maintained Victorian proprieties in public, calling him Mr. Buxbaum[39] and in her diaries, "Mr. B." Nevertheless, she liked the man, and expressed fondness and gratitude for his many kindnesses, including his generosity in bringing provisions from his grocery store to stock the larder at "The Pines," sometimes without charge, sometimes at cost.[40] He also made repairs and improvements in the house, doing some himself and paying for others to do them as well.[41]

DURING THE WINTER OF 1926, Amy Beach joined the Daughters of the American Revolution, proposed by members of the Hillsborough chapter.[42] In the 1920s the D.A.R., which had been apolitical, became a conservative organization increasingly allied not only to the Republican party but also to patriotic organizations like the American Legion.[43] Amy Beach was a product of her time, her region, her class, and her white Anglo-Saxon heritage — except when it came to her career. As noted elsewhere, her musical talent had led her into pathways that her family heritage and political and social conservatism might otherwise incline her to reject. But her politics remained those of the prevailing opinions in the D.A.R. and Hillsborough.

After a summer at "The Pines" in Centerville, 1 September 1926 found her at the MacDowell Colony, where she expected to spend the month working hard.[44] But she was taken ill on her birthday, necessitating a "slight" operation, and spent ten days at the Fenway Hospital in Boston.[45] She recovered in time to make a brief trip to New York for a meeting of the Society of American Women Composers on 5 November, and a rehearsal for the group's next concert, at which the two songs, op. 100, would have their premiere.[46]

Free to travel at last, she had decided to go on an eight-month tour of Europe. It would be her second European trip, very different from the first — involving no career goals, only pleasure, rest, and the restoration of her energies. On 20 November 1926, accompanied by Mary Hunt and Elizabeth Rothwick, she set sail from Boston on the SS *Martha Washington*.[47] Although she planned a "complete rest from musical work," Beach could not be without music making; thus, during the Italian portion of the trip, she played solo recitals and accompanied singers in private homes and hotel salons on several occasions. There was much concert going as well, especially during her extended stays in Rome and Rapallo. The winter in Italy, she wrote, did "wonders" for her.[48]

The French portion of her tour began on 7 April in Nice and progressed city by city until her arrival in Paris on 30 April.[49] During her six weeks there, Beach combined sight-seeing with hearing all the "fine music" she could fit in; she attended a recital by Albert Spalding and heard a "superb service" by the organist Lawrence K. Whipp, choirmaster and organist at the American Cathedral in Paris. Afterward, she chatted with him and stimulated his interest in her church music; following their meeting, she asked Schmidt to send Whipp the *Service in A*, op. 63, and three anthems at her expense.[50] As a result of her travels, her preference for France over Germany was strengthened—a marked change from her Munich days.[51] Finally, after a side trip to Belgium, on 12 July 1927 she embarked from Cherbourg toward home on the SS *Leviathan*.[52] After landing on 17 July, she took a boat to Fall River and train to West Barnstable, where she was met by Lillian Buxbaum, her son David, and the cousins Mabel Pierce and Fannie Lord, all of whom had prepared her Centerville home for her return.[53]

Beach's life settled into a new pattern: winters in Hillsborough, June or September or both at the MacDowell Colony, and summers in Centerville. She not only wanted people with her but, in Centerville especially, she needed their help. Her cousin Fannie Lord did most of the cooking, assisted by the Buxbaums when they were there; Mabel Pierce was the poor relation of the family who also helped out at The Pines and during the rest of the year did custom dressmaking for Beach and other family members. Beach did no cooking, housekeeping, or sewing. Later when Fannie Lord was no longer able to work, Beach hired housekeeper-cooks. Never having learned to drive, she had to rely for transportation on Lillian Buxbaum or other guests with cars who came in succession all summer; otherwise, she hired local people to chauffeur her and her companions around.

She reveled in the constant stream of visitors but reserved to herself the use of a one-room studio between the house and Long Pond where she went to compose, to correct proofs, and even to read. However, when she practiced piano in the big house, she was happy to have as an informal audience anyone who wished to listen, whether children or adults. Indeed, she assured them that she would not even mind if they talked during that time.[54] Now that she had resumed touring, summers were the time to prepare, and whether or not the house was full, the work had to go on.

Her solo tour of the South and Midwest in February and March of 1928 began in Burlington, North Carolina, and continued in several other cities where she played for clubs and colleges. As usual, her audiences were composed of women and their guests, most of whom came from social strata similar to her own. The high point of that trip was in Atlanta where she played three concerts, including one at Agnes Scott College in nearby Decatur, Georgia. Nan Bagby Stephens (1883–1946), who taught at Agnes Scott, may have arranged the recital there.[55] Musician, playwright, and fellow at the MacDowell Colony beginning in 1927, Stephens would later write the libretto for Beach's opera, *Cabildo*.

From Atlanta, she went north to play the piano quintet with the National Quartet in Washington, with the Lenox String Quartet in Pittsburgh, and with the Marianne Kneisel Quartet in New York, this last on a chamber music program by members of Society of American Women Composers on 22 April at Steinway Hall.[56] On 12 May Beach gave the piano quintet over radio station WJZ in New York with the Lenox String Quartet, perhaps the first of her many radio broadcasts.[57] A reviewer of the quintet who wrote approvingly of it neglected to point out that the work was twenty years old. He assumed that nothing about her style had changed in the interim: "the fresh sound and the invigorating declaration came from a composer who uses the old methods. Mrs. Beach may not be progressive as a technician, but her music is all progress."[58] Such reviews helped fix Beach in the public mind as a fine but outdated composer.

June 1928—following the usual routine—found Beach at the MacDowell Colony, where she finished sketching two commissioned works. She wrote *Benedicite, omnia opera Domini*, op. 121, for David McKay Williams and the St. Bartholomew's Choir. Based on Psalm 148, it is a festive work framed by fanfares for chorus and organ, with dramatic contrast between lush harmonies and choral unisons.[59] She at once sent a copy to Williams, whose immediate and enthusiastic response was noted by the composer.[60]

Communion Responses, op. 122, which Beach wrote as a complement to the *Service in A*, op. 63, are choral settings for the Episcopal service commissioned by Raymond Nold of the Church of St. Mary the Virgin, New York.[61] She also completed a fair copy of *The Canticle of the Sun*, op. 123, which she prepared for publication.[62] In addition, by the end of her stay she had written three piano pieces, op. 128,[63] that were descriptive of the Peterborough woods and dedicated to Marian MacDowell, and a piano solo, *Out of the Depths*, her op. 130, which was inspired by Psalm 130.

This was a substantial amount of work for a month; and it was accomplished despite an interruption for an important event in her life. Beach and Marian MacDowell, driven by the Parkers, traveled to Durham to attend ceremonies at the University of New Hampshire, which awarded them honorary master's degrees on 18 June. Edward M. Lewis, president of the university, read Beach's citation:

> Amy Marcy Cheney Beach, pianist of distinction, and the most eminent of American women composers. Your songs are classics in the repertory of the world's greatest singers, and your essays in larger forms have met with a success as complete and as unqualified.
>
> Native of the State of New Hampshire, and life long resident, the old Granite State is immensely the richer for what you have achieved and for what you are.
>
> It is with great pride therefore, that I . . . hereby confer upon you the degree of Master of Arts.[64]

Not long afterward, President Lewis called Beach to express his regret that the university had not awarded her an honorary doctorate rather than a master's degree. That, however, ended the matter.[65]

The rest of the summer was spent in Centerville. Preparations to open the house had begun in late May when Beach wrote to Mr. Johnson, her gardener, landscaper, and general helper, to start the pump—the only source of running water in the house—and arrange for the phone to be connected. Up to that time, too, the house lacked electricity; but that summer it was wired and Beach rejoiced in being able to read in the evening.

She was especially pressured that summer of 1928, since she was preparing for a second and more extended concert tour through the South. In addition, she read proofs of three sacred choruses for Schmidt.[66]

But Beach also made time for relaxation, reporting to Mabel Daniels in a letter, "It is heavenly quiet here and we are luxuriating in the daily 'swim.' No tonic helps me like that!"[67] Swimming was not only a pleasure and her only exercise but it was a religious experience as well, as Beach wrote in a note to herself: "To me there is no sensation comparable to the joy of feeling the ground go from under my feet when beginning a swim. The resting upon the waves letting them support my weight and help me to force my way along. Why can I not realize in exactly the same way the presence of God, resting upon Him as upon the water and feeling absolute confidence that I cannot sink while He holds me up?"[68]

The six-week fall tour began on 26 October when Beach left Hillsborough for Boston and then visited a dizzying succession of cities for rehearsals, recitals, and receptions. As if that were not enough, she made several side trips to visit friends and colleagues.[69] This required elaborate advance planning, constant moving, packing and unpacking, adjusting to the various pianos, indeed all the pressures of playing on tour. Yet Beach seemed to thrive on the regime — and on the many old friends she saw and new friends she made.

Her time in Atlanta was particularly notable. There, she was welcomed with a poem by Louise Barili (1880–1963), "To One Who Walks with Beauty," which was dedicated to the composer. The last three lines particularly conveyed Beach's credo:

And those who seek an uplift in the maze
Life has become, in these too strident days,
Shall find it in the presence of art!

The poem appeared in a local newspaper along with considerable advance press for Beach's programs.[70] Barili, whose "Artless Maid" Beach set in the early 1920s,[71] was a mezzo-soprano and the great-niece of the famous diva Adelina Patti; her father, Alfredo Barili, was the director of a music school and a leader of Atlanta's musical community.[72] Beach's first program on 7 November, with Barili assisting, was a substantial one. Of particular interest was her performance of the two new piano works she had written the previous June at the MacDowell Colony: the sparkling and descriptive "Humming Bird," and *Out of the Depths*. A reviewer thought that the latter was "expressive of [Edward] MacDowell's style and temperament" and praised Beach's rhythmic verve, technique, and "profundity of feeling."[73]

The Atlanta engagements also included a lecture recital for the children of the Atlanta Junior Music Club, during which Beach talked about the bird calls she had used in her music and played the two "Hermit Thrush" pieces, among others. An interview was reported in the following day's newspaper, which presented Beach as a strong advocate for teaching children music in the public schools : "Much of the callousness of youth today is due to the lack of inherent love of the beautiful which can only be had when one is taught the fundamentals of music," she said. She remarked that although jazz was popular especially for dancing, only the best music was worthy of study, a claim she backed up with Social Darwinian logic: "There are certain permanencies essential in all the arts . . . and classical music will last forever. It is always a matter of the survival of the fittest." She further singled out for praise the role of radio in promoting classical music, which she stated was ever more in demand.[74]

After a stop in Asheville, North Carolina, Beach went on to Chicago, where she capped off the strenuous trip with concerts, receptions, and banquets at which she both spoke and played.[75] Lyon and Healy, the organ and piano company, which mounted a large display of Beach's music, held a reception in her honor.[76] The Amy Neill Quartet, with Beach at the piano, played a broadcast of her piano quintet on 24 November, which she reported was a "remarkable" performance, "a positive thrill."[77] She heard two movements of her symphony played by the Women's Symphony Orchestra of Chicago and on the 26th gave a program for the Musicians Club of Women that included her piano quintet as well as violin and vocal music.[78] The reviews of all these events were "exceptionally fine."[79]

Her tour continued to Washington, D.C.,[80] and finally to New York, where on 9 December at St. Bartholomew's she heard the first performance of her new sacred choruses, *Benedicite, omnia opera Domini*, op. 121, and—most momentous—*The Canticle of the Sun*. Although complicated by preparations for sailing for Italy the next day, this was an exciting day for Beach and a milestone in the growth of an important professional friendship with David McKay Williams, organist of St. Bartholomew's, and with his soprano soloist, Ruth Shaffner.

Amy Beach had arranged to spend the winter and spring of 1928–29 in Rome. On 10 December she sailed out of the New York harbor on the SS *Saturnia*, destined for Naples, where she arrived eleven days later. With Mary Hunt and Elizabeth Rothwick, her traveling companions of three years earlier,[81] Beach took the train to Rome, where Helen Gifford, a cousin of Henry Beach, met her. Gifford's home at Via Cornelio Celso, 22, was Beach's residence for the duration of her stay in Rome.[82] She found Gifford's apartment beautiful and happily noted that it had a good piano.

Gifford, who was well established in Roman society, immediately introduced Beach into her social circle by giving a tea for one hundred people in Beach's honor.[83] Thereafter, she went to luncheons, dinners, and teas, played mah jongg (only once, for it bored her) and bridge, and began Italian lessons.[84] At many of these events she played for guests, sometimes offering entire programs.[85] The concerts that she attended almost daily included much contemporary music, which she noted in her diary with capsule reviews: she found Respighi's *Feste romane* "superbly brilliant,"[86] Lazare Saminsky's "Hebrew music" "deeply interesting"[87]— perhaps her euphemism for dull or overly complex—words she also used for Don Licinio Refice's *Trittico Francescano*.[88] A work by Prokofiev was "ultra modern but strong," and one by Malipiero "hideous,"[89] as was Hindemith's Concerto for brass and wind.[90] But she liked Bartók's *Rhapsody* for piano and orchestra.[91]

Gifford and her upperclass friends were apparently supporters of Mussolini, then at the height of his power. He had ended constitutional government in 1925. For those who wished—or were forced—to see, the events of 1928–29 had shown the hand of Fascist tyranny through brutal suppression of the opposition. That very year, when Mussolini signed the treaty with the Vatican, he fully consolidated his Fascist regime.[92] Beach became an admirer of Il Duce after she and Helen read aloud Mussolini's autobiography, which Beach declared was "wonderful."[93] Through Gifford, she even offered to play for him: he declined, however, stating that he had too many engagements.[94]

Gifford was busy on Beach's behalf in other ways as well. Through the British embassy, she arranged for Beach to give a concert to benefit the American Hospital in Rome.[95] Held on 23 March, it was one of two high points of the season for Beach.[96] Gifford had been energetic in selling tickets, and the flower-bedecked embassy was crowded and hot. Because it was for charity, there were no reviewers present; but Beach reported that the audience, among them many "diplomats and other distinguished people," was brilliant. The baritone Edwin Alonzo Bartlett had a "lovely voice and style" and "sang superbly." "The Year's at the Spring" had to be repeated. She viewed the concert as highly successful, both in terms of audience reaction and the large sum of money raised for the hospital.[97]

During this time Beach completed the *Quartet for Strings in One Movement*, op. 89. Its premiere, at a chamber music concert at the American Academy, was the high point of Beach's busy winter in Rome, a time filled with people and music, "beneficial" as well as "enjoyable" for her.[98] Beach, however, was not yet ready to return home, for she had one more mission to accomplish: a visit to Marcella Craft.

On 30 April, three weeks after the performance of her string quartet, Beach left Rome by train for Munich, where Marcella Craft met her. That evening they had supper together in Craft's old studio at Finkenstrasse 2, in the same pension where Beach had stayed during her first sojourn in Europe. Craft, who had had a busy schedule in the United States as a recitalist, sang with leading orchestras, and toured with the San Carlo Opera, nevertheless had not found a position with a major American opera company. She had returned to Munich in 1922, where she had a career as a concert singer and teacher of voice and acting to singers.[99]

Beach spent two nostalgic weeks in Munich. She revisited museums, churches, gardens, and palaces—now empty of their royal inhabitants as this was the time of the Weimar Republic.[100] Beach also found the trunk and three boxes that had been seized in 1914 and held for fifteen years in a storage warehouse in Munich.[101] In them were many souvenirs of the prewar time that she had shared with Craft; but—most important—there were several scores.[102] The visit made clear to her that Craft was living in the past; Beach, the older of the two, was the one who looked optimistically toward the future.

She left Munich by train for Bremerhaven on 13 May; the next day she boarded the SS *America*, which sailed for the United States via Southampton, Cherbourg, and Cobh, Ireland. On board, Beach heard a fellow passenger, Carrie Coleman Duke, sing "On a Hill," a spiritual Duke had learned "from her old Mammy." Beach notated it and wrote a fine, idiomatic accompaniment.[103] She dedicated the song to the singer Anna Hamlin, who was on board. Hamlin, who eventually became a leading voice teacher, was the daughter of George Hamlin, a concert and opera singer for whom Beach had written two songs — "Deine Blumen" and "Wind o' the Westland." Anna Hamlin gave a reading of the spiritual on shipboard and later sang it in concert as well.[104]

The boat docked in Hoboken on the morning of 25 May. Beach spent two hours in customs and paid forty-eight dollars in duty, for she had come back with dozens of gifts as well as many purchases for herself. That afternoon a boat of the Merchants Line brought her to Boston. She was in the Copley Square Hotel by 10 P.M.[105] on the eve of momentous changes for herself, the country, and the world.

21

A

FASCINATING

NEW YORK LIFE

IN THE FALL OF 1930 BEACH WROTE to her friend Lillian Buxbaum,

This New York life never seemed more fascinating and certainly I never felt more enthusiasm. I am having marvelous performances of my church music at St. Bartholomew's and Sunday night heard my Two-piano Suite at the MacDowell Club played by the Sutro sisters to whom it is dedicated. Next week I have to give a half hour program for the Nat[iona]l Opera Club of which I have been made Hon[orary] Vice President. Later I shall broadcast my Quintet for piano and strings and then there will be still more programs. So it goes. Meanwhile I go constantly to concerts, occasional theaters, and see friends daily, besides practicing 2 hours. Rather a full life![1]

Amy Beach's move to New York in the fall of 1930 followed a difficult year. In September of 1929 she had a gallbladder attack while at the MacDowell Colony and was operated on at Massachusetts General Hospital; later she had to return because of complications.[2] Predictably, people took care of her when she was discharged—her old friend Amy Brigham for the fall and winter, and her cousins the Wheelers in Short Hills, New Jersey, in the spring.[3] She considered moving to New York that spring but decided it was too risky, perhaps because of her health since she had not completely recovered her strength.[4] By mid-June she was at the MacDowell Colony for a very productive two weeks.[5]

During that summer at Centerville, Beach decided to take the plunge. She engaged a studio at the American Women's Association (AWA) Club House, at 353 West 57 Street in New York. She rented it for only three months, beginning 1 November,[6] which gave her the opportunity to test the waters without making a commitment. After settling in, she announced that she was ready to work.[7] With her strength regained at long last, she responded eagerly to New York's challenges and excitements.

Despite the economic crisis—ironically, perhaps because of it—this was a propitious time to move to New York. The Great Depression would soon bring a turning away from the radical avant-garde in music and toward an "American" style—in particular one based on Anglo-American folk tunes—and perhaps there would be a renewed audience for Beach's more conservative as well as her folk-based music. Government funding through the Federal Music Project, established in 1935 as part of the Works Progress Administration, helped fuel resurgent Americanism in music by supporting presentation of works by American composers.[8] In Europe, during the 1930s, interest in "authentic" American music also was at a high: Herman Neuman, the music director of radio station WNYC, who took an orchestra on a radio tour of Europe, included on his programs of American music Beach's From Blackbird Hills, op. 83, based on an Omaha melody.

As a result, the "Gaelic" Symphony, forgotten during the 1920s, made a comeback in the 1930s and 1940s. The Manhattan Symphony Orchestra's performance, conducted in 1931 by the American composer and conductor Henry Hadley,[9] was followed by women's symphony orchestras in Hollywood under Anna Priscilla Risher,[10] Boston under Alexander Thiede,[11] and Chicago under Ebba Sundstrom.[12] The New York Civic Symphony, under Eugene Plotnikoff, gave it three times with Beach as commentator;[13] the Chautauqua Orchestra played it under Stoessel;[14] and in the early 1940s the Harrisburg Symphony gave it two readings under George Raudenbusch.[15] None of those orchestras, however, were among the majors, in contrast to those orchestras that had given the symphony from 1896 to 1918.

From 1930 on, Beach's other works were frequently performed by local and national presenting groups as well as by instrumental and vocal soloists in concert and on the radio.[16] In addition, there were many given by Beach herself, among them more than ten radio broadcasts of her compositions. To these must be added the many performances of her sacred works in churches all over the country. That Beach's music had a wider public than ever before is reflected in her increasing ASCAP checks—attributable in part to being in New York.

Her new home was a studio on the eleventh floor of the twenty-four-story residence for women.[17] Four thousand women—students, business, and professional—occupied the studio apartments. For musicians, there were practice rooms on the top floor. Beach found the pianos fine; however, after the first year she was given the privilege of having a piano in her room.

On the day of her arrival she made a tour of the public rooms and signaled her approval of the parlors, the restaurant, the library, and the ballroom-cum-concert hall—all on the first three floors.[18] Men were welcomed there but prohibited from going into the studios. Beach had a special dispensation in view of her age and eminence: both male and female guests were allowed to visit her in her studio.[19]

The accommodations suited Beach's needs perfectly: a reasonably priced pied-à-terre in a central location, and providing everything, including meals.[20] She was especially intrigued by her view of the Hudson River and the Palisades and by the constant activity of ocean liners docking at the piers below. Most important, at the age of sixty-three she had finally settled in New York, the uncontested American musical metropolis.

The women's residence offered companionship and, with a few tenants, close friendship. Among the latter were Caroline B. Parker, hymnal editor for Appleton-Century[21] and communicant at St. Bartholomew's Episcopal Church;

Anna Addison Moody, poet and head of the arts department at St. Bart's Community Center;[22] and a group of young music students and professionals for whom Beach was patron and mentor. Thanks to these women and many others as well, Beach rarely ate a meal alone at the AWA.

St. Bartholomew's, on Fiftieth Street between Madison and Park avenues, was the other pole of Beach's New York life. She had always sought out brilliant preachers and found one in St. Bart's rector. Author and poet as well as minister, Robert Winkworth Norwood (1874–1932) was called there in 1925. A magnetic speaker, he had "a musical voice, unusual dramatic vividness in utterance and gesture, and the gift of putting his thoughts into flashing pictorial form. Moreover, he was one of those rare persons who possess a mystical experience . . . a man who was in touch with an invisible world."[23]

In one of his sermons, entitled "The Hiding God," he could have been describing Beach when he wrote that full dedication to both work and the people to whom one is close leads to a "clear knowledge of God."[24] Dr. Norwood's definition of human striving toward divinity, as well as his mysticism, fitted her own beliefs and way of living. As a tribute to him, Beach set three poems of his, one of which was performed with Beach at the piano as a surprise for the minister on a Sunday afternoon program on 20 November 1931.[25] The Reverend Norwood's sudden death at the age of fifty-nine, on 28 September 1932, was a loss long grieved over by Beach. His successor, George Paull Torrence Sargent, may not have been quite as inspirational, but Beach soon became his admirer and friend.

In addition to a charismatic preacher, she required a fine music program. If an organist also scheduled her music for services, then Beach would have a true home. Obviously the combination was not an easy one to find and was one of the inducements for moving to New York. Although her music had been given there for two decades, before 1931 it was attributed to "H. H. A. Beach"—a suppression of her gender—and it was only after Beach was a regular physical presence that Mrs. finally appeared before her name in the service leaflets, a belated admission that a woman could write fine music for worship.

When Hyde was desperately ill in 1920, he told Rector Leighton Parks that when he died, he wished David McKay Williams to play at his funeral, symbolically passing the torch. Tragically, on his death at the age of forty-five, his wish was granted; Williams, who resembled Hyde in that he, too, was a bachelor, darkly good-looking, and a gifted organist who also composed, was appointed to fill Hyde's place.[26] There were differences, however. Williams was more "colorful and dramatic," Hyde modest and unassuming, attributes that were reflected in their music.[27] Following Williams's appointment, the offerings of Beach's music increased severalfold despite the fact that Beach spent little time in New York in the twenties.

The year 1923 marked the beginning of her "wonderful friendship with D[avid]."[28] At that time he wrote asking her to set a text from the Palm Sunday Epistle, Let This Mind Be in You. This became her op. 105, for soprano and bass soli, mixed choir, and organ.[29] Beach, always alert to the dramatic possibilities of a text, set the verses in two contrasting sections. The opening Lento con molto espressione, for bass and soprano solos accompanied by organ, is permeated with chromaticism, its low register and dark quality setting the stage for the closing reference to "the death of the Cross." The second section, for mixed choir, anticipates the Risen Christ, with a choralelike setting, serene in its scalewise motion, with hardly a hint of chromaticism. Singing unaccompanied, the choir moves up sequentially three times, reaching its highest point on the text "To the Glory of God the Father." The effect is indeed dramatic. Due in part to Williams's many performances, it became Beach's most popular anthem. Eventually, Williams presented twenty-seven of her compositions, among them several that he commissioned. This made her virtually a composer in residence. She, in turn, could not have been more pleased with his conducting and playing.

In church, Beach habitually sat on the left side of the sanctuary and as far back as possible so that she could watch Williams at the organ.[30] She treasured every moment she spent with him, often recording in her diary the precise duration of their meeting or shared meal or evening of bridge and music. She also enjoyed contact with his organ students, who called her Aunt Amy and eventually took her music with them to their posts as organists and choirmasters.[31]

It did not take too long for Beach, in her great love for people and need for closeness, to create a surrogate family with David McKay Williams the son. Born in Wales in 1887, Williams was twenty years younger than Beach. Over the years, she mothered him, fussed over him, worried about his every health problem, even worried that he, like Hyde, would die young. In fact he lived to the age of ninety-one. Beach treated him like an adored son, although there are numerous suggestions in the diary that her feelings, at least for several years, were not entirely maternal. Indeed, her comments in her diaries and her frequent references to him in conversations with mutual acquaintances suggest an infatuation that may have had elements of fantasy.

Williams, whose primary interest was in young men, may have responded to the mothering but not wanted more than that. He avoided being alone with her, usually bringing others with him when they had appointments. She preferred otherwise, as she wrote in her diary: "D[avid] dined with me. For once alone! Such a good talk."[32] Nevertheless, Williams valued their friendship, telling Beach, when she was recovering from a serious illness, "You've meant a lot to me."[33] Ruth Shaffner, soprano soloist at the church, found it necessary to assure Williams that Beach "felt for him as her son."[34]

There is no doubt that the salient element in her relationship with Williams was music, as it was with all the people closest to her. People still talk with awe about his way of accompanying hymns, improvising illustrative accompaniments for individual verses, and his brilliant organ arrangements of orchestrations when accompanying the choir. Needless to say, nothing moved her more than David's conducting and playing of her own works, in which he specialized. For a composer, it is the most natural reaction to love the person who not only loves your music but also recreates it with artistry and commitment. For Beach, in the words of her song "Ariette," music and feeling were one. Unfortunately for her, this was not true for David, who was being asked for more than he could or would give. The imbalances in their relationship, particularly regarding their ages and gender preferences, rendered her need for more attention from Williams, as expressed in diaries and letters, inappropriate and unrealistic.

Ruth Shaffner was the second member of Beach's surrogate family and, along with Lillian Buxbaum, a second "daughter." Soprano soloist at St. Bart's, Shaffner became a devoted friend and musical collaborator. One of their earliest joint programs—the half-hour program for the National Opera Club mentioned above—took place on 11 December 1930 just after Beach settled in New York. Eight years later Beach noted that they had given over two hundred joint recitals.[35]

Shaffner's performances called forth letters of appreciation from Beach for her interpretations and for the beauty of her voice, a dramatic soprano of Wagnerian proportions. Among the many letters Shaffner saved was one written following a performance of Handel's *Messiah*, in January 1931, at St. Bart's. Beach wrote to her, "Dearest Ruth. . . . I have *never* heard either you or anyone else in my life give a more angelic bit of singing than was yours yesterday."[36] Hard pressed to top this praise, Beach wrote again following a rehearsal of her *Canticle of the Sun*, "No angel in heaven could have sung that *Canticle solo* [doubly underlined] as you did!"[37]

Shaffner (1897–1981), who grew up in Los Angeles, began as a piano accompanist and organist.[38] A voice scholarship brought her to the Juilliard Graduate School (1925–30), where she studied with Anna Schoen-René, who also trained Risë Stevens, Paul Robeson, and other famous singers.[39] Under her tutelage, Shaffner, a tall blond woman of generous proportions, developed into a dramatic soprano of power, extended range, sympathy, and warmth, who "would have made a great Brunnhilde."[40] Williams, then on the faculty at Juilliard, hired Shaffner as a soloist for St. Bart's soon after she entered the conservatory. She continued there for ten years, at the same time teaching voice in her New York studio. Like Williams, Shaffner had a volatile personality—up one day, down the next. Beach was the most stable of the three. Both Shaffner and Williams reacted like adult children to Beach's maternal feelings, Shaffner by her nurturance and protectiveness toward Beach, Williams by a simultaneous attraction to and withdrawal from their relationship.

Shaffner was somewhat jealous of Beach's relationship to Lillian Buxbaum and did not want her place in Beach's life taken by anyone else.[41] Because they were geographically separated, Buxbaum shared Beach's personal and musical life in New England, Shaffner in New York. The quality of the relationships differed because Buxbaum was a part-time musician who enfolded Beach into her family circle, while Shaffner, who had been married very briefly and then divorced, was a totally committed professional.[42]

Toward the end of April 1931, Lillian Buxbaum joined Beach in a program broadcast by WEEI in Boston. Afterward, in a letter to Shaffner, Beach described Buxbaum's voice, "a mezzo with contralto coloring," and noted that "some of her phrases were simply luscious."[43] But it was hard for her to hear anyone, even Buxbaum, sing songs that she had come to associate with Shaffner, "especially just now when my heart is so torn to pieces at the prospect of a long summer without you—and David—and the church—and all the lovely winter life there. I am clinging to the thought of November."[43]

Beach agreed to attend the orchestral performance of *The Canticle of the Sun* given by Albert Stoessel at the Worcester Festival. Although disappointed that Shaffner would not be the soprano soloist, she looked forward to her first hearing of the work with her orchestration.[44] There would be other compensations, including the mezzo-soprano Rose Bampton, who, two years later, would make her Metropolitan Opera debut as Laura in *La Gioconda*.

A reporter who interviewed her in advance had trouble associating "the eminent woman pianist and composer" with the "little lady in black lace who chats very rapidly and punctuates her remarks with delighted little gurgles";[45] but Beach was not interested in setting up the imposing distance affected by celebrities. After the performance, however, a reviewer had no such problem, calling the *Canticle* "one of the highlights of the Festival," the orchestration "most effective and well-balanced," and the festival choir brilliant.[46] Contrary to her expectations, Beach was "thrilled."[47]

The following year, Beach and Shaffner went to Washington for the biennial meeting of the National League of American Pen Women, 22–28 April 1932.[48] Beach joined in a performance of the piano quintet, accompanied Shaffner and played solo at several events; she also heard a good performance of *The Canticle of the Sun* with Shaffner as the soprano soloist at the Mount Vernon Methodist Episcopal Church. Social events included Beach's visit at the White House with First Lady Lou Henry Hoover.

The most memorable collaborations between Beach and Shaffner took place in Washington in 1934 and 1936. The first was part of a celebration by the National League of American Pen Women of the fiftieth anniversary of Beach's debut, her "Golden Jubilee."[49] Beach's music was performed, and she was guest of honor at entertainments and official meetings. The high point, however, came with a musicale at the White House.

On 23 April 1934, with a recently installed administration and a First Lady who was a member of the Pen Women,[50] Beach and Shaffner took part in a command performance in the East Room of the White House that had been arranged by Phyllis Fergus Hoyt, chair of music programs for the biennial convention of the Pen Women. Hoyt had written to Mrs. Roosevelt that "[t]he Dean of American Women Composers, the outstanding musician for the last fifty years, Mrs. H. H. A. Beach, is attending this convention, and I . . . would like so much to have the honor fall to our beloved member of appearing at the White House for the First Lady! . . . She is older and we cherish the time she comes to us."[51]

During the half hour program at the White House, Shaffner sang four songs and Beach played "Young Birches" and "Scherzino: A Peterborough Chipmunk" from her descriptive *Three Pianoforte Pieces*, op. 128.[52] Four hundred guests stood "gladly" in the East Room to hear the program.[53] The next day Beach wrote a warm thanks to Eleanor Roosevelt, stating that the event was "one of the most beautiful experiences" of her life.[54] Beach noted the strong resemblance between Eleanor Roosevelt and her aunt, Corinne Roosevelt Robinson, whose son-in-law was distantly related to Henry Beach.[55] She concluded her letter by offering to play for the First Lady some pieces that Robinson loved. Despite her lifelong Republican commitment, Beach preserved and displayed in her studio the autographed photos of President and Mrs. Roosevelt commemorating her "command performance."

On 17 April 1936, the members of the league were again guests at the White House, where Eleanor Roosevelt greeted Beach warmly.[56] Shaffner sang "The Year's at the Spring," after which Beach reminisced about the MacDowell Colony—for which she was always in search of new support. She then played the three pieces of op. 128, two of which she had played at the previous White House concert.[57]

On occasion, to escape New York and get some rest, Shaffner would drive Beach out to Coney Island, Brooklyn, for an overnight stay at the Half Moon Hotel, where they would walk on the boardwalk, and watch the ocean.[58] In addition, the singer often brought Beach to her vacation home in Patterson, New York, or drove up to the Cape to spend time there with Beach, usually late in the summer after the Buxbaums had left.

Shaffner was a member of the P.E.O., a nonacademic sorority that supported higher education for girls and which owned and administered Cottey Junior College in Nevada, Missouri. On 2 February 1935, Beach joined the New York chapter, thus acquiring another avenue for helping younger women. Beach and Shaffner—joined by Virginia Duffey (later Pleasants), a pianist and organist who also became a member, and Eugenie Limberg (later Dengel), violinist and violist—frequently gave short programs for the chapter. They soon became famous throughout the organization, both through their performances at conventions and later as a result of Beach's contribution of the *Ballad of the P. E. O.*, the official song of the sorority. Beach's last composition, the Ballad is a thoroughly singable *pièce d'occasion* that was written during the summer of 1944.[59]

Beach called Limberg and Duffey "the children"; they constituted the third generation of Beach's "family." They were her favorites among a group of young musicians who lived at the AWA and for whom she served as patron and mentor. In fall 1933, as a result of a recommendation from the Juilliard Graduate School, Limberg brought Duffey with her to play at a Young People's Service at St. Bartholomew's. Shaffner heard them play and recommended Limberg for future events at St. Bart's, at the same time hiring Duffey to be her studio accompanist.

Eugenie Limberg, a native of Austin, Texas, studied at the Busch Conservatory, the Cincinnati Conservatory, and the Juilliard School—the last, on full scholarship. Her violin teacher at Juilliard was Louis Persinger, who had been the first violinist of the Chamber Music Society of San Francisco when it gave the world premiere of Beach's *Theme and Variations for Flute and String Quartet*. Virginia Duffey also came to New York from Cincinnati, having graduated from the college there. The two young musicians met at the Three Arts Club, a residence that they found uncomfortable and lacking sound-proof practice rooms.

Shaffner suggested that they "come over and meet Aunt Amy—everybody calls her Aunt Amy," because she became concerned about the bad conditions and hoped that Beach could help them out. In response Beach persuaded the manager of the AWA to hire them to "play little concerts four nights a week for the ladies who lived there." In exchange the two students were offered room and board, much pleasanter living arrangements, and better practice rooms.[60]

The two became advocates of Beach's music, in which Beach coached them. At a program given 24 January 1934 by the Music Committee of the American Women's Association, Beach was joined by Limberg, Shaffner, George Rasely —the tenor soloist at St. Bartholomew's—and Duffey as accompanist in a varied program that opened with a prelude by Mary Howe and closed with a group of Beach's works. The AWA's ballroom was crowded with eight hundred people; Beach's solo playing brought down the house.[61] This may have been the first program that the "children" and Beach gave together.

Limberg and Duffey soon added other of Beach's works for violin and piano to their repertory; their first performance of the Violin Sonata prompted Beach to write to Limberg praising her interpretation, glorious tone, and mastery of a difficult work.[62] As the original AWA duo of Limberg and Duffey expanded to a trio, then a quartet, and finally a quintet, they included other chamber works by Beach.[63]

Beach was generous with the "kittens," as she also called them—she said she was the "old cat"—both in New York and in Centerville: not only were they her guests for several days at a time but she made their visits possible by paying their round-trip train fare. In Centerville, they swam in Long Pond at the foot of Beach's property, accompanied the composer on her outings to the ice cream store and to nearby restaurants for shore dinners, and daily—as weather permitted—they swam in the surf at Craigville Beach. According to Eugenie Dengel, Beach was a surprisingly strong swimmer, so buoyant that she "bobbed like a cork."[64]

As noted earlier, the "children" were not the end of Beach's family. In addition to her "nephews," Beach had a number of "nieces"—the members of the Society of American Women Composers. All of them were younger and were instructed by Beach to call her Aunt Amy. For them she served as advocate, role model, pathfinder. The composer Mabel Wheeler Daniels had a relationship to her that went back to the Boston days. Daniels had preceded her at the Mac-Dowell Colony by several years: she was one of the earliest colonists, having stayed there for the first time in 1914. They had shared the platform at the American Composer's Concert at the Panama-Pacific International Exposition in San Francisco in the summer of 1915. Beach maintained a somewhat wary relationship to Daniels, whom she occasionally found prickly and combative. Nevertheless they were on cordial terms.

In addition to arranging for Beach to play at the White House, some of her "nieces" celebrated her Golden Jubilee as a performer during the week of 11 October 1934 at the Century of Progress Exposition in Chicago, the second such celebration that year. On the first day there was a D.A.R. luncheon in honor of both Beach and Carrie Jacobs-Bond arranged by Phyllis Fergus Hoyt.

That day, the National League of American Pen Women awarded Beach a medal for her work in music, and she played an informal recital with assisting artists.

A dinner in Beach's honor for some two hundred guests was followed by a second concert by the Women's Symphony conducted by Ebba Sundstrom, concluding the day's events with Radie Britain's *Heroic Poem*, Florence Gala-jikian's prize-winning *Intermezzo*, Chaminade's *Concertstueck*, and Beach's "Gaelic" Symphony. The rest of the week continued at a similar hectic pace with luncheons, receptions, teas, dinners, recitals, opera, concerts, many given in Beach's honor. By the end of the week, Beach had to cancel all but one of the recitals she had scheduled to follow the exposition, surely from total exhaustion.[65]

This was Beach's last extended concert tour; thereafter she played single concerts out of town, most of them close to home base, whether in New York, Boston, Hillsborough, the MacDowell Colony, or Centerville. At sixty-seven, she had finally begun to slow down.

22

BEACH

THE

MODERNIST?

BEACH A MODERNIST? HOW CAN THAT BE? No discussion of her as a composer has ever judged her anything but a Victorian, a late Romantic composer and, during her later years, an anachronism in a new age. What has been almost universally ignored has been the adventurousness of some of Beach's music written during her last decades, at a time of life when creative artists are expected instead to become more conservative. It is ironic that, while exploring modernism's less extreme aspects in her music, she rejected the new music in her discourse. Perhaps nowhere in her life and work has the conflict between her Victorian mores and her musical practice been more clearly defined.

Her words about music, which had considerable currency, expressed her conservative ideology. Beach believed that many avant-garde works reflected — "perhaps unconsciously," she wrote — "the actual restlessness and chaos" of the times; and she suggested that it was inevitable that music mirror society in this way. She rejected this role for music, however, instead reaffirming the meliorist approach of the pre-1914 era: "The true mission of music is to uplift. . . . [B]eyond the earthly lies the spiritual world. To me, the greatest function of all creative art is to bring even a little of the eternal into the temporal life." In other words, the more chaotic and war-torn the world, the greater the need for music that can "elevate our mental state and help to instill courage."[1] For Beach this was not escapism but an expression both of her religious faith and her view of music's mission, the two inextricably interwoven.

Commenting on the aridity of concert music "of a purely intellectual nature, often of deep interest as problems . . . but never for a moment touching our emotions," she asked: "In order to be considered 'modern,' in other words, alive, must we . . . rule out the great inspiring force of emotion, and cling exclusively to the intellectual?" Her answer: "Surely we may be allowed to reach out in both directions — the intellectual and the emotional — in our efforts to express what is, after all the inexpressible."[2]

In addition to intellectualism, Beach objected to extreme dissonance. In 1935 she gave a paper at a conference of the Music Teachers National Association in Philadelphia. Entitled "A Plea for Mercy," the article begins with a reference to entire programs she had recently heard that were "devoted to music illustrating the complete possibilities of the piano as an instrument of percussion. . . . [attacked] with a maximum of force and rapidity that suggested a Gatling gun." Her plea for mercy was not for her own sensitive ears or those of others but for the sensitive hands of the performers. She addressed herself to "those of us who still associate [the piano] with true sentiment and deep emotional significance . . . and who still consider it worthwhile to try for real beauty of tone, with our bare hands." Although she never identifies the music that provoked this reaction, she does name performances she admires especially for beautiful tone, among them Ossip Gabrilowitsch's playing of slow movements by Beethoven and Chopin.[3]

This, of course, was a not-so-subtle attack on modernism in music, exemplified perhaps by Bartók's *Allegro barbaro* (1911),[4] Copland's *Piano Variations* (1930), or Henry Cowell's piano pieces that call for clusters of notes held down by fists or forearms, the earliest being *The Tides of Maunaunaun* (1912).[5] Women, however, were not among those committing that sin: "The lady-pianists are honorably conspicuous by their absence from my list" of offenders, Beach wrote. Nor, she implied, did they write music that was an assault on the listening ear. If we need proof that she understood the way gender had come to define the schism that had split the music world apart in the 1920s, it is in that statement.[6]

Her observations contrasting men's with women's practices have great resonance, since with the exception of a few composers—notably Ruth Crawford Seeger and her student Vivian Fine, Marion Bauer, and Beach's colleague Ethel Glenn Hier—women tended to reject much of modern music, while men of the new music movement rejected anything that was redolent of the parlor, of sentiment, of music as moral uplift. Indeed, as Catherine Parsons Smith has asserted in "A Distinguishing Virility," in the 1920s and early 1930s, many male composers chose the intellectual and the harsh to simultaneously establish their musical "virility" and lock women out.

An overview of Beach's late works points up the contrast between ideology and practice. In her credo, published in 1942, she states that "the use of unceasing dissonance" is destructive, tearing down rather than building up the social fabric.[7] Yet her later works contain more and more dissonance, even to the point of emancipating them from the tonal imperative of resolution. Or again, consider Beach's simultaneous rejection of Malipiero's string quartet and appropriation of some of its procedures in composing her own quartet. Consciously or unconsciously, Beach absorbed elements of the new music, applying them to her more adventurous pieces, her ears leading her in directions that contradicted her discourse. Again, despite ideology, she wished to be considered a contemporary composer by her peers and urged performance of her late rather than her early works.[8]

Her first modernizing experiments followed well behind those of European colleagues. Her earliest composition in French modern style came in 1914 with *The Lotos Isles*, composed during her stay in Munich: having an ocean between herself and Boston may have had its liberating aspects. Her experiments with dissonant nontonal harmonies began in 1921 with the first draft of the string quartet, a watershed composition in which she first normalized dissonance.

In her expressionist music, Beach worked in a twentieth-century style situated between late Romanticism and twelve-tone serialism. Here, too, Beach was slightly behind the times: works by others in this style are mainly from the first quarter of the twentieth century. Her interest was aroused in 1912, however, by a performance of Richard Strauss's *Salome*. Her reaction was intense (previously noted, but significant enough to repeat here): "Orchestrally it is a glowing mass of beautiful color, like a rich tapestry or stained glass window. The weaving of the motives, with the transcendent beauty of the modulations, was overwhelming."[9] This proto-expressionist opera is marked by "discontinuous textures and large melodic leaps," and "extreme, prolonged, and unresolved dissonance" as well as chromaticism, "tone clusters . . . whole-tone scales . . . purposefully distorted declamation" and otherwise daring innovations.[10]

Her *Canticle of the Sun*, op. 123, composed in 1924, exhibits many characteristics of expressionism. In it, she reverses harmonic function, making dissonance the norm, with consonance reserved for moments of high drama. The work's distortions, especially her use of diminished and augmented intervals, are found in both vocal and choral declamations and vertical collections of pitches.

Her last published work and only composition originally written for solo organ, the *Prelude on an Old Folk Tune (The Fair Hills of Eiré, O)* (1942), is a setting of the Irish melody she had used for the piano piece *The Fair Hills of Éiré, O!*, op. 91. She recomposed it, giving it a second distinctly un-folklike—often highly chromatic—harmonization. In this work, Beach deliberately misuses harmonic language by dislocating the harmonies so that they produce sharp dissonances on strong beats, with resolutions in one voice that come at the same time as the other contrapuntal voice is sounding another dissonance. Thus, while the writing is perfectly logical according to voice-leading principles, the piece has a great tension produced not only by persistent dissonance but also by the conflict between the lilting folk melody and its disturbing harmonization (ex. 22.1). She completed it on or before 21 September 1942, a few days after she began, renaming the piece to distinguish it from the piano composition on the same tune.[11]

Such Wagnerian destabilizing elements as chromaticism and frequent, occasionally breathtaking modulations to remote keys are important in *Hearken Unto Me*, op. 139 (1934), a dramatic setting of texts from Isaiah.[12] On the other hand, the long mounting climax driven by pulsating triplets in the organ, beginning with the line "They that wait upon the Lord," is a retrospective feature that recalls "The Year's at the Spring" in its urgency.

In several late works Beach begins in one key and ends in another, a feature associated with a number of nineteenth- and twentieth-century compositions that use tonality for expressive rather than structural purposes.[13] That places Beach among the many composers—Schubert, Schumann, Chopin, Wolf, Wagner, Brahms, Strauss, and Mahler—who used "directional" or "progressive

EXAMPLE 22.1 *Prelude on an Old Folk Tune (The Fair Hills of Eire, O!)*, mm. 5–8 (H. W. Gray, 1942; used by permission of Warner Brothers Music Corporation).

tonality" to suggest transcendence or "a sudden change of direction in the flow of the narrative, or . . . a definitive change of mood."[14]

In one sense the use of progressive tonality weakens the tonic and thus attacks the tonal system. But the practice affirms the power of tonality to evoke a sense of place—an eventual movement to a distantly related key can send a potent message of change. Where Beach uses progressive tonality, the associated text usually begins with conflict or suffering but ends with transcendence or movement from the earthly to the heavenly spheres. The first such instance is in an otherwise conservative work, Beach's "Lord of the Worlds Above," op. 109 (1925). The text contrasts God's earthly and heavenly temples, descriptions of the latter sung to the tune of the Lutheran hymn "A Mighty Fortress is Our God." Each two-part verse is in a new key, as if to describe the progress from earth to heaven: it begins in the "violet" key of D♭ major, moves to F major, then to F♯ major, and finally to the bright and triumphant D major.[15]

A further example of progressive tonality occurs in a secular work, Beach's controversial 1936 revision of the *Variations on Balkan Themes*, op. 60, of 1906, for piano solo. The original version begins and ends in C♯ minor and has an extensive and virtuosic cadenza. In her revision, she made several changes that helped make the music more current: she eliminated repeats, believing that people no longer needed so much repetition,[16] and—of greater importance—

cut the cadenza with its audience-grabbing brilliance. Most significantly, rather than ending in the original key of C♯, she transposed the last section, consisting of the extended *Marcia funerale* and a shortened coda, into E♭ minor. These changes emphasize the tragic messages of the associated folk-song texts. In her two-piano versions of 1937 and 1942, Beach retains the progressive tonality she introduced in the revision of 1936.[17]

Beach's use of progressive tonality was conscious and deliberate, and exhibits an awareness of its use by composers before her. Indeed, Brahms's *Schicksalslied*, given at the 1931 Worcester Festival, which she attended in order to hear her *Canticle of the Sun* with orchestra, would have reminded her of that tradition had she forgotten it.[18] Her use of progressive tonality also has its source in her perfect pitch and acute reaction to keys, many of which from her early childhood she associated with specific colors—and perhaps with the seasons, with emotional states, or even with specific locales or states of mind. The practice is also an extension of modulations found within her otherwise tonal pieces, employed not to strengthen the tonic through explorations of the most closely related keys but for expressive, often dramatic, ends.

Some late works display other means of destabilizing tonality. *Christ in the Universe*, Beach's op. 132 (1931), is second only to *The Canticle of the Sun* in its length, its vocal challenges, and its Wagnerian harmonies. Whereas much of the anthem faces the late-Romantic past, the opening recitative is forward-looking. Beach composed out an unpublished piano solo, "A September Forest," to create this anthem.[19] In its opening line, "With this ambiguous earth," she used the initial phrase of the piano work, with its tonal ambiguity and distorted gestures, to illustrate the Crucifixion.[20] Melodic and harmonic materials are drawn from the whole-tone and chromatic scales and a variety of seventh chords (ex. 22.2). The theme, which in the anthem is announced unaccompanied by the contralto soloist, is heard after the opening recitative and then taken up by the chorus. Only at the end of the following instrumental interlude is A major, the tonic of the piece, clarified. This feature is found in several of Beach's tonal pieces, where harmonic ambiguity may be resolved only at the end of a section or an entire piece.[21]

Some of Beach's pieces verge on atonality. The first of a set of three pieces for the piano, "Scherzino: A Peterborough Chipmunk," op. 128, no. 1 (1932), has a distinctly modern sound that is created in the beginning by a series of arpeggiated seventh chords that are without tonal implication (ex. 22.3). Elements of tonal harmony in the B section are combined with destabilizing chromatic progressions. At the close Beach returns briefly to the music of the nontonal opening before ending in G major. The piece also has a transparent texture typical of several late works beginning with the quartet.

In a letter to Marion Ralston, Beach wrote that the *Five Improvisations*, op. 148 (1938)[22] were "really improvised" and each one is a vignette that "seemed to come from a different source."[23] She claimed that the second, a bittersweet waltz, recalled events of "many years ago [when she] sat with friends in an out-door garden outside Vienna and heard Strauss waltzes played." A memento of "the old sweet life 'over there,'" Beach described it to Jeanne Behrend as a

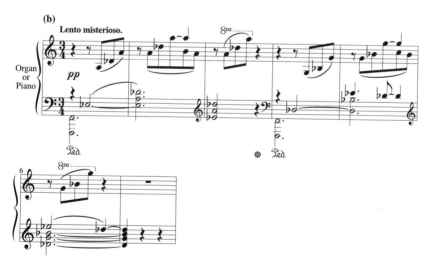

EXAMPLE 22.2 (a) "A September Forest," holograph, mm. 1–8. (University of New Hampshire, Durham) (b) *Christ in the Universe*, op. 132, mm. 1–7 (H. W. Gray, 1931; used by permission of Warner Brothers Music Corporation).

EXAMPLE 22.3 "Scherzino: A Peterborough Chipmunk," op. 128, no. 1, mm. 1–6 (Theodore Presser, 1932; used by permission).

"little, tender old Viennese slow waltz . . . sad beyond words for it represents so much happy life and recreation gone out of the world.[24] Unfortunately, this was the only one of the set for which Beach identified the recalled event and locale. The fourth, marked *Molto lento e tranquillo*, may evoke the peace and quiet of the woods at the MacDowell Colony, where Beach wrote down these improvisations. The fifth, *Largo maestoso*, is in a mazurka rhythm that is made distant by the slow tempo.

The third improvisation, marked *Allegro con delicatezza* and in G major, features parallel fourths, spikey rhythms, and overlapping harmonies that create strong clashes. The piece recalls textures and dissonant harmonies Beach used in *From Blackbird Hills*, op. 83 (1922). The fragmentary melodic line and drone fifths suggest Native American music as the inspiration. In this composition Beach may have taken her cue from the new style that came to maturity in her string quartet.

The first of the op. 148 set, *Lento molto tranquillo, A Major*, may be the most advanced piece Beach wrote. Both lyrical and dissonant, it might well have been an homage to Brahms: Beach's treatment recalls the texture and rhythm of his "Intermezzo," op. 119, no. 1 (ex. 22.4a). She translated it, however, to a dissonant and partially atonal idiom. In the A section (mm. 1–14) the falling arpeggios outline a collection of notes drawn from whole-tone scales, while the outer voices trace a series of expanding and contracting chromatic wedges with no suggestion of a key center (ex. 22.4b). In the B section, however, Beach flirts briefly with the key of A minor, yet ends up suggesting F♯. After a return to the atonal A section, the piece finally arrives at a cadence in the key promised by the title, *Lento, molto tranquillo, A Major*, although a key signature is lacking.[25]

EXAMPLE 22.4 (a) Johannes Brahms, "Intermezzo," op. 119, no. 1, mm. 1–8. (b) Beach, *Five Improvisations*, no. 1, mm. 1–8 (Composers Press, 1938; used by permission).

THIS OVERVIEW OF BEACH'S LATE WORKS reveals a range of styles, her choices depending not only on the text but also on the intended performers and audience. Occasionally she uses a variety of styles within one work, as noted above with regard to *Christ in the Universe* and other works.

Two late, large-scale works display that eclecticism. Beach wrote in her diary on 2 June 1938, the day she began work on the Trio, op. 150, for piano, violin, and violoncello, "Trying a trio from old material. Great fun." Her pleasure in making do with old material grew out of both her Yankee thrift and her awareness that materials written earlier had further developmental possibilities. Beach incorporates in this one work, French modern, late Romantic, and folk elements, perhaps guided by narrative concerns.

She composed the trio at the MacDowell Colony in fifteen days, completing it on 18 June 1938.[26] While the work is eclectic, it is also distinctly tonal. In the first movement, the Debussyan rising arpeggiated figures in the piano recall Beach's "Morning Glories," op. 97, no. 1. The cello plays a sustained first theme against these figurations. The second theme is a development of the first and is introduced by the violin against the same accompaniment. At the repetition of the theme, the accompaniment changes to slower moving arpeggios, evoking the style of a Romantic waltz. These two ideas and styles are explored in the development section. In the recapitulation, the opening figuration returns to accompany the theme and both reappear in the closing measures in A major.

For the second movement, *Lento espressivo*, Beach returns to the form she created in the "Gaelic" Symphony, presenting a scherzo section in duple meter embedded between lyrical outer sections. Her source for the outer sections is her song of 1897, the dramatic "Allein" (Alone), op. 35, no. 2 (see ex. 13.2). Beach's reworking of the song shows surprisingly little change from her original setting (ex. 22.5). There is, however, an increased level of dissonance and chromaticism, as well as a floating tonality in several places before the tonic, F♯ minor, is reestablished. An inconclusive ending leads to the central scherzo.

The scherzo section of the second movement could not stand in starker contrast to its opening. Marked *Presto*, it is based on Beach's own setting of the Inuit song "The Returning Hunter," found under the same title in her piano suite, *Eskimos*. "The Returning Hunter" filled Beach's prescription for a scherzo theme—the Inuit tune is harmonically uncomplicated, light in texture and, most important, in duple meter. In this Presto section, Beach keeps the texture transparent, but begins with a feint toward G♯ minor before settling temporarily in F♯ major. The transition from the opening section to the scherzo is simply a long pause; the retransition in F♯ minor, however, covers thirty-four measures during which motifs from the folk song gradually evolve into the opening theme of the art song. The movement closes with a brief coda based on "The Returning Hunter."

Beach may also have found inspiration for the third and final movement in the same collection of Inuit melodies, perhaps basing her first theme on the fragments of the "Song of a Padlimio" (ex. 22.6a).[27] Most of the elements of the theme—the succession of melodic thirds, the syncopated rhythm, and the final leap of a fifth—come from the bracketed measures in the song. Beach's theme, introduced by the strings and set against an ostinato pattern in the piano's bass, hews closely to the character of the Inuit song (ex. 22.6b). So also does her syncopated continuation of the theme.

Marked *meno mosso*, a second, lyrical theme is heard beginning at m. 44 in the upper notes of the left hand of the piano, and soon repeated by the violin (ex. 22.6c). After a brief section in which the first theme is developed, a *maestoso* version of the second theme, introduced by the piano, provides the cli-

EXAMPLE 22.5 Trio for Piano, Violin, and Violoncello, op. 150, II, mm. 1–8 (Composers Press, 1939; used by permission).

(a)

(b)

(c)

EXAMPLE 22.6 (a) "Song of a Padlimio." Beach, Trio, III: (b) mm. 5–8; (c) mm. 43–47, melody is in left hand.

max of the movement, which then closes with a coda based on the first theme. The themes, though very different, are nevertheless based on the interval of a third—open in the first theme but filled in for the second, thus emphasizing its *espressivo* character. In this manner, Beach knits together three disparate styles in her last major work—the last—in which she quotes Native American melodies.

Her most ambitious work of the 1930s, however, was a one-act chamber opera, *Cabildo*, op. 149, written between 1 and 18 June 1932 during a stay at the MacDowell Colony.[28] Beach had been talking about writing an opera for many years but claimed that she put it off because of the pressures of concert life and the lack of a suitable libretto. In 1915, she recommended as a libretto "picturesque moments in our history," such as "the old New York legends of Rip Van Winkle and Ichabod Crane"—"really American" subjects.[29] By 1932, her ethnocentric bias had undergone a sea change, for she found a libretto that mixed history and fantasy in a story that drew on both the Creole roots of New Orleans culture and the romantic, yet violent, aura surrounding the notorious pirate Pierre Lafitte. The librettist was Nan Bagby Stephens, a successful novelist and playwright as well as trained musician whom Beach met at the MacDowell Colony.[30] Stephens based the libretto on her play of the same name, given in New Orleans in 1926 at the Little Theater on Jackson Square directly opposite the Cabildo itself (a combined governor's palace and jail), now a museum.[31] Her story, set in New Orleans, concerns a cross-class relationship between a French aristocrat and an outlaw pirate; the latter, however, is based on an historic figure who was ostracized by polite New Orleans society, yet assisted General Andrew Jackson in lifting the siege of the city during the War of 1812.

The cast consists of the Barker (a speaking part), tourists (mixed chorus), two more tourists—the newlyweds Tom (tenor) and Mary (mezzo)—Pierre Lafitte (baritone), the Gaoler (bass), Dominique You (tenor), and Lady Valerie (soprano). A piano trio provides the instrumental accompaniment. A play within a play, the opera opens in the present with a guided tour of the Cabildo. The Barker, or tour guide, tells a group of tourists, as they stand in the very cell where Pierre had been imprisoned, the story of the pirate's incarceration and mysterious escape.[32] The Barker recounts the fictional love story of Pierre and Valerie: they met at the governor's ball in New Orleans and fell in love. As a token of their love, Valerie gave Pierre her bracelet. She was soon ordered back to France by her father, who had found a more suitable spouse for his aristocratic daughter. Her ship, Lafitte's frigate, the Falcon, was attacked by some of Lafitte's men turned traitor. The Falcon sank and Valerie drowned.

Mary's romantic imagination is captured by the Barker's story of Pierre and Valerie. As the other tourists and then Tom leave the cell to see the rest of the Cabildo, she remains behind, falls asleep, and dreams an explanation of Pierre's escape from the Cabildo. In the dream scene that follows, Dominique You, a lieutenant of the Lafittes, visits Pierre in prison. Pierre asks Dominique repeatedly for "news"; and finally but reluctantly, he tells Pierre that the ship sank and Lady Valerie drowned. The Governor, who had seized the bracelet as a means of framing Pierre, accused the pirate of stealing it and ordering the sinking to cover his theft; he sentenced Pierre to be executed. As Dominique leaves the cell, he slips Pierre the bracelet, which he surreptitiously had taken from the Governor's desk.

Pierre, alone, laments Valerie's death and sings of his love for her. Soon the ghost of Lady Valerie appears to comfort him. She tells of the drowning, and Pierre vows that he will pay for her death with his own. Valerie argues against

EXAMPLE 22.7 (a) *Cabildo*, op. 149, Overture, mm. 1–4. (b) "Mouché Mazireau." (c) Beach, *Cabildo*, Overture, mm. 47–51.

this, urging him to accept General Andrew Jackson's offer of clemency in return for fighting the British. They declare their love in a passionate and extended duet, the climax of the opera. She convinces Pierre to escape and fight alongside General Jackson. Before disappearing, she unlocks the cell door through which he escapes. The brief final scene returns to the present: Mary, awakening, assures Tom that her dream was real. The opera ends as the two celebrate the power of love, their own and that of Pierre and Valerie.

The libretto has two problems. The first is that the story is told twice: first in the opening scene, in which it is presented as past history, and again, in the dream scene, in which the story is enacted and is the dramatic crux of the opera. But because the action is a presented as dream rather than reality, the audience is asked to suspend not merely one but two levels of disbelief. Andrew Porter noted the weaknesses of the libretto in a review of a recent performance but nevertheless found the music "fluent and tuneful," carrying the drama forward.[33]

Beach, faced with a new genre and a fanciful tale, settled on a combination of folk songs for local color, one of her own art songs to provide the emotional climax, and a style that ranged from folk idioms to expressionism, especially in her use of distorted declamation. Wagnerian influence is apparent in Beach's ample use of leitmotifs and of continuous recitative.

Beach's compositional challenge in the opera was to mediate between the harmonically simple black Creole melodies she quoted, and her highly expressive post-Romantic compositional style, hardly a new problem for the composer. As a result of her study of the musical characteristics of the folk repertory, she was prepared to write in that idiom.[34] In the overture, Beach seamlessly combines her own folklike melodies with quotations from a Creole song, "Mouché Mazireau," harmonizing both with primary chords and an occasional chromatic inflection (ex. 22.7a-c).[35] Soon after the Barker enters with the tourists, however, chromaticism and dissonance escalate—particularly in the recitatives—as the story turns dramatic.

(b)

Mouché Ma-zi - reau dan sou- vié bi - reau le sem- blé cra - peaud dans niou baye do   lo

(c)

EXAMPLE 22.7 (continued)

Similar distortions are heard in music derived from Creole folk melodies. Beach quotes them at appropriate moments: as instrumental background to the speaker, as sung recitative, as choral interjections, occasionally as arioso, infrequently to accompany brief set pieces for soloists or chorus, and especially as recurring motives. As an example, "Belle Layotte" (ex. 22.8a) is heard in the accompaniment when Pierre the pirate is mentioned, as distinct from Pierre ennobled by love.[36] The folk-song text says, in translation, "I have sailed along the shore; there is none like my belle Layotte." At this point the chorus picks up the rhythm but not the melody of "Belle Layotte." A few measures later the tune is heard, but it is distorted by chromatic intervals and dissonant harmonizations (ex. 22.8b).

In the dream scene, when the Gaoler brings Dominique to see Pierre, "Mouché Mazireau" is again heard; its original words mock the Governor, "who sits in his old office like a bullfrog in a pail of water."[37] The Gaoler, after receiving a bribe from Pierre's lieutenant, Dominique You, sings "When I was on a highway," a translation of the Creole song "Quan' mo 'te d'un grand chimin," about a beggar who cadges "a pinch of snuff, a bandanna, and cognac sweet." This is the only direct and unchanged quotation of a folk song in the opera.[38] "Belle Layotte" is again invoked in the dream sequence—but in a distorted version—as Pierre blames himself for Valerie's drowning.[39]

There are several set pieces in the opera in addition to the Gaoler's, some of them folk-based, some original. "Caroline," for example, provides the melody for the only set piece for mixed chorus (mm. 324 ff.). An original duet for Tom and Mary that is reminiscent of a Gilbert and Sullivan patter song closes the first scene as they sing "Together, together, no matter what the weather"

EXAMPLE 22.8 (a) "Belle Layotte" (b) Beach, *Cabildo*, holograph, mm. 183–97 (University of Missouri Library, Kansas City).

EXAMPLE 22.9 *Cabildo* (a) mm. 365–73; (b) mm. 1034–39.

(mm. 413–27). The effect is ironic: no sooner do they finish the duet than they part, Mary to remain in Pierre's cell and Tom to see the Cabildo's model ship exhibit.

Initial presentations of fragments of these folk songs are usually in folk style. But as Beach composes them out, they become more and more distorted and harmonically complex, with the introduction of tritones and other dissonant intervals, chromaticism, floating tonality, and distant modulations—in other words, elements noted above as typically expressionist. Thus Beach bridges the stylistic gap between borrowed folk tune and original music.

Not all the leitmotifs are from folk songs. The first few notes of Beach's art song "When Soul is Joined to Soul," op. 62, are sounded whenever Valerie's name is mentioned, often in a remote key, as if simultaneously invoking her image and her distance (ex. 22.9a; see ex. 13.4). A leitmotif original to the opera, a series of rising three-note phrases, is the music for Pierre's escape. Beach again uses that motive to segue into a heroic *Alla marcia* when the narrative describes Pierre's decision to join the fight to save New Orleans (m. 265 ff.). The

EXAMPLE 22.9 (continued)

same heroic phrase is heard several times thereafter when a patriotic defense of
New Orleans is mentioned. Thus there are three styles for Pierre—as the pirate, when folk-songs are invoked; as "a very prince of a pirate" ennobled by
his love for Valerie, when art music is heard; and as the defender of New Orleans, when the martial music is introduced. Pierre has two set pieces in art-
song style—the first, "She is like a flower" (mm. 768 ff.); and the second, the
love duet with Valerie, based on Beach's song *When Soul Is Joined to Soul*, op. 62,
but with a new text, beginning "Ah love is a jasmine vine" (m. 994 ff.).[40] Its
soaring lines and ecstatic quality provide the climax of the dream scene and of
the opera as a whole (ex. 22.9b).

Beach uses tonality to separate the contemporary from the dream scenes.
The key of G major and its closely related keys are used in the outer scenes,
while keys with many flats, especially D♭ and G♭, are for the dream scene. As
a result, a piece that begins and ends in G major reaches its climax in the
dream scene in the key of G♭ which is, not coincidentally, the original key of
the art song. Furthermore, a specific musical style may be associated with a
character's social class. Simpler or lower-class characters are represented by
folk or folklike music, while more complex and upper-class characters are depicted by music in art-song style. Both these practices have precedents found
in Mozart operas.[41]

Cabildo was premiered on 27 February 1945 in the Pound Auditorium of the

University of Georgia in Athens by a cast of faculty and students, only two months after Beach's death. The conductor was Hugh Hodgson, whom Stephens recommended to Beach in 1940.[42] The delay was caused in part by wartime restrictions on travel and Hodgson's unavailing hope that Beach would be able to attend. With Beach's approval, Hodgson expanded the accompanying ensemble to sixteen, including viola, double-bass, and French horn. The extra parts have been lost.[43]

After a hiatus of nearly forty years, there have been at least five recent productions. The most recent, at Lincoln Center on 13 May 1995—staged with costumes and lighting but without scenery—proved the viability of the opera even as it demonstrated Beach's wit and vitality.[44]

Estimates of Beach as a composer must take into account not only her pre-1910 compositions but those from her later life as well. Neither her public statements nor her lingering image as a Victorian should obscure the musical changes in style to which her musical gifts led her.

23

RECKONINGS

BEACH'S COMPLEX LIFE REQUIRED prodigies of organization. Every winter was spent in New York. At the end of April, she returned her piano to the Steinway Company and emptied her room of all her belongings in anticipation of giving it up for the next six months (thus saving on rent), and packed trunks to send variously to Hillsborough, the MacDowell Colony, and Centerville. Although she occasionally traveled by train, many moves were made in Ruth Shaffner's or Lillian Buxbaum's car—or sometimes those of others—all of which had to be arranged in advance. The early part of May she spent in a hotel in Boston seeing doctors and dentists, her investment advisers, her cousin Mabel Pierce who made and repaired her clothes, and her friends the Buxbaums, Amy Brigham, cousin Helen Gifford, and others. The Boston connection was important to her and Boston did not forget her either.[1]

The balance of May she spent in Hillsborough; June, at the MacDowell Colony. Before leaving for Centerville, she arranged for Lillian Buxbaum to transport not only herself but her two cousins. It also was necessary to arrange for the Morris Steinert Company to deliver a piano to "The Pines." The moves of the late spring were reversed in the fall, with an occasional return to the MacDowell Colony, then to Hillsborough, back to Boston, and finally to New York. In advance of that last move, a piano had to be sent to her new room at AWA. As her health waned, others were increasingly involved in preparing for her arrivals and departures both in New York and in Centerville. Along with personal effects, each time she also had to move whatever music she might need in the coming months as well as a practice keyboard and clothes for performance.

These were only the beginnings of her travels. During the year there were recital tours, trips to see friends and relatives, vacations, and trips to Europe. Each location had its social pleasures and responsibilities. All told, this was a strenuous regime for a woman during her sixties and early seventies. Beach certainly satisfied her love of travel. Indeed, she seemed to have spent the second half of her life compensating for the confinement of the first half.

In 1935 Beach's New York "family" had a serious crisis which shook Williams, Shaffner, and Beach to the core. On 21 September 1935, Beach, who was in Boston, received letters from both Williams and Shaffner, which reported that the organist had given the singer notice that she was to leave at the end of the church season, on 1 May, and that there was "heartbreak on both sides."[2] Beach at once wrote to both and spent a sleepless night worrying about them. Williams later explained to Beach that "he could not fight any longer against so much criticism."[3]

Caught in the middle, Beach decided to be supportive of both but also was aware that the one who needed the most emotional support was Ruth Shaffner.[4] She immediately invited her to Boston, where they had long talks, at times "heart-breaking."[5] The season promised to be a painful one for all because Shaffner remained soprano soloist until May, with many services to sing and shared church and social events to attend along with David Williams. Repercussions of the disruption of the "family" reverberated throughout the season, with Shaffner often depressed, occasionally tearful, at times even out of control. Williams, almost as upset, was looking for acceptance by Beach of his decision. Nevertheless, being disciplined professionals, all three carried through with their work, functioning at the usual high level. The season ended on 26 April, with the first hearing of Beach's anthem, O Lord God of Israel, op. 141, dedicated to Williams. Beach reported that it went well, including Shaffner's climactic soprano solo. Afterward Williams, Shaffner, and Beach had a difficult lunch together. Beach commented in her diary, "Kept things going as well as possible."[6] Their long hard year at St. Bart's was about over. To tide Shaffner over a difficult transition following the church season's end, Beach had invited the singer to accompany her on a trip to England.[7] Not only that, but Beach paid for her passage, a generous gesture of recognition that Shaffner's economic future was uncertain and that Beach cared about her.

It is amazing that Beach managed to see as much as she did on the trip, considering that she suffered from both arthritis and foot trouble. They left on 8 May, sailing on the SS American Farmer at 4 P.M., and spent the first week in London.[8] At the end of the week they attended communion service at St. Paul's Cathedral, where they heard a "great boy choir." Kneeling on a stone step was a painful experience for Beach, who had to be helped down and up.

On the 25th they left London by car, with Shaffner at the wheel, and headed for Stratford-upon-Avon. From there they went south to Wells Cathedral in Somerset and made stops in towns along the coast of Devon. By the time they reached Winchester in Hampshire, Beach's feet just about gave out, and she occasionally had to wait in the car while Ruth walked the stone floors of cathedrals. But throughout, she reveled in the landscapes, the flowers, the ancient and history-laden buildings, the charming villages, and awe-inspiring coastline.

Back in London, Beach enjoyed the exhibits at the Victoria and Albert Museum, which she saw from a wheelchair. But she managed to get to a performance of the Mikado at Sadler's Wells that evening and to three short plays of Noel Coward the next, before sailing for home. Later, Beach declared that the trip gave them both the very rest they needed! On their return, it became clear that Shaffner had not forgiven Williams, nor would she. Rather, over the next years she teetered between anger and forgiveness even after her appointment as head of the Vocal Department at the Drew Seminary, as Beach noted with pleasure in her diary, on her "own terms."[9]

Beach's 1936–37 season began badly. Hardly had she been at the MacDowell Colony a week when she was taken to the Peterborough Hospital for still another operation. The condition required a two-week stay in the hospital followed by several months of rest and recuperation.[10] On her return to New York escorted by a nurse, friends were more than usually attentive: there was much phoning and visiting, her room filled up with flowers, there was more frequent sending of chauffeurs to drive her to engagements or simply take her out for rides, along with the usual invitations for luncheons and dinners. She was able to do some desk work but not play. Nevertheless, she listened to the radio and attended the usual round of concerts and church services, hearing several of her own works. Finally on 14 March 1937, Beach was ready to play a half hour program on W2XR (later WQXR) including songs, violin pieces, and perhaps a piano solo.[11] This was her only performance that spring.

On 4 March, Beach had sent a wire to Arthur Foote for his eighty-fourth birthday.[12] He wrote to her,

> You and I have seen many extraordinary changes (I won't say "developments" a word that fits Wagner, for instance, but hardly Hindemith e.g.) while I remember so well the evening you first played with the orchestra in the old Music Hall. Those were good days indeed—in fact the time from 1880 to 1900 was a golden time.[13]

Proud of Beach's record and envious that she was still composing while he felt quite written out, he singled out for praise her "Scottish Legend," which he found charming and played to everyone. He died the following month, the latest to go of the group of Boston composers that had included Paine and MacDowell. Chadwick and Clara Rogers had died in 1931, and Arthur Whiting in 1936.[14] Three women—Hopekirk, who would outlive Beach by a year; Lang, who lived to an amazing hundred and four; and Beach herself—were the survivors.

At the colony for the month of June, Beach revised and rearranged a number of works. The most demanding was the preparation of a two-piano arrangement of the *Variations on Balkan Themes*, op. 60, based on her 1936 revision, for which she also wrote a new variation and incorporated one written in c. 1906 for the orchestral version, never performed.[15] In addition there were daily sittings for fellow colonist Bashka Paeff, who in New York on 6 April had begun working in clay on a bust of Beach.[16] At the end of the month at the MacDowell Colony, Ruth Shaffner arrived to take Beach to the house in Centerville. On 5 September 1937 Beach quietly celebrated her seventieth birthday with Fannie Lord, Mabel Pierce, and her housekeeper, Mrs. Cheney.[17]

Arriving at MacDowell Colony in mid-September, she finished making a cello arrangement of "Dreaming"—the piano solo from *Sketches*, op. 15, no. 3;[18] corrected proofs of the two-piano version of the Balkan Variations;[19] wrote out the *Five Improvisations* for piano, op. 148; and a new anthem, *Lord of All Being*, op. 146, on a poem by Oliver Wendell Holmes, dedicating it to David Williams.[20] As ever, her dedications reflected her major preoccupation, the church and its staff: all told, four works are dedicated to Ruth Shaffner, two to David Williams, and one each to the Reverend Norwood, to Anna Addison Moody, and to St. Bart's itself in commemoration of its 100th anniversary.

By the end of 1937 she was back in stride after a long recuperation. The most important event of the new year was a concert in Boston in honor of Nadia Boulanger. The leading music teacher of the twentieth century, Boulanger was making her second trip to the United States, where she would be the first woman to conduct the Boston Symphony Orchestra.[21] The Musical Guild of Boston, with an impressive list of patrons, among them leading musicians and socialites, gave a luncheon at the Hotel Vendôme on 22 February at which both Beach and Boulanger were guests of honor. Beach noted in her diary that many in attendance were old friends of hers.

This was followed the next evening by a program also at the Vendôme at which Boulanger was guest of honor and Beach was guest artist. The first half featured music by Mozart, Duparc, Saint-Saëns, Elgar, and the song *Reflets* by Nadia Boulanger's gifted younger sister, Lili, who had died at the age of twenty-five. The second half consisted of compositions by Beach, played by Beach and sung by the lyric soprano Pearl Bates Morton[22] and by Lillian Buxbaum. Beach chose late works for herself and Morton and placed her two most famous songs at the end, where Lillian Buxbaum and Beach brought the concert to an exciting finish. She wrote of the event: "Songs by Morton (only fair) and Lillian (superb). I gave 6 pieces. Great enthusiasm. Lovely flowers. Reception. Met many friends. A great ovation."[23] This was an historic occasion when the illustrious teacher heard the music of the dean of American women composers. Boulanger's reaction is not known, however.

Beach and Amy Brigham were scheduled to sail for France on 2 March 1938 with Paris their destination and rest Beach's intention.[24] However, a fire in the ship's lounge caused a cancellation of what would have been her last trip to Europe.[25] In its stead, Shaffner arranged for a two-week vacation for Beach at the Haddon Hall Hotel in Atlantic City, which she thoroughly enjoyed.

She had been invited by the Composers' Forum-Laboratory to share a program on 20 April with the composer, conductor, and flautist Otto Luening (1900–1996), who was then the chairman of the Music Department at Bennington College. Luening's music was eclectic, modern without being entirely tonal or atonal, with "the juxtaposition of styles an essential forming principle"; his first electronic composition was not written until 1953.[26] Sponsored by the Federal Music Project of the Works Progress Administration, the Composers' Forum-Laboratory regularly offered concerts of American music followed by post-concert discussions in which composers and the audience participated. Its director, Ashley Pettis, a writer on music and a left-winger, had a fair-minded policy of presenting American composers of all stripes, "old and young, academic and 'modern,' ultra-dissonant and ultra-consonant, famous and obscure composers ranging from Mrs. H. H. A. Beach to David Diamond."[27]

On the first half of the program were Luening's third quartet and a group of songs. Beach's half opened with three songs sung by Louise Taylor, which were followed by a solo piano group that offered a range from the folk-inspired, through impressionist, to dissonant works. The *Theme and Variations for Flute and String Quartet*, op. 80, played—beautifully, according to Beach—by Carleton Sprague Smith, flautist, and the Oxford String Quartet, concluded the program. In a letter of thanks to Pettis, there are echoes of Beach's staunch Republicanism: "In the conversations held with you and the others in authority I have learned much about the workings of the project of which I had previously a very dim conception. It seems to me a very remarkable development . . . in the furtherance of musical culture in America, as well as keeping many musicians at work."[28]

Much of Beach's time at the colony in June was devoted to the composition of her Trio, op. 150, for piano, violin, and cello, her last major work, which has been discussed in chapter 22. After completing it on 17 June, she spent two days copying and practicing the work; and on 21 June she played both the Trio and her *Improvisations*, op. 148, for Haubiel, who accepted them for publication by his Composers Press.[29] Beach immediately gave him the *Improvisations* but withheld the Trio for tryouts in performance and final revisions.[30] A composer and fellow colonist, Haubiel ran the press as a cooperative venture in which composers and press shared costs equally, an arrangement that made publication possible under Depression conditions.[31]

After her summer at Centerville, on 21 September 1938 Beach left with the Buxbaums, experiencing a trip that just skirted disaster. On the way to the Buxbaum home in Newton Centre, they encountered high winds, which escalated into the destructive hurricane of 1938. "We drove up from [Centerville], arriving just *five* minutes before the big trees fell across our roads and chimneys from neighboring houses!"[32] Electricity went out, and the noise of trees falling was terrifying. Roads were impassable. Beach, who also was worried about the effects of the storm on the MacDowell Colony and on the Parkers' house in Hillsborough, had no choice but to remain at the Buxbaums' until the roads were cleared.[33]

Finally, she made her way to the colony, where she was appalled at the destruction. The storm had cut a swath through the woodlands, felling an enormous number of trees, and damaging two studios.[34] The cleanup of the land was costly and time-consuming, leaving the colony with a large deficit.[35] Marian MacDowell, then eighty-one and seemingly fragile, swung into action; she "begged, borrowed and bought the power saws she needed, bossed the gangs of lumberjacks she gathered from somewhere and, with her directors a little breathless behind her, raised the forty thousand dollars that the devastation exacted."[36] Beach, of course, was one of the contributors to the fund, giving her own money and exhorting others to do the same. Even a year after the colony reopened, Beach made a plea in the *Musical Courier* for contributions in the name of the hermit thrush that once sang outside her studio.[37]

In New York for the fall season, politics and world affairs engaged Beach. She rejoiced over the many Republican victories in the 1938 election and approved heartily of Neville Chamberlain's address from London on 9 November 1938, in which he justified the Munich appeasement after the Nazis took

Czechoslovakia.[38] Yet hers was the first signature on a letter of 3 January 1939 from the Musicians Committee to Aid Spanish Democracy, which urged the recipient, in this case Serge Rachmaninoff, to join in a campaign to have the United States lift the arms embargo against the Republicans in Spain. The other signatories on the letterhead constituted a roll-call of leading musicians.[39] On 30 January 1939 she heard Hitler's Berlin speech and commented that it contained "nothing definite except snarling."[40] The world was on the brink of war, yet the signposts for her seemed, confusingly, to point in all directions.

In December 1938 Beach was invited to the High School of Music and Art in Manhattan, one of the pet projects of New York's mayor, Fiorello H. LaGuardia. The school, then in its second year, provided basic training for many of the city's gifted music professionals. Beach visited classes, played for the students, and talked to them about the MacDowell Colony. For the students, she was the cause of some amazement, because they did not know that there were any women composers and her appearance did not match their image of a composer in any way.[41]

The first performance of the new Trio took place at the MacDowell Club in New York on 15 January 1939 on a program sponsored by the National Association of American Composers and Conductors (NAACC). The players were Eugenie Limberg, violin, Phyllis Kraeuter, cello, with Beach at the piano.[42] Beach also introduced her *Five Improvisations*, op. 148, on 12 March 1939 at a concert of the NAACC.[43]

On 16 March at a festive occasion attended by friends and colleagues, Bashka Paeff unveiled her plaster bust of Beach in her studio in Carnegie Hall. Beach also was heard on two radio programs that spring,[44] and on 6 April talked about the colony and played a program for the Piano Teachers Convention held at Steinway Hall. On 22 April Shaffner gave a choral program at Carmel High School, at which Beach played several works, and Shaffner's chorus of girls sang the premiere of Beach's rousing march, *We Who Sing Have Walked in Glory*.

Shortly after, at the end of April, Beach fell ill with a respiratory infection, an attack that was a harbinger of more serious health problems to come. She hardly had time to recover before she was notified on 9 May of the death of Fannie Lord. Beach managed to make the trip to Boston to attend the funeral on 12 May. This was the first loss from the company of regulars at her Centerville home.

That summer, Beach went early to "The Pines" as the MacDowell Colony was closed. Her most important task, with two performances of the Trio behind her, was to enter final changes in the work and send it off to Haubiel's Composers Press.[45]

War moved ever closer, and Beach followed the momentous happenings on the radio. England and France finally abandoned the appeasement stance defended the previous year by Chamberlain. On 3 September 1939 the two countries declared war following Hitler's invasion of Poland, while the United States maintained its official neutrality.

The World's Fair had opened in New York on 30 April 1939 with an ambitious music program planned, including symphonic music at the fair's music hall and sacred choral music to be given in the Temple of Religion.[46] These plans were very soon canceled as a result of a shortage of funds. More modest plans were implemented. On 26 October a pre-recorded half-hour program of Beach's vocal music was broadcast on station WNYC as a World's Fair offering sponsored by the Composers Forum-Laboratory of the Works Progress Administration.[47] Beach, who planned the program, was not involved in the recording and was disappointed with the result. Finding the performances not very good, she nevertheless wrote a letter to Pettis the following day thanking those responsible. This was the sixth world's fair at which her music was played.

In 1940 a study long in preparation finally materialized—Burnet C. Tuthill's article on Beach in the *Musical Quarterly*.[48] Beach had first heard from Tuthill, a composer and conductor (1888–1982), in 1924 when he was compiling an annotated catalogue of American chamber music for the National Federation of Music Clubs.[49] At that time, Beach had given him a copy of her *Theme and Variations for Flute and String Quartet*, op. 80, the Sonata in A Minor for Piano and Violin, op. 34, and the Piano Quintet, op. 67. He wrote to Beach again in 1937, stating that he was preparing an article on the composer and her music, and asked for biographical data and a catalogue of her works.[50] This would be his third article on American composers for the *Musical Quarterly*—the previous ones were on Leo Sowerby and Howard Hanson—and the only article about Beach to appear in a scholarly journal before 1973.[51]

Because Tuthill both rose above and yet reflected attitudes about music prevalent in the late thirties, his evaluations of Beach's music are significant. He identifies Beach as part of the New England group and notes the pervasive German influence, but he also believes that the works of all the New England composers "took on an American flavor" because of their common background.[52] Tuthill went further, recommending that their works be revived:

> [A] few champions of American music have, under the leadership of Howard Hanson, recently taken it up out of historical rather than strictly musical considerations, only to find more real value in this sincere if stylized type of expression than they had expected. With the growing interest in native music, the works of this whole school of composers will find a definite place in the repertory because of the sureness of their construction, the warmth of their melodies and harmonies, and the convincing directness of their appeal.[53]

He concluded his introduction by suggesting that "it might not be at all a bad idea for the several organizations of contemporary writers, most of whose product is extreme and without immediate public appeal, to turn to this spurned style of music for guidance in working towards their own goal of a wider recognition for American music in general."[54] It is unfortunate that only in the twilight of the modernist movement and with the emergence of a neo-Romantic period has a reevaluation of the music of the Second New England School finally begun. Tuthill's opinions were time-bound, reflecting anti-Romantic attitudes current at the time. Nevertheless, his article was a serious attempt to come to grips with Beach's work and in many ways sympathetic.

This alone made it all but unique at a time when most critics and male composers dismissed music by the Second New England School as old-fashioned and derivative—and music by women, in particular, as having little value.

The season of 1939–40 offered the usual mix of venues for Beach's music, with St. Bart's and other local churches at the top of the list. Her secular music was given as well: in December on WNYC, Virginia Duffey, Eugenie Limberg, and an unnamed cellist played the Trio and Beach herself played *Five Improvisations* as well as "Young Birches," op. 128, no. 2.[55] In March, Beach traveled to Boston to attend a concert of the Women's Symphony of Boston, conducted by Alexander Thiede. Although they gave the "Gaelic" Symphony with cuts of which she did not approve, otherwise Beach found the performance "brilliant."[56]

She returned to New York in time to rehearse the Trio with violinist Carl Tollefsen and cellist Willem Durieux for a concert in Brooklyn on 19 March at the Neighborhood Club. Beach reported that the work went well and there was much applause, but she complained that a photographic session was "tedious."[57] Undoubtedly her energy was diminishing, a more frequent occurrence during the past two years.

Soon after the Brooklyn recital, on 22 March, Beach became seriously ill. "I was stricken suddenly with terrific bronchitis," she wrote, "and for weeks fought for breath as well as life."[58] She was diagnosed as having a severe heart condition, which, although seeming to improve slightly, would be permanent for her remaining years. The Brooklyn recital was, in fact, her last performance. Afterward, she was forbidden to play the piano altogether. She was forced to turn down, with immeasurable regret, MacDowell's invitation to spend June at the colony.[59]

By 8 May, however, Beach was able to attend a signal event in her honor, a testimonial dinner at the Town Hall Club. Two hundred people came, from Washington, Boston, and places in between. In her tribute to Beach, Marian MacDowell recalled remarks of the late poet Edwin Arlington Robinson, "that June [at the MacDowell Colony] would not be complete without Mrs. Beach's unfailing interest in and encouragement to young artists who might be there—in fact of her understanding and help to all the workers at the Colony."[60] Dr. Sargent, Rector of St. Bartholomew's, spoke of Beach's major contribution to the spiritual life of the parish through her music and her person. The organist and composer, T. Tertius Noble, who was ill and could not attend, sent a letter praising Beach's compositions, of which he singled out the *Canticle of the Sun* for special appreciation.

Olga Samaroff-Stokowski sounded a strong feminist note, emphasizing that, according to an unsigned report, "women were handicapped in music as well as in other fields." The pianist credited Beach with giving her hope, despite the persistent economic discrimination she encountered as a woman artist. She concluded by asserting that "Mrs. Beach . . . had not faltered in courage and had become a great composer thus setting an example to other women in music."[61]

Beach's response touched on the need for art to counteract the gloom that had descended on the world:

The world picture is not one of harmony tonight, but an occasion like this, where you have met together to do honor in the cause of Art, is playing its bright counterpoint against the darkness across the seas. It is well that this should be. We need these bright spots. It is through such light that we solve our problems—so very difficult at this time.[62]

A program of Beach's works, including her *Romance* and the *Trio*, was performed by Virginia Duffey, Eugenie Limberg, and Phyllis Kraeuter. The contralto Saida Knox, accompanied by David McKay Williams, sang one of her most affecting songs, "Ah, Love, but a Day."[63] This event marked the end of an exciting, productive, and gratifying decade of creative work and widespread performances of Beach's music; it was a fitting tribute to that person and that life.

Whatever others may have thought, Beach herself did not view the May testimonial dinner as a retirement event. Indeed, in the following years she would turn down all invitations to public ceremonies that marked her personal retirement; perhaps she feared the physical and emotional strain—or that they would simultaneously "retire" her compositions.

The decade that began with her move to New York in 1930 was marked at midpoint by the trauma of David Williams's announcement that he was firing Shaffner in 1935 and closed in 1940 with Beach's heart attack and the testimonial dinner. By now Beach was thoroughly superstitious about the power of years divisible by five.[64] She was painfully aware that the year 1940 also marked the end of her musical career.

HARVEST

TIME

ONLY WITH GREAT RELUCTANCE DID Amy Beach admit that her performing life was at an end. In June 1941 she declared, "I have taken no formal farewell from public performances, nor do I intend to do so. But I face the fact that I shall never again be strong enough for it."[1]

There were very real limitations on her existence. She was not allowed to play the piano, and much of the time she had no energy for composition. Nevertheless, in the next four years, she would write several short pieces: the hymn "Prayer for Peace," the sacred chorus for women's voices *Pax nobiscum*, an anthem for the P.E.O., the piece for organ *Prelude on an Old Folk Tune*, and the song *Though I Take the Wings of Morning*, op. 152. The last, a folklike setting of a devotional poem by Robert Nelson Spencer, Episcopal bishop of Missouri, is dedicated to Ruth Shaffner. During these years, also, she turned an earlier draft for flute, cello, and piano into the woodwind quintet *Pastorale*, op. 151; made a few new editions of earlier works; and revised the two-piano version of the *Balkan Variations*. Not a bad record for someone seriously ill.

In the spring of 1941, she apparently felt well enough to visit Hillsborough, where she saw "friends who had eagerly awaited [her] coming for three years."[2] Thereafter at the colony, for what turned out to be her final stay, she reported in a letter to Ruth Shaffner, "I have loved working again."[3] But soon a weak spell kept her confined at the Eaves, unable to work. Shaffner rescued her and drove her to Centerville as planned. Although later that summer she rallied, there were no more visits to Boston, to Hillsborough, or to the MacDowell Colony; following doctor's orders, her life was divided only between New York and Centerville.

What made the last few years of her life more than bearable—indeed joyful—were the many friends who visited with her, joined her for lunch or dinner, for concerts and theater, or just to talk, a social schedule that continued the pattern established long before. It was a rare day when she was alone.

Practical concerns of living were also taken care of. For years, her cousins Mabel Pierce and Fannie Lord had run the house at the Cape in summer. After Fannie Lord fell ill and subsequently died, Mabel Pierce was joined by a hired housekeeper.[4] Moves between Centerville and New York were stressful, but there were always other women who took care of them. Friends packed for her, met her with wheelchairs, readied her quarters for her, and saw to the unpacking—did everything but wrap her in cotton wool. Once settled in New York, everything she needed was provided by the AWA.

In 1942 the American Women's Association moved from the old address on Fifty-seventh Street to the Hotel Barclay, at Forty-eighth Street and Lexington Avenue, only two blocks from St. Bartholomew's. Beach decided to move with the AWA even though rentals would be higher in the new hotel. For her, the added convenience of being close to St. Bartholomew's would mean that with minimal expenditure of energy she could get to as many events at the church as her health and the weather allowed.

Ruth Shaffner, in these last years, spent most of her holidays with Beach. The diary entry for Christmas eve, 1942, describes one made festive by an evening at the theater:

> Good ASCAP check.[5] Ruth took me to The Skin of Our Teeth, Thornton Wilder. Beautifully given. Remarkable play even for him. Theater packed. He is now Captain. Home by 5:30. Ruth dined here. Opened my gifts with her. Lovely evening. She left about 8:30.

Beach must have written an admiring note to Wilder immediately after the performance, for three days later a reply came from the playwright, her friend and fellow colonist at the MacDowell. He wrote of his gratitude for her reassurances of the play's value and effectiveness and for the pleasure of her company. At that time, Wilder was in the armed forces and stationed in California.[6]

On Christmas day, 1942, Beach brought Ruth Shaffner and David Williams together, hoping that the breach between them was finally healed. Although Beach reported that after seven years the hard feelings had softened and that Ruth was now comfortable in David's company, making Christmas a "[w]onderfully happy day," these observations may have been wishful thinking on her part.[7]

There were many performances of her works in the 1940s, most frequently of The Canticle of the Sun, the anthem Let This Mind Be in You, the Trio, and Song of Liberty, op. 49. This last, written during the First World War, had renewed popularity during the second one.

A high point of these last years was the festival in honor of her seventy-fifth birthday held in Washington, D.C., at the Phillips Gallery on 27–28 November 1942. The organizer was Elena de Sayn, violinist and music critic for the Evening Star, a supporter of American and women's music.[8] Earlier she had made history by playing the first recital of American violin works, which took place in Washington, D.C., on 4 December 1931. Included were compositions by John Powell, A. Walter Kramer, and Beach, with the composers accompanying their own works.[9] Therefore, when de Sayn suggested a festival to celebrate Beach's diamond anniversary, she was well known to Beach, who admired her interpretation of the Violin Sonata, and respected her as a diligent and careful organizer.

For the festival, de Sayn planned the programs in consultation with Beach and secured the musicians. De Sayn also lined up sponsors, headed by the violinist Leonora Jackson (Mrs. W. Duncan McKim) and including the music sorority Mu Phi Epsilon, the District of Columbia Federation of Music Clubs, and the League of American Pen Women. Among the patrons were the Czech minister Hurban and his wife, the composer Mary Howe, and Gertrude Clark Whittall, who donated a set of Stradivarius instruments to the Library of Congress.[10] De Sayn, who had secured the hall at the Phillips Gallery, also arranged for a display there of Bashka Paeff's plaster bust of Beach.[11] During the planning stages of the festival, the number of programs was increased to two, thus accommodating nearly all of Beach's chamber works. In addition to the festival, several other events—an all-Beach program given by Washington's Friday Morning Music Club on 27 November and the singing of the anthem Let This Mind Be in You by the choir of the Covenant-First Presbyterian Church during morning service on 29 November—made this a Beach week in Washington.

In part because both de Sayn and her friend Alice Eversman reviewed music for the *Washington Evening Star*, advance press coverage approached blitz proportions. Paid announcements were overshadowed by feature articles, each stressing different aspects of the event, the works, the performers, the patrons and sponsors, and Beach herself. De Sayn took care of ticket sales ($1.65 for one concert, $3 for the two) since the gallery donated its space for the concerts. Beach, impressed by the amount of hard work de Sayn had put into the festival, was, of course, mightily pleased. Although she would have given much to be able to attend, she told de Sayn that such a trip was beyond her strength.

Reviews were generally excellent. Following the first concert, Glenn Dillard Gunn viewed the sonata as well written and "a fine example of Nineteenth Century romanticism."[12] Ray C. B. Brown called it "a melodious and grateful work charged with poesy and exalted emotional feeling." He vividly recalled hearing the first performance of the *Theme and Variations for Flute and Strings* in San Francisco in 1916, and now, on second hearing, he found it "a work of imagination in content and of ingenuity in structure, a rather elegiac theme being treated in moods of nostalgic meditation, gayety [sic], romantic sentiment and humor. The alternation of moods has a charming effect, as the theme is varied to the purposes of extended reverie."[13] Alice Eversman, writing in the *Evening Star*, thought the flute quintet "one of her loveliest works from both the standpoint of melody and inventiveness."[14]

On the second program the String Quartet, still in manuscript more than a decade since its completion, came in for especial praise by both Brown and Gunn. The former called it "a beautiful work in both form and content,"[15] while the latter declared the work "of such unusual beauty that an early repetition was ardently desired by all" and recommended that, along with the piano quintet, it be done on the Library of Congress chamber music series.[16]

Beach, who complained that she had never heard a fine performance of the quartet, might have found this one to her satisfaction had she attended. Indeed, this may have been the one and only first-rate performance of the quartet given during her lifetime. The claim that this was the world premiere of the quartet needs qualification. As noted earlier, the work had a number of private or semiprivate presentations, with few if any reviews until this time.

Gunn, appreciative of having the opportunity to become better acquainted with Beach's music, viewed the composer herself as

> a significant personality of the art who, unjustly, but quite according to our national habit, has been relegated to relative obscurity. . . . The art which this remarkable woman has created . . . is many sided. Yet for all its variety it defines a musical personality which the cultured world cannot afford to ignore, despite an Anglo-Saxon origin. It is an art of active and highly original imaginative gift. It is also an art of wide and expert technical resource.[17]

The claim that Beach's work had been ignored because of her Anglo-Saxon origin reflects a notion that was current during Beach's younger years—that the English were not a musical people, and Americans of Anglo-Saxon origin partook of the same traits as their English ancestors. Or, to put it another way, that the greatest musicians were European or of European origin, especially German. Contemporary programming with few exceptions reflected that attitude. On the other hand, Beach's early acceptance by composers among her Boston colleagues came, in part, because she was one of their own, a Yankee like them.[18] Furthermore, in later years her work had been blessed with more hearings than that of most contemporary American composers.

In a letter to de Sayn, Beach commented wryly on the modest recognition she had received from the avatars of modern music as well as the relative neglect of American works:

> I naturally agree with you as to the desirability of using American compositions of larger forms on our orchestral and choral programs. It has been encouraging to see that several conductors have done this already and for some years. Only—they are apt to play (or sing) works that do not appeal to our public! I often hear complaints about such music and fear that the audiences will leave the halls when such things are given; and this music gives the word "American" [a bad name]. I have been amused here in New York, when ultra-modern societies have put something of mine at the end of the program, to hold the audience together and keep them contented![19]

Beach never read her recent neglect by major performing organizations as a gender issue. In October 1944 she received a letter from Sophie Drinker, written soon after completion of her remarkable, pioneering book, *Music and Women*.[20] Drinker apparently requested biographical material from Beach as well as the composer's opinion on the status of women in music. Beach, confined to bed in her final illness, had Ruth Shaffner write her response to Sophie Drinker:

> I have no special views at all about the success or non-success of women in any field. . . . My work has always been judged from the beginning by work as such, not according to sex. The question has rarely ever been raised. No special opinions as to what women have or have not done, or the why of it. Their record must show. . . . I have always tried to do the best possible in my creative work, and devote the same attention to the small as well as the large work, size not affecting the treatment at all.[21]

Ruth Shaffner probably took the letter down just as she heard it. Indeed, the reader can almost hear Beach struggling for breath.

Beach's dismissal of gender bias in the evaluation of her work contradicts evidence in critical reviews from 1892 on, including her own statements in defense of women as composers. Perhaps she preferred to remember the positive, not the negative reviews. Perhaps, because she thought of herself as a composer and not as a "woman composer," she was able to ignore those who did not see her that way.

During 1944, she had less and less energy for even daily activities, often skipping church even when her music was sung. The summer was spent quietly in Centerville. She returned to New York on 21 September. By November, she felt increasingly ill; only the most pressing business induced her to go out. On the third of that month she records in her diary that she "*Voted* (Repub.)" The afternoon of the next day Ruth Shaffner and Caroline Parker helped her attend her very last event, the wedding of Eugenie Limberg and William Dengel at the Holy Trinity Lutheran Church in New York.[22] On 6 November Amy Beach made her last diary entry: "Not feeling well. Hip aches." She took to her bed on 11 November, where she remained, surrounded by those who loved her and with "every possible care."[23]

At the annual meeting of the Allied Members of the MacDowell Colony in December, playwright Esther Willard Bates reported that she had just been to see Mrs. Beach.[24] Speaking to her from the door of her room, Bates found Beach

> very bright and surrounded by roses and flowers and Christmas greens. She was sitting up in bed with a lovely pink jacket on and said in a firm voice, "Give them all my love, my very dear love, my very best love; be sure to give them my love."[25]

Marian MacDowell then reported her amazement when a week later she received a call from Beach, whom she had already heard was desperately ill, declaring it a "miracle."[26]

Toward the end Beach slipped into a coma. Marian MacDowell paid a last visit, while Eugenie Dengel and Ruth Shaffner took turns holding her hand during the final few days. With Ruth Shaffner in loving attendance, she died of heart disease on 27 December.

Funeral services were held at St. Bartholomew's, which was still decorated with Christmas poinsettias and greens. The casket, covered in white flowers, stood in the middle of the chancel. David McKay Williams played a fifteen-minute organ prelude by Leo Sowerby after which the full choir entered in procession singing a hymn. After a reading from the Scriptures, the choir sang a setting of the Twenty-third Psalm (Eugenie Dengel thought it might have been "Aunt Amy's" setting).[27] The Reverend Dr. Sargent gave a brief tribute to Beach, praising both her music and herself. After a hymn and prayer the choir recessed followed by the pall-bearers carrying out the casket.[28]

Sometime later, David McKay Williams and Dr. Sargent, in a final tribute to Beach, took an urn with her ashes from New York to Boston, where it was interred in the Forest Hills Cemetery next to the graves of Henry Beach, his parents, and those of Clara and Charles Cheney.

POSTLUDE

The
Legacy

IN 1930, UNA L. ALLEN, assistant to the head of the Arthur P. Schmidt Company, described Beach's "gracious, friendly smile, her eager eyes, quick to catch all that is lovely in the world about her, the charm of her speaking voice, so unusually melodious and expressive, her warm sympathy and deep human interest which flow as readily to the humblest person about her as to her dearest friends." She concluded by declaring that Beach was "a great woman as well as a great musician."[1] While Allen's primary purpose in writing the article was to promote the sale of Beach's music, her article also brought a valuable body of work to public attention. Her opinion, which is based on long acquaintance with Beach and knowledge of her music, may not be far from the mark.

Amy Beach left two legacies, one personal and private, the other public, historical, and current. Both are enumerated in her will.[2] Twenty-nine persons received one or more pieces of jewelry, carefully selected by Beach to match their particular interests. Family mementos were given to those relatives to whom they might mean most, while professional mementos went to her musical friends. For example, to her cousin Gloria Marcy of Hillsborough she left the "old gold locket with picture of [Beach's] grandfather,"[3] while the wrist watch that was inscribed and given to her by the St. Cecilia Society of New York, the chorus that gave the first performance of The Chambered Nautilus, was given to Ruth Shaffner.[4]

A thirtieth bequest was to Emmanuel Church (Episcopal), Boston, where Beach was baptized and confirmed in 1910 and 1911. She specified that they receive the following:

> my large cross of miscellaneous jewels; also my large brooch of deep red jacinths and diamonds, with large aquamarine in the center, and my ring with large green diamond and two small white diamonds. The condition of this gift is that these three ornaments shall be used together . . . , inserted in a chalice or other vessel connected with the altar or with the service of holy communion, and kept as nearly as possible in their present design, which was made by Dr. Beach.[5]

She also provided a fund to accomplish the encrustation, stating that if the bequest were refused by Emmanuel Church, as in fact it was, the jewels were to go to St. Bartholomew's on the same conditions. The latter accepted the gift and now has a chalice decorated with Henry Beach's lavish gifts of jewelry to his wife.

Gifts of one hundred dollars each went to twenty people —"a slight token of the love and gratitude I have felt for each of them."[6] More substantial sums went to Ruth Shaffner and Beach's copyist and friend Helen Whitmore. Even larger sums went to her cousin Mabel Pierce, who received a regular income from investments. In addition, Beach left $10,000 to set up a "Dr. H. H. A. Beach Fund" at Massachusetts General Hospital.[7]

The most substantial gifts were her property and royalties. In her will of 1936, Beach left the house and land in Centerville to Emmanuel Church, specifying that it be used as a summer camp for poor children and be named the Henry Beach Home.[8] A codicil signed on 6 July 1943, however, left the entire property to Lillian Buxbaum, who kept it as a summer home for several years.[9] During that time, she made contributions to a children's hospital and a children's camp, following Beach's original intent that needy children benefit from the valuable property.[10] Eventually, after Isidore Buxbaum died, the property became a burden for her and she sold it.[11] The house was demolished.

Another substantial gift went to the MacDowell Colony. Royalties from publishers and performance fees from ASCAP and other agencies were regularly paid into the Amy Beach Fund of the Edward MacDowell Association, a bequest that yielded thousands of dollars per year for the colony in the first decade or so after Beach's death.[12] During the years in which her music was neglected by almost everyone but church musicians, the amounts declined considerably and subsequently the fund was folded into the general assets of the MacDowell Colony. Very recently, however, a startling change has occurred. While royalties have diminished markedly as more and more of her works are in the public domain, performance and recording fees have greatly increased, and thus between 1992 and 1995 the colony's income from Beach's music tripled. Amy Beach would have been delighted—staunch supporter that she was—to know that fifty years after her death her music is again earning thousands of dollars yearly for the colony.[13]

Amy Beach's public legacy is both her life and her music; the two are inseparable. She redefined, for all Americans, the role of women in music. Women might still choose to be the muse for a man's creativity, but they had in Beach an alternative, a model for realizing their own.

Of their traditional role, Virginia Woolf wrote, "Women have served all these centuries as looking-glasses possessing the magic and delicious power of reflecting the figure of man at twice its natural size."[14] Without the self-confidence generated by that enlarging mirror, how many great compositions by men would have been written—and by women, were left unwritten? In Beach's time, what, for example, did it take to write a symphony besides musical ideas and the craft to shape them into a large-scale form? Confidence that when all the hard work was done it would be deemed worth playing, that a conductor, almost always a man then, would believe in it, and that the orchestra players, who all but the harpist were men, would take the trouble to dig out the musical ideas and set them forth convincingly, perhaps even with passion. But what if those players shared the dominant thinking of late-nineteenth-century Americans—that women were less highly evolved than men—and so dismissed the music of a composer named Amy or Mrs. H. H. A. Beach?

Virginia Woolf noted how the minimizing process worked, quoting a passage from a music history book written in 1928: "Of Mme. Germaine Tailleferre, one can only repeat Dr. Johnson's dictum concerning a woman preacher, transposed into terms of music, 'Sir, a woman's composing is like a dog walking on his hind legs. It is not done well, but you are surprised to find it done at all.'"[15]

Biographers also hold up mirrors to lives, usually after much or all of the life is lived. Before "the telling revelations" of Lytton Strachey's *Eminent Victorians*,[16] they were often indistinguishable from hagiographers, for they too showed their subjects—all male except for an occasional reigning queen—at twice their natural size. But that is no longer the style in biography no matter what the gender of the subject. This biographer hopes she has neither diminished Amy Beach nor blown her up to superwoman size but rather shown her as a fallible girl and woman who exhibited courage in the face of obstacles, the possessor of enough strength to tackle the most challenging musical tasks.

Gender matters, for the typical life course of a male subject is one of conquest whether it be of a microbe or a nation. When Beach was a girl, a woman's life course was predestined no matter what her talents. Amy Cheney's experience was in most ways typical: little formal schooling, music lessons, and marriage. That was Clara and Charles Cheney's prescription for their daughter, given with full knowledge of her gifts. At issue, of course, was the denial by her parents and her husband of the right to choose a professional career.

Beach's career was facilitated by her freedom from household responsibilities before and after marriage—and the important fact that she was childless. Even during her long widowhood, she rejected a domestic role for herself, establishing a coterie of helpers who willingly took care of her practical needs so that she might concentrate on her work—and her pleasures—much as men did.

She pursued technical mastery despite the denial of advanced training and with the total focus typical of the gifted. Her products were her own—made even more so because she was her own teacher. After their completion she had the courage to put her name to them and send them out to the world. Indeed, she was eager to do so. This book honors that courage by recording the details of her life.

Even as her style is derivative, Beach's compositions are nevertheless marked by individuality—the richness of her harmonic sense, the daring of her tonal language beginning with Opus 1, and the lyricism of her melodies. Reference to the past placed her in the mainstream of music for the first half of her long creative life. Afterward, her experiments in more modern idioms produced some of her most original and compelling works.

Recognition of Beach's compositional skill came early. Singers and the public were the first to rejoice in her special qualities, most notably her well-turned melodies, grateful to the voice and the heart. Beach's abstract works, too, were vocally inspired, wherein even the most virtuosic flourishes of her piano pieces and her most complex orchestral passages are infused with her personal kind of lyricism. Having mastered the orchestra instrument by instrument and as a unit, she was able to create not only a symphony but effective orchestral accompaniments for vocal and choral pieces beginning with the Mass. Sung or played, hers is intensely communicative music.

Now, after a long hiatus, her music is again finding an audience in the present post-modern, neo-Romantic period. Singers, pianists, chamber and choral ensembles, and orchestras are playing her music. Over half of her three hundred works have been recorded, some of them multiple times.[17] Several music historians have found her a modest place in the canon.[18] More and more are drawn to the emotional and intellectual authenticity of her compositions.

Amy Beach answers Virginia Woolf's implied questions. What if a woman is born with supreme artistic gifts?[19] To what extent would the promise be realized, given the discouragement society serves up to women? Would the will to succeed match the amplitude of the gift; would its bearer possess the single-minded purpose and the total concentration necessary for her craft? Would she have the support from organized institutions and significant individuals to advance her professional development; would the support equal that given to a man of similar talent? The answer for Beach is a qualified yes.

APPENDIX

Catalog of Works

WORKS ARE LISTED BY PERIOD, medium, and chronology. Each entry includes the following: title of work, author of text (in parentheses); required forces; date of completion if known; publisher and date of publication (in parentheses); facsimiles, reprints, or editions and date of publication (in brackets). Anthologies that include short works are not listed.

Beach's music may be ordered from A-R Editions, 801 Deming Way, Madison, Wisconsin 53717; Hildegard Publishing Company, Box 332, Bryn Mawr, Pennsylvania 19010; Recital Publications, P.O. Box 1697, Huntsville, Texas 77340; Seesaw Music, 2067 Broadway, New York, New York 10023; G. K. Hall (*Three Centuries of American Music*); Walton Music Corporation, 170 N. E. 33 Street, Fort Lauderdale, Florida 33334.

Abbreviations

A	alto
arr.	arrangement
B	bass
facs.	facsimile
fl	flute
Mez	mezzo-soprano
obbl	obbligato
org	organ
orch	orchestra
osc	organ score
pf	piano
psc	piano score
Ps.	psalm
reprt.	reprint
rev.	revised
S	soprano
str qtt	string quartet
T	tenor

vn	violin
va	viola
vc	violoncello
v(v)	voice(s)
ww qnt	woodwind quintet

Juvenilia

All manuscripts are at University of Missouri, Kansas City.

Piano

"Mamma's Waltz," 1872
"Air and Variations," 1877
"Menuetto," 1877
"Romanza," 1877
"Petite valse," 1878
"Allegro appassionato," "Moderato cantabile," "Allegro con fuoco," n.d.

Vocal/Choral

"The Rainy Day" (Longfellow), 1v, pf, 1880 (Ditson, 1883)
Four Chorales: "Come Ye Faithful" (J. Hupton), "Come to Me" (C. Elliott), "O Lord, How Happy Should We Be" (J. Anstice), "To Heav'n I Lift My Waiting Eyes"; 4vv, 1882
"Whither" (W. Müller), v, pf (accompaniment: Chopin, Trois nouvelles études, no. 3)

1885–1910

All works issued between 1885 and 1910 were published by Arthur P. Schmidt, Co., Boston, unless otherwise indicated.

Orchestral

Opus 17   *Eilende Wolken, Segler die Lüfte* (F. von Schiller), A, orch, 1892; psc [1892]

      22   *Bal masque* (see also *Keyboard*)

      32   Symphony in E Minor, "Gaelic," 1894–96; score [1897; facs., G. K. Hall, 1992]

      45   Concerto for Piano and Orchestra in C♯ Minor, 1899; arr. 2 pf [1900; facs., Hildegard, 1995]

      53   *Jephthah's Daughter* (Mollevaut, after Judges 11.38; It. trans., I. Martinez; Eng. trans., A. M. Beach), S, orch; vsc [1903]

Chamber

23 Romance, vn, pf [1893; Hildegard, 1994]

34 Sonata in A Minor for Piano and Violin, 1896 [1899; reprt. Hildegard, 1994]; arr. va, pf [C. F. Peters, 1984]; arr. fl, pf [Hildegard, 1994]

40 *Three Compositions:* "La Captive"; "Berceuse"; "Mazurka"; vn, pf, 1898, [1899; Hildegard, 1994]; arr. vc, pf [1903; Hildegard, 1995]

55 *Invocation,* vn, pf/org, vc obbl (1904); arr. vn, pf [Hildegard, 1994]

67 Quintet for Piano and Strings in F♯ Minor, 1907 [1909; facs. Hildegard, 1997]

Keyboard

3 Cadenza to Beethoven, Piano Concerto No. 3, op. 37, 1st mvt. [1888]

4 *Valse-Caprice* [1889]

6 *Ballad* [1894]

15/1–4 *Four Sketches* (1892): "In Autumn," "Phantoms," "Dreaming," also arr. vc, pf [Hildegard, 1995]; "Fireflies"

22 *Bal masque* [1894], arr. orch

25/1–6 *Children's Carnival* [1894; Hildegard, 1990]

28/1–3 *Trois morceaux caractéristiques:* "Barcarolle" [1894; reprt., Hildegard, 1994]; also arr. vn, pf, 1936 [Hildegard, 1994]; "Minuet italien" [1894]; "Danse des fleurs" [1894]

36 *Children's Album* [1897; Hildegard, 1990]

47 *Summer Dreams,* pf 4 hands [1901]

54/1–2 "Scottish Legend"; "Gavotte fantastique" [1903]

60 *Variations on Balkan Themes,* 1904 [1906]; arr. orch, 1906; rev. [1936]; arr. 2 pf [1937; rev. 1942]

64/14 Eskimos, Four Characteristic Pieces [1907]: "Arctic Night"; "The Returning Hunter"; "Exiles"; "With Dog-teams"

65 *Les rêves de Colombine: Suite française:* "La Fée de la fontaine"; "Le prince gracieux"; "Valse amoureuse"; "Sous les étoiles"; "Danse d'Arlequin" [1907]

70 "Iverniana," 2 pf, 1910, lost; rev. as op. 104

Sacred Choral
(4vv, organ, unless otherwise indicated)

5 Mass in E♭, S, A, T, B, 4vv, org, orch, 1890; osc [1890; facs. Walton, 1995; facs. Recital Publications, 1997]

[5] *Graduale:Thou Glory of Jerusalem,* T, orch, insertion in Mass, op. 5; psc [1892]

7 *O Praise the Lord, All Ye Nations* (Ps. 117) [1891]

8/1–3 *Choral Responses:* "Nunc dimittis" (Luke 2.29); "With Prayer and

Supplication" (Phil. 4.6–7) "Peace I Leave with You" (John 4.27) [1891]

17 Festival jubilate (Ps. 100), 7vv, orch, 1891; psc [1892; facs. psc, Recital Publications, 1997]

24 Bethlehem (G. C. Hugg) [1893]

27 Alleluia, Christ Is Risen (after M. Weisse, C. F. Gellert, T. Scott, T. Gibbons) [1895]; arr. with vn obbl [1904]

33 Teach Me Thy Way (Ps. 86.11–12), 1895

38 Peace on Earth (E. H. Sears) [1897]

50 Help Us, O God (Pss. 79.9, 5; 45.26), 5vv [1903]

63 Service in A: "Te Deum," "Benedictus" [1905], "Jubilate Deo," "Magnificat," "Nunc dimittis" [1906]; S, A, T, B, 4vv, org

Secular Choral

9 The Little Brown Bee (M. Eytinge), women's chorus 4vv [1891]

16 The Minstrel and the King: Rudolph von Hapsburg (F. von Schiller), T, B, men's chorus 4vv, orch, psc [1890; facs., Recital Publications, 1997]

— "An Indian Lullaby" (Anon.), women's chorus 4vv [n. p., 1895]

30 The Rose of Avon-town (C. Mischka), S, A, women's chorus 4vv, orch, psc [1896; facs. Recital Publications, 1997]

31/1–3 Three Flower Songs (M. Deland), women's chorus 4vv, pf [1896]: "The Clover"; "The Yellow Daisy"; "The Bluebell"

39/1–3 Three Shakespeare Choruses: "Over hill, over dale"; "Come unto these yellow sands"; "Through the house give glimmering light"; women's chorus, 4vv, pf [1897]

42 Song of Welcome (H. M. Blossom), 4vv, orch; osc [1898]

46 Sylvania: A Wedding Cantata (F. W. Bancroft, after W. Bloem), S, S, A, T, B, 8vv, orch, psc [1901]

49 A Song of Liberty (F. L. Stanton), 4vv, orch, 1902; psc [1902]; arr. men's chorus 4vv, pf [1917]

57/1–2 "Only a Song" (A. L. Hughes); "One Summer Day" (Hughes) women's chorus 4vv [1904]

59 The Sea-Fairies (A. Tennyson), 1904, S, A, women's chorus 4vv, orch, psc [1904; facs., Hildegard, 1996]

66 The Chambered Nautilus (O. W. Holmes), S, A, women's chorus 4vv, orch, org ad lib, psc [1907; org part laid in, Hildegard, 1994]

Songs
(1v, pf, unless otherwise indicated)

1/1–4 Four Songs: "With Violets" (K. Vannah) [1885]; "Die vier Brüder" (F. von Schiller) [1887]; "Jeune fille et jeune fleur" (F. R. Chateaubriand) [1887]; "Ariette" (P. B. Shelley) [1886; facs., Recital Publications]

2/1–3   *Three Songs* (H. H. A. Beach): "Twilight" [1887]; "When Far from Her" [1889]; "Empress of Night" [1891; facs. Recital Publications]

10/1–3   *Songs of the Sea*: "A Canadian Boat Song" (T. Moore), S, B, pf; "The Night Sea" (H. P. Spofford), S, S, pf; "Sea Song" (W. E. Channing), S, S, pf [1890]

11/1–3   *Three Songs* (W. E. Henley): "Dark Is the Night!" [1890]; "The Western Wind" [1889]; "The Blackbird" [1889; facs., Recital Publications]

12/1–3   *Three Songs* (R. Burns): "Wilt Thou Be My Dearie?"; "Ye Banks and Braes O' Bonnie Doon"; "My Luve Is Like a Red, Red Rose"; 1887 [1887; facs. nos. 1–2, Recital Publications]

13   *Hymn of Trust* (O. W. Holmes), [1891]; rev. with vn obbl [1901; facs., Recital Publications]

14/1–4   *Four Songs*: "The Summer Wind" (W. Learned), "Le Secret" (J. de Resseguier), "Sweetheart, Sigh No More" (T. B. Aldrich), "The Thrush" (E. R. Sill); 1890 [1891; facs., Recital Publications; nos. 2–3 rev., 1901]

19/1–3   *Three Songs* (1893): "For Me the Jasmine Buds Unfold" (F. E. Coates); "Ecstasy" (A. M. Beach), 1v, pf, vn obbl [1895; facs., Recital Publications]; "Golden Gates"

20   *Villanelle: Across the World* (E. M. Thomas) [1894]; also with vc obbl [1894]

21/1–3   *Three Songs*: "Chanson d'amour" (V. Hugo), with vc obbl, 1899; "Extase" (Hugo); "Elle et moi" (F. Bovet) [1893; Hildegard, 1994]

26/1–4   *Four Songs* (1894): "My Star" (C. Fabbri); "Just for This" (Fabbri) [facs. Recital Publications]; "Spring" (Fabbri); "Wouldn't That Be Queer" (E. J. Cooley) [Hildegard, 1994]

29/1–4   *Four Songs*: "Within Thy Heart" (A. M. Beach); "The Wandering Knight" (anon., Eng. trans., J. G. Lockhart); "Sleep, Little Darling" (Spofford); "Haste, O Beloved" (W. A. Sparrow) 1894 [1895; facs. nos. 1, 2, and 4, Recital Publications]

35/1–4   *Four Songs*: "Nachts" (C. F. Scherenberg); "Allein!" (H. Heine); "Nähe des Geliebten" (J. W. von Goethe); "Forget-me-not" (H. H. A. Beach) 1896 [1897; facs. nos. 1 and 4, Recital Publications]

37/1–3   *Three Shakespeare Songs*: "O Mistress Mine"; "Take, O Take Those Lips Away"; "Fairy Lullaby" [1897; Hildegard, 1994; facs., Recital Publications]

41/1–3   *Three Songs*: "Anita" (Fabbri), [facs. Recital Publications]; "Thy Beauty" (Spofford); "Forgotten" (Fabbri) [1898]

43/1–5   *Five Burns Songs*: "Dearie"; "Scottish Cradle Song"; "Oh Were My Love Yon Lilac Fair!"; "Far Awa'" arr. org and pf [1938]; "My Lassie" [1899; facs. nos. 3–4 Recital Publications]

44/1–3   *Three [R.] Browning Songs*: "The Year's at the Spring," also with vn obbl; "Ah, Love, But a Day," also with vn obbl; "I Send My Heart Up to Thee" [1900; no. 1 Hildegard, 1994]

48/1–4   Four Songs: "Come, Ah Come" (H. H. A. Beach); "Good Morning" (A. H. Lockhart); "Good Night" (Lockhart); "Canzonetta" (A. Sylvestre) [1902; facs. no. 3, Recital Publications]

51/1–4   Four Songs (1903): "Ich sagete nicht" (E. Wissman); "Wir drei" (H. Eschelbach); "Juni" (E. Jansen), also with vn obbl [1920; Hildegard, 1994; facs., Recital Publications]; "Je demande à l'oiseau" (Sylvestre)

56/1–4   Four Songs (1904): "Autumn Song" (H. H. A. Beach), 1903; "Go Not Too Far" (F. E. Coates); "I Know Not How to Find the Spring" (Coates); "Shena Van" (W. Black), 1904, also with vn obbl [1919], arr. men's vv [1917], arr. women's vv [1917], arr. mixed vv [1932]

61   "Give Me Not Love" (Coates), S, T, pf [1905]

62   "When Soul Is Joined to Soul" (E. B. Browning) [1905; Hildegard, 1994]

68   "After" (Coates), [1909] also vn obbl, n.d.

69/1–2   Two Mother Songs: "Baby" (G. MacDonald), (Springfield, Ohio, 1908); "Hush, Baby Dear" (A. L. Hughes) [1908]

71/1–3   Three Songs (1910): "A Prelude" (A. M. Beach); "O Sweet Content" (T. Dekker); "An Old Love-Story" (B. L. Stathem)

1914–1944

Opera

149   Cabildo, 1 act (N. B. Stephens), solo vv, chorus, speaker, vn, vc, pf, 1932; solo vv, chorus, speaker, pf, 1932

Chamber

80   Theme and Variations for Flute and String Quartet, 1916 [G. Schirmer, 1920; facs. score, G. K. Hall, 1991; facs., Hildegard, 1995; facs., Recital Publications, 1997]

89   Quartet for Strings in One Movement, 1929 [A-R Editions, 1994]

90   Pastorale, fl, vc, pf, 1921; arr. vc, org/pf [Hildegard, 1995]

—   Caprice, The Water Sprites, fl, vc, pf, 1921

125   Lento espressivo, vn, pf [Hildegard, 1995]

150   Trio for Piano, Violin, and Violincello, 1938 [Composers Press, 1939]

151   Pastorale, ww qnt [Composers Press, 1942]

Keyboard
(pf unless otherwise indicated)

81   Prelude and Fugue, 1917 [G. Schirmer, 1918]

83   From Blackbird Hills [Schmidt, 1922], also for orch

87   *Fantasia fugata* [Presser, 1923]

91   *The Fair Hills of Éiré, O!* (Old Irish melody) [Schmidt, 1922]

92/1–2   "The Hermit Thrush at Eve"; "The Hermit Thrush at Morn," 1921 [Schmidt, 1922]

97/1–5   *From Grandmother's Garden:* "Morning Glories"; "Heartsease"; "Mignonette"; "Rosemary and Rue"; "Honeysuckle" [Schmidt, 1922]

102/1–2   "Farewell Summer"; "Dancing Leaves" [Ditson, 1924]

104   *Suite for Two Pianos Founded upon Old Irish Melodies* [Church, 1924]

106   *Old Chapel by Moonlight* [Church, 1924]

107   *Nocturne* [Church, 1924]

108   *A Cradle Song of the Lonely Mother* [Church, 1924]

111   *From Olden Times: Gavotte* [Schmidt]

114   *By the Still Waters* [Art Publications, 1925]

116   *Tyrolean Valse-Fantaisie,* 1911 [Ditson, 1926]

119   *From Six to Twelve:* "Sliding on the Ice"; "The First May Flowers"; "Canoeing"; "Secrets of the Attic"; "A Camp-fire Ceremonial"; "Boy Scouts March" [Ditson, 1927]

—   *A Bit of Cairo* [Presser, 1928]

128/1–3   *Three Pianoforte Pieces:* "Scherzino: A Peterborough Chipmunk"; "Young Birches"; "A Humming Bird" [Presser, 1932]

130   *Out of the Depths* (Ps. 130) [Schmidt, 1932]

148   *Five Improvisations,* 1934 [Composers Press, 1938; rev. Seesaw, 1996]

—   *Prelude on an Old Folk Tune* ("The Fair Hills of Eiré, O"), org [H. W. Gray, 1943]

Sacred Choral
(for mixed choir, org, unless otherwise indicated)

74   *All Hail the Power of Jesus' Name* (E. Perronet) [G. Schirmer, 1915], alternate text for *Panama Hymn*—see *Secular Choral*

76   *Thou Knowest, Lord* (J. Borthwick), T, B, 4vv, org/pf [G. Schirmer, 1915]

78/1–4   *Canticles:* "Bonum est, confiteri" (Ps. 92.1–4), S, 4vv, org; "Deus misereatur" (Ps. 67); "Cantate Domino" (Ps. 98); "Benedic anima mea" (Ps. 103) [G. Schirmer, 1916]

84   *Te Deum,* T, men's chorus 3vv, org, 1921 [Presser, 1922]

95   *Constant Christmas* (P. Brooks), S, A, 4vv, org [Presser, 1922]

96   *The Lord Is My Shepherd* (Ps. 23), women's chorus 3vv, org [Presser, 1923]

98   *I Will Lift Up Mine Eyes* (Ps. 121), 4vv [Presser, 1923]

103/1–2   "Benedictus es, Domine"; "Benedictus" (Luke 1.67–81), B, 4vv, org [Ditson, 1924]

105   *Let This Mind Be in You* (Phil. 2.5–11), S, B, 4vv, org [Church, 1924]

109   *Lord of the Worlds Above* (I. Watts), S, T, B, 4vv, org [Ditson, 1925]

115   *Around the Manger* (R. Davis), 4vv, org/pf [Ditson, 1925]

121 Benedicite omnia opera Domini (Dan. 3.56–8) [Schmidt, 1928]

122 Communion Responses: "Kyrie," "Gloria tibi," "Sursum corda," "Sanctus," "Agnus Dei," "Gloria" (supplement to *Service in A*); S, A, T, B, 4vv, org [Schmidt, 1928]

123 *The Canticle of the Sun* (St. Francis of Assisi, trans. Matthew Arnold), S, Mez, T, B, 4vv, orch; osc [Schmidt, 1928]

125/2 *Evening Hymn: The Shadows of the Evening Hours* (A. Procter, arr. op. 125, no. 2), S, A, 4vv, 1934 [Schmidt, 1934]

132 *Christ in the Universe* (A. Meynell), A, T, 4vv, orch; osc [Gray, 1931]

134 *God Is Our Stronghold* (E. Wordsworth), S, 4vv, org

139 *Hearken Unto Me* (Is. 51.1, 3; 43.1–3; 40.28, 31), S, A, T, B, 4vv, orch; osc [Schmidt, 1934]

141 *O Lord God of Israel* (1 Kgs. 8.23, 27–30, 34), S, A, B, 4vv, 1936

— Hymn: *O God of Love, O King of Peace* (H. W. Baker), 1941 [Appleton-Century, 1941]

146 *Lord of All Being* (O. W. Holmes) [Gray, 1938]

147 *I Will Give Thanks* (Ps. 111), S, 4vv, org [Schmidt, 1939]

— *Pax nobiscum* (E. Marlatt), women's chorus 3vv; men's chorus 3vv/4vv, org [Schmidt, 1939]

Secular Choral
(mixed chorus, pf, unless otherwise indicated)

74 *Panama Hymn* (W. P. Stafford), 4vv, orch; arr. 4vv, org/pf; with alternate text for *All Hail the Power of Jesus' Name* [G. Schirmer, 1915]

82 *Dusk in June* (S. Teasdale), women's chorus 4vv [G. Schirmer, 1917]

— *A Song of Liberty* [? 1918]

86 *May Eve*, 1921 [Silver, Burdett, 1933]

94 *Three School Songs*: "The Arrow and the Song" (H. W. Longfellow), "Clouds" (E. H. Miller), "A Song for Little May" (F. D. Sherman) 1922, 4vv [Hinds, Hayden and Eldridge, 1933]

101 *Peter Pan* (J. Andrews), women's chorus 3vv, pf [Presser, 1923]

110 *The Greenwood* (W. L. Bowles), 4vv [Birchard, 1925]

118/1–2 *Two Children's Choruses*: "The Moon Boat" (E. D. Watkins), unison chorus; "Who Has Seen the Wind" (C. G. Rossetti), chorus 2vv [Silver, Burdett, 1938]

126/1–2 "Sea Fever" (J. Masefield); "The Last Prayer"; men's chorus 4vv, pf [Schmidt, 1931]

127 *When the Last Sea Is Sailed* (Masefield), men's chorus 4vv [Schmidt, 1931]

129 *Drowsy Dreamtown* (R. Norwood), S, women's chorus 3vv, pf [Schmidt, 1932]

140 *We Who Sing Have Walked in Glory* (A. S. Bridgman), 1934 [Ditson, 1934]

— *A Bumblebee Passed by My Window*, 1935, women's chorus 3vv, pf

144   *This Morning Very Early* (P. L. Hills), women's chorus 3vv, pf [1937]
—   *The Ballad of the P.E.O.* [Gray, 1943]

Songs

72/1–2   *Two Songs:* "Ein altes Gebet" (anon.); "Deine Blumen" (L. Zacharias) [G. Schirmer, 1914]

73/1–2   *Two Songs* (Zacharias): "Grossmütterchen," "Der Totenkranz" [G. Schirmer, 1914; Hildegard, 1994]

75/1–4   "The Candy Lion" (A. F. Brown); "A Thanksgiving Fable" (O. Herford); "Dolladine" (Brown); "Prayer of a Tired Child" (Brown) 1914 [G. Schirmer, 1914; Hildegard, 1994]

76/1–2   *Two Songs:* "Separation" (J. L. Stoddard); "The Lotos Isles" (Tennyson) [G. Schirmer, 1914]

77/1–2   *Two Songs:* "I" (C. Fanning); "Wind o' the Westland" (D. Burnett) 1916 [G. Schirmer, 1916]

78/1–3   *Three Songs:* "Meadowlarks" (I. D. Coolbrith); "Night Song at Amalfi" (S. Teasdale); "In Blossom Time" (Coolbrith) [G. Schirmer, 1917]

85   *In the Twilight* (Longfellow) [Schmidt, 1922]

88   *Spirit Divine* (A. Read), S, T, org [Presser, 1922]

93   *Message* (S. Teasdale) [Presser, 1922]

99/1–4   *Four Songs:* "When Mama Sings" (A. M. Beach); "Little Brown-Eyed Laddie" (A. D. O. Greenwood); "The Moonpath" (K. Adams); "The Artless Maid" (L. Barili) [Presser, 1923]

100/1–2   *Two Songs:* "A Mirage" (B. Ochsner); "Stella Viatoris" (J. H. Nettleton), S, vn, vc, pf [Schmidt, 1924]

112   *Jesus My Saviour* (A. Elliott) [Presser, 1925]

113   *Mine Be the Lips* (L. Speyer) [Ditson, 1921]

115   *Around the Manger* (K. Davis), 1v, pf/org [Presser, 1925]

117/1–3   *Three Songs* (M. Lee): "The Singer," "The Host," "Song in the Hills" [Church, 1925]

120   *Rendez-vous* (L. Speyer), 1v, pf, vn obbl [Ditson, 1928]

—   *Mignonnette* [n. p., 1929]

—   *Birth* (F. L. Knowles), 1929

124   *Springtime* (S. M. Heywood) [G. Schirmer, 1929]

125/1–2   *Two Sacred Songs:* "Spirit of Mercy" (anon.) [Schmidt, 1930]; "Evening Hymn: The Shadows of the Evening Hours" (A. Procter) [Schmidt, 1934]

131   *Dark Garden* (L. Speyer) [Schmidt, 1932]

135   *To One I Love* (S. R. Quick), 1932

136   *Fire and Flame* (A. A. Moody), 1932 [Schmidt, 1933]

—   *My Love Came through the Fields* (R. Norwood), 1932

—   *A Light That Overflows* (Norwood), 1932

137/1–2   *Two Mother Songs:* "Baby" (S. R. Quick); "May Flowers" (A. Moody), 1932 [Schmidt, 1933]

—   Evening Song, 1934
—   The Deep-Sea Pearl (E. M. Thomas), 1935
142   I Sought the Lord (anon.), 1v, org, 1936 [Schmidt, 1937]
143   I Shall Be Brave (K. Adams), 1931 [Schmidt, 1932]
145   April Dreams (K. W. Harding), 1935
—   Jesus, Tender Shepherd, 1936
152   Though I Take the Wings of Morning (R. N. Spencer), 1v, org/pf, 1941
        [Composers Press, 1941]
—   The Heart That Melts
—   The Icicle Lesson
—   If Women Will Not Be Inclined
—   Time Has Wings and Swiftly Flies

Other Works

—   Arr. Beethoven, Piano Concerto No. 1, 2nd movt, 4 hands, 1887
—   St. John the Baptist (St. Matthew, St. Luke), 1889 (Libretto)
—   Arr. Berlioz: Les Troyens, act 1, scene 3; 1v, pf, 1896
—   R. Strauss, Ständchen, pf transcription [Schmidt, 1902]
—   Arr. On a Hill: Negro Melody (trad.), 1v, pf [Schmidt, 1929]
—   Fragment: Du sieh'st, das ist nicht so, B, pf, n.d.

Music's Ten Commandments
as Given for Young Composers
Mrs. H. H. A. Beach

SPARE NEITHER TIME NOR STRENGTH in the perfecting of the technic of composition, beginning with the simplest rudiments. Your musical material must be perfectly under control as is language in the case of a writer of literature. One must never be compelled to pause in the development of an idea through lack of knowledge of spelling or grammar.

Begin with small things—ideas that can be expressed in small form.

Study how best to develop all the possibilities of a small form. A small gem may be just as brilliantly cut as one weighing many carats.

Learn to employ as much variety in form as possible. Above all things, avoid becoming stereotyped in the expression of melodic, harmonic or rhythmic ideas.

Subject yourself to endless labor in the analysis of works by the old masters, especially using, as illustration for the form upon which you are now engaged, a master's work in the same form. There is no better way to learn how to write a fugue than by dissecting one by Bach, preferably one from "The Well-Tempered Clavichord."

Begin early to study the scores of stringed [sic] quartet music by Haydn and Mozart and the early Beethoven. It is well to select one work and subject it to the most careful analysis, studying it until it is learned by heart.

Use every possible opportunity to hear a good stringed quartet, if possible at rehearsals, as well as at concerts. Take a score of the composition and study it while it is being played.

Hear as much choral music as possible. The study of voice writing, as illustrated in the master works, is of the greatest importance.

The crowning glory of music study is familiarity with the master works in symphony, played by a fine, modern symphony orchestra. Carry into the study of symphonic compositions the same thoroughness with which you have analyzed works for the piano, stringed quartet and chorus, beginning with the simpler and earlier composers.

Remember that technic is valuable only as a means to an end. You must first have something to say—something which demands expression from the depths of your soul. If you feel deeply and know how to express what you feel, you make others feel.[1]

Los Angeles Examiner, 28 June 1915, 5. Reprinted as "How Mrs. Beach Does It," Musical Courier, 7 July 1915.

ABBREVIATIONS

Libraries

DLC-APS	Library of Congress, Music Division, Arthur P. Schmidt Collection
DLC-Ms	Library of Congress, Manuscript Division
DLC-Mu	Library of Congress, Music Division
ICHi	Chicago Historical Society
ICN	Newberry Library, Chicago
MBCM	New England Conservatory of Music, Boston
MB-Ms	Boston Public Library, Rare Books and Manuscripts Department
MB-Mu	Boston Public Library, Music Department
MoKU-Be	University of Missouri at Kansas City, Special Collections, Beach Collection
NJNPL	Newark Public Library, Newark, N.J.
Nh	New Hampshire State Library, Concord, N.H.
Nh-TFL	Tucker Free Library, Henniker, N.H.
NhU-Be	University of New Hampshire, Dimond Library, Beach Collection 51
NhU-FPL	University of New Hampshire, Dimond Library, Beach Collection 51A (Fuller Public Library deposit)
NN-L	New York Public Library, Lincoln Center Library for the Performing Arts, Music Research Division

Bibliographical References

DAB	Dictionary of American Biography, eds. Allen Johnson and Dumas Malone (New York: Charles Scribner's Sons, 1930).
EB	Encyclopedia Britannica
NCAB	National Cyclopaedia of American Biography (New York: James T. White and Co., 1916).
Grove-6	The New Grove Dictionary of Music and Musicians, ed. Stanley Sadie (London: Macmillan, 1980).

Grove-American	*The New Grove Dictionary of American Music*, ed. H. Wiley Hitchcock and Stanley Sadie (London: Macmillan, 1985).
Grove-Women	*The New Grove Dictionary of Women Composers*, ed. Julie Anne Sadie and Rhian Samuel (London: Macmillan, 1994)
S1	Amy Beach, Scrapbook, 1883–1914, NhU-Be.
S2	Amy Beach, Scrapbook, 1889–1906, NhU-Be.
S3	Amy Beach, Scrapbook, 1914–1918, NhU-FPL.
S4	Amy Beach, Scrapbook, 1885–1917, NhU-FPL.

NOTES

Chapter 1. *A Prodigy's New England Upbringing*

1. The time of Amy Cheney's birth is from Clara Imogene Cheney, [Biography of her daughter], 26 February 1892 (MacDowell Colony Papers, DLC) 1. The marriage of Charles Abbott Cheney and Clara Imogene Marcy and the birth of Amy Marcy Cheney are registered in New Hampshire Vital Records, Concord. The same information, plus biographical data on all three, is found in the following genealogies: Charles Henry Pope, comp., *The Cheney Genealogy* (Boston: Charles H. Pope, 1897), 531, 547–48; Clarence Winthrop Bowen, Donald Lines Jacobus, and William Herbert Wood, *The History of Woodstock, Connecticut*, vol. 7, *Genealogies of Woodstock Families* (Worcester, Mass.: American Antiquarian Society, 1943), 376; D. L. Jacobus and Edgar Francis Waterman, *The Waterman Family*, vol. 3, *Descendants of Richard Waterman of Providence, Rhode Island* (Hartford: Connecticut Historical Society, 1954), 403. Local histories further confirm these dates: see George Waldo Browne, *The History of Hillsborough, New Hampshire, 1735–1921*, vol. 1, *History and Description* (Manchester, N. H.: John B. Clarke Co., 1921), 406; Leander W. Cogswell, *History of the Town of Henniker, Merrimack County, New Hampshire, 1775 to 1880 with a Genealogical Register* (Concord: Republican Press Assn., 1880), 497.

2. Report, U.S. Bureau of the Census, State of New Hampshire, Merrimack County, Town of Henniker, 1870. Also included was the information that Moses and Charles Cheney were both worth $8,000, probably including only the value of the house, out-buildings, and farmland since the mill had burned down by the time the census was taken.

3. The marriage took place on 28 April 1867 (New Hampshire Vital Records). Genealogies cited above, n. 1, also give vital statistics for Emma Frances ("Franc") Marcy and Lyman H. Clement.

4. Letter, Amy Beach to Mrs. Edwin H. Wiggers, 24 August 1935 (P.E.O. Archives, New York City). Note also that Moses Cheney is listed as a farmer in *The Hillsborough, Henniker, Dunbarton, New Boston, etc. Citizen's Directory, 1889–1890* (Haverhill, N.H.: W. E. Shaw, n.d.), 28.

5. Pope, 490–91.

6. "Mrs. H. H. A. Beach," printed biographical essay and catalogue of works through op. 45, with additions in Beach's hand (Nh), [1–6].

7. Clara Imogene Cheney, [Biography of her daughter], 26 February 1892 (MacDowell Colony Papers, DLC-Ms, holograph); "Mrs. H. H. A. Beach" (Nh). Similar biographical details appear in a number of other contemporary sources of which the following are the most important: Amy Beach, "Why I Chose My Profession: The Autobiography of a Woman Composer," interviewed by Ednah Aiken, *Mother's Magazine* 11 (February 1914), 7–8; Louis C. Elson, *The History of American Music* (1915; rev. 1925; reprint, New York: Burt

Franklin, 1971), 294–305; "Mrs. H. H. A. Beach," *Musikliterärische Blätter* 14 (Vienna, 21 May 1904), 1–4; Agnes Lockhart Hughes, "Mrs. H. H. A. Beach, America's Foremost Woman Composer," *The Simmons Magazine* 4 (October 1911): 476–78.

8. Beach, "Why I Chose My Profession," 7. The list is probably lost.

9. Cheney [Biography], 1–2. The lines "The moon shines full at His command/And all the stars obey" are from the hymn by Isaac Watts (1720) that begins, "I sing th'almighty power of God," *The Book of Praise* from the Best English Hymn Writers, ed. Roundell Palmer (Boston: D. Lothrop, n.d.), 19 (text only).

10. Beach to Wiggers.

11. Cheney [Biography], [3]; Elson, 294.

12. Cheney [Biography], [1].

13. Ibid., [3–4].

14. Ibid., [3]. On the jubilee, see Sarah B. Lawrence, "The Great Peace Jubilee of 1869," *The Many Voices of Boston*, ed. Howard Mumford Jones and Bessie Zaban Jones (Boston: Little, Brown, 1975), 281.

15. Cheney [Biography], [3]; Biographical essay of Beach (earlier versions of "Mrs. H. H. A. Beach," Nh) and catalog in Beach's hand, which includes only piano works (Nh-TFL, typescript, n.d.), [1–9]; Elson, 294–95. "See, the Conquering Hero" a chorus with children's choir, is from part 3, no. 35, of Handel's oratorio *Judas Maccabeus*. Amy Cheney probably heard her mother practicing for the jubilee and accurately learned the song by rote as she did many other tunes.

16. Cheney, [Biography], [4].

17. Clara Cheney to "Cousin Anna," 27 April 1898 (NhU-Be, typed copy). Cheney, [Biography], 1, places this feat even earlier, at one year.

18. Gerald Stanley Lee, in *The Lost Art of Reading* (New York: G. P. Putnam, 1902), 77: "First. Decide what the owner of the mind most wants in the world. Second. Put this thing, whatever it may be, where the owner of the mind cannot get it unless he uses his mind. Take pains to put it where he can get it, if he does use his mind. Third. Lure him on. It is education."

19. Beach, "Why I Chose My Profession," 7.

20. Hazel Gertrude Kinscella, "'Play No Piece in Public When First Learned,' Says Mrs. Beach," *Musical America* 28 (7 September 1918): 9.

21. Frank H. Armstrong, "An Historical and Technological Perspective," *The American Baptist Churches of New Hampshire: The Bicentennial Historical Papers*, including two papers prepared for the 200th Anniversary of the Freewill Baptist Denomination, 1780–1980, unpaginated, New Hampshire Historical Society, Concord.

22. The Cheneys were married in Hillsborough Bridge by the Reverend Stephen S. Morrill (New Hampshire Bureau of Vital Records). Morrill was minister of the Congregational Church in Hillsborough, according to Browne, 404.

23. Horace Bushnell, *Christian Nurture* (New York: C. Scribner, 1863), reprinted in Philip J. Greven, Jr., *Child-Rearing Concepts, 1626–1861, Historical Sources* (Itasca, Ill.: F. E. Peacock, 1973) 137–81.

24. Ibid., 20.

25. Ibid., 244.

26. Ibid., 245.

27. Ibid., 247.

28. Beach, "Why I Chose My Profession," 7.

29. Ibid., 7.

30. Nancy B. Reich, "Women as Musicians: A Question of Class," in *Musicology and Difference*, ed. Ruth Solie (Berkeley: University of California Press, 1993), 125–46.

31. The *Boston City Directory*, 1870–72, lists Charles A. Cheney as a salesman with his business address as 36 Merchants Row. In 1873 he was an agent, at 23 Merchant Street; in 1874, a clerk at the same address, and in 1875 a clerk at 36 Merchant Street.

32. According to the Boston City directories, Charles's home was in Chelsea from 1870 to 1875; no address was given for 1870–73; for 1874, the address was 36 Marlborough Street; for 1875, 38 Marlborough Street. A search for deeds of ownership of property in Chelsea (1871–75) and Boston (1875–95) by the Cheneys yielded no results.

33. Beach, "Why I Chose My Profession," 7.

34. Beach to Wiggers.

35. Cheney, [Biography], [5].

36. Gertrude F. Cowen, "Mrs. H. H. A. Beach, the Celebrated Composer," *Musical Courier* 60 (8 June 1910): 14.

37. Cheney, [Biography], [4–5]; Elson, 295.

38. Cheney, [Biography], [5]; Biographical essay (Nh-TFL), [2].

39. Illus. Hammett Billings (Boston: Fields, Osgood, 1871).

40. John S. C. Abbott, "On the Mother's Role in Education (1833)," in Greven, *Child-Rearing Concepts*, 129.

41. Eileen McCann, "Dean of American Women Composers Recalls her Early Days in Chelsea," [c. 1932] (Beach Clipping File, NN-L).

42. Biographical essay (Nh-TFL), [3].

43. Beach to Wiggers; "Mrs. H. H. A. Beach" Nh-TFL and Nh disagree on the location of the farm; the manuscript biographies, however, show no corrections by Beach.

44. Beach, "Why I Chose My Profession," 7.

45. Ibid., 7.

46. Kinscella, "'Play No Piece,'" 9.

47. Elson, 295.

48. Beach, "Why I Chose My Profession," 7.

49. Amy undoubtedly heard her mother practicing the chorales for the 1869 Peace Jubilee, which included "great choruses of . . . Mendelssohn" (*History of the Handel and Haydn Society, of Boston, Massachusetts*, vol. 1 [1883–1893; reprint, New York: Da Capo Press, 1977], 287.

50. The "Spirit Waltz," from a set of *Six Valses et une Marche Funèbre* (Mayence: B. Schott, c. 1828); see Georg Kinsky, *Das Werk Beethovens. Thematisch-bibliographisches Verzeichnis*, ed. Hans Halm (Munich: G. Henle, 1955), 727–28. Kinsky cites another piece called "Spirit Waltz" (New York: n.p., n.d.), which may also be spurious. There is no indication which one Amy Beach played.

51. "How Mrs. Beach Did Her First Composing," 22.

52. Ibid., 22.

53. Beach, "Why I Chose My Profession," 7.

54. Philip J. Greven, Jr., *The Protestant Temperament: Patterns of Child-Rearing, Religious Experience, and the Self in Early America* (New York: Knopf, 1977), 282. See also Deborah Gorham, *The Victorian Girl and the Feminine Ideal* (London: Croon Helm, 1982), 69, who gives the age of dress differentiation for English children as between three and four years old.

55. Gorham, 72–75.

56. Ibid., 76–77.

57. Cheney, [Biography]; see also Cheney to "Cousin Anna," NhU.

58. Beach, "Why I Chose My Profession," 7. Note that in later years, Beach had only praise for her mother's teaching.

59. "Education of Girls," *Concord Monitor*, 26 January 1866.

60. *Boston Conservatory Method for the Piano-forte* (Boston: White-Smith, 1878). There must

have been an earlier edition, for in 1875 an article, "A Young Pianist," in Folio 12 (April 1875): 123, states that she has already mastered the method.

61. Letter to Wiggers.

62. Beach, "Why I Chose My Profession," 7; Cheney, [Biography], [10–11].

63. Cheney, [Biography], [10].

64. Cheney, [Biography], [10].

65. "A Young Pianist," 123; Cheney, [Biography], [10].

66. Beach to Wiggers. Cheney, [Biography], does not mention any offers by managers.

67. "Mrs. H. H. A. Beach," Nh, [4]; Biographical essay, Nh-TFL, [6].

68. Beach to Wiggers.

69. Cheney [Biography], [11], identifies the neighborhood to which they moved as "Boston Highlands," not Roxbury, as stated in the street directory.

70. *Growing Up in Boston's Gilded Age: The Journal of Alice Stone Blackwell, 1872–74*, ed. Marlene Deahl Merrill (New Haven: Yale University Press, 1990), is a record of Blackwell's years between fourteen and sixteen and demonstrates a different kind of rearing by Lucy Stone and her husband, Henry Blackwell, both feminists.

Chapter 2. The Cheneys and the Marcys

1. Clara Cheney to "Cousin Anna," 27 April 1898 (NhU-Be, typed copy).

2. *DAB* 5: 422–24. See also Cushman to "Dear Friend," Paris, 25 May, n.y. (NhU-Be).

3. Charles Henry Pope, comp., *The Cheney Genealogy* (Boston: Charles H. Pope, 1897), 199–209.

4. Inscription on the flyleaf of the Cheney family bible, "made by Cheney and Morison at Peterborough, N.H. about the year 1842" (NhU-Be). According to Sherman Grant Bonney, *Calvin Fairbanks Bonney and Harriet Cheney Bonney, A Tribute* (Concord, N.H.: Rumford Press, 1930), 18, the paper on which the inscription is printed was made by Moses Cheney, Amy Cheney's great-grandfather. The Moses Cheney who ran a singing school and is mentioned by Gilbert Chase in *America's Music*, rev. 3rd ed. (Urbana: University of Illinois Press, 1987), 34, was a distant cousin.

5. Bonney, 18.

6. Pope, 530.

7. Pope, 532–33.

8. *Bulletin of the Phillips Exeter Academy* (September 1907): 52. The *Catalogue of the Officers and Students of the Maine State Seminary, Lewiston,* (Lewiston, Me.: Journal Office, 1858 and 1859) lists Charles A. Cheney of Stratham, N.H., as a student during his fourteenth and fifteenth years.

9. Leander W. Cogswell, *History of the Town of Henniker*, reprint of 1880 edition with a new foreword by Francis Lane Childs (Somersworth: New Hampshire Publishing Co., 1973), 497.

10. Records of the Superior Court, Merrimack County, N.H.

11. Rebecca Rundlett lived until 1888, nineteen years after the divorce, which Pope, 531, carefully obscures, as follows: "His wife died, and he m.2, Oct. 26 1871, Martha . . . Smith," 531. The same statement appears in Bonney, 31–32.

12. The family bible includes the following entry for a younger brother who died in infancy: "James Rundlett Cheney was born 19 November 1846." His death is not recorded there. No further reference to James has been found.

13. Pope, 547.

14. Letter to the author from Edouard Desrochers, archivist, Phillips Exeter Academy, 21 November 1988.

15. *Bulletin of the Phillips Exeter Academy* (September 1907), 52.

16. "The American Baptist Churches of New Hampshire: The Bicentennial Historical Papers," prepared for the 200th Anniversary of the Freewill Baptist Denomination, 1780–1980, New Hampshire Historical Society, Concord, N.H. (NhHi).

17. *Catalogue of the Maine State Seminary*, 23.

18. The first-year curriculum at the seminary included Latin, English, algebra, physiology, geography, natural philosophy, and Greek. In the second year, French (including Mme de Sevigné's letters), botany, and ancient history were added. This was a strenuous curriculum for which Charles may have had little or no preparation except for Latin.

19. Biographical essay of Beach (earlier version of "Mrs. H. H. A. Beach," Nh) and catalogue in Beach's hand, which includes only piano works (Nh-TFL, typescript, n.d.), [1–9]. See also "Mrs. H. H. A. Beach" (S2, 55).

20. Cogswell, *History of the Town of Henniker*, 421.

21. "Charles A. Cheney," *The Paper Trade Journal*, 24 (3 August 1895): 717. Boston city directories for the years 1870–1895, however, give seemingly contradictory information as follows: 1876–78, salesman for Eager, Cheney; 1879–82, agent for Butterworth and Smalley, Boston; 1882–95, agent for Butterworth and Griffith, Boston.

22. Information about the Marcy family is found in George Waldo Browne, *The History of Hillsborough, New Hampshire, 1735–1921*, vol. 2, *Biography and Genealogy* (Manchester, N. H.: John B. Clarke, 1922): 401, 404–06, 445–46; Oliver Marcy, "Record of the Marcy Family," in *The New England Historical and Genealogical Register*, vol. 19 (Boston: David Clapp and Sons, 1875), 300–14. See also Clarence Winthrop Bowen, Donald Lines Jacobus, and William Herbert Wood, *The History of Woodstock Connecticut*, vol. 7, *Genealogies of Woodstock Families*, (Worcester, Mass.: American Antiquarian Society, 1943): 342–43, 349, 362, 376–77; and D. L. Jacobus and Edgar Francis Waterman, *The Waterman Family* vol. 3, *Descendants of Richard Waterman of Providence, Rhode Island* (Hartford: Connecticut Historical Society, 1954), 402–403.

23. Jacobus and Waterman, 403, give her name as Ann Eliza, probably her birth name. Her death certificate (New Hampshire Division of Public Health Services Bureau of Vital Records, Concord) gives her name as Amy E. Marcy; the 1870 Bureau of the Census for the Town of Henniker, Merrimack County, lists Amy Marcy as one of the residents in the Cheney household.

24. Amy Beach is quoted in a press release by Mary Thornton McDermott [1934], that Chester Marcy "was one of the gold pioneers of '49, but he died on his way west from New Hampshire" (NhU-Be, typescript). Although other sources, including Browne (405), give the date of Chester Marcy's death as 9 May 1849, Jacobus and Waterman (403) give the date as 6 August 1871, in agreement with Bowen (376–77).

25. "Mrs. H. H. A. Beach," *Musikliterärische Blätter*, Vienna 1 (21 May 1904), 2.

26. The marriage is recorded in the New Hampshire Vital Records.

27. Excerpt from address by Colonel Leander Cogswell, delivered 4 July 1868, quoted in *Forget New Hampshire?*, booklet prepared by residents of the town based on privately held documents (Henniker, 1968).

28. Cogswell, *History of the Town of Henniker*, 321–24.

29. Ibid., 321–24.

30. Ibid., 332.

31. Ibid., 333.

32. *Concord Monitor*, 1 March 1866.

33. Dorothy VanHouten, comp., "A History of Music in New Hampshire" (New Hampshire Writers Project no. 2354, 1941, typescript), 62–63.

34. "The Musical Convention," *Concord Monitor*, 5 January 1865.

35. Advertisements, Manchester *Daily Union*, 20 September and 3 October 1865.

36. VanHouten, 63.

37. "The May Festival," *Concord Monitor*, 4 May 1866.

38. *Forget New Hampshire?*

39. "Mrs. H. H. A. Beach," biographical essay and catalog of works through op. 45 with additions in Beach's hand (Nh), [1]; Louis C. Elson, *The History of American Music* (1915; rev. 1925; reprint, New York: Burt Franklin, 1971), 297.

40. Browne, 405.

41. A search through newspapers in Concord and Manchester for the two years before Amy was born yielded no information about Clara's musical activities.

42. Clara Imogene Cheney, [Biography of her daughter], 26 February 1892 (MacDowell Colony Papers, DLC-Ms, holograph), 10. The manuscript is signed at the end, p. 13, "Clara Imogene Cheney, Hotel Bellevue. 17 Beacon St[reet], Boston, Mass. February 26, 1892."

43. For a discussion of the mother's loss of subjectivity and the problem of maternal silence as the daughter develops, see Marianne Hirsch, *The Mother/Daughter Plot: Narrative, Psychoanalysis, Feminism* (Bloomington: Indiana University Press, 1989), 162–63.

44. The photographs are identified only by the names and addresses of photographers. Two views of the same person were taken by photographers in Concord where Clara Cheney lived: W. G. C. Kimball's is presumably of Clara Cheney before marriage, since her hair was well below her waist—women usually wore their hair up after marriage—(NhU-Be, box 5, folder 91); he took a picture of Amy Cheney when she was about two years old (NhU-Be, box 5, folder 1). A second photo of the same woman, again presumably Clara Cheney, was taken by J. P. Morgan of Concord (NhU-Be, box 5, folder 41).

45. I am grateful to Dr. Anna Burton for her psychoanalytical insights on the relationship between Amy and her mother.

46. A search of the Boston city directories for the period when Franc Marcy was in Boston yields no address for her. She may have boarded in a private home or stayed with relatives.

47. *Boston City Directory*, 1865, p. 91.

48. San Francisco city directories, 1868–1922.

49. "Jubilee Sheet," *Boston Daily Evening Transcript*, 17 June 1872.

50. Hirsch, 64.

51. *Grove-American*, s.v., "San Francisco."

Chapter 3. *A Prodigy Despite Her Mother*

1. Wilma Reid Cipolla, *A Catalog of the Works of Arthur Foote 1853–1937* (Detroit: Information Coordinators, for College Music Society, 1980), xvii. Victor Fell Yellin, *Chadwick, Yankee Composer* (Washington, D.C.: Smithsonian Institution Press, 1990), 22–23.

2. Clara Cheney continued singing with the Handel and Haydn Society until 1883, missing only the 1878–79 season, which suggests that she stayed in San Francisco with her daughter (Soprano Roll Books, Handel and Haydn Society Collection MB-Ms).

3. This episode is described in Gertrude F. Cowen, "Mrs. H. H. A. Beach, the Celebrated Composer," *Musical Courier* 60 (8 June 1910): 14; Agnes Lockhart Hughes, "Mrs. H. H. A. Beach," *The Simmons* 4 (October 1911): 476; "Mrs. H. H. A. Beach," biographical essay and catalog of works through op. 45 with additions in Beach's hand (Nh); and Biographical essay of Beach (earlier version of "Mrs. H. H. A. Beach," Nh) and catalog in Beach's hand, which includes only piano works (Nh-TFL, typescript, n.d.). The names of the German musicians are not given in any of the sources.

4. Mrs. H. H. A. Beach, "Music after Marriage and Motherhood," *Etude* 28 (August 1909): 520.

5. See Carolyn G. Heilbrun, *Writing a Woman's Life* (New York: W. W. Norton, 1988), 97–98, on the rarity of female friendships for gifted young women.

6. Summarized from Karen A. Shaffer and Neva Garner Greenwood, *Maud Powell, Pioneer American Violinist* (Ames: Iowa State University Press, 1988).

7. These or similar words appear in "Mrs. H. H. A. Beach" (Nh); Cowen, 14; Agnes Lockhart Hughes, "Mrs. H. H. A. Beach, America's Foremost Woman Composer," *Simmons*, 4 (October 1911): 476.

8. Ednah Dow Cheney, a distant relative by marriage, wrote of the educational opportunities for girls, (see "The Women of Boston," in the *Memorial History of Boston*, ed. Justin Winsor [Boston: James R. Osgood, 1880–81], 4: 344–45) that the Latin School for girls opened January 1, 1878, the very year Amy turned thirteen. She mentions further that colleges and professional schools were in 1880 "largely open to women."

9. See, for example, Ann Douglas Wood, "The Fashionable Diseases: Women's Complaints and Their Treatment in Nineteenth-Century America," in *Clio's Consciousness Raised: New Perspectives on the History of Women*, ed. Mary Hartman and Lois M. Banner (New York: Harper and Row, 1974), 2.

10. Dr. Edward Clark of Harvard, in his influential *Sex in Education* (1873), stated that "higher education was destroying the reproductive functions of American women, by overworking them at a critical time in their physiological development" (quoted in Elaine and English Showalter, "Victorian Women and Menstruation," *Victorian Studies* 14 [September 1970]: 87). See also, *Victorian Women: A Documentary Account of Women's Lives in Nineteenth-Century England, France, and the United States*, ed. Erna Olafsen Hellerstein, Leslie Parker Hume, and Karen M. Offen (Stanford, Calif.: Stanford University Press, 1981), 69–70: "Any strain upon a girl's intellect is to be dreaded, and any attempt to bring women into competition with men can scarcely escape failure."

11. The quote is from "Women's Musical Influence," *Message Bird* 2 (1 August 1850): 409. Nineteenth-century literature on the tradition of music as an accomplishment for middle-class girls and women is extensive. See Judith Tick, *American Women Composers Before 1870* (Ann Arbor, Mich.: UMI Research Press, 1983), 21–31. Note especially Tick's summary statement, "Tradition simultaneously encouraged them to take up music, yet discouraged them from aspiring to any meaningful standard and repressed artistic ambition" (30).

12. Carroll Smith-Rosenberg, *Disorderly Conduct: Visions of Gender in Victorian America* (New York: Alfred A. Knopf, 1985), 33.

13. (Johann) Ernst Perabo (1845–1920) was born in Wiesbaden, Germany. At the age of five, he began piano lessons with his father. The family emigrated to the United States in 1852; Perabo returned to Germany to study in Leipzig (1858–65) with funds raised by John Sullivan Dwight from a group of Boston supporters, and by William Scharfenberg in New York. Returning to this country, he made his mark in Boston and remained there to teach and perform. See Elson, 289, and Dwight-Scharfenberg Correspondence (MB-Ms).

14. *Johann Ernst Perabo: Compositions, Arrangements and Transcriptions* (Boston: Sparrell Print, n.d.).

15. See the recital program and a letter regarding "For Amy" in Perabo's scrapbook (Allen A. Brown Collection, MB-Mus). Persistent search has not as yet located "For Amy," which Perabo stated was published in Leipzig in 1881.

16. Amy Beach, "Why I Chose My Profession: The Autobiography of a Woman Composer," interviewed by Ednah Aiken, *Mother's Magazine* 11 (February 1914), 7.

17. *History of the Handel and Haydn Society* (1883–1893; reprint, New York: Da Capo Press, 1977), 1: 356–75.

18. Siegmund Levarie, "Hans von Bülow in America," *Newsletter, Institute for Studies in American Music* 11 (November 1981): 8.

19. William Armstrong, "New Gems in the Old Classics: A Talk with Mrs. H. H. A. Beach," *Etude* 22 (February 1904): 52.

20. Amy Fay, *Music Study in Germany*, with a new introduction by Edward O. D. Downes (1898; reprint, New York: Da Capo Press, 1979).

21. Marta Milinowski, *Teresa Carreño: "By the Grace of God."* (New Haven: Yale University Press, 1940).

22. Autograph Album, 1877–1909 (NhU-Be), 21. The album includes sixty-six items among which are communications from Darwin, pianists Busoni, Baermann, Bloomfield-Zeisler, Carreño, Essipoff, Richard Hoffman, Liszt, Joseffy, William Mason, Moriz Rosenthal, and Scharwenka; conductors Gericke, Henschel, Listemann, Neuendorff, Paur, Thomas, and Zerrahn; singers Blauvelt, Cary, Farrar, Hegermann-Lindencrone, Emma Nevada, Clara Kathleen Rogers, Scalchi, Sembrich, and Myron Whitney; violinists Bull, Liebe, and Powell; composers Chadwick, Foote, Paine, Parker, and Reinecke; writers Boucicault, Coates, Deland, Oliver Wendell Holmes, Longfellow, Nora Perry, Wendell Phillips, Harriet Spofford, Celia Thaxter, and Whittier; and the actors Edwin Booth and John Gilbert.

23. "Woman Composer Praises Philadelphia Orchestra," *Philadelphia Public Ledger*, 28 February 1915 (S4).

24. Kinscella, "'Play No Piece in Public When First Learned,' Says Mrs. Beach," *Musical America* 28 (7 September 1918): 10.

25. See Diary entry, 12 May 1930 (NhU-Be), in which Beach notes that this was the "52nd anniversary of going to San Francisco." See also letter from Beach to Jessica Fredricks, librarian of the Music Collection, San Francisco Public Library, 6 February 1939 (San Francisco Public Library, Bernard Osher Foundation Art and Music Center, Musicians' Letters: An Autograph Collection).

26. "A Medley of Choral Societies (1849–1906)," in History of Music in San Francisco Series, 15 (Works Projects Administration, City and County of San Francisco, June 1941, typescript), 55–59.

27. [Robert L. Stevenson], "Liszt's 'Favorite' California Pupil: Hugo Mansfeldt (1844–1932)," *Inter American Music Review* 7 (spring–summer 1986): 50.

28. Copy of letter from Zerrahn to Arthur P. Schmidt, undated, in German, on four sheets of Henry Beach's prescription forms, translated into English on four additional sheets of prescription forms; both are in Amy Beach's hand (NhU-Be).

29. "A Medley of Choral Societies," 55–57.

30. "Liszt's 'Favorite' California Pupil": 50.

31. "The May Festival," *Daily Alta California*, 31 May 1878, p. 1.

32. That Clara returned home soon after their arrival in San Francisco is suggested by the photographs taken in San Francisco during Amy's visit, none of which include Clara. On the other hand, there is no listing of a residence for 1878 under Charles Cheney's name in the Boston City Directory. Clara Cheney may have stayed in San Francisco with her daughter and the Clements or she and her husband may have lived in a hotel or other commercial lodging that year. However, see note 2 above.

33. Pencil manuscript, NhU-Be.

34. I am grateful to Susan C. Cook for the information that bustles were the latest fashion in 1878.

35. Sill (1841–87) was a poet whose thought and style were compared to Emerson. See Rockwell D. Hunt, "Edward Roland Sill," *California and Californians*, vol. 4 (San Francisco:

Lewis Publishing, 1926), 124–25. See also *NCAB*, s.v. "Sill, Edward Roland." To date, all efforts to locate such a book on California song birds have failed. Perhaps the book was never published.

36. Beach, "Why I Chose My Profession," 7.

37. Biographical esssay (Nh-TFL), 6.

38. Jane Holtz Kay, *Lost Boston* (Boston: Houghton Mifflin, 1980), 113.

39. Burnet C. Tuthill, "Mrs. H. H. A. Beach," *Musical Quarterly* 26 (July 1940): 301. Although Tuthill does not document this anecdote or anything else in the article, he had close cooperation from Beach in its preparation.

40. Obituary, William L. Whittemore, *Boston Evening Transcript*, 5 July 1911. Whittemore (1824–1911) was a first-class educator whose preparatory school in Boston turned out "some of the leading lawyers, business men and statesmen of New England."

41. Kinscella, 10.

42. M. Eloise Talbot, "A Brief Résumé of the History of the Attic Club," 2 May 1953, 3 (Attic Club Papers, Boston Athenaeum, typescript).

43. Letter to Edith Brown, 6 November 1940 (Attic Club Papers, Boston Athenaeum).

44. Talbot, 3.

45. Heilbrun, 98.

46. Talbot, 2.

47. Alice Bryant, "Little Sketch of Noted Guest," *Riverside Press*, 19 April 1915. Longfellow's letter is in Autograph Album, 1877–1909, 2.

48. Kinscella, 9.

49. The song is described as "very beautiful . . . full of pathetic sadness, yet rare dramatic quality," untitled clipping, *San Francisco Chronicle*, 13 May 1900 (S1, 132). As noted below, the melody is borrowed from the fourth movement of Beethoven's "Pathétique" Sonata. Her other settings of Longfellow texts are "The Arrow and the Song" (manuscript, 3 June 1922, MoKU-Be), which is published in an unidentified collection for children by Hinds, Hayden, and Eldridge (see "Amy M. Beach Estate: MacDowell Colony Papers, DLC-Ms, 2), and the dramatic song *In the Twilight*, op. 85.

50. Longfellow to Perabo, 20 November 1880 (Beach Correspondence, NhU-Be).

51. Autograph Album, 1877–1909.

52. Louis C. Elson, *The History of American Music* (1915; rev. 1925; reprint, New York: Burt Franklin, 1971), 298.

53. Louis C. Elson, *A Review of the Baermann Society*, (Boston 1913); "At the Breakfast Table," Allen A. Brown Scrapbook (MB-Mu).

54. Beach, "Why I Chose My Profession," 7.

55. Elson states that before Beach's debut "the intention . . . was to continue the studies in Europe and to develop a concert virtuoso"; he does not state whose intention it was. See Louis C. Elson, "Mrs. Beach, the American Composer," *Henniker Weekly Courier* 28 January 1896, p. 50.

56. Myrna Garvey Eden, *Energy and Individuality in the Art of Anna Huntington, Sculptor, and Amy Beach, Composer* (Metuchen, N. J.: Scarecrow Press, 1987), 38, quoting from a 1975 interview with Walter S. Jenkins.

57. Talbot, 3.

58. "Lohengrin," Margaret Ross Griffel, *Opera in German: A Dictionary* (Westport, Conn.: Greenwood Press, 1990), 149.

59. *Grove-American*, s.v. "Neuendorff, Adolph."

60. An American-born and trained soprano, Kellogg had made her debut in New York in 1861 as Marguerite in *Faust*, a role she sang many times thereafter. Esteemed as a singer in

Europe, as well as in the United States, she also had managed two opera companies, touring the United States at a time when permanent resident opera companies did not exist. Now, four years short of retirement, she was a favorite on the Handel and Haydn Society's programs, and a regular on Peck's Boston concerts. See *Grove-American*, s.v. "Kellogg, Clara Louise," and *History of the Handel and Haydn Society*, vol. 1, 373, 375–6, 383–4, 403, *et passim*.

61. *Grove-American*, s.v. "Adamowski, Timothée." The following year Adamowski joined the violin section of the Boston Symphony Orchestra, where he played for over twenty seasons. A soloist with the orchestra an astounding eighty-two times between 1885 and 1907, he also led the Adamowski String Quartet; from 1908, he taught at the New England Conservatory.

62. Mildred Aldrich, "Mrs. Amy Marcy Cheney Beach" (clipping, n.d., S1, 83), states that Cheney played her first recital at seven from memory. See also J[ohn] S[ullivan] D[wight], "First Piano Recital of Mrs. H. H. A. Beach," *Boston Transcript*, 29 February 1891 (S1, 58).

63. Olin Downes, "Mrs. H. H. A. Beach of Boston, Now Noted as Composer," unidentified clipping, 1907.

64. "Musical Notes," *Boston Gazette*, 25 October 1883 (S1, 3).

65. "Mr. Peck's Anniversary Concert," *Boston Transcript*, 28 October 1883 (S1, 2).

66. "Music and the Drama," *Boston Advertiser*, 25 October 1883 (S1, 2).

67. Beach, "How I Chose My Profession," 7.

68. The assisting artists were Lillian Bailey Henschel, who was accompanied at the piano by her husband Georg Henschel, conductor of the Boston Symphony, and Charles Martin Loeffler, violinist with the symphony who would soon become one of America's leading composers.

69. "Music and the Drama," *Boston Advertiser*, 10 January 1884 (S1, 8).

70. "Miss Amy Cheney's Recital," *Boston Transcript*, 10 January 1884.

71. "Music and the Drama," *Boston Advertiser*, 10 January 1884 (S1, 8).

72. Agnes Lockhart Hughes, "Mrs. H. H. A. Beach—America's Foremost Composer," *Boston Times*, 13 March 1915 (S4).

73. "Miss Amy Marcy Cheney's Recital," *Boston Globe*, 20 March 1884 (S1, 16).

74. Beach to Sembrich, 26 November 1906 (Sembrich Correspondence, NN-L).

75. Perry, untitled clipping (S1, 19).

76. *Boston Evening Traveller*, 30 March 1885 (S1, 26).

77. "The Boston Symphony Concert," *Boston Courier*, 29 March 1885 (S1, 25).

78. "Theatres and Concerts: Boston Symphony Orchestra," *Boston Evening Transcript*, 30 March 1885 (S1, 25).

79. *Boston Beacon*, 4 April 1885 (S1, 25).

80. "The Second Thomas Concert," *Boston Advertiser*, 30 April 1885 (S1, 28).

81. Beach, "How I Chose My Profession," 7; Burnet C. Tuthill, "Mrs. H. H. A. Beach," *Musical Quarterly* 26 (July 1940): 299.

82. "The Second Thomas Concert," *Boston Advertiser*, 30 April 1885 (S1, 28); "The Thomas Concerts," *Boston Beacon*, 2 May 1885 (S1, 23); "The Thomas Concerts," *Boston Transcript*, 1 May 1885 (S1, 28).

83. Emily Constant, "Women Who Have Succeeded, 1: Mrs. H. H. A. Beach," *New England Home Magazine* (5 March 1898): 408.

Chapter 4. The Making of a Composer: I

1. A manuscript of "Mamma's Waltz" is at MoKU-Be. On the composition, see "America's Woman Composer," *Boston Beacon* (S1, 99), which states that she wrote out "Snowflake

Waltz" at the same time. In a letter dated 24 August 1935, Beach noted that the "Snowflake Waltz" is "quite a brilliant little waltz which I sometimes now play to friends but not in public." See also her letter to Mrs. Edwin H. Wiggers.

2. Agnes Lockhart Hughes, "Mrs. H. H. A. Beach, America's Foremost Woman Composer," *Simmons* 4 (October 1911): 476.

3. Holographs of these pieces are at MoKU-Be.

4. "Wohin" is from Schubert's *Die Schöne Müllerin* (Wilhelm Müller) of 1823. A variety of hands are apparent in these manuscripts, all at MoKU-Be; "Romanza," and the "Air and Variations" are in Amy Cheney's hand.

5. Hill (1840–1916) had graduated from Boston's English High School and then went to Leipzig to study at the conservatory with Moscheles and Reinecke before returning to Boston.

6. Biography from Wellesley College Archives. See also Laurel Stavis, "The Story of Music: Nineteenth-Century Boston and College Music Passions Coincide," *Wellesley College Realia* 77 (winter 1988): 2. Hill headed the music department of Wellesley College from 1884 to 1897. There he upgraded the curriculum to offer rigorous training to the women students in theory, harmony, and analysis. He also encouraged students to study violin and other stringed instruments—long considered improper for females—and to play chamber music. In his advocacy of stringed instruments for women, Hill followed in the footsteps of Julius Eichberg at the Boston Conservatory; see Adrienne Fried Block, assisted by Nancy Stewart, "Women in American Music, 1800–1918," in *Women and Music: A History*, ed. Karin Pendle (Bloomington: Indiana University Press, 1991), 154–56.

7. Neither poet nor composer, both female, seemed concerned that the speaker in the poem is male. This seems consistent with the practice of singers of Lieder, who usually select songs without consideration of the gender of the poetic speaker.

8. *Mrs. H. H. A. Beach* (Boston: Arthur P. Schmidt, 1906), 8.

9. Letter to Louise Barili, Patti's great-niece, 4 April 1913, Georgia Department of Archives and History. Beach recalled the performance of *Traviata* forty-five years later; see Diary, 6 June 1930. See *Grove-American*, s.v. "Patti, Adelina."

10. An unidentified clipping (S1, 19) indicates that the dedication was for Cheney's unpublished "Romanza" for piano, written in 1877 (manuscript at MoKU-Be). The words *for pianoforte* are crossed out, however, which suggests that the wrong work was identified. "With Violets" is the only composition that she dedicated to Patti.

11. Clara Kathleen Rogers, *The Story of Two Lives* (Norwood, Mass.: privately printed, 1932), 81.

12. Stella Reid Crothers, "Women Composers of America—14: Madame Helen Hopekirk," *Musical America* 10 (4 September 1909): 15.

13. Judith Ann Cline, "Margaret Ruthven Lang: Her Life and Songs" (Ph.D. diss., Washington University, 1993), 11–12.

14. John N. Burk, "Wilhelm Gericke: A Centennial Prospect," *Musical Quarterly* 31 (April 1945): 170, 173–75.

15. See chapter 3, "The Establishing under Wilhelm Gericke, 1884–89" in Mark A. De Wolfe Howe, *The Boston Symphony Orchestra, 1881–1931*, rev. John N. Burk (Boston: Houghton Mifflin, 1931), 59–87. Information on the works Gericke conducted is culled from appendix B. Further see Burk, "Wilhelm Gericke," 163–87.

16. Telephone call by the author to Jeanne Morrow, head of the Music Library, New England Conservatory, 19 December 1988, who reported that Chadwick, James C. D. Parker, and Louis Maas taught composition there in 1884, and Maas, Stephen A. Emery, and George H. Howard taught theory.

17. "Mrs. H. H. A. Beach," *Boston Home Journal*, 19 April 1902, (S1).

18. Chadwick wrote in 1898 after a second hearing of the "Gaelic" Symphony: "What remarkable things this lady might have accomplished if she had had any training!" See [Chadwick Family Memoir], unpaginated sheets in a spiral notebook, private collection of Theodore Chadwick, Duxbury, Massachusetts. Compare Beach's course of self-study with the experience of Sergei Prokofiev: at the age of 10 when he arrived at the Moscow Conservatory carrying the manuscript of an opera, he was immediately given a composition teacher to prevent him from developing bad habits; see Harlow Robinson, *Sergei Prokofiev: A Biography* (New York: Viking, 1987).

19. Barbara Welter, *Dimity Convictions: The American Woman in the Nineteenth Century* (Athens, Ohio: Ohio University Press, 1976), 77–78, quotes from a list published in 1843 assigning the intellectual qualities to males, the intuitive to females.

20. George P. Upton, *Woman in Music* (Boston: J. R. Osgood, 1880), cited in Judith Tick, "Passed Away Is the Piano Girl," in *Women Making Music: The Western Art Tradition,* 1150–1950, ed. Jane Bowers and Judith Tick (Urbana: University of Illinois Press, 1986), 333.

21. Cited in Tick, 333.

22. Cited in Tick, 334.

23. Benjamin Brooks, ed., "The 'How' of Creative Composition: A Conference with Mrs. H. H. A. Beach," *Etude* 61 (March 1943): 151, 208.

24. H. Wiley Hitchcock has referred to this group of Boston composers of the late nineteenth and twentieth centuries as the Second New England School (*Music in the United States: A Historical Introduction,* 3rd edition [Englewood Cliffs, N.J.: Prentice Hall, 1988], 143–51).

25. For further discussion of Schmidt's role in the promotion of American music and especially works by American women, see Adrienne Fried Block, "Arthur P. Schmidt, Music Publisher and Champion of American Women Composers," in *The Musical Woman: An International Perspective*, vol. 2, 1984–85, ed. Judith Lang Zaimont, Catherine Overhauser, and Jane Gottlieb (Westport, Conn.: Greenwood Press, 1987), 144–76.

Chapter 5. Two Ways of Looking at a Marriage

1. "Life Sketch of H. H. A. Beach, M. D." Countway Medical Library, Boston, Mass.; s.v. "Beach, Henry Harris Aubrey"; *Biographical History of Massachusetts* (Boston: Massachusetts Biographical Society, 1911), s.v. "Henry Harris Aubrey Beach"; "Henry Harris Aubrey Beach," *The Harvard Medical School: A History, Narrative and Documentary,* 1782–1905, vol. 3, ed. Thomas Francis Harrington and James Gregory Mumford (New York and Chicago: Lewis Publishing Co., 1905): 1528. Obituaries are in *Boston Medical and Surgical Journal* 163 (14 July 1910): 71–72; *Boston Herald,* 29 June 1910, p. 8; *Boston Globe,* 29 June 1910, p. 8; and an unidentified clipping by Gertrude F. Cowen, in S4. See also *Harvard University Quinquennial Catalogue of Officers and Graduates,* 1630–1930 (Cambridge, Mass.: Harvard University, 1930); Frederick A. Washburn, M.D., *The Massachusetts General Hospital: Its Development,* 1900–1935 (Boston: Houghton Mifflin, n.d.); Grace Whiting Myers, *History of the Massachusetts General Hospital, June* 1872 *to December* 1900 (n.p., 1929).

2. With regard to the date of her engagement, Beach's recollections are contradictory, as her later diary entries suggest: on 13 August 1935, she wrote, "50th Anniversary of engagement"; on 13 August 1937, "Engagement announced in 1884!"; and on 12 August 1942, "Engagement (1885) out." The date of the wedding, however, is confirmed in numerous sources, including the marriage license.

3. Dr. Beach to Brooks, 25 and 30 May 1892, in Phillips Brooks Correspondence, Houghton Library, Harvard University. On Henry Beach's attendance as physician during Brooks's fatal illness, see Raymond W. Albright, *Focus on Infinity: A Life of Phillips Brooks* (New

York: Macmillan, 1961), 391. Regarding Amy Beach's possible relationship to Brooks, see Myrna Garvey Eden, *Energy and Individuality in the Art of Anna Huntington, Sculptor, and Amy Beach, Composer* (Metuchen, N.J.: Scarecrow Press, 1987), 41. Eden states, without documentation, that the Reverend Brooks and Amy Cheney had had frequent discussions on religious and philosophical ideas. She also states that Amy Cheney was a member of Trinity Church; however, the parish records do not list the Cheneys as pew holders, communicants, or recipients of the sacraments. Indeed, Amy Beach was not baptised as an Episcopalian until 1911.

4. "Obituaries, Marriage Notices, and Related Legal Documents," *Boston Beacon*, 5 December 1885. Drs. Henry Cutler Baldwin and Otis Kimball Newell were both Harvard Medical School graduates, and the latter became Henry Beach's assistant demonstrator of anatomy in 1887. The wedding date of 2 December 1885 is documented in the Massachusetts Department of Health and Vital Statistics, vol. 363, p. 202.

5. Clipping, Brooklyn *Daily Standard Union*, 25 May 1898, sec. 2, p. 41.

6. The description is on Henry Beach's United States Army discharge paper, 15 March 1866. He had enlisted on 23 July 1864 and was given the rank of hospital steward (NhU-Be).

7. Edith Gertrude Kinney, "Mrs. H. H. A. Beach," *The Musician* 4 (September 1899), 355.

8. A. M. B., "America's Chief Woman Composer," *Chicago Times-Herald* 28 November 1897 (S1, 119).

9. Kinney, 355.

10. "Massachusetts Vital Records," vol. 420, p. 265.

11. Ibid., vol. 402, p. 211.

12. "Connecticut Vital Records: Middletown Births, Marriages and Deaths, 1651−1854," p. 40, lists both Elijah and Lucy Beach's marriage and Henry's birth.

13. Home and business were at 52 School Street. Addresses and occupations were listed in the annual issues of the Cambridge city directories. There is no residential address for 1868.

14. *Biographical History of Massachusetts*, s.v. "Beach, Henry Harris Aubrey."

15. Genealogist Melinde Lutz Sanborn traced the Beach-Roosevelt connection through the marriage of Douglas Robinson, whose mother was a Beach, to Corinne Roosevelt, sister of President Theodore Roosevelt (letter from Sanborn to author, 25 July 1986).

16. *Biographical History of Massachusetts*; *The Harvard Medical School: A History*, 1528; Obituary, *Boston Medical and Surgical Journal*, 163.

17. Louis C. Elson, *The History of American Music* (1915; rev. 1925; reprint, New York: Burt Franklin, 1971), 269. *The Parish of the Advent in the City of Boston: A History of One Hundred Years, 1844−1944* (Boston, 1944), 124−26. See also Leonard Ellinwood, *The History of American Church Music*, rev. ed., (New York: Da Capo Press, 1970), 82.

18. Henry Beach's contemporary, Henry James (1843−1916), traveled from Cambridge to Boston by trolley. See *Henry James: An Autobiography*, ed., Frederick W. Dupee (New York: Criterion Books, 1956), 412. On music at the Church of the Advent, see J. Wallace Goodrich's chapter in *The Parish of the Advent in the City of Boston*, 124, 126, *et passim*. A boys' choir was established in 1849; by 1855 the adult choir was enlarged from a quartet to a double choir of men and boys and money was appropriated for them as well. A photograph of former members of the choir includes Henry Matson, choirmaster, and Henry Harris Aubrey Beach among others. It appears in Ann Maria Mitchell, "The Advent Parish, Boston: Pioneer of the Catholic Revival," *Living Church* (14 December 1935): 653.

19. Handel and Haydn Society Records, vol. 7 (MB-Ms). His name, given in the records as Henry H. Beach, tends to confirm the author's conjecture that "Aubrey" was added when he was baptised later that same year (see below).

20. The two sponsors for Henry were Mrs. Ruth L. Morey and Edmund Aubrey Matson, identified as an organist in the Boston City Directory, 1863, and possibly a relation of the choirmaster, Henry Matson (Church of the Advent, Parish Register, no. 885). According to Carlton Russell, Wheaton College, who is a musician and an ordained minister, it was common practice in England to add a name of one of the sponsors at the time of a christening. Ritual at the Church of the Advent was modeled on English Anglo-Catholic practice.

21. Parish Register, Church of the Advent, 20, lists Henry Harris Aubrey Beach among those confirmed by Bishop Manton Eastburn on 21 March 1864.

22. Mitchell, "The Advent Parish," 53. See also Mark J. Duffy, ed. *The Episcopal Diocese of Massachusetts, 1789–1984* (1984), 151. The date of establishment of the Church of the Advent was 14 September 1844.

23. *A Sketch of the History of the Parish of the Advent in the City of Boston, 1844–1894* (Boston: George H. Ellis, 1894), p. 23. George Cheyne Shattuck (1813–1894) attended Boston Latin School and Harvard Medical School (1835). According to the *Dictionary of American Medical Biography*, s.v. "Shattuck," he introduced into the United States the case method for teaching medicine. He also became the city's foremost Episcopal layman and was founder and financier of the Church of the Advent; *Pro Bono Publico: The Shattucks of Boston* (Boston: Massachusetts Historical Society, 1971). The other two physicians were William Edward Coale and Richard H. Salter, the latter an army surgeon during the Civil War.

24. Certificate of Appointment by the Army of the United States to the rank of hospital steward, 23 July 1864. A letter of appointment signed by George S. Gibson, captain, is in the archives of Massachusetts General Hospital.

25. In *A Memoir of Henry Jacob Bigelow* (Boston: Little, Brown, 1900), 50–51, Beach is identified as house surgeon of Massachusetts General Hospital, a position he held much later; in 1865, Beach was still in the army.

26. *A Memoir of Henry Jacob Bigelow*, 15, 47, *et passim*.

27. Discharge paper, Army of the United States, indicates that he enlisted as a clerk and was discharged from the position of hospital steward. His evaluation is "excellent in all respects . . . a highly efficient steward" (NhU-Be).

28. The addresses for 1867 to 1870 are found in Cambridge city directories.

29. *The Harvard Medical School: A History*, 1528; Obituary, *Boston Medical and Surgical Journal*, 163.

30. Holmes had gone to Paris, where he had the most advanced training in clinical medicine and diagnosis; he returned to complete his degree in medicine at Harvard in 1836. Eleven years later, he was appointed to Harvard, at which he taught until 1882. See Edwin P. Hoyt, *The Improper Bostonian Dr. Oliver Wendell Holmes* (New York: William Morrow, 1979), especially pp. 104–108, on his work on child-bed fever. See also Martin Kaufman, Stuart Galishoff, and Todd L. Savitt, *Dictionary of American Medical Biography*, vol. 1 (Westport, Conn.: Greenwood Press, 1984), 63 ff. Holmes tried unsuccessfully to win entrance of women and blacks into the medical school over the strenuous objections of his good friend and colleague Henry Bigelow.

31. Barry Menikoff, "Holmes, Oliver Wendell," *Dictionary of Literary Biography* 1, *The American Renaissance in New England*, ed. Joel Myerson (Detroit: Gale Research Co., 1978), 106–113.

32. Joe Lee David, John T. Frederick, and Franc Luther Mott, eds. *American Literature: An Anthology and Critical Survey*, vol. 2, *From 1860 to the Present* (New York: Charles Scribner's Sons, 1949), 186.

33. E. Digby Baltzell, *Puritan Boston and Quaker Philadelphia* (Boston: Beacon Press, 1979), 353.

34. Letter from Oliver Wendell Holmes, Beverly Farms, Mass., 25 June 1884, addressed to "My dear Sir," Holmes Papers, Countway Medical Library, Boston.

35. NCAB, vol. 15, p. 164.

36. The report of U.S. Bureau of the Census, State of Massachusetts, Suffolk County, Boston, Ward 10, 16 June 1870, p. 371, shows Henry Beach still living at home with his parents, brother, and an Irish servant and reports that Elijah owned $10,000 in real estate and had personal funds of $5,000.

37. *New Bedford Evening Standard*, 7 June 1871. Edward Mandell's wealth came from his law practice, extensive real estate holdings, and especially from whaling, then at its most prosperous; see Leonard Bolles Ellis, *History of New Bedford and Its Vicinity* (Syracuse, N.Y.: D. Mason, 1892), 461, 473−74, 485, 512, 517−18.

38. Deed on file, Suffolk County Courthouse, Boston, Mass.

39. The deed of purchase in Henry's name, 1 March 1879, states that the Massachusetts Hospital Life Insurance Co. held a mortgage for $20,000 (Suffolk County Courthouse, Boston, Mass.).

40. *One Boy's Boston, 1887−1901* (Boston: Houghton Mifflin, 1962), 24, 63.

41. Massachusetts Vital Records, Deaths, vol. 321, p. 182.

42. Myrna Garvey Eden, *Energy and Individuality in the Art of Anna Huntington, Sculptor, and Amy Beach, Composer* (Metuchen, N.J.: Scarecrow Press, 1987), 42, quoting 1975 interview with Jenkins. Walter Jenkins does not give the approximate date of Henry's and Amy's first meeting but quotes second-hand anecdotes from two of Beach's friends, both known only in her later life, to confirm this early friendship. One of them concerns the so-called stained-glass window that Dr. Beach gave Amy "'for her hotel bedroom because she complained of looking out on a brick wall'" (Walter S. Jenkins, *The Remarkable Mrs. Beach: American Composer* [Warren, Mich.: Harmonie Park Press, 1994], 12, 14). This could only have occurred in 1882 when the Cheneys lived in the Hotel Winthrop (Boston City Directory, 1882). Amy was fifteen, not ten, in 1882. The story is attributed to Esther Willard Bates, a fellow at the MacDowell Colony whom Beach knew in the 1930s and '40s. Eden interviewed Jenkins in 1975.

43. E. Lindsey Merrill, "Mrs. H. H. A. Beach: Her Life and Music" (Ph.D. diss., University of Rochester, 1963), 5.

44. "Already Composed a Mass," *Boston Globe*, 24 April 1892 (S2, 9). See also Emily Constant, "Women Who Have Succeeded: I. "Mrs. H. H. A. Beach," *The New England Home Magazine*, 5 March 1898, pp. 407−8.

45. Henry H. Beach joined the Handel and Haydn Society on 18 February 1863 (Handel and Haydn Society Records, vol. 7, MB-Ms).

46. Arthur Foote Scrapbook, MBCM.

47. Letter from Henry Beach to Francis H. Jenks, 10 November 1885 (MB-Ms).

48. Letter from Henry Beach, 27 September 1880, on resigning from the club, shortly after the death of Alice Beach (St. Botolph Club Archives).

49. Letter from Mason to Dr. Beach, in Autograph Album, 1877−1909, no. 53 (NhU-Be).

50. According to Jenkins, p. 15, Henry Beach sang one of her songs, "Jeune fille et jeune fleur," op. 1, no.3, still in manuscript, at a recital of pupils of L. M. Wheeler (printed program, 16 January 1885, NhU-Be).

51. Gertrude F. Cowen, "Mrs. H. H. A. Beach, the Celebrated Composer," *Musical Courier* 60 (8 June 1910): 14.

52. Author's interview, Cleveland, 8 January 1986, with Lillian Buxbaum Meredith, daughter of the singer and Beach's friend and heir. Meredith (now deceased), had been given the plates and told the story by Beach herself.

53. "Woman's First Symphony," *New York Press*, 27 February 1898, (S2, 35).

54. H. A. S., "At 74, Mrs. Beach Recalls Her First Critics," *Musical Courier*, 123 (15 May 1941): 7.

55. Cheney, "The Women of Boston," in *The Memorial History of Boston*, vol. 4, ed. Justin Winsor (Boston: Ticknor, 1881), 332, 350.

56. Told to the author by Eugenie Limberg Dengel (31 November 1988).

57. Arthur Wilson, "Mrs. H. H. A. Beach: A Conversation on Musical Conditions in America," *Musician* 17 (January 1912): 9; also H. A. S., "At 74, Mrs. Beach Recalls Her First Critics."

58. H. A. S., "At 74."

59. "The Etude Master Study Page: Famous Women Composers," *Etude* 35 (April 1917): 237.

60. Beach to Mrs. Edwin H. Wiggers, 24 August 1935 (P.E.O. Archives, New York, N.Y.).

61. Amy Beach, "Why I Chose My Profession: The Autobiography of a Woman Composer," interviewed by Ednah Aiken, *Mother's Magazine* 11 (February 1914): 7−8.

62. For a brief summary of Schmidt's career as a publisher, see Christine Merrick Ayars, *Contributions to the Art of Music in America by the Music Industries of Boston 1640−1936* (New York: H. W. Wilson, 1937), 38−41. See also Wilma Reid Cipolla, "Marketing the American Song in Edwardian London," *American Music* 8 (spring 1990): 84−94.

63. Beach to Arthur P. Schmidt, 5 October 1910, (Papers of the Arthur P. Schmidt Company, DLC-Mu).

64. The holograph is at MB-Mu.

65. Amy M. Beach, last will and testament, 6 July 1943, p. 4 (photocopy of will held by David Buxbaum).

66. Kinney, in "Mrs. H. H. A. Beach," makes note of Beach's "jewelled fingers," suggesting that she enjoyed wearing several rings at once. In her later life, however, Beach was more conservative in her use of jewelry.

67. Letter from Beach to Marcella Craft, New York, 8 May 1939, states that the dog is fifty-four years old and resides at her summer home in Centerville. The statue now belongs to David Buxbaum and sits on the porch of his summer home on Chebeague Island, Maine.

68. Carl N. Degler, *At Odds: Women and the Family in America from the Revolution to the Present* (New York: Oxford University Press, 1981), 385. Degler also concludes that 90 percent "of the wives of professional men practiced some form of birth control" between 1892 and 1920 (222).

69. Mrs. H. H. A. Beach, "How Music Is Made," *Keyboard* (winter 1942): 11, 38.

70. Ticknor, "The Symphonies," *Boston Globe*, 22 April 1888 (S1, 46).

71. Beach, "How Music Is Made," 11.

72. Eden, 86, based on a letter from Walter S. Jenkins. This statement is without documentation.

73. Beach, "Why I Chose My Profession," 7.

74. Beach to John Tasker Howard, 3 May 1930, NN-L.

75. H. A. S., "At 74," 7.

76. Beach, "Why I Chose My Profession," 7.

Chapter 6. The Making of a Composer: II

1. Hazel Gertrude Kinscella, "'Play No Piece in Public When First Learned,' Says Mrs. Beach," *Musical America* 28 (7 September 1918): 9.

2. A. M. B., "America's Chief Woman Composer," *Chicago Times-Herald*, 28 November 1897 (S1, 118−19).

3. Kinscella, 9.

4. Amy Beach, Notebook, 21 April 1887 to July 1894, Boston (MB-Mu, holograph), no folios.

5. Kinscella, 9.

6. Beach, Notebook, [20].

7. Ibid., [6]. Beach's citations in this workbook usually give only authors, with occasional page numbers. Among the authors she cites are the following (titles in parentheses are the present author's suggestions as to Beach's probable sources): George Grove (*A Dictionary of Music and Musicians*, 4 vols. [1890]) and William Foster Apthorp (probably *Scribner's Cyclopedia of Music and Musicians*, eds. Apthorp and John Denison [1888–90]); on theory and harmony, Wallace Goodrich, Weitzmann (probably Carl Friedrich Weitzmann with E. M. Bowman, *Weitzmann's Manual of Musical Theory* [New York, 1877]), and Banister (Henry C. Banister, *Lectures on Musical Analysis* [London, 1887]); texts on fugue include Ernst Friedrich Richter (*Treatise on Canon and Fugue* [London, 1878]), Karl August Haupt (*Haupt's Theory of Counterpoint, Fugue, and Double Counterpoint*, tr. H. Clarence Eddy [New York, 1876]), James Higgs (*Fugue* [London, 1878]), and Frederic Arthur Gore Ouseley (*A Treatise on Counterpoint, Canon, and Fugue, based on Cherubini* [Oxford, 1869]); on orchestration, François-Auguste Gevaert (*Cours méthodique d'orchestration* [Brussels, 1890]), Berlioz, (*Traité d'instrumentation*, 1843) and "C. M.," probably Charles Maclean (unidentified work); on composition, Percy Goetschius (*The Material Used in Musical Composition* [Stuttgart, 1882] or *The Theory and Practice of Tone-relations* [Boston, 1882]), and John Stainer (*Composition* [London, 1880]).

8. Harriette Brower, *Piano Mastery*, 2nd series (New York: Frederick A. Stokes, [1917]), 186–87. Further, see Kinscella, 9; Rupert Hughes, *Contemporary American Composers* (Boston: L. C. Page, 1900), 426.

9. Kinscella, 9.

10. Brower, *Piano Mastery*, 186–87.

11. Amy Beach, "Music Reviews," vol. 2, October 1894 (NhU-Be, holograph).

12. The Boston Symphony under Emil Paur gave the local debut on 18 December 1896; see Mark A. De Wolfe Howe, *Boston Symphony Orchestra: 1881–1931*, rev. John N. Burk (Boston: Houghton Mifflin, 1931), 196.

13. Beach, "Music Reviews," 88–90.

14. Beach, "Music's Ten Commandments," appendix 2.

15. 215. Benjamin Brooks, ed., "The 'How' of Creative Composition: A Conference with Mrs. H. H. A. Beach," *Etude* 61 (March 1943): 208.

16. *John Keats and Percy Bysshe Shelley: The Complete Poetical Works* (New York: The Modern Library, n.d.), 711–12. Beach omitted the first stanza.

17. As Ruth Solie has noted, nineteenth-century composers often set texts with a male protagonist to music written for a female voice. Beach followed this convention, but later, when she was widowed and on her own, she set many poems by women that were in a woman's voice.

18. H. H. A. B[each]., *Sketches* (Boston: Henry Beach, 1889). Amy Beach borrowed his title for a set of four piano pieces, op. 15 (1891).

19. For a discussion of op. 2, nos. 1 and 3, see chapter 12.

20. Hazel Gertrude Kinney, "Mrs. H. H. A. Beach," *Musician* 4 (September, 1899): 354.

21. Untitled article, *Boston Globe*, 1 March 1896 (S2, 17).

22. Kinscella, 9.

23. Untitled article, *Boston Globe*, 1 March 1896 (S2, 17).

24. It was published as *Cadenza to the First Movement of the Third Concerto for the Pianoforte in C minor, op. 37, by Ludwig van Beethoven*, op. 3 (Arthur P. Schmidt, 1888).

25. "Music: Twenty-third Symphony Concert," *Boston Post*, 23 April 1888 (S1, 48).

26. Untitled article, *Boston Beacon*, 22 April 1888 (S1, 47).

27. "Music," *Boston Home Journal*, 22 April 1888 (S1, 49).

28. Howard Malcom Ticknor, "The Symphonies," *Boston Globe*, 22 April 1888 (S1, 46).

29. "Mrs. Beach's Concert," *Boston Beacon*, n.d. (S1, 54).

30. "Mrs. Beach's Recital," *Boston Times* (S1, 54).

Chapter 7. *Becoming Mistress of her Craft*

1. *Grove-American*, s.v. "Paine, John Knowles."

2. "Women in Music," *Etude* (April ? [after 1913]) in S3.

3. Earlier composers of masses include Isabella Leonarda (1620–1704), Anna Amalia, Princess of Prussia (1723–1787), Sister Delia Bonita (fl. 1723), Josephine von Flad (1778–1843); see Barbara Garvey Jackson, *"Say Can You Deny Me": A Guide to Surviving Music by Women from the 16th through the 18th Centuries* (Fayetteville: University of Arkansas Press, 1994) 246, 249. Marianna Martines wrote five masses; see Irving Godt, "Marianna in Italy: The International Reputation of Marianna Martines (1744–1812)," *Journal of Musicology* 13 (fall 1995): 555. Ethel Smyth completed her Mass in D two years after Beach, in 1891; *Grove-Women*, s.v. "Smyth, Dame Ethel (Mary). Beach, however, knew of none of their works. See her response in the *Boston Daily Traveller*, 10 December 1892 (S1, 84–85), to "Women Can't Help. Dvořák says They Have No Creative Talent. He's Talking about Music," *Boston [Morning] Post*, 30 November 1892.

4. Amy Beach to Mrs. Edwin H. Wiggers, 24 August 1935 (P.E.O. Archives, New York City).

5. "Music's Ten Commandments," appendix 2.

6. Her scores of Beethoven's overtures are in the Ira F. Brilliant Center for Beethoven Studies, University of California, San Jose. Her scores of the Beethoven symphonies are at NhU-Sp, a donation of Arnold Steinhardt, first violinist of the Guarnieri Quartet. Otherwise, her score collection appears to be lost or dispersed.

7. On 5 May 1878 they broke tradition and gave Verdi's *Manzoni Requiem*. Mozart's Requiem Mass followed in 1881. However, the text for a requiem mass differs significantly from a solemn mass in the Roman Catholic ritual and could not have provided Beach with a model. For a list of the society's works in performance, see *History of the Handel and Haydn Society, of Boston Massachusetts*, vol. 1 (1883–1893; reprint, New York: Da Capo Press, 1977), [App.], xxi.

8. Ibid., xxii.

9. The only difference between the two is that the third chorus begins at a different place in the Gloria text—the Cherubini at *Gratias agimus tibi*, the Beach two lines earlier on *Laudamus te*.

10. Beach's Mass in E♭ Major, which opens and closes in the tonic key, has movements in B♭ and G♭ major, C minor, and C major.

11. "Handel and Haydn Society Performs Mrs. Beach's Mass in E Flat," *American Art Journal*, February 1893 (S2, 8).

12. Clara Imogene Cheney, [Biography of her daughter], 26 February 1892 (MacDowell Colony Papers, DLC-Ms, holograph), 13.

13. "Personal and Miscellaneous," unidentified source (S1, 67).

14. A letter from Zerrahn to Arthur P. Schmidt, undated, states that he has received the score of Beach's Mass and will do it with the Handel and Haydn Society. The letter, in German, was translated on Henry Beach's prescription blanks in Amy Beach's hand (DLC-APS).

15. Walter S. Jenkins, *The Remarkable Mrs. Beach: American Composer* (Warren, Mich.: Harmonie Park Press, 1994), 26, n. 37.

16. These revisions are discussed in Ruth Ochs's untitled preliminary study of Beach's Mass (see pp. 10–11 and musical example 1, Harvard University), a copy of which was presented to the author. Ochs's conclusions are based on a comparison of the incomplete holograph full score at the Houghton Library, the copyist's full score at the New England Conservatory, and the piano-vocal score published in 1890 by Arthur P. Schmidt.

17. 30 January 1892 (S2, 4).

18. *History of the Handel and Haydn Society*, vol. 2, part 1, 17.

19. The New York contralto Mrs. Carl (C. Katie) Alves sang in church, oratorio, and concert performances. She soon had a national reputation ("Mrs. Carl Alves," *The Chicago Mail*, 20 December 1892 (S1, 78). In the 1890–91 season, Jennie Patrick Walker was soprano soloist in *Messiah* with the Oratorio Society of New York, Walter Damrosch, conductor. Italo Campanini (1845–1896) made his debut in his native Parma in 1863 and thereafter had an international career singing leading operatic roles, including Don José in *Carmen* at the Academy of Music in New York. Emil Fischer, a German bass (1838–1914), made his debut in Graz in 1853 and sang at the Metropolitan Opera in 1883–98, specializing in Wagnerian roles.

20. Franz Kneisel, a violinist (1865–1926), was born in Bucharest and made his solo debut in Vienna in 1882; after serving as concertmaster in several German orchestras, he was recruited by Wilhelm Gericke to be concertmaster and assistant conductor of the Boston Symphony in 1885. He soon organized the Kneisel Quartet, consisting of himself as first violinist and three other first-desk men of the Boston Symphony. The quartet became a leading American ensemble, disbanding in 1917.

Benjamin Johnson Lang, pianist, conductor, organist, teacher, and composer (1837–1909) was one of the leading musicians of Boston. Born in Salem, Massachusetts, he studied in Boston and Germany, returning to Boston in 1858, where he became active as a concert pianist and organist. He was organist and assistant conductor of the Handel and Haydn Society from 1859 to 1895, after which he succeeded Carl Zerrahn as conductor. As the conductor of the Cecilia and Apollo choruses, he introduced several of Beach's compositions. His daughter was the composer Margaret Ruthven Lang (1867–1972).

21. Program booklet, Handel and Haydn Society, 7 February 1892.

22. Other soloists received fees as follows: Jennie Patrick Walker, $60; Emil Fischer, $200; Mrs. Carl Alves, $125; Italo Campanini, $275, and Priscilla White, $5 (Records of the Handel and Haydn Society, MB-MS).

23. *Liber usualis* (Tournai: Desclée, 1947), 1317.

24. Amy Beach, "Why I Chose My Profession: The Autobiography of a Woman Composer," interviewed by Ednah Aiken, *Mother's Magazine* 11 (February 1914): 8.

25. The "Graduale" is scored for pairs of woodwinds, two horns, one trumpet, three trombones, harp, and strings; score and parts at MBCM. It was sung by Charles B. Stevens, 23 February 1899, in Detroit (see "Many-sided Music of Mrs. H. H. A. Beach," *Detroit Journal*, 24 February 1899, in S2, 44); by Leo Lieberman, at the Women in Music Grand Concert, Baltimore, 14 March 1901 ("Women's Progress in Music Aptly Shown," *Baltimore Morning Herald*, 15 March 1901, NhU-Be); perhaps by Lambert Murphy at the Worcester Festival in 1919 (Arthur P. Schmidt to Beach, 30 September 1919, DLC-APS); by Arthur Hackett on a program at the Art Society of Pittsburgh, 25 February 1921.

26. C. F. Dennée, "The Handel and Haydn Concert—The Symphony Concert," *Boston Advertiser*, 8 February 1892 (S2, 6).

27. "Handel and Haydn," *Boston Daily Globe*, 8 February 1892 (S1, 69).

28. "Mrs. Beach's Mass," *Boston Beacon*, 13 February 1892 (S2, 4).

29. Untitled clipping, *Boston Gazette*, 14 February 1982 (S2, 7).

30. C. F. Dennée, "Handel and Haydn Concert."

31. C. F. Dennée, "Musical Matters," *Boston Daily Advertiser*, 8 February 1892 (S1, 70). "The Beach Mass," *Boston Home Journal*, 8 February 1892, (S1, 73). "First Production of the Beach Mass at Music Hall." *Boston Herald*, 8 February 1892 (S1, 68).

32. Among the many reviews that discuss gender issues, see F. H. Jenks, "A Grand Mass by Mrs. H. H. A. Beach," *Boston Transcript*, 23 May 1891 (S2, 2), and C. F. Dennée, "The Handel and Haydn Concert."

33. "A Noble Mass by an American Composer," *Boston Times*, n.d. (S1, 72).

34. F. H. Jenks, "A Grand Mass."

35. J. W. H., "Mrs. Beach's Mass," *The Woman's Journal*, 13 February 1892 (S2, 5).

36. Letter from Howe to Henry Beach, 8 February 1892 (Autograph Album, 33).

37. Anton Rubinstein, *A Conversation on Music*, trans. Mrs. John P. Morgan (New York: Charles F. Tretbar, 1892), 118−19.

38. "Women Can't Help. Dvořák Says They Have Not Creative Talent. He's Talking about Music," *Boston Post*, 30 November 1892.

39. "American Music . . . Some Testimony on Woman's Ability as a Composer," *Boston Daily Traveller*, 10 December 1892, p. 13. Others quoted include Julius Eichberg, director of the Boston Conservatory of Music, and Carl Faelten, dean of the New England Conservatory, who agreed that "[i]t is only a short time since women have begun to make those serious studies which composers must all make"; Estelle M. Merrill, a journalist, Anna C. Fall, a lawyer, and Alice Stone Blackwell, suffragist and editor of *The Woman's Journal*.

40. George P. Upton, *Women in Music* (Chicago, 1880).

41. 4 vols. (London: Macmillan, 1879−1889).

42. Beach, "American Music . . . Some Testimony on Woman's Ability as a Composer," *Boston Daily Traveller*, 10 December 1892 (S1, 84−85). In addition, Beach praised Chaminade, Holmès, and Señora da Lodi, who also had commissions from the Board of Lady Managers at the Chicago Fair. Regarding the achievements of the leading men of the Boston School, Beach suggested that Dvořák read the 1890 article by Francis H. Jenks ("Boston Musical Composers," *New England Magazine*, New Series, 1 [January 1890]: 475−83), which might lead him to the understanding that a school of composition existed before the Bohemian composer's arrival in New York. Finally, Beach noted brilliant performances of Dvořák's and Rubinstein's works by women musicians.

43. Beach, "American Music."

44. H. F. P., "Believes Women Composers Will Rise to Greater Heights in World Democracy," *Musical America* 25 (21 April 1917): 3.

45. Ibid.

46. Letter from Alves to Beach, 15 February 1892, NhU-Be.

47. Beach's English title.

48. *Schiller's Maria Stuart*, ed. Lewis A. Rhoades (Boston: D. C. Heath, 1894), act 3, scene 1, 96 ff.

49. "Dank diesen freundlich grünen Bäumen,/Die meines Kerkers Mauern mir verstecken!/Ich will mich frei and glücklich träumen/Warum aus meinem süssen Wahn mich wecken?/ Umfängt mich nicht der weite Himmelschooss?/Die Blicke frei und fessellos,/Ergehen sich in ungemessnen Räumen," piano-vocal score (Arthur P. Schmidt, 1892). The text is in both German and English; Beach was probably the translator.

50. Amy Beach, "Why I Chose My Profession: The Autobiography of a Woman Composer," interviewed by Ednah Aiken, *Mother's Magazine* 11 (February 1914): 8.

51. George Martin, *The Damrosch Dynasty: America's First Family of Music* (Boston: Houghton Mifflin, 1983), 102. "Auld Rob Morris," by Robert Burns is in John Greig, ed., *Scots Minstrelsie: A National Monument of Scottish Song* (Edinburgh: T. C. and E. C. Jack, 1893), 110−11.

52. "Dort, wo die grauen Nebelberge ragen,/Fängt meines Reiches Grenze an."

53. The score and parts are at MBCM. For a list of Beach's compositions using folk music, see the author's "Dvořák, Beach, and American Music" in *A Celebration of American Music: Words and Music in Honor of H. Wiley Hitchcock*, ed. Richard Crawford, R. Allen Lott, and Carol J. Oja (Ann Arbor: University of Michigan Press, 1990), 280, n. 8.

54. Letter from Alves to Beach, 29 April 1892, NhU-Be. Beach to Theodore Thomas, 12 July 1892, from Quissett, Mass., states that she has just completed the Mary Stuart aria and hopes that Thomas will consider doing it. The letter, signed "Mrs. H. H. A. Beach," is in Henry Beach's hand (ICN).

55. "Zweite Symphonie Konzert," *New-Yorker Staats-Zeitung*, 3 December 1892, trans. in *Boston Daily Transcript* (S2, 10). "New York Symphony Society," *American Art Journal*, 10 December 1892 (S2, 10).

56. Untitled clipping, S2, 11. A handwritten entry at the bottom adds, "R. de Koven, *Harper's Weekly*, December 17." In another review, Rupert Hughes simultaneously dismisses both George Frederic Handel and Beach's *scena ed aria* in one brief sentence: "The long 'Eilende Wolken' has a jerky recitative of Handelian *naïveté*, to which the Aria is a welcome relief," Rupert Hughes ("Music in America 9—The Women Composers," *Godey's Book* [January 1896]: 33; see also Rupert Hughes, *Contemporary American Composers* [Boston: L. C. Page, 1900], 432).

57. In May 1894 Beach gave a concert of her own works at Wellesley College at the invitation of Professor Junius Welch Hill, her former harmony teacher; the contralto Mrs. Homer E. Sawyer sang the Mary Stuart aria to Beach's accompaniment (unidentified clipping, S1, 89). The same singer repeated the work on 18 March 1903 at Steinert Hall, Boston, at Beach's annual recital, with the composer at the piano (S. C. Williams, "Musical Matters," *Boston Advertiser*, 19 March 1903, called the work "very significant" (S2, 62). There may also have been a performance by Mme Hesse-Sprotte in St. Paul, Minn. in 1910.

58. The aria was sung by contralto Grace Preston, with the Baltimore Symphony Orchestra conducted by Ross Jungnickel, on 14 March 1901 at the same Women's Progress in Music Grand Concert in which her Graduale was sung (see note 25 above). Included, in addition to Beach's, were works by Margaret Ruthven Lang, Cécile Chaminade, and Liza Lehmann.

Chapter 8. Reaching Out to the World

1. William Dean Howells, quoted in Howard Pollack, *Skyscraper Lullaby: The Life and Music of John Alden Carpenter* (Washington: Smithsonian Institution Press, 1995), 12–13.

2. The architect was Sophia Hayden of Boston. There had been a Woman's Pavilion designed by a man at the Centennial Exposition held in Philadelphia in 1876. See Jeanne Madeline Weimann, *The Fair Women: The Story of the Woman's Building, World's Columbian Exposition, Chicago, 1893* (Chicago: Academy, 1981), 1–4.

3. For a description of opening day at the Woman's Building, see Weimann, 246–55.

4. Regarding Social Darwinism, the racial ideology that animated many of the fair's anthropological displays, see Robert W. Rydell, *All the World's a Fair: Visions of Empire at American International Expositions, 1876–1916* (Chicago: University of Chicago Press, 1984); Burton Benedict, "The Anthropology of World's Fairs," in Benedict et al., *The Anthropology of World's Fairs: San Francisco Panama Pacific International Exposition, 1915* (London and Berkeley: Lowie Museum of Anthropology in association with Scolar Press, 1983), 43–52; Richard Hofstadter, *Social Darwinism in American Thought*, rev. ed. (New York: George W. Braziller, 1955); and George W. Stocking, Jr., *Race, Culture, and Evolution* (New York: The Free Press, 1968), especially 110–123.

5. Daniel T. Miller, "The Columbian Exposition of 1893 and the American National Character," *Journal of American Culture* 10 (summer 1987): 18. American cultural autonomy has remained a controversial issue in music for much of the current century.

6. Darwinian theories applied to society had their strongest influence in the United States between 1870 and 1910, according to Richard Hofstadter, *Social Darwinism in American Thought*, 4. On the influence of Darwinian theories on music at the World's Columbian Exposition, see this author's unpublished paper, "Music and Ideology at the World's Columbian Exposition, Chicago, 1893," Sonneck Society for American Music, Madison, Wisc., April 1995. Theodore Thomas's statement outlining his mission to present a survey of Western art music is one of many expressions of Darwinian thought regarding music at the fair ("World's Fair Music," *Etude* 10 [August 1892]: 149).

7. Amy Beach, "Why I Chose My Profession: The Autobiography of a Woman Composer," interviewed by Ednah Aiken, *Mother's Magazine* 11 (February 1914): 8.

8. Palmer to Beach, 19 March 1892, in "Mrs. Potter Palmer, President of the Lady Board of Managers, Letters," vol. 12, 564–65, ICHi. The fair was scheduled to open on the newly named Columbus Day, 12 October 1892, but delays in construction postponed the opening until May.

9. Palmer also let Mary MacMonnies know that her commissioned mural for the rotunda of the Woman's Building would be a donation (Weimann, 193–97).

10. As noted earlier, Beach had an agreement with her husband that she would accept no fees for performances but would collect royalties on her published works. There is no information about her acceptance or rejection of fees for commissioned works.

11. *Notable American Women* and *DAB*, s.v. "Palmer, Bertha Honoré."

12. Weimann, 215–17.

13. "Mrs. H. H. A. Beach" to Theodore Thomas, 28 May and 12 July 1892 (ICN). The signature on the former, which is otherwise typed, and the handwriting on the latter, including the signature, are Henry Beach's. *The Minstrel and the King* is a dramatic cantata for solo tenor and baritone, male chorus, and orchestra (Arthur P. Schmidt Co. 1894). There is no record of its performance by a chorus or by Thomas's or any other orchestra.

14. On plans for music at the fair as outlined by the Bureau of Music, see "World's Fair Music," *Etude* 10 (August 1892): 149. A bound volume of music programs given at the fair is at NN-L.

15. Not Ps. 65 as stated in Weimann, 215.

16. Louis C. Elson, *The History of American Music* (1915; rev. 1925; reprint, New York: Burt Franklin, 1971), 301. Of course the psalms are original to the Hebrew tradition, although this was not mentioned.

17. Reference to Beach's use of "an antique tone of the Church" is in a review in the *Boston Evening Transcript*, 13 May 1893 (S2, 11). Beach's opening phrase resembles the end of the first psalm tone with termination on A, *Liber Usualis*, ed. Benedictines of Solesmes (Tournai: Desclée, 1947), 113. An even closer resemblance is found in "Christ Our Passover," Canticle no. 683, for Easter Day, *The Hymnal of the Protestant Episcopal Church in the United States of America*, 1940 (New York: The Church Pension Fund, 1943).

18. *The Hymnal* . . . 1940, no. 682. Its termination, no. 683, also matches Beach's first theme, "O be joyful in the Lord."

19. Elson, *History*, 30.

20. Beach to Thomas, 28 May 1892 (ICN).

21. Letter from Mrs. Potter Palmer to Miss Willard, Chicago, 6 April 1892. (Correspondence of the Board of Lady Managers, World's Columbian Exposition, President's Letters, vol. 13, ICHi).

22. *Addresses and Reports of Mrs. Potter Palmer, President of the Board of Lady Managers, World's Columbian Exposition* (Chicago: Rand McNally, 1894), 104–6.

23. Letter to Amy Starkweather from Bertha Palmer, 2 August 1892 (Palmer Letters, vol. 12, no. 107, ICHi).

24. Paine's contribution was the *Columbus March and Hymn* (Boston: Oliver Ditson, 1892) for orchestra and chorus. Theodore Thomas also asked MacDowell, who refused, to write the music for Harriet Monroe's "Commemoration Ode." Chadwick, Thomas's second choice, accepted the commission; see Margery Morgan Lowens, "The New York Years of Edward MacDowell" (Ph.D. diss., University of Michigan, 1971), 58–59. Chadwick's piece for chorus and orchestra was called simply *Ode* (John W. Church, 1892).

25. Weimann, 216–17.

26. *Addresses and Reports of Mrs. Potter Palmer*, 104. See also Weimann, 216–17 *et passim*.

27. "Address Delivered at the Dedicatory Ceremonies of the World's Columbian Exposition . . . October 21, 1892," *Addresses and Reports of Mrs. Potter Palmer*, 114–15.

28. Weimann, 217.

29. Ibid., 217.

30. On the history of architecture at the fair, see Thomas S. Hines, *Burnham of Chicago: Architect and Planner* (New York: Oxford University Press, 1974), 92–138.

31. Quoted in Lawrence W. Levine, *Highbrow Lowbrow: The Emergence of Cultural Hierarchy in America* (Cambridge, Mass.: Harvard University Press, 1988), 212.

32. On circumstances leading up to the opening ceremonies in the Woman's Building, see "The First Columbian Letter," *Musical Courier* 26 (10 May 1893): 14. See also the untitled clipping ascribed by Beach to Mrs. Crosby Adams, *Music Review?* 1893 (S2, 15).

33. Bronsart (1840–1913), born in St. Petersburg of Swedish parents, studied piano with Liszt in Weimar, and was the composer of several operas as well as orchestral and chamber music. Ellicott (1857–1924), an English pianist who had studied at the Royal Academy of Music (1875–76), had written music on commission for the Cheltenham and Gloucester festivals.

34. "Dedicate the Home: Woman's Building Formally Completed and Opened," *Chicago Tribune*, 2 May 1893, p. 4.

35. "Music Admirable and Effective," *Chicago Tribune*, 2 May 1893 (S1, 86).

36. Clipping, *The Woman's Journal*, 6 May 1893, quotes from the *Chicago Inter-Ocean* (S2, 11).

37. Rupert Hughes, *Contemporary American Composers* (Boston: L. C. Page, 1900), 427.

38. "First Columbian Letter."

39. An announcement of Chadwick's commission for the *Columbian Ode* was reported in the *Boston Journal*, 7 March 1892. Chadwick worked on the score, 17 May–10 July (Steven Ledbetter to the author, by telephone, 6 February 1991).

40. [Mrs. Crosby Adams], *Music Review* (June 1893), in S2, 15.

41. Mildred Aldrich, "Mrs. Amy Marcy Cheney Beach," *Chicago Press*, n.d., but datelined Boston, 27 April 1893 (S1, 83–84).

42. Mrs. George B. Carpenter, who was in charge of the Woman's Musical Congresses, gave a party after the last session at which both Beaches, Maud Powell, Fanny Bloomfield Zeisler, Amy Fay, the diva Emma Thursby, and others were listed as guests. See "A Rare Musicale," *Chicago Inter-Ocean*, 9 July 1893 (Maud Powell Scrapbooks, NN-L). For further on Carpenter, see Florence Ffrench, comp., *Music and Musicians in Chicago* (Chicago: Florence Ffrench, 1899), 84–85; Pollack, *Skyscraper Lullaby*, 5–7.

43. The large attendance may be explained in part by the fact that during the period from 1890 to 1910 women's participation in the census category "music and music teaching" reached its highest level in American history; see Judith Tick, "Women in Music," *Grove-American*, vol. 4, 550–51.

44. Other works played on 5 July were by Gertrude Griswold, "What the Chimney Sang"; Maud Valerie White (1855–1937), of London, "The Throstle"; Eleanor Smith, head of the music department at Hull House in Chicago, "The Quest"; and Cécile Chaminade (1857–1944), "Rosemonde" and "Summer Song." Information on Smith is in Hilda Satt Polacheck, *I Came a Stranger: The Story of a Hull-House Girl*, ed. Dena Polacheck Epstein (Chicago: University of Illinois Press, 1989), 105.

45. Clippings from the *Chicago Times*, 7 July 1893, and the *Chicago Record*, 7 July 1893 (S2, 14). Other works given on 6 July were by Clara Kathleen Rogers (1844–1931), "Ah, Love, But a Day," "Summum bonum," "Out of My Own Great Woe," and "Apparitions"; Kate Vannah, "Good-bye, Sweet Day"; Hope Temple (1859–1938), Irish composer and pianist, "You Called to Me"; Helen Hood (1863–1949), Boston pianist, composer, and teacher, "Shepherdess," "The Violet," and "Expectation"; Julia Lois Caruthers, children's songs; and Adele Lewing (1866–1943), German-born composer and pianist residing in Boston, "Scherzino," "Wandering Waves," "French Suite," "Greeting," "Wanderer's Night Song," and "Springtime." For information on Lewing, see Christine Ammer, *Unsung: A History of Women in American Music* (Westport, Conn.: Greenwood Press, 1980), 93–94.

46. Other music offered on that day included works by White, "Ici bas," Temple, "Auf Wiedersehn"; Genevra Johnston Bishop, "Entreaty"; Mary Knight Wood (1866–1943), of Boston, "Thou," and "Ashes of Roses"; and Chaminade, "Amour d'automne." See also *Women at an Exposition*, Ann Feldman, producer, a recording of music by women given at the Chicago Fair that includes some of the compositions listed here (Koch International Classics, 3-7240-2H1).

47. *Harper's Weekly*, 29 April 1893 (S1, 85). Claire Munger wrote in the *Boston Home Journal* that Beach was "the greatest composer among women in this country or Europe" (S2, 14).

48. Clipping, *Boston Post*, 10 July 1893 (S1, 86).

49. Powell played the Bruch G-Minor Concerto on 18 July and the Mendelssohn Concerto on 4 August in the Music Hall (World's Columbian Exposition Programs, NN-L. For a review, see "Music at the Fair," clipping, 19 July 1893, in Frederick Grant Gleason Scrapbook, 423, ICN.

50. Other soloists for the Triple Concerto were Max Bendix, violin, and Bruno Steindl, cello. Zeisler played Helen Hopekirk's Sonata for Violin and Piano with Currie Due on 21 May on a program for the World's Representative Women, a meeting that took place 15–21 May at the Memorial Art Palace. This and other information about programs at the congress are in *The World's Congress Auxiliary of the World's Columbian Exposition of 1893: Official Program of the Department of Music* (Frederick Grant Gleason Scrapbook, ser. I, vol. 10, 1890–93, laid in, ICN).

51. "Sample Programs of May Music at the Fair," *Music* 4 (June 1893): 234.

52. Sandy R. Mazzola, "Bands and Orchestras at the World's Columbian Exposition," *American Music* 4 (winter 1986): 412–15.

53. The meager receipts for symphony concerts led the directory to question their heavy commitment to the 120-member Festival Orchestra. Immediately after Thomas resigned, the number of orchestra personnel was reduced, and all were let go several weeks before the fair closed. For further on this, see Ezra Schabas, *Theodore Thomas* (Urbana: University of Illinois Press, 1989), 195 ff. W. S. B. Mathews, "End of Art Music at the Fair," *Music* (September 1893): 531–40; and Mazzola, 412–17.

54. Mazzola, 417.

55. The World's Folklore Congress took place in the Memorial Art Palace. It included lecture-demonstrations of folk music and the playing of field recordings of the Navajo made by Dr. Washington Matthews.

56. See Stuart Feder, *Charles Ives: My Father's Song* (New Haven: Yale University Press, 1992), 122, 123; see also Pollack, *Skyscraper Lullaby*, 12, where he states that the World's Columbian Exposition was a "seminal event in the composer's life."

57. Further see Frederick Douglass and Ida B. Wells, *The Reason Why the Colored American Is Not in the World's Columbian Exposition* (without imprint).

58. During one visit, from 10 to 17 August, Dvořák was the hero of Bohemian Day and conducted his Symphony No. 8, three Slavonic Dances, and the overture to *My Home.* See the author's unpublished paper, "Dr. Dvořák Goes to the Fair," Dvořák Conference, Iowa City, 8 August 1993.

Chapter 9. *"One of the Boys"*

1. George P. Upton, *Woman in Music* (Boston: J. R. Osgood, 1880), 27.

2. Louis C. Elson, *The History of American Music* (1915; rev. 1925; reprint, New York: Burt Franklin, 1971), 294.

3. The term *man-tone*, is in Rupert Hughes, "Music in America IX—The Women Composers," *Godey's Book* (January 1896), 30, as follows: "what [women] write in man-tone is sometimes surprisingly strong."

4. Harriette Brower, *Piano Mastery*, 2nd series (New York: Frederick A. Stokes, [1917]), 187.

5. Philip Hale, "With Musicians: Women in the List of Symphony Makers," *Boston Journal*, 4 November 1896 (S1, 101).

6. "The Real Value of Negro Melodies," *New York Herald*, 21 May 1893, p. 28. On the authorship of the article, see Michael Beckerman, "The Real Value of Yellow Journalism," *Musical Quarterly* 77 (winter 1993): 749–68, excerpted in John C. Tibbetts, ed., *Dvořák in America 1892–1895* (Portland, Ore.: Amadeus Press, 1993), 355–59.

7. "Real Value of Negro Melodies."

8. This same attitude becomes explicit later in the writings of Daniel Gregory Mason: see MacDonald Smith Moore, *Yankee Blues: Musical Culture and American Identity* (Bloomington, Ind.: Indiana University Press, 1985), 128–60.

9. Charles Hamm, *Yesterdays: Popular Song in America* (New York: W. W. Norton, 1979), 42–61, traces the influence following publications of Thomas Moore's Irish songs and Robert Burns's Scottish melodies. There was also an Anglo–American folk tradition, but little if anything was known of it in 1893. Its later retrieval would have a profound influence on American music in the 1930s and '40s.

10. Victor Yellin, "Chadwick, American Musical Realist," *Musical Quarterly* 61 (January 1975): 95–96.

11. John Clapham, "The Evolution of Dvořák's Symphony 'From the New World'," *Musical Quarterly* 44 (1958): 168–69, 175, 177, 180 *et passim*. See also Michael Beckerman, "The Master's Little Joke: Antonin Dvořák and the Mask of Nation," in *Dvořák and His World*, ed. Michael Beckerman (Princeton, N. J.: Princeton University Press, 1993), 134–54.

12. Amy Beach, "Music Reviews," vol. 2, October 1894 (NhU-Be, holograph), 33–34.

13. Caryl B. Storrs, "Program Notes" [1917] (Beach Clipping File, NN-L).

14. In Henry Hudson, comp. "Old Irish Airs," Ms. in MB-Mu. For the provenance of the manuscript volumes and publication of selected songs from them in *The Citizen*, Dublin, 1841, see Block, "Dvořák, Beach, and American Music," in *A Celebration of American Music: Words and Music in Honor of H. Wiley Hitchcock*, ed. Richard Crawford, R. Allen Lott, and Carol J. Oja (Ann Arbor: University of Michigan Press, 1990), 264–69.

15. See Carl Dahlhaus, who wrote, "It is possible to regard nationality [in music] . . . as a quality which rests primarily in the meaning invested in a piece of music or a complex

of musical characteristics by a sufficient number of people who make and hear the music, and only secondarily, if at all, in its rhythmic and melodic substance," *Between Romanticism and Modernism*, trans. Mary Whittall (Berkeley: University of California Press, 1989), 91–92.

16. Entire scherzi in $\frac{2}{4}$ time are found in Beethoven's Piano Sonata, op. 31, no. 3, and in his Sonata, op. 110; in the second movement of Mendelssohn's "Scottish" Symphony, op. 56; and in the third movement, Allegro giocoso, of Brahms's Fourth Symphony, op. 98. All four have persistent sixteenth–note motion.

17. A holograph of the symphony, in pencil with corrections in ink, is at NhU-Be. Dates where given are at the head and the close of each movement. There are separate paginations for each movement, listed here in order of composition. Page numbers refer to the holograph in ink at DLC-Mu. Second movement, *Alla Siciliana*, begun January (?) 1894, completed 22 March 1894 (p. 32). The movement begins with what is now m. 5. Third movement, *Lento con molto espressione*, completed 14 November 1894 (p. 36). First movement, *Allegro con fuoco*, begun 21 November 1894, finished 9 June 1895 (p. 86), is bound with the one page introduction to the second movement. Fourth movement. *Allegro di molto*, begun 13 June 1895, completed 16 February 1896 (p. 84). See also untitled article, in S2, 17. The score was published in Leipzig with a German title page (Boston and Leipzig: Arthur P. Schmidt, 1897).

18. Donal O'Sullivan, *The Life and Times of an Irish Harper*, vol. 1 (London: Routledge and Kegan Paul, 1958). The song is credited to Carolan, whose full name was Turlough or Terence Carolan (1670–1738). For a biography, see 36–38. I am also grateful to Mary Deady of the Consulate General of Ireland in New York for information about Carolan and for the translation of this title, which Hudson did not supply in his edition or in the manuscript collection; see "The Native Music of Ireland," *The Citizen*, Dublin, 3 (March 1841). The same tune is found in a different arrangement in Henry Hudson, "Old Irish Airs," vols. 3, p. 123, and 6, p. 768, as well as in *Crosby's Irish Musical Repository* (1816), 38–39.

19. *The Citizen* 3 (January 1841): 1; Hudson, vols. 4, p. 3, and 5, p. 97; J. L. Hatton and J. L. Molloy, *The Songs of Ireland: Including the Most Favourite of Moore's Irish Melodies and a Large Collection of Old Songs and Ballads*, new and enl. ed. (London: Boosey, n.y.), 62.

20. "The Native Music of Ireland," *The Citizen* 3 (January 1841): 64.

21. Caryl B. Storrs, "Program Notes."

22. During the years 1894 to 1896 Beach published the following songs: *Villanelle*, op. 20: "My Star," "Just for This," "Spring," and "Wouldn't That Be Queer," op. 26; and "Within my Heart," "The Wandering Knight," "Sleep, Little Darling," and "Haste, O Beloved," op. 29. Piano works include *Bal masque*, op. 22; *Children's Carnival*, op. 25, a suite of teaching pieces; "Barcarolle," "Minuet italien," and "Danse des fleurs," op. 28; Choral works include "Alleluia, Christ is Risen," op. 27; *The Rose of Avon-Town*, op. 30; *Three Flower Songs*, op. 31; and "Teach Me Thy Way," op. 33.

23. See clipping, *Boston Beacon*, 17 November 1894 (S2, 15). The Manuscript Society of New York, which merged with the Choral Composers Association, gave the following works of Beach: "Chanson d'amour," op. 21, no. 1 (see "The Manuscript Society," *New York Sun*, 9 February 1893, in S2, 10); *Bal Masque*, op. 22, 12 December 1893, a simple little waltz which Beach may have orchestrated as an exercise. On 11 April 1898 the society gave the second performance of Beach's *Festival jubilate*, op. 17 (see review from the *New York Commercial Advertiser*, 12 April in S2, 41), and "The Festival jubilate" (a review in *Boston Beacon*, 23 April 1898, in S1, 99). On 17 November 1908, F. X. Arens, President of the Manuscript Society of New York, invited Beach to give an all-Beach concert at the National Arts Club in New York in early December (see letter in S3). Later, Beach also accepted membership in the Manuscript Society of Chicago (Beach to Frederic Grant Gleason, 2 November 1897, Manuscript Division, ICN.)

24. William Ernest Henley, *A Book of Verses* (New York: Scribner and Welford, 1889), 65. The title is Beach's.

25. Rupert Hughes, "Music in America, IX—The Women Composers," *Godey's Book* (January 1896), reprinted in *Contemporary American Composers* (Boston: L. C. Page, 1900), 431.

26. Beach, "Analytical Review of Symphony in E Minor (`Gaelic'), Op. 32," typescript bound with the edition of the work in the Allen A. Brown Collection, MB-Mu.

27. "Conor O'Reilly," is in O'Sullivan, vol. 1, no. 139, the Gaelic title and translation into English are in vol. 2, 86–87.

28. Interview with Mary Thornton McDermott in advance of a performance of the quintet in Brooklyn on 4 January 1934, NhU-Be, in which she quotes Beach: "The place on Cape Cod was bought with the early proceeds of my song 'Ecstasy,' and my husband built the house." The deed is in her name in the County Records Department, Barnstable, Mass., Book 214: 316. For a contrary assertion that Henry Beach paid for both the land and the house, see E. Lindsey Merrill, "Mrs. H. H. A. Beach: Her Life and Music," (Ph.D. diss., University of Rochester, 1963), 10.

29. Edith Gertrude Kinney, "Mrs. H. H. A. Beach," *Musician* 4 (September 1899): 355.

30. Ibid.

31. Concerning the naming of the house, Merrill states, "She would have named her home Ecstasy, according to Ruth Shaffner, but there was another home in Centerville so named," Ibid., 10.

32. Caryl B. Storrs, Program Notes, Beach Clipping File, NN-L.

33. "It was the nineteenth century which chose to believe—on very shaky grounds— that national character was the primary and essential quality of folk music . . . and that folk music expresses the spirit of a people (understood as the spirit of a nation, first and most clearly manifested in the culture of the lower classes)" (Carl Dahlhaus, "Nationalism and Music," in *Between Romanticism and Modernism*, 94).

34. Beach, "Analytical Review," 13.

35. Ibid., 16.

36. Clipping, *Boston Globe*, 1 March 1896 (S2, 17).

37. "Music Hall: Boston Symphony Orchestra," *Boston Evening Transcript*, 14 February 1898 (S1, 118).

38. "Campanari Soloist at the Symphony Concert," *Boston Sunday Globe*, 1 November 1896 (S1, 103).

39. Clipping, S1, 103.

40. "A Work of Decided Worth," *Boston Sunday Herald*, 1 November 1896 (S1, 102).

41. Hale, "With Musicians."

42. "Music," *Boston Home Journal*, 7 November 1896 (S1, 104–105; S2, 24).

43. "Mrs. Beach's Symphony," *American Art Journal*, 7 November 1896 (S1, 106); "Music and Musicians," *Boston Globe*, 15 February 1898 (S2, 36).

44. *Boston Courier*, 1 November 1895, S1, 101.

45. Hale, "With Musicians." See also, "Symphony Orchestra Matinee," *Brooklyn Daily Eagle*, 28 March 1897 (S2, 31).

46. Henry Edward Krehbiel, "Mrs. Beach's Symphony," *New York Tribune*, 27 March 1897 (S2, 31). See also his *Afro–American Folksongs: A Study in Racial and National Music* (1914; reprint, New York: Frederick Ungar, 1962), v–vii.

47. Between 1896 and 1898 the Boston Symphony Orchestra also gave the "Gaelic" a second time in Boston. During those years it was given by orchestras in Buffalo, Kansas City, and Chicago.

48. "Music Hall: Boston Symphony Orchestra," *Boston Transcript*, 14 February 1898 (S1, 118).

49. Clipping, *Boston Courier*, 13 February 1898 (S1, 117).

50. Quoted in "Mrs. Beach's Gaelic Symphony Receives Enthusiastic Praise from Kansas City Critics," *Music Courier*, 11 (May 1916), in Beach Clipping File, NN-L.

51. Hale, "With Musicians."

52. "A Work of Decided Worth."

53. Translation in Beach's hand, NhU-Be.

54. "The Boston Symphony Orchestra," *New York Sun*, 18 February 1898 (S2, 37).

55. See Judith Tick's table 6, "'Femininity' and 'Masculinity' in Music, c. 1900," in "Passed Away Is the Piano Girl," *Women Making Music*, ed. Jane Bowers and Tick, 337.

56. *Journal of Fine Arts*, March 1897 (S2, 29).

57. T. H. G., "Mrs. Beach's Symphony," *The Woman's Journal*, 7 November 1896 (S2, 26).

58. *Time and the River* 4 (9 January 1897). The poem is in the Gould Collection, MB-Ms.

59. Untitled article, attributed by Beach to C. L. Capen, *Boston Home Journal*, 7 November 1896 (S2, 24).

60. Autograph Album, no. 68 (NhU-Be).

61. There are two recordings of the Symphony in E Minor ("Gaelic"), op. 32: the first, with substantial cuts, was issued by the Society for the Preservation of American Music in the series Music in America, Karl Krueger conducting the Royal Philharmonic Orchestra (MIA 139, 1968), and reissued by the Library of Congress, in the series Our Musical Past (OMP–105); the second, complete and uncut, was recorded by the Detroit Symphony Orchestra, Neeme Järvi, conductor (Chandos Chan 8958, 1991).

Chapter 10. Amy Beach's Boston

1. Mrs. H. H. A. Beach, "How Music Is Made," *Keyboard* (winter 1942): 11, 38.

2. See *Grove-American*, s.v. "Paine, John Knowles." His students included John Alden Carpenter, Frederick S. Converse, Arthur Foote, Edward Burlingame Hill, Daniel Gregory Mason, and Walter Spalding and critics Richard Aldrich, William Apthorp, Olin Downes, and Henry T. Finck.

3. See *Grove-American*, s.v. "Chadwick, George Whitefield." His students included Horatio Parker, Mabel Daniels, Margaret Ruthven Lang, Arthur Farwell, Florence Price, Arthur Shepherd, and William Grant Still.

4. See *Grove-American*, S.V. "Foote, Arthur William."

5. Judith Ann Cline, "Margaret Ruthven Lang: Her Life and Songs" (Ph.D. diss., Washington University, 1993), 172. Lang's last work was *Three Pianoforte Pieces for Young Players*, op. 60 (1919).

6. Constance R. Hall and Helen Tetlow, *Helen Hopekirk, 1856–1945* (Cambridge, Mass.: privately printed, 1954).

7. Irving Lowens, "Writings about Music in the Periodicals of American Transcendentalism (1835–1850)," *Journal of the American Musicological Society* 10 (summer 1957): 75. Further, Lowens writes, quoting Dwight, "it was the holy mission of music to remedy the defect [of a society focused only on money and power] by 'familiarizing men with the beautiful and the infinite.'"

8. *Dwight's Journal of Music* 26 (1 September 1866): 302.

9. Joseph A. Mussulman, *Music in the Cultured Generation: A Social History of Music in America, 1870–1900* (Evanston: Northwestern University Press, 1971), 89.

10. Mussulman, 47–51. He locates the source of this belief in "[t]he Platonic doctrine of the ethical value of music [which was] revived during the middle decades of the century [and] appealed more widely than any other proposition relating music to American life," 48.

11. Mussulman, 89.

12. Quoted in Mark A. De Wolfe Howe, *The Boston Symphony Orchestra, 1881–1931*, rev. with John N. Burk (Boston: Houghton Mifflin, 1931), 16.

13. *The Music Lover's Calendar*, 1 (December 1905): 27.

14. Cleveland Amory, *The Proper Bostonians* (Orleans, Mass.: Parnassus Imprints, 1947), 20–21, 17.

15. Howe, 175.

16. Cleveland Amory, 17; E. Digby Baltzell, *Puritan Boston and Quaker Philadelphia* (Boston: Beacon Press, 1979), 221–22, 227.

17. According to a private communication from Wayne D. Shirley, "Boston" is a corruption of "St. Botolph's town."

18. Archives of the St. Botolph Club, Boston.

19. On Brooks, see Samuel Eliot Morison, *One Boy's Boston, 1887–1901* (Boston: Houghton Mifflin, 1962), 64.

20. List of members of the St. Botolph Club from the club's archives.

21. For information on exhibits at St. Botolph's, see Erica Hirschler's "Artist Biographies," in *The Bostonians: Painters of an Elegant Age, 1870–1930*, ed. Trevor J. Fairbrother et al. (Boston: Museum of Fine Arts, 1986), 198–230. On Perry, see *Lilla Cabot Perry: An American Impressionist*, ed. Meredith Martindale, with the assistance of Pamela Moffat (Washington, D.C.: The National Museum of Women in the Arts, 1990), 49.

22. Arthur Foote, "A Bostonian Remembers," *Musical Quarterly* 23 (January 1937): 41. Musicians who belonged to St. Botolph include Josef and Timothée Adamowski, George Chadwick, Julius Eichberg, Carl Faelten, Arthur Foote, Wilhelm Gericke, B. J. Lang, Malcolm Lang, Bernhard Listemann, Charles Martin Loeffler, Arthur Nikisch, John Knowles Paine, James Cutler Dunn Parker, Horatio Parker, Arthur B. Whiting, and Carl Zerrahn.

23. Joan D. Hedrick, *Harriet Beecher Stowe: A Life* (New York: Oxford University Press, 1994), 289 ff., describes the development of exclusively male clubs and the role they played in the increasingly male control of literature. St. Botolph's may have provided similar opportunities for male direction of musical life in Boston in addition to that described by Foote.

24. Quoted in Baltzell, 284.

25. Beach to Gould (MB-Ms), in which Beach responds to Gould's championing of Whitman, especially in a letter dated 2 January 1906, by admiring such poems as "When Lilacs Last in the Dooryard Bloom'd," which she declined to set, stating that she feels "much too little for such a task" (emphasis is Beach's).

26. Trevor J. Fairbrother, "Painting in Boston, 1870–1930," in *The Bostonians*, 61.

27. Bernice Kramer Leader, "The Boston Lady as a Work of Art: Paintings by the Boston School at the Turn of the Century" (Ph.D. diss., Columbia University, 1980), 179.

28. Alicia Ostriker, "The Thieves of Language: Women Poets and Revisionist Mythmaking," in Elaine Showalter, ed., *The New Feminist Criticism: Essays on Women, Literature, and Theory* (New York: Pantheon Books, 1985), 315.

29. Reproductions of these works are in Fairbrother et al., *The Bostonians*, "Catalogue of the Exhibition," 110, 95, 164.

30. Ednah Dow Cheney, "The Women of Boston," in *The Memorial History of Boston, including Suffolk County, Massachusetts, 1630–1880*, vol. 4, ed. Justin Winsor (Boston: James R. Osgood and Co., 1880–81), 332.

31. Cheney, 350.

32. F. H. Sanborn, address, *Ednah Dow Cheney. Memorial Meeting. New England Women's Club*, February 2, 1905 (Boston: George H. Ellis, 1905), 6.

33. *NAW*, s.v. "Cheney, Ednah Dow Littlehale."

34. Deland to Beach, 14 August, (Correspondence, no. 41, NhU-Be). Deland also refers to two other members, Miss Carey and Miss Felton. Further see Diana C. Reep, *Margaret Deland* (Boston: Twayne Publishers, 1985).

35. Amory, 126.

36. On Fields, see Judith A. Roman, *Annie Adams Fields: The Spirit of Charles Street* (Bloomington: Indiana University Press, 1990), 42 ff., on her role as a "true woman," and 105 ff., on her Boston marriage with Jewett. See also Hedrick, 394, who points out that the salon of Annie Adams Fields and Sara Orne Jewett was one of the few places in the latter half of the nineteenth century where men and women still met to talk about literature and politics.

37. Margaret Deland, *The Old Garden and Other Verses* (Boston: Houghton, Mifflin, 1887), pp. 17−19.

38. The songs were published by Arthur P. Schmidt in 1896.

39. Christine Ammer, *Unsung: A History of Women in American Music* (Westport, Conn.: Greenwood Press, 1980), 93.

40. Deland to Beach, n.d., NhU-Be.

41. Leader, 184.

42. Ammer, 93.

Chapter 11. *The Composer at the Keyboard*

1. See, on this subject, R. Allen Lott, "'A Continuous Trance': Hans von Bülow's Tour of America," *Journal of Musicology* 12 (fall 1994): 548−49. The pianist played 139 concerts between 18 October 1875 and 31 March 1876.

2. "Musical: Boston Symphony Concert," *Boston Gazette*, 20 February 1886 (S1, 34).

3. Clipping, *Boston Beacon* (S1, 38).

4. "Theatres and Concerts. Mrs. Beach's Recital," *Boston Evening Transcript*, 1 April 1886 (S1, 40).

5. "Theatres and Concerts. Mrs. Beach's Recital," *Boston Evening Transcript*, 10 March 1887 (S1, 42).

6. "Music," *Boston Courier*, 10 June 1897 (S1, 109). Drew opened that night in *Rosemary* by Louis W. Parker and Murray Carson at the Hollis Street Theater in Boston.

7. The title page reads, *Sonate in A moll für Pianoforte und Violine*. The German title may have been Schmidt's preference, or a result of the work's being engraved in Leipzig. The dates for the composition of the sonata are in Beach's handlist of compositions dating from 5 September 1891 to 5 September 1900 (NhU-Be). Louis C. Elson, *The History of American Music* (1915; rev. 1925; reprint, New York: Burt Franklin, 1971), 301−2, states that it was written in six weeks, not in twelve as Beach gives.

8. Louis C. Elson, "The Kneisel Quartette Concert More Than Ever Interesting," *Boston Daily Advertiser*, 5 January 1897 (S1, 110).

9. "Kneisel Quartet Concert," *Boston Daily Globe*, 5 January 1897 (S1, 109).

10. Elson, "The Kneisel Quartette Concert."

11. "Kneisel Quartet Concert," *Boston Daily Globe*, 5 January 1897 (S1, 109). On the conflict between critical and audience reactions, see Claudia MacDonald, "Critical Reception and the Woman Composer: The Early Reception of Piano Concertos by Clara Wieck Schumann and Amy Beach," *Current Musicology* 55 (1993) 24−55. On applause between movements, there is ample evidence of this practice in the nineteenth century; see Lawrence Levine, *Highbrow/Lowbrow: The Emergence of Cultural Hierarchy in America* (Cambridge, Mass.: Harvard University Press, 1988), 192.

12. Percy Goetschius, "Mrs. H. H. A. Beach and Mademoiselle Cécile Chaminade: Their Works, 1: Mrs. H. H. A. Beach," *Musician* 4 (September 1899), in S1, 132. See also

Walter Frisch, *Brahms and the Principle of Developing Variation* (Berkeley: University of California Press, 1984), 1–18.

13. This probably was the New York trip to which Beach referred in her story of the creation of her song "The Year's at the Spring." The collaboration between Beach and the Kneisel Quartet would be long lasting: between February 1899 and March 1901, they played six concerts together in which she played her own works, Brahms's Quintet, op. 34, and Beethoven's Cello Sonata, op. 69; and in 1916 she toured with them.

14. It is doubtful that Finck, who was a champion of German Romantic music, was being critical of German textbooks or German influence on American musical life. Rather he was more likely attacking Beach for acting like a student who, out of inexperience, adhered to the rules religiously.

15. [Krehbiel], "Music: The Kneisel Quartet," *New York Daily Tribune*, 29 March 1899 (S1, 123); [Finck], untitled, *New York Evening Post*, 29 March 1899 (S2, 46).

16. Henderson, "The Kneisel Quartet," *New York Times*, 29 March 1899 (S2, 46).

17. Percy Goetschius to Beach, copy of letter, 11 October 1899 (NhU-Be).

18. Copy of letter in Clara Cheney's hand from Carreño to Beach, Berlin, 18 (or 17) December 1899 (S6).

19. Clipping, *Boston Evening Transcript*, 22 December 1905 (S1, 122). Program, 24 April 1900, Salle Pleyel, Paris (S2, 56). The reviews were reprinted in the Boston and New York newspapers.

20. "Mrs. H. H. A. Beach's Sonata," *New York Commercial Advertiser*, 26 December 1901 (S1, 134). Sigmund Beel also played the sonata with Beach during her California tours of 1915–16. See also "Praise for a Boston Composer," *Boston Sunday Herald*, 22 December 1901 (S1, 134).

21. Henry Beach to Schmidt, 19 December 1901 (DLC-APS).

22. "Praise for a Boston Composer." The reviews were reprinted in *The Sunday Herald*, 22 December 1901, and the *New York Commercial Advertiser*, 26 December 1901.

23. Joseph Silverstein, violin; Gilbert Kalish, piano, NW-268.

24. These include, to 1897, the *Cadenza to the First Movement of the Third Concerto for Pianoforte [by] Beethoven*, Beach's op. 3; the *Valse-Caprice*, op. 4; the *Ballad*, op. 6; the four pieces in *Sketches*, op. 15; *Bal masque*, op. 22; and *Three Pieces*, op. 28.

25. In September 1937, Beach arranged "Dreaming" for cello and piano. The holograph manuscript is at NhU-Be.

26. Beach to Schmidt, 8 March 1902, in which she suggests that he publish her "new transcription of Richard Strauss's 'Serenade.'" She also notes that "the work seems to be much liked by musicians who have heard it," probably at Wednesday afternoon "at-homes" (DLC-APS).

27. "Recital by Mrs. Beach," *Brooklyn Daily Eagle*, 19 March 1902 (S1, 135). Later, while in Europe, Beach played this work several times for Strauss (clipping, "Noted Artist Wins Triumph," S4).

28. Beach to Coolidge, 26 April 1904 (in the private collection of Dr. John C. Coolidge).

29. Wilson, "Mrs. H. H. A. Beach," *Musician* 17 (January 1912): 10. Myrna Garvey Eden consulted the ethnomusicologist Miloš Velimirović about the four themes Beach used; see her *Energy and Individuality in the Art of Anna Huntington, Sculptor, and Amy Beach, Composer*. Composers of North America, no. 2. (Metuchen, N.J.: Scarecrow Press, 1987), 211.

30. This text and other information about Beach's folk song sources are given in the preface to the printed edition of the music (Schmidt, 1907) and reprinted in later editions. The translation of "O Maiko moyá" should be, according to Miloš Velimirović, "O my mother," but it may be a metaphor for motherland, as quoted in Eden, 277. Velimirović also

questions the authenticity of the melody and suggests that there was a fault in the transmission of the final cadence.

31. "Stara planina" (according to Beach, an ancient hymn to the mountains) and "Nasadil ye Dadó" ("Grandpa has planted a little garden") may be Bulgarian, although Beach believed they were Romanian. "Balkan Folk Songs: Mrs. Beach's New [sic] Work," *Musical Courier*, 71 (25 November 1915): 39. Beach, in her Preface to the 1906 edition, states that these songs are "heard everywhere in the vicinity of the mountains and villages." E. Douglas Bomberger found versions of two of the four songs in an edition of Nikolai Kaufman, *Bulgarski gradski pesni* (Bulgarian urban songs; Sofia, 1968): nos. 31, "Makedoneu halno Pee," and 38 and 38a, "Stara Planina"; see Bomberger's "Motivic Development in Amy Beach's *Variations on Balkan Themes*, op. 60," *American Music* 10 (fall 1992): 327–30. "Nasadil ye Dadó" is a light-hearted, dancelike melody in duple meter that begins in G major and only turns to the relative minor, E, at the final cadence. It resembles the themes Beach created for scherzolike movements and is the only one that contrasts with the other serious, even tragic, songs. The final theme, "Macedonian," she identified as an "appeal for help, made centuries ago to a neighboring country," probably Bulgaria. However, the song may have been no older than the last quarter of the nineteenth century. See Bomberger, 328.

32. R. C. DeW., untitled fragment, *Boston Transcript*, 9 February 1905 (S2, 66).

33. Goetschius to Beach, copy in Clara Cheney's hand (S4).

34. Arthur Farwell Scrapbook, in private collection of Brice Farwell.

35. For further information on this work and its relationship to the nationalist movement in American music, see this author's "Amy Beach's Music on Native American Themes," *American Music* 8 (summer 1990): 141–66.

36. Franz Boas, *The Central Eskimo*, Bureau of Ethnology Sixth Annual Report, Smithsonian Institution (Washington, D. C., 1888).

37. See also the introduction to Block, ed., Amy Beach. *Quartet for Strings in One Movement*, Opus 89, vol. 3 of *Music of the United States of America* (Madison, Wisc.: A-R Editions, for the American Musicological Society, 1994), xxiv–xxv.

38. Goetschius to Beach, 18 February 1907, copy in Clara Cheney's hand (Correspondence no. 62, NhU-Be).

39. Arthur Wilson, "Mrs. H. H. A. Beach: A Conversation on Musical Conditions in America," *Musician* 17 (January 1912): 10.

40. Beach to Arthur P. Schmidt, 15 March 1907 (DLC-APS). Between 1894 and 1908, Beach gave at least ten recitals devoted entirely to her own music.

41. Clipping, *Boston Budget and Beacon*, undated (S1, 146).

42. Program in the Harvard University Chamber Concerts series, by the Kneisel Quartet with Beach, on 13 February 1900. Although some have claimed this to be the American premiere of the Brahms Piano Quintet, the pianist Rafael Joseffy played the Brahms work with the Kneisels at a memorial concert for the composer on 5 April 1897. See Kneisel Quartet programs, NN-L.

43. On chromaticism and tonality in mm. 1–34 of the second movement, see Rose Marie Chisholm Flatt, "Analytical Approaches to Chromaticism in Amy Beach's *Piano Quintet in F♯ Minor, Indiana Theory Review* (spring 1981): 41–58.

44. Other works on the program included Schumann's String Quartet, op. 41, no. 2, in F major, and Debussy's String Quartet, op. 10, of which only the second and third movements were played.

45. Reviews in S1, 147–49, are from the *Boston Times, Boston Globe, Boston Advertiser, Boston Herald*, and *Boston Transcript*. Schmidt published the quintet in 1909.

46. "Hoffman Quartette Concert," *Boston Advertiser*, 28 February 1908 (S1, 148).

47. Clipping, *Boston Transcript*, 1908 (S1, 149).

48. A. F., *High Fidelity Magazine*, n.d., review of the 1974 recording of the piano quintet by Mary Louise Boehm, piano; Kees Cooper and Alvin Rogers, violins; Richard Maximoff, viola; and Fred Sherry, cello (Turnabout TV-S 34556).

Chapter 12. "A Veritable Autobiography?"

1. The four movements of the concerto, including the full score and piano part, were written in order between 5 September 1898 and 5 September 1899. The following year Beach revised the score as noted in her handlist of compositions by year, 1891–1900 (NhU-Be). This chapter is a revised version of Adrienne Fried Block, "'A Veritable Autobiography'? Amy Beach's Piano Concerto in C♯ Minor, op. 45," *Musical Quarterly* 78 (summer 1994): 394–416.

2. For a discussion of other possible influences on the concerto, see Claudia MacDonald, "Critical Perception and the Woman Composer: The Early Reception of Piano Concertos by Clara Wieck Schumann and Amy Beach," *Current Musicology* 55 (1993): 37–40.

3. Abraham Veinus, *The Concerto* (London: Cassell, 1948), 251, writes a dramatic description of the Tchaikovsky concerto, characterizing the relationship between orchestra and soloist as a duel, and concludes that "[t]here is a battle royal for a while, which is as it should be, for this, after all, is a concerto."

4. Mrs. H. H. A. Beach, "To the Girl Who Wants to Compose," *Etude*, 35 (November 1918): 695.

5. The concerto is scored for 3 flutes (piccolo), 2 oboes, 3 clarinets (bass clarinets), 2 bassoons, 4 horns, 2 trumpets, 3 trombones, tuba, timpani, solo piano, and strings. Score and parts are in the Fleisher Collection, Free Library of Philadelphia.

6. "Some Women in the Public Eye," *San Francisco Chronicle*, 13 May 1900, Sunday Suppl., 30.

7. Benjamin Brooks, "The 'How' of Creative Composition. A Conference with Mrs. H. H. A. Beach," *Etude* 61 (March 1943): 151.

8. Translation of the third stanza of "Jeune fille et jeune fleur": "You sleep, poor Elisa, of so few years;/You feel neither the heat nor the weight of the day,/You have lived only to the cool morning of your life,/Young girl and young flower."

9. "Californians Fête Mrs. H. H. A. Beach," *Musical Courier* 71 (14 July 1915): 7.

10. In addition to Amy Cheney and Sembrich, Mr. Peck's Annual Concert, April 23, 1884, featured the tenor Charles Adams, the mezzo-soprano Sofia Scalchi, and the Beethoven Club ensemble.

11. "Charles A. Cheney," *Paper Trades Journal* 24 (3 August 1895): 717. The death certificate (Boston Vital Records: Deaths 1895, no. 6334) gives the length of illness as four weeks.

12. Probate Report no. 99500, 15 August 1895, vol. 704, p. 354, Suffolk County, Mass.

13. Agnes Lockhart Hughes, "Mrs. H. H. A. Beach—America's Foremost Woman Composer," *Boston Times*, 13 March 1915.

14. Beach, "Music after Marriage and Motherhood," *Etude* 27 (August 1909): 520.

15. See chap. 1. Beach's associations of colors and keys are reported in several publications, including Amy Beach, "Why I Chose My Profession: The Autobiography of a Woman Composer," interviewed by Ednah Aiken, *Mother's Magazine* 11 (February 1914): 7; Louis C. Elson, *The History of American Music* (1915; rev. 1925; reprint, New York: Burt Franklin, 1971), 295; and "Mrs. H. H. A. Beach," printed biographical essay and catalog through op. 45, with annotations in Beach's hand, Nh.

16. See, for example, the opening of the last movement of Mozart's Concerto in D Minor (K. 466), where the piano, unaccompanied, introduces the first theme.

17. Howard Malcom Ticknor, "Music," *Boston Courier*, 7 April 1900 (S1, 129).

18. Louis C. Elson, "Musical Matters," *Boston Daily Advertiser*, 9 April 1900 (S1, 129−30).

19. Philip Hale, "Symphony Night," n.d. (S2, 51).

20. "The Symphony Concert," *Boston Herald*, 8 April 1900 (S2, 52).

21. Carreño to Beach, 25 May 1900, NhU-Be.

22. According to Brian Mann, in "The Carreño Collection at Vassar College," *Notes* 47 (June 1991): 1073−74, Carreño was scheduled to play a MacDowell concerto but was asked by her manager to play something new instead. She chose the Beach concerto; this choice was vetoed by her manager. In the end, on 14 October 1901 Carreño played Rubinstein's Concerto no. 4, in D Minor, with the Berlin Philharmonic for the second time.

23. Dagmar de Corval Ruebner of New York gave a performance of the concerto with the Washington Symphony Orchestra under the direction of Heinrich Hammer on 17 January 1911 at the Columbia Theatre, Washington, D.C. (program, Washington Symphony Orchestra Papers, DLC-Mu). As a result, Herbert Putnam, Librarian of Congress, requested that a copy of the score be made for the library at the library's expense, a request that was fulfilled (Beach to Herbert Putnam, Librarian of Congress, 20 January 1911, DLC-APS). The only other pianist who played the concerto during Beach's lifetime was the young pupil of Mrs. Crosby Adams, Helen Pugh; in a letter to Schmidt, 1 December 1928 (DLC-APS), Beach asked Schmidt to send the score and parts to Pugh, who "plays it superbly."

24. Between 1913 and 1917, Beach played the concerto with the following orchestras: Winderstein Orchester, Leipzig, 22 November 1913; the Orchester des Vereins Hamburgischer Musikfruende, 2 December 1913; the Berlin Philharmonic, 18 December 1913; the Los Angeles Symphony Orchestra, 28 June 1915; the Exposition Orchestra of the Panama-Pacific International Exposition, San Francisco, 1 August 1915; the Chicago Symphony Orchestra, 4 February 1916; the St. Louis Symphony Orchestra, 12−13 January 1917; the Boston Symphony Orchestra, 2−3 March 1917; and the Minneapolis Symphony Orchestra, 14−15? December 1917.

Chapter 13. *The Composer's Workshop*

1. See, for example, "Concert Record of Works by Some of Our Best American Composers," *Musical Courier* 42 (2 January 1901):9, a listing of performances of compositions by Beach, Foote, Frank Lynes, and MacDowell, on which Beach's list of works—mostly songs—is the longest of all. See also "Their Ten Favorite American Songs," *Musical America* 23 (20 November 1915): 9. The many opera singers who gave Beach's songs in concert—and later over the radio—kept her music in the public ear, thus stimulating sales. Although the sales figures for her songs are not available, we do know that with the $500 earned from royalties for her earliest "hit," "Ecstasy," published in 1893, Beach purchased land on Cape Cod in 1894. As she received five cents for every copy sold (at fifty cents each), we can assume that at least 10,000 copies were sold in less than two years.

2. Hazel Gertrude Kinscella, "'Play No Piece in Public When First Learned,' Says Mrs. Beach," *Musical America* 28 (7 September 1918): 9.

3. Mrs. H. H. A. Beach, "Enjoyment of Song," *Music on the Air*, ed. Hazel Gertrude Kinscella (Garden City, N.Y.: Garden City Publishing, 1934), 25.

4. Beach, "The Mission of the Present-day Composer," *Triangle of Mu Phi Epsilon* 36 (February 1942): 71.

5. All of the translations up to and including "Canzonetta," op. 48, no. 4 (1902), were unsigned and either her own or a collaboration between Henry and Amy Beach. There-

after, she found professional translators whose work pleased her, including Mme Isadora Martinez, a singer, conductor, and linguist, of Boston, who translated Italian, French, and German texts beginning with op. 51, and John Bernhoff, Beach's translator in Munich, for German texts beginning with op. 72, no. 1. See Beach to Arthur P. Schmidt, 27 February 1902, DLC-APS.

6. Edward T. Cone, *The Composer's Voice* (Berkeley: University of California Press, 1974), 21.

7. "'The Rose of Avontown,' Cantata Composed by Mrs. H. H. A. Beach of Boston," *Brooklyn Times*, 8 March 1896 (S1, 97).

8. This is one of three songs in opus 11 based on Henley's poems and includes the onomatopoetic "Blackbird" and the sea song "Dark Is the Night" that Beach quoted in the "Gaelic" Symphony.

9. Amy Beach, "Why I Chose My Profession: The Autobiography of a Woman Composer," interviewed by Ednah Aiken, *Mother's Magazine* 11 (February 1914): 7. Although to this date there is no trace of a manuscript collection of bird songs by Beach, her article "Bird Songs," *The Designer* (Standard Fashion Co., New York), May 1911, includes several transcriptions of bird calls.

10. Author's interview with Virginia Duffey Pleasants, 25 June 1985.

11. This was one of three French songs in the opus that Beach dedicated to the Baroness de Hegermann-Lindencrone, *née* Lillie Greenough from Cambridge, Massachusetts, an amateur singer with an extraordinarily beautiful voice who acted as a European ambassador for Beach's music. According to information told to the author by Hegermann-Lindencrone's grandson, Andreas Holm, of Copenhagen, neither the "de" nor the title of baroness was accurate. The family, although noble, were never landed and thus not titled. Greenough lived as a girl in Fay House, now part of the Radcliffe College complex. At sixteen, she went to Europe to study voice with Manuel Garcia. After marrying Charles Moulton, an American banker in Paris, she was a regular at the court of Louis Napoléon, where she was much admired for both her voice and her beauty. Some time after Moulton's death in 1871, she married Johan Hegermann-Lindencrone, then Danish Ambassador to the United States, later successively posted to Stockholm, Paris, and Berlin. She wrote two volumes of memoirs.

12. The Victor Hugo text reads: "Je t'adore ange, et t'aime femme./Dieu qui par toi m'a complété/A fait mon amour pour ton âme,/Et mon regard pour ta beauté."

13. Amy Beach, "Why I Chose My Profession: The Autobiography of a Woman Composer," interviewed by Ednah Aiken, *Mother's Magazine* 11 (February 1914): 7–8.

14. "Pippa Passes," in *The Poems and Plays of Robert Browning* (New York: Modern Library, 1934), 368.

15. Eames to Beach, 9 December 1904, NhU-Be.

16. Copy of letter in Clara Cheney's hand from Emma Eames to Beach, Paris, 14 September 1904, NhU, quoted by permission of Clare Le Corbeiller, great-niece of Emma Eames.

17. Other songs with triplets throughout in the accompaniment include: "The Summer Wind," op. 14, no. 1; "For Me the Jasmine Buds Unfold," op. 19, no.1; "Spring," op. 26, no. 3; "Haste, O Beloved," op. 29, no. 4; "Good Morning," op. 48, no. 2; and "Juni," op. 51, no. 3. Those that introduce reiterated triplet chords only to build a climax include the vocal duet "Sea Song," op. 10, no. 3; "Dark Is the Night," op. 11, no. 1; "Sweetheart, Sigh No More," op. 14, no. 3; "The Thrush," op. 14, no. 4; "My Star," op. 26, no. 1; "The Wandering Knight," op. 29, no. 2; "Ah, Love, But a Day," op. 44, no. 2; "I Send My Heart Up to Thee," op. 44, no. 3; and "When Soul Is Joined to Soul," op. 62. This technique is also used in abstract works, as in, for example, third and fourth movements of the sonata,

op. 34, and the second and third movements of the piano quintet, op. 67. Such passages are frequently marked *appassionato*.

18. "Elle et moi" is by Félix Bovet; "Le Secret" is by Le Comte Bernard Marie Jules de Resseguier (1789-1862).

19. The first page of "Elle et moi" is reproduced in *Grove-American*, s.v., "Beach, Amy."

20. Beach probably did not know the setting by Clara Schumann, which has a title from the poem's first line, "Ich stand in dunklen Träumen," op. 13, no. 1 (1840).

21. The idea was articulated by John Sullivan Dwight in his pamphlet *Address Delivered Before the Harvard Musical Association*, 25 August 1841 (n.p.), 12-13. Irving Lowens, "Writings about Music in the Periodicals of American Transcendentalism (1830-50)," *Journal of the American Musicological Society* 10 (summer 1957): 75, summarized Dwight's belief that "[t]he society which had for its standard of excellence money or power was a defective one, and it was the holy mission of music to remedy the defect by 'familiarizing men with the beautiful and the infinite'" by means of "the greatest music performed by the greatest artists." See also Ora Frishberg Saloman, *Beethoven's Symphonies and J. S. Dwight: The Birth of American Music Criticism* (Boston: Northeastern University Press, 1985), who focuses on Dwight's early writings before he launched *Dwight's Journal of Music*.

22. Henry Edward Krehbiel, *Music and Manners in the Classical Period*, 3rd ed. (New York: Charles Scribner's, 1899), 237. Webern apparently found this trinity essential to his creative work; see Anne C. Shreffler, "'Mein Weg geht jetzt vorüber': The Vocal Origins of Webern's Twelve-Tone Composition," *Journal of the American Musicological Society* 47 (summer 1994): 329.

23. Harriette Brower, *Piano Mastery*, 2nd series (New York: Frederick A. Stokes, [1917]), 183.

24. Beach, "The Twenty-Fifth Anniversary of a Vision," *Proceedings of the Music Teachers National Association*, 27th Series, 1932 (Oberlin, Ohio: MTNA, 1933), 46.

25. Eames to Beach, 17 February [1905], NhU-Be.

26. "Inclusions," *Oxford Book of Victorian Verse* (Oxford: Clarendon Press, 1919), 134.

27. For a detailed discussion of this song, see this author's Introduction to Amy Beach, *Quartet for Strings in One Movement, Op. 89*, vol. 3 of *Music of the United States of America* (Madison: A-R Editions, 1994), xvi-xvii, xx-xxi.

28. Author's interview with David Buxbaum, Chebeague Island, Me., 21 August 1986.

29. *Collected Poems of Florence Earle Coates*, vol. 2 (Boston: Houghton Mifflin, 1916), 64.

Chapter 14. Choral Music

1. See Arthur Wilson, ed., "Mrs. H. H. A. Beach: A Conversation on Musical Conditions in America," *The Musician*, 17 (January 1912): 10.

2. The poet Henry Martyn Blossom Jr. (1866-1919), was the librettist of *Mlle Modiste*, *The Red Mill*, and other operettas; see *Who Was Who in America* 1, 1897-1942 (Chicago: Marquis Who's Who, 1943), 110.

3. "Music at the Trans-Mississippi Exposition," *Musical Courier* 36 (8 June 1898): 27.

4. Ibid.

5. Ibid., 8

6. "By a Gifted Woman: Cantata 'Sylvania' Has a Notable Presentation," *Boston Globe*, 8 April 1905 (S2, 66).

7. Ibid.

8. Paine to Beach, 11 April 1905, copy in Clara Cheney's hand, NhU-Be.

9. However, a decade later Chadwick changed his mind. In his tone-poem *Tam O'Shanter*, op. 22 (1914-15), based on a narrative poem by Robert Burns, while he uses themes of distinctly Scottish flavor, he also borrows sonorities from Debussy.

10. Chadwick to Beach, copy in Clara Cheney's hand, 12 April 1905, NhU-Be.

11. Beach, "The Mission of the Present-day Composer," *Triangle of Mu Phi Epsilon* 36 (February 1942): 71.

12. At this time, there is only one recording of the complete *Service in A*: Music and Arts, CD 921, cond. Nick Strimple.

13. Beach's notes suggest that she consulted the entry "Time" in Sir George Grove's *Dictionary of Music and Musicians* 4 (London: Macmillan, 1890), 118−19; she copied out part of the discussion on "Alla breve," including the statement that "three-two time is consistently used in modern [English] church music as well as that of the sixteenth century."

14. Beach copied out the famous chant from the first edition of Grove, vol. 4, 67. Her pencil holograph of the Te Deum includes three versions of the chant—from Marbecke, from Glareanus's *Dodecachordon*, and from a Roman version that is in the supplement to the Ratisbon Gradual. Beach also copied part of the discussion of the history of the chant. All sources are at NhU-Be.

15. This is not the Emmanuel Church on Copley Square but the church at 15 Newbury Street between Arlington and Berkeley.

16. There is no record of a performance of this work. The English translation may have been by Beach herself.

17. This list includes only those works originally for male choir. Beach made numerous arrangements of her songs and choruses for various voice groups.

18. "Woman's Work in Music," *Etude*, 16 (February 1898): 36.

19. Several writers on Beach allege without documentation, that music clubs all over the country were named after Beach by members. To this date, I have located only the three named here.

20. Krehbiel, "Mrs. Beach's Symphony," *New York Tribune*, 27 March 1897 (S2, 31), deplored the clubs' support not of Beach but of women's music in general and their taking control of music in the larger cities. He also believed that Beach's music suffered by being presented by the clubs along with music of "inferior" women composers. See "Music: The Kneisel Quartet," *New York Daily Tribune*, 29 March 1899 (S1, 123).

21. Linda Whitesitt, "The Role of Women Impresarios in American Concert Life, 1871−1933," *American Music* 7 (summer 1989): 159−60. See also her "'The Most Potent Force' in American Music: The Role of Women's Music Clubs in American Concert Life," *The Musical Woman: An International Perspective*, vol. 3, 1986−1990, eds. Judith Lang Zaimont with Jane Gottlieb, Joanne Polk, and Michael T. Rogan (New York: Greenwood Press, 1991), 663−81.

22. Ada B. Douglass, "A Plea for More Serious Work among the So-called Music Clubs," *Etude* 16 (February 1898): 36.

23. See Judith Tick, *American Women Composers before 1870* (Ann Arbor: Michigan Research Press, 1979), 171.

24. "The Rose of Avontown," *Brooklyn Times*, 28 March 1896 (S2, 18).

25. Clipping, *Brooklyn Standard-Union*, 23 April 1896 (S2, 19).

26. Philip Hale, *Boston Journal*, 29 September 1898 (S2, 43); "Music," *Boston Journal*, 5 February 1897 (S2, 28).

27. Full score is at New England Conservatory of Music, Boston. In a letter to Harry Austin at Arthur P. Schmidt Co., 22 January 1940, Beach approves of an alternate orchestration for strings and piano, in which the piano is assigned the wind parts (DLC-APS).

28. *The Autocrat of the Breakfast Table* (London: J. M. Dent, 1906), 92; originally published serially in the *Atlantic Monthly* in 1857−58).

29. Vernon L. Parrington, *The Romantic Revolution in America* 1800−1860, vol. 2 of *Main Currents in American Thought* (New York: Harcourt Brace, 1927), 453.

30. See, however, Joan Hedrick's report on the one meeting of the Saturday Club to

which women, including Harriet Beecher Stowe and Harriet Prescott (Spofford) came, in *Harriet Beecher Stowe, A Life* (New York: Oxford University Press, 1994), 290. The men were made so self-conscious by the presence of the women that their usual witty and voluble conversation was completely stifled.

31. Beach to Arthur P. Schmidt, 10 May 1907 (DLC-APS).

32. Beach to Schmidt, 31 October 1907 (DLC-APS).

33. Goetschius to Beach, 15 December 1907, copy in Clara Cheney's hand, NhU-Be.

34. Goetschius to Beach, copy in Clara Cheney's hand, 26 March 1909, S5.

Chapter 15. *The Chambered Nautilus*

1. Mrs. H. H. A. Beach, "How Music Is Made," *Keyboard* 4 (winter 1942): 38.

2. Chromatic Club Scrapbooks, private collection of Marella MacDill, Boston.

3. Program, Thursday Morning Musical Club, the Club Room, 126 Massachusetts Ave. (S4).

4. Records of the Boston Browning Society, MB-Ms.

5. Russell (1871–1937) was a voice teacher and an opera director. He headed the Boston Opera Company from 1909 to 1914, after which the company dissolved.

6. Arthur Whiting, Boston composer and author, quoted in Quaintance Eaton, *The Boston Opera Company* (New York: Appleton Century, 1965; reprint, New York: Da Capo Press, 1980), 41. The Opera House was torn down in 1958 to clear the land for Northeastern University.

7. The box is missing, but an inventory of its contents is in the archives, Northeastern University, Boston.

8. Steinert's instrument collection is now housed at Yale University.

9. Clipping, *Boston Beacon*, 22 March 1884 (S1, 16).

10. Mrs. H. H. A. Beach, "Cristofori redivivus," *Music* 16 (May 1899): 4.

11. Howard Malcom Ticknor, "Music," *Boston Courier*, 7 April 1900 (S1, 129).

12. Letter from Beach to Marian MacDowell, 27 November 1906 (DLC-APS). Edward MacDowell died on 23 January 1908.

13. "Mrs. Beach's Recital," *Boston Herald*, n.d. (S1, 153).

14. Gertrude F. Cowen, "Boston and New England," *Musical Courier* 60 (16 February 1910): 44.

15. Cowen, "Boston and New England." See also "Mrs. Beach Gives Recital: Old and Modern Piano Music Is Played at Steinert Hall," *Boston Herald*, 11 February 1910, 7.

16. "Woman's Progress in Music Aptly Shown," *Baltimore Morning Herald*, 15 March 1901.

17. On the implications of tokenism, see Minnich's review essay, "Friendship between Women: The Act of Feminist Biography," *Feminist Studies* 11 (1985): 305, in which she states, "The 'Exception Woman' exists in a crack between women and men, granted status superior to her own kind by the very same people who deny her entrance to theirs. She exists to be the exception that proves the rule—several 'rules,' actually. She proves that womankind is not as capable/bright/hard-driving/whatever as men are and as she, the exception, is, because if we were, she would not be all alone where she is. She thereby proves that men are not prejudiced against women, because they hired/promoted/recognized her. The phrase itself reminds us that it is not exceptions to the prevailing rules we need, but control over rulemaking."

18. See clippings in S1, 137–39.

19. Das Comite des Richard Wagner-Denkmal, Berlin, to Beach, 1 October 1903 (S4).

20. Gertrude F. Cowen, "Mrs. H. H. A. Beach, the Celebrated Composer," *Musical Courier* 60 (8 June 1910), 15.

21. "New Gems in the Old Classics: A Talk with Mrs. H. H. A. Beach," William Armstrong, *Etude* 22 (February 1904): 51.

22. Beach, "Music after Marriage and Motherhood," *Etude* 27 (August 1909): 520.

23. To this date I have found neither written confirmation nor denial of this story.

24. Beach to Arthur P. Schmidt, 2 May 1910 (DLC-APS).

25. Gertrude F. Cowen, "Obituary: Dr. Henry H. A. Beach," *Musical Courier* 61 (6 July 1910): 23.

26. Massachusetts Vital Records, 1910 deaths, 14: 236.

27. "Obituary, H. H. A. Beach, M.D.," *Boston Medical and Surgical Journal*, 163 (14 July 1910): 71–72.

28. Gertrude F. Cowen, "Obituary, Henry H. A. Beach," *Musical Courier* 61 (6 July 1910): 23.

29. Beach to Schmidt, 1 October 1910 (DLC-APS).

30. Probate Court, Suffolk County, Commonwealth of Massachusetts, file no. 149729. The document carries the final date of 22 October 1910. Not included in the total given here were his professional books and instruments, clothing, and household items. The investments yielded only a modest amount, while Beach had the double burden of paying off the mortgage and interest on the house and the living expenses at the hotel where she and her mother were staying.

31. The original mortgage on the house, when it was purchased in 1879, was $20,000. Suffolk County Deeds show that on 27 June 1899 Henry Beach refinanced the mortgage on 28 Commonwealth Avenue.

32. Beach to Schmidt, 5 October 1910 (DLC-APS).

33. Beach to Schmidt, 5 January 1911 (DLC-APS).

34. Sacramental Records of the Active and Closed Churches of the Episcopal Diocese of Massachusetts, Boston: Emmanuel Church, p. 146.

35. Arthur Wilson, "Mrs. H. H. A. Beach," *Musician*, 17 (January 1912): 9.

36. Beach to Schmidt, 13 February 1911 (DLC-APS). She offered to return a "Rose of Sharon" (marble), "La Poésie" (marble), bronze Arab on horseback, Moorish Minstrel, carved wooden stags, a plant stand, and a Sèvres vase.

37. Massachusetts Vital Records, 1911 deaths, 8: 288.

38. The bequest was for $8,000. She may have been able to keep this sum because Henry Beach had assumed responsibility for Clara's support after she moved in with him and her daughter in 1895, following her husband's death. In a 1905 codicil to his will, Henry Beach made Clara Cheney his heir should Amy Beach predecease him.

39. Wilson, 10.

40. Beach to Schmidt, 8 March [1911] (DLC-APS).

41. Wilson, 10.

42. Beach to Schmidt, 28 August 1911 (DLC-APS).

Chapter 16. Europe and a New Life

1. Arthur Wilson, "Mrs. H. H. A. Beach: A Conversation on Musical Conditions in America," *Musician* 17 (January 1912): 9.

2. Agnes Lockhart Hughes, "Mrs. H. H. A. Beach, America's Foremost Woman Composer," *Boston Times*, 13 March 1915 (S3). Hughes was a close personal friend of Beach's, as well as a journalist, and her information probably came from the source, in contradiction to Walter S. Jenkins, *The Remarkable Mrs. Beach: American Composer* (Warren, Mich.: Harmonie Park Press, 1994), 71, which has an undocumented statement that Beach went to Europe with Amy Brigham.

3. "Musical Visitors," 5 and 11 May 1909 (NhU-Be).

4. "World's Foremost Woman Composer to Be Honor Guest at Reception," *Riverside Enterprise*, 19 April 1915 (S3).

5. See Araxie P. Churukian, "Marcella Craft," *Books at UCR* 15 (fall 1990).

6. Henry Beach to Nahan Franko, 11 May 1904 (Metropolitan Opera Archives, New York). Franko was concertmaster of the Metropolitan Opera Orchestra from 1883 to 1905 and conductor from 1899 to 1912. See also Henry Beach to Franko, 19 May 1904, Nahan Franko Correspondence, NN-L.

7. Edward T. Heyn, "American Opera Singers on German Stages," *Burr McIntosh Monthly* 12 (February 1907).

8. Tom Patterson, "Exhibit to Focus on Life of Singer from Riverside," *Riverside Press-Enterprise*, 15 April 1990, sec. B, p. 4.

9. Carolyn G. Heilbrun, in *Writing a Woman's Life* (New York: W. W. Norton, 1988), 100, uses these words to describe the friendship of the writers Vera Brittain and Winifred Holtby.

10. "Marcella Craft at Home," *Musical Courier* (25 September 1914): 13.

11. Edwin Hughes, "The Outlook for the Young American Composer: An Interview with the Distinguished American Composer, Mrs. H. H. A. Beach," *Etude* 33 (January 1915): 13.

12. Ibid.

13. "Mrs. Beach's Return," *Boston Transcript*, 23 October 1914, Beach Clipping File (NN-L).

14. "Mrs. Beach Fêted Abroad," *Musical Courier* 64 (6 March 1912): 28.

15. Aus der Ohe to Beach, 27 September 1911, NhU-Be. Adele Aus der Ohe (1864–1937) was a child prodigy who became a favorite pupil of Liszt. She made seventeen tours of the United States and played fifty concerts with the Boston Symphony Orchestra. Further, see Christine Ammer, *Unsung: A History of Women in American Music* (Westport, Conn.: Greenwood Press, 1980), 61.

16. Beach to Craft, postcard from Torbole on Lake Garda, Italy, in Marcella Craft Papers, Historic Resources Department, Riverside, Calif.

17. Sgambati (1841–1914), composer, pianist, and conductor, founded the Liceo de Santa Cecilia in Rome, later renamed the Conservatorio. Sgambati to Beach, 28 March 1912 (NhU-Be). Clare P. Peeler, "American Woman Whose Musical Message Thrilled Germany," *Musical America*, 20 (17 October 1914): 7, includes Beach's report on her visit to Sgambati.

18. Francis Marion Crawford (1854–1909), novelist, was born in Italy but was partly educated in the United States, spending a year at Harvard.

19. Peeler, "American Woman Whose Musical Message Thrilled Germany."

20. Craft sang Salome twice in 1912, on 8 February and 25 April, and a total of 11 times (Archives of the Royal Opera, Bibliothek der Bayerischen Staatsoper, Munich). She Made her debut as Salome on 20 December 1910, after which she claimed that she had problems portraying such a sexually uninhibited character. After hearing her objections to Salome's character, to the more gruesome aspects of the plot, and even to some of the music, Strauss revised the role to satisfy her. ("Marcella Craft Chats About her Art," *Pacific Coast Musical Review*, 28 [25 September 1915]: 52; and "New Idea of Salome," *Musical Leader* 32 [21 September 1916]: 293).

21. Beach to Craft, dated "Friday morning," Marcella Craft Papers.

22. Beach to Arthur P. Schmidt, 5 October 1912 (DLC-APS).

23. Kitty Peavy, "Music Is Advocated for Public Schools," *Atlanta Sunday American*, 4 November 1928 (Scrapbook, Atlanta Historical Society, Atlanta).

24. Program with Beach's inscription in S3.

25. Translation of excerpt in "Mrs. H. H. A. Beach's Musical Encomiums," *Musical Courier* 66 (7 May 1913): 49 (advertisement).

26. Beach to Arthur P. Schmidt, 30 November 1912, DLC-APS.

27. Translation of excerpt in "Mrs. H. H. A. Beach's Musical Encomiums."

28. Es bleibt ein Rätsel, wie die Komponistin in ihren Liedern so ganz ihre hohen Ziele vergessen und in die Sybäre des Hildach und Meyer-Helmund geraten konnte, in jene leichte Gefühlsseligkeit der Salonmusik, von der man in der Violonsonate verspürt. Nur das Lied "I dreamt, I loved a Star" steht merklich über diesem Niveau. . . . Ihre pianistischen Fähigkeiten sind nicht so durchgebildet wie ihre musikalischen; ihre Technik ist nicht immer klar, und die Kultur des Anschlags mangelt ihr ganz empfindlich. Aber sie verleugnet in Phrasierung und Rhythmus nie die gute Musikerin, und deshalb hört man ihr mit Interesse zu. (Alexander Berrsche, "Münchener Konzerte," *Münchener Zeitung und des Wochenschrift Propylaen*, 21 January 1913, p. 2.)

Eugen Hildach (1849–1924) and Erik Meyer-Helmund (1861–1932) were both skillful composers of lightweight songs. I am grateful to Nancy B. Reich for her expert assistance in this and the following translations from the German.

29. "Theater und Musik," *Münchener Neueste Nachrichten*, 14 January 1913, p. 2.

30. Beach to Schmidt, 2 February 1913 (DLC-APS).

31. Beach to Schmidt, 30 November 1912 (DLC-APS).

32. H.A.S., "At 74, Mrs. Beach Recalls Her First Critics," *Musical Courier* 123 (15 May 1941): 7.

33.

Über das Klavierspiel wäre nur das zu wiederholen, was bei jener früheren Gelegenheit gesagt wurdet sehr gewandt, glänzend in der Technik, aber kalt und grob im Anschlag. Als Komponistin zeigt das Quintett Mrs. Beach von ihre besten Seite. Wie schon damals die Violonsonate an musikalischem Wert die Gesänge weit übertroffen hatte, so gewann Mann auf von diesem Quintett—das vielleicht sogar noch etwas höher steht als die Sonate—den Eindruck eines ganz respektablen Könnens: und da die Komposition nicht sehr hoch hinaus will mit ihrer Musik vielmehr stets in den Grenzen hat unmittelbar Gefälligen sund leicht Eingänglichen bleibt, so darf sie auch stets einer gewissen äusseren Wirkung sicher sein. . . . Aber doch muss man wohl fragen, ob es gerade nötig war, dass die 'Münchner' die so ausserst sparsam? mit Neuheiten sind, sich des Werkes einer Amerikanerin annahmen, die als Komponistin wie als Klavierspielerin ganz brav, aber gewiss in keiner Weise bedeutend und jedenfalls nicht bedeutender ist als Dutzende von Komponisten, die uns darum so viel näher stehen müssten, weil sie Deutsche sind" ("Theater und Musik," *Münchener Neueste Nachrichten*, 24 January 1913, p. 2.

For a more complimentary appraisal, see Jacques Meyer, "Munich Premiere for American Work," *Musical America* 17 (15 February 1913): 33.

34. A statement from B. Schotts Söhne, of Arthur P. Schmidt Co. agent in Mainz, 30 June 1913, shows that they sold thirty-nine copies of Beach's song "Juni," op. 51, no. 3, but nothing else.

35. Mabel Daniels, "Memoirs," Daniels papers, Schlesinger Library, Radcliffe College, Cambridge, Mass.

36. On 31 December 1915, Schmidt sold the firm to his former assistants, Henry R. Austin, Harry B. Crosby, and Florence J. Emery, who became partners in the firm. See Arthur P. Schmidt Co. Corporate Records, box 1, Sibley Library, Eastman School of Music, Rochester, N.Y.

37. Reviews appeared in four papers, the *Breslauer Zeitung* (9 February 1913), the *Schlesische Zeitung* (14 February 1913), the *Schlesische Volkszeitung* (18 February 1913), and the *Breslauer General-Anzeiger* (15 February 1913).

38. "American Composers in Berlin," *Musical Courier* 66 (12 March 1913): 22.

39. Spiering conducted works by other American composers as well. For example, his third concert with the Berlin Philharmonic included Henry Hadley's rhapsody *The Culprit Fay*, op. 62, of 1908. He was engaged to conduct a woman's orchestra, the Neues Berliner Tonkünstlerinnen Orchester, in the fall of 1914, as reported in the *Musician*, August 1914, but instead returned to New York when war broke out. Thereafter he founded and trained the forty-member Woman's Orchestral Club of Brooklyn, N.Y., who gave a recital on 12 April 1915; see "Spiering Players in Admirable Concert," *Musical America* 21 (17 April 1915), 39. For a brief biography of Spiering, see "Theodore Spiering's Versatility," *Musical Courier* 67 (29 October 1913): 17.

40. "Stray Notes from Munich," *Musical Courier* 67 (22 October 1913): 7, has a photograph of Beach in a pony cart at the foot of the Kjendal Glacier. Jenkins, 75, states that Beach's traveling companion was her niece Elizabeth Stone, who was Henry Beach's niece by his first marriage; see Sidney D. Smith, comp., *Descendants of John Mendall, Sr., ca. 1638–1720, of Marchfield, Mass., by ca. 1660* (Baltimore: Gateway Press, 1984), 243–44).

41. H. O. Osgood, "Munich," *Musical Courier* 67/2 (9 August 1913): 7.

42. "Stray Notes from Munich."

43. Beach to Louise Miller Abell, 4 November 1913 (Arthur M. Abell Collection, NN-L).

44. *Musical Leader*, 28 November 1913 (Beach clipping file, NN-L).

45. Eugene R. Simpson, "A Draeseke Symphony Revived in Leipsic. Mrs. Beach and Theodore Spiering in Joint Concert," *Musical Courier* 67 (31 December 1913): 8.

46. 24 November 1913, translated in "Mrs. Beach's Leipsic Tributes," *Musical Courier* 68 (4 February 1914): 38.

47. H. F. P., "Believes Women Composers Will Rise to Greater Heights in World Democracy," *Musical America* 25 (21 April 1917): 3.

48. "American Art in Germany," *Berlin Continental Times*, n.d. (S3); Dr. Ferdinand Pfohl, *Hamburger Nachrichten*, 3 December 1913, quoted in an advertisement entitled, "Amy Beach (Mrs. H. H. A. Beach) in Hamburg," *Musical Courier* 67 (31 December 1913): 50.

49. Pfohl, "Amy Beach," 50.

50. [Arthur Abell], "American Composers in Berlin," *Musical Courier* 66 (12 March 1913): 22. "Berlin Choir Sings Bach's Passion Music . . . Spiering Reception in Honor of Mrs. H. H. A. Beach," *Musical Courier* 67 (10 December 1913): 6.

51. "Strauss Hearings Set a New Berlin Record," *Musical Courier* 68 (14 January 1914): 8–9.

52. O. P. Jacob, "Mrs. Beach's New Concerto Played," *Musical America* 19 (10 January 1914): 35.

53. "Berlin's Praise of Mrs. Beach," *Musical Courier* 68 (25 February 1914): 13, an advertisement that includes translated excerpts from nine Berlin reviews.

54. Edwin Hughes, "The Outlook for the Young American Composer," *Etude* 33 (January 1915): 13.

55. Peeler, "American Woman Whose Musical Message Thrilled Germany," 7.

56. Beach to Louise Abell, 16 January 1914 (Arthur M. Abell Collection (NN-LC). Her traveling companion was again Mary Hunt, who would also travel with Beach to Italy in 1926 and 1929.

57. "Lost Manuscripts," *Musical Courier* 69 (2 September 1914): 37.

58. "American Composer Returns from Europe," unidentified clipping, S3.

59. Harriette Brower, *Piano Mastery* (New York: Frederick A. Stokes, 1915), 184. For an analysis of the Prelude, see Tina Bakowski, "Structural and Contrapuntal Technique: As Found in the *Prelude and Fugue*, op. 81, by Amy Beach," unpublished paper, University of Kansas, Lawrence, November 1988. I am grateful to Mary Louise Boehm for pointing out that the theme spells Beach's name.

60. That is was not published by Oliver Ditson until 1926, twelve years after its completion, may have been due to anti-German sentiment, which by the mid-1920s, had died down.

61. The score-sketch is at NhU-Be. The introduction is undated, but the "Tempo di Valse" (p. 5) is inscribed "Rothenberg, 24 November 1911"; at the end, "Garmisch, 29 December 1911." I am indebted to Nancy B. Reich for her assistance in identifying the following folk songs: "Rosestock Holderblüh," a Swabian folk song published in an 1837 collection arranged by Friedrich Silcher; the text of "Kommt ein Vogel geflogen," published in 1822.

62. The song is dedicated to the singer Elena Gerhardt.

63. "Marcella Craft Tells of Her Lucky Escape," *Musical America* (5 August 1914): 5. "Marcella Craft in New York," *Musical Courier* 69 (16 September 1914): 38.

64. "Mrs. Beach Safe in Munich," *Musical America* 20 (5 September 1914): 3.

65. "American Composer Returns from Europe: Mrs. H. H. A. Beach," unidentified clipping (S3).

66. S1, laid in.

67. "American Composer Returns from Europe."

68. "Lost Manuscripts."

69. "American Composer Returns from Europe."

70. "American Woman Whose Musical Message Thrilled Germany."

71. "Mrs. Beach Safe in America," *Musical Courier* 69 (23 September 1914): 28.

Chapter 17. "Lion of the Hour"

1. "Mrs. Beach Caught by Camera," *Musical Courier* 70 (13 January 1915): 11.

2. Emilie Frances Bauer, "Music in New York," *Musical Leader* 29 (4 February 1915): 122.

3. "Mrs. Beach in the West," *Musical Courier* 69 (9 December 1914): 13.

4. Kitty Peavy, "Music Is Advocated for Public Schools," *Atlanta Sunday American*, 4 November 1928.

5. "American Composer Returns from Europe," unidentified clipping, S3.

6. Postcard, Beach to Ethel Clement, 24 November 1914 (DLC-APS). According to "Boston Welcomes Mrs. Beach," *Musical Courier* 69 (25 November 1914): 11, there were 900 people at the reception and concert. The name *Shena* comes from her song "Shena Van," op. 56, no. 4, the text by the Scottish writer William Black and the song's dedication to her cousin Ethel. Beach explained in a letter to Arthur P. Schmidt Co., 22 November 1939 (DLC-APS), that *Shena Van* means *darling*.

7. "Boston Welcomes Mrs. Beach."

8. "News of Music: Mrs. Beach's Concert of Her Own Compositions," *Boston Evening Transcript*, 17 December 1914 (S3).

9. Downes, "Mrs. Beach in Concert," *Boston Post*, 17? December 1914 (S4); "News of Music," *Boston Transcript*, 17 December 1914 (S3).

10. "News of Music"; Downes, "Mrs. Beach in Concert"; "Mrs. Beach's Concerto," *Boston Globe*, 17 December 1914 (S4).

11. 28? December 1914, Brighton, Mass. (S1, 63).

12. Program, 11 February 1909; see S4 for this and other programs and reviews of May (Mrs. Lafayette) Goodbar's recitals.

13. Beach gave the following recitals: Pittsburgh, 1 December 1914; Kansas City, 16 December, with Craft; Brighton, Mass., 28 December, with Craft; Portland, Me., with Craft; 8 January 1915, with Goodbar; Columbus, 3 February, with Craft; Detroit, 5 February, with Myrna Sharlow of the Boston Opera Company; Columbus, 9 February, with Craft; New York, 25 February, for the Granberry School; New York, Colony Club, 9 March, with Craft; Brooklyn, 14 March, with the Olive Mead Quartet. There were four receptions in Beach's honor in New York and one in Philadelphia.

14. "Finds New York's Music of Highest," *New York Sun*, 15 March 1915 (S3).

15. "Woman Composer Praises Philharmonic Orchestra," *Philadelphia Public Ledger*, 28 February 1915 (S4).

16. Stokowski to Beach, 6 March 1915 (NhU-Be).

17. Subsequent performances of the symphony were given by the Kansas City Orchestra, cond. Carl Busch, 4 April 1916; by the Minneapolis Symphony, cond. Emil Oberhoffer, 14 December 1917; the Philadelphia Orchestra, cond. Stokowski, 26 February 1918; and the Detroit Symphony, cond. Ossip Gabrilowitsch, 30 December 1918.

18. *Philadelphia North American* and *Philadelphia Evening Bulletin*, 27 February 1915 (S3).

19. *Philadelphia Record* and *Philadelphia Press*, 27 February 1915 (S3); "Mrs. Beach's Symphony," *Musical Leader*, n.d. (S4).

20. "Mrs. Beach's Music," *New York Times*, 17 March 1915 (Beach Clipping File, NN-L).

21. Sigmund Spaeth, "Mrs. H. A. [sic] Beach Presents Her Own Compositions," *New York Evening Mail*, 17 March 1915 (S3).

22. Author's interview with Eugenie Limberg Dengel, 14 February 1985, New York.

23. Emilie Frances Bauer, "Music in New York," *Musical Leader* 29 (25 March 1915): 336.

24. "Woman Has Achieved Little in Musical Spheres," in Walter Damrosch Scrapbooks, vol. 1, 1881–1927, NN-L.

25. Quoted in Jean Mahan Planck, "Music and the Feminine Mind," *Musical Monitor*, 4 (February 1915): 170. Planck notes that Beach answered Damrosch in the same publication in which Damrosch's interview appeared, the *National Sunday Magazine*. However, to this date, neither the original of Damrosch's nor Beach's article has been located. Other articles in response to Damrosch include J. Keeley, "Why Have We No Really Great Women Composers," *San Francisco Chronicle*, 5 September 1916, magazine section, 5; Arthur Selwyn Garbett, "Music in the Home," unidentified publication from Philadelphia, n.d. (S3).

26. H. F. P., "Believes Women Composers Will Rise to Greater Heights in World Democracy," *Musical America* 25 (21 April 1917): 3.

27. "Personalities," *Musical America* 25 (16 December 1916): 26.

28. "Pilgrims Journey to Mountain Shrine for Sunrise Concert," *Musical America* 21 (17 April 1915): 17.

29. ". . . Welcome Easter Morn," unidentified clipping, S4.

30. The Panama-Pacific International Exposition opened on 20 February 1915 and closed on 4 December 1915.

31. "Mrs. Beach's Hymn for Big Exposition," *Musical America* 21 (30 January 1915): 27, states that the Handel and Haydn Society gave the premiere of the *Panama Hymn* on 14 February 1915. This however was canceled, allowing the premiere to take place at the exposition on its opening day, 20 February 1915.

32. *Official Program, Panama-Pacific International Exposition, San Francisco*, 1915, 4–5.

33. Redfern Mason, "Masterly Work of Mrs. Beach and Haydn's 'Creation' Give Day's Musical Setting," *San Francisco Examiner*, 21 February 1915, S5.

34. "California Honors Mrs. Beach," 30 June 1915 (Beach Clipping File, NN-L).

35. Walter Anthony, "Music Season Is of Epochal Importance," *San Francisco Chronicle*, 13 June 1915, 24.

36. "Musical Importance of Mrs. Beach," *Pacific Coast Musical Review* 28 (12 June 1915): 1, 3.

37. H. F. P., "Believes Women Composers Will Rise to Greater Heights," 3.

38. "National Federation of Musical Clubs," *Pacific Coast Musical Review* 28 (19 June 1915): 3. See also "American Music Will Prevail at Coming Festival" (S4). Composers whose works were given at the biennial included Beach, Carrie Jacobs Bond, Carl Busch, Charles Wakefield Cadman, George Whitefield Chadwick, Mabel Daniels, Arthur Farwell, Arthur Foote, Adolph M. Foerster, Edgar Stillman Kelley, Ernest R. Kroeger, Edward MacDowell, W. J. McCoy, Arne Oldberg, Horatio Parker, and David Stanley Smith. In addition, women composers of songs, choruses, and instrumental solos included Faith Helen Rogers, who won the prize for the best song, Mary Turner Salter, Ella May Smith, Mary Carr Moore, Marion Bauer, and Gena Branscombe.

39. Postcard to Ethel Clement, S4.

40. "The Los Angeles Music Fiesta," *Musical Courier* 71 (7 July 1915): 24.

41. Schallert, "Musical Facts and Fancies," *Los Angeles Times*, n.d. (S4).

42. Beach to Ethel Clement, S4.

43. Mrs. H. H. A. Beach, "Los Angeles 'Fairyland' Marks an Epoch in American Music," n.d. (Scrapbook, Horatio Parker Papers, MS 532, Yale University, Music Library). Edwin F. Schallert, "'Fairyland' and Realities," *Los Angeles Daily Times*, 4 July 1915.

44. Alfred Metzger, "American Composers' Day Proves Artistic Triumph at Exposition," *Pacific Coast Musical Review*, n.d. (S4).

45. L. C. S. "A Chat with Mrs. Beach," *Musical Leader*, n.d. (S4).

46. Among the events during the 1915–1916 concert season were performances of Beach's *Ballad* for piano, op. 6, by Fannie Bloomfield Zeisler, to whom it was dedicated; her cantata *The Sea-Fairies*, op. 59, by the North Shore Festival Chorus of Chicago; and "The Year's at the Spring," at a concert at the White House for the Wilsons by Olga Samaroff and a singer.

47. "Mrs. H. H. A. Beach," *Musical Leader* 30 (16 September 1915): 27.

48. *San Francisco Chronicle*, 31 October 1915 (S3). The program took place in the colonial ballroom of the St. Francis Hotel, with Louis W. Ford and Emile Rossett, violins; Clarence B. Evans, viola; and Victor de Gomez, cello.

49. Alfred Metzger, "Coast to Have Exemplary Chamber Music," *Pacific Coast Musical Review* 30 (15 July 1915): 1, 3.

50. "Composers Praise the St. Cecilia Club," *Musical Courier* 72 (3 February 1916): 18. Beach's letter, which is quoted, was written from the Great Northern Hotel, 19 January 1916. The program was repeated on 18 January, at the Waldorf Astoria Hotel. Among the several reviews, see, "'Surprise' Concert at People's Series," *Musical America* 23 (22 January 1916): 39; and "Splendid Evening of Choral Singing," *Musical Courier* 72 (27 January 1916): 45.

51. Felix Borowski, "The Symphony Concert," *Chicago Herald*, 5 February 1916 (S3).

52. Karleton Hackett, untitled, *Chicago Evening Post*, 5 February 1916 (S3).

53. Edward C. Moore, "With the Musicians," *Chicago Evening Journal*, n.d. (S3).

54. Eric de Lamarter, "Chicago Symphony at Orchestra Hall," n.d. (S3).

55. Beach to Stanley K. Faye, undated, Mary Flagler Cary Collection, Pierpont Morgan Library, New York.

56. Stanley K. Faye, "Erudition Rules Symphony Program," *Chicago Daily News*, 5 February 1916 (S3).

57. "Beach Songs Given Trans-Continental Hearing," *Musical America*, 22 April 1916 (Beach Clippings, NN-L).

58. Alfred Metzger, "San Francisco Press Club Hears Caruso Sing Three Thousand Miles Away," *Pacific Coast Musical Review* 30 (6 May 1916): 1.

59. "Beach Day at San Diego," *Musical Courier*, 18 May 1916 (S3).

60. Ibid.

61. Voter registration rolls, 1916, Precinct 2, Assembly District 26, San Francisco. Beach gave her new address as 1104 Fulton.

62. Coolbrith was the niece of Joseph Smith, founder of the Church of Jesus Christ of the Latter Day Saints. She was born Josephine Donna Smith in a Mormon settlement in Illinois. Her mother remarried and moved west during the Gold Rush, settling with her daughter in Los Angeles. Coolbrith married, lost a child, and divorced. Renaming herself Ina Donna Coolbrith, she settled in San Francisco and began publishing her poems. At the time she and Beach met, Coolbrith ran a famous literary salon (see *NAW* 1, 379–80).

63. Redfern Mason, "Mrs. Beach Glad Hertz Will Remain as Director," *San Francisco Examiner*, 9 July 1916 (S3).

64. Beach to Coolbrith, 9 October 1920, Coolbrith Papers, Bancroft Library, University of California, Berkeley.

65. For this evaluation I am grateful to ethnomusicologist Judith Vander as well as to Judith A. Grey, reference librarian of the American Folklife Center, DLC.

66. Another setting of the same text, W. H. Anderson's *Indian Lullaby* (Western Music Co., 1948) attributes the poem to "McKellar." The music is unrelated to that by Beach.

67. "1100 Hear First Pacific Concert," *San Francisco Chronicle*, 29 September 1916 (S3). See also Alfred Metzger, "Third Chamber Music Society Concert," *Pacific Coast Musical Review*, 30 December 1916 (S4).

68. "Mrs. Beach Praises Chamber Music Society," *Pacific Coast Musical Review* 30 (16 August 1916): 4. Members of the quintet, in addition to Hecht, were Louis Persinger and Louis Ford, violins; Nathan Firestone, viola; and Horace Britt, cello.

69. For an excellent critical notice, see the review of the published edition, "New Music Vocal and Instrumental," *Musical America* 33 (26 February 1921): 38.

70. Beach to Ina Donna Coolbrith, 3 August 1916, in Henry E. Huntington Library and Art Gallery, San Marino, Calif.

71. Beach to Coolbrith, 9 October 1920, in Coolbrith Papers, Bancroft Library, University of California, Berkeley.

72. Report from the Department of Veterans Affairs, Veterans Home of California, Yountville, Calif., 12 September 1990. Lyman Clement died 1 March 1922, at the age of 78. His wife was nearest of kin. He had enlisted 9 September 1861 as a private, H Company, 4th Vermont Infantry, but saw no action. He was discharged 28 April 1862 with a disability, although he sustained no injuries.

73. "Short Items of Interest," *Pacific Coast Musical Review* 30 (19 August 1916): 5.

74. "Mrs. Beach Honors Two Young Musicians," unidentified clipping (S4). "Noted Woman Composer Makes Stop in City," *Seattle Post Intelligencer*, 8 August 1916 (S4). Agnes Lockhart Hughes was one of Beach's ardent admirers who on several occasions wrote laudatory articles about the composer. Beach set five of her poems, the earlier ones written under the poet's maiden name.

75. "Mrs. H. H. A. Beach in the East," *Musical Leader* 32 (10 August 1916): 129.

76. "Likes Our State," *Los Angeles Times*, n.d. (S3).

Chapter 18. My Old New Hampshire Home

1. Harrison C. Baldwin, *The History of Hillsborough, New Hampshire 1921–1963* (Peterborough, N.H.: Transcript Printing Co., n.d.), 16; George Waldo Browne, *The History of Hillsbor-*

ough, *New Hampshire, 1735–1921*, vol. 2, *Biography and Genealogy* (Manchester, N.H.: John B. Clarke Co., 1922), 405–6.

2. H.F.P., "Believes Women Composers Will Rise to Greater Heights in World Democracy," *Musical America* 25 (21 April 1917): 3.

3. Browne, 2, 405, possibly incorrectly, dates her teaching in Hillsborough as 1906–1907 rather than 1916–17.

4. Information from Ethel Clement's records, Art Students League of New York.

5. Interview with Paul Scruton, Hillsborough Nursing Home, 21 August 1987. Scruton had been the first president of the Hillsborough Historical Society; see Baldwin, 131.

6. Beach to Ina Coolbrith, 13 March 1921, Coolbrith Papers, Bancroft Library, University of California, Berkeley.

7. Beach to Coolbrith, 13 March 1921, Coolbrith Papers.

8. Reviews include "Kneisel Quartet," *Boston Globe*, 29 November 1916 (S3); untitled, *Chicago Post*, 22 January 1917, Beach Clipping File, NN-L; "Mrs. Beach with Kneisels," *Philadelphia Record*, 2 February 1917 (S3).

9. Richard L. Stokes, "Mrs. H. H. A. Beach Triumphs as Composer and Pianist," *St. Louis Post-Dispatch*, 13 January 1917, 3.

10. Albert F. Wegman, "Foremost Woman Composer Plays Own Work at the Odeon," *St. Louis Times* (S3).

11. Stokes, "Mrs. H. H. A. Beach Triumphs." As encores, Beach played "Fireflies," op. 15, no. 4, at the first performance and "Scottish Legend," op. 54, no. 1, at the second.

12. Beach had initated the engagement; in a letter to Mrs. Karl Muck, 15 May 1916, she expresses her pleasure that Dr. Muck has accepted her offer to play the concerto with the Boston Symphony next season (NhU-Be).

13. "Music Lovers Ready to Greet Mrs. Beach," *Boston Advertiser*, 1 March 1917 (S3).

14. Goodbar to "Dearest Nellie," 10 March 1917, NhU-Be; H[enry] T[aylor] P[arker], "The Symphony Concert," *Boston Transcript*, 4 March 1917 (S3).

15. P[arker], "The Symphony Concert," *Boston Transcript*.

16. Mark A. DeWolfe Howe, *The Boston Symphony Orchestra, 1881–1931*, rev. and ext., with John N. Burk (Boston: Houghton Mifflin, 1931), 131–32, describes the "state of perfection" to which Muck had brought the orchestra.

17. Barbara L. Tischler, "One Hundred Percent Americanism and Music in Boston during World War I," *American Music* 4 (summer 1986): 170–71.

18. For a description of the incident in Providence, see Howe, *Boston Symphony Orchestra*, 130–36.

19. Mrs. H. H. A. Beach, "America's Musical Assertion of Herself Has Come to Stay," *Musical America* 28 (19 October 1918): 5.

20. Kinscella, "'Play No Piece in Public When First Learned,' says Mrs. Beach," *Musical America* 28 (7 September 1918): 9. See also Adrienne Fried Block, "Amy Beach's Music on Native American Themes," *American Music*, 8 (summer 1990): 141–66.

21. "Mrs. Beach Gives Recital," *Musical America* 26 (4 August 1917): 29.

22. Society for the Publication of American Music, Scrapbook, Carnegie Library, Pittsburgh, Pa.

23. An indication of its continued popularity after the Armistice is its performance at the Syracuse Music Festival in April 1920, for which the conductor Howard Lyman requested that the orchestration be sent to the Chicago Symphony, which played at the festival (Arthur P. Schmidt Co. to Beach, 25 November 1919, DLC-APS). Beach scored the work for woodwinds, 2 cornets, timpani, and strings.

24. A. Walter Kramer, "Mrs. Beach's 'Song of Liberty' Expresses Spirit of the America of Today," *Musical America* 28 (8 June 1918): 5. The word *healthy* may refer to an apparent

lack of French influence, which Chadwick and Goetschius both condemned as decadent and unhealthy.

25. H. F. P., "Believes Women Composers Will Rise."

26. Beach's 1917–18 concert calendar included performances in Attleboro, 18 October; Jordan Hall, Boston, 15 November; Philadelphia, Bellevue Stratford, 4 December; St. Paul and Minneapolis, by the Minneapolis Symphony, 14–15 December; Grand Rapids, by the St. Cecilia Society, 4 January 1918; Toronto, with the Academy String Quartet, 10 January.

27. Victor Nilsson, *Minneapolis Journal*, 15 December 1917 (Rebekah Crawford Scrapbook, DLC-Mu).

28. Caryl B. Storrs, *Minneapolis Morning Tribune*, 15 December 1917 (S3).

29. "Mrs. Beach Will Devote Energies to War Work," *Musical America* 27 (2 February 1918): 27.

30. Ibid.

31. Beach to Arthur P. Schmidt Co., 13 June 1918, DLC-APS. By the time she completed the revision the following year, however, Schmidt was no longer interested in it. Following the end of the war, the plates for the concerto, piano quintet, violin sonata, *Variations on Balkan Themes*, and *Valse-Caprice* were located in Germany and eventually sent to the publisher in Boston. In anticipation of their return, the publisher felt no need to issue a revised edition of *Valse-Caprice*: see Beach to Arthur P. Schmidt Co., 22 and 30 September 1919, DLC-APS. There is no trace of the revision.

32. Background information on Coolidge's patronage is from Anne M. Woodward, "Notes on the Coolidge Competition of 1919," a copy of a typescript provided by Cyrilla Barr.

33. For a review of Coolidge's performance, see "Music at the World's Fair: Eighth Columbian Letter," *Musical Courier* 27 (1 July 1893): 21.

34. Their correspondence regarding Coolidge's compositions began on 27 February 1902 and culminated with Beach's letter of 13 December 1909, in which she enclosed a letter to Goetschius recommending Coolidge as a potential student (Elizabeth Sprague Coolidge Papers, DLC-Mu, and personal collection of Dr. John C. Coolidge of Cambridge, Mass.).

35. *Philadelphia Public Ledger*, 27 February 1918 (S3).

36. Gabrilowitsch to Beach, 31 December 1918, NhU-Be.

37. "Personalities," *Musical America* 30 (31 May 1919): 24.

38. beach to Arthur P. Schmidt Co., 25 November 1919, DLC-APS.

39. Beach to Coolbrith, 9 October 1920, Coolbrith Papers.

40. Beach to Coolbrith, 13 March 1921, Coolbrith Papers.

41. For a review of Hyde's performance of *The Chambered Nautilus*, see "Thursday Morning Club," *Boston Times*, 25 April 1908 (S1, 137). See also Arthur Wilson, "Mrs. H. H. A. Beach: A Conversation on Musical Conditions in America," *Musician* 17 (January 1912): 10.

42. Author's handlist of performances of Beach's music, from 11 December 1910 through 30 November 1919, St. Bartholomew's Episcopal Church, New York, when Hyde gave twenty-seven performances of Beach's sacred choral works.

43. Royalty agreement with G. Schirmer, Inc., dated 24 August 1916. See "Amy M. Beach Estate," Certificates of royalty, covering the years 1914 to 1938 and including all publishers but Arthur P. Schmidt Co. (Beach Miscellany, MacDowell Colony Papers, DLC-Ms).

44. Mary Katherine Kelton, "The Songs of Mrs. H. H. A. Beach" (D.M.A. diss., University of Texas, Austin, 1992), 248. See also "Obituaries: Grace Kerns," *Musical America* 56 (10 October 1936): 32.

45. Sara Teasdale, *The Collected Poems* (New York: Macmillan, 1937), 58.

46. *In Memoriam: Arthur Sewell Hyde, 1875–1920* (privately printed, 1920) includes a brief biography, eulogies delivered by two ministers under whom he served, and letters addressed to Hyde's sister written during his years of army service.

47. A. W[alter] K[ramer], "Interesting Artist Trio in Rubinstein Musicale" (S4).

48. "The Rev. Elwood Worcester, Extract of Sermon Preached at Emmanuel Church, Boston, 29 February 1920," *In Memoriam: Arthur Sewell Hyde, 1875–1920*, 21.

49. *In Memoriam: Arthur Sewell Hyde*, 5–17.

50. Beach to Coolbrith, 13 March 1921, Coolbrith Papers.

51. Beach diary, 1931–36, p. [2], NhU-Be.

52. Beach to Coolbrith, 13 March 1921, Coolbrith Papers.

53. Beach to Coolbrith, 8 July 1925, Coolbrith Papers.

Chapter 19. At the MacDowell Colony: "Solitude in Silence"

1. Una L. Allen, "The Composer's Corner: Wherein Contemporary Writers of Teaching Material Express Views Regarding Certain of Their Own Compositions. No. 10: Mrs. H. H. A. Beach" *Musician* 35 (July 1930): 21. Una Allen was the assistant to Henry Austin, head of Arthur P. Schmidt Co. from 1916 to 1958.

2. In Una L. Allen, "Composer's Corner," Beach recommended that "Hermit Thrush at Morn" be played very freely, even out of time, with the bird calls in the foreground and everything else subordinated. In the "Hermit Thrush at Eve," "the accompaniment gives the effect of a vague, cloudy twilight, growing darker and darker."

3. Robinson's poem, "Hillcrest," dedicated to Marian MacDowell, takes its title from the MacDowells' home at the colony. Beach quotes from the poem in her letter to the editor, "Mrs. H. H. A. Beach Asks MacDowell Colony Aid: Appeals in Name of 'Hermit Thrush' for Rebuilding Work," *Musical Courier* 123 (1 April 1941): 7.

4. Beach, "The Twenty-Fifth Anniversary of a Vision," in *Proceedings of the Music Teachers National Association, 1932*, 27th Series (Oberlin, Ohio: Music Teachers National Association, 1933), 46.

5. The bust is now at the University of New Hampshire.

6. "The Moonpath," op. 99, no. 3, was published by Theodore Presser in 1923; "Christ in the Universe," op. 132, was published by H. W. Gray in 1931.

7. The piano version was published by Presser in 1922; Beach's reworking for organ was published by Gray as *Prelude on an Old Folk Tune* in 1943.

8. Beach to Marian MacDowell, 27 November 1906 and 15 February 1908, DLC-APS. The recitals took place on 7 February 1907 and 12 February 1908 at Steinert Hall (S1, 143–45).

9. Beach to Marian MacDowell, 8 March 1908, DLC-APS.

10. Emilie Frances Bauer, Marion Bauer's sister, was New York correspondent for *Musical Leader*. She composed under the name of Francesco Nogero; see "Emilie Frances Bauer Dies in New York," *Musical Digest* 11 (16 March 1926), 1. The four men were Harold Henry, W. H. Humiston, Lewis M. Isaacs, and Arthur Nevin, composer of the Indianist opera *Poia* and brother of Ethelbert. Note also that several of the women were fellows for many years: Mabel Daniels (1914–47), Frances Marion Ralston (1917–44), Ethel Glenn Hier (1918–40), Marion Bauer (1919–44), Fannie Charles Dillon (1921–42), Beach (1921–41), and Mary Howe (1926–52).

11. Beach to Walter S. Jenkins, 25 April 1935, published as an endpaper in Jenkins, *The Remarkable Mrs. Beach* (Warren, Mich.: Harmonie Park Press, 1994).

12. Author's telephone interview with Prentiss Taylor, 30 November 1987.

13. Ibid.

14. Martha Weinman Lear, "Ping-Pong, Box Lunches, and the Muse: A Colonist at MacDowell," *New York Times Book Review*, 6 March 1988, p. 3.

15. On the patrons who funded this and other studios, see *The Edward MacDowell Association, Incorporated: Report for the Year 1922* (New York: Burr Printing House, 1923), 15; "The Edward MacDowell Fund, Bulletin no. 4," unidentified clipping, 4 March 1907. Regina Watson (1845-1913) was a Chicago composer and highly regarded piano teacher. Of the nineteen studios listed, most were funded by women, by music students of women, or by women's clubs with whom Marian MacDowell's fund-raising lecture-concert tours were very successful.

16. Mary Howe, *Jottings* (Howe, 1959), 100.

17. Beach's Diary, 12 June 1935.

18. Bauer (1877-1955) may have been working with her co-author, Ethel Peyser, on *How Music Grew: From Prehistoric Times to the Present Day* (New York: G. P. Putnam's Sons, 1925), the first of several books in which she considers the modernist changes in music beginning with Debussy. For comments on Beach in *How Music Grew*, see 515-46. Bauer in "Mrs. Beach Just Ahead," *Musical Leader* 32 (31 August 1916): 202, states that "the noble work she [Beach] has done in big form should be an incentive to all women working in musical composition."

19. Jenkins, *The Remarkable Mrs. Beach*, 88.

20. Introduction, *By the Still Waters*, Art Publication Society, St. Louis, 1925.

21. See Carl Dahlhaus, "Nationalism in Music," in *Between Romanticism and Modernism*, trans. Mary Whittall (Berkeley: University of California Press, 1980), 79-101, especially 94-95.

22. Edward Walsh, *The Minstrelsy of Ireland*, ed. Alfred Moffat (London: Augener, 1897), 22-24.

23. Una L. Allen, "The Composer's Corner."

24. In contradiction, Beach suggested years later that op. 104 was a brand new work: "in 1925 [sic], I went to the wonderful MacDowell Colony in Peterborough, New Hampshire, to write a suite for two pianos" (Benjamin Brooks, "The 'How' of Creative Composition: A Conference with Mrs. H. H. A. Beach, Distinguished and Beloved American Composer," *Etude* 61 [March 1943]: 151). According to records of the Amy M. Beach Estate, she signed the royalty agreement with John Church Co. on 17 November 1923 (MacDowell Colony Collection, box 59, Administrative Papers, Estate Bequests, Beach miscellany, DLC-Ms.).

25. There are other examples of Beach's method of revising by making changes in existing manuscripts or editions: see, for example, the 1937 copyright deposit of the two-piano version of the Balkan Variations, in which there are changes and additions for the 1942 revision.

26. Now on deposit at NhU-Be, the list was compiled by Beach between 19 and 23 June 1937. See her diary entries for those days.

27. Arthur Wilson, ed., "Mrs. H. H. A. Beach: A Conversation on Musical Conditions in America," *Musician*, 17 (January 1912): 10. The article is in error on the number of quotations in the symphony. There are five tunes from the same collection in the two-piano suite.

28. The Gaelic melodies used in the four movements of op. 104 were first identified in this author's lecture "A Lost Work of Amy Beach Found." Sources of the Gaelic tunes, corresponding to the order of their appearance in the suite, are in the following issues of *The Citizen*: May, February, February, June, and February 1841. I am grateful to Beverly Crawford for locating the source for the second melody in movement II, "Fuaim na Dtonn, or The Sound of the Waves," *The Citizen* (February 1841). See her "Folk Elements in

the Music of Amy Beach" (master's thesis, Florida State University, 1993), 77, and examples 49–50. On Beach's other use of Irish folk melodies from this source, see the author's "Dvořák, Beach and American Music," in *A Celebration of American Music: Words and Music in Honor of H. Wiley Hitchcock*, ed. Richard Crawford, Carol Oja, and R. Allen Lott (Ann Arbor: University of Michigan Press, 1990), 264.

29. Gertrude F. Cowen, "Boston and New England," *Musical Courier* 60 (16 February 1910): 44–45, describes the suite in some detail.

30. "Mrs. Beach Gives Sorority Recital," *Washington Sunday Star*, 8 March 1925, 37.

31. According to Martha Cox of the Theodore Presser Company, Beach signed the contract for the suite in 1923 and Presser issued it in 1924.

32. Sydney Dalton, "New Publications Include Distinctive Work by Mrs. Beach," *Musical America* 61 (6 December 1924): 42; Clarence Lucas, "Paris Hears Wagner 'Dutched': The Sutro Sisters in New Works," *Musical Courier* 89 (20 November 1924): 7.

33. The Sutro Sisters played op. 104 at the Washington Club on 2 December 1928; at the MacDowell Club, New York, before 2 December 1930 (letter from Beach to Lillian Buxbaum, NhU-Be); and at Steinway Hall, New York, 6 April 1937 (Jenkins, 138–39). Cornelia Smissaert and Gertrude Cleophas, duo-pianists, gave the work for the Glendale (Calif.) Music Club on or about 11 July 1925; see "Mrs. Beach's Two-Piano Suite Applauded on Coast," *Musical America* 42 (25 July 1925): 16; Mary T. McDermott and Helen M. Wright played the prelude at a concert presented by the MacDowell Club, New York, 28 March 1926.

34. Mrs. H. H. A. Beach, "The Mission of the Present-day Composer," *Triangle of Mu Phi Epsilon* (February 1942): 71–72.

35. Other works Beach published between 1926 and 1928 are *From Six to Twelve*, op. 116 (1927); "Ah, Love, But a Day," op. 44, no. 2, arr. for women's voices (1927); *Communion Responses*, op. 122, for mixed chorus and organ, a supplement to the *Service in A*, op. 63 (1928).

36. "Rendez-vous" is in Speyer, *A Canopic Jar* (New York: E. P. Dutton, 1921), 6–7. Beach may have met Speyer in 1892 or 1893 when she played solo violin with the Boston Symphony Orchestra under her maiden name, von Stosch. Later she put her violin aside for poetry. Beach set two other poems of hers, *Mine Be the Lips* and *Dark Garden*, as op. 113 (1921) and op. 131 (1932).

37. The performers were Margaret Winthrop, soprano; Joseph Gingold, violin; and Beach at the piano. The performance occurred shortly after 7 November 1926.

38. Brooks, "The 'How,'" 151. In this article Beach errs in dating the composition of *Canticle* as 1925 if, as she states, it was composed just before she worked on the Suite for Two Pianos, op. 104, in 1923.

39. Beach to Arthur P. Schmidt Co., 20 June 1928, DLC-APS. The score was completed and copied by 17 July 1928, Beach to Mabel Daniels, 17 July 1928, Mabel Daniels Papers.

40. I am grateful to Constance Beavon for bringing this resemblance to my attention.

41. Chicago Symphony Orchestra Scrapbook, Carnegie Library, Pittsburgh. The chorus and orchestra also performed Beach's arrangement of "The Year's at the Spring."

42. Quoted in Betty Buchanan's program notes for *The Canticle of the Sun*, sung by the Capitol Hill Choral Society, under the direction of Buchanan, at a meeting of the Sonneck Society for American Music, 23 March 1996, Washington, D.C.

43. "Music Program," *Chautauquan Daily*, 14 August 1930, p. 9.

44. Arthur P. Schmidt Co. to Beach, 21 September 1937, DLC-APS.

45. Beach's correspondence and diaries indicate that there were fifty-five performances in fifteen cities from New York to Tacoma, Washington, with thirty-five in New York alone.

46. This discussion of the quartet is a very much shortened and revised version of this author's preface to *Amy Beach, Quartet for Strings in One Movement, op. 89*, vol. 3 of *Music of the United States of America* (Ann Arbor: A-R Editions, 1993). See pp. 39 ff. for a description of the draft score and p. 33 for a description of the holograph. For an earlier version of the introduction, see this author's "Amy Beach's Music on Native American Themes," *American Music* 8 (summer 1990): 141–66.

47. Ann M. Woodward, "Notes on the Coolidge Competition and Berkshire Festival of 1919," *The American Viola Society* [Newsletter] no. 28 (April 1985): 12–16.

48. Beach to Coolidge, 12 October 1920, Elizabeth Sprague Coolidge Papers, DLC-MU.

49. Beach to Coolidge, 4 January 1921 and 14 January 1921, Elizabeth Sprague Coolidge Papers.

50. Malipiero's *Rispetti e Strambotti* is a sectionalized one-movement work based extensively on string tunings, with long passages in parallel fifths. The refrain, which ends several sections as well as the piece as a whole, is chordal and hymnic. Melodies are often rhapsodic in character, and the rhythms vary from free to dancelike. Some passages exhibit Stravinsky-like sharp dissonances that arise from the superimposition of elaborate, often Middle Eastern sounding melodic lines over drones and ostinati. It is an effective and affecting piece.

51. The draft score is in NhU-Be, 51A. The edition includes a facsimile of the draft score.

52. For a detailed description of these changes, see apparatus, *Amy Beach, Quartet for Strings in One Movement, op. 89*.

53. See Beach's letters of declination to Coolidge of 3 August 1921, 22 August 1922, 23 August 1923, 9 August 1924, 9 August 1925, 27 August 1926, 14 August 1928, 11 August 1934, and 19 August 1938, DLC-APS.

54. See diary entries for 17 to 22 January 1929. In the upper right-hand corner of p. 1 of the holograph, Beach wrote "22, Via Cornelio Celso, Rome Jan. 22/29."

55. Copyist's score at DLC-Mu. Descriptions of the score and parts are in *Amy Beach: Quartet for Strings in One Movement*, 34–35.

56. Diary, 11 April 1929. Also on the program was a quartet by Robert Sanders, then a winner of the Prix de Rome and a fellow at the American Academy. See also postcard, Beach to Mrs. Wiegand, Rome, 11 April 1929, NhU-Be: "I have finished a string quartet and heard it last week." At the time Wiegand was alto soloist at St. Bartholomew's Church; see Diary, 9 December 1928.

57. Diary, 24 January 1931.

58. Beach to Arthur P. Schmidt Co., 20 February 1932, DLC-APS. Beach gave concerts in Cincinnati in 1920, 1921, and 1922. Roedter may have arranged these programs, as she did an all-Beach concert in 1932.

59. Beach to Arthur P. Schmidt Co., 25 June 1933, DLC-APS.

60. The concert took place between 16 and 18 March 1937; see diary entries for those dates. Beach was a member of NAACC since at least 1934, when she was listed on the letterhead of the organization as first vice-president and a member of the board of directors (Elizabeth Sprague Coolidge Papers).

61. Burnet C. Tuthill, "Mrs. H. H. A. Beach," *Musical Quarterly* 26 (July 1940): 303.

62. Ibid.

Chapter 20. Caring

1. Beach to Elizabeth Sprague Coolidge, 30 August 1921, Elizabeth Sprague Coolidge Papers, DLC-Mu.

2. Beach to Coolbrith, 9 October 1920 and 8 July 1925, Coolbrith Papers, Bancroft Library, University of California, Berkeley.

3. "Where Is Jazz Leading America? Opinions of Famous Men and Women In and Out of Music," *Etude* 42 (August 1924): 517.

4. Beach to Arthur P. Schmidt Co., 9 May 1921, DLC-APS.

5. Beach to Arthur P. Schmidt Co., 4 November 1921, DLC-APS. Schmidt issued the two "Hermit Thrush" pieces the following winter; *The Fair Hills of Eiré, O!, From Blackbird Hills*, and the song "In the Twilight" (Longfellow) in fall 1922.

6. Report of estate bequests, Beach miscellany, Administrative Papers, the MacDowell Colony, box 59, DLC-Ms. Her other publishers were G. Schirmer, Theodore Presser, Oliver Ditson, John Church, H. W. Gray, and Composers Press.

7. Beach appeared at the Piano Teachers Association on 22 April 1922. Her piano pieces for children include *Children's Carnival*, op. 25, nos. 1–6 (1894); *Children's Album*, op. 36, nos. 1–5 (1897); *Summer Dreams*, op. 47, nos. 1–6 (1901), for piano four hands; *Eskimos*, op. 64, nos. 1–4 (1907); *From Blackbird Hills*, op. 83 (1922); *From Six to Twelve*, op. 119, nos. 1–6 (1927); and *A Bit of Cairo* (1928). Choral works include "Singing Joyfully," for two treble voices, from *The Children's Souvenir Song Book*, ed. by William L. Tomlins (London: Novello, 1893), 50–51; *Three School Songs*, Op. 94, nos. 1–3, (Hinds, Hayden, and Eldridge, 1933); *Two Choruses:* "The Moonboat," for unison chorus, and "Who Has Seen the Wind," for two treble voices (Silver, Burdett Co., 1938), 124–25, 228–29. Further on teaching materials, see "Worth-While American Composers: Mrs. H. H. A. Beach," *Musician* 29 (September 1924): 37; Una L. Allen, "The Composer's Corner: Wherein Contemporary Writers of Teaching Materials Express Their Views Regarding Certain of Their Own Compositions. No. 10: Mrs. H. H. A. Beach," *Musician* 35 (July 1930): 21–22.

8. Mrs. H. H. A. Beach, "Work Out Your Own Salvation," *Etude* 36 (January 1918): 11. Other articles that she wrote on this subject include "The Outlook for the Young American Composer," *Etude* 33 (January 1915): 13–14; "Common Sense in Pianoforte Touch and Technic," *Etude* 34 (October 1916): 701–2; "To the Girl Who Wants to Compose," *Etude* 35 (November 1918): 695. Beach also gave two interviews on similar topics: H.F.P., "Believes Women Composers Will Rise to Greater Heights in World Democracy," *Musical America* 25 (21 April 1917): 3; and Hazel Gertrude Kinscella, "'Play No Piece in Public When First learned,' Says Mrs. Beach," *Musical America* 28 (7 September 1918): 9–10.

9. In an interview with the author, 27 August 1986, Emma Yeaton Wheeler said that it was Beach's idea to start the club. For further information on the history of the clubs, see Harrison C. Baldwin, *The History of Hillsborough, New Hampshire 1921–1963* (Peterborough: Transcript Printing, n.d.), 120–21.

10. "Mrs. H. H. A. Beach Sets an Example," *Etude* 42 (April 1924): 274. The article is accompanied by a picture of the club members and includes the letter from Lisabel Gay from which the above is quoted.

11. Some of these pieces are discussed in Una L. Allen, "The Composer's Corner."

12. Beach's support of McLain is apparent in letters in DLC-APS. See especially Beach to McLain, 25 July 1924.

13. "Mrs. Beach Gives Sorority Recital," *Washington Sunday Star*, 8 March 1925. "Personalities," *Musical America* 41 (28 March 1925): 20.

14. Beach and Howe probably met for the first time at a convention of the National League of American Pen Women. Soon thereafter, Beach was instrumental in bringing Howe and her work to Marian MacDowell's attention. In 1926, Beach invited Howe to a dinner at Hillcrest to meet Mrs. MacDowell and then proposed her as a colonist. Howe attended for the next twenty years, and with her three children—they called themselves "The Four Howes"— she gave recitals to raise funds for the colony (Dorothy Indenbaum,

"Mary Howe: Composer, Pianist, and Music Activist," [Ph.D. diss., New York University, 1993]).

15. "Mrs. H. H. A. Beach Saturday," *Washington Post*, 1 March 1925. Mary Howe (1882–1964), who came from a socially prominent Virginia family, grew up in Washington, D.C. She studied piano and composition at Peabody Conservatory and had a career as a duo-pianist with fellow Washingtonian Anne Hull. After her graduation from Peabody at the age of forty, Howe turned out a significant body of compositions, including some for orchestra that had repeated performances.

16. Beach to Arthur P. Schmidt Co., 11 August 1922, DLC-APS.

17. Arthur P. Schmidt Co. apparently pressed Marion Bauer to change her writing style. In response, Bauer wrote that she could not change her style on order, although she wished she could; Schmidt returned the manuscripts. Bauer to Arthur P. Schmidt Co., 10 May 1918, Bauer Correspondence, DLC-APS.

18. Beach first attended a meeting of the NLAPW on 23–28 April 1922. On the 1924 meeting, see "Many Cities to Hear Mrs. Beach," *Musical America* 39 (5 April 1924): 47. The article also lists her upcoming engagements: Chaminade Club of Manchester, 7 April; Beaver College, 11 April; Art Museum Series, Cleveland, 13 April; Pen Women, Washington, D. C., 23–25 April; North Easton, Mass., 29 April. See also Beach to Arthur P. Schmidt Co., 5 April 1924, DLC-APS.

19. Beach to Arthur P. Schmidt Co., 5 April 1924, DLC-APS. See also program, 23 April 1924, including works by Beach, Hier, Branscombe, Salter, and Ware; and "Composers to Hold Forth in D.C.," unidentified clipping, Society of American Women Composers, NN-L. Gena Branscombe (1888–1977), a native of Canada, was a choral conductor and composer especially of choral music. Ethel Glenn Hier (1889–1971), an American of Scottish origin, was also a teacher and pianist; she wrote in a style that combined impressionist, popular, and jazz elements that occasionally moved toward atonality. Mary Elizabeth Turner Salter (1856–1938) wrote songs in the parlor song tradition; these included *The Cry of Rachel*, the favorite encore of the contralto Ernestine Schumann-Heink, who measured its success by the tears it drew from audiences. Harriet Ware (1877–1962) composed for orchestra, opera, voice, and chorus; she wrote the "Women's Triumphal March" for the General Confederation of Women's Clubs. See articles in *Grove-Women* on these composers. On Harriet Ware, see Christine Ammer, *Unsung* (Westport, Conn.: Greenwood Press, 1980), 96.

20. Ulric Cole (1905–1992) was a composer, teacher, and editor. She studied composition at the Juilliard School and with Nadia Boulanger; her orchestral and instrumental works are characterized by elegant design and forceful rhythms.

21. Beach to Rosalie Housman, 26 September 1925, Housman Correspondence, DLC-Mu.

22. Beach to Fannie Charles Dillon, 26 September 1925, Dillon Collection, Special Collections, Research Library, University of California, Los Angeles.

23. The founding members of the Society of American Women Composers were Beach, Marion Bauer, Gena Branscombe, Elizabeth Merz Butterfield, Ulric Cole, Mabel W. Daniels, Fay Foster, Phyllis Fergus Hoyt, Florence Parr Gier, Ethel Glenn Hier, Mabel Wood Hill, Rosalie Housman, Mary Howe, Marion Frances Ralston, Gertrude Ross, Mary Turner Salter, Helen Sears, and Louise Souther (Society of American Women Composers, NN-L).

24. Bauer had been, in 1906, Nadia Boulanger's first American student, exchanging lessons in harmony for those in English. Later she spent three years in France studying with André Gedalge. Initially she was strongly influenced by modern French music. Bauer's style remained tonal in the 1920s but became post-tonal beginning in the 1930s and serial in the 1940s; see Ellie M. Hisama, "Gender, Politics, and Modernist Music:

Analyses of Five Compositions by Ruth Crawford (1901–1953) and Marion Bauer (1887–1955)" (Ph.D. diss., City University of New York, 1996), 7–8. A champion of modern music in her books, articles, and lectures, she was a founder and leader of the League of Composers and later of the American Composers Alliance.

25. Recitals were given in New York in November 1926 and on 9 April 1927, 9 and 22 April 1928, and 24 January and 23 November 1931.

26. Beach's diary entry, 23 April 1928. The meeting was attended as well by Mildred Wood-Hill, Phyllis Fergus Hoyt, Rosalie Housman, Hier, and Hull. News of the dissolution of S.A.W.C. came to Beach in a letter from Hier (see Diary, 25 August 1932).

27. According to figures for 1926 to 1944 compiled by Walter S. Jenkins from Beach's notations in her diaries, her income from ASCAP alone skyrocketed from the low of $1,300 in 1926 to a high of $8,000 in 1939 (NhU-Be).

28. Deed of sale, Suffolk County Deeds, 4644: 93–94. Beach turned over the mortgage of $7,500 to the new buyer, reducing the unspecified sale price of the house by that amount. The house had been rented probably since 1918, allowing Beach to pay off much of the mortgage that she inherited from her husband.

29. Beach to Margaret Starr McLain, 25 July 1924, McLain Collection, Boston University Library.

30. Clement was buried in the Deering Cemetery, Deering, N.H., where her daughter Ethel was also buried. Her will, which was probated 17 November 1925, left all but stock in the Martin-Camm Co., of San Francisco, to Beach, who was also sole executrix. See Hillsborough County Courthouse, Probate #40236.

31. Beach to Arthur P. Schmidt Co., 28 November 1925, DLC-APS.

32. Following the entries of 31 December in her 1926–31 diary, she lists annual expenses, including $288 for the annual rental of "Rooms Hibby."

33. The Parkers drove Beach to Durham, N.H., when she was awarded an honorary degree (see below), took her on tours to see autumn leaves at their most colorful (Beach's diary entries, 8–9 and 12 October 1930), and brought her back from the MacDowell Colony to Hillsborough (Diary, 1 October 1930).

34. Beach to Shaffner [1932], NhU-Be.

35. Beach to the Californian violinist Hother Wismer, in which she introduces Goodbar, 2 March 1924, Hother Wismer Papers, Music Library, University of California, Berkeley.

36. Text by Adelaide Procter (1825–1864). See Samuel L. Rogal, *Sisters of Sacred Song* (New York: Garland Publishing, 1981), 62. A source for this text has not been located.

37. Beach to Elizabeth Sprague Coolidge, from Chebeague Island, 9 August 1924, Elizabeth Sprague Coolidge papers, DLC-Mu. The first reference to Lillian Buxbaum in Beach papers appears in a letter (1 March 1922) from Beach to Arthur P. Schmidt Co. asking that copies of several songs be sent to Mrs. I. Buxbaum, 281 Ward Street, Newton Center, Mass., DLC-APS.

38. The progress of their relationship is reflected in gifts of music from Beach to Buxbaum. Beach signed a copy of her song "When Mama Sings," op. 99, no. 1 (1923), "For dear Mrs. Buxbaum with love from Amy M. Beach." *Around the Manger*, op. 115 (1925), bears the inscription "For Lillian with loving Christmas greetings to her and all the dear family from Amy, 1925." Such informality of address was unusual for Beach, who always addressed Marion MacDowell as Mrs.; MacDowell addressed Beach, in turn, as Mrs. Beach.

39. Author's telephone interview with Lillian Buxbaum Meredith, 10 August 1993.

40. See, e.g., Diary, 10, 25 July 1937.

41. See, e.g., Diary, 21 July 1929 and 10 July 1931.

42. Application for membership in the National Society of the Daughters of the Rev-

olution, Washington, D.C. Beach was nominated by Lisabel Gay and Lillian M. Allan of the Eunice Baldwin Chapter, Hillsborough, N.H. Beach's national no. is 220657, assigned on 13 February 1926. Nowhere does Beach disclose her reasons for joining the society. Baltzell, however, connects the origin of the D.A.R. and similar groups "with anti-immigrant and anti-Semitic sentiments" (115).

43. Nancy F. Cott, *The Grounding of Modern Feminism* (New Haven, Conn.: Yale University Press, 1987), 255–60. Cott traces the D.A.R.'s change from an apolitical to a conservative group strongly supportive of the military.

44. Beach to Arthur P. Schmidt Co., 21 August 1926, DLC-APS; diary entry for 5 September 1926 (NhU-Be).

45. Beach to Una L. Allen at Arthur P. Schmidt Co.; the first letter is undated, the second, 9 September 1926, DLC-APS. According to her diary, she discovered the problem on 5 September 1926 and entered Fenway Hospital on 12 September. The operation, a hemorrhoidectomy, took place the next day.

46. Dinner and meeting held at the National Arts Club, New York, 5 November 1926, see Diary and Beach to Marion Ralston, 17 November 1926, reporting on the meeting of the S.A.W.C.; Mendiito Collection, Claremont Graduate School, Claremont, California. The program, of which the date is missing, included the following: Branscombe, *The Dancer of Fjaard*, for chorus and small orchestra, conducted by the composer; Mary Howe, *Fantasia* (Emmeran Stoeber, cello; and Anne Hull, piano) and *The Prinkin' Laddie* (Zelina Bartholomew, soprano; the Lenox [String] Quartet); Beach, *Mine Be the Lips*, op. 113, and *Rendez-vous*, op. 120, both to words by Leonore Speyer, and the latter with violin obbligato; Marion Bauer, Two Movements for String Quartet (Lenox Quartet); Ethel Glenn Hier, *The Lonely Cabin* (James Sorber, tenor; Alderson Mowbray, piano) and *Sextet* (Sarah Possell, flute; Beatrice Oliver, oboe; Edwin Ideler, violin; Herbert Borodkin, viola; Emmeran Stoeber, cello [other player missing]).

47. Diary, 20 November 1926.

48. Beach to Arthur P. Schmidt Co., 27 April 1927 from Tours, France, DLC-APS.

49. Ibid.

50. The anthems were *Peace on Earth*, op. 38; *O Praise the Lord, All Ye Nations*, op. 7; and *Alleluia, Christ Is Risen*, op. 27. Beach to Arthur P. Schmidt Co., 6 June 1927, DLC-APS.

51. Mabelle S. Wall, ". . . d Commentary," 18 March 1928, fragment clipping, Atlanta Music Club Scrapbook 3, [2], Atlanta Historical Society. Beach expressed enthusiasm for Debussy, Ravel, Honegger, and Franck.

52. Beach to Arthur P. Schmidt Co., 6 June 1927, DLC-APS.

53. Diary, 18 July 1927.

54. Author's telephone interview with David Buxbaum, 10 August 1993.

55. The tour lasted from 28 February to 19 April 1928: See Diary for those dates. Program courtesy of the Georgia Department of Archives and History. Beach played a program with several substitutions at Converse College for the Women's Club of Spartanburg, S.C. (information in letter from Carlos Moseley to author, 19 November 1987). For further information on Stephens, see Leslie Petteys, "*Cabildo* by Amy Marcy Beach," *Opera Journal* 22 (March 1989): 13–14.

56. Beach to Austin, 22 May 1928, DLC-APS. Marianne Kneisel, daughter of Franz Kneisel, founded and for twenty-five years led the all-female quartet.

57. As a result of these performances, Beach reported to Arthur P. Schmidt Co. that she had many requests from musicians who wished to have a copy of the work, which had gone out of print. She herself had only her one copy and asked if some could be located in Germany or if Schmidt would consider putting out a second edition. Beach also noted that the radio station of the National Broadcasting Company has "practically *every* work of

American composers (as they assured me there and also of their wish to make special use of American compositions) and only my work unrepresented": Beach to Arthur P. Schmidt Co., 22 May 1928. They replied on 25 May that copies were located in Germany and would soon be shipped to them (DLC-APS).

58. Winthrop Tryon, "Two American Modernists," *Christian Science Monitor*, 26 April 1928.

59. See Diary, 6 June 1928, the date of completion of the draft of op. 121. Beach began work on a fair copy the following day. Beach to Arthur P. Schmidt Co., 20 June 1928, states that this is the shortened version of the work.

60. Diary, 12 and 16 June 1928.

61. Diary, 11–14 June 1928. Beach to Arthur P. Schmidt Co., 20 June 1928, states that the "Kyrie" and "Gloria tibi" were performed for several years, while still in manuscript, by Emmanuel Church, Boston.

62. Beach to Arthur P. Schmidt Co., 20 June 1928, DLC-APS. See also Beach to Mabel Daniels, 17 July 1928, in which she writes, "I completed a copy of a 51-page orchestral score this morning." That is the length of the full score of *The Canticle of the Sun*; the letter is in the Daniels Papers, Schlesinger Library, Radcliffe College, Cambridge, Mass.

63. Diary, 21–22 June 1928, the dates of sketches of op. 128, nos. 1–3 (1932).

64. Copy of citation, Archives, NhU.

65. Diary, 27 June 1928.

66. By mid-October, the sacred works were published and ready for distribution. Beach prepared a list of twenty-three church musicians to receive her new music (DLC-APS).

67. Beach to Daniels, 17 July 1928, Daniels Papers.

68. Beach's note to herself, 5 September 1931, NhU-Be.

69. Diary, 1 November 1928, when Beach left Boston by train for Atlanta.

70. Unidentified clipping, Atlanta Music Club Scrapbook, Atlanta Historical Society. Beach had set Barili's poem, "The Artless Maid," as her op. 99, no. 4 (1923).

71. For further information on Barili, see "Nana Tucker Writes of Mrs. Beach, Pianist, to Be Heard Wednesday," *Atlanta Journal*, 8 November 1928, p. 22.

72. N. Lee Orr, "Alfredo Barili: Atlanta Musician, 1880–1935," *American Music* 2 (spring 1984): 49 ff.

73. Mabelle S. Wall, "Mrs. H. H. A. Beach Unique Figure in American Music," *Atlanta Journal*, 8 November 1928, p. 22. Beach reported from Chicago that she also played *Valse-Caprice*, op. 22; *From Blackbird Hills*, op. 83; "Gavotte fantastique," op. 54, no. 2; "Minuet italien," op. 28, no. 2; and "In Autumn," op. 15, no. 1, over and over again during her tour (Beach to Arthur P. Schmidt Co., 1 December 1928).

74. Kitty Peavy, "Music Is Advocated for Public Schools," *Sunday American*, 4 November 1928. Atlanta Woman's Music Club Scrapbook, 182. See also Beach's Diary, 3 November 1928.

75. Beach to Austin, 1 December 1928, DLC-APS.

76. Diary, 22 November 1928.

77. Beach to Arthur P. Schmidt Co., 1 December 1928, DLC-APS.

78. Diary, 26 November 1928. Beach to Arthur P. Schmidt Co., 9 October 1928, written in advance of her concert tour (DLC-APS).

79. Beach to Austin, 1 December 1928, DLC-APS.

80. Beach to Austin, 7 December 1928, DLC-APS.

81. Diary, 21 December 1928.

82. In her diary, Beach regularly records her monthly payments to Gifford. The first month's room and board was 3,378 [lire] (Diary, 1 February 1929).

83. Diary, 29 December 1928.

84. Ibid., 7 February 1929.

85. Ibid., 9–10 January 1929.

86. Ibid., 17 March 1929.

87. Ibid., 5 April 1929.

88. Ibid., 20 January 1929.

89. Ibid., 13 January 1929. Both works were on the same program.

90. Ibid., 3 March 1929.

91. Ibid., 14 April 1929.

92. Laura Fermi, *Mussolini* (Chicago: University of Chicago Press, 1961), 245 ff.

93. Diary, 27 December 1928.

94. Ibid., 12 April 1929.

95. Ibid., 17 January 1929.

96. Ibid., 23 March 1929.

97. Beach to Austin, 23 April 1929, DLC-APS.

98. Ibid.

99. Tom Patterson, "Exhibit to Focus on Life of Singer from Riverside," *Riverside Press-Enterprise*, 15 April 1990, sec. B, p. 4.

100. Beach to Arthur P. Schmidt Co., 11 June 1929, DLC-APS.

101. Diary, 10 May 1929.

102. Beach found the following music in the warehouse: *Eilende Wolken*, op. 18; *Jephthah's Daughter*, op. 53; a complete set of parts for the piano concerto, op. 45; and three copies of the score of her piano quintet, op. 67. She sent everything to Schmidt. (Beach to Arthur P. Schmidt Co., 6 September 1929, DLC-APS.) Beach was informed by her publisher of the discovery of the lost manuscripts several months before she left for Italy (Beach to Arthur P. Schmidt Co., 28 August 1928, DLC-APS).

103. Samuel A. Floyd, Jr., Director of the Center for Black Music Research in Chicago, told the author that Beach's arrangement was the finest he had heard.

104. Diary, 23–24 May 1929.

105. Ibid., 25 May 1929.

Chapter 2 1. *A Fascinating New York Life*

1. Beach to Lillian Buxbaum, 2 December 1930, NhU-Be.

2. Diary, 21 September 1929, reports the attack; ibid., 7 October 1929, the day she entered Phillips House of Massachusetts General Hospital, where she stayed for a month.

3. She left Brigham's on 3 March, and then stayed in Short Hills until 11 April 1930. See diary for those dates.

4. Diary, 1 April 1930.

5. According to her diary, from 17 to 28 June, Beach worked on an anthem, probably *I Will Give Thanks* (Psalm 111), commissioned by the Reverend Hugh V. White, pastor of a church in Stockton, Calif., for the dedication of new church building. Delay in the construction of the building led to cancellation of the commission. Originally numbered op. 126, Beach changed the opus number to 147 and crossed out the dedication. The work is for soprano solo, chorus, and organ. She also arranged two works for violin—*When Soul Is Joined to Soul*, op. 62, and *The Fair Hills of Éiré, O!*, op. 91 (both arrangements are lost)—and wrote two sacred songs, "Spirit of Mercy" and "Evening Hymn," op. 125, nos. 1 and 2, and the men's chorus, "The Last Prayer," op. 126, no. 2.

6. Diary, 28 August 1930.

7. Beach to Austin, 12 November 1930, DLC-APS.

8. S.v. "Works Progress Administration," *Grove-American*. The Federal Music Project gave work to 10,000 musicians by 1938, according to H. Wiley Hitchcock, *Music in the United States*, 3rd ed. (Englewood Cliffs, N.J.: Prentice Hall, 1988), 219.

9. Diary, 25 January 1931, the date of the concert.

10. Arthur P. Schmidt Co. to Beach, 21 November 1933, DLC-APS.

11. Diary, 12 March 1940.

12. Ibid., 11 October 1934.

13. Ibid., 3 February 1935.

14. Arthur P. Schmidt Co. to Beach, 23 May 1935, DLC-APS. The Chautauqua program was on 27 July 1935. The symphony shared the program with Beethoven's Piano Concerto No. 2 and Mabel Daniels's *Pirate's Island* (review in *Chautauquan Daily*, 29 July 1935, p. 3).

15. Beach to Arthur P. Schmidt Co., 22 November 1942, DLC-APS.

16. During the seven years from 1930 to 1937, Beach records in her diary an average of forty-one programs per year that include or are devoted to her music; from 1937 to 1940, the average drops to twenty-five programs per year. The change probably is a reflection of Beach's declining health, during which she relied on others to play her music.

17. Diary, 1 November 1930. There were several such residences for women in New York City, the most famous being the Barbizon Plaza. Beach was in room 1128 that first year at the A.W.A. (the bulding is now the Henry Hudson Hotel). Her studio room changed from year to year.

18. Diary, 1 November 1930.

19. Unidentified clipping, 26 February 1932, Beach file, NN-L.

20. Beach to Buxbaum, 9 March 1933, NhU-Be, states that "[t]he lowest priced room at the club is $2.50 [per night]. Surely you could do no better in any respectable place! The price of meals in the dining-room has been reduced somewhat, and between the Cafeteria and the drug store food can be had here for very little."

21. Beach contributed hymn no. 316, a prayer for peace entitled "Norwood," to *Worship in Song*, ed. by Caroline Bird Parker (New York: Appleton-Century, 1942). Beach noted (Diary, 9 and 19 June 1934) that she sketched two children's hymns for Parker for which she received twenty-five dollars each.

22. Beach set two poems of Moody's, *Fire and Flame*, op. 136, also dedicated to Moody, and "May Flowers," op. 137, no. 2.

23. *Dictionary of American Biography*, s.v. "Norwood, Robert Winkworth."

24. Robert W. Norwood, *The Hiding God: Divinity in Man* (New York: Charles Scribner's Sons, 1933), 15–16.

25. Beach set three of his poems. *Drowsy Dreamtown*, op. 129, for soprano and a trio of women's voices, is dedicated to Mrs. Norwood. "A Light That Overflows" and "My Love Came through the Fields," were written on 15 June 1932 and copied the following day (see diary entries); they were first performed at a Memorial Meeting for Dr. Norwood on 30 November 1932 at Roerich Museum, New York. See *The Edward MacDowell Association. Report for the Year 1932* (Peterborough: Transcript Printing, 1933), 8. Beach revised the second song on 10 and 12 June 1941; see Diary entry.

26. David McKay Williams (1887–1978), who came to this country as an infant, grew up in Denver. Later, he studied in Paris at the Schola Cantorum and with the composers and organists Vincent D'Indy and Charles-Marie Widor.

27. According to Jack Ossewaarde, successor to Williams at St. Bart's (author's telephone interview, 1 April 1995), this was the way Williams described the personality differences between himself and Hyde.

28. Postcard, Beach to Eugenie Limberg (Dengel), 23 June [1923], the author's personal collection.

29. Epistle to Phillipians, ii.5, from *The Book of Common Prayer* . . . Use of the Protestant Episcopal Church in the United States of America (New York: The Church Pension Fund, n.d.), 134. The only sacred work of Beach's that has remained in print, it is for soprano and bass soli, mixed choir, and organ. The first performance was on Palm Sunday, 13 April 1924, at St. Bartholomew's.

30. Interview with Eugenie Limberg Dengel, 14 February 1985. However, when Vernon de Tar (author's interview 19 September 1986) asked Beach why she sat where she did, she said it was in order to save money. He and his fellow students all reacted as follows: "What a fine thing that St. Bart's services are enriched by her music, but she has to pay for her seat and can only afford one on the side."

31. Williams, who taught organ at both the Juilliard School and the Union Theological Seminary, had a number of students who later also presented Beach's music in their churches: Jack Ossewaarde, St. Bartholomew's from 1959 to 1982; Vernon de Tar, Church of the Ascension on lower Fifth Avenue; and Robert Baker, St. James's Episcopal Church and dean of the School of Sacred Music at Union Theological Seminary in New York. William Strickland, Williams's assistant, 1936–39, and later an orchestral conductor and champion of American music, was the editor for Beach's last published composition; he also conducted the U.S. Army School Choir in Beach's "Song of Liberty" and perhaps other men's choruses while at Fort Myer, Virginia, during World War II. Telephone interview with Ossewaarde, 1 April 1995; interview with de Tar, 17 October 1986; letter from Baker to author, 3 May 1991; telephone interview with Strickland, 3 January 1986; see also Beach to Strickland, 12 April 1943, DLC-Mu; interview with Charles N. Henderson, former choirmaster and organist of St. George's Episcopal Church, 5 December 1987, who also studied organ with Williams but did not perform Beach's music.

32. Diary, 15 January 1934.

33. Ibid., 9 November 1936.

34. Ibid., 3 October 1931.

35. "A Beach-Shaffner Musicale," undated clipping, Chapter R, P.E.O., Scrapbook.

36. Beach to Shaffner [before 24 January 1931]; see also Beach to Shaffner, 5 February 1931, both in private collection of Arnold T. Schwab.

37. Beach to Shaffner [1936], Schwab Collection.

38. Obituary, *Juilliard News Bulletin*, 20 (October–November 1981). Shaffner died 3 May 1981 in Santa Barbara, Calif., at the age of eighty-four (death certificate from Santa Barbara County, no. 4200 81–853). See also Sigmund Spaeth, *Who Is Who in Music* (Chicago: Who Is Who in Music, 1929), 253.

39. Shaffner's student records, Registrar's office, Juilliard School of Music. On Anna Eugenie Schoen-René, see Obituary, *Etude* 61 (January 1943): 1.

40. Author's telephone interview with Eugenie Dengel, 8 March 1993.

41. Ibid.

42. According to Shaffner's death certificate, she had been married and divorced. Eugenie Dengel confirmed that Shaffner's husband was a lawyer and a warden at St. Bart's and that their marriage was quite brief.

43. Beach to Shaffner, [31 May 1931]; photocopy of fragment written from the Copley Square Hotel, Boston: "Ruth darling, I have begun to find myself." Schwab Collection.

44. Beach to Shaffner, 10 July 1931, Schwab Collection.

45. "A Housewife-Composer," [1 October 1931], clipping, Rebekah Crawford Scrapbook, DLC-Mu.

46. "The Worcester Festival," *Musical Leader* 61 (15 October 1931): 15.

47. Beach to de Sayn, 27 October 1931, De Sayn-Eversman Correspondence, DLC-Mu. But in a letter to Shaffner, Worcester, 9 October [1931], Beach praises everything, noting

only its lack of occasional repose and stateliness, qualities that typify performances of the work at St. Bart's (NhU-Be).

48. Diary, 23–28 April 1932 (NhU-Be). See also "American Women Composers Hold Festival in Washington," *Musical America* 51 (10 May 1932), 20.

49. This celebration was a year late as Beach's debut as a pianist took place in 1883. However, the Pen Women met only during even years.

50. According to Mary Latka, membership secretary of the N.L.A.P.W., Eleanor Roosevelt was a "very active member" (Author's telephone conversation, 14 September 1994). Elizabeth Simons Tilton, *The League of American Pen Women in the District of Columbia* (no bibliographic data given), 244, states that Eleanor Roosevelt was a member-at-large of the league and describes Beach's and Shaffner's recitals at the White House in 1934 and 1936.

51. Phyllis Fergus Hoyt to Eleanor Roosevelt, 19 March 1934, Eleanor Roosevelt Papers, Franklin D. Roosevelt Library, Hyde Park, New York.

52. Diary, 23 April 1934. See also Fergus Hoyt to Roosevelt, 19 March 1934, and the reply from Edith Helm, secretary to Eleanor Roosevelt (unsigned copy of typed letter) to Fergus Hoyt, Chicago, 3 April 1934 (Eleanor Roosevelt Papers).

53. Fergus Hoyt to Helm, 14 April [1936], Eleanor Roosevelt Papers.

54. Letter from Beach at the Raleigh Hotel, Washington, dated only Tuesday, Eleanor Roosevelt Papers. According to her diary, Beach met Robinson on 6 January 1931 at the home of Laurie Merrill, where "Mrs. Corinne Roosevelt Robinson and Mrs. Anne Floyd read poems" and Beach played piano.

55. For evidence of the relationship to Henry Beach, see L. G. Pine, *Burke's Genealogical and Heraldic History of the Landed Gentry*, 17th ed. (London: Burke's Peerage, Ltd., 1952), 2171–72; see Winthrop family charts in Ellery Kirke Taylor, *The Lion and the Hare: One Thousand Descendents of John Winthrop*, 1939.

56. Tilton, 244; Diary, 17 April 1936; "Mrs. Beach Appears in Own Works at White House," *Musical Leader* 68 (9 May 1936): 10.

57. Beach to Una Allen, 8 May 1936, DLC-APS.

58. Beach to Lillian Buxbaum, 8 January 1941, Buxbaum Correspondence, NhU.

59. According to Beach's diary entries, *Ballad* was composed 25 August–1 September 1944; the text is by Ruth Comfort Mitchell (© P.E.O. 1945). Information on Beach's participation comes from the archives of Chapter R, housed at the home of Carol Jacobson, in New York.

60. Author's interview with Eugenie Dengel, 14 February 1985.

61. "Mrs. H. H. A. Beach at A.W.A." *Musical Leader* 66 (3 February 1934): 7, 12.

62. Undated postcard signed "Aunt Amy," given to the author by Eugenie Limberg Dengel.

63. The following are some of the programs Limberg and Duffey gave of Beach's music: Beach, Shaffner, and Limberg played a recital for the Town Hall Club, 23 February 1936; Limberg and Duffey gave Beach's *Sonata for Piano and Violin*, op. 34, at the MacDowell Club, New York, 14 February 1937, on a program of works by American composers; Beach, Shaffner, Limberg, and Duffey gave a program sponsored by the P.E.O. at the MacDowell Club, 31 January 1938, including Dohnanyi's Sonata, op. 21, a group of songs sung by Shaffner, and in the second half, piano solos and songs, some with violin obbligati and all by Beach. See F. W. R., "Mrs. Beach's Works Featured," Beach Clipping File, NN-L.

64. Author's telephone interview with Dengel, 5 March 1993.

65. "Eventful Day at Century of Progress Honoring Mrs. H. H. A. Beach," *Music News* 26 (18 October 1934): 3. "Mrs. Beach in Chicago," same issue: 5. The programs she canceled were in Cleveland and Columbus, Ohio, and Buffalo and Jamestown, New York.

Chapter 22. Beach the Modernist?

1. Beach, "The Mission of the Present-day Composer," *Triangle of Mu Phi Epsilon* (February 1942): 72.

2. *Proceedings of the Music Teachers National Association*, 1931 (Oberlin: Music Teachers National Association, 1932): 17–19.

3. Beach, "A Plea for Mercy," *Proceedings of the Music Teachers National Association*, 1935 (Oberlin: Music Teachers National Association, 1936): 163–65.

4. William W. Austin, *Music in the 20th Century from Debussy through Stravinsky* (New York: W. W. Norton, 1966), 233.

5. Michael Hicks, "Cowell's Clusters," *Musical Quarterly* 77 (fall 1993): 433. The year 1917 is given for *The Tides of Maunaunan* in *Grove-American*, s.v. "Cowell, Henry (Dixon)."

6. "Beach, "A Plea for Mercy." For discussions of the coupling of dissonance and gender, see Catherine Parsons Smith, "'A Distinguishing Virility': Feminism and Modernism in American Art Music," *Cecilia Reclaimed: Feminist Perspectives on Gender and Music*, ed. Susan C. Cook and Judy S. Tsou (Urbana: University of Illinois Press, 1994), 90–106, a groundbreaking investigation of the destructive effect of modernism on women composers. See also Stuart Feder, *Charles Ives: "My Father's Song"* (New Haven: Yale University Press, 1992), who quotes Ives in "Memos" about "the way some of the 'old ladies' purred about playing the piano with a stick," 313. Judith Tick points out that Charles Ives, who argued against "effeminacy" in music while praising dissonance as an expression of manliness, discussed not music by women—which he completely ignored—but music by men; see "Charles Ives and Gender Ideology," *Musicology and Difference*, ed. Ruth Solie (Berkeley: University of California Press, 1993), 98.

7. Beach, "The Mission of the Present-day Composer": 72.

8. On her disinclination to have others perform the concerto, see Beach to de Sayn, 13 August 1942. On her preference for her recently published rather than early piano solos, see Beach to de Sayn, 7 August 1942. About desiring performances of the "Gaelic" Symphony but not of the *Eilende Wolken*, the Mary Stuart aria, see Beach to de Sayn, 12 August 1942, all in De Sayn-Eversman Correspondence, DLC-Mu.

9. Beach to Craft, dated "Friday morning," Marcella Craft Papers, Historic Resources Department, Riverside, Calif.

10. John C. and Dorothy L. Crawford, *Expressionism in Twentieth-Century Music* (Bloomington: Indiana University Press, 1993), 30, 33–34.

11. Beach to Strickland, 21 September 1942, begins, "The piece is completed." See also Beach to Strickland, 2 December 1942 (Strickland Correspondence, DLC-Mu). Vernon de Tar, choirmaster and organist of the Church of the Ascension, New York, played the piece as a Prelude to Evensong, 29 November 1942. See the church's file of service leaflets. The piece was still in manuscript at the time; publication took over a year, probably slowed by the war. David McKay Williams gave the work on an organ recital 1 March 1944; see diary for that date.

12. The choir of St. Bartholomew's gave the premiere on 13 January 1935 and sang the work three additional times before the end of the 1940s.

13. For a discussion of directional tonality in relation to *Variations on Balkan Themes*, op. 60, see this author's "On Beach's *Variations on Balkan Themes*," *American Music* 11 (fall 1993): 368–71.

14. Karl Geiringer, *Brahms: His Life and Work*, 2nd ed., rev. and enl. (Garden City, N.Y.: Anchor Books, 1961), 286. For a discussion of Brahms's *Schicksalslied* and progressive tonality, see John Daverio, "The *Wechsel der Töne* in Brahms's *Schicksalslied*," *Journal of the American Musicological Society* 46 (spring 1993): 84–113, who connects the tonal design to the narrative

and Brahms's intense reaction to it. See also Harald Krebs, "Alternatives to Monotonality in Early Nineteenth-Century Music," *Journal of Music Theory* 25 (spring 1981): 14.

15. See also her "Agnus Dei," a reworking of the opening of the last movement of the Mass, op. 5, here with English text and published in 1936 as a supplement to op. 122, and *O Lord God of Israel*, op. 141 (unpublished), given its first performance on 26 April 1936; see diary for that date.

16. In a parallel instance, Beach to de Sayn, 15 [November] 1931, states that she is "making some cuts in the Sonata which will add much to its present-day value." She then goes on to detail the cuts. De Sayn-Eversman Correspondence, DLC-Mu.

17. There are in fact five versions of *Variations on Balkan Themes*. The first was published by Arthur P. Schmidt in 1906; in 1934 Beach made no change but simply renewed the copyright in her own name. In 1906 Beach also prepared a shortened version for orchestra, which remains in manuscript, Collection 51A, NhU. In 1936 Schmidt published her revision of the 1906 edition and in 1937, her edition for two pianos. In 1942 Schmidt prevailed upon Beach to divide the 1937 edition into two volumes, arranging the work so that it could be played as a whole or either of the two parts could be given separately. In order to do so, Beach repeated the theme at the beginning of the second volume and recomposed variations 9 and 10.

18. "Worcester Festival," *Musical Leader* 6 (15 October 1931): 1, 11, 15. Some performers, unaware of both the nineteenth-century tradition of progressive tonality and Beach's usage of the procedure in other late works, have been disturbed by the conflict in the revision between the opening in C# minor and the ending in E♭, advancing that as a reason to prefer the 1906 version. See E. Douglas Bomberger, "Motivic Development in Amy Beach's *Variations on Balkan Themes*, op. 60," *American Music* 10 (fall 1992): 326–47; and this author's response, "On Beach's *Variations on Balkan Themes, op.* 60," noted above, n. 13.

19. On 25 May 1931, Beach exults in her diary that she used all of "A September Forest" as source material for *Christ in the Universe*.

20. Manuscript is at NhU-Be. "A September Forest" was probably written 28–30 September 1930; see diary. Note, however, that as Beach worked on the piano piece, its name evolved from the "'deep woods' piece," to the "'pines' piece," to "September Woods," and, finally, to "A September Forest."

21. In the later sections, however, organ pedals define the tonality that the upper parts simultaneously contest by their relentless chromaticism. The closing section is accompanied by throbbing triplets that lead to the final, quiet cadence on A. The work is dedicated to Williams and the St. Bartholomew Choir, which gave its first performance on 17 April 1932 at the church. In 1938 the Oratorio Society of New York gave the premiere with orchestra, Albert Stoessel conducting.

22. Composed on 23, 24, and 30 September 1937; see diary entry for those dates.

23. Undated letter to Ralston. Beach also advises her to patronize Composers Press, a cooperative that issued op. 148 (Ralston Correspondence, Mendiito Collection, Claremont Graduate School).

24. In a letter to Jeanne Behrend, 7 January 1941 (Jeanne Behrend Collection, Free Library of Philadelphia), Beach congratulates the pianist on her recent recording on RCA Victor of the "Allegretto grazioso e capriccioso, A major," *Improvisations*, op. 148, no. 2.

25. Beach played all five pieces of op. 148 on 12 March 1939 in New York at a concert sponsored by the National Association of American Composers and Conductors. The program also included works by Herbert Inch, Paul Creston, and Charles Tomlinson Griffes. See the program file of the National Association of American Composers and Conductors, NN-L.

26. Diary entries, 2–18 June 1938; and letter to Burnet Tuthill, 24 June 1938. She must have decided on some changes, however, for in a second letter to Tuthill, on 6 August 1938, she mentions that the trio was not finished. At that time, Tuthill was preparing his article for the *Musical Quarterly* and expressed interest in seeing this latest work as well as many of her earlier ones. Beach again denied him the trio, writing to him on 9 August that she wanted to perform it before sending Tuthill a copy. All three letters are in DLC-APS. The first performance, on 15 January 1939 at the MacDowell Club in New York, was given by violinist Eugenie Limberg, cellist Phyllis Kraeuter, and Beach. The program also included works by other composers who were members of the club: Lolita Cabrera Gainsborg, Hans Barth, Ernest Carter, Walter Golde, Philip Heffner, and Lewis Lane. See also Beach to de Sayn, 21 October 1942, De Sayn-Eversman Correspondence, DLC-Mu.

The Trio was published in 1939 by Composers Press, which also published *Pastorale for Woodwind Quintet*, op. 151 (1942) and *Though I Take the Wings of Morning*, op. 152 (1941).

27. Boas, *The Central Eskimo*, Sixth Annual Report, Smithsonian Institution, 1884–85 (Washington, D.C., 1888): Tune no. 12: 655. Beach quoted from this song in "Arctic Night," op. 64, no. 1.

28. There are three manuscripts of the opera, an incomplete pencil score consisting of pp. 1–15 and 20–23, NhU-FPL; a full holograph score in ink for voices, chorus, spoken part, and piano trio, 95 pp.; and a copyist's piano vocal score, 75 pp., the last two at MoKU-Be. The opera is one of the few works of Beach that has not been published. See also Leslie Petteys, "Cabildo by Amy Marcy Beach," *Opera Journal* 22 (March 1989): 10–19.

29. Edwin Hughes, "The Outlook for the Young American Composer: An Interview with the Distinguished American Composer, Mrs. H. H. A. Beach," *Etude* 33 (January 1915): 14.

30. Stephens was a fellow at the colony in 1927 and 1932; during the summer of the latter Beach composed the opera. Her play *Roseanne*, about an African American woman, had had a successful run in New York in 1924; see *Atlanta Journal*, 20 January 1924: 16.

31. See the review of the student production in "Blackfriars Present Midwinter Programs," *Atlanta Constitution*, 2 March 1930, sec. B, p. 11.

32. According to John Smith Kendall, *History of New Orleans*, vol. 1 (Chicago: Lewis Publishing Co., 1922) 91–109, the actual events were as follows: In 1814, the port of New Orleans was blocked by the British. Commander Nicholls offered Jean Lafitte a captaincy in the British army and $30,000 to join forces with the British. Lafitte, who hated the British, stalled Nicholls and reported the offer to General Andrew Jackson, who was in command of the defense. Lafitte offered to help defend New Orleans in return for pardons for past crimes and land. The British were defeated, the siege broken, and the pirates were pardoned, but Jackson reneged on the land grants.

33. Andrew Porter, "Musical Events. A 'Ring' and two Rarities," *New Yorker* 66 (21 May 1990): 93. The concert performance was given by the After Dinner Opera Company on 31 March 1990 at the Bruno Walter Auditorium, Lincoln Center, New York.

34. Beach's study of the folk genre is summarized in "Notes on Creole Folk Music," a three-page paper with musical examples, that discusses the rhythmic influences—African drumming and Spanish dance, and in particular the habañera—on Creole music, the instruments of the Creole orchestra, and the role of the guitar and percussion. Beach may have presented the paper at a meeting of the Hillsborough Music Club, according to Rita Morgan, former librarian of the Fuller Public Library (letter to Leslie Petteys, 13 April 1991, NhU-FPL).

35. For the folk song, see George W. Cable, "The Dance in Place Congo," *Century Magazine* 31 (February 1886): 528. A variant version of the same song, under the title "Mouché Mazireau," is in Clara Gottschalk Peterson, *Creole Songs from New Orleans in the Negro Dialect* (New Orleans: L. W. Grunewald, [1902]): 4.

36. Cable, "Place Congo": 530–31; Maud Cuney Hare, *Six Creole Folk* Songs (New York: Carl Fischer, 1921), 12–13.

37. Peterson, 4.

38. Cable, "Creole Slave Songs," *Century Magazine*, 31 (April 1886): 824; Peterson, 3.

39. Hare, 22–24. The tune appears in the accompaniment in m. 668 ff.

40. See chapter 13 for discussion of "When Soul Is Joined to Soul," on Elizabeth Barrett Browning's text.

41. See, for example, *The Magic Flute*, in which the birdcatcher Papageno's introductory aria, "Der Vogelfänger bin ich ja," is in G major but the aristocratic Tamino's introductory aria, "Dies Bildnis ist bezaubernd schön," is in E♭ major.

42. Stephens to Beach, 4 June 1940, NhU-Be. Review by Marguerite Bartholomew, "Opera Librettoed by Atlantan Thrills Athens at Premiere," *Atlanta Constitution*, 4 March 1945, sec. A, p. 11.

43. Petteys, 12–13.

44. Previous performances were given by the Conservatory of Music, University of Missouri, Kansas City; at the University of Kansas, Lawrence, Kansas, on March 23–24 and 2 April 1982; and the aforementioned After Dinner Opera Co. at Queensborough Community College of the City University of New York and at Lincoln Center on 30–31 March 1990 (see n. 33 above). The Brooklyn College Opera Theater gave *Cabildo* on 29–30 January 1994. The 1995 production in Alice Tully Hall, Lincoln Center, New York, is recorded on Delos DE 3170.

Chapter 23. *Reckonings*

1. Beach was guest of honor at the 120th anniversary celebration of the Handel and Haydn Society on 24 October 1935, also the fifty-second anniversary of Beach's debut. That afternoon there was a recital of her works at the New England Conservatory by student performers, including Eleanor Steber, who would later sing with the Metropolitan Opera.

2. Diary, 21 September 1935.

3. Ibid., 26 October 1935.

4. Ibid., 31 October 1935.

5. Ibid., 30 September, 1–2 October 1935.

6. Ibid., 26 April 1936.

7. Ibid., 25 April 1936.

8. The trip is covered in Beach's diary entries, beginning 17 May, en route to England, and ending 4 June 1936, NhU-Be.

9. Diary, 29 August 1937.

10. Ibid., 20 September–2 November 1936.

11. Beach to Austin, 13 February 1937, DLC-APS.

12. Diary, 4 March 1937.

13. 6 March [1937], from 158 Ridge Ave., Newton, Mass., Correspondence no. 58, NhU-Be.

14. Beach to Austin, 10 April 1937, DLC-APS. Beach also notes in that letter that Bashka Paeff, whose sister had studied with Foote, had done a "superb bas-relief of him." Paeff was then working on a bust of Beach; see below.

15. Diary, 5 June 1937. Beach added a new variation on 9–10 June. During that month she noted in the diary the completion of work begun the previous September. She also finished revisions of a song to words by Robert Burns, "Far Awa'," op. 43, no. 4, in arrangements for organ (sketchbook, NhU-Be, pencil sketch, 17 September 1936) and for

piano (ink holograph of transcription, Kinscella Collection, Washington State University, Seattle); the "Barcarolle," op. 28, no. 1, for violin and piano (sketchbook, NhU-Be, inscribed "same day," previous work dated 21 September 1936); an arrangement of the song "After," op. 68, for chorus and organ (pencil sketch in sketchbook, NhU-Be, 20 September 1936); a revision of the two "Hermit Thrush" pieces, op. 92; and violin and cello parts as an accompaniment for *Cabildo* (holograph in ink, MoKU). Of the above, only the arrangement of the Barcarolle was published (1937).

16. Her diary entry of 4 June 1937 notes the first sitting at the colony.

17. Mrs. Cheney was not related to Beach.

18. Diary, 21–22 September 1937.

19. Ibid., 12–14 September 1937.

20. Ibid., 23–24 and 14–20 September 1937, respectively.

21. *Grove-American*, s.v. "Boulanger, Nadia (Juliette)."

22. Later, Pearl Bates Morton (Brodrick) became president of the Beach Club of Wolfeboro, N. H., for two terms after the death of its organizer, Ella Lord Gilbert. The club originated in Manchester, according to Morton, and was moved to Wolfeboro in 1940 by Gilbert. Morton changed the name of the club to "Friends of Music" because people were confused by the name Beach. In 1988, Brodrick's daughter, Jean, became president of the club. Author's interviews with Pearl Morton and Jean Brodrick, Wolfeboro, 17 August 1988.

23. Diary, 23 February 1938.

24. Beach to Irving Schwerké, 1 March 1938, DLC-Mu. A brief trip was planned, with only a week in Paris before returning home.

25. Diary, 2–3 March 1938.

26. *Grove-American*, s.v. "Luening, Otto (Clarence)."

27. Ashley Pettis, "The WPA and the American Composer," *Musical Quarterly* 26 (January 1940): 107, a quotation from Elliot Carter. See also Barbara Zuck, *A History of Musical Americanism* (Ann Arbor: UMI Research Press, 1980), 170–71.

28. Beach to Ashley Pettis, 25 April 1938, Composers' Forum Correspondence, NN-L.

29. Diary, 21 June 1938.

30. Ibid., 24 June 1938.

31. Beach to F. Marion Ralston, 29 October 1933, Mendiito Collection, Claremont Graduate School, Claremont, Calif.

32. Diary, 21 September 1938.

33. Beach to Tuthill, 30 September 1938, DLC-APS.

34. Diary, 11 October 1938.

35. "50 Years Ago . . . Hurricane of '38 and Winds of War!" MacDowell *Colony News* 15 (winter 1987–88).

36. Hermann Hagedorn, "The Grand Old Lady of Peterborough," *New York Herald Tribune*, 22 November 1948.

37. Beach to MacDowell, n.d., in which she sends a contribution to help clean up and repair damage from the hurricane. She also discusses the ensuing fire and the heroic actions of Nina Maud Richardson, MacDowell's companion (MacDowell Correspondence, DLC-Ms). See also letter from Beach to [MacDowell], n.d.,"Dearest friend, Just a look at you and the sound of your voice could coax the bark off a tree" (DLC-Ms). See also "Mrs. H. H. A. Beach Asks MacDowell Colony Aid. Appeals in Name of 'Hermit Thrush' for Rebuilding Work," *Musical Courier* 123 (1 April 1941): 7.

38. Diary, 9 November 1938.

39. Rachmaninoff Collection, DLC-Mu.

40. Diary, 30 January 1939.

41. Ibid., 7 December 1938. The reactions of the students were reported by a former student who requested anonymity.

42. Beach was a member of the NAACC. Program in NAACC file, NN-L. The Trio was repeated at the National Arts Club on 15 March 1939. Dates given for this and other events of the 1939 season come from the diary.

43. On the same day, 12 March, the pianist and composer Jeanne Behrend played the second of the *Five Improvisations*, op. 148, on a program of American works by John Powell, Leo Sowerby, John Alden Carpenter, and Charles Ives (the "Alcott" movement from the Concord Sonata). Behrend (1911–1988) was a child prodigy, the first pianist to graduate from the Curtis Institute, where she also studied composition with Rosario Scalero. Her compositional oeuvre includes a suite for piano, *A Child's Day*, given the Joseph Bearns Prize, as well as works for orchestra, chamber ensemble, voice, chorus, and piano. She stopped composing in 1944, however, out of frustration over neglect of women's music. She then became an advocate of American music, especially Gottschalk's.

Beach played the *Five Improvisations* on a concert of music by women at the Roerich Museum on 27 December 1939, and again at a luncheon of Mu Phi Epsilon on 19 January 1940.

44. On 24 March Beach spoke over station WNYC on a Mu Phi Epsilon program; on 4 April she gave a pre-recorded talk and played for three new singers on a program for WABC.

45. Diary, 5–7 June 1939.

46. *Information Manual*, New York World's Fair, 1939. *Guide*, New-York Historical Society.

47. Beach to Arthur P. Schmidt Co., 5 October 1939, DLC-APS, reports a request from Milton Brown of the Works Progress Administration for a thirty-minute program of songs to be given at the World's Fair on 26 October. She received a recording of the program in the mail on 23 October 1939; see diary for that date.

48. Tuthill, "Mrs. H. H. A. Beach," *Musical Quarterly* 26 (July 1940): 297–306.

49. Tuthill to Beach, 28 April 1924, DLC-APS.

50. Tuthill to Beach, 19 January 1938, DLC-APS. Tuthill had submitted a list of subjects to Carl Engel, the editor, who chose Beach.

51. In *Grove-American*, s.v. "Women in Music," Judith Tick characterizes the position of American women as composers in the period from 1900 to 1950 as "functionally marginal." That helps to place in perspective the appearance of a major article on Beach in a leading music journal: a virtually unique event at a time when music by most women was neglected. The reasons for their neglect—with the exception of Marion Bauer and Ruth Crawford Seeger—remain to be explored.

52. Tuthill, 297.

53. Ibid., 298.

54. Ibid., 298. Other members of the Second New England School named by Tuthill are Paine, Chadwick, MacDowell, Foote, Horatio Parker, Arthur Whiting, and Stillman Kelley.

55. Diary, 16 December 1939.

56. Ibid., 12 March 1940.

57. Ibid., 19 March 1940.

58. Beach to Elena de Sayn, 3 June 1941, De Sayn-Eversman Correspondence, DLC-Mu.

59. Beach to MacDowell, 14 May [1940], MacDowell Collection, DLC-Ms.

60. Unsigned, "Notes on the Tribute Dinner to Mrs. H. H. A. Beach at the Town Hall Club on May 8th, 1940" (NhU-Be, typescript).

61. Ibid.

62. Ibid.

63. Ibid. See also "Mrs. H. H. A. Beach Honored," *Musical Leader*, undated, Beach Clipping File, NN-L.

64. In a letter to Shaffner, 25 September 1925, NhU, Beach recounts preceding events on years ending in 5 and 0: these included the move to Boston in 1875, her debuts with the Boston Symphony Orchestra and Theodore Thomas and her marriage in 1885, Charles Cheney's death in 1895, the premiere of the piano concerto in 1900, a calamitous mystery event in 1905, Henry Beach's death in 1910, the move to California in 1915, Ethel Clement's and Arthur Hyde's deaths in 1920, and Franc Clement's death in 1925. Beach, of course, omitted the significant events in off years that do not bear out the magic of numbers.

Chapter 24. Harvest Time

1. Beach to Elena de Sayn, 3 June 1941, De Sayn-Eversman Correspondence, DLC-Mu.

2. Beach to Ruth Shaffner, [14 June 1941], Shaffner Correspondence, Arnold Schwab Collection, Westminster, Calif.

3. Ibid.

4. Beach to Buxbaum, 14 April 1939, Buxbaum Correspondence, NhU.

5. The check was a quarterly payment of $1,328. Beach's income from publishers and ASCAP in these last years averaged about $6,000 per year.

6. Thornton Wilder to Beach, 27 December 1942, NhU-Be.

7. Diary, 25 December 1942.

8. *Who's Who in the Nation's Capital*, s.v. "De Sayn, Elena." De Sayn, a Russian emigré, was a member of an aristocratic Russian family and the daughter of a lieutenant general in the czar's army. Trained at the Leipzig and St. Petersburg conservatories, she made her debut in Leipzig and London and toured Russia, the United States, and Canada. After settling in New York, in 1922 she moved to Washington, D.C., where she worked as a journalist, translator, led a string quartet, and ran a school for violin studies.

9. Beach to de Sayn, 1 June 1931, De Sayn-Eversman Correspondence.

10. For a complete list of patrons, see "Society Will Hear Music of Great Composer," *Sunday Star*, 22 November 1942.

11. "Portrait Bust Will Honor Mrs. Beach," *Washington Times-Herald*, 28 November 1942, 75th Anniversary Scrapbook, De Sayn-Eversman Collection.

12. Glenn Dillard Gunn, "Native Music Has Big Day in Washington," *Washington Times-Herald*, 28 November 1942.

13. Ray C. B. Brown, "Postlude: Concert Celebrates Jubilee of Mrs. Beach," *Washington Post*, 28 November 1942, sec. B, p. 1.

14. Alice Eversman, "Festival Program Presents Mrs. Beach's Compositions," *Washington Evening Star*, 28 November 1942, in 75th Anniversary Scrapbook, De Sayn-Eversman Collection.

15. Ray C. B. Brown, "Postlude."

16. Gunn, "Beach Works Win Applause at Concert Here," *Washington Times Herald*, 29 November 1942, sec. B, p. 11. The String Quartet has not yet been played at the Library of Congress.

17. Ibid.

18. On the belief among New England composers that they should determine the course of art music in the United States, see MacDonald Smith Moore, *Yankee Blues: Musical Culture and American Identity* (Bloomington: Indiana University Press, 1985): 128 ff.

19. Beach to de Sayn, 8 January 1943, De Sayn-Eversman Correspondence.

20. Sophie Drinker, *Music and Women: The Story of Women in their Relation to Music* (New York: The Feminist Press at the City University of New York, 1995; Coward, 1948).

21. Typed copy of letter from Beach to Drinker, 18 November 1944, in Sophie Drinker Papers, Sophia Smith Collection, Smith College, Northampton, Mass.

22. William Dengel (1908–1981), who had a law degree, taught personal finance at Rutgers, Newark, and La Guardia College, City University of New York (author's telephone interview with Eugenie Dengel, 23 February 1994).

23. Ruth Shaffner to Marcella Craft, 26 December 1944, Marcella Craft Papers, City of Riverside Historic Resources Department, Riverside, Calif.

24. Despite her physical problems, during her last years Beach had made the extra effort to attend the annual meetings of the Allied Members of the MacDowell Colony, an organization that generated support for the colony. She served as second vice-president for several years and from 1941 until her death was first vice-president. In 1942 she headed a committee to raise funds for the maintenance of the Regina Watson Studio, in which she had frequently worked while at the colony (Papers of the MacDowell Association, DLC-Ms).

25. Minutes of meeting of Allied Members of the MacDowell Colony, 16 December 1944, at the MacDowell Club, New York (MacDowell Colony Papers, DLC-Ms).

26. Ibid.

27. Eugenie Dengel to her parents, "Friday night," personal papers of Dengel.

28. Ibid.

Notes to Postlude: The Legacy

1. "The Composer's Corner: Wherein Contemporary Writers of Teaching Material Express Views Regarding Certain of Their Own Compositions," No. 10: Mrs. H. H. A. Beach," *Musician* 35 (July 1930): 21–22.

2. The will was signed on 27 February 1936, with codicils added on 19 November 1940 and 6 July 1943. It was filed in Hillsborough, New Hampshire, in the County of Hillsborough, together with the Register of Probate in the County of Nashua, New Hampshire, on 24 April 1945. Roger Pierce, of Milton, Massachusetts, was appointed as executor, according to a provision of the will. Beach's heir and copyright holder is the MacDowell Colony.

3. Beach's last will and testament, p. 2.

4. Ibid., 1.

5. Ibid., 4.

6. Ibid., 7.

7. Ibid., 10.

8. Ibid., 8–9.

9. Ibid., 4th codicil, unnumbered page.

10. Interview with David Buxbaum, Chebeague Island, 21 August 1986.

11. According David Buxbaum, after his mother inherited the property, which was valued at $10,000, she made two donations of $5,000 each to children's charities—Kiddie Camp and the Jimmie Fund of the Children's Hospital in Boston. In fact, when Lillian Buxbaum no longer could take care of the property, it was sold to a developer for $65,000. David Buxbaum reported that his mother "lived very comfortably as a result of the sale," something that Beach would have wanted. Author's interview with David Buxbaum, Chebeague Island, 21 August 1986.

12. Ibid., 10–11. Income from royalties and performance fees are entered in checkbook stubs for the Amy Beach Fund filed in the MacDowell Colony Papers, DLC-Ms.

13. The MacDowell Colony received the following payments earned as performance

fees and royalties on Beach's music: 1992, $1,584; 1993, $929; 1994, $3,592; 1995, $4,368. Figures for other years are not readily available.

14. Woolf, *A Room of One's Own* (New York: Harcourt, Brace, and World, Inc., 1929), 35. George P. Upton, *Woman in Music* (Boston: J. R. Osgood, 1880), presents arguments against the eventuality of a great woman composer and at the same time advocates women as muses for great (male) composers.

15. Woolf, 56.

16. 1918; reprint, New York: Modern Library, 1933. See also Marc Pachter, "The Biographer Himself: An Introduction," in *Telling Lives: The Biographer's Art*, ed. Pachter (Philadelphia: The University of Pennsylvania Press, 1981), 8. Leon Edel, *Writing Lives: Principia Biographica* (New York: W. W. Norton, 1984), 31, also identifies the "new biography" as the genre "we have been creating since the days of Lytton Strachey."

17. See, for example, recordings of the *Theme and Variations for Flute and String Quartet*: Diane Gold, flute, and the Alard String Quartet (Leonarda, 1979); Doriot Anthony Dwyer, flute, and the Manhattan String Quartet (Koch, 1988); and Eugenia Zukerman, flute, and the Shanghai Quartet (Delos, 1995).

18. Gilbert Chase, *America's Music*, 3rd ed. (Urbana: University of Illinois Press, 1987), 384−85, gives two pages to Beach and her music. *Grove-American, Grove-6*, and *Grove-Women* have lengthy articles on Beach with catalogues of her music.

19. Woolf, 48−50 *et passim*, discusses what might have happened if Shakespeare had had an equally gifted sister who tried to have a career as a poet and playwright.

SELECTED BIBLIOGRAPHY

Books and Dissertations

Baldwin, Harrison C. *The History of Hillsborough, New Hampshire 1921–1963.* Peterborough, N.H.: Transcript Printing Co., n.d.

Beach, Amy. Quartet For Strings in One Movement, op. 89. Edited and introduction by Adrienne Fried Block. Vol. 3 of *Music of the United States of America.* Madison, Wisc.: A-R Editions, 1994. Score and parts.

Beach, Mrs. H. H. A. "Enjoyment of Song." In *Music on the Air*, edited by Hazel Gertrude Kinscella, 24–36. Garden City, N.Y.: Garden City Publishing, 1934.

———. "A Plea for Mercy." In *Proceedings of the Music Teachers National Association, 1935*, edited by Karl W. Gehrkens, 163–65. Oberlin, Ohio: Music Teachers National Association, 1936.

———. "Emotion Versus Intellect in Music." In *Studies in Musical Education, History, and Aesthetics: Proceedings of the Music Teachers National Association, 1931*, edited by Karl W. Gehrkens, 17–19. Oberlin, Ohio: Music Teachers National Association, 1932.

———. "The Twenty-Fifth Anniversary of a Vision." In *Proceedings of the Music Teachers National Association, 1932*, 45–48. Oberlin, Ohio: Music Teachers National Association, 1933.

Beach, Henry Harris Aubrey. *Sketches.* Boston, 1889.

Benedict, Burton. *The Anthropology of World's Fairs: San Francisco's Panama-Pacific Exposition of 1915.* London and Berkeley: Lowie Museum of Anthropology in association with Scolar Press, 1983.

Biographical Sketch: Mrs. H. H. A. Beach. Hyannis, Mass.: Patriot Office, n.d.

Block, Adrienne Fried. "The Child Is Mother of the Woman: Amy Beach's New England Upbringing." In *Cecilia Reclaimed: Feminist Perspectives on Gender and Music*, edited by Susan C. Cook and Judy S. Tsou, 107–33. Urbana: University of Illinois Press, 1994.

———. Dvořák, Beach, and American Music." In *A Celebration of American Music: Words and Music in Honor of H. Wiley Hitchcock*, edited by Richard Crawford, R. Allen Lott, and Carol J. Oja, 256–80. Ann Arbor: University of Michigan Press, 1990.

———. "Two Virtuoso Performers in Boston: Jenny Lind and Camilla Urso." *New Perspectives on Music: Essays in Honor of Eileen Southern*, edited by Josephine Wright and Samuel A. Floyd, Jr., 355–71. Warren, Mich.: Harmonie Park Press, 1992.

———. Assisted by Nancy Stewart. "Women in American Music, 1800–1918." In *Women and Music: A History*, edited by Karin Pendle, 142–72. Bloomington: Indian University Press, 1991.

Boas, Franz. *The Central Eskimo.* Sixth Annual Report of the Bureau of Ethnology, Smithsonian Institution. Washington, D.C.: Smithsonian Institution, 1888.

Boston Conservatory Method for the Piano-forte: As taught at the Boston Conservatory of Music, Julius Eichberg, Director. Boston: White-Smith, 1878.

Brower, Harriette. *Piano Mastery.* 2nd series. New York: Frederick A. Stokes, 1917.

Browne, George Waldo. *The History of Hillsborough, New Hampshire, 1735– 1921.* 2 vols. Manchester, N.H.: John B. Clarke Co., 1921–22.

Cogswell, Leander W. *History of the Town of Henniker, Merrimack County, New Hampshire, 1775 to 1880, with a Genealogical Register.* Concord: Republican Press Assn., 1880. Reprint, with a foreword by Francis Lane Childs. Somersworth: New Hampshire Publishing Co., 1973.

Crawford, Beverly. "Folk Elements in the Music of Amy Beach." Master's thesis, Florida State University, 1993.

Crawford, John C., and Dorothy L. Crawford. *Expressionism in Twentieth-Century Music.* Bloomington: Indiana University Press, 1993.

Dahlhaus, Carl. *Between Romanticism and Modernism.* Translated by Mary Whittall. Berkeley: University of California Press, 1989.

Danek, Victor B. "A Historical Study of the Kneisel Quartet." D. Mus. Ed. diss., Indiana University, 1962.

Daniels, Mabel. *An American Girl in Munich.* Boston: Little, Brown, 1905.

Drinker, Sophie. *Music and Women: The Story of Women in Their Relation to Music.* New York: Coward, 1948. Reprint, with a preface by Elizabeth Wood; afterword by Ruth A. Solie. New York: The Feminist Press at the City University of New York, 1995.

Eden, Myrna Garvey. *Energy and Individuality in the Art of Anna Huntington, Sculptor, and Amy Beach, Composer.* Composers of North America, no. 2. Metuchen, N.J.: Scarecrow Press, 1987.

Elson, Louis C. *The History of American Music.* Rev. ed. New York: Macmillan, 1915, 1925. Reprint, New York: Burt Franklin, 1971.

Fairbrother, Trevor J., and others. *The Bostonians, Painters of an Elegant Age, 1870– 1930.* Boston: Museum of Fine Arts, 1986.

Flatt, Rosemary Chisholm. "Chromaticism in Beach's Quintet, Op. 67: Techniques of Analysis." Master's thesis, Indiana University, 1981.

Foote, Arthur W. *Arthur W. Foote, 1853– 1937: An Autobiography.* Norwood, Mass.: Plimpton Press, 1946. Reprinted and revised by Wilma Reid Cipolla. New York: Da Capo Press, 1979.

Forget New Hampshire? Booklet prepared by residents of Henniker, N.H., based on privately held documents. Henniker, 1968.

Goetschius, Percy. "Mrs. H. H. A. Beach: Analytical Sketch." In *Mrs. H. H. A. Beach.* Boston: Arthur P. Schmidt, 1906.

Greven, Philip J., Jr. *Child-Rearing Concepts, 1626– 1861: Historical Sources.* Itasca, Ill.: F. E. Peacock, 1973.

———. *The Protestant Temperament: Patterns of Child-Rearing, Religious Experience, and the Self in Early America.* New York: Alfred A. Knopf, 1977.

Hall, Constance R., and Helen Tetlow. *Helen Hopekirk 1856– 1945.* Cambridge, Mass., 1954.

Heilbrun, Carolyn G. *Writing a Woman's Life.* New York: W. W. Norton, 1988.

Henniker History Committee. *The Only Henniker on Earth.* Historical Society and the Town of Henniker. Canaan, N.H.: Phoenix Publishing, n.d.

The Hillsborough, Henniker, Dunbarton, New Boston, etc. Citizen's Directory, 1889– 1890. Haverhill, N.H.: W. E. Shaw, n.d.

Hirsch, Marianne. *The Mother/Daughter Plot: Narrative, Psychoanalysis, Feminism.* Bloomington: Indiana University Press, 1989.

Howe, Julia Ward. *Reminiscences 1819– 1899.* Boston, 1910.

Hoyt, Edwin P. *The Improper Bostonian: Dr. Oliver Wendell Holmes.* New York: William Morrow, 1979.

James, George Wharton. *Exposition Memories.* Pasadena, Calif.: Radiant Life Press, 1917.

Jenkins, Walter S. *The Remarkable Mrs. Beach, American Composer.* Warren, Mich.: Harmonie Park Press, 1994.

Kay, Jane Holtz. *Lost Boston.* Boston: Houghton Mifflin, 1980.

Kelton, Mary Katherine. "The Songs of Mrs. H. H. A. Beach." D.M.A. diss., University of Texas, Austin, 1992.

Krehbiel, Henry Edward. *Afro-American Folksongs: A Study in Racial and National Music.* 1914. Reprint, New York: Frederick Ungar, 1962.

Leader, Bernice Kramer. "The Boston Lady as a Work of Art: Paintings by the Boston School at the Turn of the Century." Ph.D. diss., Columbia University, 1980.

Lee, Gerald Stanley. *The Lost Art of Reading.* New York: G. P. Putnam, 1903.

Marcy, Oliver. "Record of the Marcy Family." *The New England Historical and Genealogical Register* 19. Boston: David Clapp and Sons, 1875.

Merrill, E. Lindsey. "Mrs. H. H. A. Beach: Her Life and Music." Ph.D. diss., University of Rochester, 1963.

Miles, Marmaduke Sidney. "The Solo Piano Works of Mrs. H. H. A. Beach." D.M.A. diss., Johns Hopkins University, 1985.

Milinowski, Marta. *Teresa Carreño: "By the Grace of God."* New Haven, Conn.: Yale University Press, 1940.

Morison, Samuel Eliot. *One Boy's Boston 1887–1901.* Boston: Houghton Mifflin Co., 1962.

Mrs. H. H. A. Beach. Boston: Arthur P. Schmidt, 1906.

Norwood, Robert. *The Hiding God: Divinity in Man.* New York: Charles Scribner's Sons, 1933.

The Parish of the Advent in the City of Boston: A History of One Hundred Years, 1844–1944. Boston, 1944.

Perabo, Johann Ernst. *Johann Ernst Perabo: Compositions, Arrangements, and Transcriptions.* Boston: The Sparrell Print, n.d.

Picturesque World's Fair: An Elaborate Collection of Colored Views. Chicago: W. B. Conkley, 1894.

Piscatelli, Felicia Ann. "The Chamber Music of Mrs. H. H. A. Beach, 1867–1944." Master's thesis, University of New Mexico, 1983.

Pope, Charles Henry, comp. *The Cheney Genealogy.* Boston: Charles H. Pope, 1897.

Reich, Nancy B. "Women as Musicians: A Question of Class." In *Musicology and Difference,* edited by Ruth Solie, 125–46. Berkeley: University of California Press, 1993.

Rydell, Robert W. *All the World's a Fair: Visions of Empire at American International Expositions, 1876–1916.* Chicago: University of Chicago Press, 1984.

Shaffer, Karen A., and Neva Garner Greenwood. *Maud Powell: Pioneer American Violinist.* Ames: Iowa State University Press, 1988.

Showalter, Elaine, ed. *The New Feminist Criticism: Essays on Women, Literature, and Theory.* New York: Pantheon Books, 1985.

Smith, Catherine Parsons. "'A Distinguishing Virility': Feminism and Modernism in American Art Music." In *Cecilia Reclaimed: Feminist Perspectives on Gender and Music,* edited by Susan C. Cook and Judy S. Tsou. Urbana: University of Illinois Press, 1994, 90–106.

Smith-Rosenberg, Carroll. *Disorderly Conduct: Visions of Gender in Victorian America.* New York: Afred A. Knopf, 1985.

Tick, Judith. *American Women Composers before 1870.* Ann Arbor, Mich.: UMI Research Press, 1979.

———. "Charles Ives and Gender Ideology." In *Musicology and Difference,* edited by Ruth Solie, 83–106. Berkeley: University of California Press, 1993.

Tilton, Elizabeth Simons. *The League of American Pen Women in the District of Columbia.* Washington, D.C.: League of American Pen Women, 1942.

Todd, Frank Morton. *The Story of the Exposition.* 4 vols. New York: G. P. Putnam, 1921.

Tuthill, Burnet C. "Fifty Years of Chamber Music in the United States." In *Proceedings of the Music Teachers National Association,* edited by Karl W. Gehrkens, 163–75. Hartford, Conn.: Music Teachers National Association, 1929.

VanHouten, Dorothy, comp. "A History of Music in New Hampshire." New Hampshire Writers Project No. 2354, 1941.

Weimann, Jeanne Madeline. *The Fair Women*. Introduction by Anita Miller. Chicago: Academy, 1981.

Whiting, George E. "An American School of Composition." In *Proceedings of the Music Teachers National Association: Official Report of the Eighth Annual Meeting*, 33–43. Cleveland, Ohio: Music Teachers National Association, 1884.

Whitesitt, Linda. "'The Most Potent Force' in American Music: The Role of Women's Music Clubs in American Concert Life." In vol. 3 of *The Musical Woman: An International Perspective 1986–1990*, edited by Judith Lang Zaimont with Jane Gottlieb, Joanne Polk, and Michael T. Rogan, 663–81. New York: Greenwood Press, 1991.

Winsor, Justin, ed. *The Memorial History of Boston, Including Suffolk County, Massachusetts. 1630–1880*. 4 vols. Boston: James R. Osgood and Co., 1880–81.

Wood, Ann Douglas. "The Fashionable Diseases: Women's Complaints and Their Treatment in Nineteenth-Century America." In *Clio's Consciousness Raised: New Perspectives on the History of Women*, edited by Mary Hartman and Lois M. Banner, 1–22. New York: Harper and Row, 1974.

Yellin, Victor Fell. *Chadwick: Yankee Composer*. Washington: Smithsonian Institution Press, 1990.

Articles

A. M. B. "America's Chief Woman Composer." *Chicago Sunday Times-Herald*, 28 November 1897.

Adams, Mrs. Crosby. "An American Genius of World Renown: Mrs. H. H. A. Beach." *Etude* 46 (January 1928): 34, 61, 69.

Aiken, Ednah. "Two California Songbirds in Europe." *Sunset: The Pacific Monthly* 30 (September 1914): 534–36.

Allen, Una L. "The Composer's Corner: Wherein Contemporary Writers of Teaching Material Express Views Regarding Certain of Their Own Compositions. No. 10: Mrs. H. H. A. Beach." *Musician* 35 (July 1930): 21–22.

"American Women Composers Form Group as Allies with Pen Women." *Musical America* 40 (19 May 1924): 1, 4.

Armstrong, William. "New Gems in the Old Classics." *Etude* 22 (February 1904): 51–52.

"Arthur P. Schmidt." *Musical America* 34 (28 May 1921): 22.

Baker, Emily L. "Edward Roland Sill, Poet-Teacher." *Overland Monthly and Out West Magazine* 83 (April 1925): 154–55, 175–76.

Bartholomew, Marguerite. "Opera Librettoed by Atlantan Thrills Athens at Premiere." *Atlanta Constitution*, 4 March 1945, sec. A, p. 11.

Bauer, Emilie Frances. "Music in New York." *Musical Leader* 29 (25 March 1915): 122.

Beach, Amy. "Why I Chose My Profession: The Autobiography of a Woman Composer." Interview by Ednah Aiken. *Mother's Magazine* 11 (February 1914): 7–8.

"Beach, Henry Harris Aubrey." Obituary. *Boston Medical and Surgical Journal* 163 (14 July 1910): 71–72.

Beach, Mrs. H. H. A. "America's Musical Assertion of Herself Has Come to Stay." *Musical America* 28 (19 October 1918): 5.

———. "Bird Songs." *The Designer*. New York: Standard Fashion Co., May 1911.

———. "Common Sense in Pianoforte Touch and Technique." *Etude* 34 (October 1916): 701–2.

———. "Cristofori Redivivus." *Music* 16 (May 1899): 1–5.

————. "Don't Give Up Music at the Altar: Mrs. H. H. A. Beach." *Etude* 37 (July 1919): 407–8.

————. "How Music Is Made." *Keyboard* (winter 1942): 11, 38.

————. "The Mission of the Present-day Composer." *Triangle of Mu Phi Epsilon* 36 (February 1942): 71–72.

————. "Mrs. H. H. A. Beach Asks MacDowell Colony Aid: Appeals in Name of 'Hermit Thrush' for Rebuilding Work." Letter to the editor. *Musical Courier* 123 (1 April 1941): 7.

————. "Music after Marriage and Motherhood." *Etude* 27 (August 1909): 520.

————. "Music's Ten Commandments As Given for Young Composers." *Los Angeles Examiner*, 28 June 1915, 5. Reprinted as "How Mrs. Beach Does It." *Musical Courier* 71 (7 July 1915): 25.

————. "Must Music Forsake Emotion?" *Musician* (February 1932): 6.

————. "The Outlook for the Young American Composer: An Interview with the Distinguished American Composer Mrs. H. H. A. Beach." Interview by Edwin Hughes. *Etude* 33 (January 1915): 13–14.

————. "To the Girl Who Wants to Compose." *Etude* 35 (November 1918): 695.

————. "The Uplift of Music." *The Music Lover's Calendar* 1 (December 1905): 26–27.

————. "Work Out Your Own Salvation." *Etude* 36 (January 1918): 11–12.

————. "The World Cries Out for Harmony." *Etude* 62 (January 1944): 11.

Beckerman, Michael. "The Real Value of Yellow Journalism." *Musical Quarterly* 77 (winter 1993): 749–68.

Block, Adrienne Fried. "Amy Beach's Music on Native American Themes." *American Music* 8 (summer 1990): 141–66.

————. "On Beach's *Variations on Balkan Themes*, op. 60." *American Music* 11 (fall 1993): 368–71.

————. "'A Veritable Autobiography'? Amy Beach's Piano Concerto in C♯ Minor, Op. 45." *Musical Quarterly* 78 (summer 1994): 394–416.

————. "Why Amy Beach Succeeded as a Composer: The Early Years." *Current Musicology* 36 (1983): 41–59.

Bomberger, E. Douglas. "Motivic Development in Amy Beach's *Variations on Balkan Themes*, op. 60." *American Music* 10 (fall 1992): 326–47.

Boston Beacon, 5 December 1885. Marriage Notice.

Brooks, Benjamin, ed. "The 'How' of Creative Composition: A Conference with Mrs. H. H. A. Beach." *Etude* 61 (March 1943): 151, 208–9.

Brower, Edith. "Is the Musical Idea Masculine?" *Atlantic Monthly* 73 (March 1894): 332–39.

Brower, Harriette. "A Personal Interview with Mrs. H. H. A. Beach." *Musical Observer* 12 (May 1915): 273–74.

Brown, Ray C. B. "Concert Celebrates Jubilee of Mrs. Beach." *Washington Post*, 28 November 1942, sec. B, p. 1.

————. "Beach Works Win Applause at Concert Here." *Washington Times-Herald*, 29 November 1942, sec. B, p. 1.

Cable, George W. "Creole Slave Songs." *Century Magazine* 31 (April 1886): 807–28.

————. "The Dance in Place Congo." *Century Magazine* 31 (February 1886): 517–29.

"Charles A. Cheney." Obituary. *Paper Trade Journal* 24 (3 August 1895): 717.

Cipolla, Wilma Reid. "Marketing the American Song in Edwardian London." *American Music* 8 (spring 1990): 84–94.

"Concert Record of Works by Some of Our Best American Composers." *Musical Courier* 42 (2 January 1901): 9.

Constant, Emily. "Women Who Have Succeeded: I. Mrs. H. H. A. Beach." *The New England Home Magazine* (5 March 1898): 407–8.

Conway, Jill. "Stereotypes of Femininity in a Theory of Sexual Evolution." *Victorian Studies* 14 (September 1970): 47–61.

Cowen, Gertrude F. "Mrs. H. H. A. Beach, the Celebrated Composer." *Musical Courier* 60 (8 June 1910): 14–15.

———. "Obituary: Dr. Henry H. A. Beach." *Musical Courier* 61 (6 July 1910): 23.

"Dedicate the Home." *Chicago Tribune*, 2 May 1893, p. 4.

"Don't Give Up Music at the Altar: A Symposium by Noted Women in Music." *Etude* (July 1919): 407–8, 420.

Douglass, Ada B. "A Plea for More Serious Work among the So-called Music Clubs." *Etude* 16 (February 1898): 36.

Dvořák, Antonín. "Music in America." *Harper's Magazine* 40 (February 1895): 429–34.

"Education of Girls." *Concord Monitor*, 26 January 1866.

"The Education of Girls." *The Woman's Journal* 22 (3 January 1891): 1.

Elson, Louis C. "Musical Boston: Its Orchestras, Clubs, and Musical Institutions." *Music and Drama* 2 (3 June 1882): supplement, 1–8.

"Eventful Day at Century of Progress Honoring Mrs. H. H. A. Beach." *Music News* 26 (18 October 1934): 3.

Fay, Amy. "Women and Music." *Music* 18 (October 1900): 505–7.

Finck, Henry T. "Woman's Conquest of Music." *Musician* 7 (June 1902): 186.

Flatt, Rose Marie Chisholm. "Analytical Approaches to Chromaticism in Amy Beach's *Piano Quintet in F♯ Minor*." *Indiana Theory Review* (spring 1981): 41–58

Foote, Arthur W. "A Bostonian Remembers." *Musical Quarterly* 23 (January 1937): 37–44.

Goetschius, Percy. "Mrs. H. H. A. Beach and Mlle. Cécile Chaminade: Their Works, I. Mrs. H. H. A. Beach." *Musician* 4 (September 1899): 355.

Gould, Elizabeth Porter. "To Mrs. H. H. A. Beach." *Time and the Hour* 4 (9 January 1897).

Gunn, Glenn Dillard. "Beach Works Win Applause." *Washington Times-Herald*, 29 November 1942, sec. B, p. 11.

H. A. S. "At 74, Mrs. Beach Recalls Her First Critics." *Musical Courier* 123 (15 May 1941): 7.

H. F. P. "Believes Women Composers Will Rise to Greater Heights in World Democracy." *Musical America* 25 (21 April 1917): 3.

"How Mrs. Beach Did Her First Composing." *Musical America* 20 (8 August 1914): 22.

Howe, Mary. *Jottings*. 1959.

Hughes, Agnes Lockhart. "Mrs. H. H. A. Beach: America's Foremost Woman Composer." *Simmons Magazine* 4 (October 1911): 476–78.

Hughes, Edwin. "The Outlook for the Young American Composer." *Etude* 33 (January 1915): 13–14.

Hughes, Rupert. "Music in America, IX: The Women Composers." *Godey's Book* (January 1896): 31. Reprinted in *Contemporary American Composers* (Boston: L. C. Page, 1900): 431.

"Jubilee Sheet." *Boston Daily Evening Transcript*, 17 June 1872, p. 3.

Kinney, Edith Gertrude. "Mrs. H. H. A. Beach." *Musician* 4 (September 1899): 354–55.

Kinscella, Hazel Gertrude. "'Play No Piece in Public When First Learned,' Says Mrs. Beach." *Musical America* 28 (7 September 1918): 9–10.

Kramer, A. Walter. "Mrs. Beach's 'Song of Liberty' Expresses Spirit of the America of Today." *Musical America* 28 (8 June 1918): 5.

"Life Sketch of H. H. A. Beach, M. D." Boston, Mass., n.d. Reprinted from *Biography of Ephraim McDowell, M.D.: With Life Sketches and Portraits of Prominent Members of the Medical Profession*. New York: McDowell Publishing, n.d.

"Lost Manuscripts." *Musical Courier* 69 (2 September 1914): 37.

Lowens, Irving. "Writings about Music in the Periodicals of American Transcendentalism (1835–1850)." *Journal of the American Musicological Society* 10 (summer 1957): 71–85.

MacBride, Jessie, and Dorothy DeMuth Watson. "American Women Composers Hold Festival in Washington: League of Pen Women Sponsors Hearings of Many Native Works." *Musical America* 52 (10 May 1932): 20, 40.

MacDonald, Claudia. "Critical Perception and the Woman Composer: The Early Reception of Piano Concertos by Clara Wieck Schumann and Amy Beach." *Current Musicology* 55 (1993): 24–55.

McGlinchee, Claire. "American Literature in American Music." *Musical Quarterly* 31 (January 1945): 101–19.

Mathews, W. S. B. "Instrumental Compositions by Mrs. H. H. A. Beach." *Music* 13 (February 1898): 547–48.

Metzger, Alfred. "Musical Importance of Mrs. H. H. A. Beach." *Pacific Coast Musical Review* 28 (12 June 1915): 1, 3.

Minnich, Elizabeth Kamarck. "Friendship between Women: The Act of Feminist Biography." *Feminist Studies* 11 (1985): 287–305.

Mitchell, Ann Maria. "The Advent Parish, Boston: Pioneer of the Catholic Revival." *Living Church* (14 December 1935): 653–55.

"Mrs. Beach Appears in Own Works at White House." *Musical Leader* 68 (9 May 1936): 10.

"Mrs. Beach Just Ahead." *Musical Leader* 32 (31 August 1916): 202.

"Mrs. Beach, Leading American Woman Composer, Dies at 77." *New York Times*, 28 December 1944.

"Mrs. Beach Safe in Munich." *Musical America* 20 (5 September 1914): 3.

"Mrs. Beach Will Devote Energies to War Work." *Musical America* 27 (2 February 1918): 27.

"Mrs. H. H. A. Beach." *Musikliterarische Blätter* 1 (Vienna, 21 March 1904): 1–4.

"Mrs. H. H. A. Beach in the East." *Musical Leader* 32 (10 August 1916): 129.

"Mrs. H. H. A. Beach, Renowned American Composer-Pianist." *Etude* (August 1924): 517.

"Music in the Exposition City." *Musical Leader* (12 August 1915): 78–79.

"Music in Its Larger Meanings." *Dwight's Journal of Music* 26 (1 September 1866): 302.

"The Native Music of Ireland." *Citizen* 3 (January–June 1841): 63–66, 134–38, 198–206, 260–62, 318–20. Includes music.

"New Idea of Salome." *Musical Leader* 32 (21 September 1916): 293.

Peeler, Clare P. "American Woman Whose Musical Message Thrilled Germany." *Musical America* 20 (17 October 1914): 7.

Petteys, Leslie. "*Cabildo* by Amy Marcy Beach." *Opera Journal* 22 (March 1989): 10–19.

Pettis, Ashley. "The WPA and the American Composer." *Musical Quarterly* 26 (January 1940): 107.

Porter, Andrew. "Musical Events. A 'Ring' and Two Rarities." *New Yorker* 66 (21 May 1990): 93.

"Real Value of Negro Melodies." *New York Herald*, Sunday, May 21, 1893, p. 28.

Salter, Sumner. "Early Encouragements to American Composers." *Musical Quarterly* 18 (January 1932): 76–105.

Singal, Daniel Joseph. "Towards a Definition of American Modernism." *American Quarterly* 39 (spring 1987): 7–26.

Sonneck, Oscar G. "The American Composer and the American Music Publisher." *Musical Quarterly* 9 (January 1923): 122–44.

Swayne, Egbert. "A Vermont Musical Family." *Music* 11 (December 1896): 117–33.

T. F. G. "Washington Holds a Festival of American Women Composers." *Musical Courier* 90 (28–30 May 1925): 14.

Talbot, M. Louise. "A Brief Résumé of the History of the Attic Club." Unpublished paper, Attic Club Papers. Boston Athenaeum.

"Their Ten Favorite American Songs." *Musical America* 23 (20 November 1915): 9.

Tischler, Barbara L. "One Hundred Percent Americanism and Music in Boston During World War I." *American Music* 4 (summer 1986): 164–76.

Tuthill, Burnet C. "Mrs. H. H. A. Beach." *Musical Quarterly* 26 (July 1940): 297–310.

"Where Is Jazz Leading America?" *Etude* 42 (August 1924): 517–18, 520.

Whitesitt, Linda. "The Role of Women Impresarios in American Concert Life, 1871–1933." *American Music* 7 (summer 1989): 159–80.

Whittemore, William L. Obituary. *Boston Evening Transcript*, 5 July 1911, p. 6.

Wilson, Arthur, ed. "Mrs. H. H. A. Beach: A Conversation on Musical Conditions in America." *Musician* 17 (January 1912): 9–10.

"Worth-while American Composers: Mrs. H. H. A. Beach." *Musician* 29 (September 1924): 37.

"A Young Pianist." *Boston Folio*, 12 April 1875, p. [1].

Archival Sources

Text materials

Atlanta Music Club Scrapbook. Vol. 3 [21], 1926–29. Compiled by Irene R. Smillie. Atlanta Historical Society.

Beach, Amy M. Autograph Album, 1877–1909. Beach Collection 51. Dimond Library, University of New Hampshire, Durham.

———. Diaries, 1926–1944. 5 vols. Beach Collection 51. Dimond Library, University of New Hampshire, Durham.

———. "Music Reviews." Vol. 2, October 1894. Holograph in ink, 96 pp. Beach Collection 51. Dimond Library, University of New Hampshire, Durham.

———. "Musical Visitors," 1909–1910: Holograph in ink. Beach Collection 51. Dimond Library, University of New Hampshire, Durham.

———. Notebook, 21 April 1887–July 1894. Music Department, Boston Public Library.

———. Scrapbook, 1883–1900. Signed at end, "Amy Marcy Cheney, October 24th, 1883." Beach Collection 51. Dimond Library, University of New Hampshire, Durham.

———. Scrapbook, 1892–1906. Beach Collection 51. Dimond Library, University of New Hampshire, Durham.

———. Scrapbook, 1912–18. Beach Collection 51A. Dimond Library, University of New Hampshire, Durham.

———. Scrapbook, 1885–1917. Beach Collection 51A. Dimond Library, University of New Hampshire, Durham.

Brown, Allen A. Scrapbooks. Allen A. Brown Collection. Music Department, Boston Public Library.

Cheney, Clara Imogene. Biography of Amy M. Beach. Holograph, signed 26 February 1892. MacDowell Colony Papers. Manuscript Division, Library of Congress.

[George Whitefield Chadwick's Family Memoir]. Holograph. Private Collection of Theodore Chadwick, Duxbury, Mass.

Church of the Advent. Parish Register. Boston, Mass.

Craft, Marcella. Clipping File. Music Research Division, New York Public Library.

———. Papers. Historic Resources Department, Riverside, Calif.

———. Papers, musical scores, memorabilia. Tomás Rivera Library, University of California, Riverside.

———. Records of performances. Archives of the Royal Opera. Bibliothek der Bayerischen Staatsoper, Munich.

Damrosch, Walter. Scrapbooks, vol. 1, 1881–1927. Walter Damrosch Collection. Music Research Division, New York Public Library.

Dwight, John Sullivan. Address delivered before the Harvard Musical Association, August 25, 1841. Music Research Division, New York Public Library.

Farwell, Arthur. Scrapbook, 1903–11. Microfilm. Music Research Division, New York Public Library.

Foote, Arthur W. Scrapbooks. Music Department, Boston Public Library.

"Mrs. H. H. A. Beach." Printed biographical essay and catalog of works through op. 45 with additions in Beach's hand. New Hampshire State Library, Concord.

———. Biographical essay and list of piano works in Beach's hand. Typescript draft of "Mrs. H. H. A. Beach" (Nh), 19 pp. Tucker Free Library, Henniker, N.H.

Handel and Haydn Society Collection. Rare Books and Manuscripts Department, Boston Public Library.

Kinscella Collection. Music in America Archives, Washington State University, Seattle, Washington.

Lang, Benjamin Johnson. Scrapbooks. Rare Books and Manuscripts Department, Boston Public Library.

MacDowell Colony Papers. Manuscript Division, Library of Congress.

P.E.O. Archives. Chapter R. New York.

Panama California Exposition in San Diego. Scrapbook, 1915. San Diego Historical Society, San Diego, Calif.

Perabo, Johann Ernst. Scrapbook. Allen A. Brown Collection. Music Department, Boston Public Library.

Society for the Publication of American Music. Scrapbook. Carnegie Library, Pittsburgh, Penn.

Spiering, Theodore. Clipping file. Music Research Division, New York Public Library.

Trinity Church Parish Register, Boston, Mass.

Letter Collections

Boston Athenaeum. Attic Club Papers. Beach to Edith Brown, 1940.

Boston Public Library, Rare Books and Manuscripts Department. Correspondence, 1863–1906, Amy Beach, Henry Harris Aubrey Beach, John Sullivan Dwight, Elizabeth Porter Gould, Francis Jenks, Wilhelm Scharfenberg.

Boston University. Special Collections Department. Margaret Starr McLain Papers.

Chicago Historical Society. Correspondence, 1892, Bertha Honoré (Mrs. Potter) Palmer, Miss Willard, and Amy Starkweather.

City of Riverside (California) Historic Resources Department. Marcella Craft Papers and Correspondence.

Claremont Graduate School, Claremont, California. Mendiito Collection. Amy Beach to Frances Marion Ralston, 1933.

Free Library of Philadelphia. Jeanne Behrend Manuscripts and Correspondence.

Georgia Department of Archives and History. Louise Barili Papers.

Harvard University, Countway Medical Library. Oliver Wendell Holmes Papers. Holmes to "My dear Sir," recommending Henry Beach as a physician, 1884.

———. Houghton Library. Phillips Brooks Correspondence. Henry Harris Aubrey Beach to Bishop Brooks, 1892.

Henry E. Huntington Library and Art Gallery, San Marino, California. Coolbrith Papers.

Library of Congress, Manuscript Division. Marian MacDowell Papers.

———. Music Division. Arthur P. Schmidt Company Collection. Correspondence, 1892–

1942, Marion Bauer, Amy Beach, Henry Harris Aubrey Beach, Arthur P. Schmidt, Carl Zerrahn, and representatives of the company.

―――. Music Division. Elizabeth Sprague Coolidge Papers. Amy Beach to Coolidge, 1902–1938, 22 letters.

―――. Music Division. General Correspondence. Amy Beach to Herbert Putnam, 1911; to McLain; to Rosalie Housman, 1925.

―――. De Sayn-Eversman Correspondence. Amy Beach to Elena de Sayn, 1931–1943, 9 letters.

―――. Irving Schwerké Correspondence.

―――. William Strickland Correspondence.

―――. Burnet C. Tuthill Collection.

New York Public Library, Music Research Division. Arthur M. Abell Collection.

―――. Composers' Forum Correspondence.

―――. Nahan Franko Correspondence.

―――. Marcella Sembrich Collection.

Newberry Library, Chicago. Special Collections. Correspondence, 1892–97, Amy Beach, Bertha Honoré Palmer, Frederick Grant Gleason, Theodore Thomas.

Radcliffe College, Schlesinger Library. Mabel Wheeler Daniels Collection.

Franklin D. Roosevelt Library, Hyde Park, N.Y. Eleanor Roosevelt Papers.

Smith College, Northampton, Mass. Sophie Drinker Papers. Sophia Smith Collection.

St. Botolph Club, Boston. Archives. Henry Harris Aubrey Beach Correspondence.

San Francisco Public Library, Bernard Osher Foundation Art and Music Center. Musicians' Letters: An Autograph Collection.

University of California, Berkeley. Bancroft Library. Ina Donna Coolbrith Papers.

―――. Music Library, Hother Wismer Papers.

University of California, Los Angeles. Special Collections, Research Library. Fannie Charles Dillon Collection.

University of New Hampshire, Dimond Library. Beach Collection. Correspondence, 1880–1942, C. Katie Alves, Adele Aus der Ohe, Henry Harris Aubrey Beach, Lillian Buxbaum, Clara Imogene Cheney, Charlotte Cushman, Teresa Carreño, George Whitefield Chadwick, Committee to Honor Wagner, Margaret Deland, Emma Eames, Arthur Foote, Percy C. Goetschius, Julia Ward Howe, Henry Wadsworth Longfellow, William Mason, John Knowles Paine, Johann Ernst Perabo, Arthur P. Schmidt, Ruth Shaffner, Giovanni Sgambati, Nan Bagby Stephens, Leopold Stokowski, Thornton Wilder, Carl Zerrahn. 55 letters.

Private Collections

Dr. John C. Coolidge, Cambridge, Mass.
Adrienne Fried Block, New York.
Arnold Schwab, Westminster, Calif.

Author's Interviews

Baker, Robert, telephone, 7 April 1995.
Bentley, Shirley A., Wolfeboro, N.H., 17 August 1988.
Brodrick, Pearl Bates Morton, Wolfeboro, N.H., 17 August 1988.
Brigham, Willa, Henniker, N.H., 27 August 1986.
Brodrick, Jean, Wolfeboro, N.H., 17 August 1988.
Broughton, Jane F., Concord, N.H., 14 June 1987.

David Buxbaum, Chebeague Island, Maine, 21 August 1986.

Chase, Marian, Henniker, N.H., 23 August 1986.

Cole, Ulric, by telephone, 3 November 1991.

Dengel, Eugenie, New York, 14 February 1985.

De Tar, Vernon, New York, 17 October 1986.

Farwell, Brice, Morgan Hills, Calif., 1987.

Gallagher, Sally, Concord, N.H., 14 June 1987.

Hamlin, Anna, New York, 17 November 1986.

Howe, Calderon, by telephone, 16 November 1987.

Johnson, Harry, Centerville, Mass., 19 August 1986.

Kelly, Dorothy, Hillsborough, N.H., 21 August 1987.

Lanier, Frances Brockman, by telephone, 8 November 1993.

Levey, Geoffrey, by telephone, 8 January 1990.

MacDill, Marella, by telephone, 16 November 1987, and Boston, 17 April 1988.

Meredith, Lillian Buxbaum, Cleveland, 8 January 1986.

Morton, Pearl Bates (Brodrick), Wolfeboro, N.H., 17 August 1988

Nelson, Elna, Centerville, Mass., 19 August 1986.

Ossewaarde, Jack, by telephone, 1 April 1995.

Pleasants, Virginia Duffey, New York, 25 November 1988.

Robinson, Angela, Henniker, N.H., 27 August 1986.

Scruton, Paul, Hillsborough Nursing Home, 21 August 1987.

Smith, Helen Kelley, Concord, N.H., 14 June 1987.

Smith, Julia, New York, 16 May 1985.

Strickland, William, by telephone, 7 February 1992.

Taylor, Prentiss, by telephone, 30 November 1987.

Wheeler, Emma Yeaton, Milford, N.H., 27 August 1986.

INDEX